COLLEGE CLASSICS IN ENGLISH

General Editor

NORTHROP FRYE

Shakespeare Series: Volume II

Hamlet

Edited by Marion B. Smith
Brock University

The Tempest

Edited by David Galloway
University of Waterloo

Henry the Fourth [Part One]

Edited by John F. Sullivan
University of Windsor

THE ODYSSEY PRESS • NEW YORK

Contents

General Editor's Introduction

We do not know much about Shakespeare, and a good deal of what we talk about in connection with him is fiction. The fictions begin with his birthdate, which is generally assumed to be April 23, 1564, because he probably died on that day fifty-two years later, because we have a record of his baptism on the 26th, and because April 23 is the day of St. George, the patron saint of England. We know nothing at all about him as a writer until he appears as an established dramatist in London: the gap used to be filled in by a story about his being arrested for poaching, evidently based on an interpretation of the opening scene of *The Merry Wives of Windsor*, which is now realized to be entirely wrong. His sonnets were published in 1609, probably without his consent. Most of them are concerned with a beautiful youth and some others with a female brunette. There is no real evidence that either of these figures had any existence outside the sonnets, but there is enough fiction about them to fill a library in itself. Even evidence can be misleading. There is evidence, for example, that Shakespeare wrote a play called *A Yorkshire Tragedy*. The evidence consists of an edition of the play published in Shakespeare's lifetime with his name on the title page. This is real evidence as far as it goes, but it is not good enough, and no scholar believes that Shakespeare did write this play. We have no notion what Shakespeare's religious or political views were, what he did, if anything, besides work for the stage, or whether he ever travelled abroad. The two contemporary representations of him, the frontispiece in the Folio and the bust on the Stratford monument, do not make him look at all like a proper poet: the noble brow and serene expression of the later faked portraits are much more to our taste. One would think that so great a poet must at least have realized how good he was, but though Shakespeare took some pains with his two narrative poems, *Venus and Adonis* and *The Rape of Lucrece*, he left his plays to be gathered up by two loyal friends and published seven years after his death. Nor is there any sign of his having taken any interest in the publication of the Quartos that appeared in his lifetime.

All this seems very mysterious, even sinister, to those who, like many nineteenth-century critics of Shakespeare, have been brought up to believe that writing is a form of self-expression or distilled personal experience. The simple fact that Shakespeare wrote plays throws a different light on our knowledge, or lack of knowledge, about his personality. In drama, success depends on the co-operation of a group rather than on the personality of a writer, who is sometimes, especially in spectacular or expensive productions, not very important at all. *Henry VIII*, for example, though it contains some fine scenes, is rather low-keyed in style, because this play featured an unusual amount of pageantry and costuming. It was not the custom either for dramatists in his day to publish their own works; the first to do so was Ben Jonson, in 1616. Again, drama is an objective form where the author does not speak in his own person, but has to make everything he says appropriate to the character saying it. We may like to feel that Shakespeare is lecturing us on the drama in Hamlet's speech to the players, or announcing his retirement from the stage in Prospero's "revels" speech, but when we assume this we are really assuming that, just this once, Shakespeare is indulging us and interrupting his play in order to say something to us. There are certainly many dramatists with strong personalities and definite critical views, including Ben Jonson in Shakespeare's own day. But drama is even more congenial to temperaments who prefer to disappear behind their work, including the majority of Shakespeare's contemporaries, about whom we know even less than we do about him. The lack of information about Shakespeare's early years is not surprising either, for drama, unlike lyric poetry, music, or mathematics, is not a genre for infant prodigies.

There is no clear evidence of his having written anything before his middle twenties or after his late forties, so we should be careful about ascribing qualities in early and late plays to the eager hopefulness of youth or the mellowed wisdom of old age.

We may as well make a virtue of necessity, and realize the immense advantage we have in dealing with a poet who is important to us only for his poetry. We need not bother with "Shakespeare the man" apart from the page or two of authentic but hardly breathtaking facts that can be found in any good handbook. We certainly need not investigate the attempts to show that Shakespeare's plays were really written by somebody else, as these speculations are merely documents in the psychology of obsession. The main scholarly, as distinct from critical, issues in the study of Shakespeare are: the order and dating of the plays; the sources used; the staging of the plays in Shakespeare's theatres; and the editorial and bibliographical problems connected with trying to establish the text. The editors of the plays in this volume have tried to introduce you to these issues so far as they affect the plays they are editing, and to distinguish what is definitely known about these matters from what is still controversial and unsettled.

All these questions are exceedingly difficult on advanced levels, but in the elementary stages they are quite comprehensible. The research into the dating of the plays, as established by entries in the Stationers' Register, contemporary references, and the like, confirms in general the impression of the difference between early and late plays which anyone can feel for himself with a little practice. In the early plays the rhythm is closely bound to the pentameter line, and there is a good deal of rhyming; in the late ones there are many lines with weak endings, so that the rhythm is pushed on into the next line, often with a longer pause in the middle of a line than at the end. The effect of such run-on lines is to build up larger rhythmical units. The following is typically the rhythm of an early play (*Love's Labour's Lost*):

> You may not come, fair princess, in my gates;
> But here without you shall be so received

> As you shall deem yourself lodged in my heart,
> Though so denied fair harbour in my house.
> Your own good thoughts excuse me, and farewell:
> To-morrow shall we visit you again.
>
> (2.1.172–7)

and this is typically the rhythm of a late one (*The Winter's Tale*):

> I had thought, sir, to have held my peace until
> You had drawn oaths from him not to stay. You, sir,
> Charge him too coldly. Tell him, you are sure
> All in Bohemia's well; this satisfaction
> The by-gone day proclaim'd: say this to him,
> He's beat from his best ward.   (1.2.28–33)

Again, the main sources of the plays are frequently obvious: North's Plutarch for the Roman plays; Holinshed for the histories; earlier plays, some lost and some still extant, for some of the tragedies. Shakespeare knew French, Latin, and perhaps Italian, but preferred to use sources in English: being a poet, he was constantly on the alert for phrases he could pick up or modify. It is a fascinating experience to compare a play with its main source, where known, and see the dramatist's swift selective eye passing over this, seizing on that, suppressing irrelevant details and inventing relevant ones, throwing in characters not found, or barely named, in the sources (Enobarbus, Mercutio, Gloucester) to add whole dimensions of imaginative power. We should remember that however many natural touches and glimpses of real life there may be in the plays to delight us, everything connected with the structure and shape of the play has been got out of a book, or earlier play. We know that this is true of nearly all the plays, and those for which no likely general source has yet been found (*Love's Labour's Lost, The Tempest*) look equally literary.

The general shape of what most people think of as the typical Elizabethan theatre with its projecting outer or "apron" stage, along with its upper areas, the distribution of the audience into pit and galleries, the emphasis on costume rather than scenery, the use of boy actors and singers, and even more controversial questions like the existence of an inner stage or an Elizabethan "theatre in the round", are by now fairly familiar. Two things above all should be kept in mind. In the first place, although Shakespeare's theatres were probably among the best in Europe, they were still very small and intimate structures. The physical closeness of the play to its audience, and the intensity with which that audience was able to concentrate on the language and action, are difficult to reproduce in even the most historically accurate reconstruction. Second, the energy and excitement generated by a performance, including the surge and thunder of the verse and the frequent (in some plays almost constant) accompaniment of music, bring it closer in emotional effect to opera than to most modern proscenium plays.

There is no primary text except the Folio for a good many of the plays, and where this is true, the modern editor sticks closely to it: conjectural emendations are not now much favoured. The existence of a good Quarto complicates the editing very considerably (except when the Folio reprints the Quarto text, as sometimes happens), and an immense amount of hard work has gone into establishing what the modern reader reads and the modern actor speaks. No manuscripts of Shakespeare survive, unless some handwriting experts are right who have thought that one of several hands in a manuscript of a play on Sir Thomas More is Shakespeare's.

One is best advised not to use any critic, not even the very careful and unobtrusive editors of this volume, as a guide to the understanding of the play. The best approach to Shakespeare is still the one suggested by the editors of the Folio: "Read him, therefore; and again and again; and if then you do not like him, surely you are in some manifest danger not to understand him." This means reading until we pass the stage of reading and begin to enter the stage of possession, when the characters become members of our own imaginative family, and the cadences have begun to enter our own subconscious, or wherever it is that familiar phrases are stored. One of the elements in Shakespeare's own genius was his power of possessing everything he read, though he does not appear to have been an unusually erudite or scholarly reader. People rarely read with this kind of intensity, largely because of a panicky feeling that there is so much reading to "cover" or "get through". But one first-rate work of literature possessed is worth far more to one's literary education than any amount of casual familiarity with any number of books. After we have gained some possession of the play, we can turn to the critics, and discover that they have had similar experiences to ours, and are offering to share those experiences with us. But the critic, as distinct from the teacher, is most useful when what he writes comes to us as conversation about a play we know, rather than as an introduction to a play we do not know.

Northrop Frye

HISTORICAL AND BIOGRAPHICAL DATA

We have no sure way of knowing the actual year in which any one of Shakespeare's plays was written. In the following table, each play is listed opposite the year that is the most likely date of composition, with the date of the earliest known publication in brackets after the title.

1558   Accession of Elizabeth I. Thomas Kyd, Thomas Lodge, and Robert Greene born.

1559   Act of Uniformity. Publication of first extant edition of "A Mirror for Magistrates". Probable birthdate of George Chapman.

1561   Publication of "The Book of the Courtier", Sir Thomas Hoby's translation of Castiglione's "Il Cortegiano". Francis Bacon and Sir John Harington born.

1562   Samuel Daniel born.

1563   The Thirty-nine Articles. Publication of John Foxe's "Acts and Monuments" (known as "Foxe's Book of Martyrs"). Michael Drayton born.

1564   *William Shakespeare born at Stratford-upon-Avon.* Galileo and Christopher Marlowe born. Michelangelo and John Calvin die.

1565   Publication of the first English tragedy written in blank verse, "Gorboduc", by Thomas Norton and Thomas Sackville.

1566   Probable date of publication of Nicholas Udall's "Ralph Roister Doister", earliest extant English comedy employing the classical five-act structure. James Stuart (later James VI of Scotland and I of England) born.

1567   Abdication of Mary Queen of Scots. Thomas Nashe and Thomas Campion born.

1568   Henry Wotton born. Roger Ascham dies.

1569   Sir John Davies born.

1570   Probable birthdate of Thomas Dekker and Thomas Middleton.

1571   Johannes Kepler born. Benvenuto Cellini dies.

1572   Massacre of St. Bartholomew. Tudor Poor Law declares all actors not attached to a nobleman to be "rogues and vagabonds". John Donne and Ben Jonson born. John Knox dies.

1573   Thomas Heywood and William Laud born.

1574   Formation of Earl of Leicester's company of players with James Burbage and others.

1575   The Earl of Leicester holds festivities at Kenilworth Castle in honour of Queen Elizabeth. Probable birthdate of John Marston and Cyril Tourneur.

1576   The Theater erected: the first theatre in London. Blackfriars Theatre opens with a company of boy actors.

1577   Probable date of the opening of The Curtain Theatre. Publication of Raphael Holinshed's "Chronicles". Robert Burton born.

1578   Publication of John Lyly's "Euphues, the Anatomy of Wit". William Harvey born.

1579   Publication of Sir Thomas North's translation of Plutarch's "Lives". Publication of Edmund Spenser's "Shepherds Calendar" and Stephen Gosson's "School of Abuse". (The latter work opened the Puritan pamphleteers' attack on the theatres.) John Fletcher born.

1580   Sir Francis Drake completes his voyage around the world, begun in 1577. Publication in France of the first parts of Montaigne's "Essais", and in England of John Stow's "Chronicles of England". Probable birthdate of John Webster. Probable date of the deaths of Raphael Holinshed and John Heywood.

1581   Publication in Italy of Torquato Tasso's "Gerusalemme Liberata", and in England of "Seneca, his Ten Tragedies", a collected edition of translations by various hands that had first been published separately in the fifties and sixties.

1582   *Shakespeare marries Anne Hathaway.* Plague year in London.

1583   *Shakespeare's daughter Susanna born.* Plague year in London. Formation of the Queen's company of players. Philip Massinger born.

1584   William of Orange assassinated. Sir Walter Raleigh granted a Charter of Colonization for Virginia. Francis Beaumont born.

1585   *Shakespeare's twin son and daughter, Hamnet and Judith, born.* Earl of Leicester conducts an expedition to the Netherlands. William Drummond of Hawthornden born. Pierre de Ronsard dies.

1586   John Ford born. Sir Philip Sidney killed in battle.

1587   Mary Queen of Scots executed. The Queen's Players visit Stratford. John Foxe dies.

1588   The Spanish Armada defeated. Martin Marprelate controversy (1588–9). Thomas Hobbes born.

1589   Publication of Richard Hakluyt's "Principal Navigations, Voyages and Discoveries" and Robert Greene's "Menaphon".

1590   *"2 Henry VI" (1594), "3 Henry VI" (1595), "1 Henry VI" (1623).* Publication of Thomas Lodge's "Rosalynde", Sir Philip Sidney's "Arcadia" (posthumously), and the first three books of Edmund Spenser's "The Faerie Queene".

1591   *"The Comedy of Errors" (1623), "Titus Andronicus" (1594).* Publication of Sir John Harington's translation of Ariosto's "Orlando Furioso". Publication of Robert Greene's "Notable Discovery of Cosenage". Robert Herrick born.

1592   *"Richard III" (1597).* Plague year. Probable date of the opening of the Rose Theatre. Philip Henslowe begins his Diary. Publication of Thomas Nashe's "Pierce Penniless" and Robert Greene's "Groatsworth of Wit". Probable date of the publication of Thomas Kyd's "The Spanish Tragedy". Montaigne and Robert Greene die.

1593   *"The Taming of the Shrew" (1623). Shakespeare's poem "Venus and Adonis" published.* London theatres closed because of plague. Izaak Walton and George Herbert born. Christopher Marlowe killed.

1594   *"Two Gentlemen of Verona" (1623), "Love's Labour's Lost" (1598). Shakespeare's poem "The Rape of Lucrece" published. Shakespeare's name is recorded as one of the Lord Chamberlain's Men.* The Earl of Derby's Men become the Lord Chamberlain's Men. Publication of the first parts of Richard Hooker's "Of the Laws of Ecclesiastical Polity". Thomas Kyd dies.

1595   *"Romeo and Juliet" (1597), "A Midsummer Night's Dream" (1600), "Richard II" (1597).* Sir Walter Raleigh's voyage to Guiana. Probable date of the building of the Swan Theatre. Publication of Sir Philip Sidney's "Apology for Poetry" (posthumously) and of Edmund Spenser's "Amoretti", "Epithalamion", and "Colin Clout's Come Home Again". Torquato Tasso dies.

1596   *"King John" (1623), "The Merchant of Venice" (1600). A coat of arms granted to Shakespeare's father. Shakespeare's son, Hamnet, dies.* Blackfriars Theatre purchased by James Burbage. Publication of Edmund Spenser's "The Faerie Queene (Books I–VI)", "Prothalamion", and "Four Hymns". René Descartes born. Sir Francis Drake and George Peele die.

1597   *"1 Henry IV" (1598), "2 Henry IV" (1600). Shakespeare buys New Place in Stratford.* Publication of Francis Bacon's "Essays".

1598   *"Much Ado About Nothing" (1600), "The Merry Wives of Windsor" (1602).* Edict of Nantes. Publication of first parts of George Chapman's translation of Homer. Publication of Speght's edition of Chaucer, Francis Meres' "Palladis Tamia", and John Stow's "Survey of London". Lord Burghley dies.

1599   *"Henry V" (1600), "Julius Caesar" (1623), "As You Like It" (1623). The Globe Theatre opens with Shakespeare as one of the original shareholders. Publication of "The Passionate Pilgrim" (anonymously: containing two sonnets by Shakespeare).* Oliver Cromwell born. Edmund Spenser dies.

1600   *"Twelfth Night"* (1623), *"Hamlet"* (1603). The Fortune Theatre opens. Publication of Edward Fairfax's translation of Torquato Tasso's "Gerusalemme Liberata". Publication of William Gilbert's "De Magnete", Thomas Dekker's "Shoemaker's Holiday", and Ben Jonson's "Every Man Out of His Humour". Probable date of the death of Thomas Deloney. Richard Hooker dies.

1601   *"Troilus and Cressida" (1609). Shakespeare's poem "The Phoenix and the Turtle" published in "Love's Martyr", edited by Robert Chester. Shakespeare's father dies.* The Earl of Essex is executed for rebellion. Publication of Samuel Daniel's "Works" and Ben Jonson's "Every Man in His Humour". Probable date of the death of Sir Thomas North. Thomas Nashe dies.

1602   *Shakespeare buys considerable property in Stratford.* Bodleian Library opened at Oxford.

1603   *"All's Well that Ends Well"* (1623). Death of Queen Elizabeth I. James VI of Scotland becomes James I of England. Plague year in London. The Lord Chamberlain's Men become the King's Men. Philip Henslowe concludes his Diary. Publication of John Florio's translation of Montaigne's "Essais", and of Philemon Holland's translation of Plutarch's "Morals".

1604   *"Measure for Measure"* (1623), *"Othello"* (1622). Publication of Christopher Marlowe's "Dr. Faustus" (posthumously).

1605   *"King Lear"* (1608), *"Macbeth"* (1623). Gunpowder Plot. Publication in Spain of Cervantes' "Don Quixote" (Part 1). Publication of Francis Bacon's "Advancement of Learning", William Camden's "Remains", and Ben Jonson's "Sejanus". Sir Thomas Browne born. John Stow dies.

1606   *"Antony and Cleopatra"* (1623). Pierre Corneille born. John Lyly dies.

1607   *"Coriolanus" (1623), "Timon of Athens" (1623). Shakespeare's daughter Susanna marries John Hall, gentleman, of Stratford.* Settlement of Jamestown. Publication of George Chapman's "Bussy D'Ambois",

Ben Jonson's "Volpone", Thomas Heywood's "A Woman Killed with Kindness", and Cyril Tourneur's "The Revenger's Tragedy".

1608   *"Pericles" (1609). Shakespeare's mother dies. Shakespeare's grand-daughter, Elizabeth Hall, christened. Shakespeare becomes one of the original shareholders of the Blackfriars Theatre.* John Milton and Thomas Fuller born.

1609   *"Cymbeline" (1623). Shakespeare's "Sonnets" published.* Galileo discovers the satellites of Jupiter. Publication of Thomas Dekker's "Gull's Hornbook", Ben Jonson's "Epicoene", and Edmund Spenser's "Two Cantos of Mutability" (posthumously, in a new edition of "The Faerie Queene").

1610   *"The Winter's Tale" (1623). Probable date at which Shakespeare returns to settle in his home in Stratford.*

1611   *"The Tempest" (1623).* The struggle between King James and his Parliament intensifies. Publication of the King James Version of the Bible and John Donne's "Anatomy of the World".

1612   *"Henry VIII" (1623).* Henry, Prince of Wales, dies. Princess Elizabeth marries the Elector Palatine. Publication of Thomas Shelton's translation of Cervantes' "Don Quixote" (Part 1). Publication of Ben Jonson's "The Alchemist" and John Webster's "The White Devil". Sir John Harington dies.

1613   *Shakespeare purchases property in London.* The Globe Theatre burns down. Richard Crashaw and La Rochefoucauld born.

1614   The Globe Theatre is rebuilt. Publication of Sir Walter Raleigh's "History of the World".

1615   Publication of "Cupid's Revenge" by Francis Beaumont and John Fletcher.

1616   *Shakespeare's daughter Judith marries Thomas Quiney of Stratford. Shakespeare dies on April 23.* William Harvey expounds his theory of the circulation of the blood. Publication of Ben Jonson's "Works". Francis Beaumont, Richard Hakluyt, and Cervantes die.

1618   Beginning of the Thirty Years War. Francis Bacon becomes Lord Chancellor. Richard Lovelace and Abraham Cowley born. Sir Walter Raleigh executed.

1619   Samuel Daniel dies.

1620   The Pilgrim Fathers leave for America.

1621   Publication of Robert Burton's "The Anatomy of Melancholy". Jean de La Fontaine and Andrew Marvell born.

1622   Molière and Henry Vaughan born.

1623   *Publication of the first collected edition of Shakespeare's plays (The "First Folio"), "Pericles" omitted. Publication of John Webster's "The Duchess of Malfi". Blaise Pascal born.*

Each play in this series is accompanied by an introduction, a note on the text, a bibliography, and by the following kinds of annotation: a list of textual variants or editorial emendations, glossary notes, longer notes at the end of the play.

The texts of the plays are based on the earliest editions; that is, on the First Folio of 1623 and, in some cases, on earlier Quartos. Square brackets enclose *dramatis personae*, act and scene headings, locations, and emendations of or additions to stage directions in the copy text, which have been added by later editors.

In referring to plays other than the one under discussion, the line numbering of The Globe Edition is used.

Among the abbreviations and typographical devices employed in this text are the following:

An accent (`), which indicates that the final vowel of a word is pronounced (e.g. armèd). An accent (´), which indicates that a different syllable of a word is stressed than in modern usage (e.g., convénts).

A symbol (‡) in the margin of the text, which indicates that there is a longer note at the end of the play.

Other abbreviations of a general character are: s.d. = stage directions; s.h. = speech heading; Q_0: = a lost quarto, Q or Q_1 = First Quarto, or the earliest known single edition of a play, Q_2 = Second Quarto, and so forth; F or F_1 = First Folio, or the earliest collected edition of Shakespeare's works (1623), F_2 = Second Folio (1632), and so forth.

Where a reading or interpretation from an earlier edition is offered, the name of the editor or the edition follows in brackets.

HAMLET

William Shakespeare

**Edited, with introduction and notes, by
Marion B. Smith**

INTRODUCTION

The earliest extant version of the Hamlet story is found in the *Historica Danica* of Saxo Grammaticus, Books III and IV, composed during the latter years of the twelfth century. Horwendil, the Governor of Jutland, has been murdered by his brother Fengon, who then usurps the governorship and marries Horwendil's widow, Gerutha. "The man veiled the monstrosity of his deed with such hardihood of cunning, that he made a mock pretense of goodwill to excuse his crime, and glossed over fratricide with a show of righteousness."[1] Prince Amleth, the son of Horwendil and Gerutha, pretends to be mad in order not to seem a threat to his uncle while at the same time he prepares to take revenge on him. But he puts on such a clever act that he arouses Fengon's suspicion.

The Governor's supporters arrange a seemingly accidental solitary encounter between Amleth and a loose and lovely woman, charging her to report back to them whether Amleth is indeed so mad that he fails to behave as a normal young man might be expected to under such circumstances. Forewarned of the plot by a foster-brother, Amleth manages to enjoy the lady in the privacy of a "distant and impenetrable fen" and to persuade her to keep his secret. On his return he boasts of his conquest in such fantastic terms that no one believes him.

In the next attempt to trap him, a nobleman arranges to observe Amleth's behaviour toward his mother in the privacy of her chamber. Amleth is suspicious and simulates an attack of frenzy, in the course of which he drives his sword repeatedly

[1] Oliver Elton's translation, in Israel Gollancz, ed., *The Sources of Hamlet* . . . (London, Oxford University Press, 1926).

into the wall-hangings until he has discovered and killed the spy. After disposing of the body, he returns to upbraid his mother for her bestial sensuality until, at last, she repents and promises to mend her ways.

Fengon is unable to solve the mystery of the missing courtier and becomes more suspicious than ever of his nephew. He decides to send Amleth to England with two of his retainers who bear a warrant for the Prince's death. Amleth searches their coffers as they sleep, substitutes an order that the two retainers be killed, and proceeds to England, where he wins the love of the King's daughter. A year later he returns to Jutland in the resumed guise of a madman. Playing the butler at a feast, he makes all the courtiers drunk, entangles them in the hangings of the banquet-hall, and sets fire to the palace. Thereupon he goes to the King's chamber, where he wakens Fengon and kills him with the very sword that Fengon used to murder Horwendil. After informing the people of the facts of the case, Amleth succeeds to the governorship of Jutland and holds power for several years, until the treachery of his second wife brings death upon him.

A later version of the story, which in its main outlines follows that of Saxo Grammaticus, was included in Belleforest's *Histoires Tragiques,* published in Paris in 1576. This is the probable source both for Shakespeare's *Hamlet* and an earlier Hamlet play. A translation of Belleforest's version was published in London in 1608.

The existence of another play about this Danish prince is indicated by extant contemporary references to an early revenge play called *Hamlet*, in which a ghost cried out, "Hamlet, Revenge!" Most scholars now accept the attribution of the *Ur-Hamlet,* as the old play is called, to Thomas Kyd, the most famous of the Elizabethan imitators of Seneca's classical tragedies of revenge.

During the last decade of the sixteenth century some of the London theatrical companies went on tour to Germany. One of the plays in their touring repertory was called *Hamlet*, and it was revived at Dresden in 1626 by an English acting company led by John Green. A modernized version appears to be preserved in *Der Bestrafte Brüdermord* (*Fratricide Punished*), dating from 1710. A Senecan Prologue outlining "the argument of the play" is spoken by a character named "Alecto". The court Chamberlain is called "Corambus" (he is "Corambis" in Quarto One of Shakespeare's *Hamlet*). The story is closer to Shakespeare's play than to either Saxo's or Belleforest's version and closer to that of Quarto One than to that of Quarto Two. Therefore, if *Der Bestrafte Brüdermord* is based on Kyd's *Ur-Hamlet*, it would indicate how little Shakespeare changed the incidents of the plot while transmuting the play into something rich and strange in other respects.

Scholars are in general agreement that *Hamlet*, in the form in which we know it, was written between 1598 and 1602. The absence of any mention of the play in Francis Meres' *Palladis Tamia*, published in 1598, is usually accepted as providing a limiting date in one direction, though Meres' wording of his commendation of Shakespeare would indicate that the titles he cites are exemplary rather than exhaustive. Roberts' entry in the Stationers' Register on July 26, 1602, is unimpeachable evidence that the play was written before that date. Such evidence as there is for a more specific date of composition is contradictory, some of it pointing to 1599 or shortly thereafter, some of it to 1601. It is possible that the topical allusions to the events of 1601 were added to the text during the run of the play.

In his copy of Speght's 1598 edition of Chaucer, Spenser's friend Gabriel Harvey referred to *Hamlet* in a marginal note commenting on current literary fashions at Cambridge: "The younger sort takes much delight in Shakespeares Venus, & Adonis; but his Lucrece, & his tragedie of Hamlet, Prince of Denmarke, haue it in them to please the wiser sort." On the title page and on the last page of the book Harvey signed his name and added the date 1598, which is the date he acquired the book, but not necessarily the date of his marginal note. In the same note, however, Harvey mentions in the present tense the Earl of Essex, who was executed in February 1601.

E. J. A. Honigmann argues[2] that the references to Julius Caesar (1.1.113-120) and to Polonius' acting of the role at the university (3.2.96-102) are to be taken as allusions to a performance of Shakespeare's tragedy in which the actor playing Polonius had played Brutus. *Julius Caesar* can be dated fairly precisely as having been written during the first half of 1599, and *Hamlet* must have followed not too long afterwards if the allusions were to have any point for the audience. Since Harvey's note would seem to exclude a date later than February 1601, it is probable that the play was written late in 1599 or during the year 1600.

The evidence for the dating of the play at the turn of the century is confirmed by its style, which is that of Shakespeare's middle period though examples can be found in it of the characteristics of both his earlier and his later styles. He moves with consummate deftness from verse to prose and from one sort of verse to another as the situation demands. Particular characters are distinguished by their own speech-rhythms, word-choice, images, and by devices of rhetoric that are peculiar to themselves. A variety of stylistic devices is called upon to create a special atmosphere or to modulate from one dramatic mood to another. For example, the lyricism of Marcellus' and Horatio's speeches about that season "wherein our Saviour's birth is celebrated" and the morn "in russet mantle clad" serve to lower the pitch a little after the melodramatic tension of the first encounter with the ghost of Hamlet's father. A variety of styles, from turgid to lyrical, from verbose to compressed, from limp to vigorous, is exhibited, each in its appropriate place.

In general, the verse-rhythms of *Hamlet* follow a flexible yet clearly discernible metrical pattern. Shakespeare has long since freed himself from the tyranny of the rigid, end-stopped line with its five-foot iambic beat and medial caesura, or pause, from which earlier writers of dramatic blank verse feared to stray. Sometimes the meaning and syntax carry the movement on

---

[2] "The Date of *Hamlet*", *Shakespeare Survey* 9, pp. 24-33.

from one line to another; sometimes they require a pause or stop at the line's end. The placing of the caesura, or pause within the line, varies; it may occur anywhere or be omitted altogether. Lines are split between two speakers or are left incomplete. Trochaic feet frequently replace iambic, especially at the beginning of a line, and other substitutions – anapaest, dactyl, and spondee – are used on occasion. For the most part, the rhythms appear to flow naturally, as in conversation, and where they do not they are deliberately stilted, monotonous, archaic or artificially patterned in order to indicate pomposity or artifice or to underline the formality of a theme or occasion. Flexible and varied though the verse-pattern may be, the ear can usually recognize the beginning of a line, even though no noticeable pause has preceded it. The breaking down of the blank-verse structure has not yet proceeded to the point where the visual as well as the aural memory must be relied upon if a quotation is to be set down in proper form without reference to the text. For the later plays, such as *The Winter's Tale* and *The Tempest*, the ear is an unsafe guide in such matters.

An excerpt from the opening scene will serve to illustrate these characteristics in a run-of-the-mill passage of exposition:

BERNARDO. What, is Horatio there?
HORATIO.   A piece of him.
BERNARDO. Welcome, Horatio. Welcome, good Marcellus.
HORATIO. What, has this thing appeared again to-night?
BERNARDO. I have seen nothing.
MARCELLUS. Horatio says 'tis but our fantasy,
    And will not let belief take hold of him
    Touching this dreaded sight twice seen of us.
    Therefore I have entreated him along
    With us to watch the minutes of this night,
    That if again this apparition come,
    He may approve our eyes and speak to it. (19-29)

Bernardo's question and Horatio's answer divide a line between them; the next two lines have, respectively, a double caesura and a pause in the middle of the first foot. These are followed by a half-line standing alone. As Marcellus swings into his explanation of Horatio's presence the rhythms quicken, speeded on their way by light vowels and flowing consonants. As the speaker's excitement mounts, it seems as if he could not take time to pause within the line, for in the whole speech there is not a single caesura. After the opening line, Marcellus manages twice to get through two lines without stopping; thereafter, as if breathless with anticipation, he pauses briefly at the end of each line before galloping through the next.

The simple, straightforward expression of this passage is fairly characteristic. We seldom find in *Hamlet* the compressed intellectual content and elliptical utterance accompanied by lightning shifts of imagery which are frequent in *King Lear*, for example. Time is taken to define, explain, and amplify important points and to emphasize them by a variety of verbal devices, among which parallel, antithesis, hendiadys, paired synonyms, and simple repetition of key words are prominent. Familiar instances are Horatio's "in the *gross and scope* of my opinion", Hamlet's "within the *book and volume* of my brain", and his repeated echoing of his mother's "seems" in Act 1, scene 2, lines 75 to 86.

The generally simple style is varied and enriched by a wealth of images and allusions ranging from learned to homely, from far-fetched to familiar, and their connotations are often layered like the skins of an onion. Hamlet has a particular knack for giving his ideas both a general application and a "local habitation" by his careful choice of words in which to clothe them. The Queen's funeral shoes are a famous instance of the force of a homely image associated with a learned allusion. His mother has married, he laments, "ere those shoes were old/With which she followed my poor father's body/Like Niobe, all tears" (1.2. 147-9). For Shakespeare's ability to evoke connotation in depth we cannot do better than to examine the opening lines of the most familiar of Hamlet's soliloquies:

> To be, or not to be, that is the question:
> Whether 'tis nobler in the mind to suffer
> The slings and arrows of outrageous fortune,
> Or to take arms against a sea of troubles,

And by opposing end them. To die, to sleep –
No more; and by a sleep to say we end
The heartache, and the thousand natural shocks
That flesh is heir to.   (3.1.56-63)

The "question" is formally stated, then defined in terms which associate the agonies of the spirit with those of the flesh. The desire for cessation of being in death is an unnatural impulse, since self-preservation is the first law of nature, and this unnatural death is linked with its likeness and opposite, sleep, the natural and recreative process – no sooner mentioned than seen as lost. Thus, by antithesis and parallel combined in paradox, we come back to the association of physical and spiritual torment, in which the heart physically "aches" and the flesh is subject to "shock".

Passing over the ambiguities created by uncertainty whether "in the mind" modifies "nobler" or "suffer", and those ambiguities inherent in the word "suffer" itself, we may note, first, that "slings and arrows" is not merely an example of emphasis by synonym but is an evocation of two different kinds of physical pain. The missiles delivered by "slings" bruise and break; "arrows" pierce. And these are traditionally barbaric weapons, appropriate to "outrageous" fortune. Then we are presented with the mind taking up arms against a sea of troubles, challenging the irresistible, always changing and never changed element. The Elizabethan audience would be reminded not only of Canute's lesson in humility to his sycophantic courtiers but also of the mad Roman Emperor Caligula drawing up his forces in order of battle on the shore as if he meant to mount an offensive against the deep. All of this strengthens the sense of insuperable odds against the combatant mind, as "natural shocks" invests with the force of an earthquake the sudden assaults of accident and disease upon physical being.

The extraordinary vividness of the language of *Hamlet* is not only visual but kinetic, evoking not only pictures but various kinds of physical sensation. We feel our feet struggling to "shuffle off this mortal coil"; we experience something of Hamlet's nausea at the "mildewed ear", Claudius, "blasting his wholesome brother", Hamlet's father, and at his mother's turning aside from her true and lawful lord to "prey on garbage". We wince at the gnawing pain of "rank corruption, mining all within" while rationalizations of guilt "skin and film the ulcerous place". Our palates are cloyed by the devotion which "sugars o'er the devil himself" and anticipate the bitterness of hell to follow.

The ears of Shakespeare's contemporaries were more closely attuned to the nuances of the spoken word than our own. Theirs was still largely an oral tradition. Printing in England was only a century old and books were still costly, so that oral exposition and recitation formed a much larger part of the educational experience than they do now. Sounds rather than verbal signs were the norm: the Elizabethans sang at their work, after meals, and while waiting their turn at the barber's; they listened to the town crier's proclamations, to the night watchman's announcement of the hour, to the cries of the street-vendors, to the broadside-ballad-singer's retailing of the latest news, to ritual services and prayers and homilies, and to long, long sermons. Besides, the language was changing and expanding so rapidly that it possessed a freshness and vitality which commanded attention. The sixteenth-century audience listened with care, partly in order to remember and partly because it enjoyed effective language for its own sake. It was very conscious of poetry but in no way self-conscious about it and would have been outraged by any throwing away of the best lines. But language is only one of the elements of drama, and the Elizabethans enjoyed the others as well – the plot, the characters, the spectacle, the music and dancing, and the moral, or the way in which the play "holds the mirror up to nature". That *Hamlet* has held the stage almost uninterruptedly ever since its first performance, and that it is assumed to be every actor's ambition to undertake the title role, are sufficient proof of the play's theatrical effectiveness. It is particularly effective in the sort of theatre for which it was written, one which provides several acting locales – fore-stage, rear-stage, and second level. The upper stage level, with its balcony and central chamber, serve as first-rate battlements and guard-room for the opening scene, as well as doorways for the appearance, disappearance, and reappearance of the Ghost. It will serve also as the "stage" to which Hamlet is borne "like a soldier" at the play's end. When, at the end of Act 1, scene 4, the apparition beckons Hamlet "to a more removèd ground", he probably follows it to the lower level and onto the fore-stage apron, where Horatio and Marcellus later join him to swear secrecy at Hamlet's bidding, reinforced by a ghostly voice issuing from the cellarage. The trapdoor to that cellarage can subsequently serve as Ophelia's grave.

A reverse movement from lower to upper stage may occur after *The Murder of Gonzago* has been performed beneath the canopy over the rear portion of the stage, with the courtly audience disposed as spectators at both sides of the apron. After replying to Rosencrantz and Guildenstern that he will come to his mother "by and by" and delivering his soliloquy, Hamlet goes out, ostensibly to his mother's chamber, and the focus shifts to Claudius, probably on the upper stage conversing with Rosencrantz and Guildenstern and perhaps retiring, after they have left him, into the room off the centre of the balcony in order to pray. Here Hamlet, on his way along the "gallery" to his mother's room, can pause, watch, and listen without being seen except by the audience. Alternatively, if there is an inner room off the lower stage, it may be used for this purpose, but whichever stage level is used for this scene, the other level must be used for Gertrude's "closet".

The great advantage of such a stage is its flexibility. It provides a multiplicity of entrances and exits, easy movement from one imagined locale to another, points of vantage for observation and for concealment, ample facilities for processions and rituals and all sorts of movement. On such a stage it is quite possible to present *Hamlet* without interruption from beginning to end, though that might be a little hard on the audience, as it is a very long play. In contrast, its production on a modern proscenium-arch stage is beset with all sorts of difficulties. The final scene, for example, is almost impossible to produce effectively on a crowded, picture-frame stage. But on Shakespeare's stage the courtiers would be grouped, as spectators of the fencing-match, on the covered stage-area, perhaps with a central opening exposed so that the table on which the foils and goblet are set may be placed just within. This would leave the whole area of the fore-stage apron for Hamlet and Laertes to manoeuvre in – a space which, while Shakespeare may have found it inadequate to represent the field of Agincourt, is ample for realistic fencing. To make the match, and especially the business of exchanging foils, convincing, room is essential.

Most modern producers find it necessary to cut the text of *Hamlet* more or less drastically in order to provide time for even minimal changes of set and costume, to say nothing of the conventional two intermissions. Nowadays, an audience almost never hears Polonius instructing Reynaldo to spy upon Laertes in Paris, and rarely does it get more than a tantalizing taste of the First Player's quality. Ophelia is often limited to one or the other of her two distracted appearances, and we are seldom permitted more than a glimpse of the gravediggers. Worst of all, it is common practice to cut one of the key soliloquies, "How all occasions do inform against me" (4.4.32-66). This cutting and pasting process distorts our impression of the play and its pace, which should present a judicious mingling of the leisurely and the hurried.

Other distractions may arise from the director's desire to be "original" or to emphasize a particular interpretation of the play. Under such conditions one can sometimes sympathize with Charles Lamb's doubts of the fitness of Shakespeare's tragedies for stage presentation. All such doubts vanish, however, with a single experience in the theatre of something approximating the full text of *Hamlet* presented, if not absolutely straight, at least without obvious imposition of a particular bias in cutting and direction.

There is a story, more likely than not apocryphal, that in a Vancouver cinema during the first run of Olivier's film version of *Hamlet* a power-failure occurred. After the audience had waited patiently for over half an hour for service to be restored, the theatre manager decided to call the show off and refund the price of admission. In the subsequent queue at the box-office a woman was overheard to remark to her companion, "What a pity! Now we'll never know how it turned out." Many audiences would achieve a more satisfying appreciation of a performance of *Hamlet* if they shared this woman's innocence. Hamlet and his problems, the great soliloquies, and the host of its phrases which have become common currency in our language are so familiar to us that a performance of the play cannot be for us the electrifying experience that it must have been for Shakespeare's contemporaries, as witnessed by the number of laudatory references which have come down to us. For these first audiences, *Hamlet* was a *play*, not a psychological puzzle, nor a sacred document, nor even an acknowledged literary masterpiece, though they were impressed by its quality. At the time it was written, drama was mass entertainment and was only beginning to be considered serious art or to be regarded as less ephemeral than modern television plays. While it is true that Marlowe and Shakespeare consciously courted the "censure" of the "judicious", they also wrote to make money, a circumstance which, as Northrop Frye remarks in *A Natural Perspective*, is a useful aid to the cultivation of a proper degree of artistic detachment on the part of the playwright. It may perhaps also serve to remind us that critical analysis of a work of literature is not an end in itself but a means to understanding and enjoyment. The play's the thing which catches not only the conscience but the heart.

It is easy enough to say what happens in *Hamlet*. To say what *Hamlet* is about, as four centuries of criticism have proved – if they have proved little else about this most discussed of Shakespeare's tragedies – is another matter. For the most part, the critics, like the play itself, raise more questions than they answer. For example, is *Hamlet*, in the words of Sir Laurence Olivier's film, which echo the preponderance of nineteenth-century criticism from Coleridge down, "the tragedy of a man who could not make up his mind"? Is the "mole of nature" in its hero a predominance of the contemplative over the active faculty? And is this "mole" the Aristotelian *hamartia* or "tragic flaw"? Other critics ask whether Hamlet fits the Aristotelian pattern of the tragic hero. Or are the obstacles to the accomplishment of his purpose not internal, but external, regardless of what he himself says about it?

Some critics have suggested that the disagreement of the play's interpreters reflects Shakespeare's failure to assimilate effectively into the working out of his own tragic concept some of the more recalcitrant elements of the earlier revenge tragedy which was the play's source. Among these, T. S. Eliot insists that Hamlet's emotional disturbance is disproportionate to the circumstances which caused it.

Other commentators seek to prove that Hamlet's nature is deeply tainted by the corruption of his world. To what extent does our experience of the play suggest that the rottenness of the State of Denmark infects the soul of its Prince? Is his "a spirit of health" or is he possessed by a "goblin damned"? Is Claudius the representative (for all his sins) of affirmation and ongoing life and Hamlet that of negation and death? Is the Prince merely "mad in craft", or does the mask of madness, under the stress of events, to some extent become the reality? Is Hamlet completely normal at any time during the course of the play? Is he, in the words of A. C. Bradley, suffering from "psychic shock" even before the ghost's revelations, as the result of his mother's "o'erhasty marriage" to his loathed uncle? Is this a tragedy of circumstance in that the hero finds himself in precisely the sort of situation with which his particular qualities of temperament make him unable to cope, whereas the same circumstances might have been handled successfully and with despatch by others of Shakespeare's tragic heroes – Othello, for example? If so, are the symptoms of the melancholy which inhibits him from prompt and decisive action indicative, as Ernest Jones, the eminent disciple of Freud, has argued they are, of an Oedipus complex?

These are a few of the questions raised, probed, and never

quite satisfactorily answered by the critics. However widely they may range in their interpretations of the play, most of them are in agreement in focusing their attention upon the central character and in discussing him, even when they disclaim any such intention, as if he were a real person rather than the creation of the dramatist's imagination. What is the secret of the overpowering "reality" of this characterization? What accounts for its continuing relevance for successive centuries? Each age interprets the play and its hero in the light of its own characteristic intellectual attitudes and preoccupations, each critic in the light of his own experience of life. Each tacitly seconds Coleridge's self-revealing confession, "I have a smack of Hamlet in myself, if I may say so."

If every man sees himself in Hamlet, to what extent is Hamlet Shakespeare's Everyman? Did he see Hamlet's problem as not merely the whether, how, and when to exact vengeance for his father's murder but as the larger problem of accepting, as the pattern of human existence, the mingled good and evil of this world? Are Hamlet's repeated self-examinations to be taken as microcosmic questionings of the Elizabethan "world picture", Socratic explorations, as Harry Levin suggests, of the nature of goodness, truth, and beauty, as well as of evil? Does the multiplicity of questions the play specifically asks and the paucity of answers to them reflect the enigmas of the human situation or, perhaps, if we accept Edward Dowden's view in *Shakspere, His Mind and Art*, the playwright's disillusioned state of mind?

A good case can be made for regarding *Hamlet* as the most consciously philosophical of Shakespeare's tragedies, though, as with other interpretations, the evidence marshalled in support of this one is somewhat selective. No theory has as yet succeeded in reconciling all the discordant elements of the play's many ambiguities, paradoxes, and contradictions, and in this respect also the critic finds parallels between Hamlet's problem and his own.

The pervasive ambiguity of the play is evident in its characterization. We do not find in *Hamlet* the absolute villain, the single-minded hero, and the host of flat, minor characters of the typical revenge melodrama. Instead, the conventional roles of the genre are filled by human beings who knowing the good nevertheless choose the evil. In doubt whether to behave, as well as to regard themselves, as gods or beasts, they are all to a greater or lesser degree inconsistent. Most of the major characters share Hamlet's self-awareness: the guilty are aware of their guilt, the fools confess their folly, those who pride themselves on their rationality admit their bewilderment, and sceptics reluctantly give credence to the incredible. One of the remarkable things about the play is the frequency with which characters admit their mistakes or even their deliberate deceptions, not only in soliloquies and asides, but openly. Most of them are given to generalizing upon these occasions. Polonius, for example, for all his self-assurance, confesses to Ophelia that he has misjudged Hamlet and adds the generalization that the old are as likely to be excessively opinionated as the young are to be indiscreet. Claudius, whose outstanding characteristic is shrewdness in matters of policy, goes out of his way to point out to Gertrude that his attempt to hush up the circumstances of Polonius' death has been a foolish tactical error. Sooner or later, all are sufferers from "conscience" in the older meaning of insight as well as its more familiar one of moral censorship.

Ophelia, who like Hamlet and Othello is of a "free and open nature", (though critics can be found who think otherwise on this point also) discovers that things may not always be what they seem and that events can take place in Denmark which are "much amiss" in a naturally ordered world – to the destruction of her own inner order. The hero's loving, generous-hearted, courageous mother (for, whatever her other inadequacies, these qualities cannot be denied to Gertrude) is united, and happily so, to a dastardly villain who sincerely regrets that he is one, though he is incapable of doing what is necessary for his redemption. The most highly valued of the ill-gotten gains he cannot bear to give up is his wife, and in this sense, Claudius, the calculating Machiavellian, is "passion's slave". The noble youth Laertes, to whose nobility even Hamlet attests, behaves in a most ignoble manner in what he regards as a cause of honour. Horatio, the stoic who has taken "fortune's buffets and rewards" with equal thanks, is barely dissuaded from killing himself in grief at the loss of his friend. Pirates show themselves to be "thieves of mercy", though for a price.

The paradoxes of the human situation and of human nature are also expressed in the manifold circumstantial and verbal ironies of the play. Man may be free to choose his course of action, and indeed must make choices, but destiny shapes his ends "rough-hew them" how he will. "Purposes mistook" fall on the inventors' heads. The dialogue abounds in dramatic ironies, clear to the audience if not to the speakers, in double and even triple meanings, in ironic echoes linking contrasting situations, in reason in madness, in the opposition of apparent and real significance. The conflict between what is and what should be, between being and seeming, is emphasized in such recurring images as those of clothing and disguise, acting and the theatre, blighted blossoms and unweeded gardens, and inward disease.

As a humanist, Hamlet believes that man's nature is capable of self-improvement. He has committed himself to striving after perfection, though he is aware that the taint of Adam's original sin which infects all his descendants will prevent achievement of perfection in this world. Hamlet seeks wisdom and understanding, hungers and thirsts after righteousness, and is passionately devoted to truth. Even in his disillusionment, his loss of faith in the old certainties, he continues to seek absolutes, constantly viewing the phenomena of his existence in terms of their polarities. His is a black-and-white world. Man must be either a paragon of animals or the quintessence of dust, infinite either in faculty or in arrant knavery. Sexual love is either a rose or a blister. He fears to be passion's slave and strives to govern his actions by "godlike reason", but he is driven by his greater fear of cowardice into over-valuing rash impulsiveness. He wavers between moral traditions, having lost sight of the classical ideal of "the mean" and not having attained to the Christian ideal of charity. All men deserve whipping, all are sinners not worth the breeding, including himself. Yet the least appearance of anything less than absolute integrity in the relations of others with himself is damned as treachery, and only in Horatio, whom he sees as Aristotle's "just man", can he place his complete confidence.

While the pursuit of perfection may be both praiseworthy and profitable, refusal to accept the inevitable imperfections of this fallen world is to see oneself as superior to the natural human condition and therefore to be guilty of a kind of *hubris*, an intellectual and spiritual pride. For Hamlet, as we first meet him, only perfect love, perfect innocence, perfect honesty, perfect friendship, and perfect vengeance seem to be worth having. His failure to deal effectively with his problems is occasioned not so much by paralysis of the will or reluctance to act as by his determination to do the absolutely right thing, in precisely the right circumstances, at exactly the right time. In order to discover what the right action, the right circumstances, and the right time are, he subjects each consideration to a process of analysis by dichotomies, evaluating the alternatives open to him under categories and sub-categories until not one but a multiplicity of decisions must be made. Hamlet's deliberations are conducted according to the generally accepted rules of logic, but the complex dilemmas of his situation prolong them to the point of frustration, as he recognizes when he accuses himself of "thinking too precisely". The end of all learning, in Sir Philip Sidney's words, is "virtuous action", not merely finding out what it is right to do but *doing* it. To Hamlet it is all-important that his actions be virtuous, yet, as he confesses to Ophelia, "virtue cannot so inoculate" our natures "but we shall relish" of the results of original sin, and especially of our human bondage to the desire of the flesh which is our badge of kinship with the beasts. The question which Hamlet finds most difficult to answer is, "What should such fellows as I *do*, crawling between earth and heaven?"

Denmark – or the world – is a prison and the time out of joint for one who cannot rest in the riddle of existence, who cannot come to terms with the absurdities, the fallings short, of his external as well as his internal world. By Act 5, however, it seems that Hamlet may have worked his way through to an acceptance of a significance larger than that which is bounded by the comprehension of his own individual reason, to a faith that there is a special providence in the fall of a sparrow, though why this is so passes understanding. While he still seeks Horatio's assurance that it is "perfect conscience" to avenge his father's murder, he is no longer absolute in his demands of himself or of others. He can now admit, even boast, that he loved Ophelia in spite of her weakness and her seeming rejection of him. If he cannot bear to hear Laertes, any more than a player, tearing a passion to tatters, he can – sincerely if somewhat disingenuously – apologize to him for his unintentional killing of Polonius, the man he had earlier scorned as a "wretched, rash, intruding fool". He has ceased to attempt to force events to fit his own idea of what is timely and is content to function as the instrument of divine justice whenever and however the will of heaven may dictate.

There is no "right" interpretation of *Hamlet*; each theory which has found any considerable degree of acceptance sheds some light on our understanding of the play, each is to some extent unsatisfactory, leaves something out of account. Some critics advance persuasive evidence for regarding the play as a tragedy of blood compounded of conventionally carnal and unnatural acts without any great profundity of meaning, while others regard it as Shakespeare's most philosophically speculative tragedy. Each reader brings to the play, as his predecessors have done, his own experience of life and literature, and his interpretation will be conditioned in part by that experience. But no superficial examination, no second-hand evaluation, will be accepted without question by any thoughtful reader of *Hamlet*. Nor is the play's full flavour to be derived from a single savouring of its richness, in the theatre or the study. To appreciate the depth of its insight, and above all the subtlety and vividness of its language, the reader must follow the advice of Shakespeare's first editors and "read him again and again". He will find that, as with the charms of Cleopatra, the infinite variety of *Hamlet* is not staled by custom.

The preoccupation of criticism with the character of Hamlet is dictated in part by the structure of the play and, especially, by what, if this were a novel, would be called its narrative point of view. To a very great extent the hero is isolated from his world when we first meet him, and the circumstances which have caused this isolation have occurred before the play begins. The bare facts are given in Claudius' plausible speech-from-the-throne, but it is left to the solitary, alienated, brooding Prince to explain to us why these events are so significantly "particular" for him. Because of his isolation the exposition of Hamlet's character comes almost entirely from within himself, and our estimate of the other characters is derived as much from what Hamlet says about them in his soliloquies and asides and in his supposedly mad taunting of his opponents as from the evidence provided by their own speech and action. According to Aristotle, tragedy, which represents men doing and suffering, has as its proper action the decline of a great man from happiness to misery. That this action is already well underway before the play opens, Hamlet's first bitter words make abundantly clear, though he has still greater depths to plumb. We learn what this melancholy young man had been like before the tragically critical events of his father's death and his mother's marriage from the testimony of others. That is, we view the Hamlet *of the play* from within, the Hamlet outside the play from without.

Certain glimpses of the earlier Hamlet are afforded to us as confirmation of the validity of that external evaluation. On the infrequent occasions when his melancholy is, as it were, off-guard, or sometimes surfeited, he can respond naturally to a familiar, natural stimulus. Such responses are his delight at first seeing Horatio, his initial welcome of Rosencrantz and Guildenstern, his jovial reception of the players, and even his tender, "Nymph, in thy orisons be all my sins remembered", when he first catches sight of Ophelia walking in the lobby. But these moments are short-lived. They serve to indicate that the Prince, however contemplative by temperament, is not naturally a withdrawn or solitary person but a gregarious, genial young man who has enjoyed not only his studies but also the customary exercises and diversions of the courtier. The contrast adds to the tragic impact of those circumstances which have wrought so great a change in him.

His grief and revulsion at his mother's behaviour in marrying his uncle so soon after her husband's death have turned his view inward upon himself until, as successive horrors add to the burden of his sorrow and consequently to his isolation, he can see in the external world little more than the mirror of his own problems. All occasions inform against him. Hecuba's grief for her slaughtered lord is in painful contrast to his mother's indifference, as the player's tears over this mythical sorrow are a sharp rebuke to his own lapsed passion. Gertrude's sensuality corrupts his image of Ophelia, Claudius' unnatural slaughter of his brother patterns his judgment of those foster-brothers of his childhood, Rosencrantz and Guildenstern. Fortinbras wins his admiration, Laertes his sympathy, because in their situations he sees "the portraiture" of his. The whole action of the play emanates from Hamlet or comes back to him, is seen with his eyes when it is not presenting the concern of other characters with him. So unremittingly is the focus on the hero in conjunction with Elsinore – his prison – that we do not accompany him to England but remain behind to watch with the eyes of Horatio, his surrogate, the continuing preoccupation of the court with the results of the Prince's actions, and to hear with him the news of Hamlet's further activities at sea. Our attention is rivetted to Hamlet in relation to his world and to that world's relationship to Hamlet.

Since the basis of the plot is revenge, that is retribution for an injury, the initiative of the action does not lie with the hero, as in other tragedies, but with his antagonist, the usurper king. We are given, on the whole, a favourable first impression of Claudius, while Hamlet's hostility towards him seems ill-mannered as well as ill-tempered. We are not left with this misapprehension for long, however. Claudius has put the events of the plot in train, as we learn from the Ghost, by murdering his own brother and, before or after that murder, winning "to his lust the will" of that brother's "most seeming virtuous queen". The first or "upward" movement of such a play must consist of the hero's positive reaction to the initiatory action of his antagonist. In *Hamlet* this takes the form of a search for truth. Hamlet is no Iago who "for mere suspicion . . . will do as if for surety". Before he can take action against the uncle whose villainy he has prejudged before the interview with his father's ghost, he must be convinced, to the satisfaction of his super-sensitive conscience and his keenly logical mind, that his uncle's actions have justified the retribution which his own hatred of the man and the Ghost's testimony so strongly urge. This is the course of justice, but not that of the traditional code of vengeance, and throughout most of the first four acts Hamlet is pulled in contrary directions by his desire to satisfy the claims of both vengeance and justice.

The second, or climactic, movement begins when, in the play scene, Hamlet obtains his liberating proof that the claims of justice and of vengeance are in accord. But he is not permitted to be single-minded for long. Almost immediately after he has had proof of his uncle's guilt, the opportunity to consummate his revenge is presented to him, but it is presented in such unsatisfactory terms that he cannot accept it whole-heartedly and is again torn by contrary motives. We cannot be entirely sure whether he spares the King at prayer for a single reason or for several, but we can be sure that he both does and does not wish to kill him under these circumstances. On the basis of our knowledge of his character we have some cause for suspecting that the reason he gives – that perfect vengeance demands that he send his enemy's soul to hell, not to heaven – may not be his only reason. In *Richard III*, Shakespeare had made much of Richard's threat to violate sanctuary in order to get possession of his nephew, the Duke of York. If he did not take it for granted that his audience would expect this Christian prince to hesitate to violate the sanctuary of the altar, why should he make Laertes, his foil, offer to cut his enemy's throat "i'th' church"? Does the honour of a gentleman not prohibit the stabbing in the back of an unsuspecting and defenseless foe? Hamlet does not say so, but even Saxo's Amleth woke his uncle before he slew him. Whatever his reasons for rejecting the chance to kill Claudius during his futile attempt to seek the forgiveness of heaven, the critical circumstance is that the opportunity occurred under such imperfect conditions that he could not accept it.

That the reasons he gives for not killing Claudius at prayer are not merely excuses for irresolution is made clear by his acceptance of the next opportunity for vengeance, an acceptance which turns out to be his fatal error. In killing Polonius behind the arras, Hamlet not only mistakes him for Claudius but goes against the instinct for justice which has made him insist on certainty before proceeding to action against his uncle. Still more important, his error makes it possible for the King to proceed against him openly rather than in secret, and to win applause for his seeming clemency and concern for the welfare of his step-son while plotting his destruction. In so doing, Claudius has retrieved the initiative. The downward movement begins, a change of direction which is sign-posted, according to dramatic convention, by the removal of the hero from the stage (though by no means from our attention) so that the focus of the action may rest, for a period, upon the villain.

One of the many ironies of the play is that this transition from positive to negative movement in the hero's fortunes is accompanied by what seems to be a more resolute and therefore more positive attitude on his part. But is this decisiveness which avoids decision only seemingly a change in the right direction for Hamlet? In the soliloquy "How all occasions do inform against me" (4.4.32-66), he cross-examines the very faculty of reason by which he has so repeatedly analysed his situation, and, in a supreme paradox, decides that both aspects of his human nature – "godlike reason" and "bestial oblivion" – have contributed to what he regards as his unforgivable lack of resolution in an enterprise "of great pitch and moment". In conclusion, he discards them both in favour of undirected will, rash impulse, as his future guide to action. Until his purpose is accomplished he is willing to become passion's slave. He now professes to believe that essential instinct, nature red in tooth and claw, is the only sure preserver of life in beasts and, with Fortinbras as model, of honour in men. "From this time forth,/ My thoughts be bloody, or be nothing worth" is the conclusion of his self-examination.

Hamlet has resolved his dilemma of conscience by discarding the theological and philosophical values which have pulled him in one direction and embracing the barbaric values of the revenge code which have pulled him in the contrary direction. That this, however profitable it may prove to be in terms of accomplishing his appointed task as his father's avenger, is the wrong choice for Hamlet, is made clear by the use of such words as "trick" and "straw" (echoed in the description of Ophelia's madness at the beginning of the ensuing scene), and of "puffed" and "eggshell", all of which carry connotations of triviality. Similarly, Romeo had said, "Away to Heaven, respective lenity,/And fire-eyed fury be my conduct now!" (3.1.28-9), sealing his own and Juliet's doom with those words. Similarly also, Othello and Macbeth will deny the better part of their natures, to the destruction of themselves and all that they truly value. Granville Barker comments: "Upon which negation of all he has been and believed in until now, not envious any longer of blood and judgement . . . well commingled, but just of brute capacity for deeds of blood, we part from him."

A great part of this third movement, however, is concerned not so much with Hamlet directly as with Laertes' demonstration of how a character unlike Hamlet – indeed such a character as Hamlet has newly resolved to become – deals with a problem such as Hamlet's. The King's activities are directed towards making use of the similarity of circumstances and contrast of character to bring about his nephew's destruction. No consideration of "something after death" will give Laertes pause; he is prepared to give both this world and the next "to negligence" in order to "be revenged most throughly" for his father Polonius. The degradation of his noble nature is an index to what our response to Hamlet's similar total dedication of himself and his sense of honour to vengeance is expected to be.

But the Hamlet who returns to Denmark in Act 5 is not the bloody-minded avenger that his final words in Act 4 have led us to expect. Laertes' situation may be the mirror of Hamlet's, but neither his attitude nor his actions are those of the Prince, except perhaps for the few brief moments at Ophelia's grave when Hamlet tries to outdo him in extravagance of language. But in this tirade, Hamlet is displaying his contempt for ostentation in grief. The events of the abortive voyage to England have wrought a further change in him, and while they have confirmed his conviction that rashness can be praiseworthy if heaven is "ordinant", he now sees impulse not as a means to personal honour, nor "rude will" as directed entirely by self interest. It is no longer necessary to reject either reason or passion; both aspects of man's nature may become the instruments of divine purpose in the individual who is willing to be directed by the will of heaven. The difference is most apparent, as has been suggested above, in his attitude to time. Whereas he had earlier lamented,

> I do not know
> Why yet I live to say "This thing's to do",
> Sith I have cause, and will, and strength, and means,
> To do't. (4.4.43-46)

now, when he seems to have no "means" and little time to accomplish his purpose, he is calmly confident that means and time will be provided. His reply to Horatio's warning that "It must be shortly known . . . from England/What is the issue of the business there" is, significantly, "It will be short; the interim is mine." Since he is convinced that it is "perfect conscience" to kill the King, he is convinced also that heaven has chosen him as the instrument of its justice and will appoint the occasion for retribution. For that appointment Claudius will not be spiritually ready, but Hamlet is, and the readiness is all. Therefore he makes no attempt to regain the initiative. In spite of his forebodings he is content to go along with the course of events which his enemy has set in motion and which the divine will that even Claudius has recognized as over-riding the will of human agents is shaping to the destruction of them both. Along with Hamlet and Claudius, all who have been tainted with the rottenness of Denmark are eventually purged from the body politic. And in a final irony, it is Fortinbras, the "happy warrior", the man of action with a shrewd eye on his "rights of memory" in the kingdom, who orders a hero's and a soldier's funeral for the philosopher prince who, much as he resented the usurpation of his rights, was incapable of acting effectively for his own advantage. Like Hamlet, Fortinbras shows himself capable of recognizing and admiring those qualities which he himself lacks. The contemplative personality, he realizes, is capable of its own brand of heroism and, when called upon, is as likely as the active personality to prove "most royally".

The tragic resolution of the play embraces both Hamlet and his world, for the final words of Fortinbras imply a promise of a new order for Denmark. They reveal him to us for the first time as a man of attitudes as well as actions and as something more than a rash and irresponsible adventurer. His concept of order is based not on moral absolutes but on decorum, the behaviour appropriate to particular situations. He has already shown his respect for authority in diverting his forces from Denmark to Poland, at the request of his royal uncle. Now he expresses his sense of the fitness of things:

> Such a sight as this
> Becomes the field, but here shows much amiss.
> (5.2.400-1)

Fortinbras' behaviour as governor is likely to be less rash and more responsible than his previous role as "adventurous knight" might indicate.

NOTE ON THE TEXT

During the present century, perhaps the most productive scholarly approach to the study of Shakespeare has been the application of new knowledge of the circumstances and methods of Elizabethan publishing to the task of establishing an authoritative text of the plays. This research, which has engaged the attention of many eminent scholars and is still in progress, has been devoted more to the elucidation of the textual problems of *Hamlet* than to those of any other play. To do justice to the ever-proliferating complexity of its findings would require far more space than is available here.

There are three primary texts for *Hamlet*: the "Bad Quarto" of 1603, the "Good Quarto" of 1604, and the First Folio of 1623. Briefly, the problem is to establish the extent to which each of the two more-or-less authoritative versions of the play – as printed in the Quarto of 1604 and the Folio of 1623 – represents what Shakespeare actually wrote. Since the two versions differ greatly from each other but cannot be regarded as entirely distinct and separate, the problem is not a simple one.

Moreover, it is complicated by the circumstance that the earliest published version of the play, the unauthorized Quarto of 1603, appears to have been a literary piracy, an instance of those "stolne, and surreptitious copies, maimed, and deformed by the frauds and stealthes of iniurious imposters" which the editors of the Folio, in their Preface "to the great variety of Readers", inveighed against and now claimed to offer to the view "cur'd and perfect in their limbes". The 1603 Quarto was entered in the Stationers' Register for James Roberts on July 26, 1602, as "A booke called the Reuenge of Hamlett Prince of Denmarke as yt was latelie Acted by the Lo: Chamberleyn his servantes" (Register C, fol. 84 *verso*). The attribution to James Roberts in the entry is puzzling, as Roberts, a reputable stationer who often did business with Shakespeare's company, seems to have had nothing to do with the subsequent publication of the play, which was printed the following year as "The Tragicall Historie of Hamlet, Prince of Denmarke. By William Shakespeare. As it hath beene diuerse times acted by his Highnesse Seruants in the Cittie of London: as also in the two Vniuersities of Cambridge and Oxford, and else-where At London printed for N.L. [Nicholas Ling] and Iohn Trundell. 1603."

The printing-press for the 1603 Quarto was that of Valentine Simms, a printer of bad repute who had once been deprived of the privilege of doing business; and the publication is a thoroughly "Bad" Quarto, only two-thirds as long as the "Good" Quarto of 1604 published to replace it. From the sections of the text of the 1603 Quarto which approximate and those which differ from that of the authorized version of 1604, it appears to have been reconstructed from memory by one or more actors who doubled in minor parts. When Marcellus, Voltimand, the Players, the Second Gravedigger, the Priest, or the English ambassadors are on stage, the text is reasonably close to that of the Second Quarto; otherwise it is halting and confused, as in the "To be, or not to be" soliloquy, the first few lines of which follow:

> To be, or not to be, I there's the point,
> To Die, to sleepe, is that all? I all:
> No, to sleepe, to dreame, I mary there it goes,
> For in that dreame of death, when we awake,
> And borne before an euerlasting Judge,
> From whence no passenger euer return'd,
> The vndiscouered country, at whose sight
> The happy smile, and the accursed damn'd.

The Second Quarto, of which some copies bear the date 1604, others 1605, was printed with the title page, "The Tragicall Historie of Hamlet, Prince of Denmarke. By William Shakespeare. Newly imprinted and enlarged to almost as much againe as it was, according to the true and perfect Coppie. At

London, Printed by I.R. for N.L. and are to be sold at his shoppe vnder Saint Dunstons Church in Fleetstreet." Since "I.R." is James (Iames) Roberts and "N.L." Nicholas Ling, it would appear that Roberts and Ling had arrived at a settlement of their rival claims to ownership as registrar and publisher of the play.

As the 1604 Quarto appears to have been printed from the author's "foul papers" (the final draft submitted to the Company, of which "fair copies" might be made for various purposes by a professional scrivener), its authority is very high, but that authority is somewhat diminished by the fact that the text is full of typographical errors. Professor F. T. Bowers argues that the two compositors who worked on the 1604 Quarto not only consulted the printed text of the 1603 Quarto when they could not make out the manuscript reading, but also that one of them set large portions of Act 1 (where the 1603 readings are least corrupt) directly from the First Quarto text.[1]

The 1603 Quarto, therefore, however unauthorized, is not entirely irrelevant to the establishment of an authoritative text for *Hamlet*. On rare occasions, where the Second Quarto and Folio versions are obviously corrupt, the possibility that the piratical actor's memory may have preserved the true reading must be taken into account. The First Quarto is valuable for two further reasons: its very full stage directions give some indication of how the play was performed; and its differences from the Second Quarto, in the names of some of the characters (e.g. "Corambis" for "Polonius") and in style (some passages are in an earlier tradition of stiffer, more formal, dramatic verse), suggest that it may represent either an earlier version of Shakespeare's play or a mixture of Shakespeare's with another, much earlier, Hamlet play in which the player may also have acted. More than two hundred lines which appear in the First Quarto do not appear in the other printed versions of the play.

The First Folio text of *Hamlet* appears to have been printed from a theatrical manuscript of the play, somewhat cut for act-

---

[1]Fredson T. Bowers, *On Editing Shakespeare and the Elizabethan Dramatists* (Philadelphia: University of Pennsylvania Library, 1955).

ing purposes. Some two hundred lines which appear in the Second Quarto are omitted in the Folio and some eighty-five new lines are added. But again, the Folio compositors appear to have consulted the earlier printed versions of the play, especially the Second Quarto, when they had difficulty deciphering the manuscript copy. The Folio corrects some of the Second Quarto's errors but adds misreadings of its own, though its compositors made a much better job of type-setting than did the compositors of Quarto Two.

The present edition follows the practice of recent editors in adhering fairly closely to the text of the Second Quarto except where that of the Folio is obviously better or where it supplies material omitted in the Second Quarto. In many instances, the choice of a particular reading has been necessarily subjective, since neither the Second Quarto nor the Folio has absolute authority.

Significant variations in the readings of the First Quarto, the Second Quarto, and the Folio are indicated in the textual variants, as are relevant emendations by Theobald, Pope, Johnson, and later editors which have found general acceptance.

TEXTUAL VARIANTS

1.1.43. *it* (F); Q_2 *'a*   45. *Speak to it* (Q_2); F *Question it*   73. *cast* (F); Q_1, Q_2 *cost*   93. *comart* (Q_2); F *cou'nant*   108-25. *I think ... countrymen* (Q_1, Q_2); not in F   112. *mote* (Q_4); Q_2 *moth*   127 s.d. *Spreads ... arms*; not in F; Q_1, Q_2 *It spreads his armes*   175. *conveniently* (F); Q_1, Q_2 *convenient*

1.2.9. *of* (F); Q_1, Q_2 *to*   24. *bands* (Q_1, Q_2); F *bonds*   58-60. *wrung ... consent,* (Q_2) not in F   67. *Not so, my* (F); Q_2 *not so much*   82. *shapes* (Q_3); F *shewes*   129. *sallied* (a 16th-century variant of "sullied") (Q_1, Q_2); F *solid* (See end note.)   149. *even she* (F); not in Q_2 175. *you to drink deep* (Q_1, F); Q_2 *you for to drink*   198. *vast* (Q_1); Q_2, F *waste* (The sense of both words is much the same.)   240. *warrant* (Q_1); Q_2 *war'nt*; F *warrant you*   254. *Foul* (Q_1 F); Q_2 *Fonde*

1.3.3. *is* (F); Q_2 *in*   18. *For he ... birth* (F); not in Q_1, Q_2 21. *safety* (Q_2); F *sanctity* (which makes better metre but not better sense)   49. *like* (F); not in Q_2 51 ff. (In Q_1 Polonius' precepts are printed in inverted commas, a practice of Elizabethan printers not only in marking quotations but also in setting off proverbial statements.)   63. *hoops* (Q_2, F) Pope *hooks* (i.e. grappling irons)   65. *comrade* (F); Q_1, Q_2 *courage* (i.e. "spark" or "young blood")   74. *Are most select ... that* (The text is corrupt and no suggested emendation fully satisfies the demands of metre, syntax, and meaning.)   75. *be* (F); Q_2 *boy*   76. *loan* (F); Q_2

loue 83. *invites* (F); Q₂ *invests* 109. *Running* (Collier); Q₂ *Wrong;* F *Roaming* 115. *springes* (Q₁, F); Q₂ *springs* 123. *parley* (F); Q₁, Q₂ *parle* 125. *tether* (F); Q₂ *tider* 130. *bawds* (Theobald); Q₂, F *bonds* 131. *beguile* (F); Q₂ *beguide*

1.4.17-38. *This . . . scandal* (Q₂); not in Q₁, F   36. *evil* (Keightley); Q₂ *eale* (The word has been variously emended, but "evil" fits the obvious meaning of the passage and is generally accepted.)   37. *often dout* (Collier); Q₂ *of a doubt*   49. *interred* (Q₁, Q₂); F *enurn'd*   75-8. *The very place . . . beneath* (Q₂); not in F

1.5.20. *fretful* (Q₁ F); Q₂ *fearefull*   33. *rots* (F); Q₁, Q₂ *rootes* (The F reading intensifies the sense of thriving on corruption and decay suggested by "fat weed".)   55. *lust* (Q₁, F); Q₂ *but*   56. *sate* (Q₁, F); Q₂ *sort*   84. *pursuest* (F); Q₁, Q₂ *pursues*   95. *stiffly* (F); Q₂ *swiftly*   116. *bird* (F); Q₂ *and*   122. *my lord* (Q₁, F); not in Q₂

2.1.28 *no* (F); not in Q₂   38. *fetch of wit* (Q₁, Q₂); F *fetch of warrant* (i.e. a device which is warranted)   40. *i' th'* (F); Q₂ *with*

2.2.57. *o'erhasty* (F); Q₂ *hastie* (its compositor apparently having regarded the "our o'er" of his copy as a repetition of the same word)   73. *three thousand crowns in annual fee* (F); Q₁, Q₂ *threescore* (for "three", which disturbs the rhythm of the line and would represent an enormous sum, in those times, as annual income from land)   90. *since* (F); not in Q₂   125. *above* (F); Q₂ *about*   136. *winking* (F); Q₂ *worklng*   142. *his* (F); Q₂ *her*   181. *god* (Warburton); Q₁, Q₂, F *good* (See end note.)   188. *Far gone, far gone* (Q₁, Q₂); F *'A is far gone*   208. *sanity* (F); Q₂ *sanctity*   209-10. *suddenly . . . between him and* (F); not in Q₂   212-13. *will more* (Q₁, F); Q₂ *will not more*   221. *excellent* (F); Q₂ *extent*   225. *over-happy* (F); Q₂ *ever happy*   226. *cap* (F); Q₂ *lap*   237-60. *Let me . . . attended* (F); not in Q₂   300-305. *What . . . dust* (Q₂); The punctuation in F produces a somewhat different reading: *What a piece of work is a man! how Noble in Reason? how infinite in faculty? in forme and mouing how expresse and admirable? in Action how like an Angell? in apprehension, how like a God the beauty of the world, the Parragon of Animals; and yet to me, what is this Quintessence of Dust?*   320-21. *the clown . . . sere* (F, where *tickle* reads *tickled*); not in Q₂   332-57. *How comes it . . . his load too* (F); not in Q₂   368. *lest* (F); Q₂ *let*   393-4. *tragical-historical . . . pastoral* (F); not in Q₂   436. *affectation* (F); Q₁, Q₂ *affection* (which has much the same meaning in Elizabethan English)   466. *Then . . . Ilium* (F); not in Q₂   487. *fellies* (Furness); Q₂ *follies; fallies*   551. *the cue for* (F); Q₂ *that for*   572. *villain;* F *villain!/ Oh, Vengeance!*   578. *scullion* (F); Q₁, Q₂ *stallion* (i.e. a male prostitute)

3.1.1. *conference* (Q₂); F *circumstance* (i.e. occasion or opportunity)   32. *(lawful espials)* (F); not in Q₁, Q₂   33. *Will* (F); Q₂ *wee'le*   46. *loneliness* (F); Q₂ *lowliness*   55. *Let's* (F); not in Q₂   83. *of us all* (F); not in Q₂   86. *pitch* (Q₁, Q₂); F *pith* (i.e. substance)   107-8. *your honesty should* (F); Q₂ *you should*   144. *lisp* (F); Q₂ *list*   145-6. *your ignorance* (F); Q₂ *ignorance*   151. *courtier's, scholar's, soldier's* (Q₁); Q₂, F *courtier's, soldier's, scholar's* (The Q₁ reading makes "eye, tongue, sword" applicable respectively.)   152. *expectancy* (F); Q₂ *expectation*   156. *musicked* (Q₂); F *musicke*   157. *that* (F); Q₂ *what*   158. *out of tune* (F); Q₁, Q₂ *out of time*   159. *feature* (F); Q₂ *stature*

3.2.9. *hear* (Q₁, Q₂); F *see* (The verb "seeing" is more commonly used of dramatic representations, but Hamlet attacks excesses of both voice

and gesture.)   68. *commingled* (F); Q$_1$ Q$_2$ *commedled*   111-2. *I mean ...
lord* (F); not in Q$_2$ 131 s.d. *The trumpets sound* (Q$_1$, Q$_2$); F *Hautboys*
(i.e. oboes) *play*   133. *this is miching mallecho* (F); Q$_2$ *this munching
Mallico*   138. *counsel* (F); not in Q$_2$ 162-3. *must./ For women's* (F);
Q$_2$ *For women feare too much, euen as they loue/ And womens*   164.
In neither aught (F); Q$_2$ *Eyther none, in neither aught*   165. *love* (F);
Q$_2$ *Lord*   177. *That's wormwood* (Q$_1$, Q$_2$); F *Wormwood, wormwood!*
219. *once a widow, ever I be wife* (F); Q$_2$ *once I be a widdow euer I be a
wife*   248. *must take* (Q$_1$); Q$_2$, F *mis-take*   251. *Confederate* (Q$_1$, F);
Q$_2$ *considerat*   254. *infected* (Q$_1$, F); Q$_2$ *inuected*   256. *usurp* (F); Q$_1$,
Q$_2$ *usurps* (but the imperative is required by the context)   262. *What ...
fire* (Q$_1$, F); not in Q$_2$ 272. *two* (F); not in Q$_2$ 280. *peacock* (emendation in late 17th-century quartos and Pope); Q$_1$, Q$_2$, F *paiocke*   313. *my*
(F); not in Q$_2$ 352. *thumb* (F); Q$_2$ *the vmber*   380. *"By and by" is
easily said. Leave me, friends* (F); Q$_2$ *Leave me friends./ I will, say so.
By and by is easily said*   382. *breathes* (F); Q$_2$ *breakes*

3.3.15. *cess* (Q$_1$, Q$_2$); F *cease*   19. *huge* (F); Q$_2$ *hough*   22. *ruin* (F);
Q$_2$ *raine*   73. *pat* (F); Q$_2$ *but*   79. *Why* (Q$_1$, Q$_2$); F *Oh*   *hire and salary*
(F); Q$_1$, Q$_2$ *base and silly*

3.4.5. *be round* (Q$_1$, Q$_2$); *be round with him./*HAM. *within. Mother,
mother, mother* (F);   *warrant* (F); Q$_2$ *wait*   19. *inmost* (F); Q$_2$ *most*   51.
heated (Q$_1$, Q$_2$); F *tristful*   53. *That roars ... index* (F); Q$_2$ assigns to
Hamlet   60. *heaven-kissing* (F); Q$_2$ *a heaue, a kissing*   72. *step* (Q$_2$, F);
Collier's emendation to *stoop* is accepted by many editors   79-82. *Eyes
... mope* (Q$_2$); not in F   89. *panders* (F); Q$_2$ *pardons*   91. *grainèd* (F);
Q$_2$ *greeued*   98. *tithe* (F); Q$_2$ *kyth*   103 s.d. *Enter Ghost* (Q$_2$, F); Q$_1$
Enter Ghost in his night gown (i.e. dressing gown or robe)   124. *on end*
(Pope); Q$_1$, Q$_2$, F *an end*   169. *Refrain tonight* (F); Q$_2$ *to refraine night*
173. *curb* (Malone's substitution); not in Q$_2$; Q$_4$ *maister* (which is accepted
by some editors in spite of the violence it does to the metre)   183. *Thus*
(F); Q$_1$, Q$_2$ *This* (which would seem to refer to the body of Polonius)
219. *a foolish* (F); Q$_2$ *a most foolish*

4.1.40. *so haply slander* (supplied by Capell to fill up the half line) not
in Q$_1$, Q$_2$, F   41-4. *Whose ... air* (Q$_2$); not in F

4.2.1. GENTLEMEN *within. Hamlet, Lord Hamlet* (F); not in Q$_2$
7. *Compounded* (F); Q$_2$ *compound*   18. *like an apple* (Q$_2$); F *like an ape
an apple*   30-31. *Hide, fox, and all after!* (F); not in Q$_1$, Q$_2$

4.3.25-7. *Alas ... that worm* (Q$_2$); not in F   41. *With ... quickness*
(F); not in Q$_2$

4.4.9-66. *Good sir ... nothing worth* (Q$_2$); not in F (probably an
"acting cut")

4.5.9. *aim* (F); Q$_2$ *yawn*   16. *Let her come in* (F); Q$_2$ assigns to
Horatio   38. *ground* (Q$_1$, Q$_2$); F *grave* (Since Ophelia seems to be recalling that Polonius was *not* accorded the usual funeral ceremonies,
"ground" seems slightly more appropriate.)   95. *Attend* F omits and adds
QUEEN. *Alacke, what noyse is this?*   136. *world's* (Q$_1$, Q$_2$); F *world*   141.
swoopstake (Q$_1$); Q$_2$ F *soopstake*   145. *pelican* (Q$_1$, Q$_2$); F *Politician*
150. *'pear* (Q$_1$, Q$_2$); F *pierce*   151. *Let her come in* (F); Q$_2$ assigns to
Laertes   159. *an old* (F); Q$_2$ *a poor*   160-62. *Nature ... loves* (F); not
in Q$_2$ 164. *Hey ... nonny* (F); not in Q$_2$ 197. *I pray God* (F); not in
Q$_2$

4.7.7. *criminal* (Q₁, Q₂); F *crimefull*   14. *conjunctive* (F); Q₂ *concliue*   22. *loud a wind* (F); Q₂ *loved Arm'd* (obviously corrupt)   36. *These* . . . *queen* (Q₂); F, following the entrance of the messenger, adds KING. *How now! What news?/* MESSENGER. *Letters, my lord, from Hamlet*; and continues, *This to your majesty, this to the Queen.* (Q₂ leaves the King to discover for himself the identity of the writer, thus giving greater force to his cry of shocked amazement, *From Hamlet!* in the next line.)   159. *prepared* (F); Q₂ *preferd* (Were it not that the word does violence to the metre, "proffered" might be an acceptable emendation of Q₂'s reading.)   166. *askant* (Q₁, Q₂); F *aslant*   167. *hoar* (F); Q₂ *horry*   168. *make* (Q₁, Q₂); F *come* (The Q₁ and Q₂ reading means that she made garlands of the willow and trimmed them with the other flowers.)   171. *cold* (F); Q₂ *cull-cold*   177. *tunes* (F, Q₁); Q₂ *lauds* (i.e. hymns of praise)   191. *drowns* (Q₁, Q₂); F *doubts* (probably for "douts", i.e. quenches)

5.1.9. *se offendendo* (F); Q₂ *so offended*   12. *argal* (F); Q₂ *or all*   34-7. *Why* . . . *arms* (F); not in Q₂   60. *in, and* (Q₂); F *to Yaughan and* . . . (probably Yaughan was a local tavern keeper)   65-6. *that 'a sings in* (Q₁, Q₂); F *that he sings at*   87. *mazzard* (F); Q₂ *massene*   102-3. *Is this* . . . *recoveries?* (F); not in Q₂   158. *now-a-days* (F); not in Q₂   184. *chamber* (F); Q₂ *table*   204. *Imperious* (Q₂); F *imperiall*   207. *winter's* (F); Q₂ *waters*   208. *awhile* (Q₁, Q₂); F *aside*   222. *Shards* (F); not in Q₂   228. *a requiem* (Q₂); F *a sage requiem* (i.e. a solemn requiem)   237. *treble* (F); Q₁, Q₂ *double*   267. *thou'lt* (F); Q₂ *th'owt*   291. *shortly* (F); Q₂ *thereby*

5.2.9. *pall* (Q₂); F *fall*; Pope *fail*   *learn* (Q₁, Q₂); F *teach*   17. *unseal* (F); Q₁, Q₂ *unfold*   57. *Why, man* . . . *employment* (F); not in Q₂   68-80. *To quit* . . . *passion* (F); not in Q₂   93. *Put* (F); not in Q₂   98. *sultry* (F); Q₂ *sully*   106-141. *Sir* . . . *unfellowed*; not in F, which has instead the single sentence, *Sir, you are not ignorant of what excellence Laertes is at his weapon*   125. *do't* (Johnson); Q₂ *to't*; not in F   152-3. *I knew* . . . *done*; not in F   160. *impawned* (Wilson, N.S.); F *impon'd*; not in Q₂   183. *comply* (F); Q₂ *so*   184. *bevy* (F); Q₂ *breede*   188. *fanned and winnowed* (Warburton); Q₂ *prophaned and trennowed*; F *fond and winnowed*   202. *this wager* (F); not in Q₂   216. *knows aught of what he leaves* (Johnson); Q₁, Q₂ *man of ought he leaues, knows what is't*; F *man ha's ought of what he leaues*   233. *Sir, in this audience* (F); not in Q₂   242. *precedent* (Johnson); Q₁, Q₂, F *president*   265. *union* (F); Q₂ *Vnice*   344. *shall live* (F); Q₂ *shall I leave*   382. *forced* (F); Q₂ *for no*   391. *on* (F); Q₂ *no*

The Tragical
History of Hamlet,
Prince of Denmark

[DRAMATIS PERSONAE

CLAUDIUS, *King of Denmark*

HAMLET, *son to the former and nephew to the present King*

POLONIUS, *Lord Chamberlain*

HORATIO, *friend to Hamlet*

LAERTES, *son to Polonius*

VOLTEMAND
CORNELIUS
ROSENCRANTZ
GUILDENSTERN   *courtiers*
OSRIC
A GENTLEMAN

A PRIEST

MARCELLUS
BERNARDO   *officers*

FRANCISCO, *a soldier*

REYNALDO, *servant to Polonius*

PLAYERS

TWO CLOWNS, *grave-diggers*

FORTINBRAS, *Prince of Norway*

A NORWEGIAN CAPTAIN

ENGLISH AMBASSADORS

GERTRUDE, *Queen of Denmark, and mother to Hamlet*

OPHELIA, *daughter to Polonius*

GHOST OF HAMLET'S FATHER

Lords, Ladies, Officers, Soldiers, Sailors,
Messengers, and Attendants

Scene: Denmark]

ACT 1

Scene 1. [*Elsinore. A platform before the castle.*]

Enter Bernardo and Francisco, two sentinels.

BERNARDO. Who's there?
FRANCISCO. Nay, answer me. Stand and unfold yourself.
BERNARDO. Long live the king!
FRANCISCO. Bernardo?
BERNARDO. He. 5
FRANCISCO. You come most carefully upon your hour.
BERNARDO. 'Tis now struck twelve. Get thee to bed,
    Francisco.
FRANCISCO. For this relief much thanks. 'Tis bitter cold,
  And I am sick at heart.
BERNARDO. Have you had quiet guard?
FRANCISCO.   Not a mouse stirring. 10
BERNARDO. Well, good night.
  If you do meet Horatio and Marcellus,
  The rivals of my watch, bid them make haste.

Enter Horatio and Marcellus.

FRANCISCO. I think I hear them. Stand, ho! Who is there?
HORATIO. Friends to this ground.
MARCELLUS.   And liegemen to the Dane. 15
FRANCISCO. Give you good night.
MARCELLUS.   O, farewell, honest soldier!
  Who hath relieved you?
FRANCISCO.   Bernardo hath my place.
  Give you good night.   *Exit Francisco.*
MARCELLUS.   Holla, Bernardo!

1.1.2. *me* emphasized (it is the prerogative of the sentinel on guard
to challenge the newcomer) 13. *rivals* sharers 15. *Dane* i.e. King of
Denmark

BERNARDO.   Say –
   What, is Horatio there?
HORATIO.   A piece of him.
BERNARDO. Welcome, Horatio. Welcome, good Marcellus. 20
HORATIO. What, has this thing appeared again to-night?
BERNARDO. I have seen nothing.
MARCELLUS. Horatio says 'tis but our fantasy,
   And will not let belief take hold of him
   Touching this dreaded sight twice seen of us. 25
   Therefore I have entreated him along
   With us to watch the minutes of this night,
   That if again this apparition come,
   He may approve our eyes and speak to it.
HORATIO. Tush, tush, 'twill not appear.
BERNARDO.   Sit down awhile, 30
   And let us once again assail your ears,
   That are so fortified against our story,
   What we have two nights seen.
HORATIO.   Well, sit we down,
   And let us hear Bernardo speak of this.
BERNARDO. Last night of all, 35
   When yond same star that's westward from the pole
   Had made his course t' illume that part of heaven
   Where now it burns, Marcellus and myself,
   The bell then beating one –

Enter Ghost.

MARCELLUS. Peace, break thee off. Look where it comes
   again! 40
BERNARDO. In the same figure like the king that's dead.
MARCELLUS. Thou art a scholar; speak to it, Horatio.
BERNARDO. Looks it not like the king? Mark it, Horatio.
HORATIO. Most like. It harrows me with fear and wonder.
BERNARDO. It would be spoke to.
MARCELLUS.   Speak to it, Horatio. 45

23. *fantasy* imagination 29. *approve* verify, confirm 36. *pole* pole-star
41. *figure* shape 42. *scholar* (exorcisms against evil spirits were composed in Latin) 44. *harrows* afflicts, distresses 45. *It . . . spoke to*
(ghosts could not speak until spoken to)

HORATIO. What art thou that usurp'st this time of night
    Together with that fair and warlike form
    In which the majesty of buried Denmark
    Did sometimes march? By heaven I charge thee, speak!
MARCELLUS. It is offended.
BERNARDO.   See, it stalks away.   50
HORATIO. Stay! Speak, speak! I charge thee, speak!
                                   Exit Ghost.

MARCELLUS. 'Tis gone and will not answer.
BERNARDO. How now, Horatio! You tremble and look
    pale.
    Is not this something more than fantasy?
    What think you on't?   55
HORATIO. Before my God, I might not this believe
    Without the sensible and true avouch
    Of mine own eyes.
MARCELLUS.   Is it not like the king?
HORATIO. As thou art to thyself.
    Such was the very armour he had on   60
    When he the ambitious Norway combated.
    So frowned he once when, in an angry parle,
    He smote the sledded Polacks on the ice.
    'Tis strange.
MARCELLUS. Thus twice before, and jump at this dead
    hour,   65
    With martial stalk hath he gone by our watch.
HORATIO. In what particular thought to work I know not,
    But in the gross and scope of mine opinion,
    This bodes some strange eruption to our state.
MARCELLUS. Good now, sit down, and tell me he that
    knows,   70
    Why this same strict and most observant watch
    So nightly toils the subject of the land,

---

48. *Denmark* i.e. King of Denmark   49. *sometimes* formerly   57. *sensible . . . avouch* evidence of the senses; i.e. "seeing is believing" 61. *Norway* i.e. King of Norway   62. *parle* parley   63. *sledded Polacks* Polish soldiers riding on sleds   65. *jump* exactly   *dead* precise   68. *gross and scope* (hendiadys) general drift   72. *toils* burdens, causes to toil   *subject* people

And why such daily cast of brazen cannon
And foreign mart for implements of war;
Why such impress of shipwrights, whose sore task   75
Does not divide the Sunday from the week.
What might be toward that this sweaty haste
Doth make the night joint-labourer with the day?
Who is't that can inform me?

HORATIO.   That can I.
At least, the whisper goes so. Our last king,   80
Whose image even but now appeared to us,
Was as you know by Fortinbras of Norway,
Thereto pricked on by a most emulate pride,
Dared to the combat; in which our valiant Hamlet
(For so this side of our known world esteemed him)   85
Did slay this Fortinbras; who by a sealed compact
Well ratified by law and heraldry,
Did forfeit, with his life, all those his lands
Which he stood seized of, to the conqueror;
Against the which a moiety competent   90
Was gagèd by our king; which had returned
To the inheritance of Fortinbras,
Had he been vanquisher; as, by the same comart
And carriage of the article designed,
His fell to Hamlet. Now, sir, young Fortinbras,   95
Of unimprovèd mettle hot and full,
Hath in the skirts of Norway here and there
Sharked up a list of lawless resolutes
For food and diet to some enterprise
That hath a stomach in't; which is no other,   100
As it doth well appear unto our state,

74. *mart* trade 75. *impress* conscription 77. *toward* pending 83.
emulate envious, ambitious 85. *this . . . world* the whole western
world 87. *heraldry* code of rules governing chivalric combat 89.
seized possessed (i.e. of those lands held in his own right rather than
as King) 90. *moiety competent* sufficient or comparable portion, an
equal amount 91. *gagèd* pledged, wagered 93. *comart* mutual agreement 94. *carriage* intent, import *article* term of the agreement 96.
unimprovèd unexercised; which has not been proved, i.e. tested 97.
skirts outlying parts (cf. "outskirts") 98. *Sharked up* collected hap-
hazardly (the shark's appetite was reputed to be both voracious and
undiscriminating) 100. *stomach* challenge (of adventure)

But to recover of us by strong hand
And terms compulsatory, those foresaid lands
So by his father lost; and this, I take it,
Is the main motive of our preparations,   105
The source of this our watch, and the chief head
Of this post-haste and romage in the land.
BERNARDO. I think it be no other but e'en so.
   Well may it sort that this portentous figure
   Comes armèd through our watch so like the king   110
   That was and is the question of these wars.
HORATIO. A mote it is to trouble the mind's eye.
   In the most high and palmy state of Rome,
   A little ere the mightiest Julius fell,
   The graves stood tenantless, and the sheeted dead   115
   Did squeak and gibber in the Roman streets;
   As stars with trains of fire, and dews of blood,
   Disasters in the sun; and the moist star,
   Upon whose influence Neptune's empire stands,
   Was sick almost to doomsday with eclipse.   120
   And even the like precurse of feared events,
   As harbingers preceding still the fates
   And prologue to the omen coming on,
   Have heaven and earth together demonstrated
   Unto our climatures and countrymen.   125

Enter Ghost.

   But soft, behold, lo where it comes again!
   I'll cross it though it blast me. – Stay, illusion!
                               Spreads his arms.

106. *head* source, fountainhead   107. *romage* (i) rummage, turning of things upside down as in a search, (ii) uproar or turmoil   109. *sort* be fitting   112. *mote* speck of dust (probably an echo of "the mote that is in thy brother's eye"; Matt. 7:3)   115. *sheeted* shrouded   118. *Disasters* bad omens (from the Latin for "contrary star")   *moist star* the moon, which governs the tides   119. *Neptune's empire* the seas   120. *almost to doomsday* (an allusion to the prophecy that at Christ's second coming "the moon shall not give her light"; Matt. 24:29. See also Luke 21:25-7)   121. *precurse* foreshadowing   122. *harbingers* forerunners   *still* always   123. *omen coming on* the foreshadowed event   125. *climatures* regions   127. *cross it* (i) cross its path, and/or (ii) make a figure of the cross by spreading the arms   *though . . . me* (to "cross" the path of a demon was to risk falling under its spell)

If thou hast any sound or use of voice,
Speak to me.
If there be any good thing to be done,   130
That may to thee do ease, and grace to me,
Speak to me.
If thou art privy to thy country's fate,
Which happily foreknowing may avoid,
O, speak!   135
Or if thou hast uphoarded in thy life
Extorted treasure in the womb of earth,
For which, they say, you spirits oft walk in death,
                                             The cock crows.

Speak of it. Stay, and speak. Stop it, Marcellus!
MARCELLUS. Shall I strike at it with my partisan?   140
HORATIO. Do, if it will not stand.
BERNARDO.   'Tis here.
HORATIO.   'Tis here.
MARCELLUS. 'Tis gone.   *Exit Ghost.*
We do it wrong, being so majestical,
To offer it the show of violence;
For it is as the air, invulnerable,   145
And our vain blows malicious mockery.
BERNARDO. It was about to speak when the cock crew.
HORATIO. And then it started like a guilty thing
Upon a fearful summons. I have heard
The cock, that is the trumpet to the morn,   150
Doth with his lofty and shrill-sounding throat
Awake the god of day, and at his warning,
Whether in sea or fire, in earth or air,
Th' extravagant and erring spirit hies
To his confine; and of the truth herein   155
This present object made probation.
MARCELLUS. It faded on the crowing of the cock.
Some say that ever 'gainst that season comes

133. *art privy to* have secret knowledge of   134. *happily* haply, perhaps
140. *partisan* long-handled, broad-bladed spear with one or more
cutting-edged projections 154. *extravagant* wandering abroad *erring*
straying, perhaps with the connotation of "sinning" 156. *made probation* gave proof 158. *'gainst* immediately before

Wherein our Saviour's birth is celebrated,
This bird of dawning singeth all night long,   160
And then, they say, no spirit dare stir abroad,
The nights are wholesome, then no planets strike,
No fairy takes, nor witch hath power to charm,
So hallowed and so gracious is that time.
HORATIO. So have I heard and do in part believe it.   165
But look, the morn in russet mantle clad
Walks o'er the dew of yon high eastward hill.
Break we our watch up, and by my advice
Let us impart what we have seen to-night
Unto young Hamlet, for upon my life   170
This spirit, dumb to us, will speak to him.
Do you consent we shall acquaint him with it,
As needful in our loves, fitting our duty?
MARCELLUS. Let's do't, I pray, and I this morning know
Where we shall find him most conveniently.   *Exeunt.* 175

Scene 2. [*A room of state in the castle.*]

Flourish. Enter Claudius King of Denmark, Gertrude
the Queen, Councillors [including] Polonius, and his
son Laertes, Hamlet, cum aliis [including Voltemand
and Cornelius].

KING. Though yet of Hamlet our dear brother's death
The memory be green, and that it us befitted
To bear our hearts in grief, and our whole kingdom
To be contracted in one brow of woe,
Yet so far hath discretion fought with nature   5
That we with wisest sorrow think on him,
Together with remembrance of ourselves.
Therefore our sometime sister, now our queen,

162. *wholesome* healthy (night air was commonly believed to be a
source of contagion) *strike* exert bad influence 163. *takes* bewitches
164. *gracious* full of divine grace
  1.2.8. *sometime* former

Th' imperial jointress of this warlike state,
Have we, as 'twere with a defeated joy,   10
With an auspicious and a dropping eye,
With mirth in funeral, and with dirge in marriage,
In equal scale weighing delight and dole,
Taken to wife; nor have we herein barred
Your better wisdoms, which have freely gone   15
With this affair along. For all, our thanks.
Now follows that you know: young Fortinbras,
Holding a weak supposal of our worth,
Or thinking by our late dear brother's death
Our state to be disjoint and out of frame,   20
Colleaguèd with this dream of his advantage,
He hath not failed to pester us with message
Importing the surrender of those lands
Lost by his father, with all bonds of law,
To our most valiant brother. So much for him.   25
Now for ourself, and for this time of meeting,
Thus much the business is: we have here writ
To Norway, uncle of young Fortinbras –
Who, impotent and bedrid, scarcely hears
Of this his nephew's purpose – to suppress   30
His further gait herein, in that the levies,
The lists, and full proportions are all made
Out of his subject; and we here dispatch
You, good Cornelius, and you, Voltemand,
For bearers of this greeting to old Norway,   35
Giving to you no further personal power
To business with the king, more than the scope
Of these delated articles allow.
Farewell, and let your haste commend your duty.

CORNELIUS. ⎫
VOLTEMAND. ⎭ In that, and all things will we show our duty. 40

KING. We doubt it nothing; heartily farewell.
               Exeunt Voltemand and Cornelius.

9. *jointress* widow holding a life interest in her husband's estate 20. *frame* order 21. *Colleaguèd* combined (the reference is to "supposal", 1. 18) 31. *gait* proceeding *levies* conscripted forces 32. *lists* catalogue of those enlisted *proportions* (i) forces, and/or (ii) their equipment and supplies 33. *subject* subjects, people 37. *business* negotiate 38. *delated* stated, set forth

And now, Laertes, what's the news with you?
You told us of some suit. What is't, Laertes?
You cannot speak of reason to the Dane
And lose your voice. What wouldst thou beg, Laertes,   45
That shall not be my offer, not thy asking?
The head is not more native to the heart,
The hand more instrumental to the mouth,
Than is the throne of Denmark to thy father.
What wouldst thou have, Laertes?
LAERTES.   My dread lord,   50
Your leave and favour to return to France,
From whence, though willingly I came to Denmark
To show my duty in your coronation,
Yet now I must confess, that duty done,
My thoughts and wishes bend again toward France,   55
And bow them to your gracious leave and pardon.
KING. Have you your father's leave? What says Polonius?
POLONIUS. He hath, my lord, wrung from me my slow
    leave
By laboursome petition, and at last
Upon his will I sealed my hard consent.   60
I do beseech you give him leave to go.
KING. Take thy fair hour, Laertes. Time be thine,
And thy best graces spend it at thy will.
But now, my cousin Hamlet, and my son –
HAMLET [*aside*]. A little more than kin, and less than
    kind.   65
KING. How is it that the clouds still hang on you?
HAMLET. Not so, my lord. I am too much in the sun.
QUEEN. Good Hamlet, cast thy nighted colour off,
And let thine eye look like a friend on Denmark.
Do not for ever with thy vailèd lids   70
Seek for thy noble father in the dust.

44. *Dane* i.e. King of Denmark   45. *lose your voice* waste your words,
speak in vain   47. *native* naturally linked (in the process of decision)
48. *instrumental* serviceable (in sustaining health – of body or state)
60. *hard* reluctant   64. *cousin* any kinsman outside the immediate
family   65. *kin* blood relation (Claudius is now related to Hamlet both
by blood and by marriage)   *kind* (i) generous, affectionate, (ii)
natural, i.e. characteristic of the human species and of behaviour
normal between kinsmen   70. *vailèd* downcast

Thou know'st 'tis common – all that lives must die,
Passing through nature to eternity.
HAMLET. Ay, madam, it is common.
QUEEN.   If it be,
Why seems it so particular with thee?   75
HAMLET. Seems, madam? Nay, it is. I know not "seems".
'Tis not alone my inky cloak, good mother,
Nor customary suits of solemn black,
Nor windy suspiration of forced breath,
No, nor the fruitful river in the eye,   80
Nor the dejected haviour of the visage,
Together with all forms, moods, shapes of grief,
That can denote me truly. These indeed seem,
For they are actions that a man might play,
But I have that within which passes show –   85
These but the trappings and the suits of woe.
KING. 'Tis sweet and commendable in your nature,
       Hamlet,
To give these mourning duties to your father,
But you must know your father lost a father,
That father lost, lost his, and the survivor bound   90
In filial obligation for some term
To do obsequious sorrow. But to persever
In obstinate condolement is a course
Of impious stubbornness. 'Tis unmanly grief.
It shows a will most incorrect to heaven,   95
A heart unfortified, a mind impatient,
An understanding simple and unschooled.
For what we know must be, and is as common
As any the most vulgar thing to sense,
Why should we in our peevish opposition   100
Take it to heart? Fie, 'tis a fault to heaven,

72. *common* i.e. the common lot of humanity 73. *nature* life in this
world 75. *particular* individual, especially personal 79. *suspiration
. . . breath* heart-rending sighs 81. *haviour* behaviour, i.e. expression
87. *commendable* (the stress is on the first syllable) 92. *do obsequious
sorrow* manifest grief by observing the ceremony of mourning, i.e. the
"obsequies" 93. *condolement* grieving 95. *incorrect* unchastened, i.e.
rebellious 97. *simple* foolish, naïve 99. *vulgar* ordinary

A fault against the dead, a fault to nature,
To reason most absurd, whose common theme
Is death of fathers, and who still hath cried,
From the first corse till he that died to-day,   105
"This must be so". We pray you throw to earth
This unprevailing woe, and think of us
As of a father, for let the world take note
You are the most immediate to our throne,
And with no less nobility of love   110
Than that which dearest father bears his son
Do I impart toward you. For your intent
In going back to school in Wittenberg,
It is most retrograde to our desire,
And we beseech you, bend you to remain   115
Here in the cheer and comfort of our eye,
Our chiefest courtier, cousin, and our son.
QUEEN. Let not thy mother lose her prayers, Hamlet.
I pray thee stay with us, go not to Wittenberg.
HAMLET. I shall in all my best obey you, madam.   120
KING. Why, 'tis a loving and a fair reply.
Be as ourself in Denmark. Madam, come.
This gentle and unforced accord of Hamlet
Sits smiling to my heart, in grace whereof,
No jocund health that Denmark drinks to-day   125
But the great cannon to the clouds shall tell,
And the king's rouse the heaven shall bruit again,
Respeaking earthly thunder. Come away.

        Flourish. Exeunt all but Hamlet.

HAMLET. O, that this too too sallied flesh would melt,
Thaw, and resolve itself into a dew,   130
Or that the Everlasting had not fixed
His canon 'gainst self-slaughter. O God, God,
How weary, stale, flat, and unprofitable
Seem to me all the uses of this world!

105. *corse* corpse (the "first corse", Abel's, is much on Claudius' mind;
see 3.3.37-8)   109. *most immediate* i.e. next in succession   114. *retrograde* contrary   127. *rouse* carouse, the draining of the cup in one
draught   *bruit again* echo   132. *canon* decree   134. *uses* (i) "customs",
(ii) "interest", commercially speaking (word play with "unprofitable")

Fie on't, ah, fie! 'tis an unweeded garden   135
That grows to seed. Things rank and gross in nature
Possess it merely. That it should come to this,
But two months dead, nay, not so much, not two.
So excellent a king, that was to this
Hyperion to a satyr, so loving to my mother,   140‡‡
That he might not beteem the winds of heaven
Visit her face too roughly. Heaven and earth,
Must I remember? Why, she would hang on him
As if increase of appetite had grown
By what it fed on, and yet, within a month –   145
Let me not think on't. Frailty, thy name is woman –
A little month, or ere those shoes were old
With which she followed my poor father's body
Like Niobe, all tears, why she, even she –   ‡
O God, a beast that wants discourse of reason   150
Would have mourned longer – married with my uncle,
My father's brother, but no more like my father
Than I to Hercules. Within a month,
Ere yet the salt of most unrighteous tears
Had left the flushing in her gallèd eyes,   155
She married. O, most wicked speed, to post
With such dexterity to incestuous sheets!   ‡
It is not, nor it cannot come to good.
But break my heart, for I must hold my tongue.

Enter Horatio, Marcellus, and Bernardo.

HORATIO. Hail to your lordship!
HAMLET.   I am glad to see you well.   160
   Horatio – or I do forget myself.
HORATIO. The same, my lord, and your poor servant ever.
HAMLET. Sir, my good friend, I'll change that name with
   you.
   And what make you from Wittenberg, Horatio?   ‡
   Marcellus?   165

137. *merely* wholly 140. *Hyperion* the sun-god 141. *beteem* permit
150. *wants* lacks *discourse of reason* the faculty of logical reasoning
from premises to conclusions 155. *gallèd* sore from rubbing 163.
change exchange (the word between us is "friend", not "servant")
164. *make you from* are you doing away from

MARCELLUS. My good lord!
HAMLET. I am very glad to see you. [*To Bernardo*] Good
    even, sir. –
  But what, in faith, make you from Wittenberg?
HORATIO. A truant disposition, good my lord.
HAMLET. I would not hear your enemy say so,   170
  Nor shall you do my ear that violence
  To make it truster of your own report
  Against yourself. I know you are no truant.
  But what is your affair in Elsinore?
  We'll teach you to drink deep ere you depart.   175 ‡
HORATIO. My lord, I came to see your father's funeral.
HAMLET. I prithee do not mock me, fellow-student,
  I think it was to see my mother's wedding.
HORATIO. Indeed, my lord, it followed hard upon.
HAMLET. Thrift, thrift, Horatio. The funeral baked-meats   180 ‡
  Did coldly furnish forth the marriage tables.
  Would I had met my dearest foe in heaven
  Or ever I had seen that day, Horatio!
  My father – methinks I see my father.
HORATIO. Where, my lord?
HAMLET.   In my mind's eye, Horatio.   185
HORATIO. I saw him once, 'a was a goodly king.
HAMLET. 'A was a man, take him for all in all,
  I shall not look upon his like again.
HORATIO. My lord, I think I saw him yesternight.
HAMLET. Saw who?   190
HORATIO. My lord, the king your father.
HAMLET.   The king my father?
HORATIO. Season your admiration for a while
  With an attent ear till I may deliver
  Upon the witness of these gentlemen
  This marvel to you.
HAMLET.   For God's love, let me hear!   195

---

174. *affair* business   179. *hard* closely   182. *dearest* most costly, i.e.
damaging or dangerous; hence, worst   186. *goodly* handsome   187. *'A
was . . . all* he was in every way what a man should be   192. *Season*
temper, moderate, or possibly, "Keep it until you really need it" (as
food is pickled in brine)   *admiration* amazement

HORATIO. Two nights together had these gentlemen,
  Marcellus and Bernardo, on their watch
  In the dead vast and middle of the night
  Been thus encountered. A figure like your father,
  Armèd at point exactly, cap-a-pe,   200
  Appears before them, and with solemn march
  Goes slow and stately by them. Thrice he walked
  By their oppressed and fear-surprisèd eyes
  Within his truncheon's length, whilst they, distilled
  Almost to jelly with the act of fear,   205
  Stand dumb and speak not to him. This to me
  In dreadful secrecy impart they did,
  And I with them the third night kept the watch,
  Where, as they had delivered, both in time,
  Form of the thing, each word made true and good,   210
  The apparition comes. I knew your father.
  These hands are not more like.
HAMLET.   But where was this?
MARCELLUS. My lord, upon the platform where we watch.
HAMLET. Did you not speak to it?
HORATIO.   My lord, I did,
  But answer made it none. Yet once methought   215
  It lifted up it head and did address
  Itself to motion, like as it would speak;
  But even then the morning cock crew loud,
  And at the sound it shrunk in haste away
  And vanished from our sight.
HAMLET.   'Tis very strange.   220
HORATIO. As I do live, my honoured lord, 'tis true,
  And we did think it writ down in our duty
  To let you know of it.
HAMLET.   Indeed, sirs, but
  This troubles me. Hold you the watch to-night?
ALL. We do, my lord.

200. *at point exactly* in every particular *cap-a-pe* from top to toe
203. *oppressed* overwhelmed 204. *truncheon* commander's baton *distilled* dissolved 205. *act* action 207. *dreadful* solemn 211. *knew*
(Dover Wilson suggests "recognized" which eliminates the contradiction
with "I saw him once", 1. 186) 216. *it* i.e. its ("it" was frequently
used as a possessive form) 217. *like as* as if 224. *Hold* keep

HAMLET.   Armed, say you?
ALL.   Armed, my lord.   225
HAMLET. From top to toe?
ALL.   My lord, from head to foot.
HAMLET. Then saw you not his face.
HORATIO. O yes, my lord, he wore his beaver up.
HAMLET. What, looked he frowningly?
HORATIO. A countenance more in sorrow than in anger.   230
HAMLET. Pale or red?
HORATIO. Nay, very pale.
HAMLET.   And fixed his eyes upon you?
HORATIO. Most constantly.
HAMLET.   I would I had been there.
HORATIO. It would have much amazed you.
HAMLET.   Very like.
   Stayed it long?
HORATIO.   While one with moderate haste might tell
   a hundred.   235
BOTH. Longer, longer.
HORATIO.   Not when I saw't.
HAMLET. His beard was grizzled, no?
HORATIO. It was as I have seen it in his life,
   A sable silvered.
HAMLET.   I will watch to-night.
   Perchance 'twill walk again.
HORATIO.   I warrant it will.   240
HAMLET. If it assume my noble father's person,
   I'll speak to it though hell itself should gape
   And bid me hold my peace. I pray you all,
   If you have hitherto concealed this sight,
   Let it be tenable in your silence still,   245
   And whatsomever else shall hap to-night,
   Give it an understanding but no tongue.
   I will requite your loves. So fare you well.
   Upon the platform 'twixt eleven and twelve
   I'll visit you.

228. *beaver* the helmet's movable face-guard 235. *tell* count 239.
sable silvered dark brown mingled with white 245. *tenable* keepable
(i.e. keep quiet about it)

ALL.   Our duty to your honour.   250

HAMLET. Your loves, as mine to you. Farewell.

                        Exeunt [all but Hamlet].

My father's spirit in arms? All is not well.

I doubt some foul play. Would the night were come!

Till then sit still, my soul. Foul deeds will rise,

Though all the earth o'erwhelm them, to men's eyes.   255

                               Exit.

Scene 3

Enter Laertes and Ophelia his sister.

LAERTES. My necessaries are embarked. Farewell.

And, sister, as the winds give benefit

And convoy is assistant, do not sleep,

But let me hear from you.

OPHELIA.   Do you doubt that?

LAERTES. For Hamlet, and the trifling of his favour,   5

Hold it a fashion and a toy in blood,

A violet in the youth of primy nature,

Forward, not permanent, sweet, not lasting,

The perfume and suppliance of a minute,

No more.

OPHELIA.   No more but so?

LAERTES.   Think it no more.   10

For nature crescent does not grow alone

In thews and bulk, but as this temple waxes

The inward service of the mind and soul

Grows wide withal. Perhaps he loves you now,

253. *doubt . . . play* suspect there has been some dirty work going on – not necessarily murder   254. *Foul . . . rise* (probably referring to two proverbial expressions "murder will out", and "truth crushed to earth will rise again")

1.3.3. *convoy is assistant* means of conveyance is available   4. *But . . . you* without letting me hear from you; i.e. write every day   5. *trifling . . . favour* trifling attentions he has been paying you   6. *fashion* passing fancy   *toy in blood* casual attraction   7. *primy* springtime   8. *Forward* early   9. *suppliance* pastime   11. *crescent* in the process of growth   12. *thews* sinews, strength   *temple* body, as the temple of the soul (see I Cor. 6:19)   *waxes* grows in bulk   14. *withal* along with it

And now no soil nor cautel doth besmirch   15
The virtue of his will, but you must fear,
His greatness weighed, his will is not his own,
For he himself is subject to his birth.
He may not, as unvalued persons do,
Carve for himself, for on his choice depends   20
The safety and health of this whole state,
And therefore must his choice be circumscribed
Unto the voice and yielding of that body
Whereof he is the head. Then if he says he loves you,
It fits your wisdom so far to believe it   25
As he in his particular act and place
May give his saying deed, which is no further
Than the main voice of Denmark goes withal.
Then weigh what loss your honour may sustain
If with too credent ear you list his songs,   30
Or lose your heart, or your chaste treasure open
To his unmastered importunity.
Fear it, Ophelia, fear it, my dear sister,
And keep you in the rear of your affection,
Out of the shot and danger of desire.   35
The chariest maid is prodigal enough
If she unmask her beauty to the moon.
Virtue itself scapes not calumnious strokes.
The canker galls the infants of the spring
Too oft before their buttons be disclosed,   40
And in the morn and liquid dew of youth
Contagious blastments are most imminent.

15. *cautel* deceit   16. *virtue* quality, power, perhaps with the connotation of worthiness   *will* desire   *fear* be wary   17. *weighed* considered
18. *subject* (an implied oxymoron with "prince")   20. *Carve for himself* pick and choose as he likes   23. *voice and yielding* formal assent, vote and acquiescence   25. *wisdom* prudence, discretion   27. *May . . . deed* may perform what he promises   28. *main voice* public opinion
30. *credent* trusting, credulous   *list* listen to   34. *keep . . . affection* i.e. don't get carried away by your feelings   36. *chariest* most sparing of her favours, most circumspect   37. *unmask . . . moon* (in classical myth, the moon is ruled by Diana, Goddess of Chastity)   38. *calumnious strokes* slander, malicious gossip   39. *canker* canker-worm or caterpillar which attacks the rose in the bud   *galls* injures   40. *buttons be disclosed* buds have opened   42. *blastments* blights

Be wary then; best safety lies in fear.
Youth to itself rebels, though none else near.
OPHELIA. I shall the effect of this good lesson keep　　　45
As watchman to my heart. But, good my brother,
Do not as some ungracious pastors do,
Show me the steep and thorny way to heaven,
Whiles like a puffed and reckless libertine
Himself the primrose path of dalliance treads　　　50 ‡
And recks not his own rede.
LAERTES.　　　　　　　　　O, fear me not!

Enter Polonius.

I stay too long. But here my father comes.
A double blessing is a double grace;
Occasion smiles upon a second leave.
POLONIUS. Yet here, Laertes? Aboard, aboard, for shame!　　55
The wind sits in the shoulder of your sail,
And you are stayed for. There – my blessing with thee,
And these few precepts in thy memory　　　　　　‡
Look thou charácter. Give thy thoughts no tongue,
Nor any unproportioned thought his act.　　　60
Be thou familiar, but by no means vulgar.
Those friends thou hast, and their adoption tried,
Grapple them unto thy soul with hoops of steel;
But do not dull thy palm with entertainment
Of each new-hatched, unfledgèd comrade. Beware　　　65
Of entrance to a quarrel, but being in,
Bear't that th' opposèd may beware of thee.
Give every man thy ear, but few thy voice;
Take each man's censure, but reserve thy judgement.

44. *Youth . . . near* The headstrong passions of youth overcome one's better judgement, even without an external tempter 49. *puffed* bloated *libertine* loose-living person 50. *dalliance* playing around 51. *recks . . . rede* doesn't heed his own advice *fear me not* don't worry about me 53. *double* (Laertes has already said goodbye to his father) 54. *Occasion* opportunity *leave* leave-taking 59. *charácter* inscribe (the stress is on the second syllable) 60. *unproportioned* exaggerated; contrary to good manners, reason, or the proprieties of the situation 61. *vulgar* common 62. *tried* tested 64. *dull thy palm* give the hand of fellowship undiscriminatingly 67. *Bear't that* acquit yourself in such a way that 69. *Take . . . censure* listen to the opinions of others

Costly thy habit as thy purse can buy,   70
But not expressed in fancy; rich not gaudy,
For the apparel oft proclaims the man,
And they in France of the best rank and station
Are most select and generous, chief in that.
Neither a borrower nor a lender be,   75
For loan oft loses both itself and friend,
And borrowing dulls th' edge of husbandry.
This above all, to thine own self be true,
And it must follow as the night the day
Thou canst not then be false to any man.   80
Farewell. My blessing season this in thee!
LAERTES. Most humbly do I take my leave, my lord.
POLONIUS. The time invites you. Go, your servants tend.
LAERTES. Farewell, Ophelia, and remember well
  What I have said to you.
OPHELIA.   'Tis in my memory locked,   85
  And you yourself shall keep the key of it.
LAERTES. Farewell.   *Exit Laertes.*
POLONIUS. What is't, Ophelia, he hath said to you?
OPHELIA. So please you, something touching the Lord
    Hamlet.
POLONIUS. Marry, well bethought.   90 ‡
  'Tis told me he hath very oft of late
  Given private time to you, and you yourself
  Have of your audience been most free and bounteous.
  If it be so — as so 'tis put on me,
  And that in way of caution — I must tell you,   95
  You do not understand yourself so clearly
  As it behoves my daughter and your honour.
  What is between you? Give me up the truth.
OPHELIA. He hath, my lord, of late made many tenders   ‡
  Of his affection to me.   100
POLONIUS. Affection? Pooh! You speak like a green girl,
  Unsifted in such perilous circumstance.
  Do you believe his tenders, as you call them?

74. *chief* chiefly   77. *husbandry* thrift   81. *season* preserve   83. *tend*
wait   90. *Marry* by Mary   94. *put on me* put to me   99. *tenders* offers
102. *Unsifted* untried, inexperienced

OPHELIA. I do not know, my lord, what I should think.
POLONIUS. Marry, I will teach you. Think yourself a baby   105
   That you have ta'en these tenders for true pay
   Which are not sterling. Tender yourself more dearly,
   Or (not to crack the wind of the poor phrase,
   Running it thus) you'll tender me a fool.
OPHELIA. My lord, he hath importuned me with love   110
   In honourable fashion.
POLONIUS. Ay, fashion you may call it. Go to, go to.
OPHELIA. And hath given countenance to his speech,
    my lord,
   With almost all the holy vows of heaven.
POLONIUS. Ay, springes to catch woodcocks. I do know,   115
   When the blood burns, how prodigal the soul
   Lends the tongue vows. These blazes, daughter,
   Giving more light than heat, extinct in both
   Even in their promise, as it is a-making,
   You must not take for fire. From this time   120
   Be something scanter of your maiden presence.
   Set your entreatments at a higher rate
   Than a command to parley. For Lord Hamlet,
   Believe so much in him that he is young,
   And with a larger tether may he walk   125
   Than may be given you. In few, Ophelia,
   Do not believe his vows, for they are brokers,
   Not of that dye which their investments show,
   But mere implorators of unholy suits,
   Breathing like sanctified and pious bawds,   130
   The better to beguile. This is for all:
   I would not, in plain terms, from this time forth
   Have you so slander any moment leisure
   As to give words or talk with the Lord Hamlet.
   Look to't, I charge you. Come your ways.   135
OPHELIA. I shall obey, my lord.   *Exeunt.*

110. *importuned* persistently courted   111. *fashion* way, manner   112. *fashion* passing fancy (as Laertes had used the word in l. 6)   115. *springes . . . woodcocks* snares set for proverbially foolish birds   116. *prodigal* prodigally, extravagantly   126. *In few* in a few words   133. *slander* misuse   *moment* i.e. moment's   135. *Come your ways* Come along

[Scene 4. *The platform before the castle.*]

Enter Hamlet, Horatio, and Marcellus.

HAMLET. The air bites shrewdly; it is very cold.

HORATIO. It is a nipping and an eager air.

HAMLET. What hour now?

HORATIO.   I think it lacks of twelve.

MARCELLUS. No, it is struck.

HORATIO. Indeed? I heard it not. It then draws near the   5
    season
Wherein the spirit held his wont to walk.
       A flourish of trumpets, and two pieces go off.
What does this mean, my lord?

HAMLET. The king doth wake to-night and takes his
    rouse,
Keeps wassail, and the swagg'ring up-spring reels,
And as he drains his draughts of Rhenish down,   10
The kettledrum and trumpet thus bray out
The triumph of his pledge.

HORATIO.   Is it a custom?

HAMLET. Ay, marry, is't,
But to my mind, though I am native here
And to the manner born, it is a custom   15
More honoured in the breach than the observance.
This heavy-headed revel east and west
Makes us traduced and taxed of other nations.
They clepe us drunkards, and with swinish phrase
Soil our addition, and indeed it takes   20
From our achievements, though performed at height,
The pith and marrow of our attribute.
So oft it chances in particular men,
That for some vicious mole of nature in them,

<hr>

1.4.1. *shrewdly* sharply 2. *eager* keen-edged 3. *lacks of* is a little
before 5. *season* time 6. *held . . . walk* was in the habit of appearing
8. *doth wake* is staying up late 9. *Keeps wassail* is having a wild
party *swagg'ring . . . reels* staggers through the steps of a German
dance 10. *Rhenish* Rhine wine 12. *pledge* toast 18. *traduced . . . of*
unfairly criticized and censured by 19. *clepe* call *swinish phrase* the
epithet of "swine" (i.e. they call us "pigs") 20. *addition* name or
title; here, in the sense of "good name" 22. *attribute* reputation 24.
mole blemish, defect

As in their birth, wherein they are not guilty   25
(Since nature cannot choose his origin),
By the o'ergrowth of some complexion,
Oft breaking down the pales and forts of reason,
Or by some habit that too much o'er-leavens
The form of plausive manners – that these men,   30
Carrying, I say, the stamp of one defect,
Being nature's livery or fortune's star,
His virtues else, be they as pure as grace,
As infinite as man may undergo,
Shall in the general censure take corruption   35
From that particular fault. The dram of evil
Doth all the noble substance often doubt
To his own scandal.

Enter Ghost.

HORATIO.   Look, my lord, it comes.
HAMLET. Angels and ministers of grace defend us!
Be thou a spirit of health or goblin damned,   40
Bring with thee airs from heaven or blasts from hell,
Be thy intents wicked or charitable,
Thou com'st in such a questionable shape
That I will speak to thee. I'll call thee Hamlet,
King, father, royal Dane. O, answer me!   45
Let me not burst in ignorance, but tell
Why thy canonized bones, hearsèd in death,
Have burst their cerements; why the sepulchre
Wherein we saw thee quietly interred
Hath oped his ponderous and marble jaws   50
To cast thee up again. What may this mean
That thou, dead corse, again in complete steel
Revisits thus the glimpses of the moon,

---

26. *his* its   28. *pales* fences, ramparts   29. *o'er-leavens* i.e. changes or modifies to excess (as over-active yeast in dough)   30. *plausive* pleasing 32. *nature's . . . star* a congenital defect or bad luck   33. *else* otherwise   34. *As . . . undergo* as near perfection as man can achieve   36. *dram* small amount   37. *doubt* extinguish, obliterate (the more usual spelling is "dout")   38. *his* its   46. *burst in ignorance* burst with curiosity   47. *canonized* buried according to the laws of the church *hearsèd* coffined   48. *cerements* grave-clothes

Making night hideous, and we fools of nature
So horridly to shake our disposition   55
With thoughts beyond the reaches of our souls?
Say, why is this? wherefore? What should we do?

[Ghost] beckons.

HORATIO. It beckons you to go away with it,
  As if it some impartment did desire
  To you alone.
MARCELLUS.   Look with what courteous action   60
  It waves you to a more removèd ground.
  But do not go with it.
HORATIO.   No, by no means.
HAMLET. It will not speak; then I will follow it.
HORATIO. Do not, my lord.
HAMLET.   Why, what should be the fear?
  I do not set my life at a pin's fee,   65
  And for my soul, what can it do to that,
  Being a thing immortal as itself?
  It waves me forth again. I'll follow it.
HORATIO. What if it tempt you toward the flood, my lord,
  Or to the dreadful summit of the cliff   70
  That beetles o'er his base into the sea,
  And there assume some other horrible form,
  Which might deprive your sovereignty of reason
  And draw you into madness? Think of it.
  The very place puts toys of desperation,   75
  Without more motive, into every brain
  That looks so many fathoms to the sea
  And hears it roar beneath.
HAMLET.   It waves me still.
  Go on. I'll follow thee.
MARCELLUS. You shall not go, my lord.
HAMLET.   Hold off your hands.   80
HORATIO. Be ruled. You shall not go.

---

59. *impartment* communication   65. *a pin's fee* the price of a pin   71.
beetles o'er overhangs   72. *other horrible form* i.e. the shape of a fiend
75. *toys* impulses, freakish fancies   78. *waves* beckons

HAMLET.   My fate cries out
  And makes each petty artere in this body
  As hardy as the Nemean lion's nerve.
  Still am I called. Unhand me, gentlemen.
  By heaven, I'll make a ghost of him that lets me.   85
  I say, away! Go on. I'll follow thee.
                              [*Exeunt*] *Ghost and Hamlet.*
HORATIO. He waxes desperate with imagination.
MARCELLUS. Let's follow. 'Tis not fit thus to obey him.
HORATIO. Have after! To what issue will this come?
MARCELLUS. Something is rotten in the state of Denmark.   90
HORATIO. Heaven will direct it.
MARCELLUS.   Nay, let's follow him.
                                              Exeunt.

[Scene 5. *Another part of the platform.*]

Enter Ghost and Hamlet.

HAMLET. Whither wilt thou lead me? Speak. I'll go no
    further.
GHOST. Mark me.
HAMLET.   I will.
GHOST.   My hour is almost come,
  When I to sulph'rous and tormenting flames
  Must render up myself.
HAMLET.   Alas, poor ghost!
GHOST. Pity me not, but lend thy serious hearing   5
  To what I shall unfold.
HAMLET.   Speak. I am bound to hear.
GHOST. So art thou to revenge, when thou shalt hear.
HAMLET. What?
GHOST. I am thy father's spirit,
  Doomed for a certain term to walk the night,   10
  And for the day confined to fast in fires,
  Till the foul crimes done in my days of nature
  Are burnt and purged away. But that I am forbid
  To tell the secrets of my prison house,

82. *artere* artery 85. *lets* hinders 89. *Have after* Let's go!
  1.5.12. *crimes* (in the general sense of "sins" or "faults")

I could a tale unfold whose lightest word   15
Would harrow up thy soul, freeze thy young blood,
Make thy two eyes like stars start from their spheres
Thy knotted and combinèd locks to part,
And each particular hair to stand an end,
Like quills upon the fretful porpentine.   20
But this eternal blazon must not be
To ears of flesh and blood. List, list, O, list!
If thou didst ever thy dear father love —
HAMLET. O God!
GHOST. Revenge his foul and most unnatural murder.   25
HAMLET. Murder!
GHOST. Murder most foul, as in the best it is,
But this most foul, strange, and unnatural.
HAMLET. Haste me to know't, that I, with wings as swift
As meditation or the thoughts of love,   30
May sweep to my revenge.
GHOST.   I find thee apt,
And duller shouldst thou be than the fat weed
That rots itself in ease on Lethe wharf,
Wouldst thou not stir in this. Now, Hamlet, hear.
'Tis given out that, sleeping in my orchard,   35
A serpent stung me. So the whole ear of Denmark
Is by a forgèd process of my death
Rankly abused. But know, thou noble youth,
The serpent that did sting thy father's life
Now wears his crown.
HAMLET.   O my prophetic soul!   40
My uncle!
GHOST. Ay, that incestuous, that adulterate beast,
With witchcraft of his wits, with traitorous gifts —
O wicked wit and gifts that have the power
So to seduce! — won to his shameful lust   45
The will of my most seeming virtuous queen.

18. *knotted and combinèd* curly and tangled   20. *porpentine* porcupine
21. *eternal blazon* a "blazon" is a description of armorial bearings;
hence, a list of distinguishing features or characteristics — here, of the
life to come   27. *the best* the most extenuating circumstances   33.
Lethe the river in Hades which imparted to the spirits of the dead
forgetfulness of their lives on earth   37. *process* official account

O Hamlet, what a falling off was there,
From me, whose love was of that dignity
That it went hand in hand even with the vow
I made to her in marriage, and to decline   50
Upon a wretch whose natural gifts were poor
To those of mine!
But virtue, as it never will be moved,
Though lewdness court it in a shape of heaven,
So lust, though to a radiant angel linked,   55
Will sate itself in a celestial bed
And prey on garbage.
But soft, methinks I scent the morning air.
Brief let me be. Sleeping within my orchard,
My custom always of the afternoon,   60
Upon my secure hour thy uncle stole,
With juice of cursed hebona in a vial,
And in the porches of my ears did pour
The leperous distilment, whose effect
Holds such an enmity with blood of man   65
That swift as quicksilver it courses through
The natural gates and alleys of the body,
And with a sudden vigour it doth posset
And curd, like eager droppings into milk,
The thin and wholesome blood. So did it mine,   70
And a most instant tetter barked about
Most lazar-like with vile and loathsome crust
All my smooth body.
Thus was I sleeping by a brother's hand
Of life, of crown, of queen at once dispatched,   75 ‡
Cut off even in the blossoms of my sin,
Unhouseled, disappointed, unaneled,

50. *decline* fall back 61. *secure* carefree, unsuspecting 62. *hebona* a poisonous extract variously identified as "yew", "ebony", or "henbane" 64. *leperous distilment* liquid producing effects of leprosy 68. *posset* curdle 69. *eager* acid 71. *tetter* rash, skin eruption *barked about* covered with roughness, like bark on a tree 72. *lazar-like* like a leper 76. *blossoms . . . sin* with my sins in full bloom 77. *Unhouseled* without the sacrament *disappointed* unprepared for death (cf. "appointments", meaning "equipment") *unaneled* without extreme unction

No reck'ning made, but sent to my account
With all my imperfections on my head.
O, horrible! O, horrible! most horrible!   80
If thou hast nature in thee, bear it not.
Let not the royal bed of Denmark be
A couch for luxury and damnèd incest.
But howsomever thou pursuest this act,
Taint not thy mind, nor let thy soul contrive   85 ‡
Against thy mother aught. Leave her to heaven,
And to those thorns that in her bosom lodge
To prick and sting her. Fare thee well at once.
The glowworm shows the matin to be near,
And gins to pale his uneffectual fire.   90
Adieu, adieu, adieu. Remember me.   *[Exit.]*
HAMLET. O all you host of heaven! O earth! What else?
And shall I couple hell? O, fie! Hold, hold, my heart,
And you, my sinews, grow not instant old,
But bear me stiffly up. Remember thee?   95
Ay, thou poor ghost, whiles memory holds a seat
In this distracted globe. Remember thee?
Yea, from the table of my memory
I'll wipe away all trivial fond records,
All saws of books, all forms, all pressures past   100
That youth and observation copied there,
And thy commandment all alone shall live
Within the book and volume of my brain,
Unmixed with baser matter. Yes, by heaven!
O most pernicious woman!   105
O villain, villain, smiling, damnèd villain!
My tables – meet it is I set it down   ‡
That one may smile, and smile, and be a villain.

78. *No reck'ning made* no chance to confess, repent, and do penance for my sins and thus "balance the books" before being called to the final accounting 81. *nature* natural impulse (such as affection for your father and concern for the honour of your country) 83. *luxury* lust 89. *matin* morning 97. *distracted globe* confused head (perhaps with the additional significance that only in a mad world can such things be) 98. *table* tablet, or notebook 99. *fond* foolish 100. *saws* wise sayings *forms* ideas, concepts *pressures* impressions 107. *meet* fitting

At least I am sure it may be so in Denmark.

[*Writing.*]

So, uncle, there you are. Now to my word: 110
It is "Adieu, adieu. Remember me".
I have sworn't.

Enter Horatio and Marcellus.

HORATIO. My lord, my lord!
MARCELLUS.   Lord Hamlet!
HORATIO.   Heavens secure him!
HAMLET. So be it!
MARCELLUS. Illo, ho, ho, my lord!   115
HAMLET. Hillo, ho, ho, boy! Come, bird, come.
MARCELLUS. How is't, my noble lord?
HORATIO.   What news, my lord?
HAMLET. O, wonderful!
HORATIO. Good my lord, tell it.
HAMLET.   No, you will reveal it.
HORATIO. Not I, my lord, by heaven.
MARCELLUS.   Nor I, my lord.   120
HAMLET. How say you then, would heart of man once
    think it?
But you'll be secret?
BOTH.   Ay, by heaven, my lord.
HAMLET. There's never a villain dwelling in all Denmark
But he's an arrant knave.
HORATIO. There needs no ghost, my lord, come from the
    grave   125
To tell us this.
HAMLET.   Why, right, you are in the right,
And so without more circumstance at all
I hold it fit that we shake hands and part,
You, as your business and desire shall point you,
For every man hath business and desire   130

110. *there you are* i.e. your hypocrisy is now a matter of record, or
"I've got you taped" 114. *So be it* equivalent to "Amen to that" 116.
Hillo . . . come (Marcellus' halloo reminds Hamlet of the cry of a
falconer to his hawk) 127. *circumstance* ceremony

Such as it is, and for my own poor part,
    I will go pray.
HORATIO. These are but wild and whirling words, my lord.
HAMLET. I am sorry they offend you, heartily;
    Yes, faith, heartily.
HORATIO.   There's no offence, my lord.   135
HAMLET. Yes, by Saint Patrick, but there is, Horatio,
    And much offence too. Touching this vision here,
    It is an honest ghost, that let me tell you.
    For your desire to know what is between us,
    O'ermaster't as you may. And now, good friends,   140
    As you are friends, scholars, and soldiers,
    Give me one poor request.
HORATIO. What is't, my lord? We will.
HAMLET. Never make known what you have seen to-night.
BOTH. My lord, we will not.
HAMLET.   Nay, but swear't.
HORATIO.   In faith,   145
    My lord, not I.
MARCELLUS.   Nor I, my lord, in faith.
HAMLET. Upon my sword.
MARCELLUS.   We have sworn, my lord, already.
HAMLET. Indeed, upon my sword, indeed.
                          Ghost cries under the stage.
GHOST.   Swear.
HAMLET. Ha, ha, boy, say'st thou so? Art thou there,
    truepenny?
    Come on. You hear this fellow in the cellarage.   150
    Consent to swear.
HORATIO.   Propose the oath, my lord.
HAMLET. Never to speak of this that you have seen,
    Swear by my sword.
GHOST [*beneath*]. Swear.

131. *Such as it is* (compared with his own task, the "business and
desire" of everyday concerns are insignificant)   138. *an honest ghost*
i.e. a real ghost, not a demon in my father's shape   147. *Upon my
sword* i.e. Upon the cross formed by the hilt of the sword   149. *true-
penny* honest fellow   150. *cellarage* the cellar under the stage

HAMLET. Hic et ubique? Then we'll shift our ground.   155
 Come hither, gentlemen,
 And lay your hands again upon my sword.
 Swear by my sword
 Never to speak of this that you have heard.
GHOST [*beneath*]. Swear by his sword.   160
HAMLET. Well said, old mole! Canst work i' th' earth
   so fast?
 A worthy pioneer! Once more remove, good friends.
HORATIO. O day and night, but this is wondrous strange!
HAMLET. And therefore as a stranger give it welcome.
 There are more things in heaven and earth, Horatio,   165
 Than are dreamt of in your philosophy.
 But come.
 Here as before, never, so help you mercy,
 How strange or odd some'er I bear myself
 (As I perchance hereafter shall think meet   170
 To put an antic disposition on),
 That you, at such times, seeing me, never shall,
 With arms encumbered thus, or this head-shake,
 Or by pronouncing of some doubtful phrase,
 As "Well, well, we know", or "We could, and if we
   would"   175
 Or "If we list to speak", or "There be, and if they might"
 Or such ambiguous giving out, to note
 That you know aught of me – this do swear,
 So grace and mercy at your most need help you.
GHOST [*beneath*]. Swear.   180
HAMLET. Rest, rest, perturbèd spirit! So, gentlemen,
 With all my love I do commend me to you,
 And what so poor a man as Hamlet is
 May do t'express his love and friending to you,
 God willing, shall not lack. Let us go in together,   185
 And still your fingers on your lips, I pray.
 The time is out of joint. O cursèd spite
 That ever I was born to set it right!
 Nay, come, let's go together.   *Exeunt.*

155. *Hic et ubique* here and everywhere 162. *pioneer* miner 171.
antic mad 173. *encumbered* folded 185. *lack* be lacking

ACT 2

[Scene 1. *A room in Polonius' house.*]

Enter old Polonius, with his man [Reynaldo].

POLONIUS. Give him this money and these notes,
    Reynaldo.
REYNALDO. I will, my lord.
POLONIUS. You shall do marvell's wisely, good Reynaldo,
    Before you visit him, to make inquire
    Of his behaviour.
REYNALDO.   My lord, I did intend it.   5
POLONIUS. Marry, well said, very well said. Look you, sir,
    Enquire me first what Danskers are in Paris,
    And how, and who, what means, and where they keep,
    What company, at what expense; and finding
    By this encompassment and drift of question   10
    That they do know my son, come you more nearer
    Than your particular demands will touch it.
    Take you as 'twere some distant knowledge of him,
    As thus, "I know his father and his friends,
    And in part him". Do you mark this, Reynaldo?   15
REYNALDO. Ay, very well, my lord.
POLONIUS. "And in part him, but," you may say, "not well,
    But if't be he I mean, he's very wild,
    Addicted so and so". And there put on him
    What forgeries you please; marry, none so rank   20
    As may dishonour him. Take heed of that.

2.1.3. *marvell's* marvellous 7. *Danskers* Danes 8. *how* i.e. how they happen to be there *means* financial resources *keep* resort 9. *What company* i.e. with what companions 10. *encompassment* round-about method *drift of question* letting one question lead naturally to another 11-12. *come . . . touch it* you will get to the point more easily than by direct questioning 13. *Take . . . of him* say that he is a distant acquaintance 19. *put on him* accuse him of 20. *forgeries* imaginary misdemeanours

    But, sir, such wanton, wild, and usual slips
    As are companions noted and most known
    To youth and liberty.
REYNALDO.   As gaming, my lord.
POLONIUS. Ay, or drinking, fencing, swearing, quarrelling,   25
    Drabbing — you may go so far.
REYNALDO. My lord, that would dishonour him.
POLONIUS. Faith, no, as you may season it in the charge.
    You must not put another scandal on him,
    That he is open to incontinency.   30
    That's not my meaning. But breathe his faults so
        quaintly
    That they may seem the taints of liberty,
    The flash and outbreak of a fiery mind,
    A savageness in unreclaimèd blood,
    Of general assault.
REYNALDO.   But, my good lord —   35
POLONIUS. Wherefore should you do this?
REYNALDO.   Ay, my lord,
    I would know that.
POLONIUS.   Marry, sir, here's my drift,
    And I believe it is a fetch of wit.
    You laying these slight sallies on my son,
    As 'twere a thing a little soiled i' th' working,   40
    Mark you,
    Your party in converse, him you would sound,
    Having ever seen in the prenominate crimes
    The youth you breathe of guilty, be assured
    He closes with you in this consequence,   45
    "Good sir", or so, or "friend", or "gentleman",

23. *As . . . known* as are usually associated with 24. *liberty* wild
oats 26. *Drabbing* whoring 28. *season it* qualify it 30. *open to
incontinency* openly and extravagantly licentious 31. *quaintly* artfully
32. *taints of liberty* faults you would expect from a young man on his
own 34. *unreclaimèd blood* passion untamed by "the years that bring
the philosophic mind" 35. *Of general assault* common to humanity in
general 37. *drift* intention, meaning 38. *fetch of wit* clever device
39. *sallies* blemishes 40. *soiled i' th' working* shopworn 42. *sound*
question 43. *Having . . . crimes* if he has ever seen, with regard to
the faults you have mentioned 44. *breathe of* speak of 45. *He closes
. . . consequence* he will be sure to agree and go on as follows

According to the phrase or the addition
Of man and country.
REYNALDO.   Very good, my lord.
POLONIUS. And then, sir, does 'a this – 'a does – What
    was I about to say?
By the mass, I was about to say something.   50
Where did I leave?
REYNALDO. At "closes in the consequence".
POLONIUS. At "closes in the consequence" – ay, marry,
    He closes thus: "I know the gentleman.
I saw him yesterday, or th' other day,   55
Or then, or then, with such, or such, and as you say,
There was 'a gaming, there o'ertook in's rouse,
There falling out at tennis", or perchance
"I saw him enter such a house of sale",
Videlicet, a brothel, or so forth.   60
See you, now –
Your bait of falsehood takes this carp of truth,
And thus do we of wisdom and of reach,
With windlasses and with assays of bias,
By indirections find directions out;   65
So by my former lecture and advice
Shall you my son. You have me, have you not?
REYNALDO. My lord, I have.
POLONIUS.   God buy ye; fare ye well.
REYNALDO. Good my lord.
POLONIUS. Observe his inclination in yourself.   70
REYNALDO. I shall, my lord.
POLONIUS. And let him ply his music.
REYNALDO.   Well, my lord.
POLONIUS. Farewell.   *Exit Reynaldo.*

---

47. *addition* title, i.e. form of courteous address **51.** *leave* leave off
57. *o'ertook in's rouse* passed out **58.** *falling out* quarrelling **60.**
Videlicet that is to say **63.** *we . . . of reach* we persons of discretion
and far-reaching strategy **64.** *With windlasses* by beating about the
bush to flush out game, by going round about the question ("windlass"
here does not mean "hoist") *assays of bias* indirect attempts (a
metaphor from the game of bowls, in which the ball, being weighted
on one side, does not travel in a straight line but in a curve) **68.** *God
buy ye* "God be with you," i.e. goodbye

Enter Ophelia.

       How now, Ophelia, what's the matter?
OPHELIA. O my lord, my lord, I have been so affrighted!
POLONIUS. With what, i' th' name of God?   75
OPHELIA. My lord, as I was sewing in my closet,
 Lord Hamlet with his doublet all unbraced,
 No hat upon his head, his stockings fouled,
 Ungartered and down-gyvèd to his ankle,
 Pale as his shirt, his knees knocking each other, 80
 And with a look so piteous in purport
 As if he had been loosèd out of hell
 To speak of horrors – he comes before me.
POLONIUS. Mad for thy love?
OPHELIA.   My lord, I do not know,
 But truly I do fear it.
POLONIUS.   What said he?   85
OPHELIA. He took me by the wrist, and held me hard,
 Then goes he to the length of all his arm,
 And with his other hand thus o'er his brow,
 He falls to such perusal of my face
 As 'a would draw it. Long stayed he so.   90
 At last, a little shaking of mine arm,
 And thrice his head thus waving up and down,
 He raised a sigh so piteous and profound
 As it did seem to shatter all his bulk,
 And end his being. That done, he lets me go, 95
 And with his head over his shoulder turned
 He seemed to find his way without his eyes,
 For out adoors he went without their helps,
 And to the last bended their light on me.
POLONIUS. Come, go with me. I will go seek the king. 100
 This is the very ecstasy of love,
 Whose violent property fordoes itself,
 And leads the will to desperate undertakings
 As oft as any passion under heaven

76. *in my closet* in my room 77. *unbraced* unlaced 78. *fouled* soiled
79. *down-gyvèd . . . ankle* hanging down around his ankles like a
prisoner's fetters ("gyves") 98. *adoors* of the door 101. *ecstasy*
madness 102. *property* nature *fordoes* destroys

That does afflict our natures. I am sorry.   105
What, have you given him any hard words of late?
OPHELIA. No, my good lord, but as you did command
   I did repel his letters, and denied
   His access to me.
POLONIUS.   That hath made him mad.
   I am sorry that with better heed and judgement   110
   I had not quoted him. I feared he did but trifle,
   And meant to wrack thee; but beshrew my jealousy.
   By heaven, it is as proper to our age
   To cast beyond ourselves in our opinions
   As it is common for the younger sort   115
   To lack discretion. Come, go we to the king.
   This must be known, which being kept close, might
      move
   More grief to hide than hate to utter love.
   Come.   *Exeunt.*

Scene 2. [*A room in the castle.*]

Flourish. Enter King and Queen, Rosencrantz and
      Guildenstern [and Attendants].

KING. Welcome, dear Rosencrantz and Guildenstern.
   Moreover that we much did long to see you,
   The need we have to use you did provoke
   Our hasty sending. Something have you heard
   Of Hamlet's transformation – so call it,   5
   Sith nor th' exterior nor the inward man
   Resembles that it was. What it should be,
   More than his father's death, that thus hath put him
   So much from th' understanding of himself,
   I cannot dream of. I entreat you both   10
   That, being of so young days brought up with him,

108. *repel* refuse to receive   111. *quoted* observed   112. *wrack* ruin
beshrew curse *jealousy* suspicion   113. *proper to* characteristic of
114. *cast beyond ourselves* go too far, overshoot the mark   117. *close*
secret
   2.2.2. *Moreover* besides   6. *Sith* since

And sith so neighboured to his youth and haviour,
That you vouchsafe your rest here in our court
Some little time, so by your companies
To draw him on to pleasures, and to gather   15
So much as from occasion you may glean,
Whether aught to us unknown afflicts him thus,
That opened lies within our remedy.
QUEEN. Good gentlemen, he hath much talked of you,
And sure I am two men there is not living   20
To whom he more adheres. If it will please you
To show us so much gentry and good will
As to expend your time with us awhile
For the supply and profit of our hope,
Your visitation shall receive such thanks   25
As fits a king's remembrance.
ROSENCRANTZ.   Both your majesties
Might, by the sovereign power you have of us,
Put your dread pleasures more into command
Than to entreaty.
GUILDENSTERN.   But we both obey,
And here give up ourselves in the full bent   30
To lay our service freely at your feet,
To be commanded.
KING. Thanks, Rosencrantz and gentle Guildenstern.
QUEEN. Thanks, Guildenstern and gentle Rosencrantz.
And I beseech you instantly to visit   35
My too much changèd son. Go, some of you,
And bring these gentlemen where Hamlet is.
GUILDENSTERN. Heavens make our presence and our
    practices
Pleasant and helpful to him!
QUEEN.   Ay, amen!
    *Exeunt Rosencrantz and Guildenstern [with some
                                    Attendants].*

Enter Polonius.

12. *haviour* behaviour 13. *vouchsafe your rest* consent to stay 16.
occasion opportunity, chance 18. *opened* revealed 21. *adheres* is
attached 22. *gentry* courtesy

POLONIUS. Th' ambassadors from Norway, my good lord,   40
   Are joyfully returned.
KING. Thou still hast been the father of good news.
POLONIUS. Have I, my lord? I assure you, my good liege,
   I hold my duty as I hold my soul,
   Both to my God and to my gracious king;   45
   And I do think – or else this brain of mine
   Hunts not the trail of policy so sure
   As it hath used to do – that I have found
   The very cause of Hamlet's lunacy.
KING. O, speak of that, that do I long to hear.   50
POLONIUS. Give first admittance to th' ambassadors.
   My news shall be the fruit to that great feast.
KING. Thyself do grace to them, and bring them in.
                                 [*Exit Polonius.*]
   He tells me, my dear Gertrude, he hath found
   The head and source of all your son's distemper.   55
QUEEN. I doubt it is no other but the main,
   His father's death and our o'erhasty marriage.
KING. Well, we shall sift him.

   Enter Ambassadors [*Voltemand and Cornelius, with
                Polonius*].

                    Welcome, my good friends,
   Say, Voltemand, what from our brother Norway?
VOLTEMAND. Most fair return of greetings and desires.   60
   Upon our first, he sent out to suppress
   His nephew's levies, which to him appeared
   To be a preparation 'gainst the Polack,
   But better looked into, he truly found
   It was against your highness, whereat grieved,   65
   That so his sickness, age, and impotence
   Was falsely borne in hand, sends out arrests
   On Fortinbras, which he in brief obeys,

42. *still* always 47. *Hunts . . . policy* cannot keep track of political events 52. *the fruit* the dessert course 53. *do . . . them* do them the honour of escorting them 55. *distemper* mental disorder 56. *doubt* suspect *main* principal cause 61. *first* (meeting with him) 63. *the Polack* the Polish nation 67. *borne in hand* taken advantage of *arrests* writs summoning him to court to answer to the king for his actions

Receives rebuke from Norway, and in fine,
Makes vow before his uncle never more　　　　　　　　70
To give th' assay of arms against your majesty.
Whereon old Norway, overcome with joy,
Gives him three thousand crowns in annual fee,
And his commission to employ those soldiers,
So levied as before, against the Polack,　　　　　　　　75
With an entreaty, herein further shown,

　　　　　　　　　　　　　　　　　[Gives a paper.]

That it might please you to give quiet pass
Through your dominions for this enterprise,
On such regards of safety and allowance
As therein are set down.
KING.　　　　　　　　　　　It likes us well,　　　　　80
And at our more considered time we'll read,
Answer, and think upon this business.
Meantime we thank you for your well-took labour.
Go to your rest; at night we'll feast together.
Most welcome home!　　　　　　*Exeunt Ambassadors.*
POLONIUS.　　　　　　　This business is well ended.　　85
My liege and madam, to expostulate
What majesty should be, what duty is,
Why day is day, night night, and time is time,
Were nothing but to waste night, day, and time.
Therefore, since brevity is the soul of wit,　　　　　90
And tediousness the limbs and outward flourishes,
I will be brief. Your noble son is mad.
Mad call I it, for to define true madness,
What is't but to be nothing else but mad?
But let that go.
QUEEN.　　　　　　　More matter with less art.　　　95 ‡
POLONIUS. Madam, I swear I use no art at all.
That he is mad, 'tis true: 'tis true 'tis pity,
And pity 'tis 'tis true. A foolish figure,
But farewell it, for I will use no art.

69. *in fine* in the end　71. *To . . . arms* to attempt a trial of arms　77.
pass passage　79. *regards* considerations *allowance* permission　80.
likes pleases　86. *expostulate* discuss　90. *wit* good sense　91. *flourishes*
ornaments　98. *figure* (of speech)

Mad let us grant him, then, and now remains   100
That we find out the cause of this effect,
Or rather say the cause of this defect,
For this effect defective comes by cause.
Thus it remains, and the remainder thus.
Perpend.   105
I have a daughter – have while she is mine –
Who in her duty and obedience, mark,
Hath given me this. Now gather, and surmise.
[*Reads*] "To the celestial, and my soul's idol, the most
beautified Ophelia." – That's an ill phrase, a vile phrase, 110
"beautified" is a vile phrase. But you shall hear. Thus:
[*Reads*] "In her excellent white bosom, these, etc."
QUEEN. Came this from Hamlet to her?
POLONIUS. Good madam, stay awhile. I will be faithful.
[*Reads letter*]   "Doubt thou the stars are fire;   115
        Doubt that the sun doth move;
       Doubt truth to be a liar;
       But never doubt I love.
O dear Ophelia, I am ill at these numbers. I have not
art to reckon my groans, but that I love thee best, O 120
most best, believe it. Adieu.
         Thine evermore, most dear lady, whilst
           this machine is to him, HAMLET."
This in obedience hath my daughter shown me,
And more above, hath his solicitings,   125
As they fell out by time, by means, and place,
All given to mine ear.
KING.   But how hath she
Received his love?
POLONIUS.   What do you think of me?
KING. As of a man faithful and honourable.

105. *Perpend* Consider closely   110. *beautified* endowed with beauty (Polonius appears to take the word as meaning beautified by artificial aids; see 2.2.109-23, end note)   116. *the . . . move* (according to the accepted Ptolemaic structure of the universe, all heavenly bodies, including the sun, rotated around the earth)   117. *Doubt* suspect   119. *numbers* verses   123. *machine* body (in the formal closing Hamlet relapses into verbal affectation to express "as long as I live")

POLONIUS. I would fain prove so. But what might you
　　think,　　　　　　　　　　　　　　　　　　　　　　130
　When I had seen this hot love on the wing,
　(As I perceived it, I must tell you that,
　Before my daughter told me) what might you,
　Or my dear majesty your queen here, think,
　If I had played the desk or table-book,　　　　　　135 ‡
　Or given my heart a winking, mute and dumb,
　Or looked upon this love with idle sight,
　What might you think? No, I went round to work,
　And my young mistress thus I did bespeak:
　"Lord Hamlet is a prince out of thy star.　　　　　140
　This must not be". And then I préscripts gave her,
　That she should lock herself from his resort,
　Admit no messengers, receive no tokens.
　Which done, she took the fruits of my advice;
　And he repelled, a short tale to make,　　　　　　145
　Fell into a sadness, then into a fast,
　Thence to a watch, thence into a weakness,
　Thence to a lightness, and by this declension,
　Into the madness wherein now he raves,
　And all we mourn for.
KING.　　　　　　　　　　　　Do you think 'tis this?　　150
QUEEN. It may be, very like.
POLONIUS. Hath there been such a time – I would fain
　　know that –
　That I have positively said " 'Tis so",
　When it proved otherwise?
KING.　　　　　　　　　　　Not that I know.
POLONIUS [pointing to his head and shoulder]. Take this
　　from this, if this be otherwise.　　　　　　　　155
　If circumstances lead me, I will find
　Where truth is hid, though it were hid indeed
　Within the centre.

136. given . . . winking "winked at" the affair, connived at it 137.
looked . . . sight had not taken it seriously 138. round directly 140.
star sphere 141. préscripts commands 146. sadness depression fast
loss of appetite 147. watch insomnia 148. lightness light-headedness,
mental instability declension decline 158. centre (i.e. of the earth,
and thus, in the Ptolemaic system, of the universe)

KING.   How may we try it further?
POLONIUS. You know sometimes he walks four hours
    together
Here in the lobby.
QUEEN.   So he does, indeed.   160
POLONIUS. At such a time I'll loose my daughter to him.
Be you and I behind an arras then.
Mark the encounter. If he love her not,
And be not from his reason fall'n thereon,
Let me be no assistant for a state,   165
But keep a farm and carters.
KING.   We will try it.

Enter Hamlet reading on a book.

QUEEN. But look where sadly the poor wretch comes
    reading.
POLONIUS. Away, I do beseech you both away,
I'll board him presently.
            Exeunt King and Queen with Attendants.
                  O, give me leave.
How does my good Lord Hamlet?   170
HAMLET. Well, God-a-mercy.
POLONIUS. Do you know me, my lord?
HAMLET. Excellent well, you are a fishmonger.
POLONIUS. Not I, my lord.
HAMLET. Then I would you were so honest a man.   175
POLONIUS. Honest, my lord?
HAMLET. Ay, sir, to be honest as this world goes, is to be
    one man picked out of ten thousand.
POLONIUS. That's very true, my lord.
HAMLET. For if the sun breed maggots in a dead dog, 180
    being a god kissing carrion – Have you a daughter?
POLONIUS. I have, my lord.
HAMLET. Let her not walk i' th' sun. Conception is a bless-
    ing, but as your daughter may conceive – friend, look
    to't.   185

162. *arras* wall-hanging, usually a tapestry, for which the town of Arras
was famous 169. *board* accost *presently* immediately 173. *fishmonger*
Elizabethan slang for a bawd or pimp

POLONIUS. How say you by that? [*Aside*] Still harping on
my daughter. Yet he knew me not at first. 'A said I was
a fishmonger. Far gone, far gone. And truly in my youth
I suffered much extremity for love. Very near this. I'll
speak to him again. – What do you read, my lord?   190

HAMLET. Words, words, words.

POLONIUS. What is the matter, my lord?

HAMLET. Between who?

POLONIUS. I mean the matter that you read, my lord.

HAMLET. Slanders, sir; for the satirical rogue says here that 195
old men have grey beards, that their faces are wrinkled,
their eyes purging thick amber and plum-tree gum, and
that they have a plentiful lack of wit, together with most
weak hams – all which, sir, though I most powerfully
and potently believe, yet I hold it not honesty to have it 200
thus set down, for yourself, sir, shall grow old as I am,
if like a crab you could go backward.

POLONIUS [*aside*]. Though this be madness, yet there is
method in't. – Will you walk out of the air, my lord?

HAMLET. Into my grave?   205

POLONIUS [*aside*]. Indeed, that's out of the air. How pregnant sometime his replies are! a happiness that often
madness hits on, which reason and sanity could not so
prosperously be delivered of. I will leave him, and suddenly contrive the means of meeting between him and 210
my daughter. – My lord. I will take my leave of you.

HAMLET. You cannot take from me anything that I will
more willingly part withal – except my life, except my
life, except my life.

Enter Guildenstern and Rosencrantz.

POLONIUS. Fare you well, my lord.   215

HAMLET. These tedious old fools!

POLONIUS. You go to seek the Lord Hamlet. There he is.

ROSENCRANTZ [*to Polonius*]. God save you, sir!

                       [*Exit Polonius.*]

197. *purging* discharging   200. *honesty* good manners, propriety   206-7.
pregnant full of meaning *happiness* appropriateness or felicity of
expression

GUILDENSTERN. My honoured lord!

ROSENCRANTZ. My most dear lord!   220

HAMLET. My excellent good friends! How dost thou, ✳
Guildenstern? Ah, Rosencrantz! Good lads, how do you
both?

ROSENCRANTZ. As the indifferent children of the earth.

GUILDENSTERN. Happy in that we are not over-happy;   225
On Fortune's cap we are not the very button.

HAMLET. Nor the soles of her shoe?

ROSENCRANTZ. Neither, my lord.

HAMLET. Then you live about her waist, or in the middle
of her favours.   230

GUILDENSTERN. Faith, her privates we.

HAMLET. In the secret parts of Fortune? O, most true, she
is a strumpet. What news?

ROSENCRANTZ. None, my lord, but that the world's grown
honest.   235

HAMLET. Then is doomsday near. But your news is not
true. Let me question more in particular. What have
you, my good friends, deserved at the hands of Fortune,
that she sends you to prison hither?

GUILDENSTERN. Prison, my lord?   240

HAMLET. Denmark's a prison.

ROSENCRANTZ. Then is the world one.

HAMLET. A goodly one, in which there are many confines,
wards, and dungeons, Denmark being one o' th' worst.

ROSENCRANTZ. We think not so, my lord.   245

HAMLET. Why then 'tis none to you; for there is nothing
either good or bad, but thinking makes it so. To me it is
a prison.

ROSENCRANTZ. Why then your ambition makes it one. 'Tis
too narrow for your mind.   250

224. *indifferent* ordinary, run-of-the-mill 225. *Happy* fortunate (it was
a commonplace of the time that too much happiness was likely to be
followed by disaster) 226. *button* (i.e. on the top of the cap) 231.
privates (i) in the ordinary ranks as "soldiers of fortune", (ii) intimate
acquaintances, (iii) private parts 234-5. *the . . . honest* i.e. "that
would be news!" (a stock quip) 236. *Then . . . near* Then the
millennium has arrived

HAMLET. O God, I could be bounded in a nutshell and
count myself a king of infinite space, were it not that I
have bad dreams.

GUILDENSTERN. Which dreams indeed are ambition; for
the very substance of the ambitious is merely the shadow 255
of a dream.

HAMLET. A dream itself is but a shadow.

ROSENCRANTZ. Truly, and I hold ambition of so airy and
light a quality that it is but a shadow's shadow.

HAMLET. Then are our beggars bodies, and our monarchs 260
and outstretched heroes the beggars' shadows. Shall we
to th' court? for, by my fay, I cannot reason.

BOTH. We'll wait upon you.

HAMLET. No such matter. I will not sort you with the rest
of my servants; for to speak to you like an honest man, 265
I am most dreadfully attended. But in the beaten way
of friendship, what make you at Elsinore?

ROSENCRANTZ. To visit you, my lord; no other occasion.

HAMLET. Beggar that I am, I am even poor in thanks, but
I thank you; and sure, dear friends, my thanks are too 270
dear a halfpenny. Were you not sent for? Is it your own
inclining? Is it a free visitation? Come, come, deal justly
with me. Come, come, nay speak.

GUILDENSTERN. What should we say, my lord?

HAMLET. Why anything, but to th' purpose. You were sent 275
for, and there is a kind of confession in your looks,
which your modesties have not craft enough to colour.
I know the good king and queen have sent for you.

ROSENCRANTZ. To what end, my lord?

HAMLET. That you must teach me. But let me conjure you 280
by the rights of our fellowship, by the consonancy of
our youth, by the obligation of our ever-preserved love,
and by what more dear a better proposer can charge
you withal, be even and direct with me whether you
were sent for or no.   285

ROSENCRANTZ [aside to Guildenstern]. What say you?

262. *fay* faith (from the Old French "fei")   264. *sort you* classify you
281-2. *consonancy ... youth* i.e. similarity in our age

HAMLET [*aside*]. Nay, then, I have an eye of you. – If
you love me, hold not off.

GUILDENSTERN. My lord, we were sent for.

HAMLET. I will tell you why; so shall my anticipation pre- 290
vent your discovery, and your secrecy to the king and
queen moult no feather. I have of late – but wherefore
I know not – lost all my mirth, forgone all custom of
exercises; and indeed it goes so heavily with my disposition, that this goodly frame the earth seems to me a 295 ‡
sterile promontory, this most excellent canopy the air,
look you, this brave o'er-hanging firmament, this majestical roof fretted with golden fire, why it appeareth
nothing to me but a foul and pestilent congregation of
vapours. What a piece of work is a man, how noble in 300
reason, how infinite in faculties, in form and moving,
how express and admirable in action, how like an angel
in apprehension, how like a god: the beauty of the
world, the paragon of animals. And yet to me, what is
this quintessence of dust? Man delights not me, nor 305
woman neither, though by your smiling you seem to
say so.

ROSENCRANTZ. My lord, there was no such stuff in my
thoughts.

HAMLET. Why did ye laugh, then, when I said "Man de- 310
lights not me"?

ROSENCRANTZ. To think, my lord, if you delight not in
man, what lenten entertainment the players shall receive
from you. We coted them on the way, and hither are
they coming to offer you service.   315

HAMLET. He that plays the king shall be welcome – his
majesty shall have tribute on me; the adventurous knight
shall use his foil and target; the lover shall not sigh

<hr>

287. *eye of you* eye on you 290-91. *prevent* forestall (literally: come
before) *discovery* revelation, disclosure 292. *moult no feather*
remain intact 297. *brave* splendidly adorned *firmament* the heavens
(see Gen. 1:17) 298. *fretted* decorated with carved or embossed
ornamentation (fretwork) 299. *congregation* gathering together, lot
300. *piece of work* masterpiece 301. *faculties* capacities 302. *express*
mechanically precise, suited to its function 303. *apprehension* understanding 304. *paragon* perfection (of animate nature) 313. *lenten*
scanty, meagre 314. *coted* passed

gratis; the humorous man shall end his part in peace; ‡
the clown shall make those laugh whose lungs are tickle 320
o' th' sere; and the lady shall say her mind freely, or the
blank verse shall halt for't. What players are they?

ROSENCRANTZ. Even those you were wont to take such delight in, the tragedians of the city.

HAMLET. How chances it they travel? Their residence, 325
both in reputation and profit, was better both ways.

ROSENCRANTZ. I think their inhibition comes by the means
of the late innovation.

HAMLET. Do they hold the same estimation they did when
I was in the city? Are they so followed? 330

ROSENCRANTZ. No, indeed, are they not.

HAMLET. How comes it? Do they grow rusty?

ROSENCRANTZ. Nay, their endeavour keeps in the wonted ‡
pace; but there is, sir, an eyrie of children, little eyases,
that cry out on the top of question, and are most tyran- 335
nically clapped for't. These are now the fashion, and so
berattle the common stages (so they call them) that
many wearing rapiers are afraid of goose quills and dare
scarce come thither.

HAMLET. What, are they children? Who maintains 'em? 340
How are they escoted? Will they pursue the quality no
longer than they can sing? Will they not say afterwards,
if they should grow themselves to common players (as

319. *gratis* for nothing   320-21. *tickle o' the sere* easily set off (the "sere" was a mechanism like the modern safety-catch which kept the gun at full or half cock)   322. *halt* limp   325. *How . . . travel* How do they happen to be on tour   327. *inhibition* prohibition from playing (by decree or circumstance)   328. *innovation* (an allusion to the revival of companies of boy actors, or possibly to new decrees limiting the number of theatres in the London area)   333-4. *their . . . pace* their performance is up to its usual standard   *eyrie* nest   *eyases* nestling hawks taking their first practice flight   335. *on the . . . question* louder than the other parties to the dispute   335-6. *tyrannically* outrageously   337. *berattle . . . stages* variously interpreted as "abuse", "fill with noise", and "put into confusion", the public theatres   338. *wearing rapiers* i.e. gentlemen (those entitled to bear arms)   *goose quills* pens, i.e. the satiric comments of the writers for the children's companies (on the "low tastes" of the patrons of the public theatres)   340. *Who maintains 'em* (actors' companies were required to be, nominally at least, under the patronage of some nobleman)   341. *escoted* financially supported   *quality* the art of acting   341-2. *no longer . . . sing* only until their voices have changed

it is most like, if their means are not better), their writers do them wrong to make them exclaim against their own 345 succession?

ROSENCRANTZ. Faith, there has been much to do on both sides; and the nation holds it no sin to tarre them to controversy. There was for a while no money bid for argument, unless the poet and the player went to cuffs in the 350 question.

HAMLET. Is't possible?

GUILDENSTERN. O, there has been much throwing about of brains.

HAMLET. Do the boys carry it away?   355

ROSENCRANTZ. Ay, that they do, my lord, Hercules and his load too.

HAMLET. It is not very strange, for my uncle is King of Denmark, and those that would make mouths at him while my father lived give twenty, forty, fifty, a hun- 360 dred ducats apiece for his picture in little. 'Sblood, there is something in this more than natural, if philosophy could find it out.   *A flourish.*

GUILDENSTERN. There are the players.

HAMLET. Gentlemen, you are welcome to Elsinore. Your 365 hands. Come then, th' appurtenance of welcome is fashion and ceremony. Let me comply with you in this garb, lest my extent to the players, which I tell you must show fairly outwards, should more appear like entertainment than yours. You are welcome. But my uncle-father and 370 aunt-mother are deceived.

GUILDENSTERN. In what, my dear lord?

HAMLET. I am but mad north-north-west; when the wind is southerly I know a hawk from a handsaw.

Enter Polonius.

344. *if their . . . better* if they have no better source of income   345-6. *their own succession* the profession to which they will later belong   348. *tarre them* urge them on (as in setting dogs on to fight)   359. *mouths* grimaces   361. *in little* in miniature   *'Sblood* God's blood   366. *appurtenance* the adjuncts belonging to something (e.g. weapons and a particular style of dress are among the "appurtenance" of rank)   368. *my extent* the welcome I extend   368-9. *show fairly* look good   *entertainment* hospitality, welcome

POLONIUS. Well be with you, gentlemen.   375

HAMLET. Hark you, Guildenstern – and you too – at each
ear a hearer. That great baby you see there is not yet
out of his swaddling clouts.

ROSENCRANTZ. Happily he is the second time come to
them, for they say an old man is twice a child.   380

HAMLET. I will prophesy he comes to tell me of the players.
Mark it. – You say right, sir, a Monday morning, 'twas
then indeed.

POLONIUS. My lord, I have news to tell you.

HAMLET. My lord, I have news to tell you.   385
When Roscius was an actor in Rome –

POLONIUS. The actors are come hither, my lord.

HAMLET. Buzz, buzz.

POLONIUS. Upon my honour –

HAMLET. Then came each actor on his ass –   390

POLONIUS. The best actors in the world, either for tragedy,
comedy, history, pastoral, pastoral-comical, historical-
pastoral, tragical-historical, tragical-comical-historical-
pastoral, scene individible, or poem unlimited. Seneca
cannot be too heavy nor Plautus too light. For the law 395
of writ and the liberty, these are the only men.

HAMLET. O Jephthah, judge of Israel, what a treasure
hadst thou!

POLONIUS. What a treasure had he, my lord?

HAMLET. Why –   400
       "One fair daughter, and no more,
         The which he lovèd passing well."

POLONIUS [aside]. Still on my daughter.

HAMLET. Am I not i' th' right, old Jephthah?

379. *Happily* perhaps   382. *You say right* . . . (Hamlet pretends to be
deep in conversation with Rosencrantz and Guildenstern as Polonius
approaches)   386. *Roscius* a famous actor of Cicero's time (perhaps
mentioned to indicate that Polonius' news is stale)   388. *Buzz, buzz*
i.e. What else is new? or Here we go again!   390. *Then* . . . *ass*
(probably a line from an old song, used as a barbed comment on
Polonius' "Upon my honour")   394. *scene individible* play that observes the unity of place   *poem unlimited* play that does not observe
the unities   *Seneca* a Roman writer of tragedy   395. *Plautus* a Roman
writer of comedy   397. *Jephthah* . . . *Israel* (this and the verse lines
that follow are from a popular scriptural ballad on the theme of
Judges 11)

POLONIUS. If you call me Jephthah, my lord, I have a 405
   daughter that I love passing well.
HAMLET. Nay, that follows not.
POLONIUS. What follows then, my lord?
HAMLET. Why –
           "As by lot, God wot"   410
and then, you know,
       "It came to pass, as most like it was."
The first row of the pious chanson will show you more,
for look where my abridgement comes.

Enter the Players.

You are welcome, masters; welcome, all. – I am glad to 415
see thee well. – Welcome, good friends. – O, old friend!
Why thy face is valanced since I saw thee last. Com'st
thou to beard me in Denmark? – What, my young lady
and mistress? By'r lady, your ladyship is nearer to
heaven than when I saw you last by the altitude of a 420
chopine. Pray God your voice, like a piece of uncurrent
gold, be not cracked within the ring. – Masters, you are
all welcome. We'll e'en to't like French falconers, fly at
anything we see. We'll have a speech straight. Come
give us a taste of your quality, come a passionate speech. 425
FIRST PLAYER. What speech, my good lord?
HAMLET. I heard thee speak me a speech once, but it was
   never acted, or if it was, not above once, for the play,
   I remember, pleased not the million; 'twas caviary to
   the general. But it was – as I received it, and others 430
   whose judgements in such matters cried in the top of
   mine – an excellent play, well digested in the scenes, set

---

410. *lot* chance *wot* knows 413. *row* line or stanza *pious chanson*
godly song 414. *abridgement* (i) "entertainment", in the sense of
means of making the time seem short, or (ii) "opportunity to cut
short this conversation", i.e. "I am about to be cut off" 417. *valanced*
i.e. bearded 418. *beard* challenge *my young lady* (addressed to the
boy who plays the women's parts) 421. *chopine* a shoe with a high
cork heel and thick cork sole 425. *quality* art or skill *passionate*
highly emotional; "dramatic" in the colloquial modern sense 429.
caviary caviare (then a rare delicacy appreciated only by gourmets)
430. *the general* the average (taste), i.e. the "mass audience" 431.
cried . . . top of had more authority than 432. *digested* i.e. composed

down with as much modesty as cunning. I remember
one said there were no sallets in the lines to make the
matter savoury, nor no matter in the phrase that might 435
indict the author of affectation, but called it an honest
method, as wholesome as sweet, and by very much more
handsome than fine. One speech in't I chiefly loved.
'Twas Æneas' tale to Dido, and thereabout of it especially where he speaks of Priam's slaughter. If it live in 440 ‡
your memory, begin at this line – let me see, let me see:
    "The rugged Pyrrhus, like th' Hyrcanian beast" –
'tis not so; it begins with Pyrrhus –
    "The rugged Pyrrhus, he whose sable arms,
    Black as his purpose, did the night resemble   445
    When he lay couchèd in th' ominous horse,
    Hath now this dread and black complexion smeared
    With heraldry more dismal; head to foot
    Now is he total gules, horridly tricked
    With blood of fathers, mothers, daughters, sons,   450
    Baked and impasted with the parching streets,
    That lend a tyrannous and a damnèd light
    To their lord's murder. Roasted in wrath and fire,
    And thus o'er-sizèd with coagulate gore,
    With eyes like carbuncles, the hellish Pyrrhus   455
    Old grandsire Priam seeks."
So proceed you.

POLONIUS. Fore God, my lord, well spoken, with good
accent and good discretion.

FIRST PLAYER.   "Anon he finds him   460
    Striking too short at Greeks. His antique sword,

---

433. *modesty* artistic restraint, elegance *cunning* artistic ingenuity or
skill 434. *sallets* salads, i.e. "spicy" bits, seasoned with bawdy *double
entendre* 435-6. *matter . . . affectation* far-fetched or affected use of
language *honest* appropriate, in good taste 437-8. *more . . . fine*
elegant rather than elaborate 442. *Hyrcanian beast* tiger 446. *horse*
i.e. the Trojan horse, the device by which the Greeks gained entrance
into Troy 449. *gules* (heraldic term) red *tricked* decked out 451.
Baked . . . streets hardened into a crust by the fires raging in the
streets 452. *damnèd* hellish 454. *o'er-sizèd* covered with a sealing
coat, or "size", like plaster *coagulate* clotted 455. *carbuncles* glowing
red, semi-precious stones 459. *good discretion* not overdone

Rebellious to his arm, lies where it falls,
Repugnant to command. Unequal matched,
Pyrrhus at Priam drives, in rage strikes wide.
But with the whiff and wind of his fell sword   465
Th' unnervèd father falls. Then senseless Ilium,
Seeming to feel this blow, with flaming top
Stoops to his base, and with a hideous crash
Takes prisoner Pyrrhus' ear. For, lo! his sword,
Which was declining on the milky head   470
Of reverend Priam, seemed i' th' air to stick.
So as a painted tyrant Pyrrhus stood,
And like a neutral to his will and matter,
Did nothing.
But as we often see, against some storm,   475
A silence in the heavens, the rack stand still,
The bold winds speechless, and the orb below
As hush as death, anon the dreadful thunder
Doth rend the region; so, after Pyrrhus' pause,
A rousèd vengeance sets him new awork,   480
And never did the Cyclops' hammers fall
On Mars's armour, forged for proof eterne,
With less remorse than Pyrrhus' bleeding sword
Now falls on Priam.
Out, out, thou strumpet, Fortune! All you gods,   485
In general synod take away her power,
Break all the spokes and fellies from her wheel,
And bowl the round nave down the hill of heaven
As low as to the fiends."
POLONIUS. This is too long.   490
HAMLET. It shall to the barber's with your beard. – Prithee

463. *Repugnant to command* refusing to obey orders 465. *fell* cruel
466. *senseless Ilium* i.e. the citadel, as if stunned by the blow 468.
his its 473. *like . . . matter* as if in no-man's-land between his purpose
and its accomplishment 475. *against* just before 476. *rack* cloud mass
477. *the orb below* i.e. the earth 479. *region* air (cf. 1. 570) 481.
Cyclops' The Cyclops were one-eyed giants, some of whom worked
in the smithy of Hephaestus, Olympian god of fire and metalwork
482. *Mars's* of Mars, the god of war *for proof eterne* to last for ever
486. *synod* assembly 487. *fellies* pieces forming the rim of the wheel
488. *nave* hub

say on. He's for a jig, or a tale of bawdry, or he sleeps.
Say on; come to Hecuba.

FIRST PLAYER. "But who, ah woe! had seen the mobled
  queen –"

HAMLET. "The mobled queen"?   495

POLONIUS. That's good.

FIRST PLAYER. "Run barefoot up and down, threat'ning
  the flames
  With bisson rheum, a clout upon that head
  Where late the diadem stood, and for a robe,
  About her lank and all o'er-teemèd loins,   500
  A blanket, in the alarm of fear caught up –
  Who this had seen, with tongue in venom steeped,
  'Gainst Fortune's state would treason have
    pronounced.
  But if the gods themselves did see her then,
  When she saw Pyrrhus make malicious sport   505
  In mincing with his sword her husband's limbs,
  The instant burst of clamour that she made,
  Unless things mortal move them not at all,
  Would have made milch the burning eyes of heaven,
  And passion in the gods."   510

POLONIUS. Look whe'r he has not turned his colour, and
has tears in's eyes. Prithee no more.

HAMLET. 'Tis well. I'll have thee speak out the rest of this
soon. – Good my lord, will you see the players well
bestowed? Do you hear, let them be well used, for they 515
are the abstract and brief chronicles of the time; after
your death you were better have a bad epitaph than
their ill report while you live.

POLONIUS. My lord, I will use them according to their
desert.   520

---

492. *jig* a comic dialogue or "skit" with singing and dancing (jigs were
often performed after the conclusion of a play and were very popular
with "the general") 493. *Hecuba* the Queen of Troy 494. *mobled*
muffled 498. *bisson rheum* blinding tears *clout* cloth 500. *o'er-
teemèd* worn out with child-bearing 503. *state* government 509.
milch moist (literally: milk-giving) *burning . . . heaven* the stars 511.
turned his colour changed colour 514-15. *well bestowed* properly
accommodated 516. *abstract* summary

HAMLET. God's bodkin, man, much better. Use every man
    after his desert, and who shall 'scape whipping? Use
    them after your own honour and dignity. The less they
    deserve, the more merit is in your bounty. Take them in.
POLONIUS. Come, sirs.   525
HAMLET. Follow him, friends. We'll hear a play to-mor-
    row. [*Aside to First Player*] Dost thou hear me, old
    friend, can you play "The Murder of Gonzago"?
FIRST PLAYER. Ay, my lord.
HAMLET. We'll ha't to-morrow night. You could for a   530
    need study a speech of some dozen or sixteen lines
    which I would set down and insert in't, could you not?
FIRST PLAYER. Ay, my lord.
HAMLET. Very well. Follow that lord, and look you mock
    him not.   *Exeunt Polonius and Players.* 535
    My good friends, I'll leave you till night. You are wel-
    come to Elsinore.
ROSENCRANTZ. Good my lord.
                    Exeunt [Rosencrantz and Guildenstern].
HAMLET. Ay, so God buy to you. Now I am alone.
    O, what a rogue and peasant slave am I!   540
    Is it not monstrous that this player here,
    But in a fiction, in a dream of passion,
    Could force his soul so to his own conceit
    That from her working all his visage wanned;
    Tears in his eyes, distraction in his aspect,   545
    A broken voice, and his whole function suiting
    With forms to his conceit? And all for nothing,
    For Hecuba!
    What's Hecuba to him or he to her,
    That he should weep for her? What would he do   550
    Had he the motive and the cue for passion
    That I have? He would drown the stage with tears,
    And cleave the general ear with horrid speech,

---

521. *God's bodkin* by God's dear body   540. *rogue . . . slave* one who
lacks both a sense of honour and sensitivity of feeling   543. *conceit*
concept of the mood of the speech, imaginative re-creation of the
situation   544. *wanned* paled   551. *cue* (Hamlet takes up the theatrical
metaphor)   553. *general* public

Make mad the guilty, and appal the free,
Confound the ignorant, and amaze indeed   555
The very faculties of eyes and ears.
Yet I,
A dull and muddy-mettled rascal, peak
Like John-a-dreams, unpregnant of my cause,
And can say nothing; no, not for a king   560
Upon whose property and most dear life
A damned defeat was made. Am I a coward?
Who calls me villain, breaks my pate across,
Plucks off my beard and blows it in my face,
Tweaks me by the nose, gives me the lie i' th' throat 565
As deep as to the lungs? Who does me this?
Ha, 'swounds, I should take it; for it cannot be
But I am pigeon-livered and lack gall
To make oppression bitter, or ere this
I should 'a fatted all the region kites   570
With this slave's offal. Bloody, bawdy villain!
Remorseless, treacherous, lecherous, kindless villain!
Why, what an ass am I! This is most brave,
That I, the son of a dear father murdered,
Prompted to my revenge by heaven and hell,   575
Must like a whore unpack my heart with words,
And fall a-cursing like a very drab,
A scullion! Fie upon't! foh!
About, my brains. Hum — I have heard
That guilty creatures sitting at a play,   580
Have by the very cunning of the scene
Been struck so to the soul that presently
They have proclaimed their malefactions;

554. *free* innocent 558. *muddy-mettled* poor-spirited *peak* pine away,
mope about 559. *unpregnant . . . cause* doing nothing to advance my
cause 562. *defeat* destruction 563-6. *Who . . . lungs* (a catalogue of
deadly insults to be wiped out, according to the code of honour, only
by mortal combat) 570. *'a* have *region kites* kites (scavengers) of
the air 571. *offal* guts 572. *kindless* unnatural 573. *This . . . brave*
a fine thing 575. *by . . . hell* i.e. by heavenly justice and hellish
vengeance 577. *drab* whore 578. *scullion* the lowest-ranking servant
in the kitchen hierarchy (who, having no one to "pass the buck" to,
has no outlet other than cursing) 582. *presently* at once 583. *malefactions* evil deeds

For murder, though it have no tongue, will speak
With most miraculous organ. I'll have these players   585
Play something like the murder of my father
Before mine uncle. I'll observe his looks.
I'll tent him to the quick. If 'a do blench,
I know my course. The spirit that I have seen
May be a devil, and the devil hath power   590
T' assume a pleasing shape, yea, and perhaps
Out of my weakness and my melancholy,
As he is very potent with such spirits,
Abuses me to damn me. I'll have grounds
More relative than this. The play's the thing   595
Wherein I'll catch the conscience of the king.   *Exit.*

588. *tent* probe *blench* wince 594. *Abuses* deludes 595. *relative* to
the point, conclusive

[ACT 3]

[Scene 1. *A room in the castle.*]

Enter King, Queen, Polonius, Ophelia,
Rosencrantz, Guildenstern, Lords.

KING. And can you by no drift of conference
Get from him why he puts on this confusion,
Grating so harshly all his days of quiet
With turbulent and dangerous lunacy?
ROSENCRANTZ. He does confess he feels himself
    distracted,   5
But from what cause 'a will by no means speak.
GUILDENSTERN. Nor do we find him forward to be
    sounded,
But with a crafty madness keeps aloof
When we would bring him on to some confession
Of his true state.
QUEEN.   Did he receive you well?   10
ROSENCRANTZ. Most like a gentleman.
GUILDENSTERN. But with much forcing of his disposition.
ROSENCRANTZ. Niggard of question, but of our demands
Most free in his reply.
QUEEN.   Did you assay him
To any pastime?   15
ROSENCRANTZ. Madam, it so fell out that certain players
We o'er-raught on the way. Of these we told him,
And there did seem in him a kind of joy
To hear of it. They are here about the court,
And as I think, they have already order   20
This night to play before him.

3.1.1. *drift of conference* leading questions 3. *Grating* disturbing
7. *forward to be sounded* receptive to questioning 12. *with . . .*
disposition his heart wasn't in it 13-14. *Niggard . . . reply* He didn't
have much to say for himself but answered our questions freely enough
14-15. *assay him/ To* try to interest him in 17. *o'er-raught* overtook

92

POLONIUS.   'Tis most true,
   And he beseeched me to entreat your majesties
   To hear and see the matter.
KING. With all my heart, and it doth much content me
   To hear him so inclined.   25
   Good gentlemen, give him a further edge,
   And drive his purpose into these delights.
ROSENCRANTZ. We shall, my lord.
                    Exeunt Rosencrantz and Guildenstern.
KING.   Sweet Gertrude, leave us too,
   For we have closely sent for Hamlet hither,
   That he, as 'twere by accident, may here   30
   Affront Ophelia.
   Her father and myself (lawful espials)
   Will so bestow ourselves that, seeing unseen,
   We may of their encounter frankly judge,
   And gather by him, as he is behaved,   35
   If't be th' affliction of his love or no
   That thus he suffers for.
QUEEN.   I shall obey you. –
   And for your part, Ophelia, I do wish
   That your good beauties be the happy cause
   Of Hamlet's wildness. So shall I hope your virtues   40
   Will bring him to his wonted way again,
   To both your honours.
OPHELIA.   Madam, I wish it may.
                                        [*Exit Queen.*]
POLONIUS. Ophelia, walk you here. – Gracious, so please
   you,
   We will bestow ourselves. – [*To Ophelia*] Read on
   this book,
   That show of such an exercise may colour   45
   Your loneliness. – We are oft to blame in this,

23. *matter* play   26. *give . . . edge* encourage his interest further   29.
closely secretly   31. *Affront* confront, meet face to face   32. *lawful
espials* legitimate spies (since the end, diagnosing Hamlet's madness,
justifies the under-handed means)   35. *is behaved* behaves   41. *wonted
way* normal state   43. *Gracious* "Your Grace" (addressed to the
King)   45. *exercise* act of devotion   45-6. *colour/ Your loneliness* i.e.
make it seem natural that you should be unattended

'Tis too much proved, that with devotion's visage
And pious action we do sugar o'er
The devil himself.

KING [*aside*].   O, 'tis too true.
How smart a lash that speech doth give my conscience!   50
The harlot's cheek, beautied with plast'ring art,
Is not more ugly to the thing that helps it
Than is my deed to my most painted word.
O heavy burden!

POLONIUS. I hear him coming. Let's withdraw, my lord.   55

                    [*Exeunt King and Polonius.*]

                    Enter Hamlet.

HAMLET. To be, or not to be, that is the question:
Whether 'tis nobler in the mind to suffer
The slings and arrows of outrageous fortune,
Or to take arms against a sea of troubles,
And by opposing end them. To die, to sleep —   60
No more; and by a sleep to say we end
The heartache, and the thousand natural shocks
That flesh is heir to. 'Tis a consummation
Devoutly to be wished — to die, to sleep —
To sleep, perchance to dream, ay there's the rub;   65
For in that sleep of death what dreams may come
When we have shuffled off this mortal coil
Must give us pause — there's the respect
That makes calamity of so long life.
For who would bear the whips and scorns of time,   70
Th' oppressor's wrong, the proud man's contumely,
The pangs of déspised love, the law's delay,
The insolence of office, and the spurns
That patient merit of th' unworthy takes,

56. *question* point at issue, proposition to be debated   63. *consummation* final settling up   65. *rub* obstruction (which deflects the course of the ball in the game of bowls)   67. *coil* both (i) turmoil, and (ii) something (metaphorically) like a coil of rope in which the feet are entangled, i.e. like the body impeding the upward progress of the soul   68. *respect* consideration (re-emphasizing the sense of "the rub" in l. 65)   70. *time* i.e. this temporal world   71. *contumely* contemptuous abuse   72. *déspised* (accent on first syllable)   73. *office* government officials

When he himself might his quietus make   75
With a bare bodkin? Who would fardels bear,
To grunt and sweat under a weary life,
But that the dread of something after death,
The undiscovered country, from whose bourn
No traveller returns, puzzles the will,   80
And makes us rather bear those ills we have
Than fly to others that we know not of?
Thus conscience does make cowards of us all;
And thus the native hue of resolution
Is sicklied o'er with the pale cast of thought,   85
And enterprises of great pitch and moment
With this regard their currents turn awry
And lose the name of action. – Soft you now,
The fair Ophelia. – Nymph, in thy orisons
Be all my sins remembered.
OPHELIA.   Good my lord,   90
    How does your honour for this many a day?
HAMLET. I humbly thank you, well.
OPHELIA. My lord, I have remembrances of yours
    That I have longèd long to re-deliver.
    I pray you now receive them.
HAMLET.   No, not I,   95
    I never gave you aught.
OPHELIA. My honoured lord, you know right well you did,
    And with them words of so sweet breath composed
    As made the things more rich. Their perfume lost,
    Take these again, for to the noble mind   100
    Rich gifts wax poor when givers prove unkind.
    There, my lord.
HAMLET. Ha, ha! are you honest?
OPHELIA. My lord?

75. *might . . . make* might settle his account 76. *bodkin* small dagger
fardels burdens 79. *bourn* boundary 84. *native hue* i.e. red, characteristic of the sanguine "complexion" 85. *pale . . . thought* paleness
and brooding were characteristic of melancholy (cf. 2.1.81) 86. *pitch*
height *of great . . . moment* momentous 87. *regard* consideration
currents courses 88. *the . . . action* the honourable repute of heroic
deeds 89. *orisons* prayers 103. *honest* probably both (i) honourable,
and (ii) chaste

HAMLET. Are you fair? 105

OPHELIA. What means your lordship?

HAMLET. That if you be honest and fair, your honesty should admit no discourse to your beauty.

OPHELIA. Could beauty, my lord, have better commerce than with honesty? 110

HAMLET. Ay, truly, for the power of beauty will sooner transform honesty from what it is to a bawd than the force of honesty can translate beauty into his likeness. This was sometime a paradox, but now the time gives it proof. I did love you once. 115

OPHELIA. Indeed, my lord, you made me believe so.

HAMLET. You should not have believed me, for virtue cannot so inoculate our old stock but we shall relish of it. I loved you not.

OPHELIA. I was the more deceived. 120

HAMLET. Get thee to a nunnery. Why wouldst thou be a breeder of sinners? I am myself indifferent honest, but yet I could accuse me of such things that it were better my mother had not borne me: I am very proud, revengeful, ambitious, with more offences at my beck than 125 I have thoughts to put them in, imagination to give them shape, or time to act them in. What should such fellows as I do crawling between earth and heaven? We are arrant knaves all; believe none of us. Go thy ways to a nunnery. Where's your father? 130

OPHELIA. At home, my lord.

HAMLET. Let the doors be shut upon him, that he may play the fool nowhere but in's own house. Farewell.

OPHELIA. O, help him, you sweet heavens!

HAMLET. If thou dost marry, I'll give thee this plague for 135 thy dowry: be thou as chaste as ice, as pure as snow, thou shalt not escape calumny. Get thee to a nunnery,

---

105. *fair* (a similar *double entendre*) i.e. (i) just, and (ii) beautiful
108. *admit . . . to* have nothing to do with 109. *commerce* association
122. *of sinners* i.e. of children, since all men are sinners *indifferent honest* reasonably respectable 131. *At . . . lord* (Ophelia could hardly say "Behind that arras"; Hamlet's reply strongly suggests that he knows she is lying)

farewell. Or if thou wilt needs marry, marry a fool, for
wise men know well enough what monsters you make
of them. To a nunnery, go, and quickly too. Farewell. 140
OPHELIA. Heavenly powers, restore him!
HAMLET. I have heard of your paintings well enough. God
hath given you one face, and you make yourselves another. You jig and amble, and you lisp; you nickname   ‡
God's creatures, and make your wantonness your ignor- 145
ance. Go to, I'll no more on't, it hath made me mad. I
say we will have no moe marriage. Those that are mar-
ried already, all but one, shall live. The rest shall keep
as they are. To a nunnery, go.   *Exit.*
OPHELIA. O, what a noble mind is here o'erthrown!   150
  The courtier's, scholar's, soldier's, eye, tongue, sword,   ‡
  Th' expectancy and rose of the fair state,   ‡
  The glass of fashion and the mould of form,
  Th' observed of all observers, quite quite down!
  And I of ladies most deject and wretched,   155
  That sucked the honey of his musicked vows,   ‡
  Now see that noble and most sovereign reason
  Like sweet bells jangled, out of tune and harsh;
  That unmatched form and feature of blown youth
  Blasted with ecstasy. O, woe is me   160
  T' have seen what I have seen, see what I see!

            Exit.

    Enter King and Polonius.

KING. Love! His affections do not that way tend,
  Nor what he spake, though it lacked form a little,
  Was not like madness. There's something in his soul
  O'er which his melancholy sits on brood,   165
  And I do doubt the hatch and the disclose
  Will be some danger; which to prevent,

139. *monsters* i.e. men with horns, cuckolds 148. *all but one* (Hamlet
cannot restrain his feelings about Claudius' marriage, nor resist taunting
him if he should be within earshot) 152. *expectancy* hope 153. *glass*
mirror 159. *blown youth* youth in full bloom 160. *Blasted with
ecstasy* blighted with madness 162. *affections* imbalance of mind 163.
lacked form a little was not entirely coherent 166. *doubt* suspect
hatch . . . disclose i.e. result (pursuing the "brood" metaphor)

I have in quick determination
Thus set it down: he shall with speed to England
For the demand of our neglected tribute.   170
Haply the seas and countries different,
With variable objects, shall expel
This something-settled matter in his heart
Whereon his brains still beating puts him thus
From fashion of himself. What think you on't?   175
POLONIUS.   It shall do well. But yet do I believe
The origin and commencement of his grief
Sprung from neglected love. – How now, Ophelia?
You need not tell us what Lord Hamlet said,
We heard it all. – My lord, do as you please,   180
But if you hold it fit, after the play
Let his queen-mother all alone entreat him
To show his grief. Let her be round with him,
And I'll be placed, so please you, in the ear
Of all their conference. If she find him not,   185
To England send him; or confine him where
Your wisdom best shall think.
KING.   It shall be so.
Madness in great ones must not unwatched go.

Exeunt.

[Scene 2.   *A hall in the castle.*]

Enter Hamlet and three of the Players.

HAMLET.   Speak the speech, I pray you, as I pronounced
it to you, trippingly on the tongue; but if you mouth it
as many of our players do, I had as lief the town-crier
spoke my lines. Nor do not saw the air too much with

172. *variable objects* new sights and experiences to think about   175.
fashion of himself his usual polite behaviour   176. *It . . . well* It
ought to work   183. *be round . . . him* come straight to the point   185.
find him not doesn't find out what his trouble is
    3.2.2. *trippingly* easily, naturally   *mouth it* drag it out   3. *I . . . lief*
I'd just as soon   4. *saw the air* i.e. use harsh, awkward gestures

your hand thus, but use all gently, for in the very tor- 5
rent, tempest, and as I may say, whirlwind of your
passion, you must acquire and beget a temperance that
may give it smoothness. O, it offends me to the soul to
hear a robustious periwig-pated fellow tear a passion to
tatters, to very rags, to split the ears of the groundlings, 10
who for the most part are capable of nothing but inex-
plicable dumb shows and noise. I would have such a
fellow whipped for o'erdoing Termagant. It out-herods
Herod. Pray you avoid it.

FIRST PLAYER. I warrant your honour. 15

HAMLET. Be not too tame neither, but let your own discretion be your tutor. Suit the action to the word, the word
to the action, with this special observance, that you
o'erstep not the modesty of nature; for anything so o'er-
done is from the purpose of playing, whose end both at 20
the first, and now, was and is, to hold as 'twere the
mirror up to nature, to show virtue her own feature,
scorn her own image, and the very age and body of the
time his form and pressure. Now this overdone, or come
tardy off, though it makes the unskilful laugh, cannot 25
but make the judicious grieve, the censure of the which
one must in your allowance o'erweigh a whole theatre
of others. O, there be players that I have seen play –
and heard others praise, and that highly – not to speak
it profanely, that neither having th' accent of Christians, 30
nor the gait of Christian, pagan, nor man, have so strut-
ted and bellowed that I have thought some of nature's
journeymen had made men, and not made them well,
they imitated humanity so abominably.

5-7. *very . . . passion* i.e. at the highest pitch of violent emotion
acquire and beget achieve and create *temperance* moderation 9.
robustious . . . fellow bewigged actor who throws his weight around
passion highly emotional speech 9-10. *tear . . . tatters* i.e. ruin by
overdoing it *groundlings* i.e. those who paid a penny for standing-
room 11. *are capable of* appreciate 13. *Termagant* supposed to be a
Mohammedan deity, a "ranting" part (like that of Herod) in medieval
plays 15. *warrant* promise, guarantee 18. *observance* caution 20.
from contrary to *end* aim, intention 20-21. *at the first* from the
beginning 26. *censure* judgement

FIRST PLAYER. I hope we have reformed that indifferently 35
 with us.
HAMLET. O, reform it altogether. And let those that play
 your clowns speak no more than is set down for them,
 for there be of them that will themselves laugh, to set
 on some quantity of barren spectators to laugh too, 40
 though in the meantime some necessary question of the
 play be then to be considered. That's villainous, and
 shows a most pitiful ambition in the fool that uses it.
 Go, make you ready.   [*Exeunt Players.*]

  Enter Polonius, Guildenstern, and Rosencrantz.

How now, my lord? Will the king hear this piece of 45
 work?
POLONIUS. And the queen too, and that presently.
HAMLET. Bid the players make haste. *Exit Polonius.*
 Will you two help to hasten them?
ROSENCRANTZ. Ay, my lord.   *Exeunt they two.* 50
HAMLET. What, ho, Horatio!

    Enter Horatio.

HORATIO. Here, sweet lord, at your service.
HAMLET. Horatio, thou art e'en as just a man
 As e'er my conversation coped withal.
HORATIO. O my dear lord!
HAMLET.   Nay, do not think I flatter, 55
 For what advancement may I hope from thee,
 That no revénue hast but thy good spirits
 To feed and clothe thee? Why should the poor be
  flattered?
 No, let the candied tongue lick absurd pomp,
 And crook the pregnant hinges of the knee   60
 Where thrift may follow fawning. Dost thou hear?

35. *indifferently* fairly well, more or less 41. *necessary question* important issue 43. *fool* (i) clown, and (ii) idiot 53. *just* (in the Aristotelian sense of "virtuous and temperate") 54. *conversation* acquaintance *coped* encountered 59. *candied* (used frequently in Shakespeare as a metaphor for subservient "apple-polishing"; cf. *1 Henry IV* 1.3.251-8; *Antony and Cleopatra* 4.12.22) 60. *pregnant hinges* supple joints whose bendings also prove "productive" of favours 61. *thrift* advantage, profit *follow* result from

Since my dear soul was mistress of her choice
And could of men distinguish her election,
S'hath sealed thee for herself, for thou hast been
As one in suff'ring all that suffers nothing,   65
A man that Fortune's buffets and rewards
Hast ta'en with equal thanks; and blest are those
Whose blood and judgement are so well commingled
That they are not a pipe for Fortune's finger
To sound what stop she please. Give me that man   70
That is not passion's slave, and I will wear him
In my heart's core, ay, in my heart of heart,
As I do thee. Something too much of this.
There is a play to-night before the king.
One scene of it comes near the circumstance   75
Which I have told thee of my father's death.
I prithee, when thou seest that act afoot,
Even with the very comment of thy soul
Observe my uncle. If his occulted guilt
Do not itself unkennel in one speech,   80
It is a damnèd ghost that we have seen,
And my imaginations are as foul
As Vulcan's stithy. Give him heedful note,
For I mine eyes will rivet to his face,
And after we will both our judgements join   85
In censure of his seeming.
HORATIO.   Well, my lord.
If 'a steal aught the whilst this play is playing,
And 'scape detecting, I will pay the theft.

> *Enter Trumpets and Kettledrums, King, Queen,*
> *Polonius, Ophelia, Rosencrantz, Guildenstern,*
> *and other Lords attendant.*

63. *election* choice 64. *S'hath* she hath 68. *blood and judgement*
passion and reason 69-70. *a pipe . . . please* i.e. victims of the
whims of Fortune (as those are who act on impulse or deliberate too
long) 73. *Something . . . this* i.e. I'm letting myself get carried away
78. *the very . . . soul* your keenest and complete attention 79.
occulted hidden 80. *unkennel* reveal (suggesting that Claudius is a
dog who fawns and bites, smiles and is a villain) *in one speech* (the
"dozen or sixteen lines" Hamlet has inserted; see 2.2.531) 83. *stithy*
smithy, blacksmith's forge 86. *censure* judgement *seeming* behaviour
87-8. *If . . . theft* i.e. I won't let him get away with anything (one of
Horatio's typical, mildly humorous remarks)

HAMLET. They are coming to the play. I must be idle.
   Get you a place.   90

KING. How fares our cousin Hamlet?

HAMLET. Excellent, i' faith, of the chameleon's dish. I eat
   the air, promise-crammed. You cannot feed capons so.

KING. I have nothing with this answer, Hamlet. These
   words are not mine.   95

HAMLET. No, nor mine now, my Lord. You played once
   i' th' university, you say?

POLONIUS. That did I, my lord, and was accounted a good
   actor.

HAMLET. What did you enact?   100

POLONIUS. I did enact Julius Caesar. I was killed i' the'
   Capitol; Brutus killed me.

HAMLET. It was a brute part of him to kill so capital a calf
   there. Be the players ready?

ROSENCRANTZ. Ay, my lord, they stay upon your patience. 105

QUEEN. Come hither, my dear Hamlet, sit by me.

HAMLET. No, good mother, here's metal more attractive.

POLONIUS [to the King]. O, ho! do you mark that?

HAMLET. Lady, shall I lie in your lap?
                         [Lies down at Ophelia's feet.]

OPHELIA. No, my lord.   110

HAMLET. I mean, my head upon your lap?

OPHELIA. Ay, my lord.

HAMLET. Do you think I meant country matters?

OPHELIA. I think nothing, my lord.

HAMLET. That's a fair thought to lie between maids' legs. 115

OPHELIA. What is, my lord?

HAMLET. Nothing.

OPHELIA. You are merry, my lord.

HAMLET. Who, I?

OPHELIA. Ay, my lord.   120

89. *be idle* be foolish, i.e. play the madman 105. *stay . . . patience*
are waiting until you are ready for them 107. *metal more attractive*
(Hamlet is referring to Ophelia as a magnet that draws him to her)
108. *do . . . that* (Polonius rises to the bait that Hamlet has dropped
for him in the preceding line) 113. *Do . . . matters?* i.e. Do you
think I meant I wanted to sleep with you? 118. *merry* lewd (Ophelia
is mildly protesting at the turn the conversation has taken)

HAMLET. O God, your only jig-maker! What should a man do but be merry? For look you how cheerfully my mother looks, and my father died within's two hours.

OPHELIA. Nay, 'tis twice two months, my lord.

HAMLET. So long? Nay then, let the devil wear black, for 125 I'll have a suit of sables. O heavens! die two months ago, and not forgotten yet? Then there's hope a great man's memory may outlive his life half a year, but by'r lady 'a must build churches then, or else shall 'a suffer not thinking on, with the hobby-horse, whose epitaph is 130 "For O, for O, the hobby-horse is forgot!"

The trumpets sound. Dumb Show follows.

Enter a King and a Queen very lovingly; the Queen embracing him and he her. She kneels, and makes show of protestation unto him. He takes her up, and declines his head upon her neck. He lies him down upon a bank of flowers; she, seeing him asleep, leaves him. Anon comes in another man, takes off his crown, kisses it, pours poison in the sleeper's ears, and leaves him. The Queen returns, finds the King dead, makes passionate action. The Poisoner with some three or four comes in again, seems to condole with her. The dead body is carried away. The Poisoner woos the Queen with gifts; she seems harsh awhile, but in the end accepts love.

Exeunt.

OPHELIA. What means this, my lord?

HAMLET. Marry, this is miching mallecho; it means mischief.

OPHELIA. Belike this show imports the argument of the 135 play.

Enter Prologue.

HAMLET. We shall know by this fellow. The players cannot keep counsel; they'll tell all.

121. *your only jig-maker* only your writer of comic speeches, your "gag-man" 130. *hobby-horse* figure of a horse fastened around the waist of a morris-dancer 133. *miching mallecho* to "mich" is to "sneak", and "malheco" is Spanish for misdeed; "dirty work" is a fairly close modern equivalent 135. *argument* plot 138. *keep counsel* keep a secret

OPHELIA. Will a' tell us what this show meant?

HAMLET. Ay, or any show that you will show him. Be not 140
you ashamed to show, he'll not shame to tell you what it
means.

OPHELIA. You are naught, you are naught. I'll mark the
play.

PROLOGUE.   For us, and for our tragedy,   145
                Here stooping to your clemency,
                We beg your hearing patiently.   [Exit.]

HAMLET. Is this a prologue, or the posy of a ring?

OPHELIA. 'Tis brief, my lord.

HAMLET. As woman's love.   150

Enter [the Player] King and Queen.

PLAYER KING. Full thirty times hath Phoebus' cart gone
    round
Neptune's salt wash and Tellus' orbèd ground,
And thirty dozen moons with borrowed sheen
About the world have times twelve thirties been,
Since love our hearts and Hymen did our hands   155
Unite comutual in most sacred bands.

PLAYER QUEEN. So many journeys may the sun and moon
Make us again count o'er ere love be done!
But woe is me, you are so sick of late,
So far from cheer and from your former state,   160
That I distrust you. Yet though I distrust,
Discomfort you, my lord, it nothing must.
For women's fear and love hold quantity,
In neither aught, or in extremity.
Now what my love is proof hath made you know,   165
And as my love is sized, my fear is so.

143. *naught* naughty (but with a stronger meaning than it now carries)
146. *stooping* bowing *clemency* favourable reception (which makes
allowances for deficiencies) 147. *hearing patiently* patient hearing
148. *posy . . . ring* a brief verse motto engraved inside a keepsake
ring 151. *Phoebus' cart* the chariot of the sun 152. *Neptune's salt
wash* i.e. the sea *Tellus' orbèd ground* i.e. the round earth, the globe
153. *borrowed sheen* reflected light 155. *Hymen* the Roman god of
marriage 156. *bands* bonds 161. *distrust* am worried about 163.
hold quantity occur in equal proportions 164. *In neither . . . extremity*
i.e. either no love, no worry, or much love, much worry

Where love is great, the littlest doubts are fear;
Where little fears grow great, great love grows there.
PLAYER KING. *Faith, I must leave thee, love, and shortly*
        too;
My operant powers their functions leave to do.   170
And thou shalt live in this fair world behind,
Honoured, beloved, and haply one as kind
For husband shalt thou —
PLAYER QUEEN.   *O, confound the rest!*
Such love must needs be treason in my breast.
In second husband let me be accurst!   175
None wed the second but who killed the first.
HAMLET. That's wormwood.
PLAYER QUEEN. *The instances that second marriage move*
Are base respects of thrift, but none of love.
A second time I kill my husband dead,   180
When second husband kisses me in bed.
PLAYER KING. *I do believe you think what now you speak,*
But what we do determine oft we break.
Purpose is but the slave to memory,
Of violent birth, but poor validity;   185
Which now, the fruit unripe, sticks on the tree,
But fall unshaken when they mellow be.
Most necessary 'tis that we forget
To pay ourselves what to ourselves is debt.
What to ourselves in passion we propose,   190
The passion ending, doth the purpose lose.
The violence of either grief or joy
Their own enactures with themselves destroy.
Where joy most revels, grief doth most lament;
Grief joys, joy grieves, on slender accident.   195
This world is not for aye, nor 'tis not strange
That even our loves should with our fortunes change;
For 'tis a question left us yet to prove,
Whether love lead fortune, or else fortune love.

170. *operant powers* vital forces *leave to do* cease to perform 177.
wormwood a herb noted for its bitterness (Hamlet assumes that his
mother was involved in the murder of his father) 178. *instances*
motives 179. *respects* considerations *thrift* profit 185. *validity* endurance 193. *enactures* performances (violent emotions are short-lived,
and their purposed action dies with them)

The great man down, you mark his favourite flies;   200
The poor advanced makes friends of enemies;
And hitherto doth love on fortune tend,
For who not needs shall never lack a friend,
And who in want a hollow friend doth try,
Directly seasons him his enemy.   205
But orderly to end where I begun,
Our wills and fates do so contrary run
That our devices still are overthrown;
Our thoughts are ours, their ends none of our own.
So think thou wilt no second husband wed,   210
But die thy thoughts when thy first lord is dead.

PLAYER QUEEN. *Nor earth to me give food, nor heaven*
   light,
Sport and repose lock from me day and night,
To desperation turn my trust and hope,
An anchor's cheer in prison be my scope,   215
Each opposite that blanks the face of joy
Meet what I would have well, and it destroy,
Both here and hence pursue me lasting strife,
If once a widow, ever I be wife!

HAMLET. If she should break it now!   220

PLAYER KING. *'Tis deeply sworn. Sweet, leave me here*
   awhile.
My spirits grow dull, and fain I would beguile
The tedious day with sleep.   [*Sleeps.*]

PLAYER QUEEN.   *Sleep rock thy brain,*
   And never come mischance between us twain!   *Exit.*

HAMLET. Madam, how like you this play?   225

QUEEN. The lady doth protest too much, methinks.

HAMLET. O, but she'll keep her word.

KING. Have you heard the argument? Is there no offence
   in't?

HAMLET. No, no, they do but jest, poison in jest; no of-   230
   fence i' th' world.

KING. What do you call the play?

205. *seasons him* ripens him into 213. *Sport* pleasure 215. *anchor's
cheer* the lot of an anchorite or hermit *scope* range of activity 216.
opposite adversary *blanks* blanches

HAMLET. "The Mouse-trap." Marry, how? Tropically.
   This play is the image of a murder done in Vienna. Gonzago is the duke's name; his wife, Baptista. You shall 235
   see anon. 'Tis a knavish piece of work, but what of
   that? Your majesty, and we that have free souls, it
   touches us not. Let the galled jade wince, our withers
   are unwrung.

Enter Lucianus.

This is one Lucianus, nephew to the king.   240
OPHELIA. You are as good as a chorus, my lord.
HAMLET. I could interpret between you and your love, if
   I could see the puppets dallying.
OPHELIA. You are keen, my lord, you are keen.
HAMLET. It would cost you a groaning to take off mine 245
   edge.
OPHELIA. Still better, and worse.
HAMLET. So you must take your husbands. – Begin, mur-
   derer. Leave thy damnable faces and begin. Come, the   ‡
   croaking raven doth bellow for revenge.   250
LUCIANUS. *Thoughts black, hands apt, drugs fit, and time*
      agreeing,
   Confederate season, else no creature seeing,
   Thou mixture rank, of midnight weeds collected,
   With Hecate's ban thrice blasted, thrice infected,
   Thy natural magic and dire property   255
   On wholesome life usurp immediately.

Pours the poison in his ears.

233. *Mouse-trap* (in which he'll "catch the conscience of the King")
Tropically by a "trope" or figure of speech, i.e. metaphorically 238.
galled jade horse whose saddle rubs him *withers* shoulders (of a
horse) 239. *unwrung* not chafed 243. *puppets dallying* puppets
acting a scene of dalliance 244. *keen* sharp-witted 246. *edge* desire
247. *better* as to wit *worse* i.e. as to manners (Ophelia again gently
rebukes Hamlet for his lewd talk, assuming that he is not fully
responsible for what he says) 248. *So you . . . husbands* (i.e. "for
better, for worse") 249-50. *the . . . revenge* (a parody of two lines
from *The True Tragedy of Richard III*, a revenge play printed in 1594:
"The screeking Raven sits croaking for revenge./ Whole heards of
beasts comes bellowing for revenge") 252. *Confederate . . . seeing*
i.e. night, an accessory to the crime, is the only observer 253. *midnight weeds* (the ingredients of poisons and charms were supposed to
be especially effective if collected at midnight) 254. *Hecate's ban* the
curse of Hecate, goddess of witchcraft 255. *dire property* the poison's
fatal effect

HAMLET. 'A poisons him i' th' garden for his estate. His
 name's Gonzago. The story is extant, and written in
 very choice Italian. You shall see anon how the murderer gets the love of Gonzago's wife. 260

OPHELIA. The king rises.

HAMLET. What, frighted with false fire?

QUEEN. How fares my lord?

POLONIUS. Give o'er the play.

KING. Give me some light. Away! 265

POLONIUS. Lights, lights, lights!
      Exeunt all but Hamlet and Horatio.

HAMLET. Why, let the strucken deer go weep,
  The hart ungallèd play.
  For some must watch while some must sleep;
  Thus runs the world away. 270
 Would not this, sir, and a forest of feathers – if the rest
 of my fortunes turn Turk with me – with two Provin-
 cial roses on my razed shoes, get me a fellowship in a
 cry of players?

HORATIO. Half a share. 275

HAMLET. A whole one, I.
  For thou dost know, O Damon dear,
  This realm dismantled was
  Of Jove himself, and now reigns here
  A very, very – peacock. 280

HORATIO. You might have rhymed.

HAMLET. O good Horatio, I'll take the ghost's word for
 a thousand pound. Didst perceive?

HORATIO. Very well, my lord.

262. *false fire* discharge of a gun loaded with powder only 267-8.
Why . . . play i.e. Let the guilty weep and the innocent play 269.
watch stay awake (because of a guilty conscience) 271. *forest of
feathers* bunch of plumes (a detail of theatrical costume) 272. *turn
. . . me* prove cruel or false to me 272-3. *Provincial roses* damask
roses, the "rosa Provincialis", from Provinz, a town in France; also a
term for rosettes used as ornamental shoe-ties *razed* probably "raised"
fellowship partnership 274. *cry* company 275. *Half a share* (Horatio
says Hamlet's performance isn't quite good enough to entitle him to a
full share in such a company) 277. *Damon* (the mythical Damon
and Pythias were regarded as the models of perfect friendship) 279.
Of Jove himself i.e. of my father, a Jove among men 281. *You . . .
rhymed* (i.e. by substituting "ass" for "peacock" in l. 280)

HAMLET. Upon the talk of the poisoning.   285
HORATIO. I did very well note him.
HAMLET. Ah, ha! Come, some music. Come, the recorders.
    For if the king like not the comedy,
    Why then, belike he likes it not, perdy.
Come, some music.   290

Enter Rosencrantz and Guildenstern.

GUILDENSTERN. Good my lord, vouchsafe me a word with
  you.
HAMLET. Sir, a whole history.
GUILDENSTERN. The king, sir —
HAMLET. Ay, sir, what of him?   295
GUILDENSTERN. Is in his retirement marvellous distem-
  pered.
HAMLET. With drink, sir?
GUILDENSTERN. No, my lord, rather with choler.
HAMLET. Your wisdom should show itself more richer to 300
  signify this to the doctor, for for me to put him to his
  purgation would perhaps plunge him into more choler.
GUILDENSTERN. Good my lord, put your discourse into
  some frame, and start not so wildly from my affair.
HAMLET. I am tame, sir. Pronounce.   305
GUILDENSTERN. The queen your mother, in most great
  affliction of spirit, hath sent me to you.
HAMLET. You are welcome.
GUILDENSTERN. Nay, good my lord, this courtesy is not of
  the right breed. If it shall please you to make me a 310
  wholesome answer, I will do your mother's command-
  ment. If not, your pardon and my return shall be the
  end of my business.
HAMLET. Sir, I cannot.
ROSENCRANTZ. What, my lord?   315
HAMLET. Make you a wholesome answer; my wit's dis-
  eased. But, sir, such answer as I can make, you shall

288-9. *For . . . perdy* i.e. "If he doesn't like it, he can lump it"
("perdy" = *par Dieu*) 299. *choler* i.e. anger 301-2. *put . . . purgation*
purge him of the excess of the choleric "humour" 304. *frame* order
start . . . affair stray not so far from the point I am trying to make
311. *wholesome* reasonable

command, or rather, as you say, my mother. Therefore
no more, but to the matter. My mother, you say –

ROSENCRANTZ. Then thus she says: your behaviour hath 320
struck her into amazement and admiration.

HAMLET. O wonderful son, that can so stonish a mother!
But is there no sequel at the heels of this mother's
admiration? Impart.

ROSENCRANTZ. She desires to speak with you in her closet 325
ere you go to bed.

HAMLET. We shall obey, were she ten times our mother.
Have you any further trade with us?

ROSENCRANTZ. My lord, you once did love me.

HAMLET. And do still, by these pickers and stealers.   330

ROSENCRANTZ. Good my lord, what is your cause of distemper? You do surely bar the door upon your own
liberty, if you deny your griefs to your friend.

HAMLET. Sir, I lack advancement.

ROSENCRANTZ. How can that be, when you have the voice 335
of the king himself for your succession in Denmark?

HAMLET. Ay, sir, but "while the grass grows" – the pro-   ‡
verb is something musty.

Enter the Players with recorders.

O, the recorders! Let me see one. To withdraw with
you – why do you go about to recover the wind of me, 340
as if you would drive me into a toil?

GUILDENSTERN. O my lord, if my duty be too bold, my
love is too unmannerly.

HAMLET. I do not well understand that. Will you play
upon this pipe?   345

GUILDENSTERN. My lord, I cannot.

HAMLET. I pray you.

GUILDENSTERN. Believe me, I cannot.

HAMLET. I do beseech you.

321. *admiration* wonder   330. *by . . . stealers* i.e. by this hand   331-2.
distemper disorder   338. *something musty* somewhat stale   339. *withdraw* step aside for private talk   340. *recover . . . me* get between me and
the wind (a metaphor from sailing)   341. *toil* snare   342-3. *if . . .
unmannerly* it is my love and duty which make me forget my manners
in questioning you so boldly

GUILDENSTERN. I know no touch of it, my lord.   350

HAMLET. It is as easy as lying. Govern these ventages with
  your fingers and thumb, give it breath with your mouth,
  and it will discourse most eloquent music. Look you,
  these are the stops.

GUILDENSTERN. But these cannot I command to any utt'r- 355
  ance of harmony. I have not the skill.

HAMLET. Why, look you now, how unworthy a thing you
  make of me! You would play upon me, you would seem
  to know my stops, you would pluck out the heart of my
  mystery, you would sound me from my lowest note to 360
  the top of my compass; and there is much music, excellent voice, in this little organ, yet cannot you make it
  speak. 'Sblood, do you think I am easier to be played on
  than a pipe? Call me what instrument you will, though
  you can fret me, you cannot play upon me.   365

                         [*Exeunt Players.*]
                  Enter Polonius.

God bless you, sir!

POLONIUS. My lord, the queen would speak with you, and
  presently.

HAMLET. Do you see yonder cloud that's almost in shape
  of a camel?   370

POLONIUS. By th' mass, and 'tis like a camel indeed.

HAMLET. Methinks it is like a weasel.

POLONIUS. It is backed like a weasel.

HAMLET. Or like a whale.

POLONIUS. Very like a whale.   375

HAMLET. Then I will come to my mother by and by.
  [*Aside*] They fool me to the top of my bent. — I will
  come by and by.

POLONIUS. I will say so.   *Exit [Polonius].*

351. *ventages* stops or holes of the recorder 359. *pluck out* (with a
play on "plucking" the strings of an instrument) 361. *compass*
musical range 365. *fret me* (i) irritate me, (ii) put frets (the metal
strips across the neck of a stringed instrument to guide the fingering)
on me 369-75. *Do . . . whale* (in agreeing that the cloud looks like
a variety of animals, Polonius is humouring the madman) 377. *fool
. . . bent* humour my madness (i.e. treat me like a fool) as completely
as I could wish

HAMLET. "By and by" is easily said. Leave me, friends.　　380
　　　　　　　　Exeunt Rosencrantz and Guildenstern.
　'Tis now the very witching time of night,
　When churchyards yawn, and hell itself breathes out
　Contagion to this world. Now could I drink hot blood,
　And do such bitter business as the day
　Would quake to look on. Soft, now to my mother.　　385
　O heart, lose not thy nature; let not ever
　The soul of Nero enter this firm bosom.
　Let me be cruel, not unnatural;
　I will speak daggers to her, but use none.
　My tongue and soul in this be hypocrites –　　390
　How in my words somever she be shent,
　To give them seals never, my soul, consent!　　*Exit.*

[Scene 3. *A room in the castle.*]

Enter King, Rosencrantz, and Guildenstern.

KING. I like him not, nor stands it safe with us
　To let his madness range. Therefore prepare you.
　I your commission will forthwith dispatch,
　And he to England shall along with you.
　The terms of our estate may not endure　　5
　Hazard so near us as doth hourly grow
　Out of his brows.
GUILDENSTERN.　　We will ourselves provide.
　Most holy and religious fear it is
　To keep those many many bodies safe
　That live and feed upon your majesty.　　10

383. *Contagion* (night air was supposed to breed diseases)　387. *Nero* (the Emperor Nero murdered his mother)　391. *shent* rebuked, abused 392. *give them seals* i.e. fulfil them in action

3.3.1. *I like him not* i.e. I don't like the way he's acting 5. *The terms of our estate* the circumstances of our position (Claudius is using the royal plural) 7. *his brows* i.e. his muddled head 8. *Most . . . fear* i.e. not timidity, but the sacred responsibility of the ruler to be concerned for the welfare of his subjects

ROSENCRANTZ. The single and peculiar life is bound
   With all the strength and armour of the mind
   To keep itself from noyance, but much more
   That spirit upon whose weal depends and rests
   The lives of many. The cess of majesty   15
   Dies not alone, but like a gulf doth draw
   What's near it with it. It is a massy wheel
   Fixed on the summit of the highest mount,
   To whose huge spokes ten thousand lesser things
   Are mortised and adjoined, which when it falls,   20
   Each small annexment, petty consequence,
   Attends the boist'rous ruin. Never alone
   Did the king sigh, but with a general groan.
KING. Arm you, I pray you, to this speedy voyage,
   For we will fetters put about this fear,   25
   Which now goes too free-footed.
ROSENCRANTZ.   We will haste us.
                              Exeunt Gentlemen.

                    Enter Polonius.

POLONIUS. My lord, he's going to his mother's closet.
   Behind the arras I'll convey myself
   To hear the process. I'll warrant she'll tax him home,
   And as you said, and wisely was it said,   30
   'Tis meet that some more audience than a mother,
   Since nature makes them partial, should o'erhear
   The speech, of vantage. Fare you well, my liege.
   I'll call upon you ere you go to bed,
   And tell you what I know.
KING.   Thanks, dear my lord.   35
                              Exit [Polonius].

11-13. *The single . . . noyance* for the individual, self-preservation is
the first law of nature   14. *weal* well-being   15. *cess* cessation, death
16. *gulf* i.e. whirlpool (the metaphor is that of a sinking ship)   20.
mortised attached with mortise and tenon joints   24. *Arm you* prepare
yourselves   29. *process* conversation   *tax him home* get to the heart
of the matter in her reproof   33. *of vantage* from some hidden vantage-
point, or possibly (as Dover Wilson suggests) "in addition" (to
Gertrude)

O, my offence is rank, it smells to heaven;
It hath the primal eldest curse upon't,
A brother's murder. Pray can I not,
Though inclination be as sharp as will.
My stronger guilt defeats my strong intent,   40
And like a man to double business bound,
I stand in pause where I shall first begin,
And both neglect. What if this cursèd hand
Were thicker than itself with brother's blood,
Is there not rain enough in the sweet heavens   45
To wash it white as snow? Whereto serves mercy
But to confront the visage of offence?
And what's in prayer but this twofold force,
To be forestallèd ere we come to fall,
Or pardoned being down? Then I'll look up.   50
My fault is past. But, O, what form of prayer
Can serve my turn? "Forgive me my foul murder"?
That cannot be, since I am still possessed
Of those effects for which I did the murder –
My crown, mine own ambition, and my queen.   55
May one be pardoned and retain th' offence?
In the corrupted currents of this world
Offence's gilded hand may shove by justice,
And oft 'tis seen the wicked prize itself
Buys out the law. But 'tis not so above.   60
There is no shuffling; there the action lies
In his true nature, and we ourselves compelled,
Even to the teeth and forehead of our faults,
To give in evidence. What then? What rests?

36. *rank* (i) gross, (ii) foul-smelling   37-8. *primal . . . murder* i.e. the curse of Cain for the murder of his brother Abel (see Gen. 4:10-12) 39. *Though . . . will* though desire and intention are equally strong 41. *to . . . bound* obligated to perform contradictory tasks 46-7. *Whereto . . . offence* The function of Mercy is to confront the accuser, Guilt, and secure from the Great Judge the soul's pardon 49. *To be forestallèd* not to be led into temptation 50. *pardoned being down* having our trespasses forgiven 54. *effects* advantages 55. *mine own ambition* i.e. the fulfilment of my ambition 56. *offence* i.e. benefit of crime 58. *gilded* (i.e. with ill-gotten gains) *shove by* thrust aside 61. *shuffling* double-dealing *the action lies* the suit may legally be brought to trial 62-4. *compelled . . . evidence* (contrary to the principle of law that a man cannot be required to testify against himself) 63. *to . . . faults* face to face with our sins, who are the accusers 64. *rests* remains

Try what repentance can. What can it not?   65
Yet what can it when one can not repent?
O wretched state! O bosom black as death!
O limèd soul, that struggling to be free
Art more engaged! Help, angels! Make assay.
Bow, stubborn knees, and heart with strings of steel,   70
Be soft as sinews of the new-born babe.
All may be well.   [*He kneels.*]

Enter Hamlet.

HAMLET. Now might I do it pat, now 'a is a-praying,
And now I'll do't – and so 'a goes to heaven,
And so am I revenged. That would be scanned.   75
A villain kills my father, and for that,
I, his sole son, do this same villain send
To heaven.
Why, this is hire and salary, not revenge.
'A took my father grossly, full of bread,   80
With all his crimes broad blown, as flush as May;
And how his audit stands who knows save heaven?
But in our circumstance and course of thought
'Tis heavy with him; and am I then revenged
To take him in the purging of his soul,   85
When he is fit and seasoned for his passage?
No.
Up, sword, and know thou a more horrid hent.
When he is drunk asleep, or in his rage,
Or in th' incestuous pleasure of his bed,   90
At game a-swearing, or about some act
That has no relish of salvation in't –

66. *can not repent* (the King realizes that his remorse is not true
repentance) 68. *O limèd soul* (the metaphor is that of a bird caught
in bird-lime, a sticky substance applied to twigs) 69. *assay* the
attempt 73. *pat* readily 75. *would be scanned* i.e. requires a second
look 79. *hire and salary* paying him (for killing my father) 80.
grossly, full of bread in gross condition (as opposed to in a state of
grace, prepared for by prayer and fasting) 81. *crimes broad blown*
faults in full bloom (cf. 1.5.76) *flush* as flourishing 82. *audit* final
account 83. *in our . . . thought* as far as our imperfect human
knowledge can tell 84. *'Tis heavy with him* i.e. his account is sadly
in the red 86. *fit and seasoned* thoroughly prepared 88. *hent* occasion
92. *relish* flavour

Then trip him, that his heels may kick at heaven,
And that his soul may be as damned and black
As hell, whereto it goes. My mother stays.   95
This physic but prolongs thy sickly days.   *Exit.*
KING [*rising*]. My words fly up, my thoughts remain
  below.
Words without thoughts never to heaven go.   *Exit.*

[Scene 4. *The Queen's closet.*]

Enter [Queen] Gertrude and Polonius.

POLONIUS. 'A will come straight. Look you lay home
  to him.
Tell him his pranks have been too broad to bear with,
And that your grace hath screened and stood between
Much heat and him. I'll silence me even here.
Pray you be round.
QUEEN.   I'll warrant you. Fear me not.   5
Withdraw, I hear him coming.
                [*Polonius goes behind the arras.*]

Enter Hamlet.

HAMLET. Now, mother, what's the matter?
QUEEN. Hamlet, thou hast thy father much offended.
HAMLET. Mother, you have my father much offended.
QUEEN. Come, come, you answer with an idle tongue.   10
HAMLET. Go, go, you question with a wicked tongue.
QUEEN. Why, how now, Hamlet?
HAMLET.   What's the matter now?
QUEEN. Have you forgot me?
HAMLET.   No, by the rood, not so.

3.4.1. *straight* right away *Look . . . him* see that you lay it on
thoroughly 2. *been too broad* gone too far 4. *Much heat* i.e. the
King's resentment *silence . . . here* stop talking and hide right here
5. *Fear me not* Don't worry 8-11. *Hamlet . . . wicked tongue* (such
line-for-line dialogue is termed "stichomythia") 10. *idle* foolish 13.
forgot me forgotten who I am (that you speak so rudely) *rood* cross

You are the queen, your husband's brother's wife,
And would it were not so, you are my mother.   15
QUEEN. Nay, then I'll set those to you that can speak.
HAMLET. Come, come, and sit you down. You shall not
     budge.
You go not till I set you up a glass
Where you may see the inmost part of you.
QUEEN. What wilt thou do? Thou wilt not murder me?   20
     Help, ho!
POLONIUS [*behind*]. What, ho! help!
HAMLET [*draws*]. How now, a rat?
     Dead for a ducat, dead!
            [*Kills Polonius with a pass through the arras.*]
POLONIUS [*behind*]. O, I am slain!   25
QUEEN. O me, what hast thou done?
HAMLET.   Nay, I know not.
     Is it the king?
QUEEN. O, what a rash and bloody deed is this!
HAMLET. A bloody deed! – almost as bad, good mother,
     As kill a king and marry with his brother.   30
QUEEN. As kill a king?
HAMLET.   Ay, lady, it was my word.
                         [*Parting the arras.*]
Thou wretched, rash, intruding fool, farewell!
I took thee for thy better. Take thy fortune.
Thou find'st to be too busy is some danger. –
Leave wringing of your hands. Peace, sit you down   35
And let me wring your heart, for so I shall
If it be made of penetrable stuff,
If damnèd custom have not brazed it so
That it be proof and bulwark against sense.
QUEEN. What have I done that thou dar'st wag thy tongue   40
     In noise so rude against me?

16. *those . . . speak* (i.e. with more authority. The Queen is threatening
to summon Claudius) 18. *glass* mirror 20. *What . . . do* (Hamlet is
no doubt forcibly restraining her from leaving) 31. *As kill a king*
(Gertrude's genuine amazement at Hamlet's words of accusation acquits
her of complicity in her former husband's murder) 34. *too busy* a
busybody 38. *brazed it* brazened it, armoured it (against shame) 39.
sense feeling

HAMLET.   Such an act
   That blurs the grace and blush of modesty,
   Calls virtue hypocrite, takes off the rose
   From the fair forehead of an innocent love,
   And sets a blister there, makes marriage-vows   45
   As false as dicers' oaths. O, such a deed
   As from the body of contraction plucks
   The very soul, and sweet religion makes
   A rhapsody of words. Heaven's face does glow
   O'er this solidity and compound mass   50
   With heated visage, as against the doom –
   Is thought-sick at the act.
QUEEN.   Ay me, what act,
   That roars so loud and thunders in the index?
HAMLET. Look here upon this picture and on this,
   The counterfeit presentment of two brothers.   55
   See what a grace was seated on this brow:
   Hyperion's curls, the front of Jove himself,
   An eye like Mars, to threaten and command,
   A station like the herald Mercury
   New lighted on a heaven-kissing hill –   60
   A combination and a form indeed
   Where every god did seem to set his seal,
   To give the world assurance of a man.
   This was your husband. Look you now what follows.
   Here is your husband, like a mildewed ear   65
   Blasting his wholesome brother. Have you eyes?
   Could you on this fair mountain leave to feed,
   And batten on this moor? Ha! have you eyes?

43. *rose* i.e. the emblem of true love 45. *blister* the brand of infamy
(see 4.5.116-17) 47. *contraction* the marriage contract 48-9. *sweet
... words* makes the marriage service nothing but sentimental verbiage
49. *does glow* blushes (first with shame, then with anger ["heat"])
50. *this solidity ... mass* i.e. the earth, whose matter is compounded of
the elements earth, air, fire, and water 51. *against the doom* just
before Judgement Day 52. *thought-sick ... act* nauseated by the
very thought of such an act 53. *in the index* in the very beginning,
as in a table of contents on the first pages of a book 55. *counterfeit
presentment* portrait 59. *station* bearing, posture 61. *A combination*
(i.e. of physical qualities) 65. *ear* (i.e. of grain) 66. *Blasting ...* i.e.
blighting ... 68. *batten* gorge yourself; *moor* (i) wasteland (ii) dark man

You cannot call it love, for at your age
The heyday in the blood is tame, it's humble,   70
And waits upon the judgement, and what judgement
Would step from this to this? Sense sure you have,
Else could you not have motion, but sure that sense
Is apoplexed, for madness would not err,
Nor sense to ecstasy was ne'er so thralled   75
But it reserved some quantity of choice
To serve in such a difference. What devil was't
That thus hath cozened you at hoodman-blind?
Eyes without feeling, feeling without sight,
Ears without hands or eyes, smelling sans all,   80
Or but a sickly part of one true sense
Could not so mope. O shame! where is thy blush?
Rebellious hell,
If thou canst mutine in a matron's bones,
To flaming youth let virtue be as wax   85
And melt in her own fire. Proclaim no shame
When the compulsive ardour gives the charge,
Since frost itself as actively doth burn,
And reason panders will.
QUEEN.   O Hamlet, speak no more!
Thou turn'st my eyes into my very soul;   90
And there I see such black and grainèd spots
As will not leave their tint.
HAMLET.   Nay, but to live
In the rank sweat of an enseamèd bed,
Stewed in corruption, honeying and making love
Over the nasty sty –

70. *heyday . . . blood* careless rapture of passion, the "compulsive ardour" of line 87   71. *waits . . . judgement* defers to and is the servant of reason   78. *cozened . . . hoodman-blind* cheated you at blindman's buff   80. *sans* without   82. *so mope* be so torpid, i.e. insensitive   85. *flaming youth* youth on fire with love *virtue* (i) restraint of passion, (ii) a characteristic force or quality – here the ardour of youthful love   87. *gives the charge* sounds the signal to attack   88. *frost* i.e. the "tame" desires of middle age (as contrasted with those of "flaming youth")   89. *reason panders will* reason, which should command desire, becomes subservient to it and even seeks out occasions for its indulgence   91. *grainèd spots* ingrained faults   92. *leave their tint* lose their dye   93. *enseamèd* greasy

QUEEN.   O, speak to me no more!   95
  These words like daggers enter in my ears;
  No more, sweet Hamlet.
HAMLET.   A murderer and a villain,
  A slave that is not twentieth part the tithe
  Of your precedent lord, a vice of kings,
  A cutpurse of the empire and the rule,   100
  That from a shelf the precious diadem stole
  And put it in his pocket –
QUEEN. No more.

Enter Ghost.

HAMLET. A king of shreds and patches –
  Save me and hover o'er me with your wings,   105
  You heavenly guards! What would your gracious figure?
QUEEN. Alas, he's mad.
HAMLET. Do you not come your tardy son to chide,
  That lapsed in time and passion lets go by
  Th' important acting of your dread command?   110
  O, say!
GHOST. Do not forget. This visitation
  Is but to whet thy almost blunted purpose.
  But look, amazement on thy mother sits.
  O, step between her and her fighting soul!   115
  Conceit in weakest bodies strongest works.
  Speak to her, Hamlet.
HAMLET. How is it with you, lady?
QUEEN.   Alas, how is't with you,
  That you do bend your eye on vacancy,
  And with th' incorporal air do hold discourse?   120
  Forth at your eyes your spirits wildly peep,
  And as the sleeping soldiers in th' alarm,
  Your bedded hairs like life in excrements
  Start up and stand on end. O gentle son,

---

98. *tithe* a tenth part **99.** *vice* caricature **100.** *cutpurse* pickpocket, petty thief **109.** *lapsed . . . passion* having let time slip by and righteous indignation diminish **116.** *Conceit* imagination **119.** *vacancy* emptiness **120.** *incorporal* bodiless **123.** *like . . . excrements* as if there were life in the body's outgrowths (such as hair and nails)

Upon the heat and flame of thy distemper   125
Sprinkle cool patience. Whereon do you look?
HAMLET. On him, on him! Look you how pale he glares.
His form and cause conjoined, preaching to stones,
Would make them capable. – Do not look upon me,
Lest with this piteous action you convert   130
My stern effects. Then what I have to do
Will want true colour – tears perchance for blood.
QUEEN. To whom do you speak this?
HAMLET. Do you see nothing there?
QUEEN. Nothing at all, yet all that is I see.   135
HAMLET. Nor did you nothing hear?
QUEEN. No, nothing but ourselves.
HAMLET. Why, look you there. Look how it steals away.
My father, in his habit as he lived!
Look where he goes even now out at the portal.   140

Exit Ghost.

QUEEN. This is the very coinage of your brain.
This bodiless creation ecstasy
Is very cunning in.
HAMLET. My pulse as yours doth temperately keep time,
And makes as healthful music. It is not madness   145
That I have uttered. Bring me to the test,
And I the matter will re-word, which madness
Would gambol from. Mother, for love of grace,
Lay not that flattering unction to your soul,
That not your trespass but my madness speaks.   150
It will but skin and film the ulcerous place
Whiles rank corruption, mining all within,
Infects unseen. Confess yourself to heaven,
Repent what's past, avoid what is to come,

---

125. *distemper* madness   129. *capable* (i.e. of feeling)   130. *piteous*
(i) pitying, and (ii) pitiable   *convert* change   131. *effects* i.e. intended
deeds   130-32. *you convert . . . colour* you weaken my indignation
which should "colour", i.e. justify, killing Claudius   *tears . . . blood*
so that I may perhaps shed colourless tears instead of red blood   139.
in . . . lived in his usual dress for this time and place (in contrast to
his previous appearance in armour)   142. *bodiless creation* i.e. seeing
things that aren't there   *ecstasy* madness   148. *gambol* leap away
149. *unction* ointment   152. *mining* undermining

And do not spread the compost on the weeds,   155
To make them ranker. Forgive me this my virtue,
For in the fatness of these pursy times
Virtue itself of vice must pardon beg,
Yea, curb and woo for leave to do him good.

QUEEN. O Hamlet, thou hast cleft my heart in twain.   160

HAMLET. O, throw away the worser part of it,
And live the purer with the other half.
Good night – but go not to my uncle's bed.
Assume a virtue, if you have it not.
That monster custom, who all sense doth eat,   165 ‡
Of habits devil, is angel yet in this,
That to the use of actions fair and good
He likewise gives a frock or livery
That aptly is put on. Refrain to-night,
And that shall lend a kind of easiness   170
To the next abstinence; the next more easy;
For use almost can change the stamp of nature,
And either curb the devil, or throw him out
With wondrous potency. Once more, good night,
And when you are desirous to be blest,   175
I'll blessing beg of you. For this same lord
I do repent; but heaven hath pleased it so,   ‡
To punish me with this, and this with me,
That I must be their scourge and minister.
I will bestow him and will answer well   180
The death I gave him. So, again, good night.
I must be cruel only to be kind.
Thus bad begins and worse remains behind.
One word more, good lady.

QUEEN.   What shall I do?

HAMLET. Not this, by no means, that I bid you do: 185
Let the bloat king tempt you again to bed,
Pinch wanton on your cheek, call you his mouse,
And let him, for a pair of reechy kisses,

156. *virtue* i.e. speaking unpleasant truth 157. *fatness* grossness
pursy short-winded 159. *curb* bend the knee 188. *reechy* filthy
(literally: smoky)

Or paddling in your neck with his damned fingers,
Make you to ravel all this matter out,   190
That I essentially am not in madness,
But mad in craft. 'Twere good you let him know,
For who that's but a queen, fair, sober, wise,
Would from a paddock, from a bat, a gib,
Such dear concernings hide? Who would do so?   195
No, in despite of sense and secrecy,
Unpeg the basket on the house's top,
Let the birds fly, and like the famous ape,
To try conclusions, in the basket creep
And break your own neck down.   200
QUEEN. Be thou assured, if words be made of breath
    And breath of life, I have no life to breathe
    What thou hast said to me.
HAMLET. I must to England; you know that?
QUEEN.   Alack,
    I had forgot. 'Tis so concluded on.   205
HAMLET. There's letters sealed, and my two school-
    fellows,
    Whom I will trust as I will adders fanged,
    They bear the mandate; they must sweep my way
    And marshal me to knavery. Let it work,
    For 'tis the sport to have the engineer   210
    Hoist with his own petar; and't shall go hard
    But I will delve one yard below their mines
    And blow them at the moon. O, 'tis most sweet
    When in one line two crafts directly meet.
    This man shall set me packing.   215
    I'll lug the guts into the neighbour room.

191. *essentially* in reality 194. *paddock* toad *gib* tomcat 199. *try
conclusions* make an experiment 208. *mandate* orders *sweep my way*
clear my path 209. *marshal* conduct *knavery* some dirty work
directed against me 210-13. *'tis . . . moon* the game is to blow up the
engineer with his own blasting charge, and if I have any luck at all, I
shall counter-mine underneath their tunnel and blast them off to the
moon 211. *petar* a bomb especially designed for blowing gates open
214. *crafts* (i) plots, (ii) ships 215. *This man . . . packing* (another
of Hamlet's grim puns) I shall start packing (for the journey) by
packing Polonius' body away on my back

Mother, good night. Indeed, this counsellor
Is now most still, most secret, and most grave,
Who was in life a foolish prating knave.
Come sir, to draw toward an end with you.   220
Good night, mother.

> *[Exit the Queen. Then] exit [Hamlet*
> *tugging in Polonius].*

220. *draw . . . end* (i) conclude my business, (ii) draw (drag) away
the body

[ACT 4]

[Scene 1. *A room in the castle.*]

Enter King and Queen, with Rosencrantz
and Guildenstern.

KING. There's matter in these sighs, these profound
      heaves,
    You must translate; 'tis fit we understand them.
    Where is your son?
QUEEN. Bestow this place on us a little while.
                    Exeunt Rosencrantz and Guildenstern.
    Ah, mine own lord, what have I seen to-night!   5
KING. What, Gertrude? How does Hamlet?
QUEEN. Mad as the sea and wind when both contend
    Which is the mightier. In his lawless fit,
    Behind the arras hearing something stir,
    Whips out his rapier, cries "A rat, a rat!"   10
    And in this brainish apprehension kills
    The unseen good old man.
KING.   O heavy deed!
    It had been so with us had we been there.
    His liberty is full of threats to all –
    To you yourself, to us, to every one.   15
    Alas, how shall this bloody deed be answered?
    It will be laid to us, whose providence
    Should have kept short, restrained, and out of haunt,
    This mad young man. But so much was our love,
    We would not understand what was most fit;   20
    But, like the owner of a foul disease,
    To keep it from divulging, let it feed
    Even on the pith of life. Where is he gone?

4.1.2. *translate* explain 11. *brainish apprehension* brainsick notion
16. *answered* accounted for 17. *providence* foresight 18. *out of*
haunt away from other people 22. *divulging* being discovered

QUEEN. To draw apart the body he hath killed,
 O'er whom his very madness, like some ore   25
 Among a mineral of metals base,
 Shows itself pure: 'a weeps for what is done.
KING. O Gertrude, come away!
 The sun no sooner shall the mountains touch
 But we will ship him hence, and this vile deed 30
 We must with all our majesty and skill
 Both countenance and excuse. Ho, Guildenstern!

Enter Rosencrantz and Guildenstern.

 Friends both, go join you with some further aid.
 Hamlet in madness hath Polonius slain,
 And from his mother's closet hath he dragged him. 35
 Go seek him out; speak fair, and bring the body
 Into the chapel. I pray you haste in this.
     Exeunt [Rosencrantz and Guildenstern.]
 Come, Gertrude, we'll call up our wisest friends
 And let them know both what we mean to do
 And what's untimely done; so haply slander – 40
 Whose whisper o'er the world's diameter,
 As level as the cannon to his blank,
 Transports his poisoned shot – may miss our name,
 And hit the woundless air. O, come away!
 My soul is full of discord and dismay. *Exeunt.* 45

[Scene 2. *Another room in the castle.*]

Enter Hamlet.

HAMLET. Safely stowed.
ROSENCRANTZ AND GUILDENSTERN [*within*]. Hamlet! Lord
 Hamlet!
HAMLET. But soft, what noise? Who calls on Hamlet? O,
 here they come. 5

  [*Enter*] Rosencrantz, [*Guildenstern,*] *and Others.*

32. *countenance* assume responsibility for *excuse* explain 42. *his
blank* its mark (the "blank" is the white spot in the centre of a
target) 44. *woundless* invulnerable

ROSENCRANTZ. What have you done, my lord, with the
    dead body?
HAMLET. Compounded it with dust, whereto 'tis kin.
ROSENCRANTZ. Tell us where 'tis, that we may take it
    thence
And bear it to the chapel.
HAMLET. Do not believe it.   10
ROSENCRANTZ. Believe what?
HAMLET. That I can keep your counsel and not mine own.
    Besides, to be demanded of a sponge – what replication
    should be made by the son of a king?
ROSENCRANTZ. Take you me for a sponge, my lord?   15
HAMLET. Ay, sir, that soaks up the king's countenance,
    his rewards, his authorities. But such officers do the king
    best service in the end. He keeps them like an apple in
    the corner of his jaw, first mouthed to be last swallowed.
    When he needs what you have gleaned, it is but squeez-   20
    ing you and, sponge, you shall be dry again.
ROSENCRANTZ. I understand you not, my lord.
HAMLET. I am glad of it. A knavish speech sleeps in a
    foolish ear.
ROSENCRANTZ. My lord, you must tell us where the body   25
    is, and go with us to the king.
HAMLET. The body is with the king, but the king is not
    with the body. The king is a thing –
GUILDENSTERN. A thing, my lord!
HAMLET. Of nothing. Bring me to him. Hide fox, and all   30
    after!   *Exeunt.*

[Scene 3. *Another room in the castle.*]

Enter King, and two or three.

KING. I have sent to seek him, and to find the body.
    How dangerous is it that this man goes loose!
    Yet must not we put the strong law on him.

4.2.13. *demanded of* questioned by *replication* reply 16. *countenance* favour 23-4. *A knavish . . . ear* i.e. You are too stupid to get
the point of the insult 30-31. *Hide . . . after* (cry used in a variant
of hide-and-seek probably resembling run-sheep-run)

He's loved of the distracted multitude,
Who like not in their judgement but their eyes,   5
And where 'tis so, th' offender's scourge is weighed,
But never the offence. To bear all smooth and even,
This sudden sending him away must seem
Deliberate pause. Diseases desperate grown
By desperate appliance are relieved,   10
Or not at all.

Enter Rosencrantz, [Guildenstern,] and all the rest.

How now! what hath befall'n?
ROSENCRANTZ. Where the dead body is bestowed, my lord,
  We cannot get from him.
KING.   But where is he?
ROSENCRANTZ. Without, my lord; guarded, to know your
  pleasure.
KING. Bring him before us.
ROSENCRANTZ.   Ho! bring in the lord.   15

They enter [with Hamlet].

KING. Now, Hamlet, where's Polonius?
HAMLET. At supper.
KING. At supper? Where?
HAMLET. Not where he eats, but where 'a is eaten. A certain convocation of politic worms are e'en at him. Your 20
  worm is your only emperor for diet. We fat all creatures
  else to fat us, and we fat ourselves for maggots. Your
  fat king and your lean beggar is but variable service —
  two dishes, but to one table. That's the end.
KING. Alas, alas!   25
HAMLET. A man may fish with the worm that hath eat of
  a king, and eat of the fish that hath fed of that worm.

4.3.4. *distracted* turbulent and/or foolish 6. *scourge is weighed*
punishment is considered 7. *bear . . . even* put a good face on it in
order to avoid public disturbance 9. *Deliberate pause* careful consideration 9-10. *Diseases . . . relieved* (rewording of the proverb
"Desperate ills demand desperate remedies") 14. *guarded* (Hamlet
has now lost the freedom of action he has previously enjoyed, despite
his supposed madness) 20-21. *convocation . . . diet* (probably referring
to the Diet of the Holy Roman Empire, held at Worms in 1521)

KING. What dost thou mean by this?

HAMLET. Nothing but to show you how a king may go a
  progress through the guts of a beggar.   30

KING. Where is Polonius?

HAMLET. In heaven. Send thither to see. If your messenger
  find him not there, seek him i' th' other place yourself.
  But if, indeed, you find him not within this month, you
  shall nose him as you go up the stairs into the lobby.   35

KING [to Attendants]. Go seek him there.

HAMLET. 'A will stay till you come.

                               [Exeunt Attendants.]

KING. Hamlet, this deed, for thine especial safety –
  Which we do tender, as we dearly grieve
  For that which thou hast done – must send thee hence   40
  With fiery quickness. Therefore prepare thyself.
  The bark is ready, and the wind at help,
  Th' associates tend, and everything is bent
  For England.

HAMLET.   For England?

KING.   Ay, Hamlet.

HAMLET.   Good.

KING. So is it, if thou knew'st our purposes.   45

HAMLET. I see a cherub that sees them. But come, for
    England!
  Farewell, dear mother.

KING. Thy loving father, Hamlet.

HAMLET. My mother. Father and mother is man and wife,
  man and wife is one flesh. So, my mother. Come, for   50
  England.   Exit.

KING. Follow him at foot; tempt him with speed aboard.
  Delay it not; I'll have him hence to-night.
  Away! for everything is sealed and done
  That else leans on th' affair. Pray you make haste.   55

                       Exeunt [all but the King.]

<hr>

30. *progress* state journey   39. *tender* value, cherish   42. *at help*
favourable   43. *associates tend* escort awaits you   *bent* in readiness (a
figure from archery)   45. *if . . . purposes* (Claudius is playing Hamlet's game of *double entendre*)   46. *a cherub* (Heaven's cherubim see
everything)   52. *him at foot* at his heels   *tempt* coax   55. *leans on*
pertains to this business

And, England, if my love thou hold'st at aught –
As my great power thereof may give thee sense,
Since yet thy cicatrice looks raw and red
After the Danish sword, and thy free awe
Pays homage to us – thou mayst not coldly set   60
Our sovereign process, which imports at full
By letters congruing to that effect
The present death of Hamlet. Do it, England,
For like the hectic in my blood he rages,
And thou must cure me. Till I know 'tis done,   65
Howe'er my haps, my joys were ne'er begun.   *Exit.*

[Scene 4. *A plain in Denmark.*]

Enter Fortinbras with his Army over the stage.

FORTINBRAS. Go, captain, from me greet the Danish king.
Tell him that by his licence Fortinbras
Craves the conveyance of a promised march
Over his kingdom. You know the rendezvous.
If that his majesty would aught with us,   5
We shall express our duty in his eye,
And let him know so.
CAPTAIN.   I will do't, my lord.
FORTINBRAS. Go softly on.   *Exeunt [all but the Captain.]*

*Enter Hamlet, Rosencrantz, [Guildenstern,]
and Others.*

HAMLET. Good sir, whose powers are these?
CAPTAIN. They are of Norway, sir.   10
HAMLET. How purposed, sir, I pray you?
CAPTAIN. Against some part of Poland.

58. *cicatrice* scar (of defeat) 59-60. *free awe . . . us* i.e. England,
though technically free, pays tribute in awe of her recent conqueror
coldly set treat with indifference, disregard 61. *sovereign process* royal
instructions, mandate 62. *congruing . . . effect* in agreement on this
point 64. *hectic* a persisting rather than intermittent fever 66.
Howe'er . . . begun whatever my good fortune, I can't enjoy it while
Hamlet lives
   4.4.2. *licence* permission 3. *conveyance* escort

HAMLET. Who commands them, sir?

CAPTAIN. The nephew to old Norway, Fortinbras.

HAMLET. Goes it against the main of Poland, sir,   15
    Or for some frontier?

CAPTAIN. Truly to speak, and with no addition,
    We go to gain a little patch of ground
    That hath in it no profit but the name.
    To pay five ducats, five, I would not farm it;   20
    Nor will it yield to Norway or the Pole
    A ranker rate should it be sold in fee.

HAMLET. Why, then the Polack never will defend it.

CAPTAIN. Yes, it is already garrisoned.

HAMLET. Two thousand souls and twenty thousand ducats   25
    Will not debate the question of this straw.
    This is th' imposthume of much wealth and peace,
    That inward breaks, and shows no cause without
    Why the man dies. I humbly thank you, sir.

CAPTAIN. God buy you, sir.   *[Exit.]*

ROSENCRANTZ.   Will't please you go, my Lord?   30

HAMLET. I'll be with you straight. Go a little before.

                  Exeunt [all but Hamlet.]

    How all occasions do inform against me,
    And spur my dull revenge! What is a man,
    If his chief good and market of his time
    Be but to sleep and feed? A beast, no more.   35
    Sure he that made us with such large discourse,
    Looking before and after, gave us not
    That capability and godlike reason
    To fust in us unused. Now, whether it be

15. *main* the country as a whole   17. *addition* exaggeration   19. *name* glory of fighting   20. *To . . . ducats* at a rent of five ducats a year   21-2. *Nor . . . fee* if it were sold outright to either party it would not yield more than that much a year   32. *inform against me* (i) lay an "information", i.e. a formal charge, against me; (ii) betray me to my own conscience   33. *dull* (i) poor-spirited, as of a horse; (ii) blunted   34. *market* profit   36. *discourse* ability to reason logically (the faculty that sets man apart from the beasts)   37. *Looking . . . after* relating premises to conclusions, causes to effects, past to future   38. *capability . . . reason* (hendiadys) capability *of* godlike reason   *godlike* (it is the reason that is the divine, the flesh the animal part of our natures)   39. *fust* grow stale

Bestial oblivion, or some craven scruple   40
Of thinking too precisely on th' event —
A thought which, quartered, hath but one part wisdom   ‡
And ever three parts coward — I do not know
Why yet I live to say "This thing's to do",
Sith I have cause, and will, and strength, and means,   45
To do't. Examples gross as earth exhort me.   ‡
Witness this army of such mass and charge,
Led by a delicate and tender prince,
Whose spirit, with divine ambition puffed,   ‡
Makes mouths at the invisible event,   50
Exposing what is mortal and unsure
To all that fortune, death, and danger dare,
Even for an eggshell. Rightly to be great
Is not to stir without great argument,
But greatly to find quarrel in a straw   55
When honour's at the stake. How stand I then,
That have a father killed, a mother stained,
Excitements of my reason and my blood,
And let all sleep, while to my shame I see
The imminent death of twenty thousand men   60
That for a fantasy and trick of fame
Go to their graves like beds, fight for a plot
Whereon the numbers cannot try the cause,
Which is not tomb enough and continent
To hide the slain? O, from this time forth,   65
My thoughts be bloody, or be nothing worth!   *Exit.*

---

40. *Bestial oblivion* beasts, lacking rational memory, soon forget their parents *craven scruple* timid scrupulousness 41. *thinking . . . event* being too much concerned with possible consequences 44. *This . . . do* i.e. it has not yet been done and it is to be (and must be) done 52. *dare* challenge 53. *to be great* to display true greatness of soul 54. *argument* cause 56. *When . . . stake* i.e. both personal honour and honour as a matter of principle 56-65. *How . . . slain?* (Hamlet analyses the ingredients of his "cause" to demonstrate that they constitute "great argument") 61. *fantasy* whim 62-3. *plot . . . cause* the ground is too small to settle the issue by combat; it isn't even big enough for a battlefield 64. *continent* container 66. *My . . . bloody* (i) let my reason be passionate, or (ii) let my thoughts be directed towards the bloody fulfilment of my passionate revenge

[Scene 5. *Elsinore. A room in the castle.*]

Enter Horatio, [Queen] Gertrude, and a Gentleman.

QUEEN. I will not speak with her.
GENTLEMAN. She is importunate, indeed distract.
  Her mood will needs be pitied.
QUEEN.   What would she have?
GENTLEMAN. She speaks much of her father, says she
    hears
  There's tricks i' th' world, and hems, and beats her
    heart,   5
  Spurns enviously at straws, speaks things in doubt
  That carry but half sense. Her speech is nothing,
  Yet the unshaped use of it doth move
  The hearers to collection; they aim at it,
  And botch the words up fit to their own thoughts,   10
  Which, as her winks and nods and gestures yield them,
  Indeed would make one think there might be thought,
  Though nothing sure, yet much unhappily.
HORATIO. 'Twere good she were spoken with, for she
    may strew
  Dangerous conjectures in ill-breeding minds.   15
QUEEN. Let her come in.   *[Exit Gentleman.]*
  [Aside] To my sick soul, as sin's true nature is,
  Each toy seems prologue to some great amiss.
  So full of artless jealousy is guilt,
  It spills itself in fearing to be spilt.   20

Enter Ophelia [distracted].

OPHELIA. Where is the beauteous majesty of Denmark?
QUEEN. How now, Ophelia!

4.5.6. *Spurns . . . straws* is violently angered by the merest trifles
8. *unshaped* disordered 9. *collection* putting the pieces together 10.
botch . . . thoughts patch the words to fit their own preconceptions
11. *yield* express 12-13. *there . . . unhappily* one might have grounds
for inferring some great sorrow of undetermined cause 15. *ill-breeding
minds* minds disposed to think evil 18. *toy* trifle 19. *artless jealousy*
either natural or unconcealed suspicion, or possibly both

OPHELIA. How should I your true love know   *She sings.*   ❖
          From another one?
          By his cockle hat and staff,   25
          And his sandal shoon.
QUEEN. Alas, sweet lady, what imports this song?
OPHELIA. Say you? Nay, pray you mark.
          He is dead and gone, lady,   *(Song.)*
          He is dead and gone;   30
          At his head a grass-green turf,
          At his heels a stone.

   O, ho!
QUEEN. Nay, but, Ophelia –
OPHELIA.   Pray you mark.
   [*Sings*]   White his shroud as the mountain snow –   35

                    Enter King.

QUEEN. Alas, look here, my lord.
OPHELIA.   Larded all with sweet flowers;   *(Song.)*
          Which bewept to the ground did not go
          With true-love showers.
KING. How do you, pretty lady?   40
OPHELIA. Well, God dild you! They say the owl was a   ❖
   baker's daughter. Lord, we know what we are, but know
   not what we may be. God be at your table!
KING. Conceit upon her father.
OPHELIA. Pray let's have no words of this, but when they 45
   ask you what it means, say you this:
          To-morrow is Saint Valentine's day,   *(Song.)*
          All in the morning betime,
          And I a maid at your window,
          To be your Valentine.   50

---

26. *shoon* shoes 37. *Larded* ("larding" is the insertion of bits of fat
into the surface of meat before cooking in order to make it tender.
Flowers are pinned to the shroud with similar visual effect) 41. *dild*
yield, i.e. "reward" 44. *Conceit upon* obsession with 47. *Saint Valentine's day* (the first girl a man sees on this day will be his own true
love, according to popular belief) 48. *betime* early

Then up he rose, and donn'd his clo'es,
    And dupped the chamber-door,
Let in the maid, that out a maid
    Never departed more.
KING. Pretty Ophelia!   55
OPHELIA. Indeed, without an oath, I'll make an end on't.
  [*Sings*] By Gis and by Saint Charity,
    Alack, and fie for shame!
Young men will do't, if they come to't;
    By Cock, they are to blame.   60
Quoth she "Before you tumbled me,
    You promised me to wed."
He answers:
  "So would I 'a done, by yonder sun,
    An thou hadst not come to my bed."   65
KING. How long hath she been thus?
OPHELIA. I hope all will be well. We must be patient, but
I cannot choose but weep to think they would lay him
i' th' cold ground. My brother shall know of it, and so
I thank you for your good counsel. Come, my coach! 70
Good night, ladies, good night. Sweet ladies, good night,
good night.   *Exit.*
KING. Follow her close; give her good watch, I pray you.
               Exeunt Horatio and Gentleman.
O, this is the poison of deep grief; it springs
All from her father's death, and now behold!   75
O Gertrude, Gertrude!
When sorrows come, they come not single spies,
But in battalions: first, her father slain;
Next, your son gone, and he most violent author
Of his own just remove; the people muddied,   80
Thick and unwholesome in their thoughts and whispers
For good Polonius' death; and we have done but greenly

52. *dupped* opened 57. *Gis* contraction of "Jesus" 59. *if . . . to 't* if
they can 60. *Cock* a substitute for "God" often used in oaths (the
word also has phallic connotations) 65. *An* if 73. *give . . . watch*
take good care of her 80. *remove* departure into exile 82. *greenly*
foolishly, with too little consideration

In hugger-mugger to inter him; poor Ophelia
Divided from herself and her fair judgement,
Without the which we are pictures, or mere beasts;   85
Last, and as much containing as all these,
Her brother is in secret come from France,
Feeds on his wonder, keeps himself in clouds,
And wants not buzzers to infect his ear
With pestilent speeches of his father's death,   90
Wherein necessity, of matter beggared,
Will nothing stick our person to arraign
In ear and ear. O my dear Gertrude, this,
Like to a murd'ring piece, in many places
Gives me superfluous death. Attend,   *A noise within.* 95

Enter a Messenger.

Where are my Switzers? Let them guard the door.
What is the matter?
MESSENGER.   Save yourself, my lord.
The ocean, overpeering of his list,
Eats not the flats with more impiteous haste
Than young Laertes, in a riotous head,   100
O'erbears your officers. The rabble call him lord,
And as the world were now but to begin,
Antiquity forgot, custom not known,
The ratifiers and props of every word,
They cry "Choose we, Laertes shall be king."   105
Caps, hands, and tongues, applaud it to the clouds,
"Laertes shall be king, Laertes king."

83. *In hugger-mugger* in secrecy and haste 86. *much containing*
important 88. *wonder* (i) amazement, and (ii) doubt *clouds* (i.e. of
suspicion) 89. *buzzers* gossip-mongers 91. *necessity . . . beggared*
i.e. rumour, lacking true knowledge of the affair, must necessarily make
a good story by inventing substitutes for what it does not know 92.
Will nothing stick will not hesitate *arraign* accuse 93. *In ear and ear*
(i) in one ear after another, or (ii) in both of Laertes' ears 94.
murd'ring piece cannon loaded with shot 96. *Switzers* Swiss mercenary
soldiers (who often served as bodyguards in royal courts) 98. *overpeering . . . list* towering above its limits 99. *Eats . . . flats* does not
inundate the lowlands bordering the sea 100. *head* armed force,
collected with hostile (and usually rebellious) intention 101. *O'erbears*
drives back, overcomes 104. *word* title or decree

QUEEN. How cheerfully on the false trail they cry!

A noise within.

O, this is counter, you false Danish dogs!
KING. The doors are broke.   110

Enter Laertes, with Others.

LAERTES. Where is this king? – Sirs, stand you all without.
ALL. No, let's come in.
LAERTES.   I pray you give me leave.
ALL. We will, we will.   [*Exeunt his followers.*]
LAERTES. I thank you. Keep the door. – O thou vile king,
Give me my father!
QUEEN.   Calmly, good Laertes.   115
LAERTES. That drop of blood that's calm proclaims me
bastard,
Cries cuckold to my father, brands the harlot
Even here between the chaste unsmirchèd brow
Of my true mother.
KING.   What is the cause, Laertes,
That thy rebellion looks so giant-like?   120
Let him go, Gertrude. Do not fear our person.
There's such divinity doth hedge a king
That treason can but peep to what it would,
Acts little of his will. Tell me, Laertes,
Why thou art thus incensed. Let him go, Gertrude.   125
Speak, man.
LAERTES. Where is my father?
KING.   Dead.
QUEEN. But not by him.
KING.   Let him demand his fill.
LAERTES. How came he dead? I'll not be juggled with.
To hell allegiance, vows to the blackest devil,   130

109. *counter* a hunting term, signifying pursuing a trail opposite to the
direction the game has taken 112. *give me leave* leave me 114. *Keep*
guard 121. *fear* fear for 122. *There's . . . king* the divinely appointed
nature of his office places the King under divine protection 123.
peep . . . would i.e. peep through the "hedge" of divinity at what it
would destroy

Conscience and grace to the profoundest pit!
I dare damnation. To this point I stand,
That both the worlds I give to negligence,
Let come what comes, only I'll be revenged
Most throughly for my father.   135
KING. Who shall stay you?
LAERTES.   My will, not all the world's.
And for my means, I'll husband them so well
They shall go far with little.
KING.   Good Laertes,
If you desire to know the certainty
Of your dear father, is't writ in your revenge   140
That, swoopstake, you will draw both friend and foe,
Winner and loser?
LAERTES.   None but his enemies.
KING. Will you know them, then?
LAERTES. To his good friends thus wide I'll ope my arms,
And like the kind life-rend'ring pelican,   145
Repast them with my blood.
KING.   Why, now you speak
Like a good child and a true gentleman.
That I am guiltless of your father's death,
And am most sensibly in grief for it,
It shall as level to your judgement 'pear   150
As day does to your eye.
                    A noise within: "Let her come in."
LAERTES. How now? What noise is that?   •

131. *grace* (i) regard for God's laws, (ii) state of grace, i.e. freedom
from guilt, (iii) the grace of God which confers salvation 133. *both
. . . negligence* what happens in this world or in the next are alike
without significance (his only concern is thorough-going revenge) 136.
stay stop *My will . . . world's* Only my own will, even though that of
the whole world is against it 137-8. *I'll husband . . . little* I shall make
the most of them 141. *swoopstake* clearing the board of all stakes at
the gambling table 141-2. *That . . . loser* i.e. that you will indis-
criminately draw into the net of your vengeance both innocent and guilty
143. *Will . . . then* (i) Would you like to know who they are, or (ii)
Will you be able to distinguish friends from enemies 145-6. *like . . .
blood* (the natural affections ["kind'-ness"] of the pelican were believed
to be so strong that she fed her offspring with her own heart's blood)
149. *sensibly* feelingly, painfully 150. *level* plain

Enter Ophelia.

O, heat dry up my brains! tears seven times salt
Burn out the sense and virtue of mine eye!
By heaven, thy madness shall be paid with weight   155 ‡
Till our scale turn the beam. O rose of May,
Dear maid, kind sister, sweet Ophelia!
O heavens! is't possible a young maid's wits
Should be as mortal as an old man's life?
Nature is fine in love, and where 'tis fine   160 ‡
It sends some precious instance of itself
After the thing it loves.

OPHELIA.   They bore him barefac'd on the bier;   (*Song.*)
              Hey non nonny, nonny, hey nonny;
              And in his grave rain'd many a tear –   165
Fare you well, my dove!

LAERTES. Hadst thou thy wits, and didst persuade revenge,
It could not move thus.

OPHELIA. You must sing "A-down, a-down, and you call
him a-down-a." O, how the wheel becomes it! It is the 170
false steward, that stole his master's daughter.

LAERTES. This nothing's more than matter.

OPHELIA. There's rosemary, that's for remembrance. Pray   ‡
you, love, remember. And there is pansies, that's for
thoughts.   175

LAERTES. A document in madness, thoughts and remembrance fitted.

OPHELIA. There's fennel for you, and columbines. There's
rue for you, and here's some for me. We may call it
herb of grace a Sundays. O, you must wear your rue 180

153. *heat* (extreme grief was supposed to generate a heat which dried
up the vital essences of the body, producing a condition known as
"melancholy adust")   154. *virtue* power, faculty   161. *instance* proof
170. *how . . . becomes it* how well the rhythm of the wheel fits the
time of the song (probably Ophelia is singing the refrain of a spinning
song)   171. *false steward* (the ballad has not been identified)   172.
This . . . matter This nonsense is more expressive of her grief than
sense would be   173. *rosemary* (its smell was believed to strengthen
memory)   174. *pansies* ("pansy" is derived from the French "pensée")
176. *A document* instruction (to think and remember)   178. *fennel*
(the symbol of flattery – given to the King) *columbines* (possibly
signifying ungratefulness)   179. *rue* (the bitter herb of repentance,
which is the forerunner of grace – given to the Queen)

with a difference. There's a daisy. I would give you
some violets, but they withered all when my father died.
They say 'a made a good end.
  [*Sings*]   For bonny sweet Robin is all my joy.
LAERTES. Thought and affliction, passion, hell itself,   185
She turns to favour and to prettiness.
OPHELIA.   And will 'a not come again?   (*Song.*)
        And will 'a not come again?
            No, no, he is dead,
            Go to thy death-bed,   190
        He never will come again.

        His beard was as white as snow,
        All flaxen was his poll;
            He is gone, he is gone,
            And we cast away moan: 195
        God-a-mercy on his soul!
And of all Christian souls, I pray God. God buy you.
                                             Exit.

LAERTES. Do you see this, O God?
KING. Laertes, I must commune with your grief,
Or you deny me right. Go but apart,   200
Make choice of whom your wisest friends you will,
And they shall hear and judge 'twixt you and me.
If by direct or by collateral hand
They find us touched, we will our kingdom give,
Our crown, our life, and all that we call ours,   205
To you in satisfaction; but if not,
Be you content to lend your patience to us,
And we shall jointly labour with your soul
To give it due content.
LAERTES.   Let this be so.
His means of death, his obscure funeral –   210
No trophy, sword, nor hatchment, o'er his bones,

181. *with a difference* (Ophelia's "rue" is for grief, Gertrude's is for
remorse) *daisy* (signifying deceitfulness)   182. *violets* (signifying fidelity
and modesty)   184. *For...joy* (probably from an old ballad about
Robin Hood)   193. *poll* head   203. *collateral* indirect   204. *touched*
implicated (in the death of Polonius)   211. *trophy* visual memorial of
his achievements *hatchment* coat of arms (hung over the grave of a
nobleman along with his weapons)

No noble rite nor formal ostentation –
Cry to be heard, as 'twere from heaven to earth,
That I must call't in question.
KING.   So you shall;
And where th' offence is, let the great axe fall.   215
I pray you go with me.   *Exeunt.*

[Scene 6. *Another room in the castle.*]

Enter Horatio and Others.

HORATIO. What are they that would speak with me?
GENTLEMAN. Sea-faring men, sir. They say they have let-
ters for you.
HORATIO. Let them come in.   [*Exit Gentleman.*]
I do not know from what part of the world   5
I should be greeted, if not from Lord Hamlet.

Enter Sailors.

SAILORS. God bless you, sir.
HORATIO. Let him bless thee too.
SAILOR. 'A shall, sir, an't please him. There's a letter for
you, sir – it came from th' ambassador that was bound 10
for England – if your name be Horatio, as I am let to
know it is.
HORATIO [*reads*]. "Horatio, when thou shalt have overlooked this, give these fellows some means to the king.
They have letters for him. Ere we were two days old at 15
sea, a pirate of very war-like appointment gave us chase.
Finding ourselves too slow of sail, we put on a compelled valour, and in the grapple I boarded them. On
the instant they got clear of our ship, so I alone became
their prisoner. They have dealt with me like thieves of 20
mercy, but they knew what they did; I am to do a good
turn for them. Let the king have the letters I have sent,

215. *the great axe* (of retribution)
4.6.14 *means* (of access)   18. *in the grapple* while the two ships
were held together with grappling irons   20-21. *thieves of mercy*
merciful thieves   *they . . . did* they knew what they were doing (i.e.
they expected to be rewarded)   21-2. *do . . . them* obtain pardon for
them, perhaps

and repair thou to me with as much speed as thou
wouldest fly death. I have words to speak in thine ear
will make thee dumb; yet are they much too light for the 25
bore of the matter. These good fellows will bring thee
where I am. Rosencrantz and Guildenstern hold their
course for England. Of them I have much to tell thee.
Farewell.

> He that thou knowest thine, HAMLET." 30

Come, I will give you way for these your letters,
And do't the speedier that you may direct me
To him from whom you brought them.   *Exeunt.*

[Scene 7. *Another room in the castle.*]

Enter King and Laertes.

KING. Now must your conscience my acquittance seal,   ‡
  And you must put me in your heart for friend,
  Sith you have heard, and with a knowing ear,
  That he which hath your noble father slain
  Pursued my life.

LAERTES.   It well appears. But tell me   5
  Why you proceeded not against these feats,
  So criminal and so capital in nature,
  As by your safety, greatness, wisdom, all things else,
  You mainly were stirred up.

KING.   O, for two special reasons,
  Which may to you, perhaps, seem much unsinewed,   10
  But yet to me th' are strong. The queen his mother
  Lives almost by his looks, and for myself —   ‡
  My virtue or my plague, be it either which —
  She is so conjunctive to my life and soul
  That, as the star moves not but in his sphere,   15 ‡

25-6. *are they . . . matter* (metaphor from gunnery) the matter is
more serious than words can convey *good fellows* (ambiguous; the
phrase was often used ironically for "rogues")
  4.7.3. *Sith* since 6. *feats* acts 7. *capital* punishable by death 9.
You . . . up you were strongly impelled to do 10. *much unsinewed*
very weak 14. *conjunctive* inseparably joined

I could not but by her. The other motive,
Why to a public count I might not go,
Is the great love the general gender bear him,
Who, dipping all his faults in their affection,
Work like the spring that turneth wood to stone,   20
Convert his gyves to graces; so that my arrows,
Too slightly timbered for so loud a wind,
Would have reverted to my bow again,
But not where I have aimed them.
LAERTES. And so have I a noble father lost,   25
A sister driven into desp'rate terms,
Whose worth, if praises may go back again,
Stood challenger on mount of all the age
For her perfections. But my revenge will come.
KING. Break not your sleeps for that. You must not think   30
That we are made of stuff so flat and dull
That we can let our beard be shook with danger,
And think it pastime. You shortly shall hear more.
I loved your father, and we love our self,
And that, I hope, will teach you to imagine –   35

Enter a Messenger with letters.

MESSENGER. These to your majesty; this to the queen.
KING. From Hamlet! Who brought them?
MESSENGER. Sailors, my lord, they say. I saw them not.
They were given me by Claudio; he received them
Of him that brought them.
KING.   Laertes, you shall hear them. –   40
Leave us.   [*Exit Messenger.*]

17. *count* accounting   18. *general gender* common people   21. *Convert
. . . graces* i.e. would convert his fetters (if Claudius arrested him)
from shameful symbols to honourable ones   21-4. *my arrows . . . them*
i.e. my proceedings against Hamlet, like light-shafted arrows, would be
diverted from their target by the wind of public outcry and turned
against myself   26. *terms* state   27. *if praises . . . again* if I may
praise her for what she used to be   28. *on mount* (i) set up on high;
or (ii) mounted on horseback, i.e. ready to take on all competitors
of . . . age (modifies "challenger", not "mount")   39. *Claudio* (this
character does not appear in the play as we have it)

[*Reads*] "High and mighty, you shall know I am set
naked on your kingdom. To-morrow shall I beg leave to
see your kingly eyes; when I shall, first asking your pardon thereunto, recount the occasion of my sudden and   45
more strange return.

                                             HAMLET."

What should this mean? Are all the rest come back?
Or is it some abuse, and no such thing?

LAERTES. Know you the hand?   50

KING. 'Tis Hamlet's character. "Naked"!
And in a postscript here, he says "alone".
Can you devise me?

LAERTES. I am lost in it, my lord. But let him come.
It warms the very sickness in my heart   55
That I shall live and tell him to his teeth
"Thus didest thou."

KING.   If it be so, Laertes —
As how should it be so, how otherwise? —
Will you be ruled by me?

LAERTES.   Ay, my lord,
So you will not o'errule me to a peace.   60

KING. To thine own peace. If he be now returned,
As checking at his voyage, and that he means
No more to undertake it, I will work him
To an exploit now ripe in my device,
Under the which he shall not choose but fall;   65
And for his death no wind of blame shall breathe
But even his mother shall uncharge the practice
And call it accident.

LAERTES.   My lord, I will be ruled;
The rather if you could devise it so
That I might be the organ.

KING.   It falls right.   70

43. *naked* destitute 51. *character* handwriting 53. *devise me* explain
it to me 57-8. *If it . . . otherwise* i.e. How can it be true? Yet how
can it not be true? 62. *checking at* turning aside from his course (like
a falcon turning aside from its quarry to seek some other prey) 67.
shall . . . practice will not charge anyone with evil intention in the
execution of the "device" 70. *organ* instrument

You have been talked of since your travel much,
And that in Hamlet's hearing, for a quality
Wherein they say you shine. Your sum of parts
Did not together pluck such envy from him
As did that one, and that, in my regard,   75
Of the unworthiest siege.
LAERTES.   What part is that, my lord?
KING. A very riband in the cap of youth,
    Yet needful too, for youth no less becomes
    The light and careless livery that it wears
    Than settled age his sables and his weeds,   80
    Importing health and graveness. Two months since
    Here was a gentleman of Normandy.
    I have seen myself, and served against, the French,
    And they can well on horseback, but this gallant
    Had witchcraft in't. He grew unto his seat,   85
    And to such wondrous doing brought his horse,
    As had he been incorpsed and demi-natured
    With the brave beast. So far he topped my thought
    That I, in forgery of shapes and tricks,
    Come short of what he did.
LAERTES.   A Norman was't?   90
KING. A Norman.
LAERTES. Upon my life, Lamord.
KING.   The very same.
LAERTES. I know him well. He is the brooch indeed
    And gem of all the nation.
KING. He made confession of you,   95
    And gave you such a masterly report

73. *Your . . . parts* all of your accomplishments put together 76.
siege rank 77. *a very . . . cap* a mere ornament 78-9. *youth . . .
wears* the sports of youth, like its fashionable clothing, are no less
appropriate than . . . 80. *settled . . . weeds* the sombre and dignified
apparel of the old (metaphorically, serious and sober behaviour) 84.
can well on horseback are skilled riders (Middle English "can" and its
substantive "cunning" had the force of the modern "know-how") 87.
As had . . . demi-natured as if he were one body – half man, half horse
(like a centaur) 88. *topped* excelled 89-90. *I . . . did* ("forgery"
here means "picturing", i.e. the Horseman's truth exceeds Claudius'
powers of description) 92. *Lamord* (Levin, in *The Question of
Hamlet*, p. 95, suggests that "Lamord" suggests "La Mort", the pale
horseman Death) 95. *made . . . you* admitted that he knew you

For art and exercise in your defence,
And for your rapier most especial,
That he cried out 'twould be a sight indeed
If one could match you. The scrimers of their nation   100
He swore had neither motion, guard, nor eye,
If you opposed them. Sir, this report of his
Did Hamlet so envenom with his envy
That he could nothing do but wish and beg
Your sudden coming o'er, to play with you.   105
Now out of this –

LAERTES.   What out of this, my lord?

KING. Laertes, was your father dear to you?
Or are you like the painting of a sorrow,
A face without a heart?

LAERTES.   Why ask you this?

KING. Not that I think you did not love your father,   110
But that I know love is begun by time,
And that I see in passages of proof,
Time qualifies the spark and fire of it.
There lives within the very flame of love
A kind of wick or snuff that will abate it,   115
And nothing is at a like goodness still,
For goodness, growing to a plurisy,
Dies in his own too much. That we would do,
We should do when we would; for this "would"
    changes,
And hath abatements and delays as many   120
As there are tongues, are hands, are accidents,
And then this "should" is like a spendthrift's sigh
That hurts by easing. But to the quick of th' ulcer –
Hamlet comes back; what would you undertake
To show yourself in deed your father's son   125
More than in words?

LAERTES.   To cut his throat i' th' church.

KING. No place indeed should murder sanctuarize;

97. *art . . . defence* theory and practice of fencing 100. *scrimers*
fencers 112. *passages of proof* instances of experience 116. *a like*
the same 117. *a plurisy* an excess

Revenge should have no bounds. But, good Laertes,
Will you do this? Keep close within your chamber.
Hamlet returned shall know you are come home.   130
We'll put on those shall praise your excellence,
And set a double varnish on the fame
The Frenchman gave you, bring you in fine together,
And wager on your heads. He, being remiss,
Most generous, and free from all contriving,   135
Will not peruse the foils, so that with ease,
Or with a little shuffling, you may choose
A sword unbated, and in a pass of practice
Requite him for your father.

LAERTES.   I will do't,
And for that purpose I'll anoint my sword.   140 ‡
I bought an unction of a mountebank,
So mortal that but dip a knife in it,
Where it draws blood no cataplasm so rare,
Collected from all simples that have virtue
Under the moon, can save the thing from death   145
That is but scratched withal. I'll touch my point
With this contagion, that if I gall him slightly,
It may be death.

KING.   Let's further think of this,
Weigh what convenience both of time and means
May fit us to our shape. If this should fail,   150
And that our drift look through our bad performance,
'Twere better not assayed. Therefore this project
Should have a back or second that might hold
If this did blast in proof. Soft, let me see.
We'll make a solemn wager on your cunnings –   155
I ha't.
When in your motion you are hot and dry –
As make your bouts more violent to that end –

And that he calls for drink, I'll have prepared him
A chalice for the nonce, whereon but sipping, 160
If he by chance escape your venomed stuck,
Our purpose may hold there. – But stay, what noise?

Enter Queen.

QUEEN. One woe doth tread upon another's heel,
 So fast they follow. Your sister's drowned, Laertes.
LAERTES. Drowned? O, where? 165
QUEEN. There is a willow grows askant the brook
 That shows his hoar leaves in the glassy stream.
 Therewith fantastic garlands did she make
 Of crowflowers, nettles, daisies, and long purples
 That liberal shepherds give a grosser name, 170
 But our cold maids do dead men's fingers call them.
 There on the pendent boughs her crownet weeds
 Clamb'ring to hang, an envious sliver broke,
 When down her weedy trophies and herself
 Fell in the weeping brook. Her clothes spread wide, 175
 And mermaid-like awhile they bore her up,
 Which time she chanted snatches of old tunes,
 As one incapable of her own distress,
 Or like a creature native and indued
 Unto that element. But long it could not be 180
 Till that her garments, heavy with their drink,
 Pulled the poor wretch from her melodious lay
 To muddy death.
LAERTES.   Alas, then she is drowned?
QUEEN. Drowned, drowned.
LAERTES. Too much of water hast thou, poor Ophelia, 185
 And therefore I forbid my tears; but yet
 It is our trick; nature her custom holds,
 Let shame say what it will. When these are gone,
 The woman will be out. Adieu, my lord.

161. *stuck* thrust 166. *askant* alongside 167. *hoar* grey 170. *liberal*
free-spoken 171. *cold* chaste 172. *crownet* coronet 173. *envious
sliver* malicious branch 178. *incapable* insensible 179. *indued* endowed 180. *that element* water 187. *our trick* a natural trait of
humanity 188. *these* (i.e. tears) 189. *The . . . out* I shall have shed
my gentler nature along with my tears

I have a speech o' fire that fain would blaze   190
But that this folly drowns it.   *Exit.*
KING.   Let's follow, Gertrude.
How much I had to do to calm his rage!
Now fear I this will give it start again;
Therefore let's follow.   *Exeunt.*

[ACT 5]

[Scene 1. *A churchyard.*]

Enter two Clowns.

FIRST CLOWN. Is she to be buried in Christian burial
when she wilfully seeks her own salvation?

SECOND CLOWN. I tell thee she is. Therefore make her
grave straight. The crowner hath sat on her, and finds
it Christian burial.   5

FIRST CLOWN. How can that be, unless she drowned herself in her own defence?

SECOND CLOWN. Why, 'tis found so.

FIRST CLOWN. It must be "se offendendo"; it cannot be
else. For here lies the point: if I drown myself wittingly,   10
it argues an act, and an act hath three branches – it is
to act, to do, to perform; argal, she drowned herself
wittingly.

SECOND CLOWN. Nay, but hear you, Goodman Delver.

FIRST CLOWN. Give me leave. Here lies the water; good.   15
Here stands the man; good. If the man go to this water
and drown himself, it is, will he, nill he, he goes – mark
you that. But if the water come to him and drown him,
he drowns not himself. Argal, he that is not guilty of his
own death shortens not his own life.   20

SECOND CLOWN. But is this law?

FIRST CLOWN. Ay, marry, is't; crowner's quest law.

5.1.4. *The . . . her* the coroner has held an inquest 7. *in . . .
defence* i.e. in self-defence (a justification for homicide in law) 9. *se
offendendo* (for *se defendendo*, Law Latin for "self-defence". The
Clown's verbal blunder is factual truth; the suicide kills himself in
"self-offence") 10. *wittingly* knowingly 12. *argal* the Clown's corruption of the Latin "ergo" = therefore 22. *crowner's quest* coroner's
inquest

SECOND CLOWN. Will you ha' the truth on't? If this had not been a gentlewoman, she should have been buried out o' Christian burial. 25

FIRST CLOWN. Why, there thou say'st. And the more pity that great folk should have count'nance in this world to drown or hang themselves more than their even-Christen. Come, my spade. There is no ancient gentlemen but gard'ners, ditchers, and grave-makers. They hold 30 up Adam's profession.

SECOND CLOWN. Was he a gentleman?

FIRST CLOWN. 'A was the first that ever bore arms.

SECOND CLOWN. Why, he had none.

FIRST CLOWN. What, art a heathen? How dost thou under- 35 stand the Scripture? The Scripture says Adam digged. Could he dig without arms? I'll put another question to thee. If thou answerest me not to the purpose, confess thyself –

SECOND CLOWN. Go to. 40

FIRST CLOWN. What is he that builds stronger than either the mason, the shipwright, or the carpenter?

SECOND CLOWN. The gallows-maker, for that frame out-lives a thousand tenants.

FIRST CLOWN. I like thy wit well, in good faith. The gal- 45 lows does well. But how does it well? It does well to those that do ill. Now thou dost ill to say the gallows is built stronger than the church. Argal, the gallows may do well to thee. To't again, come.

SECOND CLOWN. Who builds stronger than a mason, a 50 shipwright, or a carpenter?

FIRST CLOWN. Ay, tell me that, and unyoke.

SECOND CLOWN. Marry, now I can tell.

FIRST CLOWN. To't.

SECOND CLOWN. Mass, I cannot tell. 55

23-5. *if this . . . burial* (the old complaint that there is one law for the rich, another for the poor) 26. *there thou say'st* "you said it!" 27. *count'nance* allowance or privilege 28-9. *even-Christen* fellow Christians 43. *frame* structure 46. *does well* is a pretty good answer 52. *and unyoke* and then you can relax

FIRST CLOWN. Cudgel thy brains no more about it, for your dull ass will not mend his pace with beating. And when you are asked this question next, say "a grave-maker". The houses he makes lasts till doomsday. Go, get thee in, and fetch me a stoup of liquor. 60

[*Exit Second Clown.*]

Enter Hamlet and Horatio [*as Clown digs and sings*].

> In youth, when I did love, did love, (*Song.*)
> Methought it was very sweet,
> To contract the time for-a my behove,
> O, methought there-a was nothing-a meet.

HAMLET. Has this fellow no feeling of his business, that 'a 65 sings in grave-making?

HORATIO. Custom hath made it in him a property of easiness.

HAMLET. 'Tis e'en so. The hand of little employment hath the dantier sense. 70

FIRST CLOWN. But age, with his stealing steps,   (*Song.*)
> Hath clawed me in his clutch,
> And hath shipped me intil the land,
> As if I had never been such.

[*Throws up a skull.*]

HAMLET. That skull had a tongue in it, and could sing 75 once. How the knave jowls it to the ground, as if 'twere Cain's jawbone, that did the first murder! This might be the pate of a politician, which this ass now o'erreaches; one that would circumvent God, might it not?

HORATIO. It might, my lord. 80

HAMLET. Or of a courtier, which could say "Good morrow, sweet lord! How dost thou, sweet lord?" This might be my Lord Such-a-one, that praised my Lord Such-a-one's horse, when 'a went to beg it, might it not?

60. *stoup* half-gallon tankard   67-8. *Custom . . . easiness* Habit has made it second nature with him (he doesn't think about it, but sings at his work like any other labourer)   70. *dantier* daintier   73. *intil* into   76. *jowls* hurls (with an obvious and ironic play on the "jowls" of flesh which are no longer attached to the skull)   78. *o'erreaches* (i) gets the better of, or better (ii) gets ahead of   79. *circumvent* get around, cheat

HORATIO. Ay, my lord.   85

HAMLET. Why, e'en so, and now my Lady Worm's, chapless, and knock'd about the mazzard with a sexton's spade. Here's fine revolution, an we had the trick to see't. Did these bones cost no more the breeding but to play at loggats with them? Mine ache to think on't.   90

FIRST CLOWN. A pick-axe and a spade, a spade, (*Song.*)
      For and a shrouding sheet:
      O, a pit of clay for to be made
      For such a guest is meet.
                [*Throws up another skull.*]

HAMLET. There's another. Why may not that be the skull 95
of a lawyer? Where be his quiddities now, his quillets, his cases, his tenures, and his tricks? Why does he suffer this mad knave now to knock him about the sconce with a dirty shovel, and will not tell him of his action of battery? Hum! This fellow might be in's time a great 100 buyer of land, with his statutes, his recognizances, his fines, his double vouchers, his recoveries. Is this the fine of his fines, and the recovery of his recoveries, to have his fine pate full of fine dirt? Will his vouchers vouch him no more of his purchases, and double ones too, than 105 the length and breadth of a pair of indentures? The very conveyances of his lands will scarcely lie in this box, and must th' inheritor himself have no more, ha?

HORATIO. Not a jot more, my lord.

HAMLET. Is not parchment made of sheepskins?   110

HORATIO. Ay, my lord, and of calves' skins too.

HAMLET. They are sheep and calves which seek out assurance in that. I will speak to this fellow. Whose grave's this, sirrah?

86-7. *chapless* with the lower jaw missing   *mazzard* head   88. *revolution* turning (probably an allusion to the Wheel of Fortune)   *trick* knack   90. *loggats* small billets of wood for throwing at a target   96. *quiddities* subtle arguments   *quillets* legal quibbles   98. *sconce* head   99-100. *tell . . . battery* lay a charge of assault and battery against him   101. *buyer of land* (for the purpose of elevating himself into the class of "landed gentry"; cf. ll. 132-5)   *recognizances* legal bonds defining debts   102-3. *fine of his fines* end of his fines   104. *fine pate* clever head (which in life was preoccupied with land and in death is filled with earth)   107. *conveyances* deeds   108. *inheritor* owner   110. *parchment* (on which legal documents were inscribed)

FIRST CLOWN.   Mine, sir.   115

[*Sings*]   O, a pit of clay for to be made –

HAMLET. I think it be thine indeed, for thou liest in't.

FIRST CLOWN. You lie out on't, sir, and therefore 'tis not yours. For my part, I do not lie in't, yet it is mine.

HAMLET. Thou dost lie in't, to be in't and say it is thine. 120 'Tis for the dead, not for the quick; therefore thou liest.

FIRST CLOWN. 'Tis a quick lie, sir; 'twill away again from me to you.

HAMLET. What man dost thou dig it for?

FIRST CLOWN. For no man, sir.   125

HAMLET. What woman, then?

FIRST CLOWN. For none neither.

HAMLET. Who is to be buried in't?

FIRST CLOWN. One that was a woman, sir; but, rest her soul, she's dead.   130

HAMLET. How absolute the knave is! We must speak by the card, or equivocation will undo us. By the Lord, Horatio, this three years I have took note of it, the age is grown so picked that the toe of the peasant comes so near the heel of the courtier, he galls his kibe. How long 135 hast thou been a grave-maker?

FIRST CLOWN. Of all the days i' th' year, I came to't that day that our last King Hamlet overcame Fortinbras.

HAMLET. How long is that since?

FIRST CLOWN. Cannot you tell that? Every fool can tell 140 that. It was that very day that young Hamlet was born – he that is mad, and sent into England.

HAMLET. Ay, marry, why was he sent into England?

FIRST CLOWN. Why, because 'a was mad. 'A shall recover his wits there; or, if 'a do not, 'tis no great matter there. 145

HAMLET. Why?

FIRST CLOWN. 'Twill not be seen in him there. There the men are as mad as he.

131. *absolute* precise 131-2. *speak . . . equivocation* i.e. be precise in our choice of words or we will be thrown off course by the grave-digger's quickness in picking up double meanings *card* (on which the points of the compass are marked) 134. *picked* refined

HAMLET. How came he mad?

FIRST CLOWN. Very strangely, they say. 150

HAMLET. How strangely?

FIRST CLOWN. Faith, e'en with losing his wits.

HAMLET. Upon what ground?

FIRST CLOWN. Why, here in Denmark. I have been sexton
here, man and boy, thirty years. 155

HAMLET. How long will a man lie i' th' earth ere he rot?

FIRST CLOWN. Faith, if 'a be not rotten before 'a die – as
we have many pocky corses now-a-days that will scarce
hold the laying in – 'a will last you some eight year or
nine year. A tanner will last you nine year. 160

HAMLET. Why he more than another?

FIRST CLOWN. Why, sir, his hide is so tanned with his trade
that 'a will keep out water a great while; and your water
is a sore decayer of your whoreson dead body. Here's a
skull now hath llen you i' th' earth three and twenty 165
years.

HAMLET. Whose was it?

FIRST CLOWN. A whoreson mad fellow's it was. Whose do
you think it was?

HAMLET. Nay, I know not. 170

FIRST CLOWN. A pestilence on him for a mad rogue! 'A
poured a flagon of Rhenish on my head once. This same
skull, sir, was, sir, Yorick's skull, the king's jester.

HAMLET [*taking the skull*]. This?

FIRST CLOWN. E'en that. 175

HAMLET. Alas, poor Yorick! I knew him, Horatio – a fellow of infinite jest, of most excellent fancy. He hath
bore me on his back a thousand times, and now how
abhorred in my imagination it is! My gorge rises at it.
Here hung those lips that I have kissed I know not how 180
oft. Where be your gibes now, your gambols, your songs,
your flashes of merriment that were wont to set the table
on a roar? Not one now to mock your own grinning?

---

158. *pocky* infected with pox (syphilis)

Quite chap-fall'n? Now get you to my lady's chamber,
and tell her, let her paint an inch thick, to this favour 185
she must come. Make her laugh at that. Prithee, Horatio,
tell me one thing.

HORATIO. What's that, my lord?

HAMLET. Dost thou think Alexander looked o' this fashion
i' th' earth? 190

HORATIO. E'en so.

HAMLET. And smelt so? Pah!   [*Throws down the skull.*]

HORATIO. E'en so, my lord.

HAMLET. To what base uses we may return, Horatio! Why
may not imagination trace the noble dust of Alexander 195
till 'a find it stopping a bung-hole?

HORATIO. 'Twere to consider too curiously to consider so.

HAMLET. No, faith, not a jot, but to follow him thither
with modesty enough, and likelihood to lead it. Alexander died, Alexander was buried, Alexander returneth to 200
dust; the dust is earth; of earth we make loam; and why
of that loam whereto he was converted might they not
stop a beer-barrel?

> Imperious Caesar, dead and turned to clay,
> Might stop a hole to keep the wind away. 205
> O, that that earth which kept the world in awe
> Should patch a wall t' expel the winter's flaw!

But soft, but soft awhile! Here comes the king,
The queen, the courtiers.

*Enter King, Queen, Laertes, and a Coffin with
[Priest and] Lords attendant.*

>   Who is this they follow?
And with such maimèd rites? This doth betoken 210
The corse they follow did with desperate hand
Fordo it own life. 'Twas of some estate.

184. *chap-fall'n* (i) with the lower jaw fallen away, (ii) "down in the
mouth" 185. *favour* appearance 197. *curiously* over-ingeniously 199.
with modesty enough without exaggeration *likelihood . . . it* following
a logical and credible sequence 204. *Imperious* imperial (as he was
emperor in all but name); since he "kept the world in awe", he was
also "imperious" in the other sense of the word 207. *flaw* gust of
wind 212. *Fordo it* destroy its

Couch we awhile and mark.   [*Retires with Horatio.*]
LAERTES. What ceremony else?
HAMLET [*to Horatio*]. That is Laertes, a very noble youth.
  Mark.   215
LAERTES. What ceremony else?
PRIEST. Her obsequies have been as far enlarged
  As we have warranty. Her death was doubtful,
  And but that great command o'ersways the order,
  She should in ground unsanctified have lodged   220
  Till the last trumpet. For charitable prayers,
  Shards, flints, and pebbles, should be thrown on her.
  Yet here she is allowed her virgin crants,
  Her maiden strewments, and the bringing home
  Of bell and burial.   225
LAERTES. Must there no more be done?
PRIEST.   No more be done.
  We should profane the service of the dead
  To sing a requiem and such rest to her
  As to peace-parted souls.
LAERTES.   Lay her i' th' earth,
  And from her fair and unpolluted flesh   230
  May violets spring! I tell thee, churlish priest,
  A minist'ring angel shall my sister be
  When thou liest howling.
HAMLET.   What, the fair Ophelia!
QUEEN. Sweets to the sweet. Farewell!

                              [*Scatters flowers.*]

  I hoped thou shouldst have been my Hamlet's wife.   235
  I thought thy bride-bed to have decked, sweet maid,
  And not have strewed thy grave.

213. *Couch we* let us conceal ourselves 219. *but . . . order* i.e. had
the King's order not overruled the usual order of procedure (in cases
of suspected suicide) 222. *Shards* broken pottery (used in ostracism
procedures in classical Greece) 223. *crants* garland (singular) 224.
strewments flowers strewn over the bier *bringing home* bringing to
her "long home", the grave (the dead maiden is decked with garlands
as if being escorted home from the marriage ceremony) 225. *bell
and burial* the ringing of the passing bell as the corpse is carried into
the churchyard for burial

LAERTES.   O, treble woe
 Fall ten times treble on that cursèd head
 Whose wicked deed thy most ingenious sense
 Deprived thee of! Hold off the earth awhile,   240
 Till I have caught her once more in mine arms.

         Leaps into the grave.

 Now pile your dust upon the quick and dead,
 Till of this flat a mountain you have made
 T' o'er-top old Pelion or the skyish head
 Of blue Olympus.

HAMLET [*coming forward*]. What is he whose grief 245
 Bears such an emphasis, whose phrase of sorrow
 Conjures the wand'ring stars, and makes them stand
 Like wonder-wounded hearers? This is I,
 Hamlet the Dane.   [*Leaps into the grave.*]

LAERTES. The devil take thy soul!

         [*Grappling with him.*]

HAMLET.   Thou pray'st not well. 250
 I prithee take thy fingers from my throat,
 For though I am not splenitive and rash,
 Yet have I in me something dangerous,
 Which let thy wisdom fear. Hold off thy hand.

KING. Pluck them asunder.   255

QUEEN. Hamlet! Hamlet!

ALL. Gentlemen!

HORATIO. Good my lord, be quiet.

    [*The Attendants part them, and they come
        out of the grave.*]

HAMLET. Why, I will fight with him upon this theme
 Until my eyelids will no longer wag.   260

QUEEN. O my son, what theme?

HAMLET. I loved Ophelia. Forty thousand brothers
 Could not with all their quantity of love
 Make up my sum. What wilt thou do for her?

KING. O, he is mad, Laertes.   265

239. *ingenious sense* quick and subtle perception 247. *Conjures* casts
a spell on 247-8. *stand . . . hearers* i.e. stand still, as if in amazement
252. *splenitive* quick-tempered (the spleen was thought to be the seat
of anger) 254. *wisdom* prudence 260. *wag* flutter, the last sign of
life in the dying

QUEEN. For love of God, forbear him.

HAMLET. 'Swounds, show me what thou'lt do.
Woo't weep, woo't fight, woo't fast, woo't tear thyself,
Woo't drink up eisel, eat a crocodile?
I'll do't. Dost come here to whine?   270
To outface me with leaping in her grave?
Be buried quick with her, and so will I.
And if thou prate of mountains, let them throw
Millions of acres on us, till our ground,
Singeing his pate against the burning zone,   275
Make Ossa like a wart! Nay, an thou'lt mouth,
I'll rant as well as thou.

QUEEN.   This is mere madness;
And thus awhile the fit will work on him.
Anon, as patient as the female dove
When that her golden couplets are disclosed,   280
His silence will sit drooping.

HAMLET.   Hear you, sir.
What is the reason that you use me thus?
I loved you ever. But it is no matter.
Let Hercules himself do what he may,
The cat will mew, and dog will have his day.   285

KING. I pray thee, good Horatio, wait upon him.

                    Exit Hamlet and Horatio.

[*To Laertes*] Strengthen your patience in our last night's
  speech.
We'll put the matter to the present push. —
Good Gertrude, set some watch over your son. —
This grave shall have a living monument.   290
An hour of quiet shortly shall we see;
Till then in patience our proceeding be.   *Exeunt.*

269. *eisel* vinegar   275. *burning zone* (the belt or zone of the heavenly
sphere bounded by the tropics of Cancer and Capricorn)   280.
couplets fledglings (the dove lays only two eggs at a time)   281.
drooping moping, melancholy contemplation   284. *Let . . . may* (the
hero of Seneca's *Hercules Furens* in his madness gave vent to bombastic
ranting and raging)   285. *The . . . mew* (Laertes' bombastic speech is
like the mewing of a cat in comparison with Hercules' ranting)   *dog
. . . day* (if Hamlet sees *himself* as the proverbial dog, this may be a
veiled threat directed against the King)   290. *a living monument* (i)
(for Gertrude) a life-like memorial, and (ii) (for Laertes) not a stone
effigy but Hamlet's life exacted as a penalty for Ophelia's death

[Scene 2. *A hall in the castle.*]

Enter Hamlet and Horatio.

HAMLET. So much for this, sir; now shall you see the
    other.
    You do remember all the circumstance?
HORATIO. Remember it, my lord!
HAMLET. Sir, in my heart there was a kind of fighting
    That would not let me sleep. Methought I lay   5
    Worse than the mutines in the bilboes. Rashly,
    And praised be rashness for it – let us know,
    Our indiscretion sometimes serves us well,
    When our deep plots do pall; and that should learn us
    There's a divinity that shapes our ends,   10
    Rough-hew them how we will –
HORATIO.   That is most certain.
HAMLET. Up from my cabin,
    My sea-gown scarfed about me, in the dark
    Groped I to find out them, had my desire,
    Fingered their packet, and in fine withdrew   15
    To mine own room again, making so bold,
    My fears forgetting manners, to unseal
    Their grand commission; where I found, Horatio –
    Ah, royal knavery! – an exact command,
    Larded with many several sorts of reasons,   20
    Importing Denmark's health, and England's too,
    With, ho! such bugs and goblins in my life,
    That on the supervise, no leisure bated,
    No, not to stay the grinding of the axe,
    My head should be struck off.
HORATIO.   Is't possible?   25

5.2.6. *mutines . . . bilboes* mutineers in the stocks ("bilboes" were
portable iron stocks carried on ships) *Rashly* on a sudden impulse
9. *pall* lose their effectiveness 13. *my sea-gown . . . me* muffled up in
my seaman's cloak 15. *Fingered* "pinched" 20. *Larded* stuffed 22.
bugs . . . life horrifying perils in allowing me to live 23. *on the
supervise* as soon as the document has been read *no leisure bated* no
time for delay to be deducted from the speed of execution 24. *stay*
wait for

HAMLET. Here's the commission; read it at more leisure.
  But wilt thou hear now how I did proceed?
HORATIO. I beseech you.
HAMLET. Being thus benetted round with villainies,
  Or I could make a prologue to my brains,   30
  They had begun the play. I sat me down,
  Devised a new commission, wrote it fair.
  I once did hold it, as our statists do,
  A baseness to write fair, and laboured much
  How to forget that learning; but sir, now   35
  It did me yeoman's service. Wilt thou know
  Th' effect of what I wrote?
HORATIO.   Ay, good my lord.
HAMLET. An earnest conjuration from the king,
  As England was his faithful tributary,
  As love between them like the palm might flourish,   40
  As peace should still her wheaten garland wear
  And stand a comma 'tween their amities,
  And many such like as's of great charge,
  That on the view and knowing of these contents,
  Without debatement further more or less,   45
  He should those bearers put to sudden death,
  Not shriving-time allowed.
HORATIO.   How was this sealed?
HAMLET. Why, even in that was heaven ordinant,
  I had my father's signet in my purse,
  Which was the model of that Danish seal,   50
  Folded the writ up in the form of th' other,
  Subscribed it, gave't th' impression, placed it safely,
  The changeling never known. Now, the next day
  Was our sea-fight, and what to this was sequent
  Thou knowest already.   55

30-31. *Or . . . play* before I could make a plan I started putting it into
action 33. *statists* statesmen 34. *baseness* vulgar accomplishment (a
gentleman's handwriting was supposed to be casual, without the
precision of the professional scrivener) 42. *comma* i.e. connective
43. *as's . . . charge* as was of great import (with a play on "asses"
with great burdens) 48. *ordinant* operative

HORATIO. So Guildenstern and Rosencrantz go to 't.

HAMLET. Why, man, they did make love to this
    employment.
  They are not near my conscience; their defeat
  Does by their own insinuation grow.
  'Tis dangerous when the baser nature comes   60
  Between the pass and fell incensèd points
  Of mighty opposites.

HORATIO.   Why, what a king is this!

HAMLET. Does it not, think thee, stand me now upon –
  He that hath killed my king and whored my mother,
  Popped in between th' election and my hopes,   65
  Thrown out his angle for my proper life,
  And with such coz'nage – is't not perfect conscience
  To quit him with this arm? And is't not to be damned
  To let this canker of our nature come
  In further evil?   70

HORATIO. It must be shortly known to him from England
  What is the issue of the business there.

HAMLET. It will be short; the interim is mine.
  And a man's life's no more than to say "one".
  But I am very sorry, good Horatio,   75
  That to Laertes I forgot myself;
  For by the image of my cause I see
  The portraiture of his. I'll court his favours.
  But sure the bravery of his grief did put me
  Into a tow'ring passion.

HORATIO.   Peace; who comes here?   80

Enter [Osric,] a courtier.

56. *to 't* to their death 59. *insinuation* meddling 60. *baser* of lower rank 61. *pass* thrust (in fencing) *fell* fierce 63. *Does . . . upon* don't you think, now, that it is up to me (to kill the King) 65. *Popped . . . hopes* (see 3.4.100, "cutpurse . . . rule", end note) 66. *angle* fishing line *proper* own 67. *coz'nage* underhanded treachery (with a play on "cousinage", i.e. kinship) *perfect conscience* so completely justified as not to trouble the most scrupulous conscience 68. *quit him* pay him back 69. *canker . . . nature* blight (or ulcer) of humanity 70. *In . . . evil* into still more crime 74. *a man's . . . "one"* i.e. you can thrust a man through as quickly as you can say "one!" (cf. *Romeo and Juliet* 2.4.22-3: "one, two, and the third in your bosom") 79. *bravery* extravagant style

OSRIC. Your lordship is right welcome back to Denmark.

HAMLET. I humbly thank you, sir. [*Aside to Horatio*] Dost know this water-fly?

HORATIO [*aside to Hamlet*]. No, my good lord.

HAMLET [*aside to Horatio*]. Thy state is the more gra- 85 cious, for 'tis a vice to know him. He hath much land, and fertile. Let a beast be lord of beasts, and his crib shall stand at the king's mess. 'Tis a chough, but as I say, spacious in the possession of dirt.

OSRIC. Sweet lord, if your lordship were at leisure, I should 90 impart a thing to you from his majesty.

HAMLET. I will receive it, sir, with all diligence of spirit. Put your bonnet to his right use. 'Tis for the head.

OSRIC. I thank your lordship, it is very hot.

HAMLET. No, believe me, 'tis very cold; the wind is north- 95 erly.

OSRIC. It is indifferent cold, my lord, indeed.

HAMLET. But yet methinks it is very sultry and hot for my complexion.

OSRIC. Exceedingly, my lord; it is very sultry, as 'twere — 100 I cannot tell how. My lord, his majesty bade me signify to you that 'a has laid a great wager on your head. Sir, this is the matter —

HAMLET. I beseech you, remember.

               [*Hamlet moves him to put on his hat.*]

OSRIC. Nay, good my lord; for my ease, in good faith. 105 Sir, here is newly come to court Laertes; believe me, an absolute gentleman, full of most excellent differences, of very soft society and great showing. Indeed, to speak feelingly of him, he is the card or calendar of gentry, for you shall find in him the continent of what part a 110 gentleman would see.

---

83. *water-fly* a large, iridescent, insubstantial insect that skims the surface of the water   87-8. *Let . . . king's mess* i.e. any lord, however much a beast, will be accepted at the King's table   87. *crib* pen   88. *chough* any noisy bird, such as a jackdaw   97. *indifferent* rather   99. *complexion* temperament, constitutional make-up   107. *differences* distinctions   109. *card or calendar* i.e. chart or listing to which one refers for accurate guidance for one's actions   110. *continent* i.e. container

HAMLET. Sir, his definement suffers no perdition in you, though I know to divide him inventorially would dozy th' arithmetic of memory, and yet but yaw neither in respect of his quick sail. But in the verity of extolment, 115 I take him to be a soul of great article, and his infusion of such dearth and rareness as, to make true diction of him, his semblable is his mirror, and who else would trace him, his umbrage, nothing more.

OSRIC. Your lordship speaks most infallibly of him.   120

HAMLET. The concernancy sir? Why do we wrap the gentleman in our more rawer breath?

OSRIC. Sir?

HORATIO. Is't not possible to understand in another tongue? You will do 't sir, really.   125

HAMLET. What imports the nomination of this gentleman?

OSRIC. Of Laertes?

HORATIO [*aside*]. His purse is empty already. All's golden words are spent.   130

HAMLET. Of him, sir.

OSRIC. I know you are not ignorant –

HAMLET. I would you did, sir; yet, in faith, if you did, it would not much approve me. Well, sir.

OSRIC. You are not ignorant of what excellence Laertes 135 is –

HAMLET. I dare not confess that, lest I should compare with him in excellence; but to know a man well were to know himself.

OSRIC. I mean, sir, for his weapon; but in the imputation 140 laid on him by them, in his meed he's unfellowed.

HAMLET. What's his weapon?

OSRIC. Rapier and dagger.

112. *definement* definition *perdition* loss or damage 113. *dozy* stagger 114. *yaw* veer unsteadily with the wind (in contrast to Laertes' swifter, steadier course) 116. *article* scope *infusion* essence 118. *semblable* likeness 121. *concernancy* purport 124-5. *Is't . . . tongue* Can't you understand your own jargon in another's mouth *do 't* i.e. beat him at his own game 126. *nomination* naming 140. *imputation* reputation 141. *meed* worth, desert *unfellowed* unequalled

HAMLET. That's two of his weapons – but well.

OSRIC. The king, sir, hath wagered with him six Barbary 145
horses, against the which he has impawned, as I take it,
six French rapiers and poniards, with their assigns, as
girdle, hangers, and so. Three of the carriages, in faith,
are very dear to fancy, very responsive to the hilts, most
delicate carriages, and of very liberal conceit. 150

HAMLET. What call you the carriages?

HORATIO [*aside to Hamlet*]. I knew you must be edified by
the margent ere you had done.

OSRIC. The carriages, sir, are the hangers.

HAMLET. The phrase would be more germane to the mat- 155
ter if we could carry a cannon by our sides. I would it
might be hangers till then. But on! Six Barbary horses
against six French swords, their assigns, and three liberal
conceited carriages; that's the French bet against the
Danish. Why is this all impawned, as you call it? 160

OSRIC. The king, sir, hath laid, sir, that in a dozen passes
between yourself and him he shall not exceed you three
hits; he hath laid on twelve for nine, and it would come
to immediate trial if your lordship would vouchsafe the
answer. 165

HAMLET. How if I answer no?

OSRIC. I mean, my lord, the opposition of your person in
trial.

HAMLET. Sir, I will walk here in the hall. If it please his
majesty, it is the breathing time of day with me. Let the 170
foils be brought, the gentleman willing, and the king
hold his purpose, I will win for him an I can. If not, I
will gain nothing but my shame and the odd hits.

OSRIC. Shall I deliver you so?

HAMLET. To this effect, sir, after what flourish your nature 175
will.

146. *impawned* pledged   147. *assigns* appendages   148. *hangers* straps
from which the sword hangs   150. *liberal conceit* fancy design   152-3.
edified . . . margent instructed by a marginal note   155-6. *The . . .
sides* (the term is more appropriately used in referring to cannons,
which are borne on gun-carriages)   164-5. *vouchsafe the answer* i.e.
consent to meet Laertes in response to this challenge   170. *the . . .
with me* my time for exercise   172. *an* if

OSRIC. I commend my duty to your lordship.

HAMLET. Yours.   *Exit Osric.*
He does well to commend it himself; there are no
tongues else for's turn.   180

HORATIO. This lapwing runs away with the shell on his
head.

HAMLET. 'A did comply, sir, with his dug before 'a sucked
it. Thus has he, and many more of the same bevy that
I know the drossy age dotes on, only got the tune of the 185
time; and out of an habit of encounter, a kind of yesty
collection which carries them through and through the
most fanned and winnowed opinions; and do but blow
them to their trial, the bubbles are out.

Enter a Lord.

LORD. My lord, his majesty commended him to you by 190
young Osric, who brings back to him that you attend
him in the hall. He sends to know if your pleasure hold
to play with Laertes, or that you will take longer time.

HAMLET. I am constant to my purposes; they follow the
king's pleasure. If his fitness speaks, mine is ready; now 195
or whensoever, provided I be so able as now.

LORD. The king and queen and all are coming down.

HAMLET. In happy time.

LORD. The queen desires you to use some gentle entertainment to Laertes before you fall to play.   200

HAMLET. She well instructs me.   *Exit Lord.*

HORATIO. You will lose this wager, my lord.

HAMLET. I do not think so. Since he went into France I
have been in continual practice. I shall win at the odds.

180. *for's turn* to do it for him   181-2. *This . . . head* This newly
hatched courtier is trying so hard to get ahead that he is running
before he's quite out of the shell   183-4. *'A did . . . it* He flattered
the breast before he sucked it; i.e. from birth he knew on which side
his bread was buttered   *bevy* flock of birds   185. *drossy* brassy   186.
habit of encounter customary style of polite greeting   *yesty* yeasty,
frothy   188. *fanned and winnowed* threshed, i.e. sifted and refined
(their collection of others' fine phrases makes an impression even on
persons of judgement, but their bubbles collapse when you put them
to the test)   195. *fitness* convenience   199-200. *use . . . Laertes* greet
Laertes politely

But thou wouldst not think how ill all's here about my 205
heart. But it is no matter.
HORATIO. Nay, good my lord –
HAMLET. It is but foolery, but it is such a kind of gaingiving as would perhaps trouble a woman.
HORATIO. If your mind dislike anything, obey it. I will fore- 210
stall their repair hither, and say you are not fit.
HAMLET. Not a whit, we defy augury. There is special
providence in the fall of a sparrow. If it be now, 'tis not
to come; if it be not to come, it will be now; if it be not
now, yet it will come. The readiness is all. Since no man 215
knows aught of what he leaves, what is't to leave betimes? Let be.

> *A table prepared. [Enter] Trumpets, Drums, and*
> *Officers with cushions; King, Queen, [Osric] and*
> *all the State, [with] foils, daggers, and Laertes.*

KING. Come, Hamlet, come, and take this hand from me.
        [The King puts Laertes's hand into Hamlet's.]
HAMLET. Give me your pardon, sir. I have done you
   wrong,
But pardon 't as you are a gentleman.   220
This presence knows, and you must needs have heard,
How I am punished with a sore distraction.
What I have done
That might your nature, honour, and exception,
Roughly awake, I here proclaim was madness.   225
Was 't Hamlet wronged Laertes? Never Hamlet.
If Hamlet from himself be ta'en away,
And when he's not himself does wrong Laertes,
Then Hamlet does it not, Hamlet denies it.
Who does it then? His madness. If't be so,   230
Hamlet is of the faction that is wronged;
His madness is poor Hamlet's enemy.
Sir, in this audience,

205-6. *how . . . heart* how uneasy I feel about it   208-9. *gaingiving*
misgiving   221. *this presence* i.e. the King and Queen (as "the royal
presence")   224. *exception* objection

Let my disclaiming from a purposed evil
Free me so far in your most generous thoughts   235
That I have shot my arrow o'er the house
And hurt my brother.
LAERTES.   I am satisfied in nature,
Whose motive in this case should stir me most
To my revenge. But in my terms of honour
I stand aloof, and will no reconcilement   240
Till by some elder masters of known honour
I have a voice and precedent of peace
To keep my name ungored. But till that time
I do receive your offered love like love,
And will not wrong it.
HAMLET.   I embrace it freely,   245
And will this brother's wager frankly play.
Give us the foils.
LAERTES.   Come, one for me.
HAMLET. I'll be your foil, Laertes. In mine ignorance
Your skill shall, like a star i' th' darkest night,
Stick fiery off indeed.
LAERTES.   You mock me, sir.   250
HAMLET. No, by this hand.
KING. Give them the foils, young Osric. Cousin Hamlet,
You know the wager?
HAMLET.   Very well, my lord;
Your Grace has laid the odds o' th' weaker side.
KING. I do not fear it, I have seen you both;   255
But since he is bettered, we have therefore odds.
LAERTES. This is too heavy; let me see another.
HAMLET. This likes me well. These foils have all a length?
                    [They] prepare to play.

OSRIC. Ay, my good lord.

___

242. *voice . . . peace* judgement, based on precedent, that a reconciliation will be regarded as honourable   243. *name ungored* reputation as
a gentleman undamaged   246. *frankly* without rancour or reservation
248. *I'll . . . foil* I'll enhance your performance by contrast   250. *Stick
fiery off* display its lustre   256. *is bettered* has the reputation of being
better   258. *have . . . length* are all the same length

KING. Set me the stoups of wine upon that table.   260
   If Hamlet give the first or second hit,
   Or quit in answer of the third exchange,
   Let all the battlements their ordnance fire.
   The king shall drink to Hamlet's better breath,
   And in the cup an union shall he throw,   265
   Richer than that which four successive kings
   In Denmark's crown have worn. Give me the cups,
   And let the kettle to the trumpet speak,
   The trumpet to the cannoneer without,
   The cannons to the heavens, the heaven to earth,   270
   "Now the king drinks to Hamlet". Come, begin –
                           Trumpets the while.
   And you, the judges, bear a wary eye.
HAMLET. Come on, sir.
LAERTES.   Come, my lord.   *[They play.]*
HAMLET.   One.
LAERTES.   No.
HAMLET.   Judgement?
OSRIC. A hit, a very palpable hit.
   Drums, trumpets and shot. Flourish; a piece goes off.
LAERTES. Well, again.   275
KING. Stay, give me drink. Hamlet, this pearl is thine.
   Here's to thy health. Give him the cup.
HAMLET. I'll play this bout first; set it by awhile.
   Come.   *[They play.]*
   Another hit; what say you?   280
LAERTES. I do confess't.
KING. Our son shall win.
QUEEN.   He's fat, and scant of breath.
   Here, Hamlet, take my napkin, rub thy brows.
   The queen carouses to thy fortune, Hamlet.
HAMLET. Good madam!   285
KING. Gertrude, do not drink.

262. *quit in answer* gives as good as he gets (i.e. if the third bout is a draw) 264. *better breath* second wind 265. *union* i.e. a particularly fine pearl 268. *kettle* kettledrum 277. *Here's . . . health* (the King drinks and then drops the poison into the cup)

QUEEN. I will, my lord; I pray you pardon me.

KING [*aside*]. It is the poisoned cup; it is too late.

HAMLET. I dare not drink yet, madam; by and by.

QUEEN. Come, let me wipe thy face.   290

LAERTES. My lord, I'll hit him now.

KING.   I do not think't.

LAERTES [*aside*]. And yet it is almost against my
    conscience.

HAMLET. Come, for the third, Laertes. You do but dally.
  I pray you pass with your best violence;
  I am afeard you make a wanton of me.   295

LAERTES. Say you so? Come on.   [*They play.*]

OSRIC. Nothing, neither way.

LAERTES. Have at you now!

     [*Laertes wounds Hamlet: then*] *in scuffling, they*
       change rapiers [*and Hamlet wounds Laertes.*]

KING. Part them. They are incensed.

HAMLET. Nay, come again.   [*The Queen falls.*] 300

OSRIC. Look to the queen there, ho!

HORATIO. They bleed on both sides. How is it, my lord?

OSRIC. How is't, Laertes?

LAERTES. Why, as a woodcock to mine own springe,
    Osric.
  I am justly killed with mine own treachery.   305

HAMLET. How does the queen?

KING. She swoons to see them bleed.

QUEEN. No, no, the drink, the drink! O my dear Hamlet!
  The drink, the drink! I am poisoned.   [*Dies.*]

HAMLET. O, villainy! Ho! let the door be locked.   310
  Treachery! seek it out.   [*Laertes falls.*]

LAERTES. It is here, Hamlet. Hamlet, thou art slain;
  No med'cine in the world can do thee good.
  In thee there is not half an hour's life.
  The treacherous instrument is in thy hand,   315
  Unbated and envenomed. The foul practice
  Hath turned itself on me. Lo, here I lie,

295. *make a wanton of* are just playing with   304. *as a . . . springe* I
have fallen into my own trap (woodcocks were sometimes trained to
serve as decoys)

Never to rise again. Thy mother's poisoned.
I can no more. The king, the king's to blame.
HAMLET. The point envenomed too?   320
   Then, venom, to thy work!   *Hurts the King.* ‡
ALL. Treason! treason!
KING. O, yet defend me, friends. I am but hurt.
HAMLET. Here, thou incestuous, murd'rous, damnèd
    Dane,
   Drink off this potion. Is thy union here?   *King dies.* 325
   Follow my mother.
LAERTES.   He is justly served.
   It is a poison tempered by himself.
   Exchange forgiveness with me, noble Hamlet.
   Mine and my father's death come not upon thee,
   Nor thine on me!   *[Dies.]* 330
HAMLET. Heaven make thee free of it! I follow thee.
   I am dead, Horatio. Wretched queen, adieu!
   You that look pale and tremble at this chance,
   That are but mutes or audience to this act,
   Had I but time, as this fell sergeant Death   335
   Is strict in his arrest, O, I could tell you –
   But let it be. Horatio, I am dead:
   Thou livest; report me and my cause aright
   To the unsatisfied.
HORATIO.   Never believe it.
   I am more an antique Roman than a Dane.   340 ‡
   Here's yet some liquor left.
HAMLET.   As th'art a man,
   Give me the cup. Let go. By heaven, I'll ha't.
   O God, Horatio, what a wounded name,
   Things standing thus unknown, shall live behind me!
   If thou didst ever hold me in thy heart,   345
   Absent thee from felicity awhile,   ‡
   And in this harsh world draw thy breath in pain,
   To tell my story.   *A march afar off.*
            What warlike noise is this?

325. *union* (i) pearl, (ii) marriage   334. *mutes* (i) non-speaking actors,
(ii) ceremonial mourners not personally involved with the dead   335.
fell cruel   *sergeant* law officer who served summonses

OSRIC. Young Fortinbras, with conquest come from
    Poland,
  To th' ambassadors of England gives   350
  This warlike volley.
HAMLET.   O, I die, Horatio!
  The potent poison quite o'er-crows my spirit.
  I cannot live to hear the news from England,
  But I do prophesy th' election lights
  On Fortinbras. He has my dying voice.   355
  So tell him, with th' occurrents, more and less,
  Which have solicited – the rest is silence.   *Dies.*
HORATIO. Now cracks a noble heart. Good night, sweet
    prince,
  And flights of angels sing thee to thy rest!

                               [March within.]
  Why does the drum come hither?   360

      Enter Fortinbras, with the Ambassadors [and
          with drum, colours, and Attendants].

FORTINBRAS. Where is this sight?
HORATIO.   What is it you would see?
  If aught of woe or wonder, cease your search.
FORTINBRAS. This quarry cries on havoc. O proud death,
  What feast is toward in thine eternal cell
  That thou so many princes at a shot   365
  So bloodily hast struck?
AMBASSADOR.   The sight is dismal;
  And our affairs from England come too late.
  The ears are senseless that should give us hearing
  To tell him his commandment is fulfilled,
  That Rosencrantz and Guildenstern are dead.   370
  Where should we have our thanks?
HORATIO.   Not from his mouth,
  Had it th' ability of life to thank you.

---

352. *o'er-crows* triumphs over (cf. "crow over") 355. *voice* vote
356. *occurrents* occurrences 357. *solicited* brought this about 363.
quarry heap of bodies *cries on havoc* ("Havoc" was the battle cry
for "no quarter", as in *Julius Caesar* 3.1.273) 364. *toward* in preparation

He never gave commandment for their death.
But since, so jump upon this bloody question,
You from the Polack wars, and you from England,   375
Are here arrived, give order that these bodies
High on a stage be placèd to the view,
And let me speak to th' yet unknowing world
How these things came about. So shall you hear
Of carnal, bloody, and unnatural acts;   380
Of accidental judgements, casual slaughters;
Of deaths put on by cunning and forced cause;
And, in this upshot, purposes mistook
Fall'n on th' inventors' heads. All this can I
Truly deliver.
FORTINBRAS.   Let us haste to hear it,   385
And call the noblest to the audience.
For me, with sorrow I embrace my fortune.
I have some rights of memory in this kingdom,
Which now to claim my vantage doth invite me.
HORATIO. Of that I shall have also cause to speak,   390
And from his mouth whose voice will draw on more.
But let this same be presently performed,
Even while men's minds are wild, lest more mischance
On plots and errors happen.
FORTINBRAS.   Let four captains
Bear Hamlet like a soldier to the stage,   395
For he was likely, had he been put on,
To have proved most royal; and for his passage
The soldier's music and the rite of war
Speak loudly for him.
Take up the bodies. Such a sight as this   400
Becomes the field, but here shows much amiss.
Go, bid the soldiers shoot.
          Exeunt [marching. A peal of ordnance shot off].

374. *jump* immediately 382. *put on* brought about 388. *rights of
memory* unforgotten rights 389. *my vantage* (there being no rival
claimant) 396. *put on* i.e. put to the test as King 397. *passage* (i.e.
to the next world) 401. *field* battlefield

1.1.21 *What, has this thing appeared again to-night* "This thing" indicates Horatio's skepticism about supernatural phenomena.

Contrary to popular impression, Elizabethans did not all believe unreservedly in ghosts; opinions differed widely, as we know from the extensive popular and learned literature on the subject, which formed part of one of the liveliest and most persistent controversies of the age. The stock stage ghost is described (satirically) in the Induction to *A Warning for Fair Women* (c. 1599):

> Then, too, a filthy whining ghost
> Lapt in some foul sheet or leathern pilch
> Comes screaming like a pig half-sticked,
> And cries, "Vindicta! Revenge, Revenge!"
> With that a little resin flasheth forth,
> Like smoke out of a tobacco pipe or boy's squib.

Thomas Lodge's *Wit's Misery* (1596) makes reference to the ghost in the older Hamlet play, "which cried so miserably at the Theatre like an oister wife, Hamlet revenge". This stock ghost, borrowed from Senecan drama by way of Kyd's *The Spanish Tragedy* (in which the original victim, Don Andrea, sits unseen, except by the audience, on stage, to comment occasionally on the action and complain to his companion, Revenge, of delay), is a far cry from Shakespeare's ghosts in *Julius Caesar*, *Macbeth*, and *Hamlet*. The ghosts in *Julius Caesar* and *Macbeth* may be regarded as illusions of outworn or guilt-tortured minds, but the Ghost of Hamlet's father in Acts 1 and 2, vouched for by four independent witnesses besides Hamlet, is certainly an objective phenomenon. The apparition is both real and contemporary, coming not from the classical Tartarus but from a "place of departed spirits" in which the audience, Catholic or Protestant, believed, however they may have differed about details. He wears not the blacksmith's "pilch" or apron of hell's fireman, but "his habit as he lived" – armour on the battlements, and a dressing-gown in the bedroom. Of the three main schools of thought regarding ghosts, the Catholic, with its doctrine of Purgatory, offered a logically as well as theologically acceptable explanation of the return of departed spirits for some specific purpose which, when fulfilled, would enable them to find rest. For Protestants, who had got rid of Purgatory, ghosts must come from either heaven or hell, abodes which were permanent. How and why, then, did ghosts cross that "bourn from which no traveller returns"? The orthodox Protestant view was that while some such apparitions might be angels assuming a familiar human shape, most were devils who usurped the form of a friend or relative in order to do spiritual harm to those to whom they appeared. Thus Lewis Lavater in *Of Ghosts and Spirits Walking by Night* (Zurich, 1570; London, as translated by R.H., 1572, 1596), after summing up Catholic doctrines, continues:

> Now, that the souls neither of the faithful nor of infidels wander . . . upon earth once they be severed from the bodies, I will make it plain and evident. . . . Those that go hence in a right belief, their souls are by and by in possession of life everlasting; and they that depart in unbelief do straightway become partakers of eternal damnation.
>
> . . .
>
> If it be not a vain persuasion proceeding through weakness of the senses, through fear, or from such like cause, or if it be not deceit of men, or some natural thing . . . it is either a good or evil angel. . . . For as servants stand before their masters to fulfill their commandments, even so are the angels . . . ready to serve God. . . .
> Contrariwise, evil angels are . . . enemies unto men; they follow them everywhere, to the end that they may withdraw them from the true worshipping of God.
> These appear in divers shapes.

A third school of thought, of which Reginald Scot's *Discoverie of Witchcraft* (1584) and its added *Discourse Upon Divels and Spirits* are the chief exponents, is that of the skeptics. Scot does not deny the existence of spirits, but he quite bluntly denies their ability to assume human form. Apparitions are neither devils nor angels any more than they are spirits, but are the hallucinations of melancholic minds or the lying tricks of rogues.

It has often been remarked that in *Hamlet* Shakespeare is more concerned to ask or evoke questions than to answer them, and the matter of ghosts is no exception. The problem is presented from all points of view. The Ghost himself speaks as if he had come from Purgatory, where "the foul crimes done in my days of nature/ Are burnt and purged away", but he is conveniently vague about details. Except for one oblique reference, young Hamlet says nothing of Purgatory and wonders only whether the supernatural emissary is "an honest ghost", "a spirit of health", or a "goblin damned". He appears to be a first-generation Protestant, as was his author. Until he has seen the Ghost (when he adopts the Protestant point of view), Horatio, along with Gertrude (who does not see the Ghost), belongs in the camp of Scot and those who regard ghosts as illusions.

The Ghost's purpose is also ambiguous. As the last lawful king he is entitled to demand justice against the usurper, but as the victim of murder he is not entitled to demand that a human agent execute his private vengeance at the peril of that agent's soul. "Vengeance is mine; I will repay, saith the Lord" (Romans 12:19). Yet the Ghost displays, in his "Leave her to heaven . . .", a proper Christian attitude to his erring wife. When, at his first appearance to the guards and Horatio, he fades away at cockcrow "like a guilty thing/ Upon a fearful summons", that disappearance reminds Marcellus of the hallowed time of Christmas, when no evil spirit can walk abroad. Subsequently the Ghost moves about underground, like a demon. All this dubious behaviour gives Hamlet cause, on second thought, to doubt the Ghost's authenticity and to hesitate to carry out his command.

Personal vengeance, as Laertes later makes clear, was demanded by the medieval code of honour, the assumptions of which Shakespeare and his contemporaries frequently questioned and even ridiculed as both unchristian and ir-rational. Private vengeance was prohibited by the laws of both church and state, yet that eminent jurist, Francis Bacon, termed revenge "a kind of wild justice".

Opinion was sufficiently divided, both as to the nature of ghosts and the claims of "honour" with regard to personal vengeance, to make Hamlet's desire to be sure of his facts perfectly credible to an Elizabethan audience. If the spirit he has seen is neither a heavenly messenger nor his father's honest ghost, but a devil who, out of his own weakness and melancholy, is abusing him, the consequences of acting upon its instructions would be, as Hamlet realizes, damnation. Not only would he be gratifying his own personal antagonism by slaying an innocent victim; in opposing his duly appointed sovereign he would also be going against the natural order and against St. Paul's command regarding obedience to temporal authority. The King was regarded as God's vice-regent on earth and was accountable for his stewardship to heaven alone, even in the matter of a kinsman's murder, as John of Gaunt makes clear in *Richard II*:

> God's is the quarrel, for God's substitute,
> His deputy anointed in His sight
> Hath caused his death. The which if wrongfully,
> Let Heaven revenge, for I may never lift
> An angry arm against His minister.
>
> (1.2.37-41)

If the sovereign had gained his office by regicide or usurpation, however, the case was altered, and it was the duty of all good citizens to restore, at all costs, the rightful succession. Therefore, if the Ghost is a deceiving demon, it is Hamlet's duty to hold his tongue however his heart may be breaking because the bed of Denmark is a couch for luxury and incest. If it is an honest Ghost, it is his duty as prince to set right the disjointed and corrupt state of Denmark, whether or not, in doing so, he is exacting personal vengeance as the son of a murdered father, since public justice as well as private retribution will then be involved.

The play which Hamlet later has enacted before the court in order to present the King with a mirror of his murder is therefore not a procrastinating device but a test of the Ghost's truth, which Claudius' reactions prove to Hamlet's complete satisfaction.

1.1.113-20 *In the most high . . . eclipse* This sounds rather like a modern "plug" for next week's program. It is probable that *Julius Caesar*, believed to have been written shortly before

Hamlet, was still in the active repertoire of Shakespeare's company.

1.1.128-38 Horatio lists the principal reasons for which a spirit might "walk": (1) to ease the spirit's conscience by causing some "good deed" to be done which will make amends for some evil or injustice done during its life, (2) to do some benefit to surviving friends or to impart to them its fore-knowledge of future danger, (3) to disclose the hiding place of buried treasure so that, if the wealth has been obtained by unjust means, it may be restored to its rightful owners.

All of these are honourable actions, the execution of which would "do grace" to the human agent to whom the spirit had communicated its instructions, and would indicate the "honesty" of the ghost and its intentions.

1.1.153 *Whether in sea or fire, in earth or air* All matter was believed to be constituted of the four elements – earth, air, fire, and water.

1.2.1-25 Claudius' speech to the Council after his accession is a masterpiece of political opportunism, or what the Elizabethans termed "policy". He makes it appear that everything he might be criticized for – the abridgement of the period of court mourning, his over-hasty marriage to his brother's widow – has been done for urgent reasons of state, in order to be able to deal promptly and effectively with the threat to national security posed by the activities of young Fortinbras. It seems clear that he has made use of these circumstances to persuade the nobles to elect him king, as a mature and experienced man of affairs, rather than Hamlet, the contemplative student. Their "better wisdoms" have "freely gone/ With this affair along". For the most part the speech is straightforward and business-like, but the formally rhetorical style of lines 10 to 14 is a warning to the audience that Claudius is a dissembler. Formal antithesis and oxymoron used as stylistic artifice are usually signposts of deception or self-deception in Shakespeare's plays.

1.2.67 *sun* (with a pun on "son", i.e. stepson). The sun was symbolically equated with "king", and Hamlet is too much in this king's eye.

1.2.92-105 Claudius' criticism of Hamlet's persistence in grief beyond the appropriate period for ceremonial mourning is sound if commonplace doctrine. Death, "a necessary end,/

Will come when it will come" (*Julius Caesar*, 2.2.36-7) and to refuse to accept its necessity is a rebellion against natural law, which is the expression of the will of heaven. It is also to set things temporal above things eternal, as Feste demonstrates in proving the folly of Olivia's excessive grief for her brother's death in *Twelfth Night*. If she believes her brother's soul to be in heaven she should rejoice in his eternal bliss rather than lamenting his loss.

1.2.109 *most immediate to our throne* By this formal announcement that Hamlet has his "voice" (i.e. "vote") for the succession to the throne, Claudius hopes to secure the Prince's acquiescence in the *fait accompli* of his own recent election and accession to the crown of Denmark.

1.2.129 *sallied* Recent bibliographical scholarship (see, for example, F. W. Bowers, "Hamlet's 'Sullied' or 'Solid' Flesh. A Bibliographical Case History", *Shakespeare Survey* 9, 1956) has undermined the authority of F's familiar "solid". Non-bibliographical arguments for retaining the F reading point out that "solid" leads naturally into the ensuing reference to the deliquescence and dissolution of the flesh into its constituent elements after death. The supporters of "sallied" = "sullied" insist that this soliliquy as a whole is far more concerned with the impurity of the flesh, the spiritual corruption of man by his physical lusts, than with a personal death-wish. It is not unlikely that Shakespeare, whichever word he set down in his manuscript, was consciously evoking the connotations of both "solid" and its near homonym "sullied".

1.2.140 *Hyperion* the most beautiful of the Olympian deities — again the sun-king parallel. Beauty of soul was regarded as manifesting itself in physical beauty.

1.2.140 *satyr* a woodland spirit half human, half beast in form. Hamlet sees his uncle as lacking royalty of nature, as bestial in appearance and behaviour. The satyrs, to which he likens Claudius, were companions of Bacchus, the God of Wine, as well as of Pan, the God of Animal Nature.

1.2.149 *Niobe* Queen of Thebes. She boasted of having more beautiful children than the goddess Leto, who thereupon sent her children, Apollo and Artemis, to kill Niobe's seven sons and daughters. Such was the mother's grief at her loss that Zeus changed her into a stone from which issued a spring of her tears.

1.2.157 *incestuous sheets* According to canon law, the union of a man and his deceased brother's wife was regarded as incest, though papal dispensations were sometimes granted for such marriages. Henry VIII secured such a dispensation before marrying Catherine of Aragon, who had been his brother Arthur's wife. Nevertheless he gave his alleged qualms of conscience about the moral validity of the marriage as his official reason for seeking a divorce from Catherine.

1.2.164 *what make you from Wittenberg, Horatio* One of the unresolved puzzles of the play is why Horatio, who must have been about the court for more than a month, since he came for Hamlet's father's funeral, is now meeting Hamlet for the first time since his arrival.

1.2.175 *We'll teach you to drink deep* One of Hamlet's several references to the proverbially heavy drinking of the Danes, a habit he found especially distasteful (cf. his comments on this "heavy-headed revel", 1.4.17 ff.), particularly as indulged in by his uncle. It is ironical that Claudius should attempt to curry favour with his nephew by celebrating his consenting to stay at the Danish court with the ceremony of the "rouse" which Hamlet found so repugnant.

1.2.180-81 *Thrift . . . tables* As every hostess knows, it is more economical to prepare for two parties at once. The first day's hot dinner can serve as the second's cold buffet.

1.2.241 *assume* Hamlet realizes that the apparition may be a demon masquerading as the spirit of his dead father, as Horatio has done (1.1.46-7) in addressing it as "thou that usurp'st . . . that fair and warlike form" and in referring to it later (1.1.80-81) as the image of the late king.

1.3.7 *A violet in the youth of primy nature* The repeated association of violets, the floral symbol of modesty, with Ophelia is one indication that her role is in no way that of the harlot of the source story, save in the doubts engendered in Hamlet's disillusioned imagination. She echoes this comment of Laertes in her distracted lament that the violets "withered all when my father died" (4.5.182), and Laertes, at her grave, prays, "And from her fair and unpolluted flesh/ May violets spring!" (5.1.230-31).

1.3.50 *primrose path* the broad road that leads to destruction, as opposed to the "strait and narrow" way to heaven (Matt. 7:13-14), called "the primrose way to the everlasting bonfire" in *Macbeth* (2.3.20-21).

1.3.58-80 *And these few precepts . . . any man* Similar sententious statements to a son, composed by various fathers from Sir Henry Sidney to Lord Chesterfield, have been preserved. Most of them are a combination of common sense and worldly wisdom. Polonius' advice resembles fairly closely the parting advice given by Euphues to Philautus in John Lyly's novella, *Euphues* (1578), for example:

> Be not lavish of thy tongue. . . .
> Everyone that shaketh thee by the hand, is not joyned to thee in heart. . . .
> Be not quarrelous for every lyght occasion. . . .
> It shall be better to heare what they say, then to speak what thou thinkest.

No precise analogue to the final precept of the catalogue has been identified, and whether "to thine own self be true" means "look after your own interests" or "preserve your integrity" remains a matter of controversy, the weight of critical opinion inclining toward the latter.

1.3.90 *Marry, well bethought* Polonius' selection of this mild expletive (equivalent to "By Our Lady") may be intended to suggest a perhaps still unconscious hope that he can make a match between Hamlet and his daughter.

1.3.99-109 Polonius plays on the word "tenders", using it in a number of senses, among them that of "script", a written promise to pay sometimes issued to soldiers on active service instead of coin. In "Tender yourself more dearly" the word has the force of "hold" or "regard", while in "tender me a fool" it may mean "furnish" or "supply with", i.e. Ophelia will give him a fool for a daughter by making a fool of herself. Elizabethan usage of "fool" for "baby" makes yet another interpretation possible, one which would make Ophelia's next speech an indignant rejoinder with the emphasis on "honourable".

1.3.108-9 *not to crack . . . Running it thus* The metaphor is that of a broken-winded horse, wheezing from being ridden too hard.

1.3.117-19 *blazes . . . a-making* Verbal embroidery on the proverbs "Hot love is soon cold", and "A quick fire is soon out".

1.3.122-3 *Set your entreatments . . . parley* The analogy between a woman's heart and a besieged castle or town was a common medieval and Renaissance literary "conceit". Polonius warns Ophelia not to enter into negotiations for a treaty of surrender at the first overture of the besieging forces. The stronger the show of resistance, the better the eventual terms of capitulation.

1.3.125 *larger tether* A reference to the double standard which permits greater freedom of behaviour to men than to women.

1.3.127-31 *for they are brokers . . . beguile* The complicated word-play of this passage is further complicated by textual disagreement. The Q's and F read "bonds"; "bawds" (1.130) is Theobald's emendation. The word "broker" signifies "go-between" in affairs of either business or pleasure; "investments" may be financial, sartorial, or both; "implorators of unholy suits" (with a likely pun on "suits") suggests by inversion clerical vestments, an association which is borne out by "dye" and by "sanctified and pious", and which supports the case for "bonds" in the sense of "vows". Financial contracts customarily began with a pious preamble, such as "In the name of God, Amen." Such contracts (or prospectuses), however, can hardly be referred to as "Breathing" their "unholy suits" and false promises, unlike gaudily dressed bawds, who are also in business and are equally likely to misrepresent the goods and services they have to offer.

Fortunately, the meaning of the passage is sufficiently clear despite the metaphorical tangle.

1.4.16 *More honoured . . . observance* commonly misinterpreted as meaning "more often neglected than observed". What Hamlet is saying is that it is more honourable to fail to observe this custom than to abide by it.

1.4.20-22 *it takes . . . attribute* The reputation of being a nation of drunkards diminishes the fame of our highest achievements, which are the substance of international esteem.

1.4.27 *o'ergrowth . . . complexion* According to the physiology of the time, a man's complexion was determined by the proportions of the four "humours" or bodily fluids in his physical constitution. These were blood, a predominance of which gave him a sanguine temperament, as a predominance of phlegm made him phlegmatic, of red bile (or choler), choleric, and of black bile, melancholic. A serious "o'ergrowth" of any of these predominances, it was believed, could cause mental or physical illness.

1.4.39 *Angels . . . defend us* Like Horatio, Hamlet is very careful and precise in the way he addresses the apparition, first invoking the protection of heaven and then addressing it as if it were truly the spirit of his father, the King. Thus, if it should turn out to be a demon rather than a true Ghost he will not be guilty of knowingly holding converse with evil spirits. In other words, he gives the Ghost the benefit of the doubt.

1.4.53 *glimpses of the moon* the moon shining either through the crenellation of the battlements or breaks in the clouds.

1.4.54-6 *Making . . . reaches of our souls* making us (who understand as little of the supernatural world as an idiot of the human world) agitate our minds so horribly with surmises about matters that are beyond our powers of comprehension.

1.4.73 *sovereignty of reason* an inversion. The meaning is "deprive your reason of sovereignty". The reason was supposed to rule over the other faculties of the soul, governing the will, the executive faculty which directed the actions of the individual. In madness, of course, the reason is deprived of rule.

1.4.83 *Nemean lion's nerve* the sinews of the lion of Nemea. One of the twelve labours of Hercules was to obtain the skin of this beast.

1.5.3 *sulph'rous and tormenting flames* This, and the subsequent reference to being "confined to fast in fires" and "Doomed for a certain term to walk the night" make it clear that the apparition professes to come from Purgatory.

1.5.18 *knotted and combinèd locks* This detail of Hamlet's appearance strengthens the horror the Ghost wishes to convey, in that it is more of a feat to make curly than straight hair stand on end.

1.5.30 *meditation or the thoughts of love* Meditation is not a word one would ordinarily use to suggest speed. Hamlet means "as swift as thought or (even swifter) the thoughts of love". But Hamlet does not find it easy to carry out swiftly the thoughts of hate, and what he actually does is engage in meditation in the reflective sense of the word.

1.5.40 *O my prophetic soul* Hamlet's astonished cry of "Murder" (1. 26) has made it clear that he had not suspected Claudius of this specific "foul deed", but this second exclamation expresses his realization that his antipathy to his uncle was not only soundly based but foreshadowed the Ghost's revelation.

1.5.43 *With witchcraft . . . gifts* The words serve to characterize Gertrude as well as Claudius. Hamlet's uncle is clever as well as treacherous; his mother is simple, sensuous, and materialistic. Her lack of introspection and her concern for externals are indicated in Hamlet's speech to her about "the trappings and the suits of woe" (1.2.86), and in his injunction to her:

> Lay not that flattering unction to your soul,
> That not your trespass but my madness speaks.
> It will but skin and film the ulcerous place
> Whiles rank corruption, mining all within,
> Infects unseen.   (3.4.149-53)

In the closet scene only Hamlet's extreme violence of speech avails to turn Gertrude's eyes into her "very soul".

When used against one with so limited an intellect as Gertrude's, wit is witchcraft, though as commonly used the words were paired as an alliterative antithesis, as in Iago's "Thou know'st we work by wit and not by witchcraft" (*Othello* 2.3.378). Not only has Claudius courted Gertrude with material gifts, he has abused his intelligence, the gift of God, by using it traitorously for evil purposes.

1.5.75 *Of life, of crown, of queen* Though this list reverses what might be regarded as the normal order of importance, it is intended to be a climactic progression, as in Claudius' account of "those effects for which I did the murder – / My crown, mine own ambition, and my queen." (3.3.54-5).

1.5.85-6 *Taint not thy mind . . . aught* "Taint not thy mind" probably carries over to "Against thy mother", "nor let thy soul contrive" being a restatement and extension of the same idea. The first phrase, however, is sometimes regarded as standing alone and is variously interpreted as "do not corrupt your nature in exacting vengeance" or even "do not destroy your mind" (i.e. "go mad"). Neither of these interpretations seems wholly satisfactory. The committing of even what one regards as a necessary and justified murder is bound to have an adverse effect on the character, and sanity is hardly a matter entirely in one's own control, as the Elizabethans were quite aware. Since the Ghost, ambiguous in some respects though he may be, is not given to talking nonsense, it seems reasonable to assume that he is here indulging his bent for rhetorical "amplification" and that "Taint not thy mind" governs "Against thy mother". That is, he charges Hamlet not to think evil of his mother or attempt to judge and punish her, but to leave both her judgement and her penance to God and her conscience.

1.5.107 *My tables . . . it down* In spite of his just concluded vow to erase everything save the Ghost's command from the book of his brain, force of habit impels Hamlet to reach for his actual notebook in order to record this observation about human nature.

1.5.116 *Hillo, ho, ho, boy* the call is that of a falconer to his hawk. It is the first instance of Hamlet's tendency to fall into light talk or wild jesting as what seems to be a means of relief from strain of extreme tension. Other instances are his behaviour after the play *The Murder of Gonzago*, and after his confrontation with his mother in the closet scene.

1.5.136 *Saint Patrick* An unlikely saint for a Dane to swear by. Shakespeare may have been thinking of Saint Patrick's Purgatory, the name of a cave in Ireland which was supposed to give entrance to the lower world.

1.5.140 *O'ermaster't as you may* i.e. control your curiosity as best you can. Wilson suggests that Hamlet changes his tone to Horatio and breaks off thus rudely because Marcellus has approached within earshot.

1.5.151 *the oath* The oath Hamlet proposes has three parts: "Never to speak of this that you have seen," "Never to speak of this that you have heard," and never to hint that you know why I am putting "an antic disposition on" (i.e. pretending to be mentally disturbed), if I should do so.

John Dover Wilson (*What Happens in Hamlet*, Cambridge University Press, 1962, pp. 78-86) argues that Hamlet's disrespectful language to the Ghost is motivated by a desire to persuade Marcellus that it *is* a devil. (Marcellus is assumed not to have heard Hamlet's remark to Horatio that it is "an honest ghost".) This would help to explain the shifting of ground for the three parts of the oath. It would hardly be appropriate to swear a sacred vow with a devil underfoot. But the swearing of an oath three times and shifting ground on each occasion appears to have been a common practice and occurs in Fletcher's *Woman's Prize*, Act 5, scene 3

(Bradley, *Shakespearean Tragedy*, London: Macmillan, 1950, p. 413).

Wilson also points out that the Ghost's behaviour and Hamlet's reaction to it will effectively seal Marcellus' lips. He is not likely to confess that he has three times sworn an oath at the command and in the presence of a devil.

2.1.24, 32 *liberty* Polonius is trying to make a distinction between "liberty" as the licentious behaviour of a confirmed "libertine" and as the perhaps blamable but natural and pardonable excesses of a youth who has escaped from parental discipline and has not yet taken upon himself the sobering responsibilities of adulthood. "Loose-living" is too strong and "exuberance" too weak a term for what he has in mind.

2.1.62 *Your bait . . . of truth* "Merely used to carry out the figure with Polonian thoroughness. Any other fish would do as well" (Kittredge). Not at all. The carp, as a scavenger, is the ideal fish to be taken in by the bait of slanderous gossip.

2.1.70 *Observe his inclination in yourself* The meaning is doubtful. Johnson's suggestion that Polonius is telling Reynaldo to observe Laertes' behaviour himself, as well as relying on the testimony of others, is perhaps the most satisfactory of several interpretations.

2.1.77 *with his doublet all unbraced* This and the other details of Hamlet's appearance as described by Ophelia are the conventional signs of the victim of love-melancholy. This is the first evidence of Hamlet's having "put an antic disposition on", and while his sloppy attire is the costume of the role he is playing, his manner suggests that he may have been playing it partly in jest, partly in earnest. (Cf. *As You Like It*, 3.2.392-401.)

2.1.117-18 *which being kept close . . . to utter love* That is, keeping quiet about the cause of Hamlet's madness might cause (and court) more trouble than revealing it. Polonius does not expect the King and Queen to be pleased at learning that Hamlet is in love with a girl so inferior to him in rank as Ophelia, but he believes it will cause less displeasure to make a clean breast of it now than to have the King learn of it later, perhaps from someone else, or perhaps after Hamlet's madness has driven him to some desperate undertaking such as suicide.

2.2.11 *being . . . with him* It was customary to select certain children of the nobility to be brought up with the prince and share his sports and studies.

2.2.14-15 *by your companies . . . pleasures* The provision of companionship and pleasant diversion was standard treatment for the withdrawal symptoms of melancholy. Claudius thus gives the impression that cure is his primary concern, and that curiosity is secondary.

2.2.38 *practices* A *double entendre*. Guildenstern uses the word to refer to the devices they intend to use to "draw" the prince "on to pleasures", but its more usual meaning is "plots", which would certainly accord with Hamlet's subsequent view of their activities.

2.2.95 *More matter with less art* Polonius has begun to deliver a formal speech structured on the rhetorical pattern of "exordium" (ll. 86-105), "narration" (ll. 106-146), and "peroration" (ll. 147-151). The Queen attempts to cut him short by indicating that, while his eloquence is impressive, she is anxious to get to the gist of the matter. Polonius takes her interruption as a compliment to his verbal skill and protests that this sort of thing is not "art"; it comes naturally to him.

2.2.106 *have while she is mine* Polonius hopes that, if all goes well, he may lose a daughter while gaining a son-in-law.

2.2.109-23 *"To the celestial . . . machine is to him, Hamlet"* Whatever allowances are made for the greater degree of formality and of hyperbole in Elizabethan as compared with twentieth-century love letters, there is no escaping the conclusion that Hamlet's has a touch of burlesque. Indeed, Hamlet confesses that the style is not worthy of the object of his affection and the "artlessness" of his confession absolves him of insincerity. In several places (notably Sonnet 85 and *Love's Labour's Lost* 5.2.402-13) Shakespeare insists that true love does not express itself in flowery speeches, but in "true, plain words". "Beautified" is used in the sense of "beautiful", without suggestion of artifice. There may be irony in the fact that Polonius, whose own vocabulary is over-ornate, should be so sensitive to Hamlet's choice of words as to take exception to the use of a "poetical" word in a love letter.

2.2.135 *played the desk or table-book* The meaning is doubtful. It may mean either "received the information and kept the knowledge of it locked in my own mind (as in a desk)" or "noted it down in my mental memoranda book but done nothing about it". On the other hand, Polonius may be thinking of desks and books as natural secret post-offices for lovers' letters and asking Claudius and Gertrude what they would have thought of him if he had connived at this correspondence between Hamlet and his daughter. The first interpretation seems the more likely in view of what follows.

2.2.161 *loose my daughter to him* turn her loose; i.e. release her, for the occasion, from my prohibition against seeing him. The degree of callousness in Polonius' using his daughter as bait is indicated by his use of language associated with the breeding of animals, as in "loose" the cow to the bull. The allusion is confirmed by the final lines of the speech:

> Let me be no assistant for a state,
> But keep a farm and carters.

2.2.173 *fishmonger* In calling Polonius a "fishmonger" (pimp) here, Hamlet is playing the antic and having fun at Polonius' expense, but the tone of his conversation, and that of his talk with Ophelia in the nunnery scene, have led some critics to suggest that he may have overheard Polonius' suggestion that he "loose" his daughter to him. A "fishmonger's daughter" is a prostitute. The epithet of "fishmonger" has the added suggestion of one who sells the secrets he has "fished" for.

2.2.180-1 *if the sun breed . . . god kissing carrion* The image of the sun kissing carrion is found in other Elizabethan plays. Kittredge cites *King Edward III* (2.1.438-9):

> The freshest summer's day doth soonest taint
> The loathed carrion that it seems to kisse.
> (Tucker Brooke, *Shakespeare Apocrypha*, p. 79)

and there is a reference to the sun as "common-kissing Titan" in *Cymbeline* (3.4.166), as mentioned by Warburton.

The whole conversation between Hamlet and Polonius is variously interpreted by the critics, but no part of it has aroused more controversy than this speech. Superficially, it sounds as mad as Hamlet intends it to do; yet there is method in it. The method — word-play on sun-son = royalty — provides a key of sorts. Hamlet is, in his own opinion, the rightful king, being the "son" of the late King Hamlet, and he therefore applies the conventional sun-king correspondence to himself. As the warmth of the sun-god is an agent of fertility, so it is an agent of corruption when it strikes a dead body (cf. *Measure for Measure* 2.2.165-8).

Similarly, love cherishes, lust corrupts. Hamlet proceeds to warn Polonius that if his daughter, whom Polonius has just said he will command to walk in the lobby in order to encounter Hamlet, and who is "good kissing carrion" – the F reading – walks too much in the sun of princely favour she may be seduced. Mental "conception", i.e. "intelligence", is a blessing, but physical "conception" will signify Ophelia's moral corruption. The analogy, if carried to its logical conclusion, involves equating Ophelia with a dead dog – i.e. a "bitch" who has killed Hamlet's concept of her as a love-object by betraying him. The negative aspect of his ambivalent attitude towards her in the nunnery scene lends some colour to this view, as does his earlier reference to Polonius as a "fishmonger". On the other hand, sexual obsession, then as now, was a recognized symptom of some types of mental disturbance (as it is with Ophelia later), and Hamlet may merely be encouraging Polonius in his conviction that he is love-mad, as he later encourages Rosencrantz and Guildenstern to believe that frustrated ambition is the source of his trouble.

2.2.192 *matter* Polonius means "subject-matter". Hamlet takes the question as meaning "what's wrong?" and afterwards the word "matter" as referring to a discharge from the eyes.

2.2.195-202 *Slanders, sir . . . backward* Hamlet manages to insult Polonius while seeming to defend the older generation, and at the same time to make the point that it is not "honesty" (i.e. decency or good manners) to speak unpleasant truths – at least in Denmark.

2.2.221 *My excellent good friends* Hamlet's naturally unsuspicious nature is indicated by the warmth of the welcome he extends to his old schoolfellows, whose appearance catches him off-guard. Gradually, as the implications of their presence at court dawn on him, and as they hesitate before answering his direct question as to whether they have been sent for, his suspicions are aroused, suspicions which are confirmed by their subsequent clumsy attempts to "pluck out the heart" of his "mystery". As Claudius is not the well-wisher he pretends to be, as his mother is not guiltless, as Ophelia by her rejection of him has denied her professed love, so these two are no longer the "excellent good friends" of his childhood. As he exaggerates the guilt of his mother and of Ophelia, so he assumes that Rosencrantz and Guildenstern have not merely allowed themselves (in what would seem to be all innocence) to be used by the King, but that they have "made love to the employment", that is either volunteered for or eagerly accepted the opportunity to betray their old friendship by spying for the King. As a "counter-intelligence" move, Hamlet encourages them to believe they have found a cause of his madness – thwarted ambition – which the King may find credible and which will put him off the true scent.

2.2.266 *dreadfully attended* Pursuing the theme of "ambition", Hamlet here complains that he lacks the train of attendants appropriate to his status.

2.2.295-305 *this goodly frame . . . quintessence of dust* Rejoicing in the beauty of the physical universe and in the glory and dignity of man is one of the more optimistic features of Renaissance humanism. By the opening years of the seventeenth century, however, the cosmic theories of Copernicus and the political doctrines of Machiavelli were beginning to cast doubts on both. This passage seems to echo the attitude of the sixteenth-century French writer Montaigne in his essay *Apologie de Raimond Sebond*.

2.2.319 *humorous man* an eccentric character dominated by one of the four humours, the sanguine, choleric, melancholic, or phlegmatic, or by some other obsessive characteristic. Popularized as a dramatic device by Ben Jonson in his play *Every Man in His Humour*.

2.2.333-57 *Nay, their endeavour . . . Hercules and his load too* The two most popular children's companies were known as "The Children of the Chapel Royal" and "Paul's Boys", since the members of these companies were enrolled in the choir schools of the royal chapel and St. Paul's Cathedral respectively. In the late eighties and early nineties choir-boys had given theatrical performances (notably those of the plays of John Lyly at the old Blackfriars), but the vogue for child actors, for various reasons, faded out. Then in 1599 Paul's Boys were re-established under the patronage of the Earl of Derby, playing in a private house near The Theatre, with John Marston as chief dramatist. Soon after, Nathaniel Giles, choirmaster of the Chapel Royal, re-established its company of child actors at the Blackfriars Theatre and enlisted the services of Ben Jonson as chief playwright. The upper classes flocked to these children's theatres to see good plays in genteel surroundings, to the detriment of the Globe, the Fortune, and the other public theatres. The so-called "War of the Theatres" began with a personal quarrel between Jonson and Marston, in which each used his dramatic productions to attack the other. Some of these satirical plays were also performed in the public theatres, with the result that the greater part of the theatrical world became involved on one side or the other. Thus what had begun as a rivalry between private and public theatres, between adult and child actors, was submerged in a literary vendetta between two groups of playwrights.

2.2.349-51 *There . . . question* There was no market for plays unless they contributed something to the controversy, and involved their authors in it personally. "Argument" is both the question at issue and the plot of the play. "Went to cuffs" means indulged in fisticuffs.

2.2.357 *load* i.e. the world. The sign of the Globe Theatre represented Hercules carrying the world on his shoulders. "Too" suggests that the tragedians of the city were some company other than Shakespeare's.

2.2.358-61 *It is not very strange . . . in little* An instance of Hamlet's habit of regarding general considerations (such as the fickleness of public favour) in terms of his personal and immediate problem.

2.2.365-70 *Gentlemen, you are welcome . . . You are welcome* In contrast to his warm and natural reception of Rosencrantz and Guildenstern at the beginning, Hamlet now tenders them a ceremonious welcome as they are about to leave, giving as excuse his fear lest they consider the greeting he will bestow upon the players to exceed in formal politeness the manner in which he had received *them*. Knowing that this strange behaviour will confirm their conviction that he is mad, he then confuses them further (ll. 373-4) by insisting that he is mad only on occasion.

2.2.373-4 *when the wind . . . handsaw* South winds were thought to be beneficial to sufferers from melancholy. Hamlet seems to be saying "I can tell the difference between things which do not resemble each other in the least." But "hawk" is also the name of a kind of hack-saw and "handsaw" may be a corruption of "hernshaw", i.e. "heron". If so, the speech might have the secondary meaning, "I have more powers of discrimination than you think; I can tell the prey from the predator."

2.2.394 *scene individible, or poem unlimited* Renaissance critical theory (unlike dramatic practice) supported the doctrine, as in part enunciated by Aristotle and extended by Italian critics, that plays should observe unities of action, place, and time. That is, they should have a single plot, a single locale, and the action should not occupy more than one day. Nor should they mix tragedy with comedy, "mingling", in Sidney's phrase, "Kings and clowns". Most of Shakespeare's plays do not observe all the unities, but *The Tempest* observes the unities faithfully as to time and place, and *The Comedy of Errors* and *The Merry Wives of Windsor* do so "indifferent well". While there are changes of scene in *Hamlet*, all the action, with one possible exception – the encounter with Fortinbras (4.4) – takes place at Elsinore.

2.2.394-5 *Seneca . . . heavy* Seneca's tragedies were tremendously popular with the Elizabethans and widely imitated. The revenge play was especially "Senecan" in its plot, characterization, and elevated poetic style, and in its frequent use of a Chorus.

2.2.395-6 *law . . . liberty* plays which strictly observe the classical rules of drama and those which ignore them, or, possibly, those which follow a written script and those (like the *commedia dell'arte*) performed extempore.

2.2.422 *cracked within the ring* A crack extending to the ring surrounding the sovereign's head invalidated a coin as legal tender, so that it would no longer "pass current". Hamlet, after commenting that the boy actor has grown taller since he last saw him, expresses the hope that his voice has not "cracked"; i.e. that it still "rings true" so that he can continue to play female roles.

2.2.440-510 *Priam's slaughter . . . passion in the gods* The slaying of Priam by Pyrrhus after the Greek irruption into Troy is described in Vergil's *Aeneid*. The player's speech, as befits its subject matter and source, is written in the epic or "heroic" style and would demand a declamatory style of delivery. Its "passionate" quality is contrasted with the "natural" style of the blank verse of the play, a contrast made stronger by the fact that the greater part of the scene in which it appears is in prose. No play has been found which contains this passage or anything closely resembling it, and it is likely that Shakespeare is here demonstrating that he can write in the high, formal style if he wants to. There is no reason, however, to assume that his intention in this context is satirical.

2.2.487 *her wheel* The wheel of Fortune was a favourite allegorical emblem of the middle ages and Renaissance. In classical mythology Fortune rode on her wheel, but in the medieval version of the myth she sat and turned it, carrying the human beings riding upon it either upwards or downwards, or first one and then the other. So Edmund, in *King Lear* (5.3.174), having risen from bastardy to power, comments on his fall: "The wheel is come full circle".

2.2.491 *It shall . . . your beard* A stock joking response and also (from anyone but a madman) an insult. (See also l. 564.)

2.2.508 *Unless things . . . at all* A reference to the Epicurean doctrine that the gods exist in a state of complete serenity, detached from and untroubled by the affairs of men.

2.2.534-5 *mock him not* Hamlet's mockery can be disregarded, since he is thought to be mad, but it wouldn't do for the players to follow his example.

2.2.568 *pigeon-livered and lack gall* Bitterness and resentment were supposed to reside in the gall of the liver (as love resides in the heart, etc.). Pigeons were not supposed to have any gall, and therefore to be incapable of anger. The pigeon, or dove, was as a result the logical choice as a symbol of peace.

3.1.2 *puts on this confusion* The phrase "puts on" here does not have the force of intentional deceit as it does in modern usage but is a clothing metaphor meaning simply "wears". The Prince's disturbed behaviour is thought of as "covering" or concealing his true or normal nature.

3.1.38-42 *I do wish . . . both your honours* Polonius has misjudged the situation. The Queen here makes it clear that she would have no objection to Ophelia as a daughter-in-law. (See also 5.1.235-6.)

3.1.46-9 *We are oft to blame . . . The devil himself* Polonius, in his usual sententious manner, is "pointing a moral". He does not mean that Ophelia is "to blame in this", but is generalizing that hypocrisy (i.e. the appearance of piety) is often an instrument of evil rather than, as in this instance it is supposed to be, of good.

3.1.52 *ugly . . . helps it* The haggard face is ugly compared to
the beautifying cosmetics (which also arouse the lust which
causes the ugliness).

3.1.56 *To be . . . the question* This seemingly direct, simple
statement is not, perhaps, as simple as it seems. Is the "question" merely one of whether or not to commit suicide, to
accept the Epicurean remedy for an intolerable existence, or
is it, in view of what immediately follows, a question of
whether true nobility of soul lies in the stoic endurance of
evil or in heroic resistance to it? If opposing the "sea of
troubles" is not only to risk but to court death, is not that
action tantamount to suicide? The only certain way to end
the troubles of this life is to die, and in Hamlet's state of
mind death would be welcome. But is death the end? Or is it
a sleep of the body accompanied by the nightmare-haunted
awareness of the guilty soul? In his earlier soliloquy Hamlet
expressed his longing to escape from a world given over to
fleshly corruption, but accepted the "canon 'gainst self-
slaughter". Here, as the term "question" indicates, he is
conducting a dialectical discussion not of the rights and
wrongs but of the merits and defects of suicide as a means to
an end. The "question" to be debated is not so much "shall I
kill myself?" as "is physical non-being preferable to physical
being, and if not, why not?"

3.1.70-74 *the whips . . . takes* Compare with the similar catalogue in Sonnet 66 – "Tired with all these, for restful death
I cry."

3.1.79-80 *from whose bourn . . . traveller returns* But what
about the Ghost? Hamlet is thinking here of human beings
returning alive and in the flesh, not of spirits.

3.1.80 *puzzles the will* confuses the faculty which directs our
actions. Other references to the numbing effect of contradictory impulses are to be found in the Player's speech describing
Pyrrhus, who "as a painted tyrant . . . stood,/ And like a
neutral to his will and matter,/ Did nothing", and in
Claudius' confession:

> My stronger guilt defeats my strong intent,
> And like a man to double business bound,
> I stand in pause where I shall first begin,
> And both neglect.   (3.3.43)

3.1.83 *Thus conscience . . . us all* In *Richard III* (1.4.138-43), where the Second Murderer laments that conscience makes a man a coward: "A man cannot steal but it accuseth him; he cannot swear but it checks him . . . it fills one full of obstacles", Shakespeare uses conscience in its usual sense. In this passage from *Hamlet*, however, he may have intended it to mean intellectual awareness of alternatives, the power of logical reasoning, or, as in 4.4.37, the "Looking before and after".

3.1.91 *How does . . . a day* "This many a day" is no doubt Ophelia's artless admission that the time has seemed long to her, but from Hamlet's point of view even the possibility of an implied reproach in the words must seem disingenuous, since it is she who has been refusing to see *him*.

The impression that she is being less than straightforward is confirmed when she returns his "remembrances" with the words, "Rich gifts wax poor when givers prove unkind."

Even if Hamlet did not overhear the King and Polonius plotting to spy on him, as Dover Wilson argues he does in *What Happens in Hamlet*, it is not necessary to assume that he catches sight of them now in order to account for his abrupt query, "Ha, ha! are you honest?" His disillusionment about his mother, confirmed by Ophelia's actions, is enough to account for his questioning her "honesty".

3.1.111-3 *the power of beauty . . . likeness* beauty will corrupt honesty (chastity) sooner than honesty will make beauty chaste. In the bitterness engendered by the Ghost's revelations about his mother, Hamlet sees all beautiful women as unchaste (cf. 3.4.41-5).

3.1.117-19 *virtue . . . relish of it* however we may engraft virtue on our heritage of original sin, that original, wild root-stock will make the fruit tainted or imperfect. "Relish" is frequently used with the connotation of lecherous appetite.

3.1.121 *Get . . . nunnery* i.e. get out of the way of temptation. But "nunnery" was also a slang term for "brothel", so that if Ophelia is not chaste the advice is still appropriate. Ironic *double entendre* pervades most of Hamlet's conversation with Ophelia.

3.1.122-7 *I am myself . . . act them in* Whether or not Hamlet is aware of the eavesdroppers, he runs no risk of revealing his secret but follows the course he has taken with Rosencrantz and Guildenstern, first suggesting that he is maddened by ambition and then confusing the issue.

3.1.144-6 *You jig . . . ignorance* You walk and talk affectedly instead of naturally. You give fancy names to ordinary things and pretend you don't know what they are commonly called – or, possibly, you give polite names to things polite society chooses to regard as vulgar and pretend not to know the natural "four-letter words" for them. Cf. Gertrude's reference to the flower "dead men's fingers" (4.7.171).

3.1.151 *The courtier's . . . sword* the courtier's eye, scholar's tongue, soldier's sword. Ophelia is saying that Hamlet was the ideal courtier in his outward appearance and bearing, and that he was a model of both the contemplative and the active virtues appropriate to a Renaissance prince.

3.1.152 *rose . . . state* Everything in creation is thought of as occupying a particular rank in its sphere of nature. The rose occupied the position of primacy among flowers, as did the lion among beasts, the eagle among birds, and the sun among the heavenly bodies (in the hierarchy of being). These are all sovereign in their categories and are frequently used as analogues of royalty. The "rose" is also the emblem of youth, beauty, and love.

3.1.156-8 *musicked vows . . . harsh* Hamlet no doubt actually sang his love to Ophelia, as convention demanded, but the music of lovers' tongues is proverbial (cf. "How silver-sweet sound lovers' tongues by night,/ Like softest music to attending ears", *Romeo and Juliet* 2.2.166-7). Plato's analogy between musical harmony and the orderly pattern of the universe was a commonplace of Renaissance thought as was his concept of love as a force of order. Ophelia expresses the loss of Hamlet's love *and* the disorder of his mind in terms of the change from harmony to discord – from "musicked vows" to "sovereign reason/ Like sweet bells jangled, out of tune".

3.1.171-5 *Haply the seas . . . himself* Claudius' prescription of a sea voyage, a change of scene, and new interests, is accepted Elizabethan psychotherapy for a neurotic fixation, the "something-settled matter in his heart/ Whereon his brains still beating puts him . . ./ From fashion of himself." Claudius' despatch of Hamlet to England, therefore, appears to be motivated by fatherly concern rather than enmity.

3.2.1-44 Hamlet's speech to the Players is generally accepted as embodying Shakespeare's own views of acting, though in Hamlet's mouth it is completely in character. The playwright and his hero equally uphold the ideal of naturalness and moderation in art and conduct. Similar views are expressed in Ulysses' description of Thersites in *Troilus and Cressida*:

> . . . like a strutting player whose conceit
> Lies in his hamstring, and doth think it rich
> To hear the wooden dialogue and sound
> 'Twixt his stretched footing and the scaffoldage,
> Such to-be-pitied and o'er-wrested seeming
> He acts thy greatness in. And when he speaks,
> 'Tis like a chime a-mending, with terms unsquared,
> Which, from the tongue of roaring Typhon dropped,
> Would seem hyperboles. (1.3.153-61)

3.2.14 *Herod* Traditionally, Herod "rages" (according to a Coventry miracle play's stage direction) "in the pagond", i.e. wagon-stage, when the three kings do not return to tell him where they have found the Christ child. His "raging" culminates in commanding the slaughter of the Innocents (all male children under two years of age).

3.2.23-4 *the very age . . . pressure* The metaphor shifts from the mirror, which is to show "the age", to the mould which produces a replica of the "body of the time".

3.2.24-5 *come tardy off* Probably "doesn't quite come off" rather than "is too slow-paced". Mason's emendation, "come tardy of", accepted by several editors, would mean "come short of", a neat antithesis with "overdone".

3.2.33 *journeymen* workmen newly entered into their trade, who have not achieved the status of master craftsmen. Here the word may be used in the literal sense of "day-labourers", i.e. unskilled odd-job men.

3.2.34 *abominably* The word "abominable" was mistakenly thought to be derived from *ab-homine*, i.e. "inhuman", though it was also widely used in its modern sense of "detestable". Both senses apply here.

3.2.91 *fares* The King means "How are you feeling?" Hamlet replies as if Claudius had asked "What are you eating?"

3.2.92-3 *chameleon's . . . air* The chameleon was popularly supposed to live on air, probably because it catches insects with its quick-darting tongue.

3.2.93 *promise-crammed* An allusion to Claudius' public announcement that Hamlet was his heir (see 1.2.108-12), with, possibly, an implied pun on "air".

3.2.126 *a suit of sables* Word-play on "sable" as "black", and "sable" as the costly fur used to trim robes. (If my mother doesn't mourn, why shouldn't I wear fancy clothes? I'll have a whole gown made of fur.)

3.2.131 *the hobby-horse is forgot* The hobby-horse, a traditional character in the morris-dance, was sometimes omitted in performances out of deference to Puritan opinion. The Puritans persistently attacked folk customs as relics of pagan superstition, and probably because of the bawdy jokes and loose behaviour often associated with them. "Hobby-horse" was also a slang term for a sexually promiscuous woman. (See also *Love's Labour's Lost* 3.1.30-33, *The Winter's Tale* 1.2.276, and *Othello* 4.1.160.)

3.2.131 s.d. In spite of his objections to dumb shows Hamlet has allowed this one to be retained, perhaps to provide more than one opportunity of observing how Claudius will react to the representation of his crime. But the text gives us no indication of Claudius' reaction to the dumb show. Some directors assume that he does not see it, and show him, during this part of the performance, deep in conversation with Polonius. If he does watch this mimed prologue, a possible interpretation of his silence is that he flatters himself that the resemblance to his own crime is coincidental. The part may also be played showing Claudius desperately trying to restrain himself but breaking down at last under the increasing tension of the situation as he gradually realizes that *The Murder of Gonzago* is not a coincidence but an accusation and a declaration of war.

3.2.184-9 *Purpose . . . debt* We hold to our purposes when the time is not ripe for performing them, but let them go when the occasion arises for carrying them out. It is natural to forget, in the maturity of judgement, the vows undertaken as a result of violent emotion.

3.2.226-9 *The lady . . . in't?* Gertrude's calm criticism of the Player Queen's exaggerated style seems inconsistent with a guilty conscience. Contrast the King's apprehensive "Is there no offence in't?"

3.2.249 *Leave thy damnable faces and begin* Cf. Buckingham in *Richard III*:

> Tut, I can counterfeit the deep tragedian,
> Speak and look back, and pry on every side,

Tremble and start at wagging of a straw,
Intending deep suspicion. Ghastly looks
Are at my service, like enforcèd smiles . . .
                                        (3.5.5-9)

Hamlet is too impatient to wait for the conventional "business" which accompanied the entrance of the villain. The blood-curdling "murderers' speech" with its many references to darkness and demonic evil, was equally conventional (see l. 381 below, and also *Macbeth* 2.1.49-56 and 3.2.46-55), as Hamlet's "croaking raven" reference shows.

3.2.261 *The king rises* "The Mouse-trap" has not been a complete success. The king's reaction to it convinces Hamlet and Horatio of the Ghost's truth, but to the courtiers he appears to be overcome by a sudden illness.

3.2.337 *while . . . grows* The ending of the proverb is "the horse starves". Hamlet, as in his earlier remark about capons (l. 93), makes the point that you can't fatten stock on promises.

3.2.381-92 *'Tis now . . . consent* A conventional murderer's speech (see 3.2.249, end note). The audience will expect a murder to follow immediately, and their expectation increases the force of Hamlet's sparing of Claudius.

3.4.27 *Is it the king* Hamlet thinks he has killed the King in a moment "That has no relish of salvation in't", and in his mother's bedchamber, the next best thing to "in th' incestuous pleasure of his bed".

3.4.72-82 *Sense . . . mope* Hamlet is here playing on the various meanings of "sense" and "motion". You must have the use of your physical senses, he tells his mother, since you are able to move. But sense can also mean emotional "feeling", as in line 39, and "motion" often means "emotion". He doubts the sensitivity of her emotions as demonstrated by her relationship with Claudius, as well as of her physical senses.

3.4.99 *vice* the buffoon or "stooge" of the old morality plays, a character who originally represented the general wickedness and folly of mankind rather than a particular sin.

3.4.100 *cutpurse of the empire and the rule* In most European countries, the monarch was at first elected; subsequently the candidates for election were limited to the members of the royal family, and still later the crown descended in the direct line of succession. In *Hamlet*, the Danish monarchy appears to have been in transition between the second and third stages of development. Claudius' accession to the throne – by the election of the nobles – is perfectly legal, but Hamlet feels that the natural expectation would have been for himself, rather than Claudius, to succeed his father, and that this expectation would have been fulfilled had he not been absent when the election took place. Claudius, as Hamlet later reminds Horatio (5.2.65), has "Popped in between th'election and my *hopes*". It seems to have been customary for the reigning monarch to nominate his successor, though such a nomination would be influential rather than binding. Claudius has named Hamlet as his heir (1.2.109), and in his last words Hamlet nominates Fortinbras. (See also *Macbeth*, 1.4.35-9.) Hamlet would naturally assume that his father, had he not been killed in his sleep, would have nominated his only son as his successor.

3.4.165-9 *That monster custom . . . put on* custom is a monster in that it dulls our sensitivities, i.e. we can get used to anything and become increasingly less aware of its nature. Custom is therefore a devil with regard to bad habits, since it diminishes our sense of their evil, but an angel with regard to good habits, since it makes them easy to maintain. Playing on the meaning of "habit", Hamlet goes on to speak of it as a "livery", or uniform, of good or evil behaviour.

3.4.177-9 *heaven hath . . . minister* i.e. heaven has seen fit to punish Polonius by letting me unwittingly kill him, and I must suffer punishment for his death. Hamlet knows that the King will realize that Polonius was slain in mistake for himself and will act accordingly.

It was a prevailing concept of the time that heaven made use of human agents to punish evil-doers. The distinction between heaven's "scourge" and heaven's "minister" is sometimes blurred, but generally the "scourge" was one who in attaining his own, frequently evil, ends brought about the punishment of other evil-doers as well as his own destruction. Such is the function of Richard III. The "minister" of heaven was usually one who, not seeking his own personal ends, acted as an instrument of divine retribution. Richmond (later Henry VII) performs this function in *Richard III*, as shown by his speech beginning "O Thou Whose captain I account myself" (5.3.108-17). Since Hamlet is both the appointed punisher of Claudius and is to be punished for killing Polonius by mistake while attempting to carry out his task, he is not sure which category he belongs in. His personal hatred of Claudius may also make him doubtful to what extent he is serving the will of heaven and to what extent he is gratifying his own antagonism towards his uncle.

3.4.192-5 *'Twere good . . . concernings hide* i.e. It would be fitting if you did tell the King, for who but a beautiful, serious-minded, sensible queen would keep such important business from a repulsive sensualist like Claudius? The ironic suggestion is that Gertrude can prove the sincerity of her repentance by keeping Hamlet's secret.

3.4.196-200 *No, in despite . . . down* The fable alluded to here has not been identified, but Kittredge reconstructs it thus:

> An ape finds a basket of birds on the housetop and opens it. The birds fly away. The ape gets into the basket and jumps out in attempt to fly, but falls from the roof and breaks his neck.

This is an implied threat that the Queen will get herself into trouble if she reveals the secret of Hamlet's pretended madness.

3.4.204-5 *Alack . . . concluded on* The Queen is sorry to part from her son but has no suspicion of the King's motives for sending Hamlet to England.

4.2.27-8 *The body . . . body* More madness with method. The body is with the King, in the sense that the King is still alive — cf. "whilst this machine (body) is to (with) him" (2.2.122-3) — but the King is not with the body of Polonius, i.e. dead.

4.3.56-60 *if my love . . . to us* Claudius seems to be applying the notorious doctrine of Machiavelli that it is better (i.e. more expedient) for a ruler to be feared than to be loved.

4.4.27-9 *This is th' imposthume . . . dies* an "imposthume" is an ulcer. Luxury and idleness in the state were supposed to breed political ills analogous to those produced in the body by over-eating and lack of exercise. Hamlet seems at this point to be in doubt whether to regard Fortinbras' purposeless excursion as the destructive (indeed, to some of its participants, fatal) result of the canker of corrupting sloth, or as the healthy preventive of such a canker. The ambivalence leads to and pervades the ensuing soliloquy.

4.4.42-3 *A thought . . . three parts coward* Hamlet speaks of the state of his mind as if it were an heraldic shield on which the "quarterings" depicted what the Renaissance regarded as the Aristotelian virtues of prudence (or practical wisdom), justice, temperance, and fortitude (courage). Hamlet's mental coat of arms, as the result of "thinking too precisely on th' event" seems to him to display one part "wisdom" (i.e. prudence) and three parts defect of courage. Since justice and temperance involve *action*, rather than mere deliberation or attitude, they do not appear at all; their "quarters" have been usurped by cowardice.

4.4.46 *Examples gross as earth* The obvious meaning of "gross" here is "large", i.e. inescapable. But the word echoes Hamlet's complaint in his first soliloquy (1.2.135-7) that the earth is "an unweeded garden" and that "Things rank and gross in nature/ Possess it". Is the activity of this "delicate and tender prince", Fortinbras, as he has suggested above, the result of "rankness" in the body politic of Norway, or is it something to be emulated? Does it represent "honour" in the true sense of nobility of soul, or hot-headed fame-seeking regardless of the cost to himself and others? What kind of honour is at the stake – the nobility associated with rank, which may be a grossly destructive pursuit of wordly fame, or the spiritual honour which comes from actions directed by right reason?

4.4.49 *with divine ambition puffed* "Devilish" is the adjective more frequently applied to "ambition" in Elizabethan times, and "puffed" has an unfavourable connotation. Hamlet's praise of Fortinbras is sincere enough, but it is wrong-headed. Fortinbras' expedition is irrational and therefore not admirable, since the honour it pursues is only a "trick of fame". Claudius sees more clearly the hellishness of ambition which seeks its end by lawless means however resolute. What Hamlet really admires in Fortinbras is his ability to make "mouths at the invisible event" instead of "thinking too precisely" on it.

Hamlet, in this soliloquy, is working his way through to the realization that logical reasoning cannot legislate for the future, nor even predict it with any degree of certainty. As he puts it later, "No man knows aught of what he leaves", i.e. has no knowledge of what might be his lot if he did not die at his appointed time.

4.5.20 *spills . . . spilt* "Spill" is often used in the sense of "destroy". Here, using the metaphor of the servant whose hand trembles for fear of spilling the brimming cup, the

Queen asserts that the guilty person's predisposition to suspect others often draws suspicion upon himself, to his ultimate destruction.

4.5.23-196 (Ophelia's songs) The snatches of song are represented as floating through Ophelia's distracted mind, half-remembered and pieced out. They are interspersed with "free associations" which suit the dramatist's purpose of bringing together themes of love and death, love of parents, love of the opposite sex, true love, and infidelity.

Ophelia begins with the conventional metaphor of the lover as a pilgrim and the beloved as a saint (cf. *Romeo and Juliet* 1.5.95 ff.). She sings the first two lines from a stanza of the old ballad "Walsingham": "Met you not with my true love . . .?" The pilgrim's answer to the lady's query is:

> How should I know your true love
> That have met many a one?
> (Percy's version)

The "cockle" or scallop shell was the insignia of pilgrims to the shrine of Saint James of Compostella, in Spain (cf. Raleigh's "The Pilgrimage": Give me my scallop shell of quiet/ My staff of faith to lean upon).

She goes on to other and bawdier songs whose language shows that her melancholy "sits on brood" on the warnings of Laertes and her father, as well as their result.

4.5.41-3 *They say . . . may be* The reference is to a folk-tale which recounts that Christ entered a baker's shop and asked for bread. The woman who kept the shop put a small piece of dough into the oven to bake for him, but was rebuked by her daughter, who insisted that the loaf was too large and made it even smaller. On opening the oven, the dough was found to have swollen to enormous size, which seeing, the daughter cried out "Heugh, heugh", and, upon uttering this "owl-like" sound, was changed into an owl for her meanness.

4.5.70-72 *Come, my coach . . . good night* Ophelia suddenly shifts her role from loose wench to noble lady, playing both in an exaggerated manner which is at odds with her previous "modesty" in both senses of the word. The pathos of her farewell speech depends in part on the associations it evokes.

4.5.85 *Without . . . or mere beasts* i.e. lacking reason (the essential quality of humanity), we are but the outward form,

or image, of human beings, or mere beasts (whose natures
are incapable of rational thought).

4.5.116-9 *That drop . . . mother* From here on, almost everything that Laertes says and does points up the parallels and
contrasts between his situation and attitude, and Hamlet's.
Verbal associations with earlier scenes of the play are frequent. Here Laertes refers to the harlot's "brand" (cf.
Hamlet's rebuke to his mother at 3.4.44.)

4.5.121 *Let him go, Gertrude* The Queen is attempting to hold
Laertes back from approaching the King. Her behaviour in
this scene is that of a fearless woman very much in love with
her husband.

4.5.155-6 *By heaven . . . beam* The satisfaction I shall demand
for the wrongs done to our family will be so heavy as to tip
the balance even against the weight of your madness. Grief
and melancholy were commonly referred to as "heaviness".

4.5.160-62 *Nature . . . loves* i.e. Love exalts and refines human
nature (cf. *Love's Labour's Lost* 4.3.329-36). Substances
refined are purged of their gross and heavy elements, thus
becoming lighter and more responsive to impulse and attraction; so nature, refined by love, sends some part of itself
after the object which attracts it. Laertes is given to elaborate
statement in moments of stress, as Hamlet is given to wit in
similar circumstances. Laertes is saying here that the part of
Ophelia's mind which was devoted to her father has gone in
search of him, leaving her distracted.

4.5.173-82 *There's rosemary . . . died* Ophelia appears to have
borrowed her "language of flowers" from Clement Robin-
son's anthology, *A Handfull of Pleasant Delites*, 1584.

4.5.212 *formal ostentation* due ceremony. Laertes may be
thinking specifically of the funeral eulogy or "showing forth"
of the service and achievements of the deceased.

4.7.1 *conscience* As in "conscience does make cowards of us
all" (see 3.1.83, end note), the word has its older meaning
of inner conviction or knowledge, here very close to the sense
of the Latin *conscientia* – private knowledge shared with
another – from which it is ultimately derived. Claudius is
asserting that the information he has just communicated to
Laertes must acquit him of blame for Polonius' death.

4.7.12 *Lives almost by his looks* either "is well or ill according
to the way he looks" or, more probably, "lives on looking at
him".

4.7.15-16 *as the star . . . by her* In the Ptolemaic cosmography the orbits of the heavenly bodies were regarded as occurring within concentric spheres, of which the earth was the axis. To the sun, the moon, each of the planets, and the so-called "fixed stars", separate spheres were assigned according to their differing patterns of motion about the earth. Outside these was the master-sphere, or *primum mobile*, which gave motion to them all. As the motions of the spheres were regarded as visible proof of a divine order, Claudius' testimony of his devotion to Gertrude approaches idolatry, since, as he says, his love for her directs his actions as the hand of God directs the motions of the stars in their courses.

4.7.20 *the spring . . . stone* At Knaresborough in Yorkshire, King's Newnham in Warwickshire, and other places in England, there are springs in which the limestone content is so great that they soon deposit a stone coating on objects placed beneath them.

4.7.32 *let our beard . . . danger* "Danger" here retains something of its medieval sense of "scorn" or "scornful threat", as well as having its more usual meaning, as indicated by Claudius' allusion to having his beard shaken, a deadly insult (cf. 2.2.563-4: "Who . . ./ Plucks off my beard and blows it in my face").

4.7.107 *Laertes, was your father dear to you* Claudius is so acutely aware that the treachery he is about to propose is repugnant to all the instincts of a gentleman that he hesitates to suggest it until he is sure that Laertes' motivation for revenge is strong enough to overcome any scruples of honour.

4.7.114-15 *There lives . . . abate it* like a candle, the very fire of love creates the charred wick or "snuff" which deadens its flame and dims its light.

4.7.118-23 *That we would . . . easing* The Elizabethans were preoccupied with the concept of the "moment of perfection", a concept fortified by parallels with "ripeness" in nature and by the Aristotelian doctrines of "the mean" and of virtue as the performance of the proper action at the proper time. The King may well be subconsciously recalling the "sentences" of the Player King on "ripeness" and intention (3.2.182-211).

Claudius' comments on the corruption of intention by delay are ironically similar to Hamlet's on the same topic, and prepare the ground for the more obvious irony of

Laertes' offer in line 126 "To cut his [Hamlet's] throat i'
th' church." Unlike the audience, of course, Claudius is
unaware that Laertes is echoing Hamlet and that Laertes'
shocking proof of the sincerity of his vengeance contrasts
strongly with Hamlet's decision not to kill the King at his
prayers, whatever its motive.

4.7.140 *I'll anoint my sword* Laertes' determination "greatly
to find quarrel in a straw/ When honour's at the stake"
makes him forget the honour of chivalry in his reckless
pursuit of the "honour" of vengeance, although he knows that
his father was slain in error, not in malice. (See Claudius'
assertion in ll. 4-5: "he which hath your noble father slain/
Pursued my life".) It can be argued that Laertes is here
demonstrating his loyalty to his sovereign rather than his
adherence to the code of the vendetta, which makes no
allowance for excuses, but his whole attitude suggests otherwise.

5.1.2 *she wilfully . . . salvation* i.e. she seeks to go to heaven
when *she* wills, not when God wills. To set one's own will
against the will of God is not, of course, the way to seek
salvation.

5.1.5 *Christian burial* Ophelia's death, as the Priest asserts in
line 218, was "doubtful" and, the coroner's inquest having
found no proof of suicide, she is given the benefit of the
doubt in that her body is allowed to be buried in conse-
crated ground (a rite denied to suicides).

5.1.11-12 *an act hath three branches . . . to perform* The usual
three-fold division of an action is (1) the thought or
imagination of the act, (2) the will or decision to perform
the act, and (3) the execution of the act. The Clown's
faulty logic, however, parodies legal jargon, which charac-
teristically expresses one concept in three synonyms, such
as "give, devise, and bequeath". This burlesque may have
been inspired by the report of the case of Sir James Hales
(who walked into a river while insane and drowned) which
was first published in 1571. One of the counsels analysed
the act of self-destruction according to the tri-partite scheme
given above.

5.1.29-31 *There is . . . profession* An allusion to the old song
attributed to the radical priest John Ball, one of the leaders
of the Peasants' Revolt of 1381:

> When Adam delved and Eva span,
> Who was then a gentleman?

5.1.61 *In youth . . . love* The Clown sings a mangled version of "The aged lover renounces love", printed in the first anthology of English Poetry, *Songs and Sonnets*, ed. Tottel, 1557.

5.1.102 *fines . . . recoveries* "Fine and recovery" was the legal process for ridding property of an entail so that it could be held "in fee simple", or outright possession. "Vouchers" were persons who vouched for or "warranted" titles to land.

5.1.106 *pair of indentures* "Indentures" were legal contracts cut in two on a jagged (indented) line, half being given to each party. The fitting together of the parts was proof of the genuineness of the document. Shakespeare is playing on the original meaning of the word, derived from the Latin prefix *in-* and *dens, dentis* = *tooth*. Since the prefix *in-* can mean "not" as well as "in" or "on", the term "pair of indentures" can be applied equally well to a toothless skull as to a legal document.

5.1.134-5 *the toe . . . galls his kibe* The new and increasing social mobility of Tudor England was much commented upon and often (especially by the upper classes) lamented or satirized. Hamlet asserts that it is now possible to rise in the world so fast that the peasant treads on the courtier's heel, "galling" (irritating) his "kibe" (chilblain), so that it is no wonder that a gravedigger should have learned the courtier's trick of witty repartee.

5.1.141-55 *It was . . . thirty years* The gravedigger's testimony that Hamlet is thirty accords ill with references elsewhere in the play to his extreme youth. In the sixteenth century, boys usually entered university at the age of fourteen or earlier, and Hamlet, even had he been following the English program of four years for a Bachelor's degree, three more for a Master's, would be unlikely to have remained in residence at the university much past the age of twenty.

5.1.164-78 *Here's a skull . . . a thousand times* Q_1 reads "this dozen years" in place of the "three and twenty years" which appears in Q_2 and F. Assuming that Yorick would have been unlikely to have borne Hamlet on his back much past the age of eight, this would make Hamlet's age somewhere around twenty. Many explanations for the altered time-indications of Q_2 and F have been offered, but none satisfactorily resolves the difficulty.

5.1.222 *Shards . . . thrown on her* The mere suspicion that Ophelia has committed suicide cannot account entirely for the intensity of the Priest's condemnation. His bitter assertion that she deserves stoning rather than charitable prayers is in ironic contrast to Christ's refusal to condemn the woman taken in adultery (John 8) for which offence the punishment was stoning. The analogue to Ophelia in the source story in Saxo Grammaticus was a prostitute, and this original has given a certain colouring of ambiguity to Ophelia's character, with the result that some critics, notably Rebecca West in *The Court and the Castle*, argue that Ophelia has allowed herself to be seduced by Hamlet. Laertes' reference to his sister's "unpolluted flesh" appears to refute the implication which may lie behind the Priest's words.

5.1.243-5 *Till of this . . . Olympus* The allusion is to the war of the Titans against Zeus and the other Olympian gods, in which they piled Mount Pelion on Mount Ossa in an attempt to reach the home of the gods on top of Mount Olympus. All three mountains are in Thessaly. Perhaps Hamlet also implies that Laertes has made a mountain of rhetoric out of a molehill of grief.

5.1.247 *wand'ring stars* i.e. the planets, as opposed to the fixed stars. Hamlet implies that Laertes' extravagant display of grief is unnatural, since the planets were supposed to govern the destinies of men, not vice versa.

5.1.269 *eat a crocodile* Hamlet is contemptuously showing that he can be as hyperbolical in his expression of grief as Laertes. Truly deep grief, as he has already asserted, "passes show" (1.2.85).

5.2.57-62 *Why, man . . . opposites* "Horatio has not meant to suggest that there was anything wrong in Hamlet's counter-plot. Indeed, he feels some satisfaction in the poetical justice that has overtaken the King's agents. But Hamlet, who is less calm by nature, is sensitive on that point and feels that he must justify himself to his friend, as he has already justified himself to his own conscience" (Kittredge). This subjective interpretation of Horatio's laconic comment and of Hamlet's reply to it is open to question. It would be quite in character for Horatio to consider the various implications of the incident rather carefully before making any judgement, and his musing comment may be intended to convey exactly what it says and no more. Hamlet's self-justification, however, is most revealing – his substitution of the forged document is the first-fruit of his resolve to avoid undue deliberation about the rights or wrongs of his actions – "O, from this time forth,/ My thoughts be bloody, or be nothing worth!" (4.4.65-6). In contrast to his attitude to Claudius, he has now acted against Rosencrantz and Guildenstern on presumption rather than proof of guilt, and he knows it. He may be aware (as he was aware of the possible effect upon his judgement of his antipathy towards the King) that his view of the guilt of his old schoolfellows may be influenced by the antagonism which has led him to prophesy that he will "delve one yard below their mines/ And blow them at the moon" (3.4.212-13). His assertion that "they did make love to this employment", i.e. that they actively and persistently sued to be employed as spies, is in direct contradiction to his knowledge that they were "sent for" by the King and Queen.

That Hamlet immediately proceeds to justify himself once again – for his intended action against the King – shows how little he has really changed since his departure for England. He may have acquired a fatalistic acceptance of whatever his divinely appointed destiny may be, but in matters of choice and decision his "conscience" – in both senses – is as active and as sensitive as ever. He is still concerned not with "action" as such but with *right* action.

5.2.92 *I will receive . . . spirit* Throughout his conversation with Osric, Hamlet parodies the courtier's elaborate style of formal address.

5.2.93 *Put your bonnet . . . head* The contest of courtesy about hats echoes (and parodies) a model in Guazzo's *Civil Conversation*, tr. Florio, 1591, Ch. vii, p. 111 (Second Frutes):

> G. [Giordano] Why do you stand barehedded? You do yourself wrong.
>
> E. [Edward] Pardon me, good sir, I do it for my ease.
>
> G. I pray you be covered, you are too ceremonious.

E.   I am so well, that me thinks I am in heaven.

G.   If you love me, put on your hat.

E.   I will do it to obey you, not for any pleasure that I take in it.

5.2.109-11 *card or calendar . . . see* The terminology of navigation: "card" is the card showing the points of the compass; the mariner's "calendar" gives the positions of the stars throughout the year. "Continent" brings in a third guide to navigation – the map.

5.2.119 *umbrage* shadow. Laertes is unique, and his only "double" is in his mirror. Those who would imitate him are but shadows of perfection.

5.2.219-37 *Give me . . . brother* Critics have been greatly distressed that Shakespeare makes Hamlet lie to Laertes in asserting that he has killed Polonius in a fit of madness; but Hamlet can hardly say, "I thought it was the King." It is true that he overdoes his apology a little, as he has a tendency to do when embarrassed or unsure of himself, but his main point, that he disclaims "a purposed evil" as far as Polonius' death is concerned, is the truth.

5.2.237-43 *I am satisfied . . . ungored* Another of Shakespeare's satiric treatments of the respective values of natural honour, an artificial code ("terms") of honour, and reputation.

5.2.282 *He's fat, and scant of breath* Critical antipathy to the idea of a corpulent Hamlet has brought forth a number of interpretations of this line. Kittredge suggests that "fat" may mean "not quite trained down"; i.e. as the word might be applied to a jockey. In Shakespeare's time the word did not bear as unfavourable a connotation as it does nowadays, and was more nearly equivalent to "plump" or "well-built". Wilson accepts the evidence supplied by several scholars that "fat", in Elizabethan writing, can mean merely "sweaty", a suggestion to which the Queen's "take my napkin, rub thy brows" lends support. The word is used as a synonym for "stuffy", as applied to a room, in *1 Henry IV*, and may here be no more than a synonym for "scant of breath", i.e. short-winded.

5.2.321-6 *Then, venom . . . mother* In stabbing the King with the sword he had led Laertes to poison, and then forcing him to drink the remaining poison in the cup, Hamlet has achieved his desired poetic justice, avenging his father, his mother, and himself. Claudius is certainly about an act "That has no relish of salvation in't", and is "sent to his account" with all his imperfections on his head.

5.2.340 *antique Roman* With reference to either or both of: (1) the custom by which Roman servants often chose to follow their masters in death, (2) the Roman doctrine that suicide was more honourable than living in disgrace or unhappiness.

5.2.346 *Absent thee from felicity awhile* An allusion to the ancient Greek saying "Call no man happy until he be dead", as well as to the bliss of Paradise.

BIBLIOGRAPHY

Shakespearean Tragedy

Anderson, Ruth, *Elizabethan Psychology and Shakespeare's Plays*. Iowa City: Iowa University Press, 1927.

Bethell, Samuel L., *Shakespeare and the Popular Dramatic Tradition*. London: Staples Press, 1944.

Bradbrook, Muriel C., *Themes and Conventions of Elizabethan Tragedy* (2nd ed.). Cambridge University Press, 1952.

Bush, Geoffrey, *Shakespeare and the Natural Condition*. Cambridge, Mass.: Harvard University Press, 1956.

Campbell, Lily B., *Shakespeare's Tragic Heroes: Slaves of Passion*. Cambridge University Press, 1930.

Charlton, Henry B., *Shakespearian Tragedy*. Cambridge University Press, 1948.

Fairchild, A. H., *Shakespeare and the Tragic Theme* (University of Missouri Studies xix.2). Columbia, Mo.: University of Missouri Press, 1944.

Jenkins, Harold, "The Tragedy of Revenge in Shakespeare and Webster", *Shakespeare Survey*, XIV (1961), 45-55.

Lawlor, John, *The Tragic Sense in Shakespeare*. London: Chatto & Windus, 1960.

Leech, Clifford, *Shakespeare's Tragedies and Other Studies in Seventeenth Century Drama*. London: Chatto & Windus, 1950.

Muir, Kenneth, *Shakespeare and the Tragic Pattern*. London: Oxford University Press, 1959.

——, *William Shakespeare: The Great Tragedies*. London: Published for the British Council by Longmans, Green, 1961.

Parker, Marion H., *The Slave of Life: A Study of Shakespeare and the Idea of Justice*. London: Chatto & Windus, 1955.

Ribner, Irving, *Patterns in Shakespearian Tragedy*. London: Methuen, 1960.

Siegel, Paul N., *Shakespearean Tragedy and the Elizabethan Compromise*. New York University Press, 1957.

Spencer, Theodore, *Death and Elizabethan Tragedy*. Cambridge, Mass.: Harvard University Press, 1936.

Spivack, Bernard, *Shakespeare and the Allegory of Evil*. New York: Columbia University Press, 1958.

Stewart, J. I. M., *Character and Motive in Shakespeare*. London: Longmans, Green, 1949.

Stirling, Brents, *Unity in Shakespearian Tragedy: The Interplay of Theme and Character*. New York: Columbia University Press, 1956.

Whitaker, Virgil K., *Shakespeare's Use of Learning: An Inquiry into the Growth of his Mind and Art*. San Marino, Calif.: Huntington Library, 1953.

Wilson, Harold S., *On the Design of Shakespearian Tragedy*. University of Toronto Press, 1957.

Text and Sources

Bowers, Fredson T., *On Editing Shakespeare and the Elizabethan Dramatists*. Philadelphia: University of Pennsylvania Library, 1955.

Duthie, George I., *The Bad Quarto of "Hamlet"*. Cambridge University Press, 1941.

Gollancz, Israel, *The Sources of "Hamlet", with an Essay on the Legend*. London: Oxford University Press, 1926.

Greg, Walter Wilson, *The Editorial Problem in Shakespeare: A Survey of the Foundations of the Text*. Oxford: Clarendon Press, 1942.

Warhaft, Sidney, "Hamlet's Solid Flesh Resolved", *Journal of English Literary History*, XXVIII (1961), 21-30.

Wilson, John Dover, *The Manuscript of Shakespeare's "Hamlet" and the Problems of its Transmission*. 2 vols. Cambridge University Press, 1934.

Criticism

Alexander, Peter, *Hamlet: Father and Son.* Oxford: Clarendon Press, 1955.

Babcock, Weston, *"Hamlet", A Tragedy of Errors.* Lafayette, Ind.: Purdue University Press, 1961.

Bowers, Fredson T., "Dramatic Structure in *Hamlet*", *Shakespeare 400*, ed. James G. McManaway. New York: Holt, Rinehart & Winston, 1964.

Brown, John R., and Bernard Harris (eds.), *Shakespeare's "Hamlet"* (Stratford-upon-Avon Studies 5). London: Edward Arnold, 1963.

Conklin, Paul S., *A History of "Hamlet" Criticism, 1601-1821.* London: Routledge & Kegan Paul, 1957.

Draper, John W., *The "Hamlet" of Shakespeare's Audience.* Durham, N.C.: Duke University Press, 1938.

Eliot, Thomas Stearns, *"Hamlet", Selected Essays, 1917-1932.* London: Faber & Faber, 1932. (A revision of the essay first published as "Hamlet and his Problems" in *The Athenaeum*, no. 4665 [1919].)

Elliott, George R., *Scourge and Minister: A Study of "Hamlet" as Tragedy of Revengefulness and Justice.* Durham, N.C.: Duke University Press, 1951.

Fergusson, Francis, *"Hamlet"* in *The Idea of a Theater.* Princeton University Press, 1949.

Jones, Ernest, *Hamlet and Oedipus.* New York: W. W. Norton, 1949.

Joseph, Bertram, *Conscience and the King: A Study of "Hamlet".* London: Chatto & Windus, 1953.

Joseph, Sister Miriam, "Discerning the Ghost in 'Hamlet'", *PMLA*, LXXVI (1961), 493-502.

Knight, G. Wilson, *The Imperial Theme.* London: Oxford University Press, 1931.

——, "*Hamlet* Reconsidered", *The Wheel of Fire* (4th ed., revised and enlarged). London: Methuen, 1949.

Knights, Lionel C., *An Approach to "Hamlet".* London: Chatto & Windus, 1960.

——, *Explorations.* London: Chatto & Windus, 1946.

Kott, Jan, "*Hamlet* of the Mid-Century", *Shakespeare, Our Contemporary*, tr. Boleslaw Taborski. New York: Doubleday, 1964.

Levin, Harry, *The Question of "Hamlet"*. New York: Oxford University Press, 1959.

Madariaga, Salvador de, *On "Hamlet"*. London: Hollis & Carter, 1948.

Rossiter, Arthur P., "*Hamlet*" in *Angel with Horns and Other Shakespeare Lectures*, ed. Graham Storey. London: Longmans, Green, 1961.

Tillyard, E. M. W., "*Hamlet*", *Shakespeare's Problem Plays*. University of Toronto Press, 1949.

Waldock, Arthur J. A., "*Hamlet*", *A Study in Critical Method*. Cambridge University Press, 1931.

Walker, Roy, *The Time is Out of Joint: A Study of "Hamlet"*. London: Andrew Dakers, 1948.

Weitz, Morris, "*Hamlet*" *and the Philosophy of Literary Criticism*. University of Chicago Press, 1964.

Wilson, John Dover, *What Happens in "Hamlet"*. Cambridge University Press, 1935.

THE TEMPEST

William Shakespeare

Edited, with introduction and notes, by
David Galloway

INTRODUCTION

So far as we know, there is no main source for *The Tempest* — nothing which corresponds to Holinshed's *Chronicles* (3rd. ed., 1587) which Shakespeare used for the history plays, nor to Sir Thomas North's translation (1579) of Plutarch's *The Lives of the Noble Grecians and Romanes*, used for the Roman plays.

Shakespeare undoubtedly drew on a wide and varied reading knowledge for the ideas and events in his plays. Gonzalo's two speeches on the commonwealth seem to be based on Florio's translation of Montaigne's essay *Of Cannibals* (see 2.1.145-62, end note), Prospero's speech about the "rarer action" being "In virtue than in vengeance" may owe something to Montaigne's essay *Of Crueltie*, and his famous speech, "Ye elves of hills, brooks, standing lakes . . ." echoes Ovid's *Metamorphoses* (see 5.1.33-50, end note).

In a few places *The Tempest* resembles some sixteenth-century Italian *commedia dell'arte* plays, in which actors improvised their parts from skeleton plots, and a German play *Die Schöne Sidea* (*The Fair Sidea*) by Jacob Ayrer of Nuremberg, who died in 1605. A few names and events in William Thomas's *The History of Italy* (1549) also have minor parallels in *The Tempest*. There is no proof, however, that Shakespeare used any of these so-called "sources"; but even if he did, they are of small importance.

There is little doubt, however, that Shakespeare did use certain "Bermuda" pamphlets. In the early summer of 1609, a fleet of nine ships had sailed from Plymouth for Virginia. A storm scattered the fleet, and the flagship, *Sea Venture*, carrying Sir Thomas Gates (the new Governor of the colony), Sir George Somers (the Admiral), and Captain Christopher Newport, ran aground in the Bermudas on the 28th of July. Gates, Somers, Newport, and the crew remained on the islands for about nine months, and at last reached Virginia the following May. Several narratives of their adventures were published in London after Gates and Newport returned to England, in September 1610. The three accounts which seem to be particularly relevant to *The Tempest* are Sylvester Jourdain's *A Discovery of the Barmudas* (1610), the Council of Virginia's official publication, *A True Declaration of the Estate of the Colonie in Virginia* (1610), and William Strachey's *A true reportory of the wracke . . .* (dated July 15, 1610, but not published until 1625). Shakespeare, who had friends among those interested in the colonization of Virginia, seems to have seen Strachey's letter in manuscript shortly after it was written, because there are close verbal parallels between passages in the letter and, for example, Ariel's description of his own fiery display during the storm (see 1.2.198, end note).

The wreck on the Bermudas undoubtedly suggested to Shakespeare a few ideas and events which he used in *The Tempest*, but the play is primarily a product of Shakespeare's imagination and fundamentally owes little to its "sources".

It is not easy to explain the hold which *The Tempest* has on our imagination because the play offers few focal points for discussion. We are used to discussing most of Shakespeare's plays in terms of character, but it is difficult to discuss *The Tempest* in this way because many of its characters seem to be abstractions, or symbols of something which lies beyond them. We are not involved in the personal problems of Prospero in the way that we are in those of Hamlet or Macbeth; compared to the youthful passion of Romeo and Juliet, the young love of Ferdinand and Miranda seems remote and idealized; compared to the assassination of Caesar, the plots against Prospero seem to be of minor political concern; the Stephano–Trinculo scenes in *The Tempest* seem to lack the boisterous comic zest of the Sir Andrew Aguecheek–Sir Toby Belch scenes of *Twelfth Night* and the Dogberry scenes of *Much Ado About Nothing*. Shakespeare's earlier "romantic" comedies seem to be anchored to a psychological reality of character in a way which *The Tempest* is not.

One reason for the difficulty in finding a focal point for the discussion of the play may be that it belongs to a kind of drama which is no longer popular on the stage – the romance. Shakespeare wrote with a long romance tradition behind him. Dramatizations of romances had long been popular on the English stage, and Shakespeare's last plays, *Pericles, Cymbeline, The Winter's Tale*, and *The Tempest* which was probably written in 1611, are all, on the face of it, romances – tales of improbable happenings in remote and sometimes enchanted places. There are storms and shipwrecks, miraculous escapes from death, and heroines in disguise. Families are separated, but after many perils and injustices are reunited. He that was lost is found. The end is reconciliation and forgiveness, and the older generations are brought together through the marriage of their children. The interest of these last plays seems to lie, at first sight, less in their direct appeal to our emotions than in their vague and undefinable "romantic" charm. The characters flit through the action, coming alive at one moment and turning into puppets or symbols at another.

The Tempest, however, differs from *Pericles, Cymbeline*, and *The Winter's Tale*. It preserves the unities of time and place, which are normally disregarded in the romance. The events of Shakespeare's other romances occupy many months, or even years; there are numerous changes of locale, and the plots inevitably appear disjointed. But the action of *The Tempest* all takes place in about four hours, on – or very near – "an uninhabited Island". Events so typical of the romance – the intrigues against Prospero in Milan, his banishment from his dukedom, his perilous voyage with Miranda in "a rotten carcass of a butt", his arrival on the island, his rescue of Ariel from the "cloven pine", the taming of Caliban – have all taken place before the play opens. *The Tempest*, in fact, is like the last act of a typical romance – the act in which confusions are resolved and a happy ending takes place.

It would be a mistake to assume, however, that the Jacobean audience that watched *The Tempest* and Shakespeare's other romances felt them to be as remote and unreal as, perhaps, a modern audience does. The romance was part of a literary and dramatic heritage that was deeply embedded in the Jacobean consciousness, and Jacobeans probably accepted the conventions of the romance as unquestioningly as many people today accept the strange goings-on on their movie and television screens.

If the "romance" elements of *The Tempest* make it difficult for many of us today to find a basis for a discussion of the play, the "masque" elements provide a further difficulty. As early as the fourteenth century the masque was a well-defined entertainment at court and in the houses of noblemen. Friends would visit a house in rich costumes, wearing masks, carrying torches, and bringing presents for the host. They would entertain the audience with a dance and then, perhaps, invite the spectators to join them. By the reign of James I (1603-25) the masque had become a favourite diversion at court, and had developed into a highly organized, elaborate, and expensive form of entertainment which combined poetry, drama, music, song, dance, splendid costume, and scenery. James's queen, Anne of Denmark, was particularly fond of masques. She and the ladies of the court took part in masques themselves and, indeed, there is a record of the Queen's appearing in one, not only with a black face, but in a dress not "much below the knee". Among those Queen Anne employed in creating masques were the dramatists Ben Jonson and George Chapman, the musician Robert Johnson (who probably wrote "Where the bee sucks" and "Full fathom five"), and the architect and scene-designer Inigo Jones.

Masques were particularly associated with weddings, and there is, in all masques, a feeling of order springing from chaos, of spring emerging from winter. *The Tempest* was played at court during the winter of 1612-13, as part of the round of entertainment that led up to the marriage of James I's daughter, Elizabeth, to Frederick, the Elector Palatine, on February 14, 1613. Some scholars think that the first scene of Act 4, which is pure masque – the masque of Iris, Ceres, and Juno – may have been added to *The Tempest* especially for Elizabeth's marriage celebrations, but this is not necessarily so. The influence of the masque had spread to the professional stage, and masques are fairly common in plays of the period. In any case, the masque in *The Tempest* fits perfectly into the context of the play, celebrating as it does the betrothal of Ferdinand and Miranda.

Music is important in nearly all of Shakespeare's plays, and is particularly so in *The Tempest. A Midsummer Night's Dream* and *Twelfth Night* contain more actual songs, but music is such an integral part of the conception of *The Tempest,* which perhaps demands more background and instrumental music than the other plays, that it stays in the mind as the most musical of all. In some of Shakespeare's earlier plays the songs, while important in establishing or reinforcing a mood, are nevertheless set pieces, and the action pauses while they are being sung. Two of the last plays, however, *The Winter's Tale* and *The Tempest,* contain songs which are an integral part of the dialogue and of the action itself. In "Full fathom five . . .", for example, Ariel sings to Ferdinand of Ferdinand's father, King Alonso, who, if we are to take the words of the song literally, is lying dead under five fathoms of water. Actually, of course, it is the old Alonso – Prospero's enemy – who is dead. The "sea change" suggests the new, penitent Alonso who will emerge during the course of the play.

The romance and masque elements in *The Tempest* and its musical quality may help to explain why some critics find little interest in the characters. Prospero, the leading character, is a magician; and if a magician can effortlessly manage the affairs of ordinary men, the affairs of ordinary men may not appear to be of much human or dramatic significance. Where all is pre-ordained by a power greater than themselves, the free will of the characters disappears, and with a magician pulling the strings the characters become puppets. For some critics Prospero's role as a magician is similar to Shakespeare's as a playwright, and J. W. Mackail sees not merely Prospero but Shakespeare himself planning and ordering the action.

It is perhaps this double consciousness – as though we were simultaneously in front watching the play as spectators, and behind seeing it being handled – that makes *The Tempest* not in fact . . . highly effective on the stage. The illusion or hallucination to which, in seeing a play acted, we are asked to abandon ourselves, has not its full chance. But when we read it, if we read it carefully enough, it brings us nearer than almost anything else to understanding Shakespeare's art.[1]

Many critics have said and implied that *The Tempest* lacks dramatic quality, that it does not involve us in the problems and predicaments of its characters, that perhaps it lies somewhere between drama proper and such forms as ballet or opera in which our emotions are appealed to primarily through music, movement, and colour on the stage. In fact *The Tempest* can be good entertainment, and it can be a moving experience, but some people talk about and produce the play today as though it has something in common with stage musicals, or such films as *The Sound of Music* in which the story is important enough to sustain a mild interest, but in which the high points are the moments when the characters burst into song. For the great Shakespearian scholar Sir Edmund Chambers, in fact, *The Tempest* is "to be classed as dramatic *spectacle* rather than as drama proper, and the elaboration with which it has been put upon the stage by modern managers may be regarded as not . . . wholly out of keeping with the intention of the dramatist".[2]

Most directors of *The Tempest*, from the late seventeenth century onwards, have emphasized the visual and musical effect of the play and smothered its essential humanity in layers of paint. Some modern directors, however, in trying to make the play more "human" and up-to-date, have allowed their actors to speak the verse as though it were a kind of chopped-up prose. The result is that Shakespeare's most effective instrument is blunted and, indeed, sometimes becomes imperceptible. Character is created in all of Shakespeare's plays not merely by the literal meaning of what the character says, or by what other characters in the play say about him, but by the sound of his

---

[1] *The Approach to Shakespeare* (Oxford: Clarendon Press, 1930), p. 106.

[2] *Shakespeare: A Survey* (New York: Hill and Wang, 1958), p. 304.

words and by the very rhythms of his lines. The careless manner in which the director will often allow his actors to throw away their lines means that, unlike Prospero's, the actors' "charms are all o'erthrown" as soon as they step on to the stage.

A Jacobean audience, attuned to the rhythms of dramatic verse in a way that we are not, familiar with the masque as a form of entertainment, and with the romance tradition, probably found it easier to keep the essential human interest of the play in sight than do we. A Jacobean audience, also, could probably have accepted Prospero's magical skill more easily, as the belief was then widespread that the dispositions and fortunes of men and women were determined by the planets or stars under which they were born, and that God communicated His Will to man through the movements of the heavenly bodies. King James himself took a great interest in the supernatural and had published a treatise, *Daemonologie*, in 1597. We need not assume that all the members of *The Tempest*'s first audience believed that a mortal man was literally capable of doing all that Prospero could do, but to that audience Prospero was no mere fairy-tale conjuror, and he was certainly no wizard dabbling dangerously with the devil. On the contrary, he was a benevolent magician who had defeated the forces of darkness as represented by the black magic of the witch Sycorax, and was probably regarded much as the scientist is today – as a man who has acquired his power by hard study, and who is harnessing the forces of nature for the benefit of mankind. Indeed, the stage direction (1.2.467) which describes Ferdinand's being "charmed from moving", after he has drawn his sword, might well be interpreted in a modern play as describing the result of hypnotism.

There is a kind of science-fiction quality about *The Tempest*. The voyagers' descriptions of the New World, some of which Shakespeare had undoubtedly read, described lands which may have seemed as strange and new to Shakespeare's contemporaries as the moon and Mars seem to us. Throughout the play runs a sense of wonder at the newness of things, which may have inspired Aldous Huxley to choose Miranda's famous phrase "brave new world", albeit a bit sardonically, as the title of his own science-fiction novel, published in 1932.

The sense of wonder, the enchanting and enchanted qualities of the island, and Prospero's magic powers, should not, however, lead us to think of all the visitors to the island as unreal. A cosmonaut in space is still a human being. To people listening or watching from a distance, he may appear to be acting strangely, but he may also be experiencing sensations of which the majority of men have no knowledge, and acting sensibly in relation to his surroundings. Two centuries ago, Dr. Johnson saw the essential reality of Shakespeare's characters in whatever situations they might happen to find themselves.

> *Shakespeare* has no heroes; his scenes are occupied only by men, who act and speak as the reader thinks that he should himself have spoken or acted on the same occasion: Even where the agency is supernatural the dialogue is level with life. Other writers disguise the most natural passions and most frequent incidents; so that he who contemplates them in the book will not know them in the world: *Shakespeare* approximates the remote and familiarizes the wonderful; the event which he represents will not happen, but if it were possible, its effects would probably be such that he has assigned; and it may be said, that he has not only shown human nature as it acts in real exigencies, but as it would be found in trials, to which it cannot be exposed.[3]

To appreciate *The Tempest* fully, we must realize that it is a romance in which improbable things can happen; that it has certain masque-like qualities which appeal to the eye; that most of the characters, within the context of the play, appear to be living and breathing creatures with human virtues and vices; and that it is created out of an extremely subtle verse and prose, every word of which should be distinctly heard, and every line of which should be rhythmically preserved. An ideal performance is, of course, impossible, but an exaggerated stress on one aspect of the play to the exclusion of others will bring the delicately balanced structure crashing down.

The first recorded production of *The Tempest* was in the

---

[3] *Johnson on Shakespeare*, ed. Walter Raleigh (London: Oxford University Press, 1908), p. 14.

Banqueting House at Whitehall, before "the King's Majesty", on November 1, 1611. Its subsequent stage history is largely one of distortion in which the spectacular elements of the play were exaggerated at the expense of the words. Throughout the late seventeenth, the eighteenth, and the nineteenth centuries, and on into the twentieth century, there have been many adaptations of the play for the stage – some, like John Dryden's *The Tempest, or The Enchanted Island* (1674), being frankly and spectacularly operatic. Dryden's version in fact supplied Miranda with a sister named Dorinda, and gave her a lover named Hippolito. One production so disgusted the famous critic William Hazlitt that he wrote in the magazine *The Examiner*, on July 23, 1815, of "common-place, clap-trap sentiments, artificial contrasts of situations and character, and all the heavy tinsel and affected formality" and of "anomalous, unmeaning, vulgar, and ridiculous additions".[4]

Not all twentieth-century productions have been so full of tinsel and froth, but, as one critic writes: "Time and again, the strength and violence that lie so near the surface of the play are submerged in layers of charm and hocus-pocus; the urgent directness of action, which moves from beginning to end with such narrative skill, is interrupted and weakened by exaggerated detail and peripheral fuss."[5]

There is room for a certain amount of spectacle in *The Tempest* – in, for example, the Masque (4.1) and in the vanishing banquet (3.3), which is perhaps the most elaborate stage spectacle in any of Shakespeare's plays – but directors should limit their spectacular effects to what is clearly demanded by the text and by the stage directions which in this play are unusually specific.

> While the influence of the masque may be conceded, what we should never forget is that the spectacularism in the romances

---

[4] *The Tempest*, eds. Arthur Quiller-Couch and John Dover Wilson (Cambridge University Press [The New Shakespeare], 1921), p. 111.

[5] David Williams, "*The Tempest* on the Stage", *Jacobean Theatre*, eds. John R. Brown and Bernard Harris (London: Edward Arnold, 1960), pp. 133-4.

is implied rather than stated; it is a spectacularism of the imagination rather than of reality. . . . the inherent vision which possessed Shakespeare in the composition of his romances can come to us only when the imagination is left free to create in ideal terms the dreamlike background against which his action is set.[6]

The Tempest opens with a "tempestuous noise of thunder and lightning", and a ship in difficulties at sea. This first scene is rather like the opening of a film before the credits and title appear on the screen. Who are the people on the ship? Where has the ship come from, and where is she sailing?

Short as the scene is (only 64 lines), it introduces nearly half the characters in the play, and we learn a little about the people we shall meet at greater leisure later on. Alonso tells the boatswain to "have care"; Gonzalo is humorously resigned to his fate and urges the boatswain – irrelevantly – to "remember whom thou hast aboard"; Sebastian and Antonio are arrogantly abusive; Ferdinand does not speak; and the boatswain, who has a job to do, is in no mood to listen to a lot of interfering and useless landlubbers.

The excitement of the storm scene should capture the audience's attention and make it all the more ready for the scene of exposition that follows – the scene in which Prospero tells Miranda (and the audience) how he and his daughter came to be on the island. Although this second scene provides an effective contrast to the storm scene, it should not begin in too relaxed a manner. Miranda is naturally concerned about the fate of the "poor souls" on the "brave vessel". As Prospero speaks, however, the tension relaxes somewhat. Some critics and directors see Prospero as a school-teacherish bore, delivering long speeches, showing a great deal of impatience with everyone else in the play, and – in this scene – chiding a daughter who seems to be bored with what he is saying. Perhaps, however, they do not sufficiently appreciate the fact that both Miranda and her father are in a state of excitement. Miranda has just

[6] Allardyce Nicoll, *Shakespeare* (London: Methuen, 1952), pp. 173-4.

seen – so she thinks – a ship go to the bottom of the sea and, to make matters worse, she thinks that her father has been responsible for putting it there. Even when Prospero has nearly finished his story (over 170 lines later) Miranda is still thinking of the ship and its passengers – "For still 'tis beating in my mind". Prospero too is in a state of some turmoil. After twelve years he has to explain to his beloved daughter how they both came to be on the island. He has to open old wounds with an account of the treachery of his brother, Antonio, who was aided by Alonso, King of Naples. He has to admit to Miranda that he was not a very efficient Duke of Milan. More important, perhaps, he has to bring Miranda to the threshold of her maturity quickly, for his old enemies are in his power and there is no time to lose.

> and by my prescience
> I find my zenith doth depend upon
> A most auspicious star, whose influence
> If now I court not, but omit, my fortunes
> Will ever after droop.   (1.2.180-84)

This scene, then, far from being one in which a father is telling a daughter a long and tedious story from which the daughter's mind (and perhaps the audience's) pardonably wanders, should be played full of urgency and agitation – an agitation reflected in the quickening pace of the verse, which is full of sharp twists of syntax and thought (see, for example, ll. 66-77 and the end note). Prospero is desperately anxious that Miranda shall grasp the significance of what he is saying.

Having put Miranda to sleep, Prospero calls for Ariel, whose entrance (l. 188) extends the spiritual quality of the play. There follows another long piece of exposition in which we learn how Ariel "performed" the tempest. Several critics have commented on what appears to be Prospero's harsh treatment of Ariel, who merely demands what Prospero has promised him – his liberty. It is understandable, however, that Prospero is impatient, for he has so much to do in such a very short time. Ariel's demand for liberty gives Prospero a natural opportunity to further the exposition by reminding Ariel of how he had been painfully imprisoned for a dozen years by the foul witch Sycorax.

The exit of Ariel is the signal for the entry of what is perhaps an even more interesting character – Caliban. We have already heard of Caliban from the conversation between Prospero and Ariel, but when Prospero summons him, instead of the "freckled whelp, hag-born" (1. 283), there enters Ariel "like a water-nymph". He pauses for his master's bidding and is gone.

The introduction of Caliban at this point, and the manner of his entry, of course, emphasize the contrast between Caliban and Ariel. Caliban, whose name may be an anagram of "canni-bal", is described in the Folio as "a salvage and deformed slave".[7] He is a savage in the sense that many natives of the New World were thought to be savages; he is somewhere in the Chain of Being[8] between a beast and a man; he is a "born devil", "got by the devil himself/ Upon thy wicked dam" (ll. 319-20). Being an inferior creature, he is what Aristotle called a slave by nature. He exists only at the simplest level of the senses, aware of lechery but not of love; yet he is able – like some animals – to listen to music with pleasure, and is dimly aware of its glories.

Prospero has been successful with Ariel, but with Caliban he has failed. He has tried to teach Caliban certain civilized arts and morals, but Caliban has responded by using the language he has learned to curse his teacher. The situation follows the common pattern of the white man as conqueror; after an initial period of harmony, the conqueror and conquered are at odds. The exit of Caliban (1. 374) completes the exposition. One sixth of the play is over, and the action can go forward.

[7] For a discussion of Caliban's possible origins, see the Introduction to the new Arden edition of *The Tempest*, ed. Frank Kermode (London: Methuen, 1954), pp. xxxviii-xliii.

[8] In Shakespeare's day the belief was widespread that every created thing formed a link in a great chain which stretched from God himself down to the meanest inanimate object. Below God were the archangels and angels; below the lowest angels came Man – a *microcosm*, or little world in himself – bridging the gulf between matter and spirit, bound to the animals by the flesh, but striving upwards to God through the soul. Below Man were the animals, below them vegetables and plants, and, at the bottom, inanimate objects such as liquids and metals.

A first step towards the reconciliation at the end of the play is the meeting of Ferdinand and Miranda. Ariel's song "Come unto these yellow sands" (ll. 375-87) leads Ferdinand to the lovers' meeting. Ferdinand, bemused by the music, is in a receptive mood, and "Full fathom five thy father lies" (ll. 397-405) provides a perfect accompaniment to his thoughts of his father, and enraptures him with its beauty. After the song Prospero allows Miranda's eyes to open from her sleep. Her reaction is immediate and direct:

> What is't? a spirit?
> Lord, how it looks about! Believe me, sir,
> It carries a brave form. But 'tis a spirit.
>   (1.2.410-12)

The sense of wonder and freshness, so characteristic of the play as a whole, is intensified when Ferdinand and Miranda see one another for the first time. From this moment on, lives are reborn and old enemies brought together.

Ferdinand and Miranda have often been regarded as an insipid hero and heroine. In keeping with the romance tradition, Ferdinand will undergo some ordeal for the love of his lady. Falling in love at first sight is also typical of the romance, but it is also very natural and very human, especially as Miranda has seen no other men but Prospero and the half-human Caliban. As George Bernard Shaw has written, "Prospero knows that he has only to throw Ferdinand and Miranda together and they will mate like a pair of doves."[9] Coleridge sees in the love confessions of Ferdinand and Miranda more than an echo of those of Romeo and Juliet. "There seems more passion in the one, and more dignity in the other, yet you feel that the sweet, girlish lingering and busy movements of Juliet, and the calmer more maidenly fondness of Miranda, might easily pass into each other."[10]

Act 2 reintroduces the courtiers whom we have seen, but probably not identified, on the sinking ship, although we have

[9] Edwin Wilson (ed.), *Shaw On Shakespeare: an anthology of George Bernard Shaw's Writings* (New York: Dutton, 1961), p. 250.

[10] Samuel Taylor Coleridge, *Lectures and Notes on Shakespeare*, ed. T. Ashe (London: Bell, 1897), p. 325.

learned something about them from Prospero's story to Miranda. Their arrival shatters the idyllic atmosphere of the courtship and reminds us of the evil in the world – an evil with which Miranda will come into contact all too soon. Away from "civilized" surroundings men often reveal their true characters very quickly, and it is not long before we recognize the courtiers for what they are. Alonso appears as a father grieving for a lost son, and perhaps the fact that he is inconsolable shows the possibility of his repentance. Gonzalo, in vain, tries to console Alonso for his loss, just as twelve years earlier he had shown concern for Prospero in his banishment by providing him with books and with "Rich garments, linens, stuffs, and necessaries/ Which since have steaded much" (1.2.164-5). Antonio and Sebastian are quickly isolated morally from Alonso and Gonzalo by the cynical and destructive manner in which they bait the well-meaning Gonzalo. Their smart alec humour is curiously humourless, and their cynicism is a prelude to graver crimes. They are further isolated from the other members of the party in that the "strange drowsiness" of the island does not possess them. Sleep, as in *Macbeth*, is for the innocent; and if Alonso is not exactly innocent, at least his falling asleep foreshadows the healing process that has begun.

The scene in which Antonio, the consummate villain, tempts Sebastian to agree to the murder of the sleeping Alonso is a masterpiece of stagecraft, with echoes of *Macbeth*.

> And yet methinks I see in thy face,
> What thou shouldst be. Th' occasion speaks thee, and
> My strong imagination sees a crown
> Dropping upon thy head. (2.1.202-5)

Antonio's brilliant persuasiveness begins with a studied hesitancy and a studied indirectness; then gradually it overcomes Sebastian's objections until the moment when they both draw their swords. A final hesitation on the part of Sebastian as the blow is about to fall – a standard dramatic device – provides the cue for Ariel to sing of the "Open-eyed conspiracy" in Gonzalo's ear. Gonzalo, Alonso, and the others awake. The plot is foiled, the crisis is past, and at least a faint hope seems to come

to Alonso, for he leads the party off to "make further search/
For my poor son" (ll. 319-20).

As the court party wanders away, Caliban enters cursing
Prospero. The corruption of civilized people is contrasted with
the unbridled savagery of primitive man. If we are to believe
Caliban in his speech full of invective against Prospero (2.2.
1-14), Prospero sets his spirits to torment Caliban for "every
trifle"; but it may be – in part at least – that the master is a
convenient scapegoat for all the ills that befall the slave.

With Trinculo's entrance the language drops into prose, and
there is low comedy after the near tragedy of the previous scene.
When Stephano enters with his bottle, he brings the "celestial
liquor" which will give Caliban his own drunken glimpse of a
"brave new world" – a theme being worked out in practice by
Shakespeare's contemporaries in the Americas.

The brief idyll that follows Caliban's exit with his drunken
dreams of freedom advances the love of Ferdinand and Miranda (3.1). In the scene in which they first met, Miranda was
overcome with wonder and admiration. In this scene she is
more practical. She consoles Ferdinand in his log-bearing and
offers herself to him.

> I am your wife, if you will marry me;
> If not, I'll die your maid. To be your fellow
> You may deny me; but I'll be your servant,
> Whether you will or no.   (3.1.83-6)

The parental reins have slackened. Miranda has already broken
her father's command by telling Ferdinand her name (1. 36).
In offering herself to Ferdinand she has become a woman in her
own right, and by the end of the brief scene, to the delight of
the unseen Prospero, the couple are betrothed.

In the next scene we are back with Stephano, Trinculo, and
Caliban who, now well gone in liquor, are at the quarrelsome
stage. Stephano, in his own estimation, has become the king of
the island, but Trinculo retains some sense of proportion: "The
folly of this island! They say there's but five upon this isle: we
are three of them. If th' other two be brained like us, the state
totters" (3.2.4-6). The tone is becoming darker, and the

comedy of this scene is shot through with brutality, lust, and greed for power. The plot of Caliban and his friends, in fact, provides an ironic parallel with the Sebastian–Antonio plot in Act 2, scene 1, and with the original plot against Prospero in Milan. Rulers are never safe.

Just as Ariel has thwarted the plot of Antonio and Sebastian, so he now interrupts Caliban's conspiracy by playing on his pipe and tabor. Stephano defies the unseen musician, and Trinculo sinks to his knees and begs for forgiveness; but Caliban, who is familiar with the mysterious sounds of the island, is not afraid and speaks some of the loveliest lines in the play.

> Be not afeard: the isle is full of noises,
> Sounds and sweet airs that give delight and hurt not.
> Sometimes a thousand twangling instruments
> Will hum about mine ears; and sometime voices,
> That, if I then had waked after long sleep,
> Will make me sleep again; and then, in dreaming,
> The clouds methought would open and show riches
> Ready to drop upon me; that, when I waked,
> I cried to dream again.   (3.2.133-41)

Caliban with his brutal savagery is a far more dangerous rebel than either Trinculo or Stephano, but somewhere in his brutish brain is a more sensitive strain, undulled by the "civilized" world, which responds to the beauty of music.

With the exit of Caliban, Stephano, and Trinculo, led away by Ariel's music on his pipe and tabor, the court party enters, tired out by the fruitless search for Ferdinand. Gonzalo is tired in body; Alonso is tired in body and in spirit and has given up hope of seeing his son again; Antonio and Sebastian are looking for another opportunity to murder Alonso.

From this point on there is a more formal and stately development of the action. Like a mirage in the desert beckoning the weary traveller, there is "Solemn and strange music", the prelude to "several strange Shapes, bringing in a banquet", who "dance about it with gentle actions of salutations; and, inviting the King &c. to eat, they depart" (3.3.17 s.d.).

The reactions of the courtiers to the strange spectacle are in keeping with their characters. Gonzalo sees the strange shapes as people of the island and, typically, sees their manners as being "more gentle, kind, than of/ Our human generation you shall find/ Many" (ll. 32-4). Alonso, indifferent to his general predicament, nevertheless appreciates the "excellent dumb discourse" being enacted before him. Sebastian and Antonio see the pageant as mere "living drollery" which will confirm the fantastic reports of travellers' tales.

Instead of the banquet, however, Ariel enters in the guise of a harpy (see 3.3.52 s.d., gloss), and serves the three men of sin with a condemnation of their past actions as "with a quaint device the banquet vanishes". Ariel's tremendous indictment is like the voice of Fate speaking directly. The sea has belched up the criminals and brought them to judgement. For Prospero, it is the moment when he is fully convinced that his "high charms" are really working effectively,

> And these, mine enemies, are all knit up
> In their distractions: they now are in my power;
> And in these fits I leave them . . . (3.3.89-91)

Gonzalo, as befits the innocent, has not heard the condemnation, but Alonso recognizes that

> the thunder,
> That deep and dreadful organ pipe, pronounced
> The name of Prosper; it did bass my trespass.
> (3.3.97-9)

Alonso, having seen the death of his son as a just retribution for his crime against Prospero, will be reconciled to his old enemy. Antonio and Sebastian, desperately defiant, remain outside the pale of reconciliation because in them there is no change of heart.

In this scene the formal masque-like world of the banquet in which the voice of Fate intervenes directly is brought into sharp and effective contrast with a world in which evil men plot and remain unrepentant. The two worlds are fused with remarkable power and beauty.

Prospero now has complete confidence in his own powers, and during the last two acts of the play he never leaves the stage. The first formal act of reconciliation – an act upon which the later reconciliation of the parents depends – is the betrothal of Ferdinand and Miranda. Prospero hands over his daughter with a father's blessing, and reveals to Ferdinand that

> All thy vexations
> Were but my trials of thy love, and thou
> Hast strangely stood the test . . .
>
> (4.1.5-7)

His warning to Ferdinand not to break Miranda's "virgin-knot" before the two are actually married has often been taken as further evidence that Prospero is a rather puritanical old man. There is, of course, in Prospero's speech (ll. 13-23) the formally recognized view that chastity should always precede marriage, but Prospero's fatherly regard is understandable enough. Admirable as Ferdinand undoubtedly is, he is the son of Prospero's old enemy; he has come from the outside world – a world that Prospero has little reason to trust. Miranda, whom Prospero loves better than anything else, has been his only human companion for the past twelve years and he has seen Caliban try to rape her. In human terms, Prospero is far from being a stuffy, Victorian-type father, and is behaving with remarkable tact and understanding considering all that he has suffered. He now recognizes that Miranda has grown up and is no longer his.

Having blessed the betrothal of his daughter to Ferdinand, it is appropriate that Prospero should entertain the couple with the formal masque associated with the betrothals and marriages of high-born people. The divine splendour of the masque, coming as it does after the human scene of the betrothal, should stand out in brilliant, formal, opulent contrast. If, however, the director has already overdone the scenic splendours, the masque may lose some of its effect.

After the masque we are back again in the petty, contrasting world where people plot and intrigue, as Prospero remembers

> that foul conspiracy
> Of the beast Caliban and his confederates
> Against my life: the minute of their plot
> Is almost come.   (4.1.139-42)

The thought of the conspiracy seems to move Prospero deeply, as Ferdinand observes, and possibly with this thought in mind Prospero delivers his great speech (ll. 146-58) on the "insubstantial pageant" of human life – perhaps the supreme poetic moment of the play. Some critics have seen in this speech a mood of pessimism, and certainly Prospero is troubled, but the phrase, "We are such stuff/ As dreams are made on" can be taken as an affirmation of faith in man whose creative imagination is constantly soaring (see 4.1.156-7, end note).

Prospero turns to deal with Caliban, in whose animal nature evil is rooted so deeply that Prospero's attempts at education ("nurture") have not been able to change him:

> A devil, a born devil, on whose nature
> Nurture can never stick: on whom my pains,
> Humanely taken, all, all lost, quite lost;
> And as with age his body uglier grows,
> So his mind cankers.   (4.1.188-92)

Ariel has already led the conspirators a merry dance through "Toothed briers, sharp furzes, pricking goss, and thorns" (l. 180), and has left them "I' th' filthy-mantled pool beyond your cell" (l. 182). Stephano and Trinculo waste their time stealing a lot of trashy clothes which Ariel has hung on a tree, although Caliban is anxious to get on with the job of killing Prospero. Finally, "divers Spirits in shape of dogs and hounds" (l. 254 s.d.) hunt the conspirators about the stage. Caliban, Stephano, and Trinculo are driven out, and the last plot against Prospero has failed.

In the final scene of *The Tempest*, as in so many of Shakespeare's other plays, various strands of the action are tied together and the characters are brought on to the stage for their rewards and punishments – although here there are to be no punishments. This scene especially has been regarded as a kind of formal ballet, and to some extent it is; but the humanity and vigour of the characters are retained, and it is a mistake to see it merely as a kind of musical tableau which ends the play.

The scene opens with Prospero's announcement that the moment of retribution has come:

> Now does my project gather to a head:
> My charms crack not, my spirits obey, and time
> Goes upright with his carriage.   (5.1.1-3)

For Ariel, it is now "the sixth hour; at which time, my lord,/ You said our work should cease" (ll. 4-5). Ariel describes how he has left Alonso and his companions "distracted" with "the good old Lord Gonzalo" weeping.

> Your charm so strongly works 'em,
> That if you now beheld them, your affections
> Would become tender.   (5.1.17-19)

This is the point at which Prospero clearly states that he will forgive:

> Though with their high wrongs I am struck to th' quick,
> Yet with my nobler reason 'gainst my fury
> Do I take part. The rarer action is
> In virtue than in vengeance. They being penitent,
> The sole drift of my purpose doth extend
> Not a frown further.   (5.1.25-30)

Prospero has probably intended to forgive long before this — his blessing on the betrothal of Ferdinand and Miranda suggests as much — but, like many people who may recognize the rightness of a decision intellectually, Prospero seems to find it difficult to put that decision into practice. The strain of acting on the recognition, which most people have in the abstract, that "The rarer action is/ In virtue than in vengeance" is a human one.

The use of reason, which distinguishes man from the beasts, triumphs, however. Prospero abjures his "rough magic", Alonso and the courtiers are brought in "spell-stopped", and Prospero restores them to their reason.

> The charm dissolves apace;
> And as the morning steals upon the night,
> Melting the darkness, so their rising senses
> Begin to chase the ignorant fumes that mantle
> Their clearer reason.   (5.1.64-8)

Prospero's forgiveness seems to be all-embracing, but the corresponding repentance is not. Alonso's repentance is full and genuine (ll. 118-19), Trinculo and Stephano have at least learned a lesson, and Caliban will be "wise hereafter,/ And seek for grace" (ll. 295-6). But there is no word of repentance from Antonio and Sebastian. They say very little, and what little they do say still smacks of the smart alec attitudes they showed in Act 2.

Several critics have suggested that Prospero has by no means solved his problems and still has trouble in store for himself. Dean Ebner writes:

> The possibility of rebellion is not dead. No perfect society has been attained. Yet Prospero rids himself of his magical power before he is safely back in Milan. He stands helpless before the men who have given him nothing but evil for good. He trusts the sincerity of those who have repented.[11]

Society is certainly not perfect and no one would expect Prospero to be so naïve as to assume that it can be. But does he really stand quite so "helpless before the men who have given him nothing but evil for good"? On a lonely island Prospero has mastered a difficult art; he has learned – the hard way – how to forgive; he has mastered himself; his eyes are open; and the wisdom that he has gained will serve him well in the future. His new life in Milan will be another story.

When Alonso wishes that Ferdinand and Miranda were alive as King and Queen of Naples, Prospero seems to be completely satisfied. He "discovers" the lovers at their game of chess, and the reconciliation between him and Alonso is absolute in the union of their children. Miranda's delight in the "brave new world/ That has such people in't!" (ll. 183-4), however, is tempered by Prospero's voice of experience as he observes, " 'Tis new to thee." Miranda will no doubt learn that "brave" forms may conceal evil hearts.

The play ends with Prospero's consigning Ariel to the elements: "Be free, and fare thou well!" (l. 319). A simple,

[11] *The Tempest*: Rebellion and the Ideal State", *Shakespeare Quarterly*, XVI (1965), 172.

human, "I shall miss thee" (1. 95), has already fallen from his lips. The fleet can now sail for Naples with "calm seas" and "auspicious gales".

In the Epilogue, with its echoes of the Bible and the Lord's Prayer, Prospero's final appeal is to Christian virtue.

In spite of all that has been written about *The Tempest* and about Shakespeare's other romances, most of the criticism seems to be several stages removed from our experience of the works themselves. Attempts to explain the "meaning" of *The Tempest* often seem to be trivial and only vaguely connected with the play. A much more widespread and thorough understanding of the nature of the romance and of the Jacobean audience's responses to it might help us to find more useful bases for discussion.

When Shakespeare wrote *The Tempest*, he was at the end – or very near the end – of his dramatic career. It is tempting and plausible to see the play as Shakespeare's farewell to the stage, with the dramatist at times speaking directly to his audience through the mouth of Prospero, especially in the Epilogue and in the speech "Our revels now are ended", which for many people seems to sum up Shakespeare's philosophy of life more than any other single passage in his work. Some critics hold the view that the romance plays, and especially *The Tempest*, represent the mature, wise, serene mood of a dramatist, weary of the London stage, who is preparing to pass his declining years in the quiet country town of his youth, basking in the joys of nature and surrounded by his family and friends. For other critics, however, Shakespeare, in the romances, was as usual giving the public what it wanted, and the public at that time wanted romance and spectacle. Some see *The Tempest* as being full of myth, symbol, and allegory, with everything in the play possessing an additional underlying meaning. Ariel and Caliban, especially, have been singled out as the embodiments of a variety of philosophical beliefs; Prospero, too, has been assigned a symbolic role, for instance as Divine Providence controlling a world in which men struggle for power; and the play as a whole has been seen as presenting a specifically Christian interpretation of life—a kind of extended sermon on the Sacraments.

A few critics have even detected political allegory in the play – for example, a veiled commentary on the death of Henry IV of France in 1610.

For many people *The Tempest* is an optimistic reading of life; for others it is a pessimistic one. What happens within the play itself, of course, can lead us to the conclusion that it is both optimistic and pessimistic – optimistic in the sense that things are brighter at the end than they were at the beginning; pessimistic in that some of the characters are apparently unrepentant, and evil is still at large in the world. Ultimately, however, words such as "optimistic" and "pessimistic" are irrelevant. As we leave the theatre, we are, or should be, conscious that we have experienced a great work of art in which the over-all impression is one of serenity, detachment, and a wise acceptance of the world as it is. We should have acquired an understanding that "The rarer action is/ In virtue than in vengeance", however difficult it may be to put such an understanding into practice.

The serenity of *The Tempest*, however, is not the serenity of a tired man looking forward to a well-earned retirement, but the serenity that arises from the way in which the varied elements of the play are so beautifully controlled and balanced. The total effect is rather like that of a great piece of music, such as one of Beethoven's last quartets. Nor does it matter how tired – or how rejuvenated – Shakespeare may have felt when he wrote *The Tempest*. Having portrayed in many plays all kinds of people in all kinds of situations, he has now achieved in one play alone an almost perfect statement of the great range of human experience. *The Tempest* shows him "more conscious than ever of the tangle of earthly existence, but surer than ever of what gives beauty, worth, and humanity to the lives of men".[12]

The "meaning" of *The Tempest* must lie, ultimately, in the manner in which we respond to it. Towards that "meaning" criticism may dimly point the way.

[12] Peter Alexander, *Shakespeare's Life and Art* (New York University Press, 1961), p. 216.

NOTE ON THE TEXT

The Tempest, the shortest of Shakespeare's plays with the exception of *The Comedy of Errors*, is one of eighteen plays printed for the first time in the Folio of 1623 (the earliest collected edition of Shakespeare's works), and is the first in the collection. The Folio text was carefully edited and printed, the stage directions are unusually full, and, unlike many other plays in the volume, it is divided into acts and scenes. *The Tempest* is one of only seven plays, out of the thirty-six in the Folio, to list the names of the characters, and is the only one to state clearly, in so many words, where the action takes place — on "an un-inhabited island".

Compared with most editions, the present one follows the Folio closely, but the spelling and punctuation have been modernized.

EDITORIAL EMENDATIONS

1.1.62. *furze*; F *firrs*

2.1.36. *Ha, ha, ha!*; F assigns to Sebastian   37. *So, you're paid*; F assigns to Antonio   92. *Ay!*; F *I*

3.1.15. *least*; F *lest*

3.2.120. *scout*; F *cout*

3.3.29. *islanders?*; F *Islands*

4.1.9. *off*; F *of*   13. *gift*; F *guest*   61. *vetches*; F *Fetches*   123. *wise*; some copies of F *wife*

The Tempest

NAMES OF THE ACTORS

ALONSO, *King of Naples*
SEBASTIAN, *his brother*
PROSPERO, *the right Duke of Milan*
ANTONIO, *his brother, the usurping Duke of Milan*
FERDINAND, *son to the King of Naples*
GONZALO, *an honest old councillor*
ADRIAN *and* FRANCISCO, *lords*
CALIBAN, *a savage and deformed slave*
TRINCULO, *a jester*
STEPHANO, *a drunken butler*
MASTER OF A SHIP
BOATSWAIN
MARINERS
MIRANDA, *daughter to Prospero*
ARIEL, *an airy spirit*
IRIS
CERES
JUNO } *[presented by] spirits*
NYMPHS
REAPERS

[*Other Spirits attending on Prospero*]

Scene: An uninhabited Island

ACT 1

Scene 1

A tempestuous noise of thunder and lightning heard.
Enter a Shipmaster and a Boatswain.

MASTER. Boatswain!

BOATSWAIN. Here, master. What cheer?

MASTER. Good: speak to th' mariners; fall to 't yarely, or
we run ourselves aground. Bestir, bestir!   *Exit.*

Enter Mariners.

BOATSWAIN. Heigh, my hearts! Cheerly, cheerly, my 5
hearts! Yare, yare! Take in the topsail! Tend to th'
master's whistle! Blow till thou burst thy wind, if room
enough!

Enter Alonso, Sebastian, Antonio, Ferdinand,
Gonzalo, and others.

ALONSO. Good boatswain, have care. Where's the master?
Play the men.   10

BOATSWAIN. I pray now, keep below.

ANTONIO. Where is the master, bos'n?

BOATSWAIN. Do you not hear him? You mar our labour:
keep your cabins: you do assist the storm.

GONZALO. Nay, good, be patient.   15

1.1.1. *Boatswain* (ship's officer who, under the master, directed the
duties of the seamen) 2. *master* (master mariner, captain of a merchant
vessel) 3. *Good* (the master is probably acknowledging the boatswain's
reply, but some editors place a comma after "Good", thus making it
mean "my good fellow" or "my good man") *yarely* briskly, promptly
4. *Bestir* i.e. bestir yourselves, get a move on 6. *Yare* quick *Take . . .
topsail* (the topsail was to be taken in to check the drift of the ship
towards the land) 6-7. *th' master's whistle* (used to direct sailors in the
working of the ship) *Blow . . . wind* (addressed to the storm) 7-8. *if
room enough* i.e. if we are far enough from the shore so as not to run
aground 10. *Play the men* Act the part of men, i.e. Show that you are
men; or (perhaps) "Ply" the men, i.e. Keep the men busy 13. *mar our
labour* i.e. get in the way of our work 15. *good* i.e. good man

BOATSWAIN. When the sea is. Hence! What cares these
    roarers for the name of King? To cabin! Silence! Trouble
    us not!

GONZALO. Good, yet remember whom thou hast aboard.

BOATSWAIN. None that I more love than myself. You are 20
    a councillor: if you can command these elements to
    silence, and work the peace of the present, we will not
    hand a rope more; use your authority: if you cannot,
    give thanks you have lived so long, and make yourself
    ready in your cabin for the mischance of the hour, if it 25
    so hap. Cheerly, good hearts! Out of our way, I say.

Exit.

GONZALO. I have great comfort from this fellow: methinks
    he hath no drowning mark upon him; his complexion is
    perfect gallows. Stand fast, good Fate, to his hanging:
    make the rope of his destiny our cable, for our own 30
    doth little advantage. If he be not born to be hanged,
    our case is miserable.   Exeunt.

Enter Boatswain.

BOATSWAIN. Down with the topmast! Yare! Lower, lower!
    Bring her to try with main-course! (A cry within.) A
    plague upon this howling! They are louder than the 35
    weather or our office.

Enter Sebastian, Antonio, and Gonzalo.

Yet again? What do you here? Shall we give o'er and
drown? Have you a mind to sink?

SEBASTIAN. A pox o' your throat, you bawling, blasphe-
    mous, incharitable dog!   40

---

16. *cares* (a singular verb with a plural subject is common in this and
other plays of the time) 17. *roarers* i.e. roaring waves 22. *work . . .
present* i.e. cause the storm to stop immediately 23. *hand* handle 29.
fast firm 31. *doth little advantage* i.e. does not help us very much 32.
case situation 33. *topmast* (a mast at the head of the mainmast. The
topmast was lowered to reduce the weight at the top of the ship and
lessen the drift towards the shore) 34. *Bring . . . try* i.e. try to make
the ship heave to (stationary) *main-course* mainsail 35-6. *They . . .
office* i.e. the passengers make more noise than the weather, or us in
performing our duties 37. *give o'er* give up 39. *A pox o'* a plague on
40. *incharitable* ill-tempered

BOATSWAIN. Work you, then.

ANTONIO. Hang, cur, hang, you whoreson, insolent noise-
  maker! We are less afraid to be drowned than thou art.

GONZALO. I'll warrant him for drowning, though the ship
  were no stronger than a nutshell, and as leaky as an 45
  unstanched wench.

BOATSWAIN. Lay her ahold, ahold! Set her two courses!
  Off to sea again! Lay her off!

Enter Mariners wet.

MARINERS. All lost! To prayers, to prayers! All lost!
                                        [*Exeunt.*]

BOATSWAIN. What, must our mouths be cold?   50

GONZALO. The King and Prince at prayers: let's assist
    them,
  For our case is as theirs.

SEBASTIAN.   I am out of patience.

ANTONIO. We are merely cheated of our lives by
    drunkards.
  This wide-chopped rascal – would thou mightst lie
    drowning
  The washing of ten tides!

GONZALO.   He'll be hanged yet,   55
  Though every drop of water swear against it,
  And gape at wid'st to glut him.

A confused noise within.   "Mercy on us! –
  We split, we split! – Farewell, my wife and children! –
  Farewell, brother! – We split, we split, we split!"
                                  [*Exit Boatswain.*]

ANTONIO. Let's all sink with th' King.

SEBASTIAN.   Let's take leave of him. 60
                                  Exit [with Antonio].

---

44. *warrant . . . drowning* guarantee him against drowning 46. *unstanched* i.e. loose, of low reputation 47. *Lay her ahold* bring her (the
ship) close to the wind *Set . . . courses* i.e. Set the mainsail and foresail
again (in an effort to get the ship to clear the shore) 48. *Lay her off*
i.e. Bring her away from shore 50. *must . . . cold* i.e. must we die
without a drink 52. *case* plight 53. *merely* completely 54. *wide-
chopped* wide-jawed, i.e. big-mouthed 57. *glut* swallow

GONZALO. Now would I give a thousand furlongs of sea
for an acre of barren ground – long heath, brown furze,
anything. The wills above be done, but I would fain die
a dry death. *Exit.*

Scene 2

Enter Prospero and Miranda.

MIRANDA. If by your art, my dearest father, you have
Put the wild waters in this roar, allay them.
The sky, it seems, would pour down stinking pitch,
But that the sea, mounting to th' welkin's cheek,
Dashes the fire out. O, I have sufferèd   5
With those that I saw suffer: a brave vessel
(Who had no doubt some noble creature in her)
Dashed all to pieces. O, the cry did knock
Against my very heart! Poor souls, they perished!
Had I been any god of power, I would   10
Have sunk the sea within the earth or ere
It should the good ship so have swallowed, and
The fraughting souls within her.
PROSPERO.   Be collected.
No more amazement. Tell your piteous heart
There's no harm done.
MIRANDA.   O, woe the day!
PROSPERO.   No harm. 15
I have done nothing but in care of thee,
Of thee my dear one, thee my daughter, who

61. *furlongs* (a furlong is a unit of distance equal to 220 yards) 62. *long . . . furze* (probably heather and gorse, which normally grow on waste land)
1.2.1. *art* i.e. magic art 3. *pitch* (dark substance obtained from boiling tar. The idea here is that the dark sky seems to be boiling) 4-5. *the sea . . . out* i.e. the heavy sea, mounting to the face (cheek) of the sky (welkin), extinguishes its fire. (The idea of the sea and sky meeting is a common one) 6. *brave* gallant, fine 11. *or ere* before 13. *fraughting souls* i.e. people who form the freight, or cargo (possibly suggesting also "souls fraught with care") *collected* calm, composed 14. *amazement* worrying *piteous* pitying 16. *in care of* in concern for

Art ignorant of what thou art, naught knowing
Of whence I am; nor that I am more better
Than Prospero, master of a full poor cell,   20
And thy no greater father.

MIRANDA.   More to know
Did never meddle with my thoughts.

PROSPERO.   'Tis time
I should inform thee farther. Lend thy hand
And pluck my magic garment from me. So,
Lie there, my art. Wipe thou thine eyes; have comfort. 25
The direful spectacle of the wrack, which touched
The very virtue of compassion in thee,
I have with such provision in mine art
So safely orderèd, that there is no soul –
No, not so much perdition as an hair   30
Betid to any creature in the vessel
Which thou heard'st cry, which thou saw'st sink. Sit
   down;
For thou must now know farther.

MIRANDA.   You have often
Begun to tell me what I am, but stopped
And left me to a bootless inquisition,   35
Concluding, "Stay: not yet."

PROSPERO.   The hour's now come;
The very minute bids thee ope thine ear.
Obey, and be attentive. Canst thou remember
A time before we came unto this cell?
I do not think thou canst, for then thou wast not   40
Out three years old.

MIRANDA.   Certainly, sir, I can.

PROSPERO. By what? By any other house or person?
Of any thing the image tell me, that

19. *more better* (a double form of comparison common in Shakespeare's day) 20. *full* very 21. *thy . . . father* i.e. your father who is no greater than the master of a very poor cell 22. *meddle with* enter, mingle with 25. *Lie . . . art* (Prospero is laying down his robe, which is the symbol of his magic powers) 26. *wrack* wreck 27. *virtue* essence 28. *provision* foresight 29. *no soul* no one (hurt) 30. *perdition* loss 31. *Betid* happened 35. *bootless inquisition* fruitless inquiry 38. *Obey* listen 41. *Out* fully

Hath kept with thy remembrance.

MIRANDA.   'Tis far off,
And rather like a dream than an assurance   45
That my remembrance warrants. Had I not
Four or five women once that tended me?

PROSPERO. Thou hadst, and more, Miranda. But how is it
That this lives in thy mind? What seest thou else
In the dark backward and abysm of time?   50
If thou rememb'rest aught ere thou cam'st here,
How thou cam'st here thou mayst.

MIRANDA.   But that I do not.

PROSPERO. Twelve year since, Miranda, twelve year since,
Thy father was the Duke of Milan and
A prince of power.

MIRANDA.   Sir, are not you my father?   55

PROSPERO. Thy mother was a piece of virtue, and
She said thou wast my daughter; and thy father
Was Duke of Milan; and his only heir
A princess, no worse issuèd.

MIRANDA.   O the heavens!
What foul play had we that we came from thence?   60
Or blessèd was't we did?

PROSPERO.   Both, both, my girl:
By foul play, as thou say'st, were we heaved thence,
But blessedly holp hither.

MIRANDA.   O, my heart bleeds
To think o' th' teen that I have turned you to,
Which is from my remembrance! Please you, farther. 65

PROSPERO. My brother and thy uncle, called Antonio –   ⁑
I pray thee mark me – that a brother should
Be so perfidious! – he whom next thyself

43-4. *tell . . . remembrance* describe for me what has remained in your memory 45-6. *rather . . . warrants* i.e. more like a dream than an actual recollection that my memory guarantees 50. *backward . . . time* i.e. past and abyss of time 52. *thou mayst* i.e. you may (remember) 56. *piece* masterpiece 59. *no worse issuèd* i.e. of no worse parentage than that just described 63. *holp* helped 64. *teen . . . you to* sorrow that I have caused you to remember 65. *from my remembrance* passed out of my memory *Please you, farther* If it please you, continue

Of all the world I loved, and to him put
The manage of my state, as at that time   70
Through all the signories it was the first,
And Prospero the prime duke, being so reputed
In dignity, and for the liberal arts
Without a parallel; those being all my study,
The government I cast upon my brother,   75
And to my state grew stranger, being transported
And rapt in secret studies. Thy false uncle –
Dost thou attend me?

MIRANDA.   Sir, most heedfully.

PROSPERO. Being once perfected how to grant suits,
How to deny them; who t' advance, and who   80
To trash for over-topping; new created
The creatures that were mine, I say, or changed 'em,
Or else new-formed 'em; having both the key
Of officer and office, set all hearts i' th' state
To what tune pleased his ear, that now he was   85
The ivy which had hid my princely trunk
And sucked my verdure out on't. Thou attend'st not?

MIRANDA. O, good sir, I do.

PROSPERO.   I pray thee mark me.
I thus neglecting worldly ends, all dedicated
To closeness, and the bettering of my mind   90
With that which, but by being so retired,
O'er-prized all popular rate, in my false brother

69-70. *put/ The manage* entrusted the management   71. *signories* dukedoms (of Italy)   72. *prime* first, foremost   73. *the liberal arts* i.e.
scholarship and learning generally   74. *study* occupation, interest   76.
to . . . stranger i.e. withdrew from affairs of state   *transported* carried
away (i.e. by my studies)   79. *Being once perfected* i.e. having once been
skilful in   81. *trash for over-topping* check for over-reaching themselves
81-2. *new created . . . mine* i.e. made my former supporters transfer their
allegiance to him   *creatures* dependents   83-4. *having . . . office* i.e.
having control of both officers and their offices (just as a musician can
"key" his instrument and make it obey him)   85. *what* whatever   *that*
so that   86-7. *The ivy . . . out on't* i.e. Antonio was like the parasitic ivy
which hid the trunk of the tree (Prospero) and sucked the sap out of it
89. *ends* objectives   89-90. *dedicated/ To closeness* devoted to privacy
91. *but . . . retired* but for the fact that it kept me so secluded   92. *O'er-
priz'd . . . rate* outvalued all ordinary estimation

Awaked an evil nature, and my trust,
Like a good parent, did beget of him
A falsehood in its contrary as great   95
As my trust was, which had indeed no limit,
A confidence sans bound. He being thus lorded,
Not only with what my revénue yielded
But what my power might else exact, like one
Who having into truth, by telling of it,   100
Made such a sinner of his memory
To credit his own lie, he did believe
He was indeed the Duke, out o' th' substitution,
And executing th' outward face of royalty
With all prerogative. Hence his ambition growing –   105
Dost thou hear?

MIRANDA.   Your tale, sir, would cure deafness.

PROSPERO. To have no screen between this part he played
And him he played it for, he needs will be
Absolute Milan. Me (poor man) my library
Was dukedom large enough. Of temporal royalties   110
He thinks me now incapable; confederates
(So dry he was for sway) with th' King of Naples
To give him annual tribute, do him homage,
Subject his coronet to his crown, and bend
The dukedom, yet unbowed (alas, poor Milan!)   115
To most ignoble stooping.

MIRANDA.   O the heavens!

94-6. *Like . . . limit* (alludes to the proverb "A father above the common
rate has commonly a son below it." See also l. 120)   97. *sans bound*
without limit   *lorded* i.e. made lord of the dukedom   98. *with* by means
of   99. *But . . . exact* i.e. but with what my power might exact in
addition to the normal revenues   99-102. *like . . . lie* i.e. like one who
tells a lie so often that he makes his memory false and actually believes
the lie that he tells   100. *it* i.e. his own lie   102. *To credit* so as to
believe   103-5. *out . . . prerogative* i.e. as a result of his acting as my
substitute and wielding – outwardly – my authority, with all my powers
Hence thus   107-8. *To have . . . it for* i.e. he (Antonio) was playing the
part of the Duke for me, but he wanted no screen (impediment) between
him and the real dukedom   *needs will be* feels that he must be   109.
Absolute Milan i.e. Duke of Milan in fact   *Me* as for me   110. *temporal
royalties* worldly duties of kingship   111. *confederates* makes a pact
with   112. *dry* thirsty, i.e. eager   114. *coronet* i.e. the dukedom of Milan
crown i.e. the kingdom of Naples   115. *unbowed* (Milan had not yet
been subject to any overlord)

PROSPERO. Mark his condition, and th' event; then tell me
    If this might be a brother.
MIRANDA.   I should sin
    To think but nobly of my grandmother:
    Good wombs have borne bad sons.
PROSPERO.   Now the condition. 120
    This King of Naples, being an enemy
    To me inveterate, hearkens my brother's suit;
    Which was, that he, in lieu o' th' premises
    Of homage and I know not how much tribute,
    Should presently extirpate me and mine   125
    Out of the dukedom, and confer fair Milan,
    With all the honours, on my brother: whereon,
    A treacherous army levied, one midnight
    Fated to th' purpose, did Antonio open
    The gates of Milan; and, i' th' dead of darkness,   130
    The ministers for th' purpose hurrièd thence
    Me and thy crying self.
MIRANDA.   Alack, for pity!
    I, not rememb'ring how I cried out then,
    Will cry it o'er again; it is a hint
    That wrings mine eyes to 't.
PROSPERO.   Hear a little further,   135
    And then I'll bring thee to the present business
    Which now's upon's; without the which this story
    Were most impertinent.
MIRANDA.   Wherefore did they not
    That hour destroy us?
PROSPERO.   Well demanded, wench:
    My tale provokes that question. Dear, they durst not, 140

117. *condition* i.e. the terms of his agreement (with the King of Naples)
event outcome (of the agreement) 118. *might be* could possibly be
119. *but* other than 122. *hearkens* listens to 123. *in lieu . . . premises* in
return for the guarantees 125. *presently* at once *extirpate* root out,
i.e. banish 127. *whereon* whereupon 128. *levied* raised 129. *Fated*
devoted (suggesting also that the Fates were against Prospero) 131.
ministers agents employed 134. *hint* occasion 135. *wrings . . . to't*
forces my eyes to weep 138. *impertinent* irrelevant 139. *demanded*
asked *wench* girl (often an affectionate term in Shakespeare's time)
140. *provokes* prompts

So dear the love my people bore me; nor set
A mark so bloody on the business; but
With colours fairer painted their foul ends.
In few, they hurried us aboard a bark,
Bore us some leagues to sea; where they prepared 145
A rotten carcass of a butt, not rigged,
Nor tackle, sail, nor mast; the very rats
Instinctively have quit it. There they hoist us,
To cry to th' sea that roared to us; to sigh
To th' winds, whose pity, sighing back again, 150
Did us but loving wrong.

MIRANDA.   Alack, what trouble
Was I then to you!

PROSPERO.   O, a cherubin
Thou wast that did preserve me. Thou didst smile,
Infusèd with a fortitude from heaven,
When I have decked the sea with drops full salt, 155
Under my burden groaned; which raised in me
An undergoing stomach, to bear up
Against what should ensue.

MIRANDA.   How came we ashore?

PROSPERO. By providence divine.
Some food we had, and some fresh water, that 160
A noble Neapolitan, Gonzalo,
Out of his charity, who being then appointed
Master of this design, did give us, with
Rich garments, linens, stuffs, and necessaries
Which since have steaded much. So, of his gentleness, 165

141-2. *nor set . . . business* i.e. they (the conspirators) did not dare to shed our blood over the business 142-3. *but . . . ends* i.e. but disguised their foul purposes with fair pretences 144. *In few* in a few words *bark* ship 146. *butt* tub, clumsy old boat 147-8. *rats . . . quit it* (it was a common belief that rats instinctively leave a doomed ship) *hoist us* hoisted us up, put us aboard 150-51. *whose pity . . . wrong* i.e. the winds wronged us by blowing us about, but they also showed their pity and love by sighing 152. *cherubin* little angel 154. *Infusèd* filled 155. *decked* sprinkled or adorned 156. *which* i.e. Miranda's smile 157. *undergoing stomach* courage to endure 158. *what should ensue* whatever should befall 162. *charity* generosity, Christian virtue *then* at that time 163. *Master . . . design* i.e. in charge of this plan (for putting Prospero and Miranda to sea) 165. *steaded much* been of great use *of his gentleness* out of the kindness of his heart

Knowing I loved my books, he furnished me
From mine own library with volumes that
I prize above my dukedom.
MIRANDA.   Would I might
But ever see that man!
PROSPERO.   Now I arise:
Sit still, and hear the last of our sea-sorrow.   170
Here in this island we arrived; and here
Have I, thy schoolmaster, made thee more profit
Than other princess can, that have more time
For vainer hours, and tutors not so careful.
MIRANDA. Heavens thank you for't! And now I pray you,
    sir –   175
For still 'tis beating in my mind – your reason
For raising this sea-storm?
PROSPERO.   Know thus far forth.
By accident most strange, bountiful Fortune
(Now my dear lady) hath mine enemies
Brought to this shore; and by my prescience   180 ⚑
I find my zenith doth depend upon
A most auspicious star, whose influence
If now I court not, but omit, my fortunes
Will ever after droop. Here cease more questions:
Thou art inclined to sleep: 'tis a good dulness,   185
And give it way. I know thou canst not choose.
                              [*Miranda sleeps.*]
Come away, servant, come! I am ready now.
Approach, my Ariel: come!

Enter Ariel.

169. *But ever* only *Now I arise* (he probably rises to his feet at this
point, but his words may also indicate that his fortunes are improving)
172-3. *made thee . . . can* i.e. given you a better education than other
princesses get 174. *vainer hours* less serious pursuits *careful* full of
care 176. *'tis . . . mind* i.e. the thought is constantly throbbing in my
mind 179. *(Now . . . lady)* (i.e. Fortune, who has brought his enemies
to the shore of the island) 180. *prescience* foreknowledge 181. *my
zenith* the high point of my fortunes 182. *influence* i.e. the influence of
the stars upon which man's fortunes depended 183. *court not* do not
take advantage of it *omit* neglect or ignore 185. *'tis . . . dulness* i.e.
your drowsiness is a good thing 186. *give it way* give way to it *choose*
help it 187. *Come away* (i.e. from where you are now)

ARIEL. All hail, great master! grave sir, hail! I come
 To answer thy best pleasure; be't to fly,   190
 To swim, to dive into the fire, to ride
 On the curled clouds: to thy strong bidding task
 Ariel and all his quality.
PROSPERO.   Hast thou, spirit,
 Performed to point the tempest that I bade thee?
ARIEL. To every article.   195
 I boarded the King's ship: now on the beak,
 Now in the waist, the deck, in every cabin,
 I flamed amazement: sometime I'ld divide
 And burn in many places; on the topmast,
 The yards, and boresprit would I flame distinctly,   200
 Then meet and join. Jove's lightnings, the precursors
 O' th' dreadful thunderclaps, more momentary
 And sight-outrunning were not: the fire and cracks
 Of sulphurous roaring the most mighty Neptune
 Seem to besiege, and make his bold waves tremble;   205
 Yea, his dread trident shake.
PROSPERO.   My brave spirit!
 Who was so firm, so constant, that this coil
 Would not infect his reason?
ARIEL.   Not a soul
 But felt a fever of the mad, and played
 Some tricks of desperation. All but mariners   210
 Plunged in the foaming brine, and quit the vessel,

189. *grave* reverend, dignified 190. *To answer . . . pleasure* to do whatever shall please you best 192. *task* tax, put to the test 193. *quality* i.e. probably Ariel's followers (the other spirits), but possibly Ariel's abilities — or a combination of both 194. *to point* down to the last detail 195. *article* detail, item 196. *beak* prow 197. *waist* middle (between the quarter-deck and forecastle) 198. *flamed amazement* i.e. struck terror by appearing as flames 200. *yards* (spar which juts out from a mast and supports a sail) *boresprit* bowsprit (large boom or spar which projects from the stem of a ship to help carry a sail) *flame distinctly* i.e. show myself as a flame (in several places at once) 202-3. *more momentary . . . not* were not more brief and quick to the sight *cracks* thunderous sounds 204. *Neptune* i.e. god of the sea 206. *trident* three-pronged spear *brave* fine 207. *constant* full of self-control *coil* turmoil 209. *a fever . . . mad* i.e. such a fever (fit) as madmen have 209-10. *played . . . desperation* i.e. did some strange things out of their desperation *All but mariners* i.e. all but the mariners

Then all afire with me: the King's son Ferdinand,
With hair up-staring (then like reeds, not hair),
Was the first man that leapt; cried "Hell is empty,
And all the devils are here!"
PROSPERO.   Why, that's my spirit!   215
But was not this nigh shore?
ARIEL.   Close by, my master.
PROSPERO. But are they, Ariel, safe?
ARIEL.   Not a hair perished.
On their sustaining garments not a blemish,
But fresher than before; and as thou bad'st me,
In troops I have dispersed them 'bout the isle.   220
The King's son have I landed by himself,
Whom I left cooling of the air with sighs
In an odd angle of the isle, and sitting,
His arms in this sad knot.
PROSPERO.   Of the King's ship,
The mariners say how thou hast disposed,   225
And all the rest o' th' fleet.
ARIEL.   Safely in harbour
Is the King's ship; in the deep nook, where once
Thou call'dst me up at midnight to fetch dew
From the still-vexed Bermoothes, there she's hid;
The mariners all under hatches stowed,   230
Who, with a charm joined to their suff'red labour,
I have left asleep: and for the rest o' th' fleet,
Which I dispersed, they all have met again,
And are upon the Mediterranean flote
Bound sadly home for Naples,   235
Supposing that they saw the King's ship wracked,
And his great person perish.

212. *all . . . with me* i.e. the vessel was all afire just as Ariel was   213.
up-staring standing on end   215. *that's my spirit* i.e. that's my fine spirit
220. *troops* groups   223. *odd angle of* out-of-the-way place on   224.
arms . . . knot folded sadly – like this (Ariel presumably folds his own
arms to illustrate this)   229. *still-vexed Bermoothes* perpetually storm-
ridden Bermuda Islands (which were associated with storms and en-
chantments)   230. *under hatches* below   231. *their suff'red labour* i.e.
the labour (or trouble) that they have undergone   234. *flote* there is a
sense, here, of (i) sea, (ii) afloat, (iii) rising and falling on the waves

PROSPERO.   Ariel, thy charge
   Exactly is performed; but there's more work.
   What is the time o' th' day?
ARIEL.   Past the mid season.
PROSPERO. At least two glasses. The time 'twixt six and
   now   240
   Must by us both be spent most preciously.
ARIEL. Is there more toil? Since thou dost give me pains,
   Let me remember thee what thou hast promised,
   Which is not yet performed me.
PROSPERO.   How now? moody?
   What is't thou canst demand?
ARIEL.   My liberty.   245
PROSPERO. Before the time be out? No more!
ARIEL.   I prithee,
   Remember I have done thee worthy service,
   Told thee no lies, made thee no mistakings, served
   Without or grudge or grumblings. Thou did promise
   To bate me a full year.
PROSPERO.   Dost thou forget   250
   From what a torment I did free thee?
ARIEL.   No.
PROSPERO. Thou dost; and think'st it much to tread the
   ooze
   Of the salt deep,
   To run upon the sharp wind of the North,
   To do me business in the veins o' th' earth   255
   When it is baked with frost.
ARIEL.   I do not, sir.

237. *charge* duty 239. *the mid season* noon 240. *At . . . glasses* i.e. At least two hours (as measured by an hour glass in which the sand took one hour to run its course. In the seventeenth century, however, the half-hour glass was becoming more common) 241. *most preciously* as if it were very precious 242. *pains* labours 243. *remember* remind 244. *is not . . . me* i.e. you have not yet given me 246. *time be out* i.e. period of service be finished 249. *or . . . or* either . . . or 250. *bate me* shorten my term of service 252. *ooze* slimy depths 255. *veins* subterranean streams 256. *baked* crusted, hardened

PROSPERO. Thou liest, malignant thing! Hast thou forgot
   The foul witch Sycorax, who with age and envy
   Was grown into a hoop? hast thou forgot her?
ARIEL. No, sir.
PROSPERO.   Thou hast. Where was she born? speak;
   tell me.   260
ARIEL. Sir, in Argier.
PROSPERO.   O, was she so? I must
   Once in a month recount what thou hast been,
   Which thou forget'st. This damned witch Sycorax,
   For mischiefs manifold, and sorceries terrible
   To enter human hearing, from Argier,   265
   Thou know'st, was banished: for one thing she did
   They would not take her life. Is not this true?
ARIEL. Ay, sir.
PROSPERO. This blue-eyed hag was hither brought with
   child,
   And here was left by th' sailors. Thou, my slave,   270
   As thou report'st thyself, wast then her servant;
   And, for thou wast a spirit too delicate
   To act her earthly and abhorred commands,
   Refusing her grand hests, she did confine thee,
   By help of her more potent ministers,   275
   And in her most unmitigable rage,
   Into a cloven pine; within which rift
   Imprisoned, thou didst painfully remain
   A dozen years; within which space she died

258. *Sycorax* (a name of doubtful origin, perhaps derived from the Greek "sys", meaning sow, and "korax", meaning both raven and curved) *envy* malignity, viciousness 261. *Argier* Algiers 266-7. *for one ... life* (possibly because of some good deed not mentioned here, but probably because she was pregnant) 269. *blue-eyed hag* (Sycorax may have had blue eyes, but blueness around the eyes was often regarded as a sign of pregnancy, debauchery, or of general exhaustion) *with child* pregnant 272. *for* because 272-3. *too delicate ... commands* i.e. Ariel was a spirit of the air and was too delicate (pure) to perform the earthy, unclean, and horrid commands of Sycorax 274. *grand hests* important commands 275. *her ... ministers* i.e. her agents or spirits who were more powerful than you 279. *space* period (of time)

And left thee there, where thou didst vent thy groans 280
As fast as millwheels strike. Then was this island
(Save for the son that she did litter here,
A freckled whelp, hag-born) not honoured with
A human shape.

ARIEL.   Yes, Caliban her son.

PROSPERO. Dull thing, I say so: he, that Caliban 285
Whom now I keep in service. Thou best know'st
What torment I did find thee in; thy groans
Did make wolves howl and penetrate the breasts
Of ever-angry bears. It was a torment
To lay upon the damned, which Sycorax 290
Could not again undo. It was mine art,
When I arrived and heard thee, that made gape
The pine, and let thee out.

ARIEL.   I thank thee, master.

PROSPERO. If thou more murmur'st, I will rend an oak
And peg thee in his knotty entrails till 295
Thou hast howled away twelve winters.

ARIEL.   Pardon, master.
I will be correspondent to command
And do my spriting gently.

PROSPERO.   Do so; and after two days
I will discharge thee.

ARIEL.   That's my noble master!
What shall I do? say what? what shall I do? 300

PROSPERO. Go make thyself like a nymph o' th' sea: be
subject
To no sight but thine and mine; invisible
To every eyeball else. Go take this shape
And hither come in't. Go! Hence with diligence!

                               Exit [Ariel].

280. *vent* utter   281. *millwheels strike* (the clappers on millwheels strike against a grain hopper and shake the grain down on to the grinding surfaces)   283. *whelp* young pup   *hag-born* born of a hag (witch)   286. *in service* as a servant   291. *Could . . . undo* (because she was dead) 295. *his* its   297. *correspondent* obedient   298. *do . . . gently* perform my duties as a spirit uncomplainingly

Awake, dear heart, awake! thou hast slept well;   305
Awake!
MIRANDA. The strangeness of your story put
    Heaviness in me.
PROSPERO.   Shake it off. Come on;
    We'll visit Caliban, my slave, who never
    Yields us kind answer.
MIRANDA.   'Tis a villain, sir,
    I do not love to look on.
PROSPERO.   But as 'tis,   310
    We cannot miss him: he does make our fire,
    Fetch in our wood, and serves in offices
    That profit us. What, ho! slave! Caliban!
    Thou earth, thou! speak!
CALIBAN (within).   There's wood enough within.
PROSPERO. Come forth, I say! There's other business for
    thee.   315
    Come, thou tortoise! when?

Enter Ariel like a water nymph.

Fine apparition! My quaint Ariel,
Hark in thine ear.
ARIEL.   My lord, it shall be done.   *Exit.*
PROSPERO. Thou poisonous slave, got by the devil himself
    Upon thy wicked dam, come forth!   320

Enter Caliban.

CALIBAN. As wicked dew as e'er my mother brushed
    With raven's feather from unwholesome fen
    Drop on you both! A south-west blow on ye
    And blister you all o'er!

307. *Heaviness* drowsiness   311. *miss* do without   314. *Thou earth* i.e.
you thing of earth   316. *when* i.e. when are you coming (an exclamation
of impatience)   317. *quaint* (this word had several related meanings,
e.g. ingenious, dainty, elegant, skilful)   318. *Hark . . . ear* (whispering
further orders in Ariel's ear)   319. *got* begotten   320. *wicked* poisonous,
foul   322. *fen* bog, swamp   323. *south-west* south-west wind (thought
to be foggy and unwholesome)

PROSPERO. For this, be sure, to-night thou shalt have
    cramps,   325
  Side-stitches that shall pen thy breath up; urchins
  Shall, for that vast of night that they may work
  All exercise on thee; thou shalt be pinched
  As thick as honeycomb, each pinch more stinging
  Than bees that made 'em.
CALIBAN.   I must eat my dinner.   330
  This island's mine by Sycorax my mother,
  Which thou tak'st from me. When thou cam'st first,
  Thou strok'st me and made much of me; wouldst give
    me
  Water with berries in't; and teach me how
  To name the bigger light, and how the less,   335
  That burn by day and night; and then I loved thee
  And showed thee all the qualities o' th' isle,
  The fresh springs, brine-pits, barren place and fertile.
  Cursed be I that did so! All the charms
  Of Sycorax – toads, beetles, bats, light on you!   340
  For I am all the subjects that you have,
  Which first was mine own king; and here you sty me
  In this hard rock, whiles you do keep from me
  The rest o' th' island.
PROSPERO.   Thou most lying slave,
  Whom stripes may move, not kindness! I have used thee 345
  (Filth as thou art) with humane care, and lodged thee
  In mine own cell, till thou didst seek to violate
  The honour of my child.
CALIBAN. O ho, O ho! would't had been done!
  Thou didst prevent me; I had peopled else   350
  This isle with Calibans.
MIRANDA.   Abhorrèd slave,

326. *pen . . . up* i.e. make it difficult for you to breathe *urchins* i.e.
goblins or imps in the shapes of hedgehogs 327. *vast* endless expanse
that . . . work (it was believed that evil spirits had power only during
darkness) 328. *exercise on* practise on, torment 330. *'em* them; i.e. the
cells of the honeycomb 335. *the bigger . . . the less* i.e. the sun and the
moon 337. *qualities* natural resources 340. *toads, beetles, bats* (the
evil spirits who served witches were supposed to take these forms) 342.
Which first who at first *sty me* i.e. imprison me like a pig 345. *stripes*
lashes 350. *I had . . . else* otherwise I would have populated

Which any print of goodness wilt not take,
Being capable of all ill! I pitied thee,
Took pains to make thee speak, taught thee each hour   355
One thing or other: when thou didst not, savage,
Know thine own meaning, but wouldst gabble like
A thing most brutish, I endowed thy purposes
With words that made them known. But thy vile race,
Though thou didst learn, had that in't which good
   natures
Could not abide to be with; therefore wast thou   360
Deservedly confined into this rock, who hadst
Deserved more than a prison.
CALIBAN. You taught me language, and my profit on't
  Is, I know how to curse. The red plague rid you
  For learning me your language!
PROSPERO.   Hag-seed, hence!   365
  Fetch us in fuel; and be quick, thou'rt best,
  To answer other business. Shrug'st thou, malice?
  If thou neglect'st or dost unwillingly
  What I command, I'll rack thee with old cramps,
  Fill all thy bones with aches, make thee roar,   370
  That beasts shall tremble at thy din.
CALIBAN.   No, pray thee.
  [*Aside*] I must obey. His art is of such pow'r,
  It would control my dam's god, Setebos,
  And make a vassal of him.
PROSPERO.   So, slave; hence!   *Exit Caliban.*

Enter Ferdinand; and Ariel (invisible),
playing and singing.

352. *Which . . . take* (i.e. Caliban is incapable of retaining the goodness
which Prospero has tried to teach him) 355-8. *when thou . . . known*
i.e. when you were incapable of expressing yourself, but gabbled like a
brute, I taught you to use language by which you could communicate
your intentions *race* species, nature 359. *good natures* natural virtues,
or people who are naturally good 364. *red plague* bubonic plague *rid
you* get rid of you; i.e. destroy you 365. *learning* teaching *Hag-seed*
offspring of a witch 366-7. *thou'rt . . . answer* i.e. you'd better attend
to *malice* malicious creature 369. *old cramps* (i.e. cramps such as old
people suffer) 370. *aches* (pronounced "aitches") 371. *that* so that
373. *Setebos* (a god of the Patagonian Indians, known to the Elizabethans
through the reports of voyagers)

264   THE TEMPEST 1.2

[ARIEL (*sings*).]	Come unto these yellow sands,	375

[ARIEL (*sings*).] Come unto these yellow sands, 375
      And then take hands:
     Curtsied when you have and kissed,
      The wild waves whist:
     Foot it featly here and there;
     And, sweet sprites, the burden bear. 380
      Hark, hark!
BURDEN (*dispersedly*). Bowgh, wawgh!
[ARIEL.] The watchdogs bark.
BURDEN (*dispersedly*). Bowgh, wawgh!
[ARIEL.]   Hark, hark! I hear 385
     The strain of strutting chanticleer
      Cry, cock-a-diddle-dowe.
FERDINAND. Where should this music be? I' th' air or th'
 earth?
It sounds no more; and sure it waits upon
Some god o' th' island. Sitting on a bank, 390
Weeping again the King my father's wrack,
This music crept by me upon the waters,
Allaying both their fury and my passion
With its sweet air. Thence I have followed it,
Or it hath drawn me rather; but 'tis gone. 395
No, it begins again.
[ARIEL (*sings*).] Full fathom five thy father lies;
      Of his bones are coral made;
     Those are pearls that were his eyes;
      Nothing of him that doth fade, 400
     But doth suffer a sea-change
     Into something rich and strange.
     Sea nymphs hourly ring his knell:
BURDEN.   Ding-dong.
[ARIEL.] Hark! now I hear them – Ding-dong
     bell. 405

377. *Curtsied . . . kissed* i.e. when you have curtsied to your partners and kissed them (some dances began with a formal kiss) 378. *whist* being hushed 379. *featly* nimbly, daintily 380. *burden* refrain 382 s.d. *dispersedly* (i.e. the sound of the refrain comes from different directions) 389. *waits upon* is at the service of 393. *passion* deep sorrow, passionate lamentation 394. *thence* i.e. from the water's edge 399. *pearls* i.e. pearls are now where his eyes were 400-1. *Nothing . . . sea-change* i.e. no part of him has faded or rotted, but has been transformed

FERDINAND. The ditty does remember my drowned
    father.
  This is no mortal business, nor no sound
  That the earth owes. I hear it now above me.
PROSPERO. The fringèd curtains of thine eye advance,
  And say what thou seest yond.
MIRANDA.   What is't? a spirit?   410
  Lord, how it looks about! Believe me, sir,
  It carries a brave form. But 'tis a spirit.
PROSPERO. No, wench: it eats, and sleeps, and hath such
    senses
  As we have, such. This gallant which thou seest
  Was in the wrack; and, but he's something stained   415
  With grief (that's beauty's canker), thou mightst call
    him
  A goodly person: he hath lost his fellows
  And strays about to find 'em.
MIRANDA.   I might call him
  A thing divine; for nothing natural
  I ever saw so noble.
PROSPERO [aside].   It goes on, I see,   420
  As my soul prompts it. Spirit, fine spirit, I'll free thee
  Within two days for this.
FERDINAND [seeing Miranda]. Most sure, the goddess
  On whom these airs attend! Vouchsafe my prayer
  May know if you remain upon this island,
  And that you will some good instruction give   425
  How I may bear me here. My prime request,
  Which I do last pronounce, is (O you wonder!)
  If you be maid or no?

406. *remember* (i) commemorate, or (ii) remind me of 408. *owes*
possesses 409. *fringèd curtains* i.e. eyelashes *advance* raise 415. *but*
except that *stained* marred, disfigured 416. *beauty's canker* (probably
a reference to the canker caused by the caterpillar which eats out the
heart of the rose. Ferdinand's beauty has been somewhat eaten away by
grief) 417. *goodly* fine-looking 419. *natural* (as opposed to spiritual)
420. *It goes on* i.e. (i) Miranda's love develops, or perhaps (ii) my spell
is working 421. *prompts* desires, would wish 422. *most sure* most
certainly this is 422-3. *the goddess . . . attend* (see 11. 390-91 above)
424. *remain* dwell 426. *bear me* conduct myself *prime* most important
428. *maid or no* (Ferdinand is asking whether Miranda is (i) mortal
maiden or goddess, with the secondary implication, which would undoubtedly occur to many members of an audience, of (ii) virgin or not)

MIRANDA.   No wonder, sir,
But certainly a maid.
FERDINAND.   My language? Heavens!
I am the best of them that speak this speech,   430
Were I but where 'tis spoken.
PROSPERO.   How? the best?
What wert thou if the King of Naples heard thee?
FERDINAND. A single thing, as I am now, that wonders
To hear thee speak of Naples. He does hear me;
And that he does I weep. Myself am Naples,   435
Who with mine eyes, never since at ebb, beheld
The King my father wracked.
MIRANDA.   Alack, for mercy!
FERDINAND. Yes, faith, and all his lords, the Duke of
Milan
And his brave son being twain.
PROSPERO [aside].   The Duke of Milan
And his more braver daughter could control thee,   440
If now 'twere fit to do't. At the first sight
They have changed eyes. Delicate Ariel,
I'll set thee free for this. — A word, good sir.
I fear you have done yourself some wrong: a word.
MIRANDA [aside]. Why speaks my father so ungently? This 445
Is the third man that e'er I saw; the first
That e'er I sighed for: pity move my father
To be inclined my way!
FERDINAND.   O, if a virgin,

430. *best* the highest rank (Ferdinand is now the "best" because he thinks
that he has succeeded his father who is "dead") *speech* language 433.
single (i) solitary, (ii) helpless, and possibly (iii) sincere, (iv) single-
minded, or (v) weak 434. *He does . . . me* (because, thinking his father
drowned, he believes *himself* to be King of Naples) 435. *that* because
Naples King of Naples 436. *never . . . ebb* i.e. that have never since
stopped weeping 439. *his brave son* (the Duke of Milan's son is not
mentioned elsewhere in the play) *brave* gallant 440. *control* contradict, refute 441. *'twere fit* i.e. it were a suitable time 442. *changed
eyes* exchanged looks of love, i.e. fallen in love 444. *done . . . wrong*
(polite way of saying that you have told a lie) 446. *third man* (presumably the other two are Prospero and Caliban, although later on
[3.1.50-51] she tells Ferdinand that her father is the only other man she
has seen) 447. *pity* may pity 448. *To be . . . way* to sympathize with
me, to think as I do

And your affection not gone forth, I'll make you
The Queen of Naples.
PROSPERO.   Soft, sir! one word more.   450
  [*Aside*] They are both in either's pow'rs. But this
      swift business
  I must uneasy make, lest too light winning
  Make the prize light. – One word more! I charge thee
  That thou attend me. Thou dost here usurp
  The name thou ow'st not, and hast put thyself   455
  Upon this island as a spy, to win it
  From me, the lord on't.
FERDINAND.   No, as I am a man.
MIRANDA. There's nothing ill can dwell in such a temple:
  If the ill spirit have so fair a house,
  Good things will strive to dwell with't.
PROSPERO.   Follow me. –   460
  Speak not you for him; he's a traitor. – Come;
  I'll manacle thy neck and feet together;
  Sea water shalt thou drink; thy food shall be
  The fresh-brook mussels, withered roots, and husks
  Wherein the acorn cradled. Follow.
FERDINAND.   No;   465
  I will resist such entertainment till
  Mine enemy has more power.
                    He draws, and is charmed from moving.
MIRANDA.   O dear father,
  Make not too rash a trial of him, for
  He's gentle, and not fearful.
PROSPERO.   What, I say,
  My foot my tutor? – Put thy sword up, traitor!   470

449. *gone forth* i.e. given to another 450. *Soft* not so fast 451. *either's* each other's 452. *uneasy* not easy, i.e. difficult 452-3. *lest . . . prize light* i.e. lest too easy winning make the prize (Miranda) slightly valued (with a pun on the idea that light [i.e. loose] women are easily won) 455. *ow'st* ownest 460. *Good things . . . with't* i.e. good things will strive to dwell in such a temple (as Ferdinand) 466. *entertainment* treatment 468. *Make . . . him* i.e. (i) do not judge him too hastily, or, possibly (ii) do not be too hasty in putting him to the test 469. *gentle . . . fearful* of noble birth and not cowardly 470. *My . . . tutor* i.e. Shall an inferior tell me what to do

Who mak'st a show, but dar'st not strike, thy
    conscience
Is so possessed with guilt. Come, from thy ward!
For I can here disarm thee with this stick
And make thy weapon drop.

MIRANDA.   Beseech you, father!

PROSPERO. Hence! hang not on my garments.

MIRANDA.   Sir, have pity;   475
I'll be his surety.

PROSPERO.   Silence! one word more
Shall make me chide thee, if not hate thee. What!
An advocate for an impostor? Hush!
Thou think'st there is no more such shapes as he,
Having seen but him and Caliban. Foolish wench!   480
To th' most of men this is a Caliban,
And they to him are angels.

MIRANDA.   My affections
Are then most humble: I have no ambition
To see a goodlier man.

PROSPERO.   Come on; obey:
Thy nerves are in their infancy again   485
And have no vigour in them.

FERDINAND.   So they are:
My spirits, as in a dream, are all bound up.
My father's loss, the weakness which I feel,
The wrack of all my friends, nor this man's threats,
To whom I am subdued, are but light to me,   490
Might I but through my prison once a day
Behold this maid. All corners else o' th' earth
Let liberty make use of; space enough
Have I in such a prison.

PROSPERO [aside].   It works.
         [To Ferdinand] Come on.
Thou has done well, fine Ariel! [To Ferdinand] Follow
    me.   495

472. *Come . . . ward* Drop your guard   473. *stick* i.e. wand, staff   474.
Beseech you I beseech you   476. *surety* guarantee   481. *To th' most of*
compared to most   482. *affections* tastes, inclinations   484. *goodlier*
more handsome and more worthy   485. *nerves* sinews   487. *spirits*
energies

[*To Ariel*] Hark what thou else shalt do me.
MIRANDA.   Be of comfort;
   My father's of a better nature, sir,
   Than he appears by speech: this is unwonted
   Which now came from him.
PROSPERO [*to Ariel*].   Thou shalt be as free
   As mountain winds; but then exactly do   500
   All points of my command.
ARIEL.   To th' syllable.
PROSPERO [*to Ferdinand*]. Come, follow. – [*To Miranda*]
   Speak not for him.   *Exeunt.*

496. *what . . . do me* i.e. what other service you will do for me   501. *To the syllable* To the last detail

ACT 2

Scene 1

Enter Alonso, Sebastian, Antonio, Gonzalo,
Adrian, Francisco, and others.

GONZALO. Beseech you, sir, be merry; you have cause
    (So have we all) of joy; for our escape
    Is much beyond our loss. Our hint of woe
    Is common: every day some sailor's wife,
    The master of some merchant, and the merchant,   5
    Have just our theme of woe; but for the miracle,
    I mean our preservation, few in millions
    Can speak like us. Then wisely, good sir, weigh
    Our sorrow with our comfort.
ALONSO.   Prithee peace.
SEBASTIAN. He receives comfort like cold porridge.   10
ANTONIO. The visitor will not give him o'er so.
SEBASTIAN. Look, he's winding up the watch of his wit;
    by and by it will strike.
GONZALO. Sir –
SEBASTIAN. One. Tell.   15
GONZALO. When every grief is entertained, that's offered
    Comes to th' entertainer –
SEBASTIAN. A dollar.

2.1.1. *Beseech you* I beseech you *be merry* be cheerful, cheer up 3.
hint of occasion for 5. *master . . . merchant* captain of some merchant
vessel *the merchant* (probably the owner of the merchant ship) 6. *for*
as for 8. *weigh* balance 9. *peace* (with a pun on "pease" [porridge].
The lines which follow are full of puns) 11. *visitor* spiritual adviser,
consoler (i.e. Gonzalo, compared here to a priest counselling one of his
flock) *give . . . so* give him up so easily 12-13. *he's winding . . . wit*
i.e. you can see his mind ticking 15. *One. Tell* i.e. The watch (of his
wit) has struck one. Count (and see how many more times it will strike)
16. *entertained* accepted as it comes *that's . . . entertainer* whatever
(grief) is offered comes to the recipient (of the grief) 18. *a dollar*
(Sebastian pretends to think of the entertainer as being a host or innkeeper who is paid a dollar for receiving grief as a guest)

GONZALO. Dolour comes to him, indeed: you have spoken
　　truer than you purposed.   20

SEBASTIAN. You have taken it wiselier than I meant you
　　should.

GONZALO. Therefore, my lord –

ANTONIO. Fie, what a spendthrift is he of his tongue!

ALONSO. I prithee spare.   25

GONZALO. Well, I have done: but yet –

SEBASTIAN. He will be talking.

ANTONIO. Which, of he or Adrian, for a good wager, first
　　begins to crow?

SEBASTIAN. The old cock.   30

ANTONIO. The cock'rel.

SEBASTIAN. Done! The wager?

ANTONIO. A laughter.

SEBASTIAN. A match!

ADRIAN. Though this island seem to be desert –   35

ANTONIO. Ha, ha, ha!

SEBASTIAN. So, you're paid.

ADRIAN. Uninhabitable and almost inaccessible –

SEBASTIAN. Yet –

ADRIAN. Yet –   40

ANTONIO. He could not miss't.

ADRIAN. It must needs be of subtle, tender, and delicate
　　temperance.

ANTONIO. Temperance was a delicate wench.

SEBASTIAN. Ay, and a subtle; as he most learnedly de-   45
　　livered.

---

19. *Dolour* grief (an obvious pun on "dollar") 21. *taken it wiselier*
understood my words better (Sebastian, apparently, had not expected
Gonzalo to catch even such an obvious pun) 24. *spend-thrift* (Antonio
is still labouring the pun on spending) 25. *spare* spare us your words,
i.e. keep quiet 28-9. *Which . . . crow* (Antonio wants to bet on whether
Gonzalo or Adrian will speak first) 30. *old cock* i.e. Gonzalo 31.
cock'rel i.e. Adrian 32. *Done* i.e. It's a bet 33. *A laughter* (the winner
is to have the laugh on the loser) 34. *A match* It's a deal 37. *you're
paid* i.e. you've had your laugh 41. *He . . . miss't* i.e. He could not
possibly have said anything else (both Sebastian and Antonio know, from
experience, Adrian's habits of speech) 42. *It . . . needs be* it is indeed
43. *temperance* temperature, climate 44. *Temperance* (a girl's name
common in Shakespeare's day) 45. *subtle* i.e. subtle wench 45-6.
delivered reported

ADRIAN. The air breathes upon us here most sweetly.

SEBASTIAN. As if it had lungs, and rotten ones.

ANTONIO. Or as 'twere perfumed by a fen.

GONZALO. Here is everything advantageous to life.   50

ANTONIO. True; save means to live.

SEBASTIAN. Of that there's none, or little.

GONZALO. How lush and lusty the grass looks! how green!

ANTONIO. The ground indeed is tawny.

SEBASTIAN. With an eye of green in't.   55

ANTONIO. He misses not much.

SEBASTIAN. No; he doth but mistake the truth totally.

GONZALO. But the rarity of it is – which is indeed almost
     beyond credit –

SEBASTIAN. As many vouched rarities are.   60

GONZALO. That our garments, being, as they were,
     drenched in the sea, hold, notwithstanding, their fresh-
     ness and glosses, being rather new-dyed than stained
     with salt water.

ANTONIO. If but one of his pockets could speak, would it   65
     not say he lies?

SEBASTIAN. Ay, or very falsely pocket up his report.

GONZALO. Methinks our garments are now as fresh as
     when we put them on first in Afric, at the marriage of
     the King's fair daughter Claribel to the King of Tunis. 70

SEBASTIAN. 'Twas a sweet marriage, and we prosper well
     in our return.

ADRIAN. Tunis was never graced before with such a para-
     gon to their queen.

GONZALO. Not since widow Dido's time.   75

ANTONIO. Widow? a pox o' that! How came that "widow"
     in? Widow Dido!

49. *fen* bog, swamp   53. *lush and lusty* luxuriant and vigorous   54.
tawny parched brown colour   55. *eye* touch, shade   58. *the . . . of it*
the strangest thing about it   59. *credit* belief   60. *vouched rarities* i.e.
strange tales whose truth is vouched for by their tellers   67. *pocket up*
receive without protest, suppress   73. *graced* honoured   73-4. *paragon
to* model of excellence for   75. *Dido* Queen of Carthage (see end note)
76. *a pox o'* a plague on   76-7. *How . . . "widow" in* i.e. How did that
widow get into the conversation

SEBASTIAN. What if he had said "widower Aeneas" too?
Good Lord, how you take it!

ADRIAN. "Widow Dido," said you? You make me study of 80
that: she was of Carthage, not of Tunis.

GONZALO. This Tunis, sir, was Carthage.

ADRIAN. Carthage?

GONZALO. I assure you, Carthage.

ANTONIO. His word is more than the miraculous harp.   85

SEBASTIAN. He hath raised the wall, and houses too.

ANTONIO. What impossible matter will he make easy next?

SEBASTIAN. I think he will carry this island home in his
pocket, and give it his son for an apple.

ANTONIO. And, sowing the kernels of it in the sea, bring 90
forth more islands.

GONZALO. Ay!

ANTONIO. Why, in good time.

GONZALO. Sir, we were talking that our garments seem now
as fresh as when we were at Tunis at the marriage of 95
your daughter, who is now Queen.

ANTONIO. And the rarest that e'er came there.

SEBASTIAN. Bate, I beseech you, widow Dido.

ANTONIO. O, widow Dido? ay, widow Dido.

GONZALO. Is not, sir, my doublet as fresh as the first day I 100
wore it? I mean, in a sort.

ANTONIO. That "sort" was well fished for.

79. *how you . . . it* what a fuss you are making (i.e. about Gonzalo's
calling Dido a widow)   80-81. *You make . . . that* you make me think
carefully of that   82. *Tunis . . . Carthage* (Gonzalo is wrong. Tunis was
near, but not on, the site of the ancient city of Carthage)   85. *the
miraculous harp* (Amphion, by playing on his miraculous harp, was said
to have raised the walls of Thebes. Antonio says that Gonzalo's word is
even more miraculous because it has rebuilt Carthage)   92. *Ay* (The
exact meaning is not easily explained. Gonzalo may simply be stressing,
after a pause, that Tunis was indeed Carthage)   93. *Why . . . time*
(perhaps an ironical rejoinder to Gonzalo: "That's an opportune remark", or perhaps simply a way of trying to close the matter: "All in
good time")   98. *Bate* with the exception of, less   100. *doublet* a tight-
fitting jacket, with or without sleeves, worn by men in Shakespeare's day
101. *in a sort* more or less, comparatively   102. *That . . . for* (Gonzalo's
qualification ["in a sort"] of his statement that his doublet is as fresh
as the first day that he wore it was a lucky catch in the sense that he
added it in time to make his statement more or less true)

GONZALO. When I wore it at your daughter's marriage.
ALONSO. You cram these words into mine ears against
    The stomach of my sense. Would I had never   105
    Married my daughter there! for, coming thence,
    My son is lost; and, in my rate, she too,
    Who is so far from Italy removed
    I ne'er again shall see her. O thou mine heir
    Of Naples and of Milan, what strange fish   110
    Hath made his meal on thee?
FRANCISCO.   Sir, he may live:
    I saw him beat the surges under him,
    And ride upon their backs; he trod the water,
    Whose enmity he flung aside, and breasted
    The surge most swol'n that met him; his bold head   115
    'Bove the contentious waves he kept, and oared
    Himself with his good arms in lusty stroke
    To th' shore, that o'er his wave-worn basis bowed,
    As stooping to relieve him. I not doubt
    He came alive to land.
ALONSO.   No, no, he's gone.   120
SEBASTIAN. Sir, you may thank yourself for this great loss,
    That would not bless our Europe with your daughter,
    But rather loose her to an African,
    Where she, at least, is banished from your eye,
    Who hath cause to wet the grief on't.
ALONSO.   Prithee peace.   125
SEBASTIAN. You were kneeled to and importuned other-
    wise
    By all of us; and the fair soul herself
    Weighed, between loathness and obedience, at   ‡
    Which end o' th' beam should bow. We have lost your
    son,

104-5. *You cram . . . sense* i.e. You force these words into my ears
although my mind has no inclination to hear them   107. *in my rate* (i)
in my opinion, (ii) so far as I am concerned   118. *his* its (referring to
shore)   *basis* base (in the sand)   119. *I not doubt* I do not doubt that
123. *loose her* let her go, mate her, prostitute her   125. *wet . . . on't*
weep over the grief resulting from her loss   126. *importuned otherwise*
persistently begged to act in a different manner   128. *Weighed* balanced
loathness reluctance   129. *th' beam . . . bow* the horizontal bar of the
balance should incline

I fear, for ever. Milan and Naples have   130
Moe widows in them of this business' making
Than we bring men to comfort them:
The fault's your own.
ALONSO.   So is the dear'st o' th' loss.
GONZALO. My Lord Sebastian,
The truth you speak doth lack some gentleness,   135
And time to speak it in: You rub the sore
When you should bring the plaster.
SEBASTIAN.   Very well.
ANTONIO. And most chirurgeonly.
GONZALO. It is foul weather in us all, good sir,
When you are cloudy.
SEBASTIAN.   Foul weather?
ANTONIO.   Very foul.   140
GONZALO. Had I plantation of this isle, my lord –
ANTONIO. He'd sow't with nettle seed.
SEBASTIAN.   Or docks, or mallows.
GONZALO. And were the king on't, what would I do?
SEBASTIAN. 'Scape being drunk for want of wine.
GONZALO. I' th' commonwealth I would by contraries   145
Execute all things; for no kind of traffic
Would I admit; no name of magistrate;
Letters should not be known; riches, poverty,
And use of service, none; contract, succession,
Bourn, bound of land, tilth, vineyard, none;   150

131. *Moe* more (an old word for "more in number") 131-2. *in them
. . . comfort them* i.e. in Milan and Naples as a result of this expedition,
than the number of men we shall bring back to comfort them (Sebastian
seems confident that he and his immediate companions will return) 133.
dear'st bitterest, worst 136. *time* i.e. suitable time 138. *chirurgeonly*
like a surgeon 139-40. *It is . . . cloudy* i.e. We all feel depressed when
you are troubled *Foul . . . foul* (Sebastian and Antonio pretend to take
Gonzalo's remark about foul weather literally) 141. *Had . . . isle* i.e.
were I to be given the task of colonizing this island 144. *'Scape . . .
wine* i.e. Keep sober because there would be nothing to drink 145.
contraries i.e. doing the opposite of what is usually done 146. *traffic*
trade 148. *Letters* i.e. learning generally 149. *use of service* having
servants, having labourers who work for a master *contract* i.e. legal
contract *succession* inheritance of property 150. *Bourn* boundary (of
property) *bound of land* boundary of land (paraphrases "bourn")
tilth tillage of the soil, agriculture

    No use of metal, corn, or wine, or oil;
    No occupation; all men idle, all;
    And women too, but innocent and pure;
    No sovereignty —
SEBASTIAN.   Yet he would be king on't.
ANTONIO. The latter end of his commonwealth forgets the 155
    beginning.
GONZALO. All things in common nature should produce
    Without sweat or endeavour: treason, felony,
    Sword, pike, knife, gun, or need of any engine
    Would I not have; but nature should bring forth,   160
    Of it own kind, all foison, all abundance,
    To feed my innocent people.
SEBASTIAN. No marrying 'mong his subjects?
ANTONIO. None, man, all idle; whores and knaves.
GONZALO. I would with such perfection govern, sir,   165
    T' excel the Golden Age.
SEBASTIAN.   Save his Majesty!
ANTONIO. Long live Gonzalo!
GONZALO.   And — do you mark me, sir?
ALONSO. Prithee no more: thou dost talk nothing to me.
GONZALO. I do well believe your Highness; and did it to
    minister occasion to these gentlemen, who are of such 170
    sensible and nimble lungs that they always use to laugh
    at nothing.
ANTONIO. 'Twas you we laughed at.
GONZALO. Who in this kind of merry fooling am nothing
    to you: so you may continue, and laugh at nothing still. 175
ANTONIO. What a blow was there given!

155-6. *The latter . . . beginning* (i.e. At the end of his speech about the commonwealth Gonzalo seems to have forgotten what he said at the beginning) 159. *engine* instrument of war 161. *it* its *foison* plentiful crop 162. *innocent* uncorrupted, simple 164. *idle* worthless 166. *T' excel* so as to excel *Golden Age* (according to the Greeks and Romans, this was the first age in the history of the world, when mankind lived in a state of happiness, free from trouble and want) *Save* God save 168. *nothing* (i.e. of any importance) 170. *minister occasion* give an opportunity 171. *sensible* sensitive *use to* are accustomed to 176. *What . . . given* (i.e. Antonio admits that he has been beaten in the exchange of words. Gonzalo has been more aware of their mockery than Sebastian and Antonio thought)

SEBASTIAN. An it had not fall'n flatlong.

GONZALO. You are gentlemen of brave mettle: you would
lift the moon out of her sphere, if she would continue in
it five weeks without changing.   180

Enter Ariel [invisible] playing solemn music.

SEBASTIAN. We would so, and then go a bat-fowling.

ANTONIO. Nay, good my lord, be not angry.

GONZALO. No, I warrant you: I will not adventure my discretion so weakly. Will you laugh me asleep, for I am
very heavy?   185

ANTONIO. Go sleep, and hear us.
                    [*All sleep except Alonso, Sebastian, and Antonio.*]

ALONSO. What, all so soon asleep? I wish mine eyes
Would, with themselves, shut up my thoughts: I find
They are inclined to do so.

SEBASTIAN.   Please you, sir,
Do not omit the heavy offer of it: 190
It seldom visits sorrow; when it doth,
It is a comforter.

ANTONIO.   We two, my lord,
Will guard your person while you take your rest,
And watch your safety.

ALONSO.   Thank you. Wondrous heavy.
                    [*Alonso sleeps. Exit Ariel.*]

SEBASTIAN. What a strange drowsiness possesses them!   195

ANTONIO. It is the quality o' th' climate.

SEBASTIAN.   Why
Doth it not then our eyelids sink? I find not
Myself disposed to sleep.

177. *An* if *flatlong* with the flat (of the sword); (i.e. the "blow" has
been harmless) 178. *brave mettle* fine quality 181. *would so* certainly
should *a bat-fowling* (i.e. catching birds at night by means of lights
and bats. Birds flew at the lights and then were struck down with bats.
Sebastian suggests that the moon would be used as a light) 183. *warrant*
assure 183-4. *adventure . . . weakly* risk my reputation for common
sense for such a weak reason 185. *heavy* drowsy 186. *Go . . . us* i.e.
Go to sleep and hear our laughter as your lullaby 189. *Please you* if it
please you 190. *Do not . . . of it* i.e. do not neglect the opportunity (for
sleep) offered by this drowsiness 191. *It* i.e. sleep 194. *watch* i.e.
watch over *Wondrous heavy* i.e. I am very drowsy 196. *quality*
peculiar property 197. *sink* cause to shut

ANTONIO.   Nor I: my spirits are nimble.
They fell together all, as by consent;
They dropped as by a thunder-stroke. What might,   200
Worthy Sebastian – O, what might? – No more: –
And yet methinks I see it in thy face,
What thou shouldst be. Th' occasion speaks thee, and
My strong imagination sees a crown
Dropping upon thy head.

SEBASTIAN.   What? Art thou waking?   205

ANTONIO. Do you not hear me speak?

SEBASTIAN.   I do; and surely
It is a sleepy language, and thou speak'st
Out of thy sleep. What is it thou didst say?
This is a strange repose, to be asleep
With eyes wide open; standing, speaking, moving,   210
And yet so fast asleep.

ANTONIO.   Noble Sebastian,
Thou let'st thy fortune sleep – die, rather; wink'st
Whiles thou art waking.

SEBASTIAN.   Thou dost snore distinctly;
There's meaning in thy snores.

ANTONIO. I am more serious than my custom: you   215
Must be so too, if heed me; which to do
Trebles thee o'er.

SEBASTIAN.   Well, I am standing water.

ANTONIO. I'll teach you how to flow.

SEBASTIAN.   Do so: to ebb
Hereditary sloth instructs me.

198. *nimble* alert 199. *They . . . consent* they all fell asleep together as if by agreement 200. *What might* i.e. "What might be", with a possible suggestion of "What might (power) could you have" 201. *Worthy* noble 203. *Th' occasion . . . thee* the opportunity summons you 205. *waking* awake (i.e. really aware of the implications of your words) 212. *wink'st* close your eyes (i.e. to the opportunity) 213. *distinctly* intelligibly, with meaning, significantly 215. *than my custom* i.e. than I usually am 216. *if heed me* if you are willing to pay attention to me 216-17. *which . . . thee o'er* which, if you do, will make you three times as great as you are now *standing water* water which is neither ebbing nor flowing (i.e. receptive to your suggestions) 218. *I'll . . . flow* I'll teach you how to rise (i.e. better your fortunes) 219. *Hereditary sloth* natural laziness

ANTONIO.   O,
  If you but knew how you the purpose cherish   220
  Whiles thus you mock it! how, in stripping it,
  You more invest it! Ebbing men indeed,
  Most often do so near the bottom run
  By their own fear or sloth.
SEBASTIAN.   Prithee say on:
  The setting of thine eye and cheek proclaim   225
  A matter from thee; and a birth, indeed,
  Which throes thee much to yield.
ANTONIO.   Thus, sir:
  Although this lord of weak remembrance, this
  Who shall be of as little memory
  When he is earthed, hath here almost persuaded   230
  (For he's a spirit of persuasion, only
  Professes to persuade) the King his son's alive,
  'Tis as impossible that he's undrowned
  As he that sleeps here swims.
SEBASTIAN.   I have no hope
  That he's undrowned.
ANTONIO.   O, out of that no hope   235
  What great hope have you! No hope that way is
  Another way so high a hope that even
  Ambition cannot pierce a wink beyond,
  But doubt discovery there. Will you grant with me
  That Ferdinand is drowned?
SEBASTIAN.   He's gone.
ANTONIO.   Then tell me,   240
  Who's the next heir of Naples?

220. *the purpose* i.e. the meaning behind my words *cherish* enrich
222. *invest it* clothe it, make it greater 225-6. *The setting . . . from
thee* i.e. the expression on your face shows that you have something
important to say 227. *throes . . . yield* costs you much effort to come
out with *Thus* i.e. this is what I have to say 228. *this lord* (probably
Francisco, whose story [ll. 111-20] Antonio does not believe, but perhaps Gonzalo) 229. *of . . . memory* as little remembered 230. *earthed*
buried 231-2. *only . . . persuade* i.e. his sole profession is to persuade
234. *As he* i.e. as that he 236-9. *No hope . . . discovery there* No hope
that way (i.e. that Ferdinand is undrowned) means that, in another way,
there is so high a hope (i.e. that Sebastian may obtain the crown) that
ambition cannot glimpse beyond it. *and is uncertain of the prospect there*

SEBASTIAN. Claribel.

ANTONIO. She that is Queen of Tunis; she that dwells
Ten leagues beyond man's life; she that from Naples
Can have no note, unless the sun were post –
The man i' th' moon's too slow – till new-born chins   245
Be rough and razorable; she that from whom
We all were sea-swallowed, though some cast again,
And, by that destiny, to perform an act
Whereof what's past is prologue; what to come,
In yours and my discharge.

SEBASTIAN. What stuff is this? How say you?250
'Tis true my brother's daughter's Queen of Tunis;
So is she heir of Naples; 'twixt which regions
There is some space.

ANTONIO. A space whose ev'ry cubit
Seems to cry out "How shall that Claribel
Measure us back to Naples? Keep in Tunis,   255
And let Sebastian wake!" Say this were death
That now hath seized them, why, they were no worse
Than now they are. There be that can rule Naples
As well as he that sleeps; lords that can prate
As amply and unnecessarily   260
As this Gonzalo; I myself could make
A chough of as deep chat. O, that you bore
The mind that I do! what a sleep were this
For your advancement! Do you understand me?

SEBASTIAN. Methinks I do.

243. *Ten . . . life* i.e. so far away that the distance is more than a lifetime away (i.e. beyond man's understanding)   244. *note* news   *post* messenger   245-6. *till . . . razorable* i.e. until new-born infants have grown to manhood   *from whom* (i.e. in travelling)   247. *though . . . again* i.e. though some of us were cast up on the shore again (note the series of theatrical puns which follow: "cast", "perform", "act", "prologue")   248. *destiny* fortune destined   250. *In . . . discharge* is yours and mine to perform (as a theatrical part)   *What . . . this* What business is this? What's all this about?   253. *cubit* (about one and a half feet)   255. *Measure us* traverse the distance across us (i.e. "ev'ry cubit")   *Keep* remain (addressed to Claribel)   257. *them* i.e. the sleeping lords   258. *be* are those   261-2. *I myself . . . chat* i.e. I myself could teach a crow, or jackdaw, to talk as profoundly (as Gonzalo); or, I could make a crow of myself if I talked as profoundly (as Gonzalo)   262-3. *O, that . . . I do* i.e. Oh, that you shared my thoughts

ANTONIO.   And how does your content   265
  Tender your own good fortune?
SEBASTIAN.   I remember
  You did supplant your brother Prospero.
ANTONIO.   True:
  And look how well my garments sit upon me,
  Much feater than before. My brother's servants
  Were then my fellows; now they are my men.   270
SEBASTIAN. But, for your conscience –
ANTONIO. Ay, sir, where lies that? if 'twere a kibe,
  'Twould put me to my slipper; but I feel not
  This deity in my bosom. Twenty consciences
  That stand 'twixt me and Milan, candied be they,   275
  And melt ere they molest! Here lies your brother,
  No better than the earth he lies upon,
  If he were that which now he's like – that's dead;
  Whom I with this obedient steel (three inches of it)
  Can lay to bed for ever; whiles you, doing thus,   280
  To the perpetual wink for aye might put
  This ancient morsel, this Sir Prudence, who
  Should not upbraid our course. For all the rest,
  They'll take suggestion as a cat laps milk;
  They'll tell the clock to any business that   285
  We say befits the hour.
SEBASTIAN.   Thy case, dear friend,
  Shall be my precedent: as thou got'st Milan,
  I'll come by Naples. Draw thy sword: one stroke
  Shall free thee from the tribute which thou payest,
  And I the King shall love thee.

265-6. *And how . . . good fortune* And how does your satisfaction (with
what I have said) cause you to estimate your good fortune   269. *feater*
more neatly   270. *fellows* companions, i.e. equals   *men* servants, i.e.
inferiors   272. *kibe* chilblain   273. *put . . . slipper* force me to wear
slippers   274. *deity* i.e. conscience   275. *candied* (i) coated with sugar,
or (possibly) (ii) frozen   276. *ere they molest* before they trouble me
280. *lay to bed* put to sleep   281. *perpetual wink* everlasting sleep (i.e.
death)   *for aye* for ever   282. *This . . . Prudence* i.e. Gonzalo   282-3.
who/ Should not so that he should not   *upbraid* reprove, condemn
284. *take suggestion* i.e. listen eagerly to our suggestions   285. *tell . . .
clock to* chime in with (i.e. agree with)   286. *befits the hour* suits the
occasion   *Thy case* your situation, your example (possibly with a legal
pun linking with *precedent* [in law], l. 287)

ANTONIO.   Draw together;   290
    And when I rear my hand, do you the like,
    To fall it on Gonzalo.   *[They draw.]*
SEBASTIAN.   O, but one word!
                       [They talk apart.]

     Enter Ariel [invisible] with music and song.

ARIEL. My master through his art foresees the danger
    That you, his friend, are in; and sends me forth
    (For else his project dies) to keep them living.   295
                     Sings in Gonzalo's ear.
         While you here do snoring lie,
         Open-eyed conspiracy
           His time doth take.
         If of life you keep a care,
         Shake off slumber and beware.   300
          Awake, awake!
ANTONIO. Then let us both be sudden.
GONZALO [*wakes*].   Now, good angels
    Preserve the King!   *[The others wake.]*
ALONSO. Why, how now? – Ho, awake! – Why are you
    drawn?
    Wherefore this ghastly looking?
GONZALO.   What's the matter?   305
SEBASTIAN. Whiles we stood here securing your repose,
    Even now, we heard a hollow burst of bellowing
    Like bulls, or rather lions: did't not wake you?
    It struck mine ear most terribly.
ALONSO.   I heard nothing.
ANTONIO. O, 'twas a din to fright a monster's ear,   310
    To make an earthquake: sure it was the roar
    Of a whole herd of lions.
ALONSO.   Heard you this, Gonzalo?
GONZALO. Upon mine honour, sir, I heard a humming,
    And that a strange one too, which did awake me.

292. *fall it* let it fall   *O, . . . word* i.e. Just a moment   294. *his friend*
i.e. Gonzalo   298. *time* opportunity   302. *sudden* quick   304. *you* i.e.
your swords   305. *looking* expression   306. *securing* guarding

I shaked you, sir, and cried. As mine eyes opened,   315
I saw their weapons drawn. There was a noise,
That's verily. 'Tis best we stand upon our guard,
Or that we quit this place: let's draw our weapons.
ALONSO. Lead off this ground, and let's make further
    search
For my poor son.
GONZALO.   Heavens keep him from these beasts! 320
For he is sure i' th' island.
ALONSO.   Lead away.
ARIEL. Prospero my lord shall know what I have done.
So, King, go safely on to seek thy son.   *Exeunt.*

Scene 2

Enter Caliban with a burden of wood.
A noise of thunder heard.

CALIBAN. All the infections that the sun sucks up
From bogs, fens, flats, on Prosper fall, and make him
By inchmeal a disease! His spirits hear me,
And yet I needs must curse. But they'll nor pinch,
Fright me with urchin-shows, pitch me i' th' mire,   5
Nor lead me, like a firebrand, in the dark
Out of my way, unless he bid 'em; but
For every trifle are they set upon me;
Sometime like apes that mow and chatter at me,
And after bite me; then like hedgehogs which   10
Lie tumbling in my barefoot way, and mount
Their pricks at my footfall; sometime am I
All wound with adders, who with cloven tongues
Do hiss me into madness.

---

317. *verily* certain   319. *off* away from
    2.2.1-2. *sun . . . flats* (mists from bogs were thought to be drawn up
by the sun)   3. *By inchmeal* inch by inch, piecemeal   4. *nor* neither   5.
urchin-shows (apparitions in the form of elves or hedgehogs)   6. *like a
firebrand* i.e. in the shape of a will-o'-the-wisp (a spirit which took the
form of a wandering light and led travellers astray in the dark)   9. *mow*
make faces   12. *pricks* prickles   13. *wound* wound around

Enter Trinculo.

                              Lo, now, lo!
Here comes a spirit of his, and to torment me   15
For bringing wood in slowly. I'll fall flat,
Perchance he will not mind me.   [*Lies down.*]
TRINCULO. Here's neither bush nor shrub to bear off any
    weather at all, and another storm brewing: I hear it sing
    i' th' wind. Yond same black cloud, yond huge one,   20
    looks like a foul bombard that would shed his liquor.
    If it should thunder, as it did before, I know not where
    to hide my head: yond same cloud cannot choose but
    fall by pailfuls. What have we here? a man or a fish?
    dead or alive? A fish: he smells like a fish; a very ancient 25
    and fishlike smell; a kind of not of the newest Poor-John.
    A strange fish! Were I in England now, as once I was,
    and had but this fish painted, not a holiday fool there but
    would give a piece of silver. There would this monster
    make a man: any strange beast there makes a man.   30
    When they will not give a doit to relieve a lame beggar,
    they will lay out ten to see a dead Indian. Legged like a   ‡
    man! and his fins like arms! Warm, o' my troth! I do now
    let loose my opinion, hold it no longer: this is no fish,
    but an islander, that hath lately suffered by a thunder-   35
    bolt. [*Thunder.*] Alas, the storm is come again! my best
    way is to creep under his gaberdine: there is no other
    shelter hereabout. Misery acquaints a man with strange
    bedfellows. I will here shroud till the dregs of the storm
    be past.   [*Creeps under Caliban's garment.*]   40

        Enter Stephano, singing [a bottle in his
                     hand].

17. *mind* notice   18. *bear off* ward off; i.e. protect me from   21. *bombard*
large leather container for liquor   *his* its   23. *cannot choose* cannot
help   26. *Poor-John* i.e. dried and salted hake   28. *painted* i.e. made
into a picture and, probably, set up outside a tent or booth at a fair
holiday fool fool on holiday   30. *make a man* be looked upon as a man
(with a pun on "make a man's fortune")   31. *doit* a Dutch coin worth a
fraction of a cent (used, generally, to denote any small coin)   33. *o' my
troth* on my faith   34. *hold* withold   35. *suffered* (i.e. death)   37.
gaberdine loose cloak   39. *shroud* shelter

STEPHANO.   I shall no more to sea, to sea;
                   Here shall I die ashore.
This is a very scurvy tune to sing at a man's funeral:
well, here's my comfort.   *Drinks.*
          The master, the swabber, the boatswain, and I,   45
               The gunner, and his mate,
          Loved Mall, Meg, and Marian, and Margery,
               But none of us cared for Kate.
               For she had a tongue with a tang,
               Would cry to a sailor "Go hang!"   50
          She loved not the savour of tar nor of pitch;
          Yet a tailor might scratch her where'er she did itch.
               Then to sea, boys, and let her go hang!
This is a scurvy tune too; but here's my comfort.
                                                     Drinks.

CALIBAN. Do not torment me: O!   55

STEPHANO. What's the matter? Have we devils here? Do
     you put tricks upon 's with savages and men of Inde,
     ha? I have not 'scaped drowning to be afeard now of
     your four legs; for it hath been said, "As proper a man
     as ever went on four legs cannot make him give 60
     ground"; and it shall be said so again, while Stephano
     breathes at nostrils.

CALIBAN. The spirit torments me: O!

STEPHANO. This is some monster of the isle, with four legs,
     who hath got, as I take it, an ague. Where the devil 65
     should he learn our language? I will give him some re-
     lief, if it be but for that. If I can recover him, and keep
     him tame, and get to Naples with him, he's a present for
     any emperor that ever trod on neat's leather.

43. *scurvy* miserable *at . . . funeral* i.e. at his own or Trinculo's 45.
swabber (low-ranking officer who saw that the ship was kept clean or,
sometimes, the sailor who actually cleaned the decks) 47. *Mall* i.e.
Moll (nickname for Mary) 49. *tongue . . . tang* i.e. sharp tongue 51.
savour smell, perfume 57. *tricks* (probably conjuror's tricks) *'s* us
men of Inde i.e. men of India or the East or West Indies, or, more
generally, any Indians, including those of North America 59. *As . . . a
man* as fine a fellow ("as proper a man as ever went on two legs" was a
proverbial saying. Stephano changes this to "four legs" to suit the strange
creature before him) 65. *ague* fever 67. *recover* cure, revive 69.
neat's leather cowhide

CALIBAN. Do not torment me, prithee; I'll bring my wood 70
    home faster.

STEPHANO. He's in his fit now and does not talk after the
    wisest. He shall taste of my bottle: if he have never
    drunk wine afore, it will go near to remove his fit. If I
    can recover him and keep him tame, I will not take too 75
    much for him; he shall pay for him that hath him, and
    that soundly.

CALIBAN. Thou dost me yet but little hurt. Thou wilt anon;
    I know it by thy trembling. Now Prosper works upon
    thee.   80

STEPHANO. Come on your ways; open your mouth; here
    is that which will give language to you, cat; open your
    mouth. This will shake your shaking, I can tell you, and
    that soundly. [*Gives Caliban drink.*] You cannot tell
    who's your friend; open your chaps again.   85

TRINCULO. I should know that voice. It should be – but he
    is drowned; and these are devils. O, defend me!

STEPHANO. Four legs and two voices – a most delicate
    monster! His forward voice now is to speak well of his
    friend; his backward voice is to utter foul speeches and 90
    to detract. If all the wine in my bottle will recover him,
    I will help his ague. Come! [*Gives drink.*] Amen! I will
    pour some in thy other mouth.

TRINCULO. Stephano!

STEPHANO. Doth thy other mouth call me? Mercy, mercy! 95
    This is a devil, and no monster: I will leave him; I have
    no long spoon.

72. *fit* fever, delirium 72-3. *after the wisest* in the most sensible way
75-6. *I will . . . for him* i.e. I will take what price I can get for him,
however high 76-7. *he shall . . . soundly* i.e. whoever buys him shall
pay handsomely for him 78. *anon* soon, presently 78-80. *Thou . . .
thee* (Caliban thinks that Prospero's magic is working on Trinculo, who
is trembling with fear) 81. *Come . . . ways* i.e. come along now 82.
cat (alludes to the proverb, "Good liquor will make a cat speak") 85.
chaps jaws 87. *defend me* i.e. God defend me 88. *delicate* rare (possibly in ironic contrast to "delicate" Ariel) 91. *detract* slander 92.
Amen (Stephano probably says "Amen" because Caliban has just
swallowed a mouthful of liquor) 97. *long spoon* (alludes to the
proverb, "He must have a long spoon that eats with the devil")

TRINCULO. Stephano! If thou beest Stephano, touch me,
  and speak to me; for I am Trinculo – be not afeard –
  thy good friend Trinculo.   100
STEPHANO. If thou beest Trinculo, come forth: I'll pull
  thee by the lesser legs: if any be Trinculo's legs, these
  are they. [*Draws him out from under Caliban's garment.*] Thou art very Trinculo indeed: how cam'st thou
  to be the siege of this mooncalf? Can he vent Trinculos?105
TRINCULO. I took him to be killed with a thunder-stroke.
  But art thou not drowned, Stephano? I hope now thou
  art not drowned. Is the storm overblown? I hid me under
  the dead mooncalf's gaberdine for fear of the storm.
  And art thou living, Stephano? O Stephano, two Nea-110
  politans 'scaped!
STEPHANO. Prithee do not turn me about; my stomach is
  not constant.
CALIBAN [*aside*]. These be fine things, an if they be not
  sprites.
  That's a brave god and bears celestial liquor.   115
  I will kneel to him.
STEPHANO. How didst thou 'scape? How cam'st thou
  hither? Swear by this bottle how thou cam'st hither. I
  escaped upon a butt of sack which the sailors heaved
  o'erboard; by this bottle, which I made of the bark of a120
  tree with mine own hands since I was cast ashore.
CALIBAN. I'll swear upon that bottle to be thy true subject,
  for the liquor is not earthly.
STEPHANO. Here; swear then how thou escapedst.
TRINCULO. Swum ashore, man, like a duck; I can swim like125
  a duck, I'll be sworn.
STEPHANO. Here, kiss the book. [*Gives him drink.*] Though
  thou canst swim like a duck, thou art made like a goose.

105. *siege* excrement *mooncalf* misshapen creature, freak (the moon
was thought to influence the birth of monsters) *vent* emit, put forth
113. *constant* steady 114. *an if* if 115. *brave* fine, impressive 119.
butt barrel *sack* (general name for Spanish white wine) 127. *kiss the
book* (Stephano gives Trinculo a drink from the bottle as if it were
kissing the Bible) 128. *like a goose* i.e. (i) with a long neck, or
possibly (ii) stupid

TRINCULO. O Stephano, hast any more of this?

STEPHANO. The whole butt, man: my cellar is in a rock by 130
th' seaside, where my wine is hid. How now, mooncalf!
How does thine ague?

CALIBAN. Hast thou not dropped from heaven?

STEPHANO. Out o' th' moon, I do assure thee: I was the
Man i' th' Moon when time was.   135

CALIBAN. I have seen thee in her, and I do adore thee.
My mistress showed me thee, and thy dog, and thy bush.

STEPHANO. Come, swear to that; kiss the book: I will
furnish it anon with new contents. Swear.

                              [*Caliban drinks.*]

TRINCULO. By this good light, this is a very shallow mon- 140
ster! I afeard of him? A very weak monster! The Man
i' th' Moon? A most poor credulous monster! — Well
drawn, monster, in good sooth!

CALIBAN. I'll show thee every fertile inch o' th' island;
And I will kiss thy foot. I prithee be my god.   145

TRINCULO. By this light, a most perfidious and drunken
monster! When's god's asleep, he'll rob his bottle.

CALIBAN. I'll kiss thy foot; I'll swear myself thy subject.

STEPHANO. Come on then; down, and swear.

TRINCULO. I shall laugh myself to death at this puppy- 150
headed monster. A most scurvy monster! I could find in
my heart to beat him —

STEPHANO. Come, kiss.

TRINCULO. But that the poor monster's in drink. An
abominable monster!   155

CALIBAN. I'll show thee the best springs; I'll pluck thee
berries;
I'll fish for thee, and get thee wood enough.
A plague upon the tyrant that I serve!

---

135. *when time was* once upon a time   137. *My mistress* i.e. Miranda
thy dog . . . bush (according to legend the Man in the Moon was a
peasant banished to the moon, with his dog and the last bush he had
picked up, for gathering sticks on a Sunday)   139. *furnish it* i.e. fill the
bottle   140. *shallow* silly   142-3. *Well drawn* i.e. well drunk (Caliban
has taken a long pull at the bottle)   *sooth* truth   154. *in drink* drunk

I'll bear him no more sticks, but follow thee,
Thou wondrous man.   160
TRINCULO. A most ridiculous monster, to make a wonder
of a poor drunkard!
CALIBAN. I prithee let me bring thee where crabs grow;
And I with my long nails will dig thee pignuts,
Show thee a jay's nest, and instruct thee how   165
To snare the nimble marmoset; I'll bring thee
To clust'ring filberts, and sometimes I'll get thee
Young scamels from the rock. Wilt thou go with me?
STEPHANO. I prithee now, lead the way without any more
talking. Trinculo, the King and all our company else 170
being drowned, we will inherit here. Here, bear my
bottle. Fellow Trinculo, we'll fill him by and by again.
                                  Caliban sings drunkenly.
CALIBAN. Farewell, master; farewell, farewell!
TRINCULO. A howling monster; a drunken monster!
CALIBAN.   No more dams I'll make for fish,   175
              Nor fetch in firing
              At requiring,
            Nor scrape trenchering, nor wash dish.
              'Ban, 'Ban, Ca – Caliban
              Has a new master: get a new man.   180
Freedom, high-day! high-day, freedom! freedom, high-
day, freedom!
STEPHANO. O brave monster! lead the way.   *Exeunt.*

163. *crabs* crabapples   164. *pignuts* i.e. (i) small nuts which grow under
the ground, or possibly (ii) peanuts   166. *marmoset* some kind of small
monkey (not necessarily the true marmoset)   167. *filberts* hazel nuts
168. *scamels* possibly (i) some kind of sea bird, or (ii) shellfish   170.
our company else the rest of our company   171. *inherit* take possession
178. *trenchering* trenchers (wooden plates)   179. *Ca – Caliban* (probably
drunken stuttering)

ACT 3

Scene 1

Enter Ferdinand, bearing a log.

FERDINAND. There be some sports are painful, and their labour
    Delight in them sets off; some kinds of baseness
    Are nobly undergone, and most poor matters
    Point to rich ends. This my mean task
    Would be as heavy to me as odious, but   5
    The mistress which I serve quickens what's dead
    And makes my labours pleasures. O, she is
    Ten times more gentle than her father's crabbèd;
    And he's composed of harshness. I must remove
    Some thousands of these logs and pile them up,   10
    Upon a sore injunction. My sweet mistress
    Weeps when she sees me work, and says such baseness
    Had never like executor. I forget;
    But these sweet thoughts do even refresh my labours,
    Most busy least, when I do it.

Enter Miranda; and Prospero [behind, unseen].

MIRANDA.   Alas, now pray you   15
    Work not so hard: I would the lightning had
    Burnt up those logs that you are enjoined to pile!

3.1.1-2. *There be . . . sets off* there are some sports which are strenuous, but the delight we take in them cancels out our pains 3-4. *most poor . . . ends* the majority of trivial matters lead to valuable results 5. *but* but that 6. *which* whom *quickens what's dead* i.e. puts life into this tedious labour 8. *crabbèd* crotchety, ill-tempered 11. *Upon . . . injunction* in obedience to a stern command 12. *such baseness* such a menial task 13. *like executor* such a (worthy) person to perform (it) *I forget* i.e. I forgot myself (in these pleasant thoughts) 15. *Most . . . do it* i.e. I seem to be least busy when I am performing my task (because of my pleasant thoughts of Miranda)

Pray set it down and rest you: when this burns,
'Twill weep for having wearied you. My father
Is hard at study; pray now rest yourself: 20
He's safe for these three hours.

FERDINAND.   O most dear mistress,
The sun will set before I shall discharge
What I must strive to do.

MIRANDA.   If you'll sit down,
I'll bear your logs the while. Pray give me that:
I'll carry it to the pile.

FERDINAND.   No, precious creature;   25
I had rather crack my sinews, break my back,
Than you should such dishonour undergo,
While I sit lazy by.

MIRANDA.   It would become me
As well as it does you; and I should do it
With much more ease; for my good will is to it,   30
And yours it is against.

PROSPERO [*aside*].   Poor worm, thou are infected!
This visitation shows it.

MIRANDA.   You look wearily.

FERDINAND. No, noble mistress; 'tis fresh morning with
    me
When you are by at night. I do beseech you,
Chiefly that I might set it in my prayers,   35
What is your name?

MIRANDA.   Miranda. – O my father,
I have broke your hest to say so!

FERDINAND.   Admired Miranda!

19. *weep* (Miranda thinks of the log as "weeping" when the sap runs
from it into the fire)   21. *safe* out of the way   24. *the while* for a while
31. *Poor worm* i.e. poor creature (here used tenderly, although, of course,
it was often used with contempt)   *thou art infected* (i.e. by love)   32.
visitation (a word often used to describe an attack of the plague, i.e.
Miranda has been infected by the plague of love)   33-4. *'tis . . . night*
i.e. your presence makes me feel as fresh at night as I do in the morning
37. *hest* command   *Admired Miranda* (Ferdinand is playing upon the
meaning of the name Miranda; i.e. "wonderful woman" or "a woman
to be admired")

Indeed the top of admiration, worth
What's dearest to the world! Full many a lady
I have eyed with best regard, and many a time   40
Th' harmony of their tongues hath into bondage
Brought my too diligent ear; for several virtues
Have I liked several women; never any
With so full soul, but some defect in her
Did quarrel with the noblest grace she owed,   45
And put it to the foil. But you, O you,
So perfect and so peerless, are created
Of every creature's best.

MIRANDA.   I do not know
One of my sex; no woman's face remember,
Save, from my glass, mine own; nor have I seen   50
More that I may call men than you, good friend,
And my dear father. How features are abroad
I am skilless of; but, by my modesty
(The jewel in my dower), I would not wish
Any companion in the world but you;   55
Nor can imagination form a shape,
Besides yourself, to like of. But I prattle
Something too wildly, and my father's precepts
I therein do forget.

FERDINAND.   I am, in my condition,
A prince, Miranda; I do think, a king   60
(I would not so), and would no more endure
This wooden slavery than to suffer
The flesh-fly blow my mouth. Hear my soul speak:
The very instant that I saw you, did
My heart fly to your service; there resides,   65

39. *What's dearest* whatever is most valuable   40. *best regard* closest
attention, the greatest approval   42. *several* various, different   44. *With
. . . soul* i.e. so wholeheartedly   45. *Did . . . owed* did mar (or contrast
with) the noblest of the qualities she possessed   46. *And . . . foil* i.e. and
make it of no effect   48. *Of . . . best* (i.e. from the best qualities of every
woman)   52. *abroad* elsewhere in the world   53. *skilless* ignorant   54.
The . . . dower i.e. the most valuable of my possessions   57. *to like of*
(i) to take delight in, (ii) as a comparison   58. *Something* somewhat
59. *condition* rank, normal situation in the world   61. *would . . . endure*
(i.e. were it not for Miranda)   62. *wooden slavery* i.e. the slavery of
carrying logs   63. *blow* blow (its eggs) into

To make me slave to it; and for your sake
Am I this patient log-man.
MIRANDA.   Do you love me?
FERDINAND. O heaven, O earth, bear witness to this
    sound,
And crown what I profess with kind event
If I speak true! if hollowly, invert   70
What best is boded me to mischief! I,
Beyond all limit of what else i' th' world,
Do love, prize, honour you.
MIRANDA.   I am a fool
To weep at what I am glad of.
PROSPERO [*aside*].   Fair encounter
Of two most rare affections! Heavens rain grace   75
On that which breeds between 'em!
FERDINAND.   Wherefore weep you?
MIRANDA. At mine unworthiness, that dare not offer
What I desire to give, and much less take
What I shall die to want. But this is trifling;
And all the more it seeks to hide itself,   80
The bigger bulk it shows. Hence, bashful cunning,
And prompt me, plain and holy innocence!
I am your wife, if you will marry me;
If not, I'll die your maid. To be your fellow
You may deny me; but I'll be your servant,   85
Whether you will or no.
FERDINAND.   My mistress, dearest;
And I thus humble ever.
MIRANDA.   My husband then?
FERDINAND. Ay, with a heart as willing
As bondage e'er of freedom: here's my hand.

69. *kind event* favourable outcome 70. *hollowly* falsely, insincerely
70-71. *invert . . . me to* turn the good fortune that is foretold for me
into 72. *Beyond . . . what* beyond the bounds of everything 75. *Of . . .
affections* i.e. fortunate meeting of two people of the rarest qualities
grace i.e. divine favour 76. *that . . . 'em* i.e. their love 77. *that* who
79. *to want* to go without (i.e. Ferdinand's love) 80. *it* i.e. my love
81. *Hence, bashful cunning* (Miranda is implying that her modesty has
made her bashful and prevents her from speaking directly and honestly
about her love) 84. *maid* probably (i) unmarried girl, and (ii) servant
fellow equal, companion 87. *thus humble ever* (Ferdinand probably
kneels) 89. *As . . . freedom* as a person in bondage wishing to be free

MIRANDA. And mine, with my heart in't; and now farewell 90
    Till half an hour hence.
FERDINAND.   A thousand thousand!
          Exeunt [Ferdinand and Miranda severally].
PROSPERO. So glad of this as they I cannot be,
    Who are surprised withal; but my rejoicing
    At nothing can be more. I'll to my book;
    For yet, ere supper time, must I perform   95
    Much business appertaining.   *Exit.*

Scene 2

Enter Caliban, Stephano, and Trinculo.

STEPHANO. Tell not me: – when the butt is out, we will
    drink water; not a drop before: therefore bear up and
    board 'em! Servant monster, drink to me.
TRINCULO. Servant monster? The folly of this island! They
    say there's but five upon this isle: we are three of them. 5
    If th' other two be brained like us, the state totters.
STEPHANO. Drink, servant monster, when I bid thee: thy
    eyes are almost set in thy head.
TRINCULO. Where should they be set else? He were a brave
    monster indeed, if they were set in his tail.   10
STEPHANO. My man-monster hath drowned his tongue in
    sack: for my part, the sea cannot drown me; I swam, ere

93. *Who . . . withal* as they are taken unawares by all that is going on
(Prospero knew what was going to happen)   96. *appertaining* relevant
(to the marriage between Ferdinand and Miranda)
    3.2.1. *Tell not me* don't talk to me (about saving the wine)   *out*
empty   2-3. *bear . . . 'em* (a sailor's phrase describing a manoeuvre in
which a ship or fleet "bears down" on enemy ships and boards them.
Stephano seems to be thinking of an attack on the bottle)   4. *The . . .
island* (i) What a foolish place this island is, or perhaps (ii) Trinculo is
thinking of Caliban as the "folly" or freak of the island   6. *th' other
two* i.e. Prospero and Miranda   *be . . . like us* have brains like ours, are
as intelligent as we are   8. *set* fixed (Caliban's eyes have the fixed,
glazed stare of a drunkard)   9. *brave* (i) fine, (ii) strange, (iii) unusual

I could recover the shore, five-and-thirty leagues off and
on. By this light, thou shalt be my lieutenant, monster,
or my standard.   15

TRINCULO. Your lieutenant, if you list; he's no standard.

STEPHANO. We'll not run, Monsieur Monster.

TRINCULO. Nor go neither; but you'll lie like dogs, and yet
say nothing neither.

STEPHANO. Mooncalf, speak once in thy life, if thou beest 20
a good mooncalf.

CALIBAN. How does thy honour? Let me lick thy shoe.
I'll not serve him; he is not valiant.

TRINCULO. Thou liest, most ignorant monster: I am in case
to justle a constable. Why, thou deboshed fish thou, was 25
there ever man a coward that hath drunk so much sack
as I today? Wilt thou tell a monstrous lie, being but half
a fish and half a monster?

CALIBAN. Lo, how he mocks me! Wilt thou let him, my
lord?   30

TRINCULO. "Lord" quoth he? That a monster should be
such a natural!

CALIBAN. Lo, lo, again! Bite him to death, I prithee.

STEPHANO. Trinculo, keep a good tongue in your head: if
you prove a mutineer – the next tree! The poor mon- 35
ster's my subject, and he shall not suffer indignity.

CALIBAN. I thank my noble lord. Wilt thou be pleased
To hearken once again to the suit I made to thee?

STEPHANO. Marry, will I: kneel and repeat it; I will stand,
and so shall Trinculo.   40

---

13. *recover* reach *five . . . leagues* (about one hundred and five miles)
13-14. *off and on* more or less *By this light* (a conventional oath)   15.
standard i.e. standard-bearer (probably an ironical pun, because Caliban
cannot stand up) 16. *list* please, like *no standard* (because he cannot
stand) 17. *run* (i.e. from the enemy), with a secondary meaning of
"make water" 18. *go* walk *lie* (i) lie down, (ii) tell lies 24-5. *I am
. . . constable* I am in fit condition (i.e. drunk enough) to jostle or push
around a constable *deboshed* debauched 32. *natural* born fool (a
monster is, of course, unnatural) 34. *good* civil, respectful 35. *the
next tree* i.e. you'll be hanged on the nearest tree 38. *suit* request 39.
Marry By the Virgin Mary (by Shakespeare's day this oath had become
a mild one corresponding roughly to our "By Jove")

Enter Ariel, invisible.

CALIBAN. As I told thee before, I am subject to a tyrant, a
sorcerer, that by his cunning hath cheated me of the
island.

ARIEL. Thou liest.

CALIBAN.   Thou liest, thou jesting monkey thou;
I would my valiant master would destroy thee.   45
I do not lie.

STEPHANO. Trinculo, if you trouble him any more in's tale,
by this hand, I will supplant some of your teeth.

TRINCULO. Why, I said nothing.

STEPHANO. Mum then, and no more. – Proceed.   50

CALIBAN. I say by sorcery he got this isle;
From me he got it. If thy greatness will
Revenge it on him – for I know thou dar'st,
But this thing dare not –

STEPHANO. That's most certain.   55

CALIBAN. Thou shalt be lord of it, and I'll serve thee.

STEPHANO. How now shall this be compassed?
Canst thou bring me to the party?

CALIBAN. Yea, yea, my lord: I'll yield him thee asleep,
Where thou mayst knock a nail into his head.   60

ARIEL. Thou liest; thou canst not.

CALIBAN. What a pied ninny's this! Thou scurvy patch!
I do beseech thy greatness give him blows,
And take his bottle from him. When that's gone,
He shall drink naught but brine, for I'll not show him   65
Where the quick freshes are.

STEPHANO. Trinculo, run into no further danger: interrupt
the monster one word further and, by this hand, I'll turn
my mercy out o' doors and make a stockfish of thee.

48. *supplant* uproot, knock out   50. *Mum* silence, keep quiet (i.e. mum's
the word)   52. *greatness* lordship   54. *this thing* i.e. Trinculo (or
possibly Caliban himself)   57. *compassed* brought about   58. *the party*
i.e. the person concerned   59. *yield . . . asleep* deliver him to you when
he is asleep   62. *pied ninny* motley fool (Trinculo is presumably wearing
the many-coloured coat of the jester)   *patch* i.e. clown (referring to
the fool's patchwork coat)   66. *quick freshes* fresh-water springs   68-9.
turn . . . doors put aside any mercy I have for you   *stockfish* salted and
dried hake or cod, which was thoroughly beaten during the drying
process

TRINCULO. Why, what did I? I did nothing. I'll go farther 70
off.

STEPHANO. Didst thou not say he lied?

ARIEL. Thou liest.

STEPHANO. Do I so? Take thou that! [*Strikes Trinculo.*]
As you like this, give me the lie another time.   75

TRINCULO. I did not give the lie. Out o' your wits, and
hearing too? A pox o' your bottle! this can sack and
drinking do. A murrain on your monster, and the devil
take your fingers!

CALIBAN. Ha, ha, ha!   80

STEPHANO. Now forward with your tale. – Prithee stand
further off.

CALIBAN. Beat him enough. After a little time
I'll beat him too.

STEPHANO.   Stand farther. – Come, proceed.

CALIBAN. Why, as I told thee, 'tis a custom with him   85
I' th' afternoon to sleep: there thou mayst brain him,
Having first seized his books; or with a log
Batter his skull, or paunch him with a stake,
Or cut his wesand with thy knife. Remember
First to possess his books; for without them   90
He's but a sot, as I am, nor hath not
One spirit to command: they all do hate him
As rootedly as I. Burn but his books.
He has brave utensils (for so he calls them)
Which, when he has a house, he'll deck withal.   95
And that most deeply to consider is
The beauty of his daughter. He himself
Calls her a nonpareil. I never saw a woman
But only Sycorax my dam and she;
But she as far surpasseth Sycorax   100
As great'st does least.

75. *give . . . lie* contradict me   78. *murrain* (a disease of cattle)   88.
paunch him stab him in the belly   89. *wesand* windpipe   90. *possess*
get hold of   91. *sot* powerless fool   93. *rootedly* firmly, deeply   *Burn
but* (i) be sure to burn, or possibly (ii) burn only   94. *brave utensils*
fine household goods   95. *Which . . . withal* with which he will furnish
his house when he has one   96. *And that . . . consider* that which is
most worth considering   98. *nonpareil* person without equal

STEPHANO.   Is it so brave a lass?

CALIBAN. Ay, lord; she will become thy bed, I warrant,
   And bring thee forth brave brood.

STEPHANO. Monster, I will kill this man: his daughter and
   I will be king and queen, – save our graces! – and Trin-[105]
   culo and thyself shall be viceroys. Dost thou like the
   plot, Trinculo?

TRINCULO. Excellent.

STEPHANO. Give me thy hand: I am sorry I beat thee; but
   while thou liv'st, keep a good tongue in thy head.   110

CALIBAN. Within this half hour will he be asleep.
   Wilt thou destroy him then?

STEPHANO.   Ay, on mine honour.

ARIEL. This will I tell my master.

CALIBAN. Thou mak'st me merry; I am full of pleasure.
   Let us be jocund: will you troll the catch   115
   You taught me but whilere?

STEPHANO. At thy request, monster, I will do reason, any
   reason. Come on, Trinculo, let us sing.   *Sings.*
               Flout 'em and scout 'em,
               And scout 'em and flout 'em;   120
               Thought is free.

CALIBAN. That's not the tune.
         Ariel plays the tune on a tabor and pipe.

STEPHANO. What is this same?

TRINCULO. This is the tune of our catch, played by the picture of Nobody.   125

STEPHANO. If thou beest a man, show thyself in thy likeness:
   if thou beest a devil, take't as thou list.

TRINCULO. O, forgive me my sins!

---

103. *brave brood* fine children   115. *troll the catch* sing the part-song (a "catch" was a song for several voices in which each singer, from the second on, began by singing the line of the previous singer)   116. *but whilere* only a short time ago   117-8. *do reason . . . reason* satisfy you, and do anything within reason   119. *Flout* deride *scout* jeer at   121. *Thought is free* (proverbial expression)   122 s.d. *tabor* (small drum worn at the side)   124-5. *the . . . Nobody* (possibly a topical allusion to pictures with heads, legs, and arms, but no bodies. A bookseller named John Trundle used such a sign over his shop)   127. *as thou list* as you like

STEPHANO. He that dies pays all debts: I defy thee.
  Mercy upon us!   130
CALIBAN. Art thou afeard?
STEPHANO. No, monster, not I.
CALIBAN. Be not afeard: the isle is full of noises,
  Sounds and sweet airs that give delight and hurt not.
  Sometimes a thousand twangling instruments   135
  Will hum about mine ears; and sometime voices,
  That, if I then had waked after long sleep,
  Will make me sleep again; and then, in dreaming,
  The clouds methought would open and show riches
  Ready to drop upon me; that, when I waked,   140
  I cried to dream again.
STEPHANO. This will prove a brave kingdom to me, where
  I shall have my music for nothing.
CALIBAN. When Prospero is destroyed.
STEPHANO. That shall be by and by: I remember the story.145
TRINCULO. The sound is going away: let's follow it, and
  after do our work.
STEPHANO. Lead, monster; we'll follow. I would I could
  see this taborer: he lays it on. Wilt come?
TRINCULO. I'll follow, Stephano.   *Exeunt.*150

Scene 3

*Enter Alonso, Sebastian, Antonio, Gonzalo,
Adrian, Francisco, &c.*

GONZALO. By'r lakin, I can go no further, sir;
  My old bones ache: here's a maze trod indeed
  Through forthrights and meanders. By your patience,
  I needs must rest me.

---

129. *He . . . debts* (because, according to proverb, you cannot collect a
debt from a dead man)   140. *that* so that   145. *I . . . story* i.e. I have
not forgotten what you have told me   149. *lays it on* i.e. thumps his
drum vigorously

  3.3.1. *By'r lakin* by our Lady (i.e. the Virgin Mary; "lakin" is shortened
form of ladykin, or little lady)   2. *maze* (shrubbery planted to form an
intricate pattern of paths among which it is very easy to get lost)   3.
forthrights straightforward paths   *meanders* twisting paths   *By your
patience* with your leave

ALONSO.   Old lord, I cannot blame thee,
  Who am myself attached with weariness   5
  To th' dulling of my spirits. Sit down and rest.
  Even here I will put off my hope, and keep it
  No longer for my flatterer: he is drowned
  Whom thus we stray to find; and the sea mocks
  Our frustrate search on land. Well, let him go.   10
ANTONIO [*aside to Sebastian*]. I am right glad that he's so
    out of hope.
  Do not for one repulse forgo the purpose
  That you resolved t' effect.
SEBASTIAN [*aside to Antonio*]. The next advantage
  Will we take throughly.
ANTONIO [*aside to Sebastian*]. Let it be to-night;
  For, now they are oppressed with travel, they   15
  Will not, nor cannot, use such vigilance
  As when they are fresh.
SEBASTIAN [*aside to Antonio*]. I say to-night. No more.

*Solemn and strange music; and Prospero on the top
(invisible). Enter several strange Shapes, bringing
in a banquet; and dance about it with gentle actions
of salutations; and, inviting the King &c. to eat,
they depart.*

ALONSO. What harmony is this? My good friends, hark!
GONZALO. Marvellous sweet music.
ALONSO. Give us kind keepers, heavens! What were these?   20
SEBASTIAN. A living drollery. Now I will believe
  That there are unicorns; that in Arabia
  There is one tree, the phoenix' throne; one phoenix
  At this hour reigning there.
ANTONIO.   I'll believe both;

5. *attached* seized, overcome 6. *To . . . spirits* i.e. to such an extent that
my energy is sapped 7-8. *I will . . . flatterer* i.e. I will give up hope (of
finding my son) and not allow it to delude me any longer 10. *frustrate*
frustrated, fruitless 12. *repulse* set-back 13. *advantage* opportunity
14. *throughly* thoroughly 15. *oppressed* worn out *travel* wandering
17 s.d. *on the top* (probably on a gallery or upper stage, depending on
the theatre or hall in which the production took place) 20. *keepers* i.e.
guardian angels 21. *A living drollery* i.e. A comic puppet show in which
the figures are alive

And what does else want credit, come to me,   25
And I'll be sworn 'tis true. Travellers ne'er did lie,
Though fools at home condemn 'em.
GONZALO.   If in Naples
  I should report this now, would they believe me
  If I should say I saw such islanders?
  (For certes these are people of the island)   30
  Who, though they are of monstrous shape, yet note,
  Their manners are more gentle, kind, than of
  Our human generation you shall find
  Many – nay, almost any.
PROSPERO [aside].   Honest lord,
  Thou hast said well; for some of you there present   35
  Are worse than devils.
ALONSO.   I cannot too much muse
  Such shapes, such gesture, and such sound, expressing
  (Although they want the use of tongue) a kind
  Of excellent dumb discourse.
PROSPERO [aside].   Praise in departing.
FRANCISCO. They vanished strangely.
SEBASTIAN.   No matter, since   40
  They have left their viands behind; for we have
     stomachs.
  Will't please you taste of what is here?
ALONSO.   Not I.
GONZALO. Faith, sir, you need not fear. When we were
     boys,
  Who would believe that there were mountaineers
  Dewlapped like bulls, whose throats had hanging at 'em   45
  Wallets of flesh? or that there were such men
  Whose heads stood in their breasts? which now we find

25. *what . . . credit* whatever else is beyond belief   30. *certes* certainly,
truly   32. *manners* characters, behaviour ("manners" had a wider meaning than it has today)   33. *human generation* human race   36. *muse*
wonder at   37. *gesture* bearing   39. *Praise in departing* (a proverbial
expression) i.e. don't give your praise too soon in case you should have
reason to change your mind; don't speak too soon   41. *for . . . stomachs*
because we have appetites   45. *Dewlapped* i.e. with folds of loose skin
hanging from the throat   46. *Wallets* pieces of fleshy skin   46-7. *men
. . . breasts* (a common travellers' tale)

Each putter-out of five for one will bring us
Good warrant of.
ALONSO.   I will stand to, and feed;
Although my last, no matter, since I feel   50
The best is past. Brother, my lord the Duke,
Stand to, and do as we.

*Thunder and lightning. Enter Ariel, like a harpy;
claps his wings upon the table; and with a quaint
device the banquet vanishes.*

ARIEL. You are three men of sin, whom destiny –
That hath to instrument this lower world
And what is in't – the never-surfeited sea   55
Hath caused to belch up you; and on this island,
Where man doth not inhabit, you 'mongst men
Being most unfit to live, I have made you mad;
And even with such-like valour men hang and drown
Their proper selves.
                    [*Alonso, Sebastian, &c. draw their swords.*]
                        You fools: I and my fellows   60
Are ministers of Fate: the elements,
Of whom your swords are tempered, may as well
Wound the loud winds, or with bemocked-at stabs
Kill the still-closing waters, as diminish
One dowle that's in my plume. My fellow ministers   65
Are like invulnerable. If you could hurt,
Your swords are now too massy for your strengths,
And will not be uplifted. But remember

48. *putter-out . . . one* traveller who insures himself against his safe
return from his travels. Five to one was a common rate   49. *warrant*
confirmation   *stand to* fall to, i.e. begin   50. *Although my last* i.e. even
if it is my last meal   51. *The best* i.e. the best part of my life   52 s.d.
like i.e. in the shape of   *harpy* (a legendary monster, with a woman's
face and body, and bird's wings and claws, supposed to be a minister of
vengeance)   *with . . . device* by an ingenious contrivance   54. *to
instrument* as its instrument   55. *what* whatever   *never-surfeited* never-
satisfied   59. *such-like valour* i.e. the valour which madness gives   60.
proper true, essential   61. *ministers* agents   62. *Of whom* of which   63.
bemocked-at stabs stabs (of the sword) which are mocked at; i.e. in-
effectual attempts to wound   64. *still-closing* constantly closing   65.
dowle small feather   66. *like* equally, similarly   67. *massy* massive,
heavy

(For that's my business to you) that you three
From Milan did supplant good Prospero;   70
Exposed unto the sea, which hath requit it,
Him and his innocent child; for which foul deed
The powers, delaying, not forgetting, have
Incensed the seas and shores, yea, all the creatures,
Against your peace. Thee of thy son, Alonso,   75
They have bereft; and do pronounce by me
Ling'ring perdition (worse than any death
Can be at once) shall step by step attend
You and your ways; whose wraths to guard you from,
Which here, in this most desolate isle, else falls   80
Upon your heads, is nothing but heart's sorrow
And a clear life ensuing.

*He vanishes in thunder; then, to soft music, enter
the Shapes again, and dance with mocks and mows,
and carrying out the table.*

PROSPERO. Bravely the figure of this harpy hast thou
Performed, my Ariel; a grace it had devouring.
Of my instruction hast thou nothing bated   85
In what thou hadst to say: so, with good life
And observation strange, my meaner ministers
Their several kinds have done. My high charms work,
And these, mine enemies, are all knit up
In their distractions: they now are in my power;   90

70. *supplant* expel   71. *requit it* requited it, i.e. paid you back (for the
crime)   73. *powers* i.e. agents of vengeance   74. *all the creatures* i.e. all
living things   76. *bereft* robbed   77. *Ling'ring perdition* slow destruction,
damnation (which)   79. *whose wraths* i.e. the wrath of the "powers"
80. *else* otherwise   81. *is nothing but* i.e. there is no alternative but   82.
clear blameless, sinless   s.d. *mocks and mows* mocking gestures and
grimaces   83. *Bravely* excellently   *figure* part   84. *a grace . . . devouring*
(i) it (your performance as a harpy) had an absorbing grace about it
(perhaps, also (ii) you performed your task of making the food vanish
very well)   85. *bated* omitted   86. *with good life* (i) with great liveli-
ness, or (ii) in a very lifelike way   87. *observation strange* remarkable
attention, exceptional care   *meaner ministers* i.e. lesser spirits (than
Ariel)   88. *Their . . . done* i.e. have performed their own particular tasks
high powerful   89-90. *knit . . . distractions* tangled up and confused in
their delusions, or fits of madness

And in these fits I leave them, while I visit
Young Ferdinand, whom they suppose is drowned,
And his and mine loved darling.   [*Exit above.*]
GONZALO. I' th' name of something holy, sir, why stand
    you
In this strange stare?
ALONSO.   O, it is monstrous, monstrous!   95
Methought the billows spoke, and told me of it;
The winds did sing it to me; and the thunder,
That deep and dreadful organ pipe, pronounced
The name of Prosper; it did bass my trespass.
Therefore my son i' th' ooze is bedded; and   100
I'll seek him deeper than e'er plummet sounded,
And with him there lie mudded.   *Exit.*
SEBASTIAN.   But one fiend at a time,
I'll fight their legions o'er.
ANTONIO.   I'll be thy second.
        Exeunt [*Sebastian and Antonio*].
GONZALO. All three of them are desperate: their great
    guilt,
Like poison given to work a great time after,   105
Now 'gins to bite the spirits. I do beseech you,
That are of suppler joints, follow them swiftly
And hinder them from what this ecstasy
May now provoke them to.
ADRIAN.   Follow, I pray you.
        Exeunt omnes.

94-5. *why . . . stare* why are you standing there with this strange look on your face (Gonzalo has not heard Ariel's speech)   *monstrous* unnatural 96. *of it* i.e. of my sin   99. *bass my trespass* proclaimed my sin in deep tones   101. *plummet* (a piece of metal, usually lead, on a string, used for sounding the depth of the sea)   102. *mudded* buried in mud   102-3. *But . . . legions o'er* i.e. If I can take on one fiend at a time, I'll fight them down to the very last one   105. *given . . . after* that takes effect long after (it is administered)   106. *Now . . . spirits* now begins to affect their vital powers   108. *ecstasy* madness, frenzy

ACT 4

Scene 1

Enter Prospero, Ferdinand, and Miranda.

PROSPERO. If I have too austerely punished you,
   Your compensation makes amends; for I
   Have given you here a third of mine own life,
   Or that for which I live; who once again
   I tender to thy hand. All thy vexations
   Were but my trials of thy love, and thou
   Hast strangely stood the test: here, afore heaven,
   I ratify this my rich gift. O Ferdinand,
   Do not smile at me that I boast her off,
   For thou shalt find she will outstrip all praise
   And make it halt behind her.
FERDINAND.   I do believe it
   Against an oracle.
PROSPERO. Then, as my gift, and thine own acquisition
   Worthily purchased, take my daughter: but
   If thou dost break her virgin-knot before
   All sanctimonious ceremonies may
   With full and holy rite be minist'red,
   No sweet aspersion shall the heavens let fall
   To make this contract grow; but barren hate,
   Sour-eyed disdain, and discord shall bestrew
   The union of your bed with weeds so loathly

4.1.1. *austerely* severely 3. *a third* i.e. Miranda (see end note) 7. *strangely* wonderfully well, to an exceptional degree 9. *boast her off* boast of her, speak with such pride of her 11. *halt* limp 12. *Against an oracle* even if an oracle were to deny it 14. *purchased* acquired, won 16. *sanctimonious* holy 18. *aspersion* sprinkling of rain (i.e. blessings) 19. *To make . . . grow* i.e. to make this betrothal develop into a fruitful and happy marriage 20. *disdain* vexation, trouble 20-21. *bestrew . . . bed* (refers to the custom of strewing the bridal bed with flowers)

That you shall hate it both. Therefore take heed,
As Hymen's lamp shall light you.
FERDINAND.   As I hope
  For quiet days, fair issue, and long life,
  With such love as 'tis now, the murkiest den,   25
  The most oppórtune place, the strong'st suggestion
  Our worser genius can, shall never melt
  Mine honour into lust, to take away
  The edge of that day's celebration
  When I shall think or Phoebus' steeds are foundered   30
  Or Night kept chained below.
PROSPERO.   Fairly spoke.
  Sit then, and talk with her; she is thine own.
  What, Ariel! my industrious servant, Ariel!

Enter Ariel.

ARIEL. What would my potent master? here I am.
PROSPERO. Thou and thy meaner fellows your last service   35
  Did worthily perform; and I must use you
  In such another trick. Go bring the rabble,
  O'er whom I give thee pow'r, here to this place:
  Incite them to quick motion; for I must
  Bestow upon the eyes of this young couple   40
  Some vanity of mine art: it is my promise,
  And they expect it from me.
ARIEL.   Presently?
PROSPERO. Ay, with a twink.

22. *hate it both* both hate it   23. *As . . . light you* i.e. as you hope that the torch carried by Hymen, the Greek god of marriage, will light up your wedding festivities. (If the torch burned clearly, it was a good omen)   24. *issue* children   25. *With . . . now* i.e. with love as strong as it is now   26. *suggestion* temptation   27. *Our . . . genius can* that our evil genius can make   28. *to take* so as to take   29. *that day's* i.e. the marriage day's   30. *or* either   *Phoebus' steeds* (the horses that pull the chariot of Phoebus, the sun-god)   *foundered* lame   31. *below* i.e. below the horizon (Night was thought to rise above the horizon as the sun went down below it)   33. *What* (a mode of calling someone, corresponding to "Come here!" or "Hullo there!")   37. *trick* (probably used here to mean an elaborate device such as that of the banquet in 3.3)   *rabble* i.e. the lesser spirits (not used contemptuously here)   41. *vanity* show, trifling exhibition   42. *Presently* At once   43. *with a twink* in the twinkling of an eye

ARIEL.   Before you can say "Come" and "Go,"
              And breathe twice and cry, "So, so,"   45
              Each one, tripping on his toe,
              Will be here with mop and mow.
              Do you love me, master? No?
PROSPERO. Dearly, my delicate Ariel. Do not approach
  Till thou dost hear me call.
ARIEL.   Well: I conceive.   *Exit.* 50
PROSPERO. Look thou be true: do not give dalliance
  Too much the rein: the strongest oaths are straw
  To th' fire i' th' blood: be more abstemious,
  Or else good night your vow!
FERDINAND.   I warrant you, sir;
  The white cold virgin snow upon my heart   55
  Abates the ardour of my liver.
PROSPERO.   Well.
  Now come, my Ariel: bring a corollary
  Rather than want a spirit: appear, and pertly!
  No tongue! all eyes! be silent.   *Soft music.*

Enter Iris.

IRIS. Ceres, most bounteous lady, thy rich leas   60
  Of wheat, rye, barley, vetches, oats, and pease;
  Thy turfy mountains, where live nibbling sheep,
  And flat meads thatched with stover, them to keep;
  Thy banks with pionèd and twillèd brims,
  Which spongy April at thy hest betrims,   65

47. *mop and mow* mocking gestures and grimaces 50. *Well: I conceive* It
is well: I understand 51. *true* i.e. true to your word *dalliance* love-
play (in modern slang, "necking") 53. *To* compared to 54. *good . . .
vow* i.e. it will be the end of the vow that you have made 55. *The . . .
snow* possibly (i) Miranda's pure breast (Ferdinand may be embracing
her), or perhaps (ii) the very idea of Miranda 56. *ardour* heat *liver*
(thought to be the seat of sexual passion) *Well* It is well 57. *a
corollary* a surplus, too many 58. *want* lack *pertly* promptly, briskly
59. *No tongue* i.e. Let no one speak (silence was necessary during
demonstrations of magic) s.d. *Iris* (a messenger of the gods who
represented the rainbow in Greek mythology; she always appeared with
multicoloured wings) 60. *Ceres* (the goddess of corn and harvests)
leas arable land 61. *vetches* a hay plant 63. *thatched . . . keep* covered
with cattle fodder to nourish them 64. *pionèd and twillèd brims* trenched
and ridged(?) 65. *spongy* showery *hest* command *betrims* bedecks
(with flowers)

To make cold nymphs chaste crowns; and thy broom-
   groves,
Whose shadow the dismissèd bachelor loves,
Being lasslorn; thy pole-clipt vineyard;
And thy sea-marge, sterile and rocky-hard,
Where thou thyself dost air – the queen o' th' sky,   70
Whose wat'ry arch and messenger am I,
Bids thee leave these, and with her sovereign grace,
Here on this grass-plot, in this very place,
To come and sport: her peacocks fly amain.
Approach, rich Ceres, her to entertain.   75

Enter Ceres.

CERES. Hail, many-coloured messenger, that ne'er
Dost disobey the wife of Jupiter,
Who, with thy saffron wings, upon my flow'rs
Diffusest honey drops, refreshing show'rs,
And with each end of thy blue bow dost crown   80
My bosky acres and my unshrubbed down,
Rich scarf to my proud earth – why hath thy queen
Summoned me hither to this short-grassed green?
IRIS. A contract of true love to celebrate,
And some donation freely to estate   85
On the blessed lovers.
CERES.   Tell me, heavenly bow,
If Venus or her son, as thou dost know,

---

66. *cold nymphs* pure (passionless) maidens *broom-groves* clumps of
gorse 67. *dismissèd* rejected *bachelor* young man, swain 68. *lasslorn*
i.e. forsaken by his sweetheart *pole-clipt vineyard* i.e. (i) a vineyard
whose poles are clasped (embraced) by the vines, or possibly (ii) a
vineyard that has been pruned 69. *sea-marge* seashore 70. *dost air* do
take the air *queen . . . sky* i.e. Juno, the wife and sister of Jupiter, who
was worshipped as the queen of the heavens and as the goddess of all
power and of riches 71. *wat'ry arch* i.e. the rainbow 72. *these* i.e. the
places just mentioned *grace* i.e. majesty 74. *peacocks* (peacocks were
sacred to Juno and drew her chariot through the skies) *amain* swiftly,
strongly 75. *entertain* greet, receive 78. *saffron* orange-red 81. *bosky*
wooded, covered with bushes *unshrubbed* bare, without shrubs *down*
rolling open expanse of upland 85. *donation* gift *estate* bestow 86.
heavenly bow i.e. Iris 87. *Venus* (goddess of love) *her son* i.e. Cupid

Do now attend the queen? Since they did plot
The means that dusky Dis my daughter got,
Her and her blind boy's scandalled company   90
I have forsworn.
IRIS.   Of her society
Be not afraid: I met her Deity
Cutting the clouds towards Paphos, and her son
Dove-drawn with her. Here thought they to have done
Some wanton charm upon this man and maid,   95
Whose vows are, that no bed-right shall be paid
Till Hymen's torch be lighted; but in vain.
Mars's hot minion is returned again;
Her waspish-headed son has broke his arrows,
Swears he will shoot no more, but play with sparrows,   100
And be a boy right out.

[*Enter Juno.*]

CERES.   Highest queen of state,
Great Juno comes; I know her by her gait.
JUNO. How does my bounteous sister? Go with me
To bless this twain, that they may prosperous be
And honoured in their issue.   *They sing.* 105
JUNO.   Honour, riches, marriage blessing,
          Long continuance, and increasing,
          Hourly joys be still upon you!
          Juno sings her blessings on you.

89. *that* by which   *dusky Dis* i.e. Pluto, god of the underworld, who
abducted Ceres' daughter Proserpine and carried her off to his kingdom
under the earth as his queen 90. *blind boy's* i.e. Cupid's *scandalled*
scandalous, disgraceful 92. *her Deity* her divine majesty, i.e. Venus
93. *Paphos* (a town on the island of Cyprus which was the centre of the
worship of Venus) 94. *Dove-drawn* (the chariot of Venus was drawn
by doves) 95. *wanton charm* lascivious trick (i.e. charming Ferdinand
and Miranda into breaking their vow of chastity before the actual
marriage ceremony) 97. *Hymen's torch* i.e. the torch of the god of
marriage 98. *Mars's hot minion* i.e. Venus, who was the lustful mistress
of Mars, the god of war *is returned again* i.e. has gone back to where
she came from 99. *waspish-headed* spiteful *son* i.e. Cupid 101. *right
out* outright, completely (i.e. Cupid will settle down to act like a real
boy and not like a god) *state* majesty 102. *gait* stately walk 108.
still ever, always

[CERES.] Earth's increase, foison plenty,   110
       Barns and garners never empty;
       Vines with clust'ring bunches growing,
       Plants with goodly burden bowing;
       Spring come to you at the farthest
       In the very end of harvest.   115
       Scarcity and want shall shun you,
       Ceres' blessing so is on you.

FERDINAND. This is a most majestic vision, and
   Harmonious charmingly. May I be bold
   To think these spirits?

PROSPERO.   Spirits, which by mine art   120
   I have from their confines called to enact
   My present fancies.

FERDINAND.   Let me live here ever!
   So rare a wond'red father and a wise
   Makes this place Paradise.

Juno and Ceres whisper, and send Iris on employment.

PROSPERO.   Sweet now, silence!
   Juno and Ceres whisper seriously.   125
   There's something else to do: hush and be mute,
   Or else our spell is marred.

IRIS. You nymphs, called Naiades, of the windring brooks,
   With your sedged crowns and ever-harmless looks,
   Leave your crisp channels, and on this green land   130
   Answer your summons; Juno does command.
   Come, temperate nymphs, and help to celebrate
   A contract of true love: be not too late.

Enter certain Nymphs.

---

110. *foison* abundance   111. *garners* granaries   114. *farthest* latest   117. *so* to that end (i.e. to make all that has just been said come true)   119. *charmingly* magically   121. *their confines* i.e. the places in which they normally live   123. *So rare . . . wise* i.e. a father who has such remarkable and wonderful powers and who is so wise   124. *Sweet now, silence* (probably addressed to Miranda, who may be about to add a comment; some editors give this phrase to Miranda and suggest that she is addressing Ferdinand)   128. *Naiades* water nymphs   *windring* (a combination of winding and wandering)   129. *sedged crowns* garlands of sedge (a reedy plant growing in marshy soil)   130. *crisp* rippling   *land* (probably) lawn   132. *temperate* chaste

You sunburned sicklemen, of August weary,
Come hither from the furrow and be merry.   135
Make holiday: your rye-straw hats put on,
And these fresh nymphs encounter every one
In country footing.

> *Enter certain Reapers, properly habited: they join
> with the Nymphs in a graceful dance; towards the
> end whereof Prospero starts suddenly and speaks;
> after which, to a strange, hollow, and confused
> noise, they heavily vanish.*

PROSPERO [*aside*]. I had forgot that foul conspiracy
Of the beast Caliban and his confederates   140
Against my life: the minute of their plot
Is almost come. [*To the Spirits*] Well done! Avoid! No
  more!
FERDINAND. This is strange. Your father's in some passion
That works him strongly.
MIRANDA.   Never till this day
Saw I him touched with anger so distempered.   145
PROSPERO. You do look, my son, in a movèd sort,
As if you were dismayed: be cheerful, sir.
Our revels now are ended. These our actors,
As I foretold you, were all spirits and
Are melted into air, into thin air;   150
And, like the baseless fabric of this vision,
The cloud-capped towers, the gorgeous palaces,
The solemn temples, the great globe itself,
Yea, all which it inherit, shall dissolve,
And, like this insubstantial pageant faded,   155
Leave not a rack behind. We are such stuff

---

134. *sicklemen* reapers 135. *furrow* (equivalent, here, to "fields of
grain") 137. *fresh* young, beautiful *encounter* meet, join 138. *footing*
dance s.d. *properly habited* suitably dressed *they heavily vanish* i.e.
they vanish in a slow, sorrowful, and dispirited manner 142. *Avoid* i.e.
Avoid my sight, Begone 144. *works* moves, agitates 145. *distempered*
violent 146. *movèd sort* troubled mood, distressed 148. *revels* pageants
(more generally, "entertainments") 151. *baseless fabric* i.e. structure
without foundation or reality 154. *it inherit* occupy it 156. *rack* wisp
of cloud or mist

As dreams are made on, and our little life
Is rounded with a sleep. Sir, I am vexed;
Bear with my weakness: my old brain is troubled:
Be not disturbed with my infirmity. 160
If you be pleased, retire into my cell
And there repose: a turn or two I'll walk,
To still my beating mind.
FERDINAND, MIRANDA. We wish your peace.
      Exit [Ferdinand with Miranda].
PROSPERO. Come with a thought. I thank thee, Ariel:
 come.

       Enter Ariel.

ARIEL. Thy thoughts I cleave to. What's thy pleasure?
PROSPERO.   Spirit, 165
 We must prepare to meet with Caliban.
ARIEL. Ay, my commander: when I presented Ceres,
 I thought to have told thee of it, but I feared
 Lest I might anger thee.
PROSPERO. Say again, where didst thou leave these varlets? 170
ARIEL. I told you, sir, they were redhot with drinking;
 So full of valour that they smote the air
 For breathing in their faces; beat the ground
 For kissing of their feet; yet always bending
 Towards their project. Then I beat my tabor; 175
 At which, like unbacked colts, they pricked their ears,
 Advanced their eyelids, lifted up their noses
 As they smelt music. So I charmed their ears
 That, calf-like, they my lowing followed through
 Toothed briers, sharp furzes, pricking goss, and thorns, 180
 Which ent'red their frail shins. At last I left them

---

158. *rounded with* rounded off by 161. *If . . . pleased* if it please you
163. *beating* agitated 164. *Come . . . thought* (i.e. Prospero has thought
of Ariel and Ariel is arriving) 165. *Thy . . . cleave to* i.e. I am firmly
attached to your thoughts 167. *presented Ceres* (i.e. either (i) played
the part of Ceres in the masque, or (ii) "presented" the masque, which
included the part of Ceres) 170. *varlets* rogues, rascals 174. *bending*
going towards 175. *their project* i.e. the murder of Prospero 176.
unbacked colts unbroken colts *pricked* (i.e. up) 177. *Advanced* raised
178. *As* as if 180. *goss* gorse

I' th' filthy-mantled pool beyond your cell,
There dancing up to th' chins, that the foul lake
O'erstunk their feet.
PROSPERO.   This was well done, my bird.
  Thy shape invisible retain thou still: 185
  The trumpery in my house, go bring it hither
  For stale to catch these thieves.
ARIEL.   I go, I go.   *Exit.*
PROSPERO. A devil, a born devil, on whose nature
  Nurture can never stick: on whom my pains,
  Humanely taken, all, all lost, quite lost;   190
  And as with age his body uglier grows,
  So his mind cankers. I will plague them all,
  Even to roaring.

    Enter Ariel, loaden with glistering apparel, &c.

             Come, hang them on this line.

    [Prospero and Ariel remain, invisible.]
    Enter Caliban, Stephano, and Trinculo, all wet.

CALIBAN. Pray you tread softly, that the blind mole may
    not
  Hear a foot fall: we now are near his cell.   195
STEPHANO. Monster, your fairy, which you say is a harm-
    less fairy, has done little better than played the Jack
    with us.
TRINCULO. Monster, I do smell all horse-piss; at which my
    nose is in great indignation.   200
STEPHANO. So is mine. Do you hear, monster? If I should
    take a displeasure against you, look you —
TRINCULO. Thou wert but a lost monster.
CALIBAN. Good my lord, give me thy favour still.

182. *filthy-mantled pool* pool covered with filthy scum   183. *that* so that
184. *O'erstunk* stank worse than   *bird* i.e. Ariel   186. *trumpery* trifles,
junk   187. *For stale* as a decoy   189. *Nurture* education, training, discipline   192. *cankers* festers (with malice)   193. *Even to roaring* until
they roar   *line* lime or linden tree   194. *blind mole* i.e. Prospero (moles
were noted for their keen hearing)   196. *your fairy* i.e. Ariel   197. *Jack*
(i) knave, joker, (ii) will-o'-the-wisp   203. *wert* would be   204. *give . . .*
still let me stay in your good books

Be patient, for the prize I'll bring thee to 205
Shall hoodwink this mischance. Therefore speak softly;
All's hushed as midnight yet.
TRINCULO. Ay, but to lose our bottles in the pool –
STEPHANO. There is not only disgrace and dishonour in
 that, monster, but an infinite loss. 210
TRINCULO. That's more to me than my wetting: yet this is
 your harmless fairy, monster.
STEPHANO. I will fetch off my bottle, though I be o'er ears
 for my labour.
CALIBAN. Prithee, my king, be quiet. Seest thou here? 215
 This is the mouth o' th' cell. No noise, and enter.
 Do that good mischief which may make this island
 Thine own for ever, and I, thy Caliban,
 For aye thy foot-licker.
STEPHANO. Give me thy hand; I do begin to have bloody 220
 thoughts.
TRINCULO. O King Stephano! O peer! O worthy Stephano,
 look what a wardrobe here is for thee!
CALIBAN. Let it alone, thou fool! it is but trash.
TRINCULO. O, ho, monster! we know what belongs to a 225
 frippery. O King Stephano!
STEPHANO. Put off that gown, Trinculo: by this hand, I'll
 have that gown!
TRINCULO. Thy Grace shall have it.
CALIBAN. The dropsy drown this fool! What do you mean 230
 To dote thus on such luggage? Let't alone,
 And do the murder first. If he awake,
 From toe to crown he'll fill our skins with pinches,
 Make us strange stuff.

206. *hoodwink this mischance* i.e. blind our eyes to this misadventure,
make us forget our recent calamity 213. *fetch off* rescue *o'er ears* i.e.
over the ears in the "filthy-mantled pool" 214. *labour* pains, trouble
217. *that good mischief* i.e. that evil deed which will make your good
fortune 222. *O King . . . worthy Stephano* (Trinculo is thinking of an
old popular song, "King Stephen was a worthy peer". Iago sings one
stanza in *Othello* [2.3.91-9]) 226. *frippery* second-hand clothes shop
230. *dropsy* (swelling caused by the accumulation of body fluids) *drown*
choke 231. *luggage* junk 234. *Make . . . stuff* turn us into strange
material

STEPHANO. Be you quiet, monster. Mistress line, is not this[235]
   my jerkin? [*Takes it down.*] Now is the jerkin under the
   line. Now, jerkin, you are like to lose your hair and
   prove a bald jerkin.
TRINCULO. Do, do; we steal by line and level, an't like
   your Grace.   240
STEPHANO. I thank thee for that jest; here's a garment
   for't. Wit shall not go unrewarded while I am king of
   this country. "Steal by line and level" is an excellent pass
   of pate; there's another garment for't.
TRINCULO. Monster, come put some lime upon your[245]
   fingers, and away with the rest.
CALIBAN. I will have none on't: we shall lose our time
   And all be turned to barnacles, or to apes
   With foreheads villainous low.
STEPHANO. Monster, lay-to your fingers: help to bear this[250]
   away where my hogshead of wine is, or I'll turn you out
   of my kingdom. Go to, carry this.
TRINCULO. And this.
STEPHANO. Ay, and this.

   *A noise of hunters heard. Enter divers Spirits in
   shape of dogs and hounds, hunting them about;
   Prospero and Ariel setting them on.*

PROSPERO. Hey, Mountain, hey!   255
ARIEL. Silver! there it goes, Silver!
PROSPERO. Fury, Fury! there, Tyrant, there! hark, hark!
   [*Caliban, Stephano, and Trinculo are driven out.*]

235. *Mistress line* (presumably referring to the lime tree on which the
"glistering apparel" was hung) 236. *jerkin* jacket 239. *Do, do* i.e. fine,
fine (Trinculo is approving Stephano's pun) *by . . . level* according to
rule, methodically (by plumb line and carpenter's level with a pun on
"line") *an't like* if it please 243-4. *pass of pate* sally of wit 245.
lime (lime was a sticky substance used for trapping birds. Stephano
probably suggests jestingly that the rest of the clothing will stick to
Caliban's fingers, since thieves were said to have "sticky" fingers) 246.
and away . . . rest i.e. and then Caliban can get away with the rest (of
the clothing) 247. *on't* of it *lose our time* waste our time, lose our
opportunity 248. *barnacles* i.e. wild geese 249. *villainous* miserably,
wretchedly 250. *lay-to your fingers* use your fingers 252. *Go to* come
on, get on with it 255-7. *Mountain, Silver, Fury, Tyrant* (the names of
hounds) *hark* (cry to encourage the hounds)

    Go, charge my goblins that they grind their joints
    With dry convulsions, shorten up their sinews
    With agèd cramps, and more pinch-spotted make them   260
    Than pard or cat o' mountain.
ARIEL.   Hark, they roar!
PROSPERO. Let them be hunted soundly. At this hour
    Lie at my mercy all mine enemies:
    Shortly shall all my labours end, and thou
    Shalt have the air at freedom. For a little,   265
    Follow, and do me service.   *Exeunt.*

259. *dry convulsions* (rheumatic condition when the joints of the bones are dry from old age)   260. *agèd cramps* cramps such as old people have   260-61. *more . . . mountain* give them more spots (from pinching them) than has a leopard or panther   265. *at freedom* at liberty

ACT 5

Scene 1

Enter Prospero in his magic robes, and Ariel.

PROSPERO. Now does my project gather to a head:
My charms crack not, my spirits obey, and time
Goes upright with his carriage. How's the day?
ARIEL. On the sixth hour; at which time, my lord,
You said our work should cease.
PROSPERO.   I did say so,   5
When first I raised the tempest. Say, my spirit,
How fares the King and 's followers?
ARIEL.   Confined together
In the same fashion as you gave in charge;
Just as you left them; all prisoners, sir,
In the line grove which weather-fends your cell;   10
They cannot budge till your release. The King,
His brother, and yours abide all three distracted,
And the remainder mourning over them,
Brimful of sorrow and dismay; but chiefly
Him that you termed, sir, "the good old Lord Gonzalo"; 15
His tears run down his beard like winter's drops
From eaves of reeds. Your charm so strongly works 'em,
That if you now beheld them, your affections
Would become tender.
PROSPERO.   Dost thou think so, spirit?
ARIEL. Mine would, sir, were I human.
PROSPERO.   And mine shall.   20

5.1.2. *crack not* show no signs of a flaw   2-3. *time . . . carriage* time
bears his burden without stooping, i.e. Prospero's plans are going according to schedule   4. *hour* (two syllables; F reads "hower")   8. *gave in
charge* commanded   10. *weather-fends* protects against the weather   11.
till your release until you release them (from the spell)   12. *yours* i.e.
your brother   *abide* remain   17. *From . . . reeds* i.e. from the eaves of a
thatched roof   *works* works on, moves   18. *affections* feelings

Hast thou, which art but air, a touch, a feeling
Of their afflictions, and shall not myself,
One of their kind, that relish all as sharply
Passion as they, be kindlier moved than thou art?
Though with their high wrongs I am struck to th' quick, 25
Yet with my nobler reason 'gainst my fury
Do I take part. The rarer action is
In virtue than in vengeance. They being penitent,
The sole drift of my purpose doth extend
Not a frown further. Go, release them, Ariel.   30
My charms I'll break, their senses I'll restore,
And they shall be themselves.
ARIEL.   I'll fetch them, sir.   *Exit.*
PROSPERO. Ye elves of hills, brooks, standing lakes, and
    groves,
And ye that on the sands with printless foot
Do chase the ebbing Neptune, and do fly him   35
When he comes back; you demi-puppets that
By moonshine do the green sour ringlets make,
Whereof the ewe not bites; and you whose pastime
Is to make midnight mushrumps, that rejoice
To hear the solemn curfew; by whose aid   40
(Weak masters though ye be) I have bedimmed
The noontide sun, called forth the mutinous winds,
And 'twixt the green sea and the azured vault
Set roaring war: to the dread rattling thunder

21. *touch* sense, sensibility 23-4. *that relish . . . they* who feel strong
emotion as intensely as they do *kindlier moved* i.e. more moved in
accordance with my humanity (human kind) 25. *their high wrongs*
the great wrongs done by them 26-7. *Yet . . . part* but I take the part
of reason against anger (in the conflict of the two within me) 27-8.
The rarer . . . vengeance i.e. It is finer (nobler) to be virtuous than to
take vengeance (the word "virtue" implies strength as well as moral
goodness) 29. *The sole . . . purpose* the whole intent of my purpose
now 30. *Not . . . further* i.e. no further in hostility than I have already
gone 33. *standing* still 35. *Neptune* i.e. sea (the picture in ll. 35-6 is
that of the elves who, like children, chase the ebbing waves and then run
back quickly so as not to wet their feet) 36. *demi-puppets* half-puppets,
fairies 37. *green sour ringlets* i.e. fairy rings (circles in the grass, unpleasant to the taste, supposed to have been formed by the dancing of
fairies) 39. *mushrumps* mushrooms 40. *curfew* (after the curfew bell,
which rang at nine o'clock, spirits could wander abroad) 41. *Weak
masters* weak forces (in contrast to the powerful spirits of the Devil)
42. *mutinous* stormy 43. *azured vault* i.e. blue sky

Have I given fire and rifted Jove's stout oak   45
With his own bolt; the strong-based promontory
Have I made shake, and by the spurs plucked up
The pine and cedar: graves at my command
Have waked their sleepers, oped, and let 'em forth
By my so potent art. But this rough magic   50
I here abjure; and when I have required
Some heavenly music (which even now I do)
To work mine end upon their senses, that
This airy charm is for, I'll break my staff,
Bury it certain fathoms in the earth,   55
And deeper than did ever plummet sound
I'll drown my book.   *Solemn music.*

*Here enters Ariel before; then Alonso, with a
frantic gesture, attended by Gonzalo; Sebastian
and Antonio in like manner, attended by Adrian
and Francisco. They all enter the circle which
Prospero had made, and there stand charmed;
which Prospero observing, speaks.*

A solemn air, and the best comforter
To an unsettled fancy, cure thy brains,
Now useless, boiled within thy skull! There stand,   60
For you are spell-stopped.
Holy Gonzalo, honourable man,
Mine eyes, ev'n sociable to the show of thine,
Fall fellowly drops. The charm dissolves apace;
And as the morning steals upon the night,   65
Melting the darkness, so their rising senses

45. *rifted* split *Jove's stout oak* (the oak tree was sacred to Jove, or
Jupiter) 46. *bolt* i.e. thunderbolt 47. *spurs* roots 50. *rough magic*
i.e. crude magic (which displays the results of Prospero's art in an
obvious manner) 51. *required* requested 53. *their senses, that* the
senses of those whom 54. *airy charm* i.e. the magical music *staff* i.e.
magic wand 55. *certain* i.e. a certain number of, many 57. *book* i.e.
the book of magic that contains Prospero's spells s.d. *gesture* bearing,
manner *the circle* i.e. the magic circle 58-9. *A solemn . . . fancy* a
solemn piece of music, which is the best comforter to a troubled imagination 60. *boiled . . . skull* i.e. Alonso's brains are in a ferment 61.
spell-stopped held motionless by my spell 62. *Holy* righteous, good 63.
ev'n . . . thine i.e. responding to the sight of yours 64. *Fall fellowly
drops* i.e. shed tears in sympathy *apace* quickly 66. *rising* i.e. returning

Begin to chase the ignorant fumes that mantle
Their clearer reason. O good Gonzalo,
My true preserver, and a loyal sir
To him thou follow'st, I will pay thy graces   70
Home both in word and deed. Most cruelly
Didst thou, Alonso, use me and my daughter:
Thy brother was a furtherer in the act.
Thou art pinched for't now, Sebastian. Flesh and blood,
You, brother mine, that entertained ambition,   75
Expelled remorse and nature; who, with Sebastian
(Whose inward pinches therefore are most strong),
Would here have killed your king; I do forgive thee,
Unnatural though thou art. Their understanding
Begins to swell, and the approaching tide   80
Will shortly fill the reasonable shore,
That now lies foul and muddy. Not one of them
That yet looks on me or would know me. Ariel,
Fetch me the hat and rapier in my cell;
I will discase me, and myself present   85
As I was sometime Milan. Quickly, spirit!
Thou shalt ere long be free.

                     [*Exit Ariel and returns immediately.*]

ARIEL (*sings and helps to attire him*).
        Where the bee sucks, there suck I;
        In a cowslip's bell I lie;
        There I couch when owls do cry.   90
        On the bat's back I do fly
        After summer merrily.
      Merrily, merrily shall I live now
      Under the blossom that hangs on the bough.

67. *ignorant fumes* i.e. fumes of delusion   *mantle* obscure (literally: cover with scum)   **69.** *true preserver* (see 1.2.160-68. Gonzalo preserved Prospero and Miranda by giving them supplies when they were cast adrift)   *sir* gentleman   **70-71.** *pay . . . Home* repay your favours and services thoroughly   **74.** *pinched* harassed, paid back   **75.** *entertained* willingly received, welcomed   **76.** *remorse* pity   *nature* natural feeling   **77.** *inward pinches* i.e. twinges of guilt   *therefore . . . strong* (because he planned to kill Alonso, who was not only his brother but his king)   **80.** *swell* increase (as the tide rises)   **81.** *reasonable shore* shore of reason   **85.** *discase me* disrobe myself, i.e. throw off my magic robe   **86.** *sometime Milan* i.e. as I was before, when I was Duke of Milan   **90.** *couch* lie (probably concealed)   **92.** *After summer* in pursuit of summer (Ariel, now that he is free, can follow summer around the globe)

PROSPERO. Why, that's my dainty Ariel! I shall miss thee, 95
  But yet thou shalt have freedom; so, so, so.
  To the King's ship, invisible as thou art:
  There shalt thou find the mariners asleep
  Under the hatches; the master and the boatswain
  Being awake, enforce them to this place, 100
  And presently, I prithee.
ARIEL. I drink the air before me, and return
  Or ere your pulse twice beat.   *Exit.*
GONZALO. All torment, trouble, wonder, and amazement
  Inhabits here: some heavenly power guide us 105
  Out of this fearful country!
PROSPERO.   Behold, sir King,
  The wrongèd Duke of Milan, Prospero.
  For more assurance that a living prince
  Does now speak to thee, I embrace thy body,
  And to thee and thy company I bid 110
  A hearty welcome.
ALONSO.   Whe'r thou be'st he or no,
  Or some enchanted trifle to abuse me,
  As late I have been, I not know: thy pulse
  Beats, as of flesh and blood; and, since I saw thee,
  Th' affliction of my mind amends, with which, 115
  I fear, a madness held me. This must crave
  (An if this be at all) a most strange story.
  Thy dukedom I resign and do entreat
  Thou pardon me my wrongs. But how should Prospero
  Be living and be here?
PROSPERO.   First, noble friend, 120
  Let me embrace thine age, whose honour cannot
  Be measured or confined.

96. *so, so, so* i.e. that will do (Ariel has now finished helping Prospero to change) 99. *Under the hatches* below deck 100. *Being awake* when they are awake *enforce them* compel them (to come) 101. *presently* immediately, right away 102. *drink the air* "devour the way" (corresponds roughly to the modern expression "eat up the miles") 103. *Or ere* before 104. *amazement* complete confusion 108. *For more assurance* to make you even more sure 111. *Whe'r* whether 112. *enchanted trifle* apparition raised by magic, trick of magic *abuse* deceive 113. *As late . . . been* as, recently, I have been (deceived) 116. *crave* call for, demand 117. *An if . . . all* if this is really happening 119. *my wrongs* i.e. the wrongs that I have done to you 121. *thine age* your old body, you who are old

GONZALO.   Whether this be,
   Or be not, I'll not swear.
PROSPERO.   You do yet taste
   Some subtleties o' th' isle, that will not let you
   Believe things certain. Welcome, my friends all.   125
   [*Aside to Sebastian and Antonio*] But you, my brace of
      lords, were I so minded,
   I here could pluck his Highness' frown upon you,
   And justify you traitors. At this time
   I will tell no tales.
SEBASTIAN [*aside*].   The devil speaks in him.
PROSPERO.   No.
   For you, most wicked sir, whom to call brother   130
   Would even infect my mouth, I do forgive
   Thy rankest fault – all of them; and require
   My dukedom of thee, which perforce I know
   Thou must restore.
ALONSO.   If thou beest Prospero,
   Give us particulars of thy preservation;   135
   How thou hast met us here, who three hours since
   Were wracked upon this shore; where I have lost
   (How sharp the point of this remembrance is!)
   My dear son Ferdinand.
PROSPERO.   I am woe for't, sir.
ALONSO. Irreparable is the loss, and patience   140
   Says it is past her cure.
PROSPERO.   I rather think
   You have not sought her help, of whose soft grace
   For the like loss I have her sovereign aid,
   And rest myself content.

123. *taste* feel   124. *subtleties* subtle effects, lingering magic (see end note)   125. *things certain* in the reality of things   127. *pluck* call down (literally: pull down)   128. *justify* prove   129. *No* (either a response to Sebastian's aside or a further stress to the promise to "tell no tales")   132. *all of them* i.e. all of your faults   *require* request, demand   133. *perforce* of necessity   139. *woe* sorry, full of woe   140-41. *patience/ . . . cure* i.e. patience cannot cure my grief   142. *her help* i.e. the help of patience   *of . . . grace* by whose gentle mercy   143. *sovereign* most potent   144. *rest myself content* manage to remain happy myself

ALONSO.   You the like loss?

PROSPERO. As great to me as late; and, supportable   145
    To make the dear loss, have I means much weaker
    Than you may call to comfort you; for I
    Have lost my daughter.

ALONSO.   A daughter?
    O heavens, that they were living both in Naples,
    The King and Queen there! that they were, I wish   150
    Myself were mudded in that oozy bed
    Where my son lies. When did you lose your daughter?

PROSPERO. In this last tempest. I perceive these lords
    At this encounter do so much admire,
    That they devour their reason, and scarce think   155
    Their eyes do offices of truth, their words
    Are natural breath. But, howsoev'r you have
    Been justled from your senses, know for certain
    That I am Prospero, and that very duke
    Which was thrust forth of Milan, who most strangely   160
    Upon this shore, where you were wracked, was landed
    To be the lord on't. No more yet of this;
    For 'tis a chronicle of day by day,
    Not a relation for a breakfast, nor
    Befitting this first meeting. Welcome, sir;   165
    This cell's my court: here have I few attendants,
    And subjects none abroad: pray you look in.
    My dukedom since you have given me again,
    I will requite you with as good a thing;

145. *As great . . . late* i.e. my loss is as great as is yours and has happened just as recently   145-6. *supportable/ . . . loss* to make the grievous loss bearable   147. *call* i.e. call on   150. *that* provided that (Alonso says that he would willingly change places with his son, whom he thinks drowned, if, by his death, he could ensure that Ferdinand and Miranda lived)   154. *encounter* meeting (with me)   *admire* wonder   155. *devour their reason* i.e. their reason is dulled by astonishment   155-6. *scarce . . . truth* i.e. can hardly believe the testimony of their own eyes   156-7. *their . . . breath* that their words are the words of ordinary human beings   *howsoev'r* however much   158. *justled* jolted   160. *of* from   162. *on't* of it   164. *relation* tale   167. *abroad* outside of my cell, or, possibly, "abroad in the island"

At least bring forth a wonder to content ye   170
As much as me my dukedom.

> *Here Prospero discovers Ferdinand and*
> *Miranda playing at chess.*

MIRANDA. Sweet lord, you play me false.

FERDINAND.   No, my dearest love,
I would not for the world.

MIRANDA. Yes, for a score of kingdoms you should
 wrangle,
And I would call it fair play.

ALONSO.   If this prove   175
A vision of the island, one dear son
Shall I twice lose.

SEBASTIAN.   A most high miracle!

FERDINAND. Though the seas threaten, they are merciful.
I have cursed them without cause.   [*Kneels.*]

ALONSO.   Now all the blessings
Of a glad father compass thee about!   180
Arise, and say how thou cam'st here.

MIRANDA.   O, wonder!
How many goodly creatures are there here!
How beauteous mankind is! O brave new world
That has such people in't!

PROSPERO.   'Tis new to thee.

ALONSO. What is this maid with whom thou wast at play? 185
Your eld'st acquaintance cannot be three hours.
Is she the goddess that hath severed us
And brought us thus together?

FERDINAND.   Sir, she is mortal;
But by immortal providence she's mine.
I chose her when I could not ask my father   190
For his advice, nor thought I had one. She
Is daughter to this famous Duke of Milan,

170. *a wonder . . . ye* a marvel to please you 171 s.d. *discovers* reveals
(possibly by drawing back a curtain on the stage) 172. *play me false*
cheat me (a light-hearted reference not only to the game of chess but to
the game of love) 174. *wrangle* (i) dispute, or possibly (ii) cheat 176.
A vision i.e. another illusion 180. *compass* embrace, surround 182.
goodly handsome 183. *brave* fine, excellent 186. *Your eld'st acquain-*
tance the longest period of your acquaintance

Of whom so often I have heard renown,
But never saw before; of whom I have
Received a second life; and second father   195
This lady makes him to me.
ALONSO.   I am hers.
But, O, how oddly will it sound that I
Must ask my child forgiveness!
PROSPERO.   There, sir, stop.
Let us not burden our remembrances
With a heaviness that's gone.
GONZALO.   I have inly wept,   200
Or should have spoke ere this. Look down, you gods,
And on this couple drop a blessèd crown;
For it is you that have chalked forth the way
Which brought us hither.
ALONSO.   I say Amen, Gonzalo.
GONZALO. Was Milan thrust from Milan, that his issue   205
Should become kings of Naples? O, rejoice
Beyond a common joy, and set it down
With gold on lasting pillars: in one voyage
Did Claribel her husband find at Tunis,
And Ferdinand her brother found a wife   210
Where he himself was lost; Prospero his dukedom
In a poor isle; and all of us ourselves
When no man was his own.
ALONSO [*to Ferdinand and Miranda*]. Give me your
     hands:
Let grief and sorrow still embrace his heart
That doth not wish you joy.
GONZALO.   Be it so! Amen!   215

*Enter Ariel, with the Master and Boatswain
           amazedly following.*

O, look, sir; look, sir! here is more of us:

193. *renown* report   196. *I am hers* i.e. I accept her; I am a second
father to her   200. *heaviness* sorrow   *inly* inwardly   203. *chalked forth*
marked out   205. *Was Milan* i.e. was the Duke of Milan   213. *When
. . . own* when no man was his real self (or in his right senses)   214.
still for ever   215 s.d. *amazedly* as in a maze, in a daze

I prophesied, if a gallows were on land,
This fellow could not drown. Now, blasphemy,
That swear'st grace o'erboard, not an oath on shore?
Hast thou no mouth by land? What is the news?   220
BOATSWAIN. The best news is that we have safely found
Our king and company; the next, our ship,
Which, but three glasses since, we gave out split,
Is tight and yare and bravely rigged, as when
We first put out to sea.
ARIEL [*aside to Prospero*]. Sir, all this service   225
Have I done since I went.
PROSPERO [*aside to Ariel*]. My tricksy spirit!
ALONSO. These are not natural events; they strengthen
From strange to stranger. Say, how came you hither?
BOATSWAIN. If I did think, sir, I were well awake,
I'ld strive to tell you. We were dead of sleep   230
And (how we know not) all clapped under hatches;
Where, but even now, with strange and several noises
Of roaring, shrieking, howling, jingling chains,
And moe diversity of sounds, all horrible,
We were awaked; straightway at liberty;   235
Where we, in all our trim, freshly beheld
Our royal, good, and gallant ship, our master
Cap'ring to eye her. On a trice, so please you,
Even in a dream, were we divided from them,
And were brought moping hither.
ARIEL [*aside to Prospero*].   Was't well done?   240
PROSPERO [*aside to Ariel*]. Bravely, my diligence. Thou
shalt be free.

217. *I prophesied* (see 1.1.27-9. During the storm Gonzalo said that the boatswain was destined to hang, not drown)   *were* i.e. existed 218. *blasphemy* i.e. you blasphemous fellow 219. *That . . . o'erboard* that drives God's grace overboard by your profanity 221. *safely* safe and sound 223. *three glasses* three hours 224. *yare* seaworthy 226. *tricksy* full of tricks, ingenious 227-8. *strengthen . . . stranger* increase more and more in strangeness 230. *dead of sleep* in a deep sleep 232. *several* various 234. *moe* more 236. *Where* whereupon, on which occasion *in . . . trim* i.e. all fit and ready *freshly* in fine condition 238. *Cap'ring* dancing for joy *On a trice* in a moment 239. *them* i.e. the rest of the crew and the ship 240. *moping* bewildered, or, possibly, sulking 241. *Bravely* splendidly *my diligence* i.e. my conscientious spirit, diligent one

ALONSO. This is as strange a maze as e'er men trod,
   And there is in this business more than nature
   Was ever conduct of. Some oracle
   Must rectify our knowledge.
PROSPERO.   Sir, my liege,   245
   Do not infest your mind with beating on
   The strangeness of this business: at picked leisure,
   Which shall be shortly, single I'll resolve you
   (Which to you shall seem probable) of every
   These happened accidents; till when, be cheerful   250
   And think of each thing well. [*Aside to Ariel*] Come
      hither, spirit.
   Set Caliban and his companions free:
   Untie the spell.   [*Exit Ariel.*]
          How fares my gracious sir?
   There are yet missing of your company
   Some few odd lads that you remember not.   255

     Enter Ariel, driving in Caliban, Stephano, and
       Trinculo, in their stolen apparel.

STEPHANO. Every man shift for all the rest, and let no man
   take care for himself; for all is but fortune. Coragio,
   bully-monster, coragio!
TRINCULO. If these be true spies which I wear in my head,
   here's a goodly sight.   260
CALIBAN. O Setebos, these be brave spirits indeed!
   How fine my master is! I am afraid
   He will chastise me.

242. *maze* i.e. bewildering series of events 243-4. *more . . . conduct of*
more than can be explained by natural causes 245. *Must . . . knowledge*
must put things straight in our minds *my liege* my lord, to whom I owe
allegiance 246. *infest* torment, trouble *beating on* dwelling on, harping
on 247. *at picked leisure* at some chosen leisure moment 248. *single
. . . you* privately (or to you alone, or all by myself) I'll clear up your
doubts 249. *Which . . . probable* which (explanation) shall seem reasonable to you 249-50. *of . . . accidents* of every one of these events that
have happened *till when* i.e. until that time 251. *And think . . . well*
i.e. and think of all that happened as being for the best 255. *odd*
unaccounted for 256-7. *let . . . himself* (the drunken Stephano inverts
the proverb "Every man for himself") *fortune* i.e. chance *Coragio*
courage 259. *spies* i.e. eyes 261. *Setebos* (see 1.2.373, gloss) 262.
fine magnificent (Prospero is dressed as Duke of Milan)

SEBASTIAN.   Ha, ha!
   What things are these, my Lord Antonio?
   Will money buy 'em?
ANTONIO.   Very like; one of them   265
   Is a plain fish and no doubt marketable.
PROSPERO.   Mark but the badges of these men, my lords,
   Then say if they be true. This misshapen knave,
   His mother was a witch; and one so strong
   That could control the moon, make flows and ebbs,   270
   And deal in her command without her power.
   These three have robbed me, and this demi-devil
   (For he's a bastard one) had plotted with them
   To take my life. Two of these fellows you
   Must know and own; this thing of darkness I   275
   Acknowledge mine.
CALIBAN.   I shall be pinched to death.
ALONSO.   Is not this Stephano, my drunken butler?
SEBASTIAN.   He is drunk now: where had he wine?
ALONSO.   And Trinculo is reeling ripe: where should they
   Find this grand liquor that hath gilded 'em?   280
   How cam'st thou in this pickle?
TRINCULO.   I have been in such a pickle, since I saw you
   last, that, I fear me, will never out of my bones: I shall
   not fear fly-blowing.
SEBASTIAN.   Why, how now, Stephano?   285
STEPHANO.   O, touch me not! I am not Stephano, but a
   cramp.
PROSPERO.   You'ld be king o' the isle, sirrah?

266. *a plain fish* clearly a fish   267. *badges . . . men* signs of these men (see end note)   268. *true* honest   270. *That* that she   271. *And . . . power* i.e. (i) Sycorax could act as the moon's lieutenant without having been empowered by the moon to do so, or (ii) Sycorax could control the seas even more than the moon   273. *For he's . . . one* (because he is the bastard child of the Devil himself)   275. *thing of darkness* i.e. Caliban, who is the Devil's offspring (with perhaps also an allusion to the dark colour of his skin)   279. *reeling ripe* i.e. so drunk that he is reeling   279-80. *where . . . Find* where can they have found   *gilded 'em* made them flushed   281. *pickle* predicament (with a play on the sense that he has been steeped in a pond and in liquor. Note the use of the word "pickled" for "drunk" in modern slang)   283-4. *I . . . fly-blowing* i.e. I am safe from the attentions of flies (having been pickled)   287. *cramp* (Stephano is full of aches and pains)   288. *sirrah* (a normal form of address to inferiors)

STEPHANO. I should have been a sore one then.

ALONSO. This is a strange thing as e'er I looked on.   290

PROSPERO. He is as disproportioned in his manners
  As in his shape. Go, sirrah, to my cell;
  Take with you your companions: as you look
  To have my pardon, trim it handsomely.

CALIBAN. Ay, that I will; and I'll be wise hereafter,   295
  And seek for grace. What a thrice-double ass
  Was I to take this drunkard for a god,
  And worship this dull fool!

PROSPERO.   Go to! Away!

ALONSO. Hence, and bestow your luggage where you
      found it.

SEBASTIAN. Or stole it rather.   300

      [*Exeunt Caliban, Stephano, and Trinculo.*]

PROSPERO. Sir, I invite your Highness and your train
  To my poor cell, where you shall take your rest
  For this one night; which, part of it, I'll waste
  With such discourse as, I not doubt, shall make it
  Go quick away – the story of my life,   305
  And the particular accidents gone by
  Since I came to this isle; and in the morn
  I'll bring you to your ship, and so to Naples,
  Where I have hope to see the nuptial
  Of these our dear-beloved solémnizèd;   310
  And thence retire me to my Milan, where
  Every third thought shall be my grave.

ALONSO.   I long
  To hear the story of your life, which must
  Take the ear strangely.

289. *sore* (i) severe, (ii) aching, (iii) sorry, (iv) poor   290. *a strange thing* as strange a thing   291. *manners* character, morals   293-4. *as you . . . To* if you expect to   *trim* prepare   296. *grace* forgiveness, favour   298. *Go to* Very well, enough said   299. *luggage* junk (i.e. the "glistering apparel" that Ariel hung on the lime tree in 4.1.193)   303. *waste* spend   306. *particular . . . by* the details of the incidents that have happened   312. *Every . . . grave* (this phrase is reminiscent of 4.1.3. The other two thoughts may be Miranda and Milan, but, in general terms, the words probably mean that Prospero, from now on, will give much thought to death)   314. *Take the ear* enthrall the listener

PROSPERO.   I'll deliver all;
And promise you calm seas, auspicious gales,   315
And sail so expeditious that shall catch
Your royal fleet far off. – My Ariel, chick,
That is thy charge. Then to the elements
Be free, and fare thou well! – Please you draw near.

Exeunt omnes.

314. *deliver all* tell everything   316. *sail so expeditious* sailing so speedy
316-17. *that . . . far off* that you shall overtake your royal fleet, which is far
away   318. *to the elements* (Ariel is to return to the elements – the air –
where he came from)

EPILOGUE

spoken by Prospero

Now my charms are all o'erthrown,
And what strength I have's mine own.
Which is most faint. Now 'tis true
I must be here confined by you,
Or sent to Naples. Let me not,   5
Since I have my dukedom got
And pardoned the deceiver, dwell
In this bare island by your spell;
But release me from my bands
With the help of your good hands.   10
Gentle breath of yours my sails
Must fill, or else my project fails,
Which was to please. Now I want
Spirits to enforce, art to enchant;
And my ending is despair   15
Unless I be relieved by prayer,
Which pierces so that it assaults
Mercy itself and frees all faults.
As you from crimes would pardoned be,
Let your indulgence set me free.   *Exit.* 20

Epilogue **4.** *confined* held captive (on this island) **8.** *by your spell* i.e. by your silence **9.** *bands* bonds **10.** *hands* i.e. hand-clapping, applause (if the audience applauds it will break the spell and the actor can leave the stage happily) **11.** *Gentle breath* kind words, approbation **12.** *project* i.e. the object of the whole piece **13.** *want* lack **16.** *relieved by prayer* i.e. relieved by the plea that I am now making **17.** *pierces* (just as prayer pierces the heavens and wins God's mercy, so here Prospero hopes that his plea will win the audience's approval, and forgiveness for any faults in the play) **18.** *frees* wins pardon for **19.** *crimes* sins, offences **20.** *indulgence* generosity

NOTES

1.1.27-9 *methinks . . . gallows* This alludes to the proverb "He that is born to be hanged will never be drowned." The boatswain's character, which Gonzalo reads in his face ("complexion"), shows that he will be hanged and not drowned.

1.1.54-5 *would thou . . . tides* The English Court of Admiralty sometimes sentenced pirates to be hanged on the shore at low water, and to remain there until three tides had passed over them. Antonio, in mentioning "ten tides", is, of course, comically exaggerating the sentence of the court.

1.2.66-77 *My brother . . . studies* i.e. "My brother who is also your uncle, Antonio – please listen to what I am saying – Oh that a brother should be so treacherous! – he (Antonio), the person whom, next to yourself, I loved better than anyone else in the world, and to whom I entrusted the control of my government, which at that time was the chief among all the dukedoms (of Italy) and I, Prospero, the chief among dukes, being generally reputed to be so in dignity, and without parallel in my knowledge of the liberal arts; these (liberal arts) being all my concern, I handed over the government to my brother and withdrew from affairs of state, carried away as I was and deeply engrossed in my private studies."

1.2.89-105 *I thus . . . prerogative* i.e. "I thus neglected worldly affairs and dedicated myself to a private life of study which was beyond the understanding and esteem of the people. My retirement brought out the evil in my brother's nature, and my trust in him gave rise to a disloyalty equally great on his part, just as it sometimes happens that a good father has a bad son. My brother thus became lord not only of my normal revenues but of what, through my power, he could exact in addition to them. Like one who tells a lie so often that he makes his memory false and actually believes the lie that he tells, my brother came to believe that he was,

in fact, the Duke, as a result of his acting as my substitute
and performing the functions of a ruler."

1.2.180-84 *by my prescience . . . droop* In Shakespeare's day the
idea that the stars influenced men's fortunes was widely held.
Here, Prospero is speaking as an astrologer who must take
advantage of the fact that his star is at its zenith. If he does
not act now his fortunes will wane. Brutus, in *Julius Caesar*,
expresses a similar idea when he says,

> There is a tide in the affairs of men
> Which taken at the flood leads on to fortune;
> Omitted, all the voyage of their life
> Is bound in shallows and in miseries.
>
> (4.3.218-21)

1.2.198 *I flamed amazement* This imaginatively describes the
effect of Ariel's appearing like lightning in different parts of
the ship. Several sixteenth- and seventeenth-century voyagers'
accounts contain descriptions of such a phenomenon, sometimes called Saint Elmo's fire. William Strachey, in his account
(1610) of the wreck of Sir George Somers on the Bermudas
(see Introduction), writes, "upon the thursday night Sir
George Summers being upon the watch, had an apparition
of a little round light, like a faint Starre, trembling, and
streaming along with a sparkeling blaze, halfe the height
upon the Maine Mast, and shooting sometimes from Shroud
to Shroud, tempting to settle as it were upon any of the foure
Shrouds: and for three or foure houres together, or rather
more, halfe the night it kept with us, running sometimes
along the Maine-yard to the very end, and then returning."

1.2.201-3 *Jove's lightnings . . . were not* i.e. "The lightnings of
Jove, the forerunners of the dreadful thunderclaps, were not
more sudden and quick to the sight (than the flames which
Ariel caused)."

1.2.212 *Then all afire with me* Depending on the punctuation,
the phrase can refer to the vessel or to Ferdinand. F reads
". . . and quit the vessell;/ Then all a fire with me the Kings
sonne *Ferdinand*/ . . ." If the F punctuation is correct, Ariel
is saying that Ferdinand was "all afire with me". Many
editors, however, place a colon after the phrase and a comma
after "the vessell", thus making the passage mean that the
vessel was "all afire".

1.2.218 *sustaining* Ariel probably means that their garments sustained them in water; i.e. helped them to keep afloat. He may mean, however, that the garments had managed to sustain their freshness in spite of their having been in the sea.

1.2.298-9 *after . . . thee* Prospero actually discharges Ariel when the action of the play comes to an end soon after six o'clock on the same day as it begins. Ariel, however, is to see that the King's ship has "calm seas" and "auspicious gales" which will enable it to overtake the rest of the fleet. His task, therefore, is probably to continue for another two days; but it is a task so congenial to Ariel's nature that he will, perhaps, not regard it as a task at all.

1.2.301-3 *Go make . . . eyeball else* Ariel, of course, would be visible to the audience and to Prospero, although supposedly invisible to the other characters in the play. Probably he would wear some conventional robe which the audience would associate with a character who was supposed to be invisible. As he is to sing songs appropriate to a nymph of the sea, he dresses as a sea nymph and thus appears in harmony with the role that he is to play. Note that Ariel also appears "invisible" at line 374 s.d.

1.2.458-60 *There's nothing . . . with't* Miranda's statement that Ferdinand's outward beauty must be an indication of his inward goodness is a conventional expression of Renaissance neo-platonic doctrine, although, of course, it is also a natural expression of what the girl, no doubt, feels. Edmund Spenser's *Epithalamion* (especially ll. 167-241) gives a fuller poetic expression of this neo-platonism.

1.2.492-4 *All corners . . . a prison* i.e. "Let those who are free have all the rest of the world. With Miranda near me, my prison is all the space that I need."

2.1.54 *The ground indeed is tawny* Antonio is still treating Gonzalo in a mock-serious manner, and has probably made an elaborate pretence of examining the grass. His conclusion is that he cannot quite agree with Gonzalo.

2.1.75-99 *Not since . . . widow Dido* The full significance of the allusions to "widow Dido" in these lines has never been explained satisfactorily, but we can be fairly certain that they meant more to Shakespeare's audience than they do to us. Dido, the daughter of the King of Tyre, became a widow when her husband, Sichaeus, was murdered. She fled to the coast of North Africa where she founded the City of Carthage. According to Vergil she fell in love with Aeneas and killed herself when Aeneas, by order of the gods, abandoned her.

2.1.128-9 *at . . . bow* i.e. Claribel hated the marriage and was torn between her reluctance and her obedience to her father; her obedience tipped the scales.

2.1.142 *He'd . . . mallows* Antonio and Sebastian again pretend to take Gonzalo's words in a more restricted sense than Gonzalo intended, and interpret "plantation" as meaning the actual planting of crops. Nettles, docks, and mallows are noxious weeds.

2.1.145-62 *I' th' commonwealth . . . innocent people* Gonzalo's two speeches on the commonwealth are based on Montaigne's essay *Of Cannibals* in John Florio's translation (1603) from the French. Montaigne and some other writers saw in a natural society of primitive peoples a happy contrast to the corruptions and complications of so-called civilized societies. Such primitive societies remind Gonzalo of the Golden Age (see l. 166, gloss).

2.1.274-6 *Twenty consciences . . . molest* The interpretation of this sentence depends on whether "candied" is taken to mean (i) "coated with sugar", or (ii) "frozen". The passage could be paraphrased: (i) "If there were twenty consciences standing between me and the dukedom of Milan, let them be coated with sugar and let that sugar melt rather than that they should trouble me", or (ii) "If there were twenty consciences standing between the dukedom of Milan and me, let them be frozen solid and then melt away rather than that they should trouble me."

2.2.32 *Indian* North American Indians had been brought back to England, occasionally from the time of the Cabots in the late fifteenth century, and frequently from about the beginning of the seventeenth century.

3.3.22-3 *in Arabia . . . throne* The phoenix was a legendary bird of Arabia which built its nest in a certain tree, lived for six hundred years, died in the nest, and was consumed by fire. From the ashes of the dead bird a new phoenix was born. There was only one phoenix alive at a time.

4.1.3 *a third of mine own life* There has been much conjecture as to what Prospero means here: Kittredge suggests that

"Life consists of past, present, and future. All that the future means to Prospero – all that henceforth he lives for – is his daughter. Therefore she *is* his future – a *third* of his own life." Northrop Frye suggests that the "third" may mean "Prospero's love, his knowledge and his power being the other two-thirds?" Frank Kermode suggests that Prospero may mean that in giving away Miranda he is giving away a third of his life – the other two-thirds being his dead wife and himself. Capell suggests that the three thirds are Miranda, Prospero, and his dukedom. A less likely suggestion is that Prospero means that Miranda's training has taken up fifteen of his forty-five years and that he has, therefore, in a sense, given up a third of his life to that point. Whether these or any other conjectures are correct or not, it is clear that Prospero, in giving up Miranda, is giving up part of himself.

4.1.114-15 *Spring . . . harvest* The meaning of these lines seems to be: "May spring, for you, follow immediately after harvest," i.e. "May there be no winter in your lives." This sentiment shows another aspect of the conventional desire for a Golden Age (see 2.1.166, gloss). "Spring" may have the additional sense of "offspring". Juno has already called on Ceres to join with her in blessing Ferdinand and Miranda "that they may . . . be . . . honoured in their issue".

4.1.156-7 *We are . . . made on* In this famous phrase most editors take the "on" to mean "of", as, indeed, it often did in Shakespeare's day. There seems to be no strong reason, however, against retaining the ordinary meaning of "on" here. The phrase would then mean that "we (mankind) are the material upon which dreams can be constructed, the material upon which the imagination works."

4.1.236-7 *Now . . . line* i.e. the jerkin, having been taken down, is now under the lime tree (the "line" was also a term for the Equator, and sailors who crossed the Equator often suffered from scurvy and lost their hair. Hence the references that follow to losing hair and proving a "bald jerkin").

4.1.248 *barnacles* Barnacles are small shellfish often found clinging to rocks and to the timbers of ships. A certain type of wild goose was supposed to hatch out of them. Caliban, here, seems to be thinking of the geese, not the shellfish.

5.1.21-30 Some editors have found difficulty with this passage, but it may be roughly paraphrased as follows: "If you (Ariel) who are mere air have been able to feel sympathy for them, shall not I who am human, and can experience emotion as strongly as they do, feel even more sympathy than you? Although I am deeply hurt by the cruel injuries that they have done me, I shall still make my reason overrule my anger. It is nobler to be virtuous than to take vengeance. Because they are now sorry for the wrongs that they have committed, I shall pursue my revenge no further."

5.1.33-50 For this famous speech, Shakespeare was indebted to a passage in Ovid's *Metamorphoses* (vii, 197-206), probably in Arthur Golding's translation, published in 1567. "Ye Ayres and windes: ye Elves of Hilles, of Brookes, of Woods alone,/ Of standing Lakes, and of the Night . . ." etc.

5.1.124 *subtleties* Apart from the primary meaning of the word subtlety, which is "subtle effect" or "magic quality", it had the more specific secondary meaning of an ornamental device, usually made out of sugar, which showed allegorical figures, temples, and chariots, and was eaten at banquets or used as a table decoration. Something of this secondary meaning may be intended here, because there has been a mock banquet (3.3) and Prospero tells Gonzalo that he does "yet *taste/* Some subtleties o' th' isle".

5.1.172-5 There are several examples in medieval romances and in the literature of Shakespeare's day of lovers playing at chess – a royal and princely game of which Queen Elizabeth was fond. The general idea in these lines is fairly clear, but the passage is not easy to understand in detail. It might, however, be paraphrased as follows: "MIRANDA. Sweet lord (Ferdinand) you are cheating me at chess (and in the game of love). FERDINAND. No, my dearest love, I would not cheat you for the whole world. MIRANDA. Yes, you would play false for the whole world; even if the score (stake) were reckoned merely in kingdoms you would play me false, and such is my love for you that I would still call it fair play."

5.1.267-8 *Mark . . . true* Prospero may simply mean, "Judge by the outward appearances of these men, whether or not they are good, honest men." A "badge", however, was a device, usually a coat of arms, worn by the retainers of a nobleman to indicate that they were in his service. Prospero may mean that the stolen garments which Caliban, Trinculo, and Stephano are wearing are "badges" of their rascality; or it may be that one of the conspirators is wearing a "badge" of Milan – an ironical comment on Antonio's own usurpation of the dukedom.

Epilogue Epilogues were common in Shakespeare's day. In them, a leading actor usually steps forward on the stage, asks the audience to forgive faults in the production, and asks for applause and favourable criticism. This epilogue has sometimes been taken as an apology to King James I "for dabbling in magic" or, like another famous speech in the play (4.1. 146-63), as Shakespeare's farewell to London and to his career as a playwright. But whether or not personal allegory is contained in the epilogue, it is quite satisfactory as it stands. Prospero addresses the audience, partly as Prospero and partly as the actor who played the part of Prospero, and, in effect, says: "Now the magic which I could work as Prospero has gone, and I stand before you as a humble actor, waiting for your applause to let me leave the stage. Now that you have seen me recover my dukedom in the play, release me from the stage ('this bare island') by the sound of your applause. If I do not succeed in obtaining your approval, my project, which was to please you, will have failed. I cannot force you to approve of me because I have renounced my magic, and I face despair unless this prayer to you succeeds. I can only appeal to you to be merciful towards me; and just as you would wish to have your sins forgiven, so let your generosity to me give me liberty to leave the stage."

BIBLIOGRAPHY

Chambers, E. K., "The Integrity of *The Tempest*", *Review of English Studies*, I (1925), 129-50. (Reprinted in *Shakespearean Gleanings*. London: Oxford University Press, 1944.)

*Coleridge, Samuel Taylor, *Coleridge's Shakespearean Criticism* (2nd ed.), ed. T. M. Raysor. 2 vols. London: Dent, 1960. (Especially I, 113-23; II, 130-40, 257-9.)

Dobrée, Bonamy, "*The Tempest*", *Essays and Studies*, 5. London: John Murray, 1952. (Reprinted in *Shakespeare: The Comedies*, ed. K. Muir. Englewood Cliffs, N.J.: Prentice-Hall, 1965.)

Ebner, Dean, "*The Tempest*: Rebellion and the Ideal State", *Shakespeare Quarterly*, XVI (1965), 161-73.

Gesner, Carol, "*The Tempest* as Pastoral Romance", *Shakespeare Quarterly*, X (1959), 531-9.

*Harbage, Alfred, *William Shakespeare: A Reader's Guide*. New York: Farrar, Straus, 1963.

Hoeniger, F. D., "Prospero's Storm and Miracle", *Shakespeare Quarterly*, VII (1956), 33-8.

Knight, G. Wilson, *The Shakespearian Tempest* (3rd ed.). London: Methuen, 1953. (Especially pp. 247-66.)

———, "The Shakespearian Superman: An Essay on *The Tempest*", *The Crown of Life*. London: Methuen, 1949.

Leech, Clifford, "*The Tempest*", *Shakespeare's Tragedies and Other Studies in Seventeenth Century Drama*. London: Chatto & Windus, 1950.

*Neilson, Francis, *Shakespeare and "The Tempest"*. West Rindge, N.H.: Richard R. Smith, 1956. (Especially pp. 126-81; the earlier pages are, for the most part, irrelevant.)

Palmer, D. J., ed., *Shakespeare: "The Tempest"*. Macmillan Casebook Series. London: Macmillan, 1968.

Pettet, Ernest C., *Shakespeare and the Romance Tradition*. London: Staples Press, 1949. (Especially pp. 161-99; the whole book is important, however, for an understanding of the romance tradition.)

*Quiller-Couch, Arthur, "The Tempest", *Shakespeare's Workmanship*. London: Fisher Unwin, 1918.

Shakespeare, William, *The Tempest*, (5th ed., revised), ed. Frank Kermode. London: Methuen (The Arden Shakespeare), 1954. (Introduction, pp. xi-lxxxviii.)

Tillyard, E. M. W., *Shakespeare's Last Plays*. London: Chatto & Windus, 1938. (Especially pp. 1-15, 48-58, 78-85.)

Traversi, Derek A., *Shakespeare: The Last Phase*. New York: Harcourt, Brace, 1954. (Especially pp. 1-18, 193-272.)

*Williams, David, "*The Tempest* on the Stage", *Jacobean Theatre* (Stratford-upon-Avon Studies 1), eds. John R. Brown and Bernard Harris. London: Edward Arnold, 1960.

*Wilson, John Dover, *The Meaning of "The Tempest"*. The Literary and Philosophical Society of Newcastle upon Tyne, 1936. (Reprinted in *His Infinite Variety*, ed. Paul N. Siegel. Philadelphia and New York: Lippincott, 1964.)

Works marked with an asterisk are particularly suitable as introductory reading.

HENRY THE FOURTH
[Part One]

William Shakespeare

Edited, with introduction and notes, by
John F. Sullivan

INTRODUCTION

The History of Henry the Fourth, now generally called "*Henry IV*, Part One*", is one of ten plays for which Shakespeare used material from English history.[1] Eight of the plays form a fairly continuous cycle, to which separate single plays serve as prelude and postlude. Representing more than a quarter of the Shakespeare canon, these ten plays constitute a vast historical pageant, perhaps the nearest approach to a national epic ever to come from an English pen.

It is not likely, however, that Shakespeare designed this group of plays with much concern for their over-all unity. They were not composed in their historical order; of the eight linked plays, the second set of four was composed first, very early in Shakespeare's career, while the four that begin the series – including *1 Henry IV* – were written some six or eight years later, when Shakespeare's artistry was considerably advanced. There is no evidence, however, that he did much in the way of revising the plays he had written earlier to make them fit in with the later ones. The group of four plays which includes *1 Henry IV* possesses a unity well enough defined that it is sometimes called the "Lancastrian Tetralogy", but even this more closely related unit may not have been planned as

[1] The plays are as follows:

Play:	Deals with events *circa*:	First produced(?):
King John	1200-1216	1595
Richard II	1398-1400	1595
1 Henry IV	1402-1403	1597
2 Henry IV	1403-1413	1598
Henry V	1414-1420	1599
1 Henry VI	1422-1453	1592
2 Henry VI	1445-1455	1592
3 Henry VI	1455-1471	1592
Richard III	1471-1485	1593
Henry VIII	1520-1533	1613

such; it has been argued that Shakespeare did not intend, while he was writing his first play on Henry IV, that there would eventually be a "Part Two".[2]

Each of the plays, then, was intended to be a complete work in itself, and it is still entirely possible to read or see any one of them and to feel, when one puts down the book or leaves the theatre, that its story has been brought to a close, that the artistic experience is complete.

None the less, the modern audience for one of these plays is at some disadvantage, compared to its Elizabethan counterpart. Shakespeare wrote in the late sixteenth century about events which had taken place for the most part in the fifteenth century; the main eight-play sequence deals fairly consecutively with the period from 1398 to 1485. Not only was the memory of those troubled times still relatively fresh in Shakespeare's day, but men had been forced to turn back to those events by the pressure of contemporary issues. In the late sixteenth century, England knew that Elizabeth I would not marry or bear a child. While open discussion of the problem was forbidden, the prospect of a disputed succession, which seemed all too likely to be the nation's lot at Elizabeth's death, could hardly be prevented from occupying men's minds. They could – and did – discuss this dire prospect in historical terms.

Shakespeare could thus count on presenting his play to an already interested and knowledgeable audience. The audience for his first play about Henry IV would probably have some knowledge of how Henry came to be king – either from what they knew of history or quite possibly from having seen Shakespeare's own *Richard II*. And though *2 Henry IV* and

---

[2] Critics have long debated the question of how the two parts of *Henry IV* are related. Modern interest in the problem was stimulated by the publication of Robert Adger Law's article, "Structural Unity in the Two Parts of *Henry the Fourth*", in *Studies in Philology*, XXIV (1927), 223-42. A convenient guide to discussions of this problem may be found in the bibliographical note appended to Harold Jenkins, *The Structural Problem in Shakespeare's "Henry the Fourth"* (London: Methuen, 1956), p. 28. A further contribution by R. A. Law is "The Composition of Shakespeare's Lancastrian Trilogy", in *Texas Studies in Language and Literature*, III (1961), 321-7.

Henry V were not yet written, perhaps not even planned, nearly everyone in England already knew how the story of Prince Hal would come out, since they knew the legend of the scapegrace prince who metamorphosed into a glorious king and won the great victory at Agincourt. There was at least one earlier play, *The Famous Victories of Henry the fifth*, which had depicted this legend, though in a bumbling way, and there may well have been others, now lost.

While the play can be successful, then, even for a modern audience which knows little or nothing of its background in history, one's understanding and enjoyment of it can be enhanced by an awareness of how it fits into the larger historical pattern. To supply some of this knowledge for the modern reader, a brief account of "The History Behind *1 Henry IV*" follows the text of the play.

It quickly becomes apparent in *1 Henry IV* that two main actions are to be depicted. In the opening scene, the King meets with his Council to discuss the problems confronting the new government; a plan to embark on a Crusade has had to be deferred because of trouble at home. There are serious threats to be met on the Welsh and Scottish borders, and a victory over the Scots, having removed one problem, promptly poses another – for the Percies, who won it, have given indications that they are growing restive and insubordinate. This is to be one of the main actions of the play: the story of a rebellion against the King and how he will cope with it.

This opening scene also introduces another problem for the King – a more personal one. He has occasion to remark on the scandal of his son's behaviour in preferring the company of roisterers and highwaymen in gamy taverns to life at court and preparation for the day when he will rule England. The other main action of the play will thus be the story of another kind of rebellion against the King.

It follows then that while other characters – Prince Hal, Hotspur, and Falstaff – may command more of our attention than the King, the play is properly his (and has his name for its title), in that he forms the centre of both actions. A complex set of relationships among the four main characters will involve them in tense, dramatic conflict. In the end, the conflict will be resolved and the relationships changed.

While both actions are to a degree introduced in the opening scene, and while subsequent scenes are seldom given over entirely to one action or the other, in the beginning of the play they tend to be separately presented. Indeed, to the extent that one action can be regarded as serious and historical, the other as comic and legendary, they are brought forward at first in alternate scenes which could be labelled: "History", "Comedy", "History", "Comedy", and so on. Shakespeare could present a dual action in this way because he wrote for a theatre that did not use massive scenery. Since he did not have to allow for scene changes, he could rapidly alternate short scenes, using a technique much like that of the motion picture or television drama. So, for example, after the first scene, with the problem of the Percy insubordination left in suspense, the action changes to introduce us to the Prince and his cronies. Again, when interest has been developed in the scheme to play a joke on Falstaff by robbing the robbers, the action turns back to the King's confrontation of the Percies. A sense of simultaneity, of several exciting actions going on at once, is generated.

An even more important structural technique made available by the feasibility of writing in short, rapidly changing scenes is that which modern film-makers call "montage". Because a film is edited – that is, "shots" are cut apart and spliced together in different arrangements – the film-maker can achieve striking effects through juxtaposing materials that might not otherwise be brought into close relationship with one another. Shakespeare's scenic technique, permitting, for example, rapid alternation of serious and comic material, made it easy for him to achieve the elementary effect of contrast, used by artists in all media. But much more than mere contrast can be achieved through montage, and in this play Shakespeare takes brilliant advantage of the possibilities. Thus, for example, by juxtaposing a plot by Prince Hal and Poins to betray Falstaff with a plot by the Percies to betray the King, each action is made to comment on the other. Falstaff, the leader of the tavern crew, is plotted against in jest by two of his associates; the prank that is meant to be only a source of passing merriment for a tavern crowd foreshadows, however, the eventual wholly serious betrayal by the Prince of Falstaff's dreams of affluence and power. On the other hand, the King is faced with a deadly threat to his leadership, but the leading rebel, Hotspur, thinks of his plot as a lark, a good joke on the stodgy King, and in this he is at one with the Prince and Poins, who bedevil Falstaff. Nor is it only that we are invited to wonder what is serious and what is not. Emotional responses are artfully controlled, sometimes devastatingly undermined. For instance, whenever someone in the play utters heroic sentiments in high-flown rhetoric, a fat old man is likely to waddle on stage a moment later to say something outrageously disrespectful. Indeed, his mere physical presence in the play is enough to render suspect all grandiose language and attitudes. A simple, brief, but striking example of this effect comes at the end of Act 3, scene 3: Hal's lines are a battle-cry,

> The land is burning, Percy stands on high,
> And either we or they must lower lie.

The fat man's response is to order his breakfast.

The montage technique considerably enhances the impact of what is surely the most remarkable of the structural effects in this play – the use of parody. There are two notable instances of it, both serving to control and qualify emotional response. The first is Hal's parody version, in Act 2, scene 4, of the relationship between Hotspur and his wife, which we have just seen "straight" in the immediately preceding scene. Hal's coarse mockery offers another possible view of this charming and tender relationship; his Hotspur is a ruffianly border lord who thinks more of his horse than of his wife, and there is enough truth in this version to prevent us from becoming too deeply entranced by Hotspur's glamour. The second and much more complex instance of parody comes later in the same scene, when we are treated to not one but two parodies of a scene that is still to come: the interview Hal must have with his father. Once more, the result is that we cannot be emotionally overwhelmed by the "serious" scene when it comes; we cannot quite clear from our minds, as we watch the King upbraid his son, the picture of Falstaff, a cushion perched absurdly on his bald pate, prosing away on the same moral.

Shakespeare's masterly exploitation of such structural devices as montage and parody gives *1 Henry IV* a general unity of structure that might otherwise have been lost in the management of dual main actions. The history plays have been censured by classically oriented critics from the time of Ben Jonson onwards[3] for their structural looseness. Many of them do encompass rather motley assortments of historical material and range over broad time-spans. But *1 Henry IV* cannot be faulted in this respect; in this play Shakespeare's architectonic power is displayed at its incomparable best. Earlier in his career, he did sometimes yield to the temptation to insert a fine speech or rig a comic plot for its own sake, without regard to the effect of the whole. By the time of *1 Henry IV*, however, his native talent was matched by a confident command of his craft. He limited the concern of this play to a coherent series of events which follow closely on one another in time. Nothing extraneous is admitted; even such scenes as Act 2, scene 1, and Act 4, scene 4, which do little to carry forward the action of the play, are none the less essential, both for their contribution to the epic quality of the histories as a whole and for their significance to the thematic design of this play. Structurally, *1 Henry IV* represents an extraordinary accomplishment upon which Shakespeare was never to improve.

All the characters of *1 Henry IV* are carefully rendered, distinct, and interesting individuals, even if their roles are no more extensive than that of Francis, the tavern boy, who has little more to say than "Anon, anon, sir." But at least four of them — the King, Prince Hal, Hotspur, and Falstaff — require special notice; indeed, Falstaff is probably better known and has been

---

[3] See Jonson's Prologue to *Every Man in His Humour*, first produced in 1598 and revised for publication in 1616; cf. also E. K. Chambers, *Shakespeare: A Survey* (London: Sidgwick & Jackson, 1925), pp. 118-19.

more often written about than any other Shakespearean character except Hamlet.

While the King is of less striking interest than the other three major characters of this play, he is none the less, as was noted earlier, a centre on which the action of the play turns. One reason why his character does not dominate this play is that his portrait is not complete within these five acts. He had for Henry IV was that of progressive revelation. In *Richard II* and he was to appear again in still another play, *2 Henry IV*. The method of character delineation which Shakespeare used for Henry IV was that of progressive revelation. In *Richard II* he was a "silent King" (4.1.290), a man revealed more in action than in words, a man never shown except as (to apply a line by Yeats) a "smiling public man". In this earlier play he has no soliloquies; he is not even shown in private conversation with intimates; his character can thus only be judged by his actions and by what others say about him. At one point in *Richard II*, Shakespeare seems to be giving us an important clue to Henry's character, though in a roundabout way. Henry has been banished by his cousin, King Richard, who describes Henry's behaviour as he takes leave of England to go into exile. At that moment, Richard himself is not a very attractive character; he is gleefully contemptuous of his adversaries and shortly will be gloating in anticipation of the death of old John of Gaunt, Henry's father. Thus, when Richard scornfully describes Henry's "courtship to the common people", assuming it to be mere political strategy on the part of a cunning opportunist, we disbelieve him. Instead, we assume that Henry's courtesy is sincere, that his modesty is unfeigned, and that he has won the love and respect of the common man by proffering his own love and respect quite guilelessly. The judgement of Henry's character thus arrived at is to be strikingly qualified, however, when, in *1 Henry IV*, the King himself recalls this incident and comments on it.

The early scenes in *1 Henry IV* also show the King only as a public man – in Council, dealing with affairs of state. There is to follow, however, a most significant scene, prepared for by the parodies of it in the tavern and given structural importance by its placement close to the mathematical centre of the play. In this scene (3.2), the King at last puts aside the mask he has always donned in public and speaks quite candidly to his son. Henry is contemptuous of the man he deposed, calling Richard "The skipping King" (l. 60), who was not sufficiently proud and haughty to be a monarch, but rather

> Grew a companion to the common streets,
> Enfeoffed himself to popularity . . .
>
> (ll. 68-9)

His own strategy, he explains, was to be sparing of public appearances, so that when he did permit himself to be seen, he was the object of all eyes. But what Richard had suspected about his "courtship to the common people" – and what we had previously disbelieved – is now borne out by Henry himself. He admits:

> And then I stole all courtesy from heaven,
> And dressed myself in such humility
> That I did pluck allegiance from men's hearts,
> Loud shouts and salutations from their mouths
> Even in the presence of the crownèd King.
>
> (ll. 50-54)

The connotations of Henry's words – particularly as they involve images of theft and disguise – are unmistakable. Hotspur had earlier called him a "vile politician" (1.3.239), and it must be admitted that there are many people today who would automatically couple Hotspur's adjective with this noun. But vile or not, Henry *is* a politician – that is, one who understands and employs successfully the techniques of gaining and holding office.

There is no other opportunity in this play to see the King alone with his thoughts or speaking candidly to his son, though such opportunities recur in the Second Part. However, the revelation of Henry's real character is further advanced in this play by different means. His treatment of the rebels is ambiguous, but, aside from the romantic figure of Hotspur (and perhaps the gentle Mortimer), the rebel leaders – oily Worcester, dilatory Northumberland, and pompous Glendower – have little to recommend themselves to us, and in the negotiations preceding the Battle of Shrewsbury Henry does appear to be trying to treat them fairly. Our judgement of Henry's character will be affected, however, by the presence in the play of parallels to the historical characters and action. Robber Falstaff plays a robber king, and Gadshill is emboldened (2.1.79-81) to prey on the commonwealth by the example of his betters.

As with the King, Prince Hal's character is depicted in more than one play; it is difficult to confine a discussion of it to those aspects that are shown in *1 Henry IV*. Yet it is not so difficult as in the instance of the King, because Shakespeare's technique with Hal is different. Instead of showing his character gradually, through progressive removal of outer façades, Shakespeare allows the audience to know Hal from the first, though other characters in the play do not know him as he is. He is given a soliloquy at the end of the very first scene in which he appears (1.2.186-208).

It must be admitted, however, that this soliloquy is at the source of most of the disagreement – which is considerable – about the character Shakespeare intended to give Prince Hal. If it is taken, as the soliloquies in later plays are often taken, to be self-revelation, perhaps unconscious, then it presents us with a Hal who is uncommonly like his father and nearly as unattractive. We can all easily forgive a young man who sows some rather harmless wild oats. We are particularly prone to forgive a little high-spirited roguery in a young man who must eventually accept, as king, a life of hard, grey responsibility. (This sort of thing has often served as material for light comedy or operetta – *The Student Prince* is likely to be the most familiar example.) What we cannot easily forgive is a deliberate course of sowing wild oats in order to stage, later on, a glittering reformation.

Hal's defenders argue that this is not a soliloquy like one of Hamlet's, but that it is rather more like the one with which *Richard III* opens – a simple exposition to the audience, not to be taken as self-revelation at all, for it is not psychologically valid. No one would say, in actuality, "I am determinèd to prove a villain", as does the villainous Richard III in his soliloquy; the character in the play is merely informing the audience, as a sort of program note, that he is to be the villain of the piece. So, too, with Hal; it is argued that he speaks as he does to permit Shakespeare to tell his audience that the Prince is not really the young idler he seems. It has also been suggested that Shakespeare took the earliest available opportunity to cancel out any memory of the truly graceless – even vicious – character that had been given the Prince in the old play, *The Famous Victories*.

Leaving aside all theorizing about the soliloquy in Shakespearean drama, and considering only this particular speech by Prince Hal, we may agree that the principal impression left by it is of a Prince no less thoughtful and purposeful in political matters than is his father, the King. The son has chosen a different (and more difficult) method of winning popular favour than his father's; it can only be effective if it is kept completely secret. Shakespeare does not like, however, to keep secrets from his audience; in this instance, by telling of Hal's plan, he opens his character to the charge of hypocrisy – as he must have realized he would. He counted, I think, on diffusing the possible impression of hypocrisy given by this speech in the more general impression of Hal's character derived from the remainder of this play and from the others in which he appears. This more general impression of Hal is that of a man who is always fully in control, fully self-knowing, fully aware of what he is doing and where he is going. This is the man who knows from the outset that some day he will banish "plump Jack" – and even tells him so to his face, though the words are perhaps lost in the commotion of the sheriff banging at the inn door (2.4.464). This is the man whose motto is encapsuled in his warning to the Douglas; he is one "Who never promiseth but he means to pay" (5.4.42).

Hal has his family's characteristics, failings as well as abilities. In the Second Part, Falstaff celebrates the virtues of sack in a famous soliloquy, during which he argues that the "cold blood" which Hal and his humourless brother, John of

Lancaster, "did naturally inherit" from their father has been warmed, in Hal's case, by addiction to sack. But Falstaff is wrong. Hal is his father's son, as Falstaff learns, to his cost, very shortly thereafter.

Perhaps the most attractive aspect of Hal's character is the one he displays on the field of Shrewsbury a moment after he has killed Hotspur when he sees Falstaff apparently lying dead as well. He exclaims:

> What, old acquaintance, could not all this flesh
> Keep in a little life? Poor Jack, farewell!
> I could have better spared a better man.
> O I should have a heavy miss of thee
> If I were much in love with vanity.

(5.4.101-5)

There is expressed in these lines a genuine, if wry sort of fondness for an old friend. This is coupled, however, with a clear-eyed recognition of the fact that the speaker is not going to waste any sentimental tears over his loss. Such a combination of a capacity for true feeling with the power always to keep emotion under control is the secret of Prince Hal's personality.

Henry Percy, for ever renowned as "Hotspur", is made by Shakespeare to serve as a splendid foil for the Prince. Just as Hamlet's character is the more compelling in that he faces such a powerful adversary, so the greatness of Prince Hal is emphasized by the quality of his foe.

Like Brutus in *Julius Caesar*, Hotspur alone of the conspirators acted not out of mean or selfish motives but "in a general honest thought". The charm of his personality, his dash and fire, are well-nigh irresistible. The eventual extinction of this brilliant flame inspires a sense of loss that is akin to the tragic; we feel the waste of human greatness almost as keenly here as at the death of Brutus – or of Hamlet.

It is common to hear that *1 Henry IV* is about honour, and that Hotspur and Falstaff represent extreme attitudes, between which the Prince chooses a posture of moderation for himself. In this view, Falstaff values honour too little and Hotspur too much, while the Prince comes to rate it at its true worth. It may be questioned, however, whether honour can properly be considered in this Aristotelian way – that is, one which accounts the true virtue to be a mean between extremes. Falstaff and Hotspur represent opposites, to be sure, since Falstaff regards honour as a meaningless word, whereas Hotspur believes that it must be plucked from the moon or the ocean depths, if necessary, so that there can be no "corrival" to share in glory (see 1.3.199-205). There is not always, however, a middle ground between negation and assertion.

It is true that Hotspur's valuation of honour, like other lofty sentiments, is sometimes rudely questioned by this play; Falstaff's "catechism" requires us to think more carefully about the matter than we might otherwise do. So, too, Hal's parody of Hotspur may remind us that this so-much-valued honour is built, after all, on thoughtless violence. Hal's renunciation, in Falstaff's favour, of the credit for his victory over Hotspur implies a criticism of Hotspur's obsession with the reputation, more than the reality, of honour. Yet most of Hal's actions in the second half of the play are designed to present him as wholly worthy to be, like Hotspur, "the theme of honour's tongue". He offers to meet Hotspur in single combat, refuses to retire from the battlefield when wounded, comes to his father's rescue, and finally triumphs over Hotspur in a fair fight. In all this he is behaving in accordance with Hotspur's code of honour, not something less.

It is perhaps not with Hal that Hotspur should be contrasted, but with others: his treacherous father and uncle and even the King, who betters his odds by dressing many men in his colours. At his best, Hotspur represents an ideal of chivalry that is always fatally vulnerable in a world of cold-blooded realists. In his characterization of Hotspur, Shakespeare touches, if lightly, on the spring that was later to energize his great tragedies; Hotspur's dying speech concerns the universally tragic condition of man – who, no matter how lofty his thoughts, how noble his deeds, is subject always to the human limitation that life and thoughts together are slaves to time – to what Shakespeare was later to call "envious and calumniating time". All men must come to know what Hotspur recognizes, that

   . . . thoughts, the slaves of life, and life, time's fool,
  And time, that takes survey of all the world,
    Must have a stop.   (5.4.80-82)

Finally, we come to that famous and troublesome character, Falstaff. Across the footlights, he has always cast an irresistible spell. His success was immediate and almost unparalleled in theatrical history; one of his first great admirers was Queen Elizabeth herself, who (so tradition tells us) demanded that Shakespeare bring Falstaff back to life and show him in love — as was done in the hastily contrived farce *The Merry Wives of Windsor*. Like the Queen, most audiences since have freely succumbed to his charm, wishing only for more of him.

Literary critics, too, have found Falstaff irresistible; some of the most celebrated pieces of Shakespearean criticism have been inspired by him. In the end, however, he eludes the critic's net as nimbly and triumphantly as he slipped the noose that Hal and Poins thought to draw tight around him in the tavern after Gadshill. One is tempted to let him off with no more than Dr. Johnson's sigh of surrender: "But Falstaff, unimitated, unimitable Falstaff, how shall I describe thee?"

He *has* been described as a coward, a fraud, the Vice of the old morality plays, and many other wicked things — not wrongly — but he must also be described as honest enough in his own unorthodox way, capable of stealing the heart of even the sternest moralist, and, as he boasts in the Second Part, not only witty in himself but the cause that wit is in other men. He is quite certainly one of the great comic creations of world literature, the stock "braggart soldier" of traditional comedy apotheosized, a character so fully created that he will fit in no convenient critical pigeonhole.

One point that can be made with reasonable certainty about Falstaff is that, whatever relationship the fully developed character may bear to the archetypes of the braggart soldier, the Vice, or even the scapegoat of primitive ritual, Shakespeare's starting point was nothing so literary or theoretical. It was undoubtedly no more than the veteran soldiers who thronged the streets of London. England was at war with Spain during the whole first half of Shakespeare's career; money and men were also being poured into the effort to subdue Ireland. In those days (as, indeed, until quite recently) old soldiers were thoroughly mistrusted by the civilian population; they could seldom find honest work once home from the wars and were thus driven to beggary or thieving. Shakespeare could not have failed to find interesting matter in the "stale Knights, and Captaines out of service"[4] who swaggered in Paul's Walk or larded their tavern conversation with strange oaths.

Critics who have not known military life themselves are apt to scold Falstaff inordinately for such supposed breaches of military decorum as carrying a bottle of sack in his pistol case or wishing, before the Battle of Shrewsbury, that it were bedtime, and all well. The first is only an example of something soldiers have probably always done; Roman legionaries were undoubtedly not the first soldiers, as G.I.s in the Second World War will not be the last, to discard cumbrous and useless equipment issued by supply services behind the lines. The Elizabethan blunderbuss, which is what Shakespeare would have had in mind for Falstaff's pistol case, was not likely to hit any target smaller than a barn door, if it discharged a bullet at all. There was more than an even chance that it would blow up in the hand of the man who tried to fire it. As for the wish that it were bedtime, this is only common humanity speaking. Half-mad characters like Hotspur may prefer the battlefield to their beds, but countless brave men have entered battle no less gallantly for the wish that it need not be, or, having to be, were done with, and all well.

That Falstaff was an old soldier explains much; it does not, by any means, explain everything. It should come as no surprise that Shakespeare, handling a story which has the familiar outlines of the Parable of the Prodigal Son, should have adapted the character of the Vice or Tempter from popular theatrical treatments of this theme. As so often in Shakespeare, however, the fascination lies not in what bits and scraps he worked with, but in what he made of them. His Falstaff is no more a stereo-

---

[4] John Earle, "Pauls Walke", in *Micro-cosmographie* (London: Printed by William Stansby, for Robert Allot, 1628), Sig. I12v.

type of the Vice than he is of the braggart soldier. Indeed, modern readers are unlikely to recognize Falstaff as a stock character from classical drama; it is much more probable that they will take him to be a stock character from modern psychological fiction: the father-substitute, standing in relation to Hal as Leopold Bloom does to Stephen Dedalus in James Joyce's *Ulysses*. There is much to be said for such a reading of the character, supported, obviously, by Falstaff's literal acting-out of the father's role in the tavern scene (2.4).

Falstaff is truly all these things, but he is more. His essence is surely his supreme versatility, his unique ability to elude every snare that is set for him.

Life sets snares for every man. Some rush headlong among them with dash and fire, like Hotspur, and are entrapped early. Some tread with enormous caution, like King Henry, enduring, though every step be dreadful. Some march quietly forward, like Prince Hal, side-stepping when they can but fighting when they must. In the end, of course, as Hotspur's dying breath concedes, there will be a snare that does its work.

Few men, however, with no other resource than human wit and ingenuity, defy the odds as long as does Falstaff. This, I think, is the secret of his appeal: he is apparent proof that, of himself, with neither wealth nor high degree to sustain him, man can make a stand against the ills that beset him. I have spoken of "life" setting snares, but of course it is not "life" that does this, but the enemies of life. Falstaff is on the side of life, whatever he may do or say. In the end, fat rogue and King alike must give up living, but Falstaff's end is not yet, not in this play. Here, he wins a fantastic round in the contest of life, capping incomparably the audacity of his response in the tavern to the thrust of Hal and Poins with that of his response at Shrewsbury: "Lord, Lord, how this world is given to lying."

Like Hal then, we have to admit that there is simply no way to answer this singular, incorrigible, mad-witted, outrageous, but immensely vital old man.

Except for a few early, apprentice-work plays, all that Shakespeare wrote is thematically rich. There is, however, an especially luxuriant thematic texture in the history plays. They were not only complete plays in themselves but also units in a larger whole, what John Masefield called a "great processional pageant".[5] There appear in them, then, not only themes of the individual play but others which course through several – or all – of the group.

One striking example of a theme which we meet thus in mid course in *1 Henry IV* is what might be called the theme of "compassing the crown" (to use a phrase from Shakespeare's *Henry V*). As was mentioned earlier, the paramount political issue of the 1590s, when Shakespeare wrote all but one of his English histories, was that of the succession to the childless Elizabeth. The Elizabethan theatre, always ready to capitalize on matters of current interest, even if they had to be disguised as history, turned often to problems connected with the succession.[6] From his first play, the first part of *Henry VI*, Shakespeare had also been presenting stories from English history of how various persons, with good or bad title to it, came to the throne, and of what happened to them. In *Richard III*, for example, he showed how an unscrupulous and determined man might get the crown for himself mainly by murdering all those who stood closer in the line of succession. This method worked, all right, but it was not one that could be much recommended; Richard did not keep the crown very long.

In *Richard II*, as we know, Shakespeare showed how Henry IV came to be king by combining support from strong nobles with popular favour, acquired through rare but spectacular public appearances, at which he made gracious, even humble gestures to the common man.

As the pivotal scene in *1 Henry IV* (3.2) makes clear, part of the reason for the estrangement between the King and Prince Hal is that the son has chosen a different method than

---

[5] *William Shakespeare* (London: Williams & Norgate, 1911), p. 120.

[6] That the succession issue was a major interest of Elizabethan drama has been shown by Gertrude Catherine Reese in a study demonstrating its significance in twenty-three plays; see "The Question of the Succession in Elizabethan Drama", University of Texas *Studies in English*, XXII (1942), 59-85.

his father's – that of the spectacular reformation. This technique depends for success on its being kept a secret, so that Henry sees in his son only a juvenile delinquent who is likely to lose the crown to Hotspur just as Richard had lost it to Henry. Though Hal gives his father reason for cheer at the end of the scene and still more demonstrates something of his real nature at Shrewsbury, the theme of "compassing the crown" cannot be fully worked out until in the two subsequent plays Hal stages his public reformation and then displays his ability to cope with the job of being king.

The estrangement between King Henry and his son suggests another theme that is prominent in both *Henry IV* plays – the eternal conflict of the generations, which makes today's fathers, no less than fifteenth-century kings, misunderstand and censure their teen-age sons. Here we arrive at the secret of Shakespeare's continuing appeal; we can perceive beneath the historical trappings characters and themes no less meaningful to us today than they were to audiences in sixteenth-century London. Those audiences were vitally concerned about who was to succeed Queen Elizabeth; modern audiences could hardly care less – the issue is decided and dead. We do need to know what contemporary political meaning the play had for Shakespeare's time – if only to clear away misconceptions – but if there were no more to it than comment on the political situation, it would remain only a quaint relic. What gives it continuing life is that the modern audience can see not only the historical personages but figures of far more general significance in it. Father and son remain in conflict across the generations; one cause of this conflict in every generation is that every father wants his son to follow in his footsteps, and every son knows that he must make his own path. The father's impulse is to pass on the wisdom he has painfully acquired, but the new generation always needs to live its own life, suffer its own pains, acquire its own untransmittable wisdom. Yet a son needs a father, and if the father of his own blood will not or does not recognize him, he must seek out a father in spirit. Each generation needs to learn this afresh, and each generation will return to *1 Henry IV* with profit.

Still another theme that takes us through both parts of *Henry IV* has to do with education – specifically, the education of a prince for his eventual kingly task. The problem of how best to educate for political leadership is not now one of the training of princes, but the change of title need not put us off; this is our problem, too. In a sense, it is the key problem of all education in a democracy, which we believe to be a workable form of government only if all citizens have been educated for their political role. In Shakespeare's day – and before – many great minds applied themselves to this problem. The traditional books on the education of princes or "governors" prescribed extensive programs for the intellectual and moral formation of the future leader; such programs were, in fact, assiduously followed in the education of Tudor and Stuart monarchs, and still constitute in large measure the humanities courses in our schools and colleges. Machiavelli shocked sixteenth-century Europe so powerfully just because he broke with the traditional assumptions about the formation of a Prince and suggested, for the prospective ruler, training based on the lessons of history and practical politics.[7] Though more subtly, Shakespeare also suggests that another sort of preparation than the traditional formal education might better equip the future king. The type of preparation he suggests is not original with him; he was working with the tradition of the unconventional behaviour of Prince Hal, and back of that lay the long tradition of a ruler who goes about in disguise, like Haroun-al-Raschid in the *Arabian Nights*, to acquire knowledge of his people. None the less, amid the welter of stuffy books on the subject, one supposes that there was freshness in the suggestion that it might be good for a prince to learn to "drink with any tinker in his own

[7] It used to be supposed that Machiavelli's ideas were known to the Elizabethans only in a grotesquely distorted form, since his major works were not published in English translations before the mid-seventeenth century, but contemporary references to these works are fairly common; they were printed in both Italian and Latin in Elizabethan London, making them easily available to educated readers. It is now known that several English translations of *The Prince* circulated in manuscript before 1600; there seems also to have been a translation of the *Discourses* (see *Notes and Queries*, V [April, 1958], 144-5).

language" (2.4.18). The suggestion is impressively endorsed by the fact that one ruler so educated was "this star of England", Henry V.

Hal's "education", however, may be quite illusory. His character seems fully formed from his first appearance on stage, and he has from the first a purpose in all that he does. None of his actions are without some flavour of calculation; the "education" may well be designed to affect the "tinker" more than the Prince. When Hal describes his drinking bout with the drawers, he is addressing Poins and is therefore a little on the defensive, but the description – and the joke on Francis which follows – have about them a hint of contempt for these lowly ones, among whom one may sound "the very bass-string of humility" (2.4.5-6). Recollection that it is the future commander at Harfleur and Agincourt who speaks may lend an ironic overtone to his exultant cry, "when I am King of England I shall command all the good lads in Eastcheap" (2.4.13-14). They have pledged him their loyalty because he seems to them a good fellow; they might be less enthusiastic if they knew he was acting a part with them, or if they knew they were to metamorphose, in *Henry V*, into Bates and Court and Williams, Shakespeare's representative English soldiers in the camp before Agincourt.

Yet another theme often regarded as central to Shakespeare's English history plays is the "Tudor myth". As E. M. W. Tillyard summarizes it, this was:

> ...a universally held and still comprehensible scheme of history: a scheme fundamentally religious, by which events evolve under a law of justice and under the ruling of God's Providence, and of which Elizabeth's England was the acknowledged outcome.[8]

It is undeniable that the Elizabethan government assiduously propagated this party line; a prime vehicle for it was the official Homilies, required to be read in all churches. A cardinal point

---

[8] *Shakespeare's History Plays* (London: Chatto & Windus, 1944), pp. 320-21.

was the appalling sinfulness of rebellion, which the 1571 Homily "Against Disobedience and Wilful Rebellion" described thus:

> How horrible a sin against God and man rebellion is, cannot possibly be expressed according to the greatness thereof. For he that nameth rebellion, nameth not a singular or one only sin, as is theft, robbery, murder, and such like; but he nameth the whole puddle and sink of all sins against God and man, against his prince, his country, his parents, his children, his kinfolks, his friends and against all men universally; all sins, I say, against God and all men heaped together, nameth he that nameth rebellion.[9]

The very passion of the appeal in such writing is testimony to the reality of the threat of rebellion – a constant menace to the Tudors from the rising of the Cornish peasants in 1497 to the attempted coup by the Earl of Essex on February 8, 1601. Indeed, this particular Homily was promulgated in the wake of a domestic revolt which was probably a more crucial event in Elizabethan history than the later attempted Spanish invasion. Nowadays we see the Elizabethan age through a romantic haze as a golden time of peace and unity, in contrast to the troubled Stuart reigns which followed. But it is wrong to suppose that the Elizabethans themselves had our perspective; they knew how narrowly they had escaped disaster in 1569, when the Northern Earls raised the standard of revolt, and they understood how religious differences might at any moment plunge the country into civil war (as, indeed, they did in 1642). Shakespeare's plays are an indication of how much a thoughtful man might be troubled by what he regarded as the disorder and moral decay of his time.

Rebellion is depicted in Shakespeare's histories because no consideration of national problems in sixteenth-century England could leave it out of account. It is not, however, automatically denounced, as it would have been had Shakespeare in-

---

[9] *Certain Sermons, Or Homilies Appointed to be read in Churches* (London: The Prayer book and Homily Society, 1852), p. 534.

tended only to dramatize the "Tudor myth". When rebellion is stupid or mismanaged, he shows this; when it is ludicrous, he exploits its comic possibilities. Even so, he does not preach on the Homily text. Indeed, his material includes some successful rebellions, such as those of Henry IV against Richard II or of Henry VII against Richard III, which receive a qualified approval. His concern, then, is not simply to condemn rebellion as such, but to show it as a symptom of a deeper disorder – symbolized for us in the early play, *3 Henry VI*, that shows a father killing his son and a son killing his father.

Increasing disorder, both political and moral, was no less paramount a concern in Shakespeare's age than in the twentieth century, about which William Butler Yeats lamented:

> Things fall apart; the centre cannot hold;
> Mere anarchy is loosed upon the world,
> The blood-dimmed tide is loosed, and everywhere
> The ceremony of innocence is drowned;
> The best lack all conviction, while the worst
> Are full of passionate intensity.[10]

In Shakespeare's age, as now, men looked to political leadership for restoration of order. But what if the political leadership is itself morally flawed?

At a fundamental level, then, the theme of Shakespeare's histories is the nature of political leadership and the moral problems posed by it. He saw kingship as a burden. Except for his Richard III, who cherished infantile illusions about the glory of being a king, all of Shakespeare's monarchs, weak and strong, good and bad, possess a sense of the oppressive weight of the crown. In attributing this sense to his kings, Shakespeare was not, I think, expressing what might be taken as the ruler's equivalent of the rich man's complaint that money cannot buy happiness. He had played at court; he had had opportunity to observe Queen Elizabeth at first hand; and Shakespeare was nothing if he was not what he calls his Cassius – "a great

[10] From "The Second Coming", in *The Collected Poems of W. B. Yeats*, 2nd ed. (London: Macmillan, 1950), pp. 210-11.

observer" who looked "quite through the deeds of men". He must have seen for himself the loneliness of the Queen – a loneliness undoubtedly sharpened by her unmarried state.[11] Shakespeare would have understood what agonizing decisions this woman faced alone – such as that to execute Mary Stuart, over which she hesitated for nearly twenty years.

If the decision to eliminate an adversary can be difficult, how much more harrowing must be the decision to sacrifice a friend. Yet it is one of the harsh realities of political life that such decisions must sometimes be taken, in the interest of the nation's good, of policy, or even of simple survival. Shakespeare's kings are all required to face this reality. Richard II, for example, vainly tried to save his crown by banishing his loyal henchman, Mowbray. After Henry had seized the crown and Richard was murdered at his all but express command, the new King disowned Exton, the murderer, exiling him to wander "like Cain". In *1 Henry IV*, while it may be too strong to say that the Percies are betrayed by Henry, and Hotspur by his father, it is undeniable that their valiant services are meanly rewarded. But the great archetype of the casting off of a friend is still to come, though it is strongly foreshadowed in Hal's soliloquy at the end of Act 1, scene 2, and in the tavern scene wherein Falstaff's defence of himself, concluding "Banish plump Jack, and banish all the world," is answered by Hal's ominous, "I do, I will."

It would be quite wrong, of course, to see at any stage of the relationship of Falstaff and the Prince a simple confrontation between a tragic victim and a hard-hearted tyrant. Both men are victims – victims of the circumstances of public life. Perhaps in recognition of this, Shakespeare later spared Falstaff the ignominious end that awaited the rest of the Boar's-Head crew and, indeed, celebrated his passing in some of the most affecting lines ever written (*Henry V*, 2.3). There is sadness in the ultimate fate of Falstaff and his companions, but Time, not Hal, is the villain. The two worlds of court and tavern, whose orbits for a brief, anarchic moment unnaturally inter-

[11] Of all the English monarchs who lived to maturity, Elizabeth I is the only one who did not marry.

sected, had eventually to spin apart again, and the dwellers in them to be estranged for ever.

In *1 Henry IV*, however, it is not yet the Prince who must bear the full moral burden of political leadership; it is the King. The play begins with Henry's description of the horrors of civil strife which have made him "so wan with care". He had hoped to unite the nation in a Crusade, but he was never to realize this hope. Instead, in this play and in its sequel, the land continues to bleed from "intestine shock" and "civil butchery", and though Henry wins his battles, as at Shrewsbury, and keeps his crown, he dies in bitter regret at the wounded peace, the quarrels and bloodshed which have been the "argument" of all his reign. Where Henry fails, his son is to succeed; Henry V unites the nation in a war of aggression against France. Its justification is that by it he can maintain the peace and order of England which is his primary responsibility. It is ironic that men must go to their deaths on foreign soil so that "gentlemen in England now abed" (*Henry V*, 4.3.64) may sleep securely. In this irony is the moral dilemma that Shakespeare's kings – and all political leaders – must confront.

The hard choice between the dictates of morality and the necessities of political reality had been forced upon the consciousness of men of Shakespeare's age by many events – the wars of religion, struggles for power among the newly emergent nations, vast social and economic upheavals, and the opening up of the New World across the Atlantic. More than anything else, however, what made men of this age conscious of the terms of the dilemma were the writings of Niccolò Machiavelli.[12] Shakespeare obviously knew the grotesque version of Machiavelli popular on the stage; his Aaron in *Titus Andronicus* is an excellent specimen of the stereotyped "Machiavel", while his Richard III is at least based on the same model, though he transcends it in some respects. However, as a literary man in the London of the 1590s, Shakespeare was almost certainly also aware of the true import of Machiavelli's teachings. He could appreciate, as did his contemporary, Francis Bacon, that

[12] See note 7 above; for a slightly different view of how Shakespeare used Machiavelli, see Tillyard, *op. cit.*, pp. 21-3.

Machiavelli described "what men do, and not what they ought to do".[13] To show what men do was Shakespeare's concern as well; Hamlet clearly speaks for his creator in declaring that the purpose of playing is to hold the mirror up to nature. In the history plays, Shakespeare, like Machiavelli, set out to show the actual behaviour of that curious political animal – man. Yet Shakespeare was far more troubled than either Machiavelli or Bacon appear to have been by the omission of what men "ought to do". He does not let us forget the moral issues which arise in a consideration of the political behaviour of men. Is the way to peace – to civil and moral order – necessarily through the transgression of moral law, the disregard of the Christian conscience? In sum, is the game worth the candle?

Shakespeare found the question no less difficult than we do today; he had no ready answer. Nor did he set the question aside when he laid down his pen after completing *Henry V* in 1599. The greatness of his greatest plays – the major tragedies – lies precisely in their concern with this eternal conflict of moral idealism and cold-blooded realism. Our play, *1 Henry IV*, mingles history and comedy and contains an unrivalled comic character. The series ends in *Henry V* with the merry wooing of the fair princess by the plain soldier, and, as is appropriate to comedy, boy gets girl. None the less, it is to these history plays that we must look for the germ of the greater tragic drama to come.

That these plays anticipate the moral concern of the later tragedies becomes evident when it is realized that their themes can be expressed in terms of the problem of the distinction between appearance and reality, a problem which also lies at the heart of the great tragic themes. All of the thematic interests of *1 Henry IV* – "compassing the crown", estrangement of father and son, education, the morality of rebellion, the morality of political leadership – represent particular aspects of this problem. The word "counterfeit", whose various senses are so tellingly explored by Falstaff (5.4.112-23), supplies the key

[13] *The Works of Francis Bacon*, ed. James Spedding, Robert Leslie Ellis, and Douglas Denon Heath (New York: Hurd & Houghton, 1869), IX, 221.

image of the play.[14] Henry, who counterfeited courtesy and humility, is a counterfeit of the true king, whom he deposed. Prince Hal is a counterfeit rogue, deceiving thereby both his real father and Falstaff, the counterfeit father. The King passes counterfeit coin on the battlefield – other men in his colours – instead of the true coin of personal valour, but Falstaff also counterfeits in the conviction that "The better part of valour is discretion" (5.4.118-19). Yet all of the characters may say with Falstaff, "I lie; I am no counterfeit." For the counterfeit kings are to prove better rulers than the true one. Honour, says Falstaff, is but a word, and truly it leaves Hotspur with his dying breath – to become, inconstantly, the scutcheon of his conqueror. In this world of shifting shapes, where honour and honesty are, with all the traditional virtues, but empty words, how can the ruler perform his task? Only, it would seem, by accommodating himself to this world. Yet in so doing, he must accept the Machiavellian dissociation of morality from politics; how then can he hope to sustain or restore moral order in his dominions?

It is plain that these are questions which still – perhaps today more urgently than ever – await an answer. Shakespeare offers none, but he continues to put before us, with terrifying cogency, the terms of our dilemma. That – not the propagation of a doctrine – is the only true function of art.

Some attention ought to be given the formal aspects – language, imagery, poetic style, and the like – of *1 Henry IV*; these aspects are likely to be overlooked simply because of the sheer excellence of structure, characterization, and theme in this play. That they are so often overlooked is perhaps more an artistic merit than a defect. In the early plays by Shakespeare we are often dazzled by language, just because there is little behind the façade of language to interest us. In the later plays, a metaphysical complexity in the language prompts us to probe the depths that are obviously there. In the middle plays,

[14] It is worth noting, too, the many references to coins in this play and the frequent use of imagery based on the minting or passing of money.

however – and none is more representative than *1 Henry IV* – Shakespeare has perfectly suited "the action to the word, the word to the action", and we take the mastery of the medium for granted.

The main impressions of the style of *1 Henry IV* are of vigour, animation, versatility, and suitability. The speech rhythms are strong and masculine; the imagery is active, frequently martial. A pleasing variety of manner is displayed, ranging from the airy trifling between Hotspur and his lady to the impassioned declamation of a commander addressing his troops. Most notable of all, perhaps, is the immense aptness of language – to the character and to the situation. So distinctive is the speech of each character that we need hear only a few lines to know who is speaking, but it varies, too, from moment to moment, as the mood of the character changes. As the most volatile of the characters, Hotspur provides the best examples of speech varying with emotional temperature. The part of Hotspur in the whole of Act 1, scene 3, is a supreme instance of how emotional characterization can be accomplished by modulation of language.

We may, perhaps, term the style of *1 Henry IV* onomatopoeic, if the sense of that word can be extended a little. It is not just that words echo the thing they stand for, but that the style as a whole – rhythm, intonation, imagery, even syntax – is imitative, both of subject and object, of the speaker and the thing talked about. Perhaps the best example of this effect is Hotspur's description of the demand for his prisoners (1.3.28-68).

Finally, attention should be called to the appearance in this play of a marvellously fluid prose. A too casual inspection of the play sometimes leads students to the naïve conclusion that prose is used to distinguish comic from serious scenes – the latter being in verse. Or it may be concluded that "low" characters speak prose and socially more elevated ones, verse. Actually, the interplay of prose and verse achieves a more subtle and basically musical effect. Like a musical composition, the whole play moves in varied rhythms – now slow, now fast, now more measured, now subtly disguised by counter-rhythms.

Verse modulates easily into prose and back again, even in the same scene, or in the speech of the same character (see, for example, 5.3.39-42). Verse and prose are combined with fluid ease, and both succeed remarkably in maintaining the rhythm of natural speech. The lines are easy to read; they virtually speak themselves. Accents fall where we would naturally put them, and the effect is almost as though actual speech had been transcribed.

This very naturalness may dispose us to underestimate the supreme art with which it has been accomplished. As one listens to the casual grace of Falstaff's prose, for instance, one may not remember that, in general, English prose style did not achieve a similar conversational ease – the goal of Dryden – until about a century after Shakespeare had worked his miracles. So, too, with other aspects of the play – structure, characterization, themes – the completely natural way in which all comes together in an incomparable whole makes us oblivious to the craft which wrought it. Analysis of this best of all well-made plays will reveal for us the pre-eminence of that craft, dispelling the old notion that Shakespeare was an untutored genius. But when the analysis is finished, we should pick up the book or go back to the theatre and surrender once again to the art that sets before us life itself.

NOTE ON THE TEXT

The First Part of *Henry IV* was entered for publication in the Stationers' Register on February 25, 1598. Of what may be supposed to have been the first publication only eight pages, containing the text from 1.3.199 to 2.2.105, have survived; they were discovered, in the nineteenth century, in the binding of an old book. The first edition to survive in a complete form was printed later in 1598, using the earlier edition as its text. The play was then reprinted in 1599, 1604, 1608, 1613, and 1622, before its appearance in the First Folio in 1623. None of these later editions has any textual authority; they were set from one another and merely multiply corruptions. The Folio text (set from a corrected copy of the 1613 edition) does introduce editorial changes; act and scene divisions are indicated, oaths are expurgated (in keeping with the Act of 1606 forbidding their use in plays), stage directions are altered, and some new readings are given.

One other early text is of interest. This is a manuscript, dating from the early seventeenth century, in which the two parts of *Henry IV* are combined to make one play, possibly for performance at Court or on tour. This manuscript contains further revisions in the hand of Sir Edward Dering (1598-1644) and has thus come to be known as the "Dering Manuscript".

Though an occasional reading from one of the later texts has sometimes been thought acceptable, the only valid foundation for a modern edition is that provided by the 1598 quartos — Q_0 for 1.3.199 to 2.2.105, and Q_1 for the remainder. The present text results from a collation of the 1598 quartos and F_1, with reference to other editions where necessary. The more interesting F_1 variants and all departures from the copy-texts are noted below, except that spelling and punctuation have been silently modernized. Act and scene divisions are as in F_1, except where noted. Additions to the directions given in Q_0, Q_1, or F_1 are shown in square brackets and are not ordinarily noted here. All locations have been supplied by editors; they are by now conventional.

TEXTUAL VARIANTS

1.1.64. *Stained*; F_1, Dering MS *strained*   76. *In faith it is* (Malone); Q_1, F_1 assign to the King

1.2 s.d. *Enter . . . Falstaff* (Q_1); F_1 *Enter Henry Prince of Wales, Sir John Falstaffe, and Pointz* (the editors of F_1 misread Falstaff's exclamatory "Poins!" at line 103 below as a speech heading and overlooked the entrance direction for Poins just preceding. Perhaps as a consequence, they added Poins's name to the entry at the head of this scene, but if Poins were on stage all along, the exchange of greetings with the Prince at lines 107-8 would be meaningless, and the actor playing Poins would have an uncomfortable time on stage with nothing to do or say)   77. *similes* (Q_5); Q_1, F_1 *smiles*   86-7. *wisdom . . . and*; not in F_1 (the expurgation from F_1 of oaths and references to the Deity extended also to some scriptural allusions)   103. *match*; F_1 *watch* 109. *Sack and Sugar? Jack,*; Q_1 *Sack, and Sugar Jack?*; F_1 *Sack and Sugar: Jack?* (the Q_1 comma may suggest a significant pause) 152 s.d. *Exit Falstaff* (F_2); not in Q_1, F_1 (but Falstaff must be off-stage when the plot against him is framed)   155. *Bardolph, Peto* (Theobald); Q_1, F_1 *Harvey, Rossill* (these names were probably changed at the same time that "Oldcastle" was changed to "Falstaff", since Harvey and Russell were family names of prominent Elizabethans, but a few references to them escaped notice)   181. *lives*; F_1 *lies*

1.3 location *Windsor. The council chamber* (Halliwell, following Holinshed and indication at 1.1.103); many eds. read *London. The palace*   9. *ne'er* (F_1); Q_1 *neare*   107. *bare*; F_1 *base*   135. *Bolingbroke* (Pope); Q_1, F_1 *Bullingbrooke* (the spelling in the original texts indicates the pronunciation)   199 s.h. HOTSPUR (F_1); not in Q_0, Q_1 (the fragment of Q_0 begins at this point, without the speech heading) 221. *hollo* (Q_3); Q_0, Q_1 *hollow*; F_1 *holla*   237. *whipped* (Q_1, F_1); Q_0 *whip*   261. *granted. [To Northumberland] You, my lord,* (Theobald); Q_0, Q_1 *granted you my Lord.*; F_1 *granted you, my Lord.* 295. *our fortunes* (Q_1, F_1); Q_0 *out fortunes*

2.1.47 s.d. *Enter Chamberlain*; follows line 46 in Q_0, Q_1, and F_1 (but whether Gadshill is calling for the Chamberlain or greeting him, he must enter very nearly upon the line)   76. *oneyers* (F_1); Q_0, Q_1 *Oneyres* (Many conjectural readings have been offered; the most plausible being Malone's *onyers*, from "to ony", a technical term of the Exchequer, and with the sense of "sheriffs responsible for money due to the King"; and Johnson's *one-yers* as a slangy expansion of "ones".)   80. *prey* (F_1); Q_0, Q_1 *pray*

2.2.20. *Bardolph* (F_1); Q_0 *Bardol*; Q_1 *Bardoll* (The quartos spell "Bardol" or "Bardoll" throughout; F has "Bardol" once but otherwise "Bardolf(e)" or "Bardolph". The Q form presumably reflects the original pronunciation, "Bardle", but the spelling "Bardolph" has now been universally accepted.)   34. *my* (Q_0); Q_1, F_1 *mine*   99-104. *Got . . . pity him* (Q_0, Q_1, F); many eds., in the eighteenth century and subsequently, print as verse   105. *fat* (Q_0); not in Q_1, F_1

2.3.1 s.h. HOTSPUR (Capell); not in Q_1, F_1 2. *in respect* (F_1); Q_1 *in the respect*   68. *What horse? A roan,* (F_1); Q_1 *What horse, Roane?*   70-72. *That roan . . . park* (Q_1, F_1); many eds. print as verse   77-81. *Out . . . you go –* (Q_1, F_1); many eds. print as verse   83-5. *Come . . . things true* (Q_1, F_1); many eds. print as verse

2.4.8. *Francis* (F_1); Q_1 *Frances* or *Fraunces* throughout (the spelling in Q perhaps indicates more precisely the original pronunciation) 32. *precedent* (Pope); F_1 *President*; Q_1 *present*   83 s.d. *Enter Poins*; follows line 82 in F_1 114. *Titan!*, Q_1, F_1 *Titan*; Theobald *Butter* 115. *sun's*; Q_1 *sonnes*; F_1 *Sunne*   136 s.h. POINS (Q_1); F_1 PRINCE 165 s.h. PRINCE (F_1, Dering MS); Q_1 GADSHILL   166 s.h. GADSHILL (F_1); Q_1 ROSS. (i.e. ROSSILL); Dering MS BARD (i.e. BARDOLPH)   168 s.h. GADSHILL (F_1); Q_1 ROSS.; not in Dering MS (which continues as Falstaff's speech)   172 s.h. GADSHILL (F_1); Q_1 ROSS.; Dering MS BARD. 181 s.h. PRINCE (Q_1); F_1 POINS   235. *eel-skin* (Hanmer); Q_1 *elsskin*; F_1 *Elfe-skin*   313 s.d. *Enter Falstaff* (F_1); follows line 325 in Q_1 328. *O,* (F_1); Q_1 *O*; Dering MS, some eds. *Owen*   380. *tristful* (Dering MS); Q_1, F_1 *trustfull*   457. *lean* (F_1); Q_1 *lane*   470 s.h. PRINCE (Q_1); F_1 FALST.; Dering MS POYN.   475. *made* (Q_1, F_1); F_3 *mad* (preferred by many eds.)   487 s.d. *Exeunt . . . Peto* (Collier); F_1 *Exit*; not in Q_1 (Q_1, F_1 assign the speeches at lines 511-12, 516, and 533 to Peto, and read "Peto" at line 532; the Dering MS has "Poins" in these places; some eds. follow Johnson in preferring Poins as the recipient of an "honourable" place.)   488-94. *Now, master . . . butter* (Q_1, F_1); many eds. print as verse   489-90. *First . . . house*; many eds. print as verse   518 s.h. PETO (F_1); Dering MS POINS; not in Q_1 s.d. *[reads]* (Capell); not in Q_1, F_1 524 s.h. PRINCE (F_1); not in Q_1

3.1 location *Wales. Glendower's castle*; most eds. follow Theobald and give the location as *The Archdeacon of Bangor's House in Wales*

(which derives from Holinshed; see 3.1 location, end note)   3-9. *Lord
Mortimer . . . heaven* (Q₁); F₁, many eds. print as verse   17-19.
Why . . . born (Q₁, F₁); Pope prints as verse, some eds. follow
66. *Booteless*; Q₁ *Booteles*; F₁ *Bootlesse*   99. *cantle* (F₁); Q₁ *scantle*
106-9. *Yea . . . from you* (Q₁); F₁, many eds. print as verse   197-9.
She . . . upon (Q₁); F₁ prints all as verse   248-51. *Not . . . as day* (Q₁);
F₁ prints as verse

3.2.59. *wan* (Q₁); F₁ *wonne*   63. *cap'ring* (Q₁); F₁ *carping*   71-2.
began/ To loathe the (T. Johnson, 1710); Q₁, F₁ *began to loath/ The*
156. *intemperance* (Q₁); F₁ *intemperature*   161 s.d. *Enter Blunt* (F₁);
follows line 162 in Q₁

3.3.34-5. *that's God's angel* (Q₃); Q₁ *that Gods Angell*; not in F₁
50 s.d. *Enter Hostess* (F₁); Q₁ has entry opposite lines 51-2   56. *tithe*
(Theobald); Q₁, F₁ *tight*   84. *sneak-up*; Q₁ *sneakeup*; F₁ *sneak-cup*
86 s.d. *and Peto* (Theobald); not in Q₁, F₁; some eds. *and Poins*
(see note on variant to 2.4.487 s.d., above)   168-71. *Hostess . . . gone*
(Q₁); F₁ prints as verse   170. *guests* (F₁); Q₁ *ghesse*   174-5. *O my . . .
again* (Q₁); F₁ prints as verse

4.1.20. *I, my Lord* (Capell); Q₁ *I my mind*; F₁ *I his mind*   54. *is*
(F₁); Q₁ *tis*   107. *dropped* (F₁); Q₁ *drop*   125. *cannot* (F₁); Q₁ *can*
126. *yet* (F₁); Q₁ *it*

4.2.3. *Sutton Co'fil'*; Q₁ *Sutton cophill*; F₁ *Sutton-cop-hill*

4.3.20. *horse* (F₁); Q₁ *horses*   27. *ours* (F₁); Q₁ *our*   81.
country's (Rowe); F₁ *Countries*; Q₁ *Countrey*

4.4.17. *a rated sinew* (Q₁); F₁ *rated firmely*

5.1.2. *bulky* (Q₁); F₁ *busky* (preferred by many eds. The choice
is between the sense of "massive" and the sense of "wooded")
121-4. *Hal . . . farewell* (Pope); Q₁, F₁ print as verse   137-8. *will it*
(F₁); Q₁ *wil*

5.2.3. *undone* (F₁); Q₁ *under one*   27 s.d. *Enter Hotspur* (F₁);
Q₁ *Enter Percy* (opposite line 25)   100 s.d. *Exeunt* (Rowe); not in
Q₁, F₁

5.3 scene division and bracketed portions of the stage direction
(Capell, made necessary by Rowe's emendation at 5.2.100 s.d., above);
Q₁, F₁ have a continuous s.d. (see 5.3, end note)   22. *A fool go*
(Capell); Q₁ *Ah foole, goe*; F₁ *Ah foole: go*   35-6. *rag-of-muffins*;
Q₁, F₁ *rag of Muffins*; Capell *ragamuffins* (preferred by many eds.)

5.4.67. *Nor* (F_1); Q_1 *Now* **80-82.** *thoughts, the slaves . . . stop;*
Q_1 *But thoughts the slaves of life, and life times fool,/ And time that
takes survey of all the world/ Must have a stop;* F_1 *But thought's
the slave of life, and life, times fool;/ And time, that takes
survey of all the world,/ Must have a stop* (preferred by many **eds.**;
see 5.4.80-82, end note) **91.** *thee dead* (Q_7); Q_1, F_1 *the dead*
156. *ours* (F_1); Q_1 *our*

5.5.36. *bend you* (F_1); Q_1 *bend, you*

The History of Henry the Fourth
[PART ONE]

[DRAMATIS PERSONAE

The King's Party

KING HENRY *the Fourth*

HENRY, *called* HAL, *Prince of Wales* ⎫
LORD JOHN OF LANCASTER ⎭ *sons to the King*

EARL OF WESTMORELAND

SIR WALTER BLUNT

Attendant Lords

Soldiers

The Rebels

HENRY PERCY, *Earl of Northumberland*

THOMAS PERCY, *Earl of Worcester, brother to Earl of Northumberland*

HENRY PERCY, *called* HOTSPUR, *son to Earl of Northumberland*

EDMUND MORTIMER, *Earl of March*

ARCHIBALD, *Earl of Douglas*

OWEN GLENDOWER

SIR RICHARD VERNON

RICHARD SCROOP, *Archbishop of York*

SIR MICHAEL, *in the Archbishop's service*

Soldiers

LADY PERCY, *called* KATE, *wife to Hotspur and sister to Mortimer*

LADY MORTIMER, *daughter to Glendower and wife to Mortimer*

The Tavern Crew

SIR JOHN FALSTAFF

POINS

GADSHILL

PETO

BARDOLPH

MISTRESS QUICKLY, *the Hostess*

FRANCIS, *a drawer*

VINTNER

Sheriff, Chamberlain, two Carriers, Ostler, Travellers, Messenger

Scene: England and Wales]

[ACT 1

Scene 1. *London. The palace.*]

Enter the King, Lord John of Lancaster, Earl of
Westmoreland, [Sir Walter Blunt,] with others.

KING. So shaken as we are, so wan with care,
 Find we a time for frighted peace to pant
 And breathe short-winded accents of new broils
 To be commenced in stronds afar remote.
 No more the thirsty entrance of this soil   5
 Shall daub her lips with her own children's blood,
 No more shall trenching war channel her fields,
 Nor bruise her flow'rets with the armèd hoofs
 Of hostile paces. Those opposèd eyes,
 Which, like the meteors of a troubled heaven,   10
 All of one nature, of one substance bred,
 Did lately meet in the intestine shock
 And furious close of civil butchery,
 Shall now in mutual well-beseeming ranks
 March all one way and be no more opposed   15
 Against acquaintance, kindred, and allies.
 The edge of war, like an ill-sheathèd knife,
 No more shall cut his master. Therefore, friends,
 As far as to the sepulchre of Christ —
 Whose soldier now, under whose blessèd cross   20
 We are impressèd and engaged to fight —
 Forthwith a power of English shall we levy,
 Whose arms were moulded in their mother's womb
 To chase these pagans in those holy fields
 Over whose acres walked those blessèd feet   25
 Which fourteen hundred years ago were nailed

1.1.2. *pant* catch her breath 3. *accents* staccato (because breathless)
reports 4. *stronds* strands, i.e. places 12. *intestine* interior 13. *close*
hand-to-hand combat

For our advantage on the bitter cross.
But this our purpose now is twelve month old,
And bootless 'tis to tell you we will go.
Therefor we meet not now. Then let me hear   30
Of you, my gentle cousin Westmoreland,
What yesternight our council did decree
In forwarding this dear expedience.

WESTMORELAND. My liege, this haste was hot in question
And many limits of the charge set down   35
But yesternight; when all athwart there came
A post from Wales, loaden with heavy news,
Whose worst was that the noble Mortimer,
Leading the men of Herefordshire to fight
Against the irregular and wild Glendower,   40
Was by the rude hands of that Welshman taken,
A thousand of his people butcherèd;
Upon whose dead corpse there was such misuse,
Such beastly shameless transformation
By those Welshwomen done, as may not be   45
Without much shame retold or spoken of.

KING. It seems then that the tidings of this broil
Brake off our business for the Holy Land.

WESTMORELAND. This, matched with other, did, my
    gracious lord,
For more uneven and unwelcome news   50 ‡
Came from the north, and thus it did import:
On Holy Rood Day the gallant Hotspur there,
Young Harry Percy, and brave Archibald,
That ever-valiant and approvèd Scot,
At Holmedon met, where they did spend   55

---

29. *bootless* useless 30. *Therefor . . . now* i.e. That is not the purpose
of this meeting 33. *dear expedience* cherished enterprise ("expedience"
has the sense of great urgency, which Westmoreland echoes in the next
line) 34. *hot in question* hotly discussed 35. *limits . . . charge* details
of the undertaking and its cost 36. *athwart* (i) across, i.e. thwarting or
frustrating, (ii) brought by mounted messenger 40. *irregular* unruly
(but also in the sense of "guerrilla leader") 43. *corpse* (here plural)
44. *transformation* probably castration (as suggested by Holinshed) 52.
Holy Rood Day September 14, Feast of the Exaltation of the Holy Cross
55. *Holmedon* now Humbleton, in Northumberland near the Scottish
border

A sad and bloody hour –
As by discharge of their artillery
And shape of likelihood the news was told –
For he that brought them, in the very heat
And pride of their contention did take horse,   60
Uncertain of the issue any way.

KING. Here is a dear, a true industrious friend,
Sir Walter Blunt, new lighted from his horse,
Stained with the variation of each soil
Betwixt that Holmedon and this seat of ours,   65
And he hath brought us smooth and welcome news.
The Earl of Douglas is discomfited;
Ten thousand bold Scots, two and twenty knights,
Balked in their own blood did Sir Walter see
On Holmedon's plains. Of prisoners, Hotspur took   70
Mordake, Earl of Fife and eldest son
To beaten Douglas, and the Earl of Athol,
Of Murray, Angus, and Menteith.
And is not this an honourable spoil?
A gallant prize? Ha, cousin, is it not?   75

WESTMORELAND. In faith it is. A conquest for a prince
        to boast of.

KING. Yea, there thou mak'st me sad, and mak'st me sin
In envy, that my Lord Northumberland
Should be the father to so blest a son,
A son who is the theme of honour's tongue,   80
Amongst a grove the very straightest plant,
Who is sweet fortune's minion and her pride –
Whilst I, by looking on the praise of him,
See riot and dishonour stain the brow
Of my young Harry. O that it could be proved   85
That some night-tripping fairy had exchanged

57. *artillery* i.e. any missile-hurling weapon, not necessarily guns 58.
shape of likelihood what seemed the likely outcome 59. *them* i.e. the
news (formerly regarded as plural) 65. *seat of ours* i.e. the official
residence of the king 69. *Balked* (i) laid out in rows ("balks" are the
ridges of unploughed land between furrows), (ii) thwarted (implied)
71. *Mordake* Murdoch (actually son to the Duke of Albany) 82.
minion favourite 86. *night-tripping fairy* (a reference to tales in which
fairies substitute an ugly "changeling" for a beautiful infant)

In cradle clothes our children where they lay,
And called mine Percy, his Plantagenet!
Then would I have his Harry, and he mine.
But let him from my thoughts. What think you, coz,   90
Of this young Percy's pride? The prisoners
Which he in this adventure hath surprised
To his own use he keeps, and sends me word
I shall have none but Mordake Earl of Fife.

WESTMORELAND. This is his uncle's teaching. This is
      Worcester,   95
Malevolent to you in all aspects,
Which makes him prune himself and bristle up
The crest of youth against your dignity.

KING. But I have sent for him to answer this:
And for this cause awhile we must neglect   100
Our holy purpose to Jerusalem.
Cousin, on Wednesday next our council we will hold
At Windsor, so inform the lords:
But come yourself with speed to us again,
For more is to be said and to be done   105
Than out of anger can be utterèd.

WESTMORELAND. I will, my liege.   *Exeunt.*

[Scene 2. *London. The Prince's lodging.*]

Enter Prince of Wales and Sir John Falstaff.

FALSTAFF. Now Hal, what time of day is it, lad?

PRINCE. Thou art so fat-witted with drinking of old sack,
and unbuttoning thee after supper, and sleeping upon
benches after noon, that thou hast forgotten to demand
that truly which thou wouldest truly know. What a devil   5
hast thou to do with the time of the day? Unless hours

were cups of sack, and minutes capons, and clocks the
tongues of bawds, and dials the signs of leaping houses,
and the blessed sun himself a fair hot wench in flame-
coloured taffeta, I see no reason why thou shouldst be　10
so superfluous to demand the time of the day.

FALSTAFF. Indeed you come near me now, Hal; for we
that take purses go by the moon and the seven stars, and
not by Phoebus, he, that wand'ring knight so fair. And
I prithee, sweet wag, when thou art a king, as, God save　15
thy Grace – Majesty I should say, for grace thou wilt
have none –

PRINCE. What, none?

FALSTAFF. No, by my troth, not so much as will serve to
be prologue to an egg and butter.　　　　20

PRINCE. Well, how then? Come, roundly, roundly.

FALSTAFF. Marry, then, sweet wag, when thou art king,
let not us that are squires of the night's body be called
thieves of the day's beauty. Let us be Diana's foresters,
gentlemen of the shade, minions of the moon; and let　25
men say we be men of good government, being governed, as the sea is, by our noble and chaste mistress the
moon, under whose countenance we steal.

PRINCE. Thou sayest well, and it holds well too; for the
fortune of us that are the moon's men doth ebb and　30
flow like the sea, being governed as the sea is by the
moon. As for proof now: a purse of gold most resolutely
snatched on Monday night and most dissolutely spent
on Tuesday morning; got with swearing "Lay by," and

8. *dials* sundials or clock-faces　*leaping houses* brothels　11. *superfluous*
(i.e. in asking an unnecessary question)　12. *near me* close to scoring off
me　13. *the seven stars* the Pleiades　14. *Phoebus* i.e. the sun　*he . . . so
fair* (probably a snatch from an old ballad)　16. *Grace – Majesty* ("Your
Grace" is the proper address for a prince; "Your Majesty" for a king.
Falstaff suggests Hal is such a scapegrace that he does not even deserve
grace before meals)　21. *roundly* to the point　22. *Marry* i.e. "By the
Virgin Mary" (a mild oath)　23-4. *squires . . . beauty* i.e. "Do not let us
who serve by night be called thieves by day" ("squires of the body" =
attendants on a nobleman; with puns on "night" and "knight", "body"
and "bawdy", "beauty" and "booty")　24-5. *Diana's . . . moon* (eu-
phemisms for thieves; criminal cant has always affected such phrases.
Diana was the Roman goddess of the moon and of the hunt)　28.
countenance (i) face, (ii) approval　29. *it holds well* i.e. the idea holds
up to inspection　34. *"Lay by"* (the highwayman's command to his
victims)

> spent with crying "Bring in"; now in as low an ebb as 35
> the foot of the ladder, and by and by in as high a flow
> as the ridge of the gallows.
>
> FALSTAFF. By the Lord, thou say'st true, lad – and is not
> my hostess of the tavern a most sweet wench?
>
> PRINCE. As the honey of Hybla, my old lad of the castle – 40
> and is not a buff jerkin a most sweet robe of durance?
>
> FALSTAFF. How now, how now, mad wag? What, in thy
> quips and thy quiddities? What a plague have I to do
> with a buff jerkin?
>
> PRINCE. Why, what a pox have I to do with my hostess of 45
> the tavern?
>
> FALSTAFF. Well, thou hast called her to a reckoning many
> a time and oft.
>
> PRINCE. Did I ever call for thee to pay thy part?
>
> FALSTAFF. No; I'll give thee thy due, thou hast paid all 50
> there.
>
> PRINCE. Yea, and elsewhere, so far as my coin would
> stretch; and where it would not, I have used my credit.
>
> FALSTAFF. Yea, and so used it that, were it not here ap-
> parent that thou art heir apparent – But I prithee, sweet 55
> wag, shall there be gallows standing in England when
> thou art king? And resolution thus fubbed as it is with
> the rusty curb of old father Antic the law? Do not thou,
> when thou art king, hang a thief.
>
> PRINCE. No, thou shalt. 60
>
> FALSTAFF. Shall I? O rare! By the Lord, I'll be a brave
> judge.

35. *"Bring in"* (command to the waiter in a tavern)   36. *ladder* (i.e. to the gallows)   40. *Hybla* a town in Sicily, famous for fine honey *old . . . castle* roisterer (see also "The History Behind *1 Henry IV*", following this play)   41. *buff jerkin* ox-hide jacket, commonly worn by sheriff's men *durance* i.e. imprisonment (with a pun on "long-wearing")   43. *quips . . . quiddities* jokes and clever word-play (quiddity came from the Latin *quidditas*, a philosophical term, and acquired the sense of "logic-chopping")   47. *called . . . reckoning* (i) asked her for the bill, (ii) called on her to give an account of herself   54-5. *here . . . heir* (pronounced alike in Elizabethan English)   57. *fubbed* fobbed, i.e. cheated, gypped (cf. "fobbed off")   58. *curb* a chain attached to a horse's bit which checks him when the reins are pulled *old father Antic* "that ancient clown"   61. *brave* fine

PRINCE. Thou judgest false already. I mean, thou shalt
have the hanging of the thieves and so become a rare
hangman.   65

FALSTAFF. Well, Hal, well, and in some sort it jumps with
my humour as well as waiting in the court, I can tell
you.

PRINCE. For obtaining of suits?

FALSTAFF. Yea, for obtaining of suits, whereof the hang-   70
man hath no lean wardrobe. 'Sblood, I am as melancholy as a gib-cat or a lugged bear.

PRINCE. Or an old lion, or a lover's lute.

FALSTAFF. Yea, or the drone of a Lincolnshire bagpipe.

PRINCE. What sayest thou to a hare, or the melancholy of   75
Moorditch?

FALSTAFF. Thou hast the most unsavoury similes, and art
indeed the most comparative, rascalliest, sweet young
prince. But Hal, I prithee trouble me no more with   80
vanity. I would to God thou and I knew where a commodity of good names were to be bought. An old lord
of the council rated me the other day in the street about
you, sir, but I marked him not; and yet he talked very
wisely, but I regarded him not; and yet he talked wisely,
and in the street too.   85

PRINCE. Thou didst well, for wisdom cries out in the
streets, and no man regards it.

FALSTAFF. O, thou hast damnable iteration, and art indeed
able to corrupt a saint. Thou hast done much harm upon

66-7. *jumps . . . humour* fits in with my mood   69. *suits* (i) favour at
court, (ii) the clothing of the criminal (which was a perquisite of the
hangman)   71. '*Sblood* by God's blood   72. *gib-cat* a male cat (thought
to be melancholy from its mournful cries on back fences; "gib" is short
for Gilbert)   *lugged bear* baited bear (i.e. one tied up and set upon by
dogs; bull and bear baiting were popular Elizabethan entertainments,
competing with theatres for cash customers)   76. *Moorditch* one of the
foul open sewers of London   78. *comparative* adept at making comparisons (disparaging ones, in this instance)   80. *vanity* worldly matters
(parodying Puritan attitudes and language)   80-81. *commodity* supply
82. *rated* berated, scolded   86-7. *wisdom . . . it* (see Prov. 1:20, 24:
"Wisdom crieth without, she uttereth her voice in the streets"; "Because
I have called, and ye refused; I have stretched out my hand, and no man
regarded")   88. *damnable iteration* damnable (because "the Devil can
quote Scripture") habit of repeating (and twisting) my words

me, Hal – God forgive thee for it! Before I knew thee, 90
Hal, I knew nothing; and now am I, if a man should
speak truly, little better than one of the wicked. I must
give over this life, and I will give it over! By the Lord,
and I do not, I am a villain! I'll be damned for never a
king's son in Christendom.   95

PRINCE. Where shall we take a purse tomorrow, Jack?

FALSTAFF. Zounds, where thou wilt, lad! I'll make one.
An I do not, call me villain and baffle me.

PRINCE. I see a good amendment of life in thee – from
praying to purse-taking.   100

FALSTAFF. Why, Hal, 'tis my vocation, Hal. 'Tis no sin
for a man to labour in his vocation.

Enter Poins.

Poins! Now shall we know if Gadshill have set a match.
O, if men were to be saved by merit, what hole in hell
were hot enough for him? This is the most omnipotent 105
villain that ever cried "Stand!" to a true man.

PRINCE. Good morrow, Ned.

POINS. Good morrow, sweet Hal. What says Monsieur
Remorse? What says Sir John Sack and Sugar? Jack,
how agrees the devil and thee about thy soul, that thou 110
soldest him on Good Friday last for a cup of Madeira
and a cold capon's leg?

PRINCE. Sir John stands to his word, the devil shall have
his bargain, for he was never yet a breaker of proverbs;
he will give the devil his due.   115

POINS. Then art thou damned for keeping thy word with
the devil.

PRINCE. Else he had been damned for cozening the devil.

POINS. But, my lads, my lads, tomorrow morning, by four
o'clock early, at Gadshill, there are pilgrims going to 120

94. *and* if (see also l. 98 and gloss below) 97. *Zounds* by God's wounds
98. *An* if *baffle* degrade from knighthood (a knight who broke his oath
was stripped of armour, his shield reversed, and his picture or effigy hung
upside down; cf. *Richard II*, 1.1.170) 103. *set a match* planned a
robbery 104. *merit* good works (which Puritans denied were efficacious
for salvation) 105. *omnipotent* almighty (used humorously), i.e. un-
mitigated 106. *true* honest 118. *cozening* cheating

Canterbury with rich offerings, and traders riding to
London with fat purses. I have vizards for you all; you
have horses for yourselves. Gadshill lies tonight in
Rochester. I have bespoke supper tomorrow night in
Eastcheap. We may do it as secure as sleep. If you will 125
go, I will stuff your purses full of crowns; if you will
not, tarry at home and be hanged!

FALSTAFF. Hear ye, Yedward, if I tarry at home and go
not, I'll hang you for going.

POINS. You will, chops?   130

FALSTAFF. Hal, wilt thou make one?

PRINCE. Who, I rob? I a thief? Not I, by my faith.

FALSTAFF. There's neither honesty, manhood, nor good
fellowship in thee, nor thou cam'st not of the blood
royal if thou darest not stand for ten shillings.   135

PRINCE. Well then, once in my days I'll be a madcap.

FALSTAFF. Why, that's well said.

PRINCE. Well, come what will, I'll tarry at home.

FALSTAFF. By the Lord, I'll be a traitor then, when thou
art king.   140

PRINCE. I care not.

POINS. Sir John, I prithee, leave the Prince and me alone.
I will lay him down such reasons for this adventure that
he shall go.

FALSTAFF. Well, God give thee the spirit of persuasion 145
and him the ears of profiting, that what thou speakest
may move and what he hears may be believed, that the
true prince may (for recreation sake) prove a false
thief; for the poor abuses of the time want countenance.
Farewell; you shall find me in Eastcheap.   150

PRINCE. Farewell, the latter spring! Farewell, All-hallown
summer!   [*Exit Falstaff.*]

---

122. *vizards* masks 125. *Eastcheap* a London district 128. *Yedward*
(dialect form of "Edward", Poins's given name) 130. *chops* jaws or
cheeks (particularly if fat) 135. *royal* (with a pun on "royal", a gold
coin worth ten shillings) 149. *want countenance* need protection and
royal favour 151. *the latter spring* (i.e. because still youthful late in
life) 151-2. *All-hallown summer* i.e. "Indian summer" (same sense as
the previous phrase; "All-hallown" = the eve of All Hallows, the modern
Hallowe'en)

POINS. Now, my good sweet honey lord, ride with us
tomorrow. I have a jest to execute that I cannot manage alone. Falstaff, Bardolph, Peto, and Gadshill shall 155
rob those men that we have already waylaid; yourself
and I will not be there; and when they have the booty,
if you and I do not rob them, cut this head off from
my shoulders.

PRINCE. How shall we part with them in setting forth? 160

POINS. Why, we will set forth before or after them and
appoint them a place of meeting, wherein it is at our
pleasure to fail; and then will they adventure upon the
exploit themselves, which they shall have no sooner
achieved but we'll set upon them. 165

PRINCE. Yea, but 'tis like that they will know us by our
horses, by our habits, and by every other appointment,
to be ourselves.

POINS. Tut! Our horses they shall not see – I'll tie them
in the wood; our vizards we will change after we leave 170
them; and, sirrah, I have cases of buckram for the
nonce, to immask our noted outward garments.

PRINCE. Yea, but I doubt they will be too hard for us.

POINS. Well, for two of them, I know them to be as true-
bred cowards as ever turned back; and for the third, if 175
he fight longer than he sees reason, I'll forswear arms.
The virtue of this jest will be the incomprehensible lies
that this same fat rogue will tell us when we meet at
supper – how thirty, at least, he fought with – what
wards, what blows, what extremities he endured – and 180
in the reproof of this lives the jest.

PRINCE. Well, I'll go with thee. Provide us all things necessary and meet me tomorrow night in Eastcheap. There
I'll sup. Farewell.

POINS. Farewell, my lord. *Exit Poins.* 185

PRINCE. I know you all, and will awhile uphold   ‡
The unyoked humour of your idleness;

167. *appointment* piece of equipment, furnishing 171. *sirrah* (form used
to address persons of lower rank, or to show contempt; here indicating
extreme familiarity) *cases of buckram* "overalls" of coarse cloth 171-
2. *for the nonce* for the occasion 173. *I doubt* I am afraid 180. *wards*
defensive postures in sword-play 187. *unyoked . . . idleness* uncontrolled
character of your frivolous carryings-on

Yet herein will I imitate the sun,
Who doth permit the base contagious clouds
To smother up his beauty from the world,   190
That, when he please again to be himself,
Being wanted, he may be more wond'red at
By breaking through the foul and ugly mists
Of vapours that did seem to strangle him.
If all the year were playing holidays,   195
To sport would be as tedious as to work;
But when they seldom come, they wished-for come,
And nothing pleaseth but rare accidents.
So when this loose behaviour I throw off
And pay the debt I never promisèd,   200
By how much better than my word I am,
By so much shall I falsify men's hopes,
And, like bright metal on a sullen ground,
My reformation, glitt'ring o'er my fault,
Shall show more goodly and attract more eyes   205
Than that which hath no foil to set it off.
I'll so offend, to make offence a skill,
Redeeming time when men think least I will.

Exit.

[Scene 3. *Windsor. The council chamber.*]

*Enter the King, Northumberland, Worcester,
Hotspur, Sir Walter Blunt, with others.*

KING. My blood hath been too cold and temperate,
    Unapt to stir at these indignities,

---

189. *contagious* (clouds were thought to breed pestilence)   192. *wanted*
missed, longed for   198. *rare accidents* exceptional and unlooked-for
events   202. *falsify men's hopes* make everyone's predictions false   203.
sullen ground dull background   206. *foil* contrast; specifically, the
metal in which a gem is set to show off its brilliance   207. *make . . . skill*
convert sinning into a useful device   208. *Redeeming time* (see Eph.
5:15-16: "See then that ye walk circumspectly, not as fools, but as wise,
Redeeming the time, because the days are evil"; verses 1-20 of this chapter
of the Epistle are relevant)

And you have found me, for accordingly
You tread upon my patience; but be sure
I will from henceforth rather be myself,　　　5
Mighty and to be feared, than my condition,
Which hath been smooth as oil, soft as young down,
And therefore lost that title of respect
Which the proud soul ne'er pays but to the proud.

WORCESTER. Our house – my sovereign liege – little
　　　deserves　　　10
The scourge of greatness to be used on it,
And that same greatness too which our own hands
Have holp to make so portly.

NORTHUMBERLAND.　　　　　　　　My lord –

KING. Worcester, get thee gone, for I do see
Danger and disobedience in thine eye.　　　15
O, sir, your presence is too bold and peremptory,
And majesty might never yet endure
The moody frontier of a servant brow.
You have good leave to leave us: when we need
Your use and counsel, we shall send for you.　　　20

　　　　　　　　　　　　　　　Exit Worcester.

You were about to speak.

NORTHUMBERLAND.　　　　　Yea, my good lord.
Those prisoners in your Highness' name demanded,
Which Harry Percy here at Holmedon took,
Were, as he says, not with such strength denied
As is deliverèd to your Majesty.　　　25
Either envy, therefore, or misprision
Is guilty of this fault, and not my son.

HOTSPUR. My liege, I did deny no prisoners,
But I remember, when the fight was done,
When I was dry with rage and extreme toil,　　　30
Breathless and faint, leaning upon my sword,

1.3.3. *found me* i.e. discovered this weakness of mine　5. *be myself*
i.e. be what I ought to be, as king　6. *my condition* my natural disposition
13. *holp* (obsolete past participle) helped　*portly* dignified, stately　18.
moody frontier i.e. sullen, defiant look (as though Worcester's forehead
["front"] were the ramparts ["frontier"] of a fortress)　26. *misprision*
misapprehension, mistake

Came there a certain lord, neat and trimly dressed,
Fresh as a bridegroom, and his chin new reaped
Showed like a stubble land at harvest home;
He was perfumèd like a milliner,   35
And 'twixt his finger and his thumb he held
A pouncet box, which ever and anon
He gave his nose, and took't away again,
Who therewith angry, when it next came there,
Took it in snuff, and still he smiled and talked;   40
And as the soldiers bore dead bodies by,
He called them untaught knaves, unmannerly,
To bring a slovenly unhandsome corse
Betwixt the wind and his nobility;
With many holiday and lady terms   45 ‡
He questioned me, amongst the rest demanded
My prisoners in your Majesty's behalf.
I then, all smarting with my wounds being cold,
To be so pest'red with a popingay,
Out of my grief and my impatience   50
Answered neglectingly, I know not what —
He should, or he should not — for he made me mad
To see him shine so brisk, and smell so sweet,
And talk so like a waiting gentlewoman
Of guns and drums and wounds — God save the mark! — 55
And telling me the sovereignest thing on earth
Was parmacity for an inward bruise,
And that it was great pity, so it was,
This villainous saltpetre should be digged
Out of the bowels of the harmless earth,   60

33. *reaped* i.e. with beard closely trimmed   37. *pouncet box* a box with perforated cover, containing perfume, which the fastidious sniffed at in the presence of foul odours   40. *Took . . . snuff* snuffed at it, with a pun on "took offense at it" (not necessarily anachronistic, since snuff of herbs or perfumes was in use before the introduction of tobacco)   43. *corse* corpse   45. *holiday and lady* flowery and effeminate   49. *popingay* popinjay (originally, a parrot; hence, one dressed in gaudy fashion who chatters idly)   50. *grief* pain (of wounds)   55. *God . . . mark* roughly equivalent to "God help us!"   56. *sovereignest* best (an instance of the kind of high-flown language to which Hotspur objects — a "holiday" term)   57. *parmacity* spermaceti, a waxlike substance from sperm whales, used in ointments

Which many a good tall fellow had destroyed
So cowardly, and but for these vile guns
He would himself have been a soldier.
This bald unjointed chat of his, my lord,
I answered indirectly, as I said,   65
And I beseech you, let not his report
Come current for an accusation
Betwixt my love and your high Majesty.

BLUNT. The circumstance considerèd, good my lord,
  Whate'er Lord Harry Percy then had said   70
  To such a person, and in such a place,
  At such a time, with all the rest retold,
  May reasonably die, and never rise
  To do him wrong, or any way impeach
  What then he said – so he unsay it now.   75

KING. Why, yet he doth deny his prisoners,
  But with proviso and exception,
  That we at our own charge shall ransom straight
  His brother-in-law, the foolish Mortimer,
  Who, on my soul, hath wilfully betrayed   80
  The lives of those that he did lead to fight
  Against that great magician, damned Glendower –
  Whose daughter, as we hear, that Earl of March
  Hath lately married. Shall our coffers, then,
  Be emptied to redeem a traitor home?   85
  Shall we buy treason? and indent with fears
  When they have lost and forfeited themselves?
  No, on the barren mountains let him starve!
  For I shall never hold that man my friend
  Whose tongue shall ask me for one penny cost   90
  To ransom home revolted Mortimer.

HOTSPUR. Revolted Mortimer?
  He never did fall off, my sovereign liege,
  But by the chance of war. To prove that true
  Needs no more but one tongue for all those wounds,   95
  Those mouthèd wounds, which valiantly he took

---

67. *Come current* be given currency, credit   86. *indent with fears* bargain
with cowards   96. *mouthèd wounds* open, bloody wounds (which look
like mouths and testify to the valour of the soldier who receives them)

When on the gentle Severn's sedgy bank,
In single opposition, hand to hand,
He did confound the best part of an hour
In changing hardiment with great Glendower.   100
Three times they breathed, and three times did they
    drink,
Upon agreement, of swift Severn's flood;
Who then affrighted with their bloody looks
Ran fearfully among the trembling reeds
And hid his crisp head in the hollow bank,   105
Bloodstainèd with these valiant combatants.
Never did bare and rotten policy
Colour her working with such deadly wounds,
Nor never could the noble Mortimer
Receive so many, and all willingly.   110
Then let not him be slanderèd with revolt.
KING. Thou dost belie him, Percy, thou dost belie him!
He never did encounter with Glendower;
I tell thee, he durst as well have met the devil alone
As Owen Glendower for an enemy.   115
Art thou not ashamed? But, sirrah, henceforth
Let me not hear you speak of Mortimer.
Send me your prisoners with the speediest means,
Or you shall hear in such a kind from me
As will displease you. My Lord Northumberland,   120
We license your departure with your son;
Send us your prisoners, or you will hear of it.
                    Exit King [with Blunt, and train].
HOTSPUR. And if the devil come and roar for them
I will not send them. I will after straight
And tell him so, for I will ease my heart,   125
Albeit I make a hazard of my head.
NORTHUMBERLAND. What? Drunk with choler? Stay, and
    pause awhile.

99. *confound* consume   100. *changing hardiment* displaying resolution
and vigour to one another   105. *crisp head* curled head (the source of a
river is called its "head", thus the personified Severn is pictured as hiding
its curled, in the sense of "rippling", head)   107. *policy* guile, scheming
108. *Colour* give an acceptable appearance to (in this instance, with the
blood of wounds)   116. *sirrah* (see 1.2.171 and gloss; used here insult-
ingly)   127. *choler* anger

Here comes your uncle.

Enter Worcester.

HOTSPUR.   Speak of Mortimer?
Zounds, I will speak of him, and let my soul
Want mercy if I do not join with him!   130
Yea, on his part I'll empty all these veins,
And shed my dear blood, drop by drop in the dust,
But I will lift the downtrod Mortimer
As high in the air as this unthankful king,
As this ingrate and cank'red Bolingbroke.   135
NORTHUMBERLAND. Brother, the King hath made your
    nephew mad.
WORCESTER. Who struck this heat up after I was gone?
HOTSPUR. He will forsooth have all my prisoners,
And when I urged the ransom once again
Of my wife's brother, then his cheek looked pale,   140
And on my face he turned an eye of death,
Trembling even at the name of Mortimer.
WORCESTER. I cannot blame him. Was not he proclaimed
By Richard that dead is, the next of blood?
NORTHUMBERLAND. He was, I heard the proclamation: 145
And then it was when the unhappy king
(Whose wrongs in us God pardon!) did set forth
Upon his Irish expedition;
From whence he, intercepted, did return
To be deposed, and shortly murderèd.   150
WORCESTER. And for whose death we in the world's wide
    mouth
Live scandalized and foully spoken of.
HOTSPUR. But soft, I pray you, did King Richard then
Proclaim my brother Edmund Mortimer
Heir to the crown?

135. *cank'red* (from the same root as "cancer") ulcerated, rotten with
disease, hence (as here) morally corrupt *Bolingbroke* i.e. the King (he
was generally called "Bolingbroke", his by-name, before he seized the
crown) 144. *next of blood* closest relative (thus heir to the throne)
147. *in us* inflicted by us 149. *intercepted* interrupted 150. *shortly*
shortly afterward 154. *brother* i.e. brother-in-law

NORTHUMBERLAND.   He did, myself did hear it.   155
HOTSPUR. Nay, then I cannot blame his cousin king,
    That wished him on the barren mountains starve.
    But shall it be that you – that set the crown
    Upon the head of this forgetful man,
    And for his sake wear the detested blot   160
    Of murderous subornation – shall it be
    That you a world of curses undergo,
    Being the agents or base second means,
    The cords, the ladder, or the hangman rather?
    O pardon me, that I descend so low   165
    To show the line and the predicament
    Wherein you range under this subtle king!
    Shall it for shame be spoken in these days,
    Or fill up chronicles in time to come,
    That men of your nobility and power   170
    Did gage them both in an unjust behalf
    (As both of you, God pardon it, have done)
    To put down Richard, that sweet lovely rose,
    And plant this thorn, this canker Bolingbroke?
    And shall it in more shame be further spoken   175
    That you are fooled, discarded, and shook off
    By him for whom these shames ye underwent?
    No – yet time serves wherein you may redeem
    Your banished honours and restore yourselves
    Into the good thoughts of the world again;   180
    Revenge the jeering and disdained contempt
    Of this proud king, who studies day and night
    To answer all the debt he owes to you
    Even with the bloody payment of your deaths.
    Therefore I say –

161. *murderous subornation* instigating another to commit murder 163-
4. *second means . . . rather* ("second means" = secondary instruments,
tools) i.e. the Percies were not judge or jury to Richard, but rather the
executioners of another's will 166. *line* (i) rank or station, (ii) occupation (i.e. hangman), (iii) the "tether" (by which the king limits your
freedom) *predicament* (i) category, from the technical term in logic,
(ii) dangerous situation 171. *gage* engage, pledge 174. *canker* wild
rose, inferior to cultivated variety (see also l. 135 and gloss above)
183-4. *debt . . . deaths* (word play made possible by the Elizabethan
pronunciation of "death" like "debt")

WORCESTER.   Peace, cousin, say no more.   185
   And now I will unclasp a secret book,
   And to your quick-conceiving discontents
   I'll read you matter deep and dangerous,
   As full of peril and adventurous spirit
   As to o'erwalk a current roaring loud   190
   On the unsteadfast footing of a spear.
HOTSPUR. If he fall in, good night, or sink, or swim!
   Send danger from the east unto the west,
   So honour cross it from the north to south,
   And let them grapple. O the blood more stirs   195
   To rouse a lion than to start a hare!
NORTHUMBERLAND. Imagination of some great exploit
   Drives him beyond the bounds of patience.
HOTSPUR. By heaven, methinks it were an easy leap
   To pluck bright honour from the pale-faced moon,   200
   Or dive into the bottom of the deep,
   Where fathom line could never touch the ground,
   And pluck up drownèd honour by the locks,
   So he that doth redeem her thence might wear
   Without corrival all her dignities;   205
   But out upon this half-faced fellowship!
WORCESTER. He apprehends a world of figures here,
   But not the form of what he should attend.
   Good cousin, give me audience for a while.
HOTSPUR. I cry you mercy.   210
WORCESTER. Those same noble Scots that are your
     prisoners –
HOTSPUR. I'll keep them all;
   By God, he shall not have a Scot of them!
   No, if a Scot would save his soul, he shall not.
   I'll keep them, by this hand!

187. *quick-conceiving* quick to understand, alert 192. *good . . . swim*
i.e. he will be lost, whether he sinks at once or is carried off by the
current 205. *corrival* an (equal) partner 206. *out . . . fellowship* curse
this half-and-half sharing (honour will not suffice for either partner if
shared; both will starve: "half-faced" = thin faced, or starving) 207.
world of figures multitude of (i) figures of speech, (ii) "shapes", "forms"
(as opposed to substance) 210. *cry you mercy* beg your pardon 214.
Scot (the "scot" was an old tax; hence used punningly here to mean "a
small payment")

WORCESTER.   You start away   215
  And lend no ear unto my purposes.
  Those prisoners you shall keep.
HOTSPUR.   Nay, I will! That's flat!
  He said he would not ransom Mortimer,
  Forbade my tongue to speak of Mortimer,
  But I will find him when he lies asleep,   220
  And in his ear I'll hollo "Mortimer!"
  Nay, I'll have a starling shall be taught to speak
  Nothing but "Mortimer," and give it him
  To keep his anger still in motion.
WORCESTER. Hear you, cousin, a word.   225
HOTSPUR. All studies here I solemnly defy,
  Save how to gall and pinch this Bolingbroke;
  And that same sword-and-buckler Prince of Wales,
  But that I think his father loves him not
  And would be glad he met with some mischance,   230
  I would have him poisonèd with a pot of ale.
WORCESTER. Farewell, kinsman: I'll talk to you
  When you are better tempered to attend.
NORTHUMBERLAND. Why, what a wasp-stung and
      impatient fool
  Art thou to break into this woman's mood,   235
  Tying thine ear to no tongue but thine own!
HOTSPUR. Why, look you, I am whipped and scourged
      with rods,
  Nettled, and stung with pismires, when I hear
  Of this vile politician, Bolingbroke.
  In Richard's time – what do you call the place?   240
  A plague upon it! It is in Gloucestershire;
  'Twas where the madcap duke his uncle kept,
  His uncle York – where I first bowed my knee
  Unto this king of smiles, this Bolingbroke –

221. *hollo* shout (same word as "holler" in modern slang, and akin to
"hello" from the French *ho là*) 226. *defy* renounce 228. *sword-and-
buckler* i.e. low, common (the rapier and dagger, not the sword and
shield, were a gentleman's weapons) 231. *ale* (additionally contemptuous, since wine, not ale, was a gentleman's drink) 238. *pismires* ants
242. *madcap duke* i.e. Edmund Langley, Duke of York, uncle to both
Richard II and Henry IV (referred to by Holinshed as pleasure-loving)
kept lived

    'Sblood! – when you and he came back from
        Ravenspurgh –   245
NORTHUMBERLAND. At Berkeley Castle.
HOTSPUR. You say true.
    Why, what a candy deal of courtesy
    This fawning greyhound then did proffer me!
    "Look when his infant fortune came to age,"   250
    And "gentle Harry Percy," and "kind cousin" –
    O the devil take such cozeners! – God forgive me!
    Good uncle, tell your tale; I have done.
WORCESTER. Nay, if you have not, to it again.
    We will stay your leisure.
HOTSPUR.   I have done, i' faith.   255
WORCESTER. Then once more to your Scottish prisoners:
    Deliver them up without their ransom straight,
    And make the Douglas' son your only mean
    For powers in Scotland – which, for divers reasons
    Which I shall send you written, be assured   260
    Will easily be granted. [*To Northumberland*] You,
      my lord,
    Your son in Scotland being thus employed,
    Shall secretly into the bosom creep
    Of that same noble prelate well-beloved,
    The Archbishop.   265
HOTSPUR. Of York, is it not?
WORCESTER. True; who bears hard
    His brother's death at Bristow, the Lord Scroop.
    I speak not this in estimation,
    As what I think might be, but what I know   270
    Is ruminated, plotted, and set down,
    And only stays but to behold the face
    Of that occasion that shall bring it on.

245. *Ravenspurgh* (in Yorkshire, where Bolingbroke landed on his return from exile and was joined by Northumberland in the enterprise against Richard II)   248. *candy deal* sugary lot   249. *then* (this meeting of Hotspur and Bolingbroke is depicted in Shakespeare's *Richard II*, 2.3.41-50)   252. *cozeners* cheats (punningly, those who call you "Cousin" in such a hypocritical way)   255. *stay your leisure* wait until you have free time   258. *mean* agent   259. *powers* (raising) troops   268. *brother's death* i.e. the execution for treason in 1399 of William Scrope, Earl of Wiltshire (actually he was cousin to the Archbishop; Shakespeare follows Holinshed's mistake in this)   *Bristow* Bristol   269. *estimation* conjecture

HOTSPUR. I smell it. Upon my life, it will do well.
NORTHUMBERLAND. Before the game is afoot thou still
    let'st slip.   275
HOTSPUR. Why, it cannot choose but be a noble plot –
  And then the power of Scotland and of York
  To join with Mortimer, ha?
WORCESTER.   And so they shall.
HOTSPUR. In faith, it is exceedingly well aimed.
WORCESTER. And 'tis no little reason bids us speed   280 ‡
  To save our heads by raising of a head,
  For, bear ourselves as even as we can,
  The King will always think him in our debt,
  And think we think ourselves unsatisfied,
  Till he hath found a time to pay us home.   285
  And see already how he doth begin
  To make us strangers to his looks of love.
HOTSPUR. He does, he does! We'll be revenged on him.
WORCESTER. Cousin, farewell. No further go in this
  Than I by letters shall direct your course.   290
  When time is ripe, which will be suddenly,
  I'll steal to Glendower and Lord Mortimer,
  Where you and Douglas, and our pow'rs at once,
  As I will fashion it, shall happily meet,
  To bear our fortunes in our own strong arms,   295
  Which now we hold at much uncertainty.
NORTHUMBERLAND. Farewell, good brother. We shall
    thrive, I trust.
HOTSPUR. Uncle, adieu. O let the hours be short
  Till fields and blows and groans applaud our sport!

                              Exeunt.

275. *let'st slip* unleash (the hunting dogs)   281. *head* army (i.e. a source
of power, as a "head" of water, steam, etc.)   285. *home* in full, i.e. with
  a fatal thrust that strikes "home"   291. *suddenly* very soon

[ACT 2

Scene 1. *Rochester. An inn yard.*]

Enter a Carrier with a lantern in his hand.

FIRST CARRIER. Heigh-ho! An it be not four by the day,
I'll be hanged. Charles' wain is over the new chimney,
and yet our horse not packed. What, ostler!
OSTLER [*within*]. Anon, anon.
FIRST CARRIER. I prithee, Tom, beat Cut's saddle, put a few   5
flocks in the point; poor jade is wrung in the withers out
of all cess.

Enter another Carrier.

SECOND CARRIER. Peas and beans are as dank here as a
dog, and that is the next way to give poor jades the bots.
This house is turned upside down since Robin Ostler 10
died.
FIRST CARRIER. Poor fellow never joyed since the price of
oats rose; it was the death of him.
SECOND CARRIER. I think this be the most villainous house
in all London road for fleas, I am stung like a tench.   15
FIRST CARRIER. Like a tench? By the mass, there is ne'er
a king christen could be better bit than I have been
since the first cock.
SECOND CARRIER. Why, they will allow us ne'er a jordan,

2.1.1. *by the day* in the morning 2. *Charles' wain* Charles' (i.e.
Charlemagne's) wagon, an old name for the constellation Ursa Major,
our "Big Dipper" 4. *Anon* immediately 5. *beat . . . saddle* (in order to
make the padding more even, thus softer) *Cut* horse's name, for his
docked tail 6. *flocks . . . point* tufts of wool in the pommel *wrung . . .
withers* galled at the part of the back between the shoulders 6-7. *out
. . . cess* excessively 9. *next* quickest *bots* a disease of horses and cattle,
caused by larvae of botflies in the stomach, here blamed on damp fodder
12-13. *price of oats* (it trebled between 1593 and 1596) 15. *tench* a
variety of fish whose red spots make it look flea-bitten (the tench and
loach are sometimes infested with a form of louse; see l. 21) 16-17.
ne'er . . . christen not even a Christian king (i.e. one who has the best of
everything, including fleabites) 19. *jordan* chamberpot

and then we leak in your chimney, and your chamber- 20
lye breeds fleas like a loach.

FIRST CARRIER. What, ostler! Come away and be hanged!
Come away!

SECOND CARRIER. I have a gammon of bacon and two
razes of ginger, to be delivered as far as Charing Cross. 25

FIRST CARRIER. God's body! The turkeys in my pannier
are quite starved. What, ostler! A plague on thee, hast
thou never an eye in thy head? Canst not hear? And
'twere not as good deed as drink to break the pate on
thee, I am a very villain. Come, and be hanged! Hast 30
no faith in thee?

Enter Gadshill.

GADSHILL. Good morrow, carriers, what's o'clock?

FIRST CARRIER. I think it be two o'clock.

GADSHILL. I prithee lend me thy lantern to see my gelding
in the stable.   35

FIRST CARRIER. Nay, by God, soft! I know a trick worth
two of that, i' faith.

GADSHILL. I pray thee lend me thine.

SECOND CARRIER. Ay, when? Canst tell? Lend me thy lantern, quoth he? Marry, I'll see thee hanged first!   40

GADSHILL. Sirrah, carrier, what time do you mean to come
to London?

SECOND CARRIER. Time enough to go to bed with a candle,
I warrant thee. Come, neighbour Mugs, we'll call up
the gentlemen, they will along with company, for they 45
have great charge.   *Exeunt [Carriers].*

GADSHILL. What ho! Chamberlain!

Enter Chamberlain.

20. *chimney* fireplace   20-21. *chamber-lye* urine   *loach* (see gloss l. 15
above)   24. *gammon of bacon* the bottom end of a side of bacon; a ham
25. *razes* roots   *Charing Cross* (then a separate village between London
and Westminster, on the far side of London from Rochester; now a part
of London)   26. *pannier* basket   29-30. *the pate on thee* your head   39.
Ay . . . tell (a proverbial retort; "when Hell freezes over" is the idea)
43. *Time . . . candle* i.e. before dark or after dark (an evasive answer by
the suspicious carrier)   46. *great charge* (responsibility for) a valuable
shipment of goods or money   47. *Chamberlain* man in charge of rooms
at an inn

CHAMBERLAIN. "At hand, quoth pickpurse."

GADSHILL. That's even as fair as "at hand, quoth the chamberlain"; for thou variest no more from picking 50 of purses than giving direction doth from labouring: thou layest the plot how.

CHAMBERLAIN. Good morrow, Master Gadshill. It holds current that I told you yesternight: there's a franklin in the wild of Kent hath brought three hundred marks 55 with him in gold, I heard him tell it to one of his company last night at supper – a kind of auditor, one that hath abundance of charge too, God knows what. They are up already and call for eggs and butter, they will away presently.   60

GADSHILL. Sirrah, if they meet not with Saint Nicholas' clerks, I'll give thee this neck.

CHAMBERLAIN. No, I'll none of it; I pray thee keep that for the hangman, for I know thou worshippest Saint Nicholas as truly as a man of falsehood may.   65

GADSHILL. What talkest thou to me of the hangman? If I hang, I'll make a fat pair of gallows; for if I hang, old Sir John hangs with me, and thou knowest he is no starveling. Tut! There are other Troyans that thou dream'st not of, the which for sport sake are content 70 to do the profession some grace, that would (if matters should be looked into) for their own credit sake make all whole. I am joined with no foot-landrakers, no long-staff sixpenny strikers, none of these mad mustachio purple-hued maltworms, but with nobility and tranquil- 75 ‡

48. *At hand . . . pickpurse* "Right here, said the pickpocket" (a slang expression, appropriate to this thieves' conversation)   50-52. *thou . . . plot how* (Chamberlains were commonly accused of "tipping off" highwaymen, as this one is doing)   53-4. *It holds current* it is still true   *franklin* wealthy farmer   55. *wild* weald (the Weald of Kent was formerly a woodland district in south-eastern England; it is now mainly agricultural) *three hundred marks* i.e. £200 or, in modern money, several thousand dollars (not a coin, the mark was worth two-thirds of a pound)   57. *auditor* tax official   61-2. *Saint Nicholas' clerks* i.e. highwaymen (perhaps so called because St. Nicholas was patron of travellers)   69. *Troyans* Trojans, i.e. good lads   73. *foot-landrakers* vagabond footpads   73-4. *long-staff sixpenny strikers* low class of thieves who knock a man from his horse with a pole to steal as little as sixpence   74-5. *mustachio purple-hued maltworms* long-mustached, red-faced ale guzzlers   75-6. *tranquillity* (Gadshill's word, to pair with "nobility", for the class that "takes its ease")

lity, burgomasters and great oneyers, such as can hold
in, such as will strike sooner than speak, and speak
sooner than drink, and drink sooner than pray – and
yet, zounds, I lie, for they pray continually to their saint,
the commonwealth, or rather, not pray to her, but prey   80
on her, for they ride up and down on her and make her
their boots.

CHAMBERLAIN. What, the commonwealth their boots?
Will she hold out water in foul way?

GADSHILL. She will, she will! Justice hath liquored her. We   85
steal as in a castle, cocksure. We have the receipt of   ‡
fernseed, we walk invisible.

CHAMBERLAIN. Nay, by my faith, I think you are more
beholding to the night than to fernseed for your walking
invisible.   90

GADSHILL. Give me thy hand. Thou shalt have a share in
our purchase, as I am a true man.   ‡

CHAMBERLAIN. Nay, rather let me have it, as you are a
false thief.

GADSHILL. Go to; "homo" is a common name to all men.   95
Bid the ostler bring my gelding out of the stable. Farewell, you muddy knave.   [*Exeunt.*]

[Scene 2. *The highway, near Gadshill.*]

Enter Prince, Poins, and Peto, etc.

POINS. Come, shelter, shelter! I have removed Falstaff's
horse, and he frets like a gummed velvet.

---

oneyers usually taken to mean simply "ones" (see 2.1.76, textual variants)
76-7. *hold in* keep quiet (about their activities and those of others)   82.
boots (with a pun on "booty")   84. *in foul way* on a wet, muddy road
85. *liquored* (i) greased, both literally, to keep out water, and in the
slang sense of "greased palm", (ii) got (her) drunk   86-7. *receipt of
fernseed* recipe for fernseed, thought to confer invisibility (see end note)
92. *purchase* (as though it were a strictly legitimate transaction)   *true*
honest   95. *"homo" . . . men* (a direct quotation from the discussion of
common nouns in Lily's *Grammar*, the standard primary textbook in
Shakespeare's time and for many years afterward)   97. *muddy* muddle-
headed
    2.2.2. *frets . . . velvet* frays like a cheap velvet which has been stiffened
with gum

PRINCE. Stand close.   [*They step aside.*]

Enter Falstaff.

FALSTAFF. Poins! Poins, and be hanged! Poins!

PRINCE [*coming forward*]. Peace, ye fat-kidneyed rascal! 5
What a brawling dost thou keep!

FALSTAFF. Where's Poins, Hal?

PRINCE. He is walked up to the top of the hill; I'll go seek
him.   [*Steps aside.*]

FALSTAFF. I am accursed to rob in that thief's company. 10
The rascal hath removed my horse and tied him I know
not where. If I travel but four foot by the squire further
afoot, I shall break my wind. Well, I doubt not but to
die a fair death for all this, if I scape hanging for killing
that rogue. I have forsworn his company hourly any 15
time this two and twenty years, and yet I am bewitched
with the rogue's company. If the rascal have not given
me medicines to make me love him, I'll be hanged. It
could not be else: I have drunk medicines. Poins! Hal!
A plague upon you both! Bardolph! Peto! I'll starve ere 20
I'll rob a foot further. And 'twere not as good a deed as
drink to turn true man and to leave these rogues, I am
the veriest varlet that ever chewed with a tooth. Eight
yards of uneven ground is threescore and ten miles afoot
with me, and the stony-hearted villains know it well 25
enough. A plague upon it when thieves cannot be true
one to another! (*They whistle.*) Whew! A plague upon
you all! Give me my horse, you rogues! Give me my
horse and be hanged!

PRINCE [*coming forward*]. Peace, ye fat-guts! Lie down, 30
lay thine ear close to the ground, and list if thou canst
hear the tread of travellers.

FALSTAFF. Have you any levers to lift me up again, being
down? 'Sblood, I'll not bear my own flesh so far afoot
again for all the coin in thy father's exchequer. What a 35
plague mean ye to colt me thus?

PRINCE. Thou liest, thou art not colted, thou art uncolted.

---

3. *Stand close* Take cover   12. *squire* i.e. square, a measuring instrument
22. *true* honest   23. *varlet* rascal   36. *colt* trick

FALSTAFF. I prithee, good Prince Hal, help me to my
  horse, good king's son.
PRINCE. Out, ye rogue! Shall I be your ostler? 40
FALSTAFF. Hang thyself in thine own heir-apparent garters! If I be ta'en, I'll peach for this. And I have not
  ballads made on you all, and sung to filthy tunes, let a
  cup of sack be my poison. When a jest is so forward –
  and afoot too! – I hate it. 45

          Enter Gadshill [and Bardolph].

GADSHILL. Stand!
FALSTAFF. So I do, against my will.
POINS. O 'tis our setter; I know his voice. [*Coming for-
  ward with Peto.*] Bardolph, what news?
BARDOLPH. Case ye, case ye! On with your vizards! There's 50
  money of the King's coming down the hill; 'tis going to
  the King's exchequer.
FALSTAFF. You lie, ye rogue! 'Tis going to the King's
  tavern.
GADSHILL. There's enough to make us all – 55
FALSTAFF. To be hanged.
PRINCE. Sirs, you four shall front them in the narrow
  lane; Ned Poins and I will walk lower: if they 'scape
  from your encounter, then they light on us.
PETO. How many be there of them? 60
GADSHILL. Some eight or ten.
FALSTAFF. Zounds, will they not rob us?
PRINCE. What, a coward, Sir John Paunch?
FALSTAFF. Indeed, I am not John of Gaunt your grand-
  father, but yet no coward, Hal. 65
PRINCE. Well, we leave that to the proof.
POINS. Sirrah Jack, thy horse stands behind the hedge.
  When thou need'st him, there thou shalt find him. Fare-
  well and stand fast.

---

42. *peach* turn informer   44. *is so forward* goes so far   48. *setter* the
man who arranges the robbery (in this instance, Gadshill)   64. *John of
Gaunt* (Hal was tall and thin, according to the chronicles; thus the
allusion to the by-name of his grandfather has punning significance)   67.
Sirrah Jack (contemptuous variation by Poins on the "Sir John Paunch"
and "John of Gaunt" interchange)

FALSTAFF. Now cannot I strike him, if I should be hanged. 70
PRINCE [*aside to Poins*]. Ned, where are our disguises?
POINS [*aside to Prince*]. Here, hard by. Stand close.
                              [*Exeunt Prince and Poins.*]
FALSTAFF. Now, my masters, happy man be his dole, say
    I. Every man to his business.

Enter the Travellers.

TRAVELLER. Come, neighbour. The boy shall lead our 75
    horses down the hill; we'll walk afoot awhile and ease
    our legs.
THIEVES. Stand!
TRAVELLER. Jesus bless us!
FALSTAFF. Strike! Down with them! Cut the villains' 80
    throats! Ah, whoreson caterpillars! Bacon-fed knaves!
    They hate us youth. Down with them! Fleece them!
TRAVELLER. O we are undone, both we and ours forever!
FALSTAFF. Hang ye, gorbellied knaves, are ye undone?
    No, ye fat chuffs; I would your store were here! On, 85
    bacons, on! What, ye knaves, young men must live. You
    are grandjurors, are ye? We'll jure ye, faith!
          Here they rob them and bind them. Exeunt.

Enter the Prince and Poins [disguised].

PRINCE. The thieves have bound the true men. Now
    could thou and I rob the thieves and go merrily to Lon-
    don, it would be argument for a week, laughter for a 90
    month, and a good jest forever.
POINS. Stand close! I hear them coming.
                              [*They step aside.*]

Enter the thieves again.

73. *happy . . . dole* i.e. good luck to us! (literally: "may it be his fate to
be a happy man") 81. *whoreson* bastard *caterpillars* rascals, particularly those with hands in the public purse (see "caterpillars of the
commonwealth" [*Richard II*, 2.3.166], and compare Gadshill's remarks
in 2.1) 84. *gorbellied* big-bellied 85. *chuffs* misers *store* total wealth
86. *bacons* pigs, i.e. fat men 87. *grandjurors* (only men of means could
serve on a grand jury) 90. *argument* topic of conversation

FALSTAFF. Come, my masters, let us share and then to
horse before day. And the Prince and Poins be not two
arrant cowards, there's no equity stirring. There's no 95
more valour in that Poins than in a wild duck.

PRINCE. Your money! *As they are sharing, the Prince*
POINS. Villains!   *and Poins set upon them. They*
                      all run away, and Falstaff, after
                      a blow or two, runs away too,
                      leaving the booty behind them.

PRINCE. Got with much ease. Now merrily to horse. The
thieves are all scattered, and possessed with fear so 100
strongly that they dare not meet each other: each takes
his fellow for an officer. Away, good Ned. Falstaff
sweats to death and lards the lean earth as he walks
along. Were't not for laughing, I should pity him.
POINS. How the fat rogue roared!   *Exeunt.* 105

[Scene 3. *Northumberland. Warkworth Castle.*]

Enter Hotspur solus, reading a letter.

[HOTSPUR.] "But, for mine own part, my lord, I could be
well contented to be there, in respect of the love I bear
your house." He could be contented – why is he not
then? In respect of the love he bears our house! He
shows in this he loves his own barn better than he loves 5
our house. Let me see some more. "The purpose you
undertake is dangerous" – why, that's certain! 'Tis
dangerous to take a cold, to sleep, to drink; but I tell
you, my lord fool, out of this nettle, danger, we pluck
this flower, safety. "The purpose you undertake is dan- 10
gerous, the friends you have named uncertain, the
time itself unsorted, and your whole plot too light for
the counterpoise of so great an opposition." Say you so,

95. *arrant* out-and-out   *no equity stirring* i.e. no justice in the world   103.
lards bastes
  2.3 s.d. *solus* alone   3. *house* family   12. *unsorted* unsuitable

say you so? I say unto you again, you are a shallow,
cowardly hind, and you lie. What a lack-brain is this! 15
By the Lord, our plot is a good plot as ever was laid; our
friends true and constant: a good plot, good friends,
and full of expectation; an excellent plot, very good
friends. What a frosty-spirited rogue is this! Why, my
Lord of York commends the plot and the general course 20
of the action. Zounds, and I were now by this rascal, I
could brain him with his lady's fan. Is there not my
father, my uncle, and myself; Lord Edmund Mortimer,
my Lord of York, and Owen Glendower? Is there not,
besides, the Douglas? Have I not all their letters to meet 25
me in arms by the ninth of the next month, and are they
not some of them set forward already? What a pagan
rascal is this, an infidel! Ha! you shall see now, in very
sincerity of fear and cold heart will he to the King and
lay open all our proceedings. O I could divide myself 30
and go to buffets for moving such a dish of skim milk
with so honourable an action! Hang him, let him tell the
King! We are prepared. I will set forward tonight.

Enter his Lady.

How now, Kate? I must leave you within these two
hours.　　　　　　　　　　　　　　　　　　　　　　35
LADY. O my good lord, why are you thus alone?
For what offence have I this fortnight been
A banished woman from my Harry's bed?
Tell me, sweet lord, what is't that takes from thee
Thy stomach, pleasure, and thy golden sleep?　　　40
Why dost thou bend thine eyes upon the earth,
And start so often when thou sit'st alone?
Why hast thou lost the fresh blood in thy cheeks
And given my treasures and my rights of thee

15. *hind* (i) peasant, (ii) female deer, typically timid　19-20. *my . . .
York* i.e. the Archbishop (see 1.3.264-8)　29. *will he . . . King* (Hotspur
does not say whose letter he reads from; Holinshed mentions that George
Dunbar, Scottish Earl of March, urged the King to attack before the
rebels' power grew)　30-31. *I . . . buffets* I could split myself in two and
set the halves to a boxing-match　40. *stomach* appetite

To thick-eyed musing and cursed melancholy?   45
In thy faint slumbers I by thee have watched,
And heard thee murmur tales of iron wars,
Speak terms of manage to thy bounding steed,
Cry "Courage! To the field!" And thou hast talked
Of sallies and retires, of trenches, tents,   50
Of palisadoes, frontiers, parapets,
Of basilisks, of cannon, culverin,
Of prisoners' ransom, and of soldiers slain,
And all the currents of a heady fight.
Thy spirit within thee hath been so at war,   55
And thus hath so bestirred thee in thy sleep,
That beads of sweat have stood upon thy brow
Like bubbles in a late-disturbèd stream,
And in thy face strange motions have appeared,
Such as we see when men restrain their breath   60
On some great sudden hest. O what portents are these?
Some heavy business hath my lord in hand,
And I must know it, else he loves me not.
HOTSPUR. What ho!

[*Enter a Servant.*]

           Is Gilliams with the packet gone?
SERVANT. He is, my lord, an hour ago.   65
HOTSPUR. Hath Butler brought those horses from the
    sheriff?
SERVANT. One horse, my lord, he brought even now.
HOTSPUR. What horse? A roan, a crop-ear, is it not?
SERVANT. It is, my lord.
HOTSPUR. That roan shall be my throne. Well, I will back   70
    him straight. O Esperance! Bid Butler lead him forth
    into the park.   [*Exit Servant.*]

---

45. *cursed* bad-tempered 50. *sallies* attacks *retires* retreats 51. *palisadoes* defensive arrays of sharp stakes *frontiers* outer parts of a fortification 52. *basilisks . . . culverin* three types of artillery piece (see end note) 54. *currents* rapid movements, swirl *heady* fierce 61. *hest* demand, order 71. *Esperance* Hope (*Esperance ma comforte* – "Hope is my strength" – was the Percy family motto, and *Esperance!* was their battle-cry; see also 5.2.96)

LADY. But hear you, my lord.

HOTSPUR. What say'st thou, my lady?

LADY. What is it carries you away?   75

HOTSPUR. Why, my horse, my love, my horse.

LADY. Out, you mad-headed ape! A weasel hath not such
a deal of spleen as you are tossed with. In faith, I'll
know your business, Harry, that I will! I fear my brother
Mortimer doth stir about his title and hath sent for you 80
to line his enterprise, but if you go –

HOTSPUR. So far afoot, I shall be weary, love.

LADY. Come, come, you paraquito, answer me directly
unto this question that I ask. In faith, I'll break thy little
finger, Harry, and if thou wilt not tell me all things true. 85

HOTSPUR. Away, away, you trifler! Love? I love thee not;
I care not for thee, Kate. This is no world
To play with mammets and to tilt with lips.
We must have bloody noses and cracked crowns,
And pass them current too. Gods me, my horse!   90
What say'st thou, Kate? What wouldst thou have
   with me?

LADY. Do you not love me? Do you not indeed?
Well, do not then, for since you love me not,
I will not love myself. Do you not love me?
Nay, tell me if you speak in jest or no.   95

HOTSPUR. Come, wilt thou see me ride?
And when I am a-horseback, I will swear
I love thee infinitely. But hark you, Kate,
I must not have you henceforth question me
Whither I go, nor reason whereabout.   100
Whither I must, I must, and – to conclude –
This evening must I leave you, gentle Kate.
I know you wise – but yet no farther wise
Than Harry Percy's wife; constant you are –
But yet a woman; and for secrecy,   105

---

78. *spleen* caprice, nervous excitement (the spleen was thought to be
responsible for emotional turbulence) 81. *line* strengthen 83. *paraquito* parakeet, parrot 88. *mammets* dolls 89. *crowns* (i) heads, (ii)
five-shilling pieces 90. *current* i.e. as currency *Gods me* God save me

No lady closer – for I well believe
Thou wilt not utter what thou dost not know,
And so far will I trust thee, gentle Kate.
LADY. How? So far?
HOTSPUR. Not an inch further. But hark you, Kate,   110
Whither I go, thither shall you go too;
Today will I set forth, tomorrow you.
Will this content you, Kate?
LADY.   It must of force.

                                        Exeunt.

[Scene 4. *Eastcheap. The Boar's Head Tavern.*]

                Enter Prince and Poins.

PRINCE. Ned, prithee come out of that fat room and lend
me thy hand to laugh a little.
POINS. Where hast been, Hal?
PRINCE. With three or four loggerheads amongst three or
fourscore hogsheads. I have sounded the very bass-string   5
of humility. Sirrah, I am sworn brother to a leash of
drawers and can call them all by their christen names,
as Tom, Dick, and Francis. They take it already upon
their salvation that, though I be but Prince of Wales,
yet I am the king of courtesy, and tell me flatly I am no   10
proud Jack like Falstaff, but a Corinthian, a lad of
mettle, a good boy (by the Lord, so they call me!), and
when I am King of England I shall command all the
good lads in Eastcheap. They call drinking deep, dyeing
scarlet, and when you breathe in your watering, they   15
cry "hem!" and bid you play it off. To conclude, I am

113. *of force* of necessity
   2.4.1. *fat room* (i) hot, stuffy room, or perhaps (ii) vat room, where
wine and ale were kept (but it is Hal, not Poins, who has been among
the hogsheads) 4. *loggerheads* blockheads 6. *leash* trio (hunting term
for a set of three hounds) 7. *drawers* literally: those who draw liquor
at a bar; here, ordinary waiters 11. *Jack* fellow *Corinthian* good sport,
young man-about-town (the people of Corinth were reputedly dissolute
Epicureans) 14-15. *dyeing scarlet* (i.e. because one turns red in the
face) *breathe . . . watering* stop for breath in your drinking 16. *play
it off* drink it down

so good a proficient in one quarter of an hour that I can
drink with any tinker in his own language during my
life. I tell thee, Ned, thou hast lost much honour that
thou wert not with me in this action. But, sweet Ned – to   20
sweeten which name of Ned, I give thee this pennyworth
of sugar, clapped even now into my hand by an underskinker, one that never spake other English in his life
than "Eight shillings and sixpence," and "You are welcome," with this shrill addition, "Anon, anon, sir!   25
Score a pint of bastard in the Half-moon," or so – but,
Ned, to drive away the time till Falstaff come, I prithee
do thou stand in some by-room while I question my
puny drawer to what end he gave me the sugar, and do
thou never leave calling "Francis!" that his tale to me   30
may be nothing but "Anon!" Step aside, and I'll show
thee a precedent.

POINS. Francis!

PRINCE. Thou art perfect.

POINS. Francis!   [*Poins steps aside.*]   35

Enter [Francis, a] Drawer.

FRANCIS. Anon, anon, sir. Look down into the Pomgarnet, Ralph.

PRINCE. Come hither, Francis.

FRANCIS. My lord?

PRINCE. How long hast thou to serve, Francis?   40

FRANCIS. Forsooth, five years, and as much as to –

POINS [*within*]. Francis!

FRANCIS. Anon, anon, sir.

18. *tinker* vagabond, gipsy, a member of the lowest order of society
(gipsies, of course, have their own cant) 22-3. *underskinker* assistant
waiter (to "skink" was to pour) 25. *Anon* (originally, "anon" meant
"at once"; like words of similar meaning [e.g. "presently"], it was often
used as these waiters were doing and came to mean "in a little while",
and then "after a while") 26. *Score* chalk up *bastard* a sweet Spanish
wine *Half-moon* the name of a room in the inn (the practice of giving
glamorous or catchy names to various bars and lounges still obtains in
modern hotels) 28. *by-room* adjacent room 32. *precedent* example
36-7. *Pomgarnet* i.e. Pomegranate, the name of another room in the inn
40. *serve* (i.e. as an apprentice, the usual term being seven years)

PRINCE. Five year! By'r Lady, a long lease for the clink-
  ing of pewter. But, Francis, darest thou be so valiant as 45
  to play the coward with thy indenture and show it a fair
  pair of heels and run from it?

FRANCIS. O Lord, sir, I'll be sworn upon all the books in
  England I could find in my heart –

POINS [*within*]. Francis! 50

FRANCIS. Anon, sir.

PRINCE. How old art thou, Francis?

FRANCIS. Let me see – about Michaelmas next I shall be –

POINS [*within*]. Francis!

FRANCIS. Anon, sir. Pray stay a little, my lord. 55

PRINCE. Nay, but hark you, Francis. For the sugar thou
  gavest me – 'twas a pennyworth, was't not?

FRANCIS. O Lord! I would it had been two!

PRINCE. I will give thee for it a thousand pound. Ask me
  when thou wilt, and thou shalt have it. 60

POINS [*within*]. Francis!

FRANCIS. Anon, anon.

PRINCE. Anon, Francis? No, Francis; but tomorrow,
  Francis; or, Francis, a Thursday; or indeed, Francis,
  when thou wilt. But, Francis – 65

FRANCIS. My lord?

PRINCE. Wilt thou rob this leathern-jerkin, crystal-button,
  not-pated, agate-ring, puke-stocking, caddis-garter,
  smooth-tongue, Spanish pouch?

FRANCIS. O Lord, sir, who do you mean? 70

PRINCE. Why then, your brown bastard is your only drink;
  for look you, Francis, your white canvas doublet will
  sully. In Barbary, sir, it cannot come to so much.

FRANCIS. What, sir?

46. *indenture* contract (of apprenticeship) 48. *books* i.e. bibles 53.
Michaelmas September 29 63. *Anon, Francis* (Hal pretends to take
Francis' answer to Poins as a response to his offer of the thousand
pounds) 67-9. *this leathern-jerkin . . . Spanish pouch* i.e. Francis' master,
the innkeeper, dressed in a leather jacket with crystal buttons, with
short-cropped hair, an agate ring, dark woollen stockings, garters of
plain tape, an ingratiating manner, and a purse of Spanish leather at his
belt 71-3. *Why then . . . so much* (double talk which totally bewilders
Francis)

POINS [*within*]. Francis!   75
PRINCE. Away, you rogue! Dost thou not hear them call?
   Here they both call him. The Drawer stands
   amazed, not knowing which way to go.

    Enter Vintner.

VINTNER. What, stand'st thou still, and hear'st such a
 calling? Look to the guests within. [*Exit Francis.*]
 My lord, old Sir John, with half a dozen more, are at
 the door. Shall I let them in? 80
PRINCE. Let them alone awhile, and then open the door.
         [*Exit Vintner.*]
 Poins!
POINS [*within*]. Anon, anon, sir.

    Enter Poins.

PRINCE. Sirrah, Falstaff and the rest of the thieves are at
 the door. Shall we be merry? 85
POINS. As merry as crickets, my lad. But hark ye, what
 cunning match have you made with this jest of the
 drawer? Come, what's the issue?
PRINCE. I am now of all humours that have showed themselves humours since the old days of goodman Adam 90
 to the pupil age of this present twelve o'clock at midnight. What's o'clock, Francis?
FRANCIS [*within*]. Anon, anon, sir.
PRINCE. That ever this fellow should have fewer words
 than a parrot, and yet the son of a woman! His industry 95
 is upstairs and downstairs, his eloquence the parcel of a
 reckoning. I am not yet of Percy's mind, the Hotspur of ‡
 the North, he that kills me some six or seven dozen of
 Scots at a breakfast, washes his hands, and says to his
 wife, "Fie upon this quiet life! I want work." "O my 100
 sweet Harry," says she, "how many hast thou killed
 today?" "Give my roan horse a drench," says he, and

76 s.d. *Vintner* i.e. the innkeeper 88. *issue* point (of the joke) 89-92.
I . . . midnight "I am now a medley of all the moods known from the
Creation to the infancy of this new day" 95-7. *His industry . . . reckon-*
ing "he does nothing but run up and down stairs (serving customers) and
he has nothing to say but the amount of a bill" 102. *drench* dose of
medicine

answers "Some fourteen," an hour after, "a trifle, a
trifle." I prithee call in Falstaff. I'll play Percy, and that
damned brawn shall play Dame Mortimer his wife. [105]
"Rivo!" says the drunkard. Call in Ribs, call in Tallow.

*Enter Falstaff, [Gadshill, Bardolph, and Peto;
Francis follows with wine].*

POINS. Welcome, Jack. Where hast thou been?
FALSTAFF. A plague of all cowards, I say, and a vengeance
too! Marry and amen! Give me a cup of sack, boy. Ere
I lead this life long, I'll sew netherstocks and mend them [110]
and foot them too. A plague of all cowards! Give me a
cup of sack, rogue. Is there no virtue extant?

             He drinketh.

PRINCE. Didst thou never see Titan kiss a dish of butter –
pitiful-hearted Titan! – that melted at the sweet tale of
the sun's? If thou didst, then behold that compound. [115]
FALSTAFF. You rogue, here's lime in this sack too! There
is nothing but roguery to be found in villainous man.
Yet a coward is worse than a cup of sack with lime in
it. A villainous coward! Go thy ways, old Jack, die
when thou wilt; if manhood, good manhood, be not for- [120]
got upon the face of the earth, then am I a shotten
herring. There lives not three good men unhanged in
England, and one of them is fat, and grows old. God
help the while! A bad world, I say. I would I were a
weaver; I could sing psalms or anything. A plague of [125]
all cowards, I say still!
PRINCE. How now, woolsack, what mutter you?
FALSTAFF. A king's son! If I do not beat thee out of thy
kingdom with a dagger of lath and drive all thy subjects
afore thee like a flock of wild geese, I'll never wear hair [130]
on my face more. You Prince of Wales?

105. *brawn* fat pig, i.e. Falstaff (also called "Ribs" and "Tallow", l. 106
below)   106. *Rivo* a drinking cry; probably no more than an exuberant
shout by the slightly tipsy Hal   110. *netherstocks* stockings (which were
at that time cut out of material and sewed, not knitted)   116. *lime*
adulterant used to give poor wine better taste and colour   121-2. *shotten
herring* herring which has discharged its roe and is therefore lean   129.
lath (the Vice, a character in the old morality plays, was equipped with
 a dagger or sword of lath)

PRINCE. Why, you whoreson round man, what's the
matter?

FALSTAFF. Are not you a coward? Answer me to that –
and Poins there?   135

POINS. Zounds, ye fat paunch, and ye call me coward,
by the Lord, I'll stab thee.

FALSTAFF. I call thee coward? I'll see thee damned ere I
call thee coward, but I would give a thousand pound I
could run as fast as thou canst. You are straight enough 140
in the shoulders; you care not who sees your back.
Call you that backing of your friends? A plague upon
such backing, give me them that will face me. Give me
a cup of sack. I am a rogue if I drunk today.

PRINCE. O villain, thy lips are scarce wiped since thou 145
drunk'st last.

FALSTAFF. All is one for that. *(He drinketh.)* A plague of
all cowards, still say I.

PRINCE. What's the matter?

FALSTAFF. What's the matter? There be four of us here 150
have ta'en a thousand pound this day morning.

PRINCE. Where is it, Jack, where is it?

FALSTAFF. Where is it? Taken from us it is – a hundred
upon poor four of us!

PRINCE. What, a hundred, man?   155

FALSTAFF. I am a rogue if I were not at half-sword with
a dozen of them two hours together. I have scaped by
miracle. I am eight times thrust through the doublet,
four through the hose; my buckler cut through and
through; my sword hacked like a handsaw – *ecce sig-* 160
num! I never dealt better since I was a man. All would
not do. A plague of all cowards! Let them speak. If
they speak more or less than truth, they are villains and
the sons of darkness.

---

156. *at half-sword* in close combat at less than a sword's length (more
cautious fighters would keep at a respectful distance)   158. *doublet*
coat   159. *hose* breeches   *buckler* small shield (Falstaff is a "sword-
and-buckler" man; see 1.3.228, gloss)   160-61. *ecce signum* behold the
sign (Latin); i.e. look for yourself   161-2. *All . . . not do* i.e. All this
valiant effort was of no avail

PRINCE. Speak, sirs, how was it? 165

GADSHILL. We four set upon some dozen –

FALSTAFF. Sixteen at least, my lord.

GADSHILL. And bound them.

PETO. No, no, they were not bound.

FALSTAFF. You rogue, they were bound, every man of 170
them, or I am a Jew else – an Ebrew Jew.

GADSHILL. As we were sharing, some six or seven fresh
men set upon us –

FALSTAFF. And unbound the rest, and then come in the
other. 175

PRINCE. What, fought you with them all?

FALSTAFF. All? I know not what you call all, but if I
fought not with fifty of them, I am a bunch of radish!
If there were not two or three and fifty upon poor old
Jack, then am I no two-legged creature. 180

PRINCE. Pray God you have not murd'red some of them.

FALSTAFF. Nay, that's past praying for. I have peppered
two of them. Two I am sure I have paid, two rogues in
buckram suits. I tell thee what, Hal – if I tell thee a lie,
spit in my face, call me horse. Thou knowest my old 185
ward: here I lay, and thus I bore my point. Four rogues
in buckram let drive at me.

PRINCE. What, four? Thou saidst but two even now.

FALSTAFF. Four, Hal, I told thee four.

POINS. Ay, ay, he said four. 190

FALSTAFF. These four came all afront and mainly thrust
at me. I made me no more ado, but took all their seven
points in my target, thus.

PRINCE. Seven? Why, there were but four even now.

FALSTAFF. In buckram? 195

POINS. Ay, four, in buckram suits.

FALSTAFF. Seven, by these hilts, or I am a villain else.

PRINCE [aside to Poins]. Prithee let him alone. We shall
have more anon.

FALSTAFF. Dost thou hear me, Hal? 200

171. *Ebrew* Hebrew   175. *other* others   186. *ward* defensive stance in
fencing (see 1.2.180, gloss)   193. *targ* shield

PRINCE. Ay, and mark thee too, Jack.

FALSTAFF. Do so, for it is worth the list'ning to. These nine in buckram that I told thee of –

PRINCE. So, two more already.

FALSTAFF. Their points being broken – 205

POINS. Down fell their hose.

FALSTAFF. Began to give me ground; but I followed me close, came in, foot and hand, and with a thought seven of the eleven I paid.

PRINCE. O monstrous! Eleven buckram men grown out 210 of two!

FALSTAFF. But, as the devil would have it, three misbegotten knaves in Kendal green came at my back and let drive at me; for it was so dark, Hal, that thou couldest not see thy hand. 215

PRINCE. These lies are like their father that begets them – gross as a mountain, open, palpable. Why, thou clay-brained guts, thou knotty-pated fool, thou whoreson obscene greasy tallow-catch –

FALSTAFF. What, are thou mad? Art thou mad? Is not the 220 truth the truth?

PRINCE. Why, how couldst thou know these men in Kendal green when it was so dark thou couldst not see thy hand? Come, tell us your reason. What sayest thou to this? 225

POINS. Come, your reason, Jack, your reason.

FALSTAFF. What, upon compulsion? Zounds, and I were at the strappado, or all the racks in the world, I would not tell you on compulsion. Give you a reason on compulsion? If reasons were as plentiful as blackberries, I 230 would give no man a reason upon compulsion, I.

201. *mark* pay attention to, but also keep score of the mounting numbers 206. *Down . . . hose* (Poins takes "points" to mean the laces holding the breeches to the doublet; with points broken, their pants would fall down) 213. *Kendal green* a poor quality cloth made at Kendal in Westmorland and worn by servants and woodsmen 219. *tallow-catch* probably either (i) a pan to catch drippings under a roast, or (ii) a "tallow-keech" – a roll of tallow supplied by butchers to candlemakers 228. *strappado* a form of torture in which victim was hoisted by a rope and then dropped, to be jerked up short 230. *reasons* (pronounced like "raisins" in Elizabethan English, thus a pun with "blackberries")

PRINCE. I'll be no longer guilty of this sin. This sanguine
coward, this bed-presser, this horseback-breaker, this
huge hill of flesh —

FALSTAFF. 'Sblood, you starveling, you eel-skin, you dried 235
neat's-tongue, you bull's pizzle, you stockfish — O for
breath to utter what is like thee! — you tailor's yard,
you sheath, you bowcase, you vile standing tuck!

PRINCE. Well, breathe awhile, and then to it again; and
when thou hast tired thyself in base comparisons, hear 240
me speak but this.

POINS. Mark, Jack.

PRINCE. We two saw you four set on four, and bound
them and were masters of their wealth. Mark now how
a plain tale shall put you down. Then did we two set on 245
you four and, with a word, outfaced you from your
prize, and have it, yea, and can show it you here in the
house. And, Falstaff, you carried your guts away as
nimbly, with as quick dexterity, and roared for mercy,
and still run and roared, as ever I heard bullcalf. What 250
a slave art thou to hack thy sword as thou hast done,
and then say it was in fight! What trick, what device,
what starting hole canst thou now find out to hide thee
from this open and apparent shame?

POINS. Come, let's hear, Jack. What trick hast thou now? 255

FALSTAFF. By the Lord, I knew ye as well as he that made
ye. Why, hear you, my masters. Was it for me to kill the
heir apparent? Should I turn upon the true prince? Why,
thou knowest I am as valiant as Hercules. But beware
instinct, the lion will not touch the true prince. Instinct 260 ‡
is a great matter. I was now a coward on instinct. I shall
think the better of myself, and thee, during my life — I
for a valiant lion, and thou for a true prince. But, by
the Lord, lads, I am glad you have the money. Hostess,

232. *sanguine* (an excess of the sanguine humour [blood] was supposed
to give a ruddy complexion, like Falstaff's, and also to make a man
courageous; a "sanguine" or ruddy-faced coward is thus a paradox)
235-8. *starveling . . . tuck* (Falstaff's rejoinder to Hal's invective on his
grossness is directed at Hal's lankiness; "neat's tongue" = ox tongue,
"stockfish" = dried cod or haddock, "standing tuck" = a rapier standing
upright on its point)   253. *starting hole* hole in which a hunted animal
seeks safety

clap to the doors. Watch tonight, pray tomorrow. Gal- 265
lants, lads, boys, hearts of gold, all the titles of good
fellowship come to you! What, shall we be merry? Shall
we have a play extempore?

PRINCE. Content, and the argument shall be thy running
away.   270

FALSTAFF. Ah, no more of that, Hal, and thou lovest me!

Enter Hostess.

HOSTESS. O Jesu, my lord the Prince!

PRINCE. How now, my lady the hostess, what say'st thou
to me?

HOSTESS. Marry, my lord, there is a nobleman of the court 275
at door would speak with you. He says he comes from
your father.

PRINCE. Give him as much as will make him a royal man,
and send him back again to my mother.

FALSTAFF. What manner of man is he?   280

HOSTESS. An old man.

FALSTAFF. What doth gravity out of his bed at midnight?
Shall I give him his answer?

PRINCE. Prithee do, Jack.

FALSTAFF. Faith, and I'll send him packing.   *Exit.* 285

PRINCE. Now, sirs. By'r Lady, you fought fair; so did you,
Peto; so did you, Bardolph. You are lions too, you ran
away upon instinct, you will not touch the true prince,
no – fie!

BARDOLPH. Faith, I ran when I saw others run.   290

PRINCE. Faith, tell me now in earnest, how came Falstaff's
sword so hacked?

PETO. Why, he hacked it with his dagger, and said he
would swear truth out of England but he would make
you believe it was done in fight, and persuaded us to do 295
the like.

265. *Watch . . . tomorrow* (see Matt. 26:41: "Watch and pray, that ye
enter not into temptation: the spirit indeed is willing, but the flesh is
weak"; but Falstaff means "sit up and drink tonight and worry about
tomorrow when it comes") 269. *argument* plot 278. *royal man* i.e. give
him enough to raise him to "royal" rank (which would be three shillings
and four pence. The "royal" was a coin worth ten shillings; the "noble"
was worth only six shillings and eight pence) 282. *gravity* i.e. a respectable older man

BARDOLPH. Yea, and to tickle our noses with speargrass
to make them bleed, and then to beslubber our garments with it and swear it was the blood of true men.
I did that I did not this seven year before – I blushed 300
to hear his monstrous devices.

PRINCE. O villain! Thou stolest a cup of sack eighteen
years ago and wert taken with the manner, and ever
since thou hast blushed extempore. Thou hadst fire and
sword on thy side, and yet thou ran'st away. What in- 305
stinct hadst thou for it?

BARDOLPH. My lord, do you see these meteors? Do you
behold these exhalations?

PRINCE. I do.

BARDOLPH. What think you they portend? 310

PRINCE. Hot livers and cold purses.

BARDOLPH. Choler, my lord, if rightly taken.

PRINCE. No, if rightly taken, halter.

Enter Falstaff.

Here comes lean Jack; here comes bare-bone. How now,
my sweet creature of bombast? How long is't ago, Jack, 315
since thou sawest thine own knee?

FALSTAFF. My own knee? When I was about thy years,
Hal, I was not an eagle's talent in the waist, I could
have crept into any alderman's thumb-ring. A plague
of sighing and grief, it blows a man up like a bladder. 320
There's villainous news abroad. Here was Sir John
Bracy from your father: you must to the court in the
morning. That same mad fellow of the north, Percy,

---

297. *speargrass* a kind of grass with long, spear-like leaves   300. *that*
that which   303. *with the manner* in the act, with the goods   304. *fire*
i.e. the alcoholic's red face, Bardolph's most notable feature   307-8.
meteors . . . exhalations i.e. the excrescences and other blemishes on
Bardolph's face (referred to as though they were meteorological phenomena)   311. *Hot . . . purses* i.e. the usual effects of excessive drinking
312. *Choler* anger (if his face is red because he is a choleric man, he is
irascible and presumably not a coward)   *rightly taken* correctly interpreted   313. *No . . . halter* (Hal's retort puns brilliantly on three separate
words: "rightly" = [i] correctly, [ii] justly; "taken" = [i] interpreted,
[ii] arrested; "halter" = collar ["choler"], the hangman's noose)   315.
bombast soft material used for padding   318. *talent* talon

and he of Wales that gave Amamon the bastinado, and
made Lucifer cuckold, and swore the devil his true [325]
liegeman upon the cross of a Welsh hook – what a
plague call you him?

POINS. O, Glendower.

FALSTAFF. Owen, Owen – the same; and his son-in-law
Mortimer, and old Northumberland, and that sprightly [330]
Scot of Scots, Douglas, that runs a-horseback up a hill
perpendicular –

PRINCE. He that rides at high speed and with his pistol
kills a sparrow flying.

FALSTAFF. You have hit it. [335]

PRINCE. So did he never the sparrow.

FALSTAFF. Well, that rascal hath good metal in him; he
will not run.

PRINCE. Why, what a rascal art thou then, to praise him
so for running! [340]

FALSTAFF. A-horseback, ye cuckoo! But afoot he will not
budge a foot.

PRINCE. Yes, Jack, upon instinct.

FALSTAFF. I grant ye, upon instinct. Well, he is there too,
and one Mordake, and a thousand bluecaps more. Wor- [345]
cester is stol'n away tonight; thy father's beard is turned
white with the news; you may buy land now as cheap
as stinking mack'rel.

PRINCE. Why then, it is like, if there come a hot June, and
this civil buffeting hold, we shall buy maidenheads as [350]
they buy hobnails, by the hundreds.

FALSTAFF. By the mass, lad, thou sayest true; it is like we
shall have good trading that way. But tell me, Hal, art
not thou horrible afeard? Thou being heir apparent,

324. *Amamon* a devil, mentioned in Reginald Scot's *Discoverie of Witchcraft* (1584)　*the bastinado* a beating with a stick (usually upon the
soles of the feet)　326. *Welsh hook* a pike with a hook below the point
(since it did not form a cross, as did a sword hilt, it could not be sworn
upon)　337. *metal* (with a pun on "mettle")　345. *bluecaps* i.e. Scots in
blue "bonnets"　347-8. *you may . . . mack'rel* (because, fearing economic
upheaval of war, landowners want to turn estates into ready money)
350-51. *we shall . . . hundreds* (because girls will be easily seduced by
soldiers going off to war)

could the world pick thee out three such enemies again 355
as that fiend Douglas, that spirit Percy, and that devil
Glendower? Art thou not horribly afraid? Doth not thy
blood thrill at it?

PRINCE. Not a whit, i' faith. I lack some of thy instinct.

FALSTAFF. Well, thou wilt be horribly chid tomorrow 360
when thou comest to thy father. If thou love me, practise an answer.

PRINCE. Do thou stand for my father and examine me
upon the particulars of my life.

FALSTAFF. Shall I? Content. This chair shall be my state, 365
this dagger my sceptre, and this cushion my crown.

PRINCE. Thy state is taken for a joined-stool, thy golden
sceptre for a leaden dagger, and thy precious rich crown
for a pitiful bald crown.

FALSTAFF. Well, and the fire of grace be not quite out of 370
thee, now shalt thou be moved. Give me a cup of sack
to make my eyes look red, that it may be thought I have
wept, for I must speak in passion, and I will do it in
King Cambyses' vein.

PRINCE. Well, here is my leg.   375

FALSTAFF. And here is my speech. Stand aside, Nobility.

HOSTESS. O Jesu, this is excellent sport, i' faith!

FALSTAFF. Weep not, sweet Queen, for trickling tears are
vain.

HOSTESS. O the Father, how he holds his countenance!

FALSTAFF. For God's sake, Lords, convey my tristful
Queen!   380
For tears do stop the floodgates of her eyes.

HOSTESS. O Jesu, he doth it as like one of these harlotry
players as ever I see!

FALSTAFF. Peace, good pint-pot, peace, good tickle-brain.

358. *thrill* (with fear, not excitement) 365. *state* throne 367. *a joined-
stool* a cheap, common wooden stool 374. *King Cambyses' vein* (an
old-fashioned bombastic style; see 2.4.384, end note) 375. *leg* ("to
make a leg" is to show respect with an elegant bow) 376. *Nobility* (as
though the crowd of ruffians were the peers of the realm) 378. *Queen*
(with a pun on "quean", or prostitute) 379. *holds his countenance*
keeps a straight face 380. *tristful* sorrowful 382. *harlotry* rascally (in
a good-humoured sense) 384. *tickle-brain* strong drink (slang)

Harry, I do not only marvel where thou spendest thy 385
time, but also how thou art accompanied. For though
the camomile, the more it is trodden on, the faster it
grows, so youth, the more it is wasted, the sooner it
wears. That thou art my son I have partly thy mother's ‡
word, partly my own opinion, but chiefly a villainous 390
trick of thine eye and a foolish hanging of thy nether lip
that doth warrant me. If then thou be son to me, here
lies the point: why, being son to me, art thou so pointed
at? Shall the blessed sun of heaven prove a micher and
eat blackberries? A question not to be asked. Shall the 395
son of England prove a thief and take purses? A question to be asked. There is a thing, Harry, which thou
hast often heard of, and it is known to many in our land
by the name of pitch. This pitch (as ancient writers do
report) doth defile; so doth the company thou keepest. 400
For, Harry, now I do not speak to thee in drink, but in
tears; not in pleasure, but in passion; not in words only,
but in woes also: and yet there is a virtuous man whom
I have often noted in thy company, but I know not his
name.   405

PRINCE. What manner of man, and it like your Majesty?
FALSTAFF. A goodly portly man, i' faith, and a corpulent;
of a cheerful look, a pleasing eye, and a most noble carriage; and, as I think, his age some fifty, or, by'r Lady,
inclining to threescore; and now I remember me, his 410
name is Falstaff. If that man should be lewdly given, he
deceiveth me; for, Harry, I see virtue in his looks. If
then the tree may be known by the fruit, as the fruit by
the tree, then peremptorily I speak it, there is virtue in
that Falstaff; him keep with, the rest banish. And tell me 415
now, thou naughty varlet, tell me where hast thou been
this month?

387. *camomile* a small plant of the aster family, used in medicine   391.
trick characteristic expression, perhaps a twitch   *nether* lower (a hanging
lower lip was thought to be a sign of wantonness)   394. *micher* truant;
here, a small boy who slips away from school to go blackberrying   412-
13. *If then . . . fruit* (see Matt. 12:33: "Either make the tree good, and
his fruit good; or else make the tree corrupt, and his fruit corrupt: for
the tree is known by his fruit")   414. *peremptorily* decisively

PRINCE. Dost thou speak like a king? Do thou stand for
me, and I'll play my father.

FALSTAFF. Depose me? If thou dost it half so gravely, so 420
majestically, both in word and matter, hang me up by
the heels for a rabbit-sucker or a poulter's hare.

PRINCE. Well, here I am set.

FALSTAFF. And here I stand. Judge, my masters.

PRINCE. Now, Harry, whence come you?   425

FALSTAFF. My noble lord, from Eastcheap.

PRINCE. The complaints I hear of thee are grievous.

FALSTAFF. 'Sblood, my lord, they are false! Nay, I'll tickle
ye for a young prince, i' faith.

PRINCE. Swearest thou, ungracious boy? Henceforth ne'er 430
look on me. Thou art violently carried away from grace.
There is a devil haunts thee in the likeness of an old fat
man; a tun of man is thy companion. Why dost thou
converse with that trunk of humours, that bolting-
hutch of beastliness, that swoll'n parcel of dropsies, that 435
huge bombard of sack, that stuffed cloakbag of guts,
that roasted Manningtree ox with the pudding in his
belly, that reverend vice, that grey iniquity, that father
ruffian, that vanity in years? Wherein is he good, but to
taste sack and drink it? Wherein neat and cleanly, but 440
to carve a capon and eat it? Wherein cunning, but in
craft? Wherein crafty, but in villainy? Wherein villainous, but in all things? Wherein worthy, but in nothing?

FALSTAFF. I would your Grace would take me with you:
whom means your Grace?   445

PRINCE. That villainous abominable misleader of youth,
Falstaff, that old white-bearded Satan.

FALSTAFF. My lord, the man I know.

PRINCE. I know thou dost.

FALSTAFF. But to say I know more harm in him than in 450
myself were to say more than I know. That he is old,
the more the pity, his white hairs do witness it, but that
he is, saving your reverence, a whoremaster, that I
utterly deny. If sack and sugar be a fault, God help the
wicked! If to be old and merry be a sin, then many an 455
old host that I know is damned. If to be fat be to be
hated, then Pharaoh's lean kine are to be loved. No, my
good lord: banish Peto, banish Bardolph, banish Poins
— but for sweet Jack Falstaff, kind Jack Falstaff, true
Jack Falstaff, valiant Jack Falstaff, and therefore more 460
valiant being, as he is, old Jack Falstaff, banish not him
thy Harry's company, banish not him thy Harry's company. Banish plump Jack, and banish all the world!

PRINCE. I do, I will.   [*A knocking heard. Exeunt*
Hostess, Francis, and Bardolph.]

Enter Bardolph, running.

BARDOLPH. O, my lord, my lord! The sheriff with a most 465 ‡
monstrous watch is at the door.

FALSTAFF. Out, ye rogue! Play out the play! I have much
to say in the behalf of that Falstaff.

Enter the Hostess.

HOSTESS. O Jesu, my lord, my lord!

PRINCE. Heigh, heigh, the devil rides upon a fiddlestick! 470
What's the matter?

HOSTESS. The sheriff and all the watch are at the door.
They are come to search the house. Shall I let them in?

FALSTAFF. Dost thou hear, Hal? Never call a true piece of
gold a counterfeit. Thou art essentially made without 475
seeming so.

457. *Pharaoh's lean kine* (an allusion to the Pharaoh's dream which
Joseph interpreted, see Gen. 41:19-21; "kine" = cattle) 466. *monstrous*
watch an exceptionally large force of citizens conscripted to help patrol
the city at night 474-6. *Never . . . seeming so* (see 2.4.475, textual
variants, and 2.4.465-82, end note)

PRINCE. And thou a natural coward without instinct.

FALSTAFF. I deny your major. If you will deny the sheriff,
so; if not, let him enter. If I become not a cart as well
as another man, a plague on my bringing up! I hope I 480
shall as soon be strangled with a halter as another.

PRINCE. Go hide thee behind the arras. The rest walk
up above. Now, my masters, for a true face and good
conscience.

FALSTAFF. Both which I have had, but their date is out, 485
and therefore I'll hide me.   *Exit.*

PRINCE. Call in the sheriff.

                    [*Exeunt all but the Prince and Peto.*]

                    Enter Sheriff and the Carrier.

Now, master sheriff, what is your will with me?

SHERIFF. First, pardon me, my lord. A hue and cry hath
followed certain men unto this house.   490

PRINCE. What men?

SHERIFF. One of them is well known, my gracious lord –
a gross fat man.

CARRIER. As fat as butter.

PRINCE. The man, I do assure you, is not here,   495
For I myself at this time have employed him,
And, sheriff, I will engage my word to thee
That I will by tomorrow dinner time
Send him to answer thee, or any man,
For anything he shall be charged withal;   500
And so let me entreat you leave the house.

SHERIFF. I will, my lord. There are two gentlemen
Have in this robbery lost three hundred marks.

PRINCE. It may be so. If he have robbed these men,
He shall be answerable; and so farewell.   505

SHERIFF. Good night, my noble lord.

478. *major* i.e. major premise in logic (with a pun on "mayor" which was
pronounced and often spelled the same) 479. *cart* i.e. the cart taking
a condemned man to the gallows 480. *bringing up* (i) training, (ii)
summoning to court 482. *arras* tapestry hung on a wall (actually, on
stage, the curtain of the recess) 489. *hue and cry* (when a crime was
discovered, a "hue and cry" was raised, and the whole town joined in the
hunt for the criminal)

PRINCE. I think it is good morrow, is it not?

SHERIFF. Indeed, my lord, I think it be two o'clock.

           Exit [with Carrier].

PRINCE. This oily rascal is known as well as Paul's. Go call him forth. 510

PETO. Falstaff! – Fast asleep behind the arras, and snorting like a horse.

PRINCE. Hark how hard he fetches breath. Search his pockets.

  He searcheth his pocket and findeth certain papers.
What hast thou found? 515

PETO. Nothing but papers, my lord.

PRINCE. Let's see what they be. Read them.

PETO [*reads*]. "Item, a capon . . . . . . 2s. 2d.
    Item, sauce . . . . 4d.
    Item, sack two gallons . . 5s. 8d. 520
    Item, anchovies and sack
      after supper . . . . 2s. 6d.
    Item, bread . . . . ob."

PRINCE. O monstrous! But one halfpennyworth of bread to this intolerable deal of sack! What there is else, keep 525 close; we'll read it at more advantage. There let him sleep till day. I'll to the court in the morning. We must all to the wars, and thy place shall be honourable. I'll procure this fat rogue a charge of foot, and I know his death will be a march of twelve score. The money shall 530 be paid back again with advantage. Be with me betimes in the morning, and so good morrow, Peto.

PETO. Good morrow, good my lord.   *Exeunt.*

---

509. *Paul's* i.e. Old St. Paul's Cathedral (one of the largest in Europe and a prominent feature of London; the medieval structure was destroyed in the Great Fire of 1666) 523. *ob.* obolus, a halfpenny 529. *charge of foot* company of infantry to command 530. *twelve score* i.e. paces 531. *advantage* interest *betimes* early

[ACT 3

Scene 1. *Wales. Glendower's castle.*]

Enter Hotspur, Worcester, Lord Mortimer, Owen
Glendower.

MORTIMER. These promises are fair, the parties sure,
  And our induction full of prosperous hope.
HOTSPUR. Lord Mortimer, and cousin Glendower, will
  you sit down? And uncle Worcester. A plague upon
  it! I have forgot the map.   5
GLENDOWER. No, here it is. Sit, cousin Percy, sit, good
  cousin Hotspur, for by that name as oft as Lancaster
  doth speak of you, his cheek looks pale, and with a ris-
  ing sigh he wisheth you in heaven.
HOTSPUR. And you in hell, as oft as he hears Owen Glen- 10
  dower spoke of.
GLENDOWER. I cannot blame him. At my nativity
  The front of heaven was full of fiery shapes
  Of burning cressets, and at my birth
  The frame and huge foundation of the earth   15
  Shakèd like a coward.
HOTSPUR. Why, so it would have done at the same season
  if your mother's cat had but kittened, though yourself
  had never been born.
GLENDOWER. I say the earth did shake when I was born.   20
HOTSPUR. And I say the earth was not of my mind,
  If you suppose as fearing you it shook.
GLENDOWER. The heavens were all on fire, the earth did
      tremble –
HOTSPUR. O, then the earth shook to see the heavens on
      fire,
  And not in fear of your nativity.   25

  3.1.2. *induction* beginning, prologue (to a play)   14. *cressets* torches
or beacons

427

Diseasèd nature oftentimes breaks forth
In strange eruptions; oft the teeming earth
Is with a kind of colic pinched and vexed
By the imprisoning of unruly wind
Within her womb, which for enlargement striving   30
Shakes the old beldame earth and topples down
Steeples and mossgrown towers. At your birth
Our grandam earth, having this distemp'rature,
In passion shook.

GLENDOWER.   Cousin, of many men
I do not bear these crossings. Give me leave   35
To tell you once again that at my birth
The front of heaven was full of fiery shapes,
The goats ran from the mountains, and the herds
Were strangely clamorous to the frighted fields.
These signs have marked me extraordinary,   40
And all the courses of my life do show
I am not in the roll of common men.
Where is he living, clipped in with the sea
That chides the banks of England, Scotland, Wales,
Which calls me pupil or hath read to me?   45
And bring him out that is but woman's son
Can trace me in the tedious ways of art
And hold me pace in deep experiments.

HOTSPUR. I think there's no man speaks better Welsh; I'll   ⸸
to dinner.   50

MORTIMER. Peace, cousin Percy, you will make him
     mad.

GLENDOWER. I can call spirits from the vasty deep.

HOTSPUR. Why, so can I, or so can any man,
     But will they come when you do call for them?

GLENDOWER. Why, I can teach you, cousin, to command   55
     the devil.

---

31. *beldame* grandmother   33. *distemp'rature* ailment   34. *passion* painful affliction   *Cousin* (Glendower is related to Hotspur only through the marriage of his daughter to Lady Percy's brother, Edmund Mortimer) 43-4. *clipped . . . Wales* i.e. in all the isle of Britain   45. *read to* instructed 47. *trace* follow in my footsteps   *tedious* difficult   *art* magic   48. *hold me pace* keep up with me   49. *Welsh* i.e. does not speak intelligible English (see 3.1.49, end note)

HOTSPUR. And I can teach thee, coz, to shame the devil –
   By telling truth. Tell truth and shame the devil.
   If thou have power to raise him, bring him hither,
   And I'll be sworn I have power to shame him hence: 60
   O, while you live, tell truth and shame the devil!
MORTIMER. Come, come, no more of this unprofitable
   chat.
GLENDOWER. Three times hath Henry Bolingbroke made
   head
   Against my power; thrice from the banks of Wye
   And sandy-bottomed Severn have I sent him   65
   Booteless home and weather-beaten back.
HOTSPUR. Home without boots, and in foul weather too!
   How scapes he agues, in the devil's name?
GLENDOWER. Come, here is the map. Shall we divide our
   right
   According to our threefold order ta'en?   70
MORTIMER. The Archdeacon hath divided it
   Into three limits very equally:
   England, from Trent and Severn hitherto,
   By south and east is to my part assigned:
   All westward, Wales beyond the Severn shore,   75
   And all the fertile land within that bound,
   To Owen Glendower: and, dear coz, to you
   The remnant northward lying off from Trent.
   And our indentures tripartite are drawn,
   Which being sealèd interchangeably   80
   (A business that this night may execute),
   Tomorrow, cousin Percy, you and I
   And my good Lord of Worcester will set forth
   To meet your father and the Scottish power,
   As is appointed us, at Shrewsbury.   85
   My father Glendower is not ready yet,

58. *Tell .... devil* (a proverbial saying) 66. *Booteless* the trisyllable
permits a three-fold sense: (i) bootless, i.e. fruitlessly, (ii) booty-less, i.e.
without plunder, (iii) boot-less, without boots (see 3.1.66, textual variants)
68. *agues* colds, fevers 69. *right* justifiably claimed property 72. *limits*
tracts 79. *indentures tripartite* contracts in triplicate 80. *sealèd inter-*
changeably i.e. each party will seal all three and keep one copy for himself

Nor shall we need his help these fourteen days.
[*To Glendower*] Within that space you may have
   drawn together
Your tenants, friends, and neighbouring gentlemen.
GLENDOWER. A shorter time shall send me to you, lords,   90
And in my conduct shall your ladies come,
From whom you now must steal and take no leave,
For there will be a world of water shed
Upon the parting of your wives and you.
HOTSPUR. Methinks my moiety, north from Burton here,   95
In quantity equals not one of yours;
See how this river comes me cranking in
And cuts me from the best of all my land
A huge half-moon, a monstrous cantle out.
I'll have the current in this place dammed up,   100
And here the smug and silver Trent shall run
In a new channel fair and evenly;
It shall not wind with such a deep indent
To rob me of so rich a bottom here.
GLENDOWER. Not wind? It shall, it must! You see it doth. 105
MORTIMER. Yea, but mark how he bears his course, and
runs me up with like advantage on the other side, geld-
ing the opposèd continent as much as on the other side
it takes from you.
WORCESTER. Yea, but a little charge will trench him
   here   110
And on this north side win this cape of land,
And then he runs straight and even.
HOTSPUR. I'll have it so, a little charge will do it.
GLENDOWER. I'll not have it alt'red.
HOTSPUR. Will not you?   115
GLENDOWER. No, nor you shall not.
HOTSPUR. Who shall say me nay?
GLENDOWER. Why, that will I.

___

95. *moiety* share 97. *cranking* winding 99. *cantle* portion 101. *smug* smooth 104. *bottom* low-lying valley 107. *advantage* i.e. disadvantage 107-8. *gelding . . . continent* cutting out of the opposite bank 110. *charge* expense *trench* cut a new channel for

HOTSPUR. Let me not understand you then, speak it in
    Welsh.   120

GLENDOWER. I can speak English, lord, as well as you,
    For I was trained up in the English court,
    Where, being but young, I framèd to the harp
    Many an English ditty lovely well,
    And gave the tongue a helpful ornament –   125
    A virtue that was never seen in you.

HOTSPUR. Marry, and I am glad of it with all my heart!
    I had rather be a kitten and cry mew
    Than one of these same metre ballad-mongers;
    I had rather hear a brazen canstick turned   130
    Or a dry wheel grate on the axletree,
    And that would set my teeth nothing on edge,
    Nothing so much as mincing poetry –
    'Tis like the forced gait of a shuffling nag.

GLENDOWER. Come, you shall have Trent turned.   135

HOTSPUR. I do not care, I'll give thrice so much land
    To any well-deserving friend,
    But in the way of bargain, mark ye me,
    I'll cavil on the ninth part of a hair.
    Are the indentures drawn? Shall we be gone?   140

GLENDOWER. The moon shines fair, you may away by
     night;
    I'll haste the writer, and withal
    Break with your wives of your departure hence.
    I am afraid my daughter will run mad,
    So much she doteth on her Mortimer.   *Exit.* 145

MORTIMER. Fie, cousin Percy, how you cross my father!

HOTSPUR. I cannot choose; sometime he angers me
    With telling me of the moldwarp and the ant,

---

125. *gave . . . ornament* perhaps (i) added to the stock of English literature, (ii) helped to develop the English language as a vehicle for poetry,
or (iii) adorned the words of poems with musical accompaniments 129.
metre ballad-mongers hawkers of street ballads (which were hurriedly
composed by hacks and hawked like modern newspapers; "metre" often
suggested the jolting rhythm of doggerel verse) 130. *canstick turned*
candlestick being scraped on a lathe 134. *forced gait* (horses were
trained to a regular gait by confining their legs, forcing them to take
smaller steps) 143. *Break with* break the news to 148. *moldwarp* mole
(see 3.1.148, end note)

Of the dreamer Merlin and his prophecies,
And of a dragon and a finless fish,   150
A clip-winged griffin and a moulten raven,
A couching lion and a ramping cat,
And such a deal of skimble-skamble stuff
As puts me from my faith. I tell you what —
He held me last night at least nine hours   155
In reckoning up the several devils' names
That were his lackeys: I cried "hum," and "well, go to!"
But marked him not a word. O he is as tedious
As a tired horse, a railing wife,
Worse than a smoky house. I had rather live   160
With cheese and garlic in a windmill, far,
Than feed on cates and have him talk to me
In any summer house in Christendom.

MORTIMER.   In faith, he is a worthy gentleman,
Exceedingly well read and profited   165
In strange concealments, valiant as a lion,
And wondrous affable, and as bountiful
As mines of India. Shall I tell you, cousin?
He holds your temper in a high respect
And curbs himself even of his natural scope   170
When you come 'cross his humour — faith, he does.
I warrant you that man is not alive
Might so have tempted him as you have done
Without the taste of danger and reproof,
But do not use it oft, let me entreat you.   175

WORCESTER.   In faith, my lord, you are too wilful-blame,
And since your coming hither have done enough
To put him quite besides his patience;

151. *moulten raven* i.e. one which has moulted, or shed its feathers   152. *couching, ramping* lying down, rearing (from the heraldic attitudes "couchant" and "rampant")   153. *skimble-skamble* nonsensical (apparently coined by Shakespeare; no earlier use of the word is known)   159-60. *a railing . . . house* (an old saying, a variant on Prov. 27:15, "A continual dropping in a very rainy day and a contentious woman are alike"; Chaucer and Langland also used the "smoky house" version)   161. *cheese and garlic* (proverbially a diet of the abject poor)   *windmill* (i.e. a creaky, unstable dwelling)   162. *cates* dainties   165-6. *profited . . . concealments* proficient in occult mysteries   171. *humour* temperament   176. *too wilful-blame* (i) to blame for being so headstrong; also perhaps (ii) to blame for your deliberate heckling

You must needs learn, lord, to amend this fault.
Though sometimes it show greatness, courage, blood –   180
And that's the dearest grace it renders you –
Yet oftentimes it doth present harsh rage,
Defect of manners, want of government,
Pride, haughtiness, opinion, and disdain,
The least of which haunting a nobleman   185
Loseth men's hearts and leaves behind a stain
Upon the beauty of all parts besides,
Beguiling them of commendation.
HOTSPUR. Well, I am schooled – good manners be your
     speed!
Here come our wives, and let us take our leave.   190

Enter Glendower with the Ladies.

MORTIMER. This is the deadly spite that angers me,
     My wife can speak no English, I no Welsh.
GLENDOWER. My daughter weeps; she'll not part with
     you,
She'll be a soldier too, she'll to the wars.
MORTIMER. Good father, tell her that she and my aunt
     Percy   195
Shall follow in your conduct speedily.
                    Glendower speaks to her in Welsh, and
                              she answers him in the same.
GLENDOWER. She is desperate here,
A peevish self-willed harlotry, one that no persuasion
can do good upon.
                    The Lady speaks in Welsh.
MORTIMER. I understand thy looks. That pretty Welsh   200
Which thou pourest down from these swelling heavens
I am too perfect in, and, but for shame,
In such a parley should I answer thee.
                    The Lady again in Welsh.

180. *blood* high spirits, mettle 184. *opinion* conceit 188. *Beguiling*
depriving 189. *good . . . speed* (a parting gibe), in effect: "let's hope
good manners do you some good in the coming battle" 191. *spite*
vexation, shame 198. *harlotry* silly wench 200-201. *pretty . . . heavens*
(extravagant expression for "those tears from these eyes") 203. *parley*
conversation (of tears)

MORTIMER. I understand thy kisses, and thou mine,
 And that's a feeling disputation,   205
 But I will never be a truant, love,
 Till I have learnt thy language, for thy tongue
 Makes Welsh as sweet as ditties highly penned,
 Sung by a fair queen in a summer's bow'r,
 With ravishing division, to her lute.   210
GLENDOWER. Nay, if you melt, then will she run mad.
       The Lady speaks again in Welsh.
MORTIMER. O I am ignorance itself in this!
GLENDOWER. She bids you on the wanton rushes lay
  you down
 And rest your gentle head upon her lap,
 And she will sing the song that pleaseth you 215
 And on your eyelids crown the god of sleep,
 Charming your blood with pleasing heaviness,
 Making such difference 'twixt wake and sleep
 As is the difference betwixt day and night,
 The hour before the heavenly-harnessed team 220
 Begins his golden progress in the east.
MORTIMER. With all my heart I'll sit and hear her sing;
 By that time will our book, I think, be drawn.
GLENDOWER. Do so, and those musicians that shall play
  to you
 Hang in the air a thousand leagues from hence, 225
 And straight they shall be here: sit, and attend.
HOTSPUR. Come, Kate, thou art perfect in lying down;
 Come, quick, quick, that I may lay my head in thy lap.
LADY PERCY. Go, ye giddy goose.   *The music plays.*
HOTSPUR. Now I perceive the devil understands Welsh, 230
 And 'tis no marvel he is so humorous,
 By'r Lady, he is a good musician.

205. *feeling disputation* conversation by (i) sense of touch, (ii) the emotions 208. *highly penned* extravagantly phrased (as are his own lines here) 210. *division* elegant or bravura variation in music 213. *wanton rushes* luxurious carpet of rushes (which were used as a floor covering instead of rugs) 220. *team* i.e. the horses of Apollo, god of the sun 223. *book* agreement 231. *humorous* capricious (this line will fit either the one before, i.e. his ability to understand Welsh proves him capricious, or the one after, i.e. his capriciousness makes him a good musician. Lady Percy takes up the second construction)

LADY PERCY. Then should you be nothing but musical,
  For you are altogether governed by humours.
  Lie still, ye thief, and hear the lady sing in Welsh.   235
HOTSPUR. I had rather hear Lady, my brach, howl in
  Irish.
LADY PERCY. Wouldst thou have thy head broken?
HOTSPUR. No.
LADY PERCY. Then be still.   240
HOTSPUR. Neither! 'Tis a woman's fault.
LADY PERCY. Now God help thee!
HOTSPUR. To the Welsh lady's bed.
LADY PERCY. What's that?
HOTSPUR. Peace! She sings.   245

Here the Lady sings a Welsh song.

HOTSPUR. Come, Kate, I'll have your song too.
LADY PERCY. Not mine, in good sooth.
HOTSPUR. Not yours, in good sooth! Heart, you swear
  like a comfit-maker's wife. "Not you, in good sooth!"
  and "as true as I live!" and "as God shall mend me!"   250
  and "as sure as day!"
  And givest such sarcenet surety for thy oaths
  As if thou never walk'st further than Finsbury.
  Swear me, Kate, like a lady as thou art,
  A good mouth-filling oath, and leave "in sooth"   255
  And such protest of pepper gingerbread
  To velvet guards and Sunday citizens.
  Come, sing.
LADY PERCY. I will not sing.
HOTSPUR. 'Tis the next way to turn tailor or be redbreast 260
  teacher. And the indentures be drawn, I'll away within
  these two hours, and so come in when ye will.   *Exit.*

236. *brach* female hunting dog 247. *sooth* truth 249. *comfit-maker's*
confectioner's 252. *sarcenet* fine, light silk 253. *Finsbury* Finsbury
Fields, a favourite resort of middle-class Londoners 256. *pepper ginger-*
bread a spiced product of the "comfit-maker" (which is not "mouth-
filling" but melts rapidly away) 257. *guards* trimmings (the Sunday
finery of middle-class Londoners was often velvet-trimmed) 260-61.
'Tis . . . teacher i.e. "All right, then, don't. Singing's not all that much,
anyway; it's the surest way to turn into a tailor or a singing teacher to
the birds" ("next" = quickest, surest; "redbreast" = robin; tailors were
noted for singing at their work)

GLENDOWER. Come, come, Lord Mortimer, you are as
    slow
  As hot Lord Percy is on fire to go:
  By this our book is drawn; we'll but seal,   265
  And then to horse immediately.
MORTIMER.   With all my heart.
                                          Exeunt.

[Scene 2. *London. The palace.*]

Enter the King, Prince of Wales, and others.

KING. Lords, give us leave: the Prince of Wales and I
  Must have some private conference, but be near at
      hand,
  For we shall presently have need of you.
                                      Exeunt Lords.
  I know not whether God will have it so
  For some displeasing service I have done,   5
  That, in his secret doom, out of my blood
  He'll breed revengement and a scourge for me;
  But thou dost in thy passages of life
  Make me believe that thou art only marked
  For the hot vengeance and the rod of heaven   10
  To punish my mistreadings. Tell me else,
  Could such inordinate and low desires,
  Such poor, such bare, such lewd, such mean attempts,
  Such barren pleasures, rude society,
  As thou art matched withal and grafted to,   15
  Accompany the greatness of thy blood
  And hold their level with thy princely heart?

3.2.6. *blood* blood relations; here, child or children 8. *passages* way
9-11. *thou . . . mistreadings* (i) you are chosen by Heaven to be the
punishment for my sins, (ii) you are marked for punishment, as retribution for my sins 12. *inordinate* improper (for one of your rank) 15.
withal with

PRINCE. So please your Majesty, I would I could
    Quit all offences with as clear excuse
    As well as I am doubtless I can purge   20
    Myself of many I am charged withal;
    Yet such extenuation let me beg
    As, in reproof of many tales devised,
    Which oft the ear of greatness needs must hear
    By smiling pickthanks and base newsmongers,   25
    I may for some things true, wherein my youth
    Hath faulty wand'red and irregular,
    Find pardon on my true submission.
KING. God pardon thee! Yet let me wonder, Harry,
    At thy affections, which do hold a wing   30
    Quite from the flight of all thy ancestors.
    Thy place in council thou hast rudely lost,
    Which by thy younger brother is supplied,
    And art almost an alien to the hearts
    Of all the court and princes of my blood.   35
    The hope and expectation of thy time
    Is ruined, and the soul of every man
    Prophetically do forethink thy fall.
    Had I so lavish of my presence been,
    So common-hackneyed in the eyes of men,   40
    So stale and cheap to vulgar company,
    Opinion, that did help me to the crown,
    Had still kept loyal to possession
    And left me in reputeless banishment,
    A fellow of no mark nor likelihood.   45
    By being seldom seen, I could not stir
    But like a comet I was wond'red at,
    That men would tell their children, "This is he!"

19. *Quit* acquit myself of 22-8. *Yet . . . submission* let me ask such extenuation that when I have refuted many false charges . . . I may be forgiven some true ones 25. *pickthanks* i.e. those who seek the king's favour (an expressive word, derived from Holinshed) *newsmongers* tattletales 30. *affections* inclinations 38. *do* (plural, from the plural sense of "every man") 40. *common-hackneyed* (with the original sense of "hackney" as a common horse for ordinary work, often for hire to anyone) 43. *possession* the possessor, i.e. Richard II

Others would say, "Where? Which is Bolingbroke?"
And then I stole all courtesy from heaven,   50
And dressed myself in such humility
That I did pluck allegiance from men's hearts,
Loud shouts and salutations from their mouths
Even in the presence of the crownèd King.
Thus did I keep my person fresh and new,   55
My presence, like a robe pontifical,
Ne'er seen but wond'red at, and so my state,
Seldom, but sumptuous, showed like a feast
And wan by rareness such solemnity.
The skipping King, he ambled up and down   60 ‡
With shallow jesters and rash bavin wits,
Soon kindled and soon burnt, carded his state,
Mingled his royalty with cap'ring fools,
Had his great name profanèd with their scorns,
And gave his countenance, against his name,   65
To laugh at gibing boys and stand the push
Of every beardless vain comparative,
Grew a companion to the common streets,
Enfeoffed himself to popularity,
That, being daily swallowed by men's eyes,   70
They surfeited with honey and began
To loathe the taste of sweetness, whereof a little
More than a little is by much too much.
So, when he had occasion to be seen,
He was but as the cuckoo is in June,   75
Heard, not regarded – seen, but with such eyes
As, sick and blunted with community,
Afford no extraordinary gaze,

58. *Seldom* (i.e. seen)   59. *wan* won (frequent form of preterite in
Elizabethan English)   61. *bavin* kindling wood   62. *carded* i.e. cheapened
(to "card" was to mix different drinks together, usually with the intention
of adulterating the mixture)   65-6. *gave his . . . boys* (i) presented a
laughing face, inconsistent with the dignity proper to his royal title, to
the jokes cracked by jesters (or street urchins), (ii) countenanced laughing at jesters, an improper use of his authority   *stand the push* i.e. submit to the impudence   67. *comparative* dealer in insulting comparisons
(see 1.2.78 and gloss)   69. *Enfeoffed* surrendered, a legal term for giving
possession of property   *popularity* a disparaging word for the people,
the lower classes, the "mob"   77. *community* familiarity

Such as is bent on sun-like majesty
When it shines seldom in admiring eyes,   80
But rather drowsed and hung their eyelids down,
Slept in his face, and rend'red such aspect
As cloudy men use to their adversaries,
Being with his presence glutted, gorged, and full.
And in that very line, Harry, standest thou,   85
For thou hast lost thy princely privilege
With vile participation. Not an eye
But is aweary of thy common sight,
Save mine, which hath desired to see thee more,
Which now doth that I would not have it do –   90
Make blind itself with foolish tenderness.
PRINCE. I shall hereafter, my thrice gracious lord,
  Be more myself.
KING.   For all the world,
  As thou art to this hour was Richard then
When I from France set foot at Ravenspurgh,   95
And even as I was then is Percy now.
Now, by my sceptre, and my soul to boot,
He hath more worthy interest to the state
Than thou the shadow of succession.
For of no right, nor colour like to right,   100
He doth fill fields with harness in the realm,
Turns head against the lion's armèd jaws,
And, being no more in debt to years than thou,
Leads ancient lords and reverend bishops on
To bloody battles and to bruising arms.   105
What never-dying honour hath he got
Against renownèd Douglas! whose high deeds,
Whose hot incursions and great name in arms
Holds from all soldiers chief majority
And military title capital   110
Through all the kingdoms that acknowledge Christ.

83. *cloudy* (i) sullen, (ii) hostile (like clouds to the royal "sun")   85.
line category (see 1.3.166)   91. *tenderness* i.e. tears   98-9. *He . . .
succession* i.e. he has a more valid claim to the kingdom (by his merit)
than you with your insubstantial one by inheritance   101. *harness* armour
109. *majority* pre-eminence   110. *capital* foremost

Thrice hath this Hotspur, Mars in swathling clothes,
This infant warrior, in his enterprises
Discomfited great Douglas, ta'en him once,
Enlargèd him, and made a friend of him,   115
To fill the mouth of deep defiance up
And shake the peace and safety of our throne.
And what say you to this? Percy, Northumberland,
The Archbishop's grace of York, Douglas, Mortimer
Capitulate against us and are up.   120
But wherefore do I tell these news to thee?
Why, Harry, do I tell thee of my foes,
Which art my nearest and dearest enemy?
Thou that art like enough, through vassal fear,
Base inclination, and the start of spleen,   125
To fight against me under Percy's pay,
To dog his heels and curtsy at his frowns,
To show how much thou art degenerate.
PRINCE. Do not think so, you shall not find it so,
And God forgive them that so much have swayed   130
Your Majesty's good thoughts away from me!
I will redeem all this on Percy's head
And in the closing of some glorious day
Be bold to tell you that I am your son,
When I will wear a garment all of blood,   135
And stain my favours in a bloody mask,
Which, washed away, shall scour my shame with it.
And that shall be the day, whene'er it lights,
That this same child of honour and renown,
This gallant Hotspur, this all-praisèd knight,   140
And your unthought-of Harry chance to meet.
For every honour sitting on his helm,
Would they were multitudes, and on my head
My shames redoubled! For the time will come
That I shall make this northern youth exchange   145

112. *swathling clothes* baby clothes 115. *Enlargèd* released 116. *To
fill . . . up* to make the voice of defiance louder 120. *Capitulate* draw up
articles of agreement *up* (i.e. in arms) 123. *dearest* (i) best-loved,
(ii) most grievous 125. *start of spleen* fit of (i) temper, or (ii)
capriciousness 136. *favours* features, but also in the sense of scarfs, etc.
worn as insignia in battle

His glorious deeds for my indignities.
Percy is but my factor, good my lord,
To engross up glorious deeds on my behalf,
And I will call him to so strict account
That he shall render every glory up, 150
Yea, even the slightest worship of his time,
Or I will tear the reckoning from his heart.
This in the name of God I promise here,
The which if He be pleased I shall perform,
I do beseech your Majesty may salve 155
The long-grown wounds of my intemperance:
If not, the end of life cancels all bands,
And I will die a hundred thousand deaths
Ere break the smallest parcel of this vow.
KING. A hundred thousand rebels die in this! 160
Thou shalt have charge and sovereign trust herein.

Enter Blunt.

How now, good Blunt? Thy looks are full of speed.
BLUNT. So hath the business that I come to speak of.
Lord Mortimer of Scotland hath sent word
That Douglas and the English rebels met 165
The eleventh of this month at Shrewsbury.
A mighty and a fearful head they are,
If promises be kept on every hand,
As ever off'red foul play in a state.
KING. The Earl of Westmoreland set forth today, 170
With him my son, Lord John of Lancaster,
For this advertisement is five days old.
On Wednesday next, Harry, you shall set forward,
On Thursday we ourselves will march. Our meeting
Is Bridgenorth, and, Harry, you shall march 175
Through Gloucestershire, by which account,

147. *factor* agent 148. *engross* gather 151. *worship . . . time* honour
gained in his (life)time 157. *bands* bonds, debts 159. *parcel* portion
162. *Thy looks . . . speed* You have an air of urgency about you 164.
Lord Mortimer of Scotland actually George Dunbar, the Scottish Earl
of March (see 2.3.29, gloss; Shakespeare seems to have assumed he was a
Mortimer, like the English Earls of March) 172. *advertisement*
information

Our business valuèd, some twelve days hence
Our general forces at Bridgenorth shall meet.
Our hands are full of business: let's away:
Advantage feeds him fat while men delay. *Exeunt.* 180

[Scene 3. *Eastcheap. The Boar's Head Tavern.*]

Enter Falstaff and Bardolph.

FALSTAFF. Bardolph, am I not fall'n away vilely since this
last action? Do I not bate? Do I not dwindle? Why, my
skin hangs about me like an old lady's loose gown. I am
withered like an old apple-john. Well, I'll repent, and
that suddenly, while I am in some liking; I shall be out 5
of heart shortly, and then I shall have no strength to
repent. And I have not forgotten what the inside of a
church is made of, I am a peppercorn, a brewer's horse:
the inside of a church! Company, villainous company,
hath been the spoil of me.   10

BARDOLPH. Sir John, you are so fretful you cannot live
long.

FALSTAFF. Why, there is it! Come, sing me a bawdy song,
make me merry. I was as virtuously given as a gentleman need to be – virtuous enough – swore little, diced 15
not above seven times a week, went to a bawdy house
not above once in a quarter of an hour, paid money that

177. *Our business valuèd* i.e. considering everything that must be done
(in the way of preparation) 180. *Advantage . . . delay* i.e. opportunity
swallows up good chances if men hesitate; in effect, "Time waits on no
man"
 3.3.1. *fall'n away* shrunk 2. *last action* (i.e. at Gadshill, as though it
were a military action) *bate* abate, i.e. decrease 3. *loose gown* shapeless
garment 4. *apple-john* apple kept over to St. John's Day (June 24) and
hence having shrivelled skin 5. *in some liking* (i) in the mood, (ii) in
good bodily condition 5-6. *out of heart* (i) out of the mood, (ii) out
of good condition 8. *peppercorn* dried berry of black pepper, once used
as a nominal rent payment, hence an insignificant trifle *brewer's horse*
(unlike the magnificent draught animals of nineteenth-century brewery
wagons, brewer's horses in Shakespeare's day were notorious as decrepit
nags) 14. *virtuously given* inclined to virtue 17. *paid* i.e. paid back

I borrowed three or four times, lived well, and in good
compass; and now I live out of all order, out of all
compass.   20

BARDOLPH. Why, you are so fat, Sir John, that you must
needs be out of all compass – out of all reasonable compass, Sir John.

FALSTAFF. Do thou amend thy face, and I'll amend my
life. Thou art our admiral, thou bearest the lantern in   25
the poop, but 'tis in the nose of thee: thou art the Knight
of the Burning Lamp.

BARDOLPH. Why, Sir John, my face does you no harm.

FALSTAFF. No, I'll be sworn, I make as good use of it as
many a man doth of a death's-head or a *memento mori*.   30
I never see thy face but I think upon hellfire and Dives
that lived in purple: for there he is in his robes, burning,
burning. If thou wert any way given to virtue, I would
swear by thy face: my oath should be "By this fire, that's
God's angel." But thou art altogether given over, and   35
wert indeed, but for the light in thy face, the son of utter
darkness. When thou ran'st up Gadshill in the night to
catch my horse, if I did not think thou hadst been an
ignis fatuus or a ball of wildfire, there's no purchase in
money. O thou art a perpetual triumph, an everlasting   40
bonfire-light! Thou hast saved me a thousand marks in

18-19. *in good compass* i.e. within reasonable limits (but Bardolph takes
it in the sense of "circumference")   25. *admiral* i.e. flagship (identifiable
by lantern carried at the stern = "poop")   26-7. *Knight . . . Lamp* (an
allusion to a character from an old romance: Amadis, Knight of the
Burning Sword)   30. *death's-head . . . mori* i.e. a skull (perhaps represented on a ring) or a similar object that brings death to mind; "*memento
mori*" = "remember that you must die"   31. *Dives* the rich man who
burns in hell (see Luke 16:19-31)   32. *purple* (because purple dye was
scarce and costly in ancient times, only the wealthy could wear purple
garments; "the purple" came to mean the acme of luxury, the symbol of
empire)   34-5. "*By . . . angel*" i.e. swearing by this fire is as good as
swearing by an angel of God (see various scriptural references to angels
as fiery, e.g. Exod. 3:2; as Kittredge notes, Falstaff may be quoting a tag
from an old play, *Misogonus, c.* 1570)   36-7. *son . . . darkness* (an
allusion to the "utter [i.e. outer] darkness" of Matt. 8:12; 22:13; and
25:30)   39. *ignis fatuus* "fools fire", i.e. marsh light or will-o'-the-wisp
ball of wildfire either (i) flaming ball of gunpowder, used as a firework or
in naval warfare, or (ii) "ball lightning"   40. *triumph* a torchlit festivity

links and torches, walking with thee in the night betwixt
tavern and tavern: but the sack that thou hast drunk me
would have bought me lights as good cheap at the dearest
chandler's in Europe. I have maintained that salamander   45
of yours with fire any time this two and thirty years,
God reward me for it!

BARDOLPH. 'Sblood, I would my face were in your belly!

FALSTAFF. God-a-mercy! so should I be sure to be heart-
burnt.   50

Enter Hostess.

How now, Dame Partlet the hen, have you enquired   ‡
yet who picked my pocket?

HOSTESS. Why, Sir John, what do you think, Sir John? Do
you think I keep thieves in my house? I have searched,
I have enquired, so has my husband, man by man, boy   55
by boy, servant by servant. The tithe of a hair was never
lost in my house before.

FALSTAFF. Ye lie, hostess. Bardolph was shaved and lost
many a hair, and I'll be sworn my pocket was picked.
Go to, you are a woman, go!   60 ‡

HOSTESS. Who, I? No, I defy thee! God's light, I was never
called so in mine own house before!

FALSTAFF. Go to, I know you well enough.

HOSTESS. No, Sir John, you do not know me, Sir John. I
know you, Sir John. You owe me money, Sir John, and   65
now you pick a quarrel to beguile me of it. I bought you
a dozen of shirts to your back.

FALSTAFF. Dowlas, filthy dowlas! I have given them away
to bakers' wives; they have made bolters of them.

42. *links* small torches, usually made of tow and pitch, carried at night
44. *good cheap* cheaply   45. *salamander* a fabulous lizard, supposed to
live in (and on) fire   48. *I . . . belly* (a proverbial retort, to which
Falstaff's reply is particularly apposite)   51. *Dame Partlet* traditional
name for a hen (Pertelote is the hen's name in Chaucer's "Nun's Priest's
Tale"), particularly appropriate to the clucking and scolding Hostess   56.
tithe tenth part (see 3.3.56, textual variants)   68. *Dowlas* cheap, coarse
linen, priced at ninepence a yard in 1550   69. *bolters* cloths for sifting
flour

HOSTESS. Now, as I am a true woman, holland of eight 70
  shillings an ell. You owe money here besides, Sir John,
  for your diet, and by-drinkings, and money lent you,
  four and twenty pound.

FALSTAFF. He had his part of it; let him pay.

HOSTESS. He? Alas, he is poor; he hath nothing. 75

FALSTAFF. How? Poor? Look upon his face. What call you
  rich? Let them coin his nose, let them coin his cheeks.
  I'll not pay a denier. What, will you make a younker of
  me? Shall I not take mine ease in mine inn but I shall
  have my pocket picked? I have lost a seal ring of my 80
  grandfather's worth forty mark.

HOSTESS. O Jesu, I have heard the Prince tell him, I know
  not how oft, that that ring was copper!

FALSTAFF. How? The Prince is a Jack, a sneak-up. 'Sblood,
  and he were here, I would cudgel him like a dog if he 85
  would say so.

Enter the Prince [and Peto], marching, and Falstaff
meets him, playing upon his truncheon like a fife.

How now, lad? Is the wind in that door, i' faith? Must
  we all march?

BARDOLPH. Yea, two and two, Newgate fashion.

HOSTESS. My lord, I pray you hear me. 90

PRINCE. What say'st thou, Mistress Quickly? How doth
  thy husband? I love him well, he is an honest man.

HOSTESS. Good my lord, hear me.

FALSTAFF. Prithee let her alone and list to me.

PRINCE. What say'st thou, Jack? 95

---

70. *holland* fine linen, usually about four shillings a yard (about half the
price quoted by the Hostess) 71. *ell* cloth measure, a yard and a
quarter 72. *by-drinkings* drinks between meals 77. *rich* (referring to
Bardolph's ruby-red face) 78. *denier* small coin worth one-tenth of a
penny *younker* youngster, here in sense of "greenhorn" 84. *Jack*
fellow, knave *sneak-up* expressive term for one who "sneaks up", a
dastard (see 3.3.84, textual variants) 86 s.d. *truncheon* club or staff,
especially one borne by a military officer 87. *Is . . . door* (proverbial
expression) i.e. "Is that the way things are going?" 89. *Newgate fashion*
i.e. manacled in pairs, like prisoners being led to Newgate prison

FALSTAFF. The other night I fell asleep here, behind the
arras, and had my pocket picked. This house is turned
bawdy house; they pick pockets.

PRINCE. What didst thou lose, Jack?

FALSTAFF. Wilt thou believe me, Hal, three or four bonds 100
of forty pound apiece and a seal ring of my grandfather's.

PRINCE. A trifle, some eightpenny matter.

HOSTESS. So I told him, my lord, and I said I heard your
Grace say so: and, my lord, he speaks most vilely of 105
you, like a foulmouthed man as he is, and said he would
cudgel you.

PRINCE. What! He did not?

HOSTESS. There's neither faith, truth, nor womanhood in
me else.   110

FALSTAFF. There's no more faith in thee than in a stewed
prune, nor no more truth in thee than in a drawn fox,
and for womanhood, Maid Marian may be the deputy's
wife of the ward to thee. Go, you thing, go!

HOSTESS. Say, what thing, what thing?   115

FALSTAFF. What thing? Why, a thing to thank God on.

HOSTESS. I am no thing to thank God on, I would thou
shouldst know it! I am an honest man's wife, and, setting
thy knighthood aside, thou art a knave to call me so.

FALSTAFF. Setting thy womanhood aside, thou art a beast 120
to say otherwise.

HOSTESS. Say, what beast, thou knave, thou?

FALSTAFF. What beast? Why, an otter.

PRINCE. An otter, Sir John? Why an otter?

FALSTAFF. Why? She's neither fish nor flesh, a man knows 125
not where to have her.

111-12. *stewed prune* i.e. prostitute (stewed prunes were a common dish
in brothels)   *drawn fox* a fox drawn from his lair and using deceit to
evade the hunters   113. *Maid Marian* a character in May-games, object
of Puritan attack, with a reputation for impudent behaviour   113-14.
the deputy's . . . ward i.e. a paragon of respectability (as the wife of the
deputy of the ward, its most responsible citizen)   125. *She's . . . flesh*
(ancient authorities debated whether the otter was properly beast or fish,
or a combination of both)

HOSTESS. Thou art an unjust man in saying so. Thou or
any man knows where to have me, thou knave, thou!
PRINCE. Thou say'st true, hostess, and he slanders thee
most grossly.   130
HOSTESS. So he doth you, my lord, and said this other day
you ought him a thousand pound.
PRINCE. Sirrah, do I owe you a thousand pound?
FALSTAFF. A thousand pound, Hal? A million! Thy love
is worth a million, thou owest me thy love.   135
HOSTESS. Nay, my lord, he called you Jack and said he
would cudgel you.
FALSTAFF. Did I, Bardolph?
BARDOLPH. Indeed, Sir John, you said so.
FALSTAFF. Yea, if he said my ring was copper.   140
PRINCE. I say 'tis copper. Darest thou be as good as thy
word now?
FALSTAFF. Why, Hal, thou knowest, as thou art but man,
I dare; but as thou art Prince, I fear thee as I fear the
roaring of the lion's whelp.   145
PRINCE. And why not as the lion?
FALSTAFF. The King himself is to be feared as the lion.
Dost thou think I'll fear thee as I fear thy father? Nay,
and I do, I pray God my girdle break.
PRINCE. O, if it should, how would thy guts fall about thy 150
knees! But, sirrah, there's no room for faith, truth, nor
honesty in this bosom of thine. It is all filled up with
guts and midriff. Charge an honest woman with picking
thy pocket? Why, thou whoreson, impudent, embossed
rascal, if there were anything in thy pocket but tavern 155
reckonings, memorandums of bawdy houses, and one
poor pennyworth of sugar-candy to make thee long-
winded – if thy pocket were enriched with any other
injuries but these, I am a villain. And yet you will
stand to it, you will not pocket up wrong. Art thou not 160
ashamed?

132. *ought* owed 147. *The King . . . lion* (see 2.4.260, end note) 154.
embossed (i) swollen, (ii) slavering (like a hunted deer) 155. *rascal*
(i) rogue, (ii) a slender young deer 159. *injuries* i.e. things whose loss
you would term "injuries"

FALSTAFF. Dost thou hear, Hal? Thou knowest in the
state of innocency Adam fell, and what should poor
Jack Falstaff do in the days of villainy? Thou seest I
have more flesh than another man, and therefore more 165
frailty. You confess then, you picked my pocket?

PRINCE. It appears so by the story.

FALSTAFF. Hostess, I forgive thee, go make ready breakfast, love thy husband, look to thy servants, cherish thy
guests. Thou shalt find me tractable to any honest rea- 170
son. Thou seest I am pacified still. Nay, prithee be gone.

                                            Exit Hostess.

Now, Hal, to the news at court: for the robbery, lad –
how is that answered?

PRINCE. O my sweet beef, I must still be good angel to
thee – the money is paid back again.   175

FALSTAFF. O I do not like that paying back! 'Tis a double
labour.

PRINCE. I am good friends with my father and may do
anything.

FALSTAFF. Rob me the exchequer the first thing thou 180 ‡
doest, and do it with unwashed hands too.

BARDOLPH. Do, my lord.

PRINCE. I have procured thee, Jack, a charge of foot.

FALSTAFF. I would it had been of horse. Where shall I find
one that can steal well? O for a fine thief of the age of 185
two and twenty or thereabouts: I am heinously unpro-
vided. Well, God be thanked for these rebels, they offend
none but the virtuous: I laud them, I praise them.

PRINCE. Bardolph!

BARDOLPH. My lord?   190

PRINCE. Go bear this letter to Lord John of Lancaster,
To my brother John; this to my Lord of Westmoreland.

                                    [Exit Bardolph.]

Go, Peto, to horse, to horse, for thou and I
Have thirty miles to ride yet ere dinner time.

                                          [Exit Peto.]

181. *with unwashed hands* (proverbial) i.e. without delay or being nice
about it   183. *charge of foot* infantry command (see 2.4.529)

Jack, meet me tomorrow in the Temple Hall   195
At two o'clock in the afternoon;
There shalt thou know thy charge, and there receive
Money and order for their furniture.
The land is burning, Percy stands on high,
And either we or they must lower lie.   [*Exit.*] 200
FALSTAFF. Rare words! Brave world! Hostess, my break-
    fast, come.
O I could wish this tavern were my drum!   [*Exit.*]

198. *furniture* equipment   202. *drum* i.e. assembly point for my soldiers

[ACT 4

Scene 1. *The rebel camp near Shrewsbury.]*

[Enter Hotspur, Worcester, and Douglas.]

HOTSPUR. Well said, my noble Scot. If speaking truth
In this fine age were not thought flattery,
Such attribution should the Douglas have
As not a soldier of this season's stamp
Should go so general current through the world.   5
By God, I cannot flatter, I do defy
The tongues of soothers, but a braver place
In my heart's love hath no man than yourself.
Nay, task me to my word, approve me, lord.
DOUGLAS. Thou art the king of honour: 10
No man so potent breathes upon the ground
But I will beard him.

Enter one with letters.

HOTSPUR.   Do so, and 'tis well.
What letters hast thou there? – I can but thank you.
MESSENGER. These letters come from your father.
HOTSPUR. Letters from him? Why comes he not himself?   15
MESSENGER. He cannot come, my lord, he is grievous sick.
HOTSPUR. Zounds! How has he the leisure to be sick
In such a justling time? Who leads his power?
Under whose government come they along?
MESSENGER. His letters bear his mind, not I, my lord.   20
WORCESTER. I prithee tell me, doth he keep his bed?

4.1.3. *attribution* praise 6. *defy* despise 7. *soothers* flatterers 9.
task . . . approve me i.e. hold me to my word, put me to the proof 12.
beard challenge 13. *I . . . thank you* (addressed to Douglas) 18.
justling turbulent 19. *government* command

450

MESSENGER. He did, my lord, four days ere I set forth,
  And at the time of my departure thence
  He was much feared by his physicians.
WORCESTER. I would the state of time had first been whole   25
  Ere he by sickness had been visited:
  His health was never better worth than now.
HOTSPUR. Sick now? Droop now? This sickness doth
    infect
  The very life-blood of our enterprise.
  'Tis catching hither, even to our camp.   30
  He writes me here that inward sickness —
  And that his friends by deputation
  Could not so soon be drawn, nor did he think it meet
  To lay so dangerous and dear a trust
  On any soul removed but on his own.   35
  Yet doth he give us bold advertisement
  That with our small conjunction we should on
  To see how fortune is disposed to us;
  For, as he writes, there is no quailing now,
  Because the King is certainly possessed   40
  Of all our purposes. What say you to it?
WORCESTER. Your father's sickness is a maim to us.
HOTSPUR. A perilous gash, a very limb lopped off —
  And yet, in faith, it is not! His present want
  Seems more than we shall find it. Were it good   45
  To set the exact wealth of all our states
  All at one cast? to set so rich a main
  On the nice hazard of one doubtful hour?
  It were not good, for therein should we read
  The very bottom and the soul of hope,   50
  The very list, the very utmost bound
  Of all our fortunes.

24. *feared* feared for 32. *by deputation* by means of a deputy 35.
removed not immediately concerned 36. *advertisement* advice 37.
conjunction combined force 40. *possessed* informed 42. *maim* (legal
term) injury to or loss of a member 46. *set* stake 47. *main* (i) army,
(ii) stake in dice game 48. *nice* precarious 50. *soul* essence (with a
play on "sole") 51. *list* selvage of cloth, hence outer boundary

DOUGLAS.　　　　　　Faith, and so we should,
　Where now remains a sweet reversion.
　We may boldly spend upon the hope of what is to
　　come in:
　A comfort of retirement lives in this.　　　　　　55
HOTSPUR.　A rendezvous, a home to fly unto,
　If that the devil and mischance look big
　Upon the maidenhead of our affairs.
WORCESTER.　But yet I would your father had been here:
　The quality and hair of our attempt　　　　　　60
　Brooks no division. It will be thought
　By some that know not why he is away,
　That wisdom, loyalty, and mere dislike
　Of our proceedings kept the Earl from hence.
　And think how such an apprehension　　　　　　65
　May turn the tide of fearful faction
　And breed a kind of question in our cause:
　For well you know we of the off'ring side
　Must keep aloof from strict arbitrement,
　And stop all sight-holes, every loop from whence　　70
　The eye of reason may pry in upon us.
　This absence of your father's draws a curtain
　That shows the ignorant a kind of fear
　Before not dreamt of.
HOTSPUR.　　　　　　You strain too far.
　I rather of his absence make this use:　　　　　　75
　It lends a lustre and more great opinion,
　A larger dare to our great enterprise,
　Than if the Earl were here; for men must think,
　If we, without his help, can make a head
　To push against a kingdom, with his help　　　　　80
　We shall o'erturn it topsy-turvy down.
　Yet all goes well, yet all our joints are whole.
DOUGLAS.　As heart can think. There is not such a word
　Spoke of in Scotland as this term of fear.

53. *reversion* prospective inheritance　55. *comfort of retirement* refuge
to fall back upon　57. *big* menacingly　60. *hair* nature　61. *Brooks* will
tolerate　66. *fearful* timid　68. *off'ring side* offensive; attacking side
69. *strict arbitrement* critical examination and judgment　70. *loop* loop-
hole　72. *draws* opens　76. *opinion* prestige　79. *a head* (i) headway,
(ii) an army

Enter Sir Richard Vernon.

HOTSPUR. My cousin Vernon, welcome, by my soul.   85
VERNON. Pray God my news be worth a welcome, lord.
  The Earl of Westmoreland, seven thousand strong,
  Is marching hitherwards; with him Prince John.
HOTSPUR. No harm. What more?
VERNON.   And further, I have learned,
  The King himself in person is set forth,   90
  Or hitherwards intended speedily,
  With strong and mighty preparation.
HOTSPUR. He shall be welcome too. Where is his son,
  The nimble-footed madcap Prince of Wales,
  And his comrades, that daft the world aside   95
  And bid it pass?
VERNON.   All furnished, all in arms;
  All plumed like estridges that with the wind
  Bated like eagles having lately bathed,
  Glittering in golden coats like images,
  As full of spirit as the month of May   100
  And gorgeous as the sun at midsummer;
  Wanton as youthful goats, wild as young bulls.
  I saw young Harry with his beaver on,
  His cushes on his thighs, gallantly armed,
  Rise from the ground like feathered Mercury,   105
  And vaulted with such ease into his seat
  As if an angel dropped down from the clouds
  To turn and wind a fiery Pegasus
  And witch the world with noble horsemanship.
HOTSPUR. No more, no more! Worse than the sun in
      March,   110
  This praise doth nourish agues. Let them come!

---

95. *daft* put off (as clothing), hence negligently tossed aside 97.
estridges (probably) ostriches (though the word also meant goshawks,
notable for fierce attack) 98. *Bated* fluttered their wings (from falconry)
102. *Wanton* sportive 103. *beaver* helmet 104. *cushes* cuisses, i.e. thigh-
armour (the spelling indicates the Elizabethan pronunciation) 105.
Mercury Roman messenger of the gods, represented as winged to denote
fleetness 108. *wind* wheel about *Pegasus* winged horse of Greek
mythology 111. *agues* colds, fevers

They come like sacrifices in their trim,
And to the fire-eyed maid of smoky war
All hot and bleeding will we offer them:
The mailèd Mars shall on his altars sit   115
Up to the ears in blood. I am on fire
To hear this rich reprisal is so nigh,
And yet not ours. Come, let me taste my horse,
Who is to bear me like a thunderbolt
Against the bosom of the Prince of Wales.   120
Harry to Harry shall, hot horse to horse,
Meet, and ne'er part till one drop down a corse.
O that Glendower were come!
VERNON.   There is more news:
I learned in Worcester, as I rode along,
He cannot draw his power this fourteen days.   125
DOUGLAS. That's the worst tidings that I hear of yet.
WORCESTER. Ay, by my faith, that bears a frosty sound.
HOTSPUR. What may the King's whole battle reach unto?
VERNON. To thirty thousand.
HOTSPUR.   Forty let it be.
My father and Glendower being both away,   130
The powers of us may serve so great a day.
Come, let us take a muster speedily –
Doomsday is near; die all, die merrily.
DOUGLAS. Talk not of dying. I am out of fear
Of death or death's hand for this one half year.   135

             Exeunt.

[Scene 2. *A road near Coventry.*]

Enter Falstaff [and] Bardolph.

FALSTAFF. Bardolph, get thee before to Coventry; fill me
 a bottle of sack. Our soldiers shall march through: we'll
 to Sutton Co'fil' tonight.

113. *fire-eyed maid* i.e. Bellona, Roman goddess of war 115. *Mars*
Roman god of war 117. *reprisal* prize, booty 128. *battle* forces
 4.2.3. *Sutton Co'fil'* Sutton Coldfield, near Birmingham, about 20 miles
beyond Coventry, though off the direct route to Shrewsbury

BARDOLPH. Will you give me money, captain?

FALSTAFF. Lay out, lay out.   5

BARDOLPH. This bottle makes an angel.

FALSTAFF. And if it do, take it for thy labour – and if it make twenty, take them all; I'll answer the coinage. Bid my lieutenant Peto meet me at town's end.

BARDOLPH. I will, captain. Farewell.   *Exit.* 10

FALSTAFF. If I be not ashamed of my soldiers, I am a soused gurnet; I have misused the King's press damnably. I have got, in exchange of a hundred and fifty soldiers, three hundred and odd pounds. I press me none but good householders, yeomen's sons; inquire me out 15 contracted bachelors, such as had been asked twice on the banes, such a commodity of warm slaves as had as lief hear the devil as a drum, such as fear the report of a caliver worse than a struck fowl or a hurt wild duck. I pressed me none but such toasts-and-butter, with hearts 20 in their bellies no bigger than pins' heads, and they have bought out their services, and now my whole charge consists of ancients, corporals, lieutenants, gentlemen of companies – slaves as ragged as Lazarus in the painted cloth, where the glutton's dogs licked his sores; and such 25 as indeed were never soldiers, but discarded unjust serving-men, younger sons to younger brothers, revolted tapsters, and ostlers trade-fall'n, the cankers of a calm world and a long peace, ten times more dishonourable ragged than an old fazed ancient; and such have I to fill 30 up the rooms of them as have bought out their services

5. *Lay out* i.e. Pay for it yourself (or perhaps a complaint: "All I hear are demands for money") 6. *makes* i.e. makes it add up to (Falstaff takes it literally, in the sense of "mints", however) *angel* a coin, with the Archangel Michael stamped on it, worth about ten shillings 8. *answer* be answerable for (private minting of coins was illegal) 12. *soused gurnet* pickled fish *press* conscripting power 16-17. *contracted . . . banes* engaged men who are very soon to marry ("banes" = banns, the announcements of intention to marry made on three successive Sundays in the parish church) *warm* comfortable, wealthy 19. *caliver* musket 23. *ancients* ensigns 23-4. *gentlemen of companies* minor officers 24-5. *Lazarus . . . sores* (referring again to the parable of Dives and Lazarus [alluded to in 3.3.31-3.], Luke 16:19-31, as pictured on a cheap painted cloth hanging) 26. *unjust* dishonest 27. *revolted* runaway 28. *trade-fall'n* unemployed *cankers* disfiguring sores 30. *fazed ancient* tattered ensign or flag

that you would think that I had a hundred and fifty tat- ‡
tered prodigals lately come from swine-keeping, from
eating draff and husks. A mad fellow met me on the
way, and told me I had unloaded all the gibbets and 35
pressed the dead bodies. No eye hath seen such scare-
crows. I'll not march through Coventry with them, that's
flat. Nay, and the villains march wide betwixt the legs,
as if they had gyves on, for indeed I had the most of
them out of prison. There's not a shirt and a half in all 40
my company, and the half-shirt is two napkins tacked
together and thrown over the shoulders like a herald's
coat without sleeves; and the shirt, to say the truth,
stol'n from my host at Saint Albans, or the red-nose
innkeeper of Daventry. But that's all one; they'll find 45
linen enough on every hedge.

Enter the Prince [and the] Lord of Westmoreland.

PRINCE. How now, blown Jack? How now, quilt?

FALSTAFF. What, Hal? How now, mad wag? What a devil
dost thou in Warwickshire? My good Lord of Westmoreland, I cry you mercy, I thought your honour had 50
already been at Shrewsbury.

WESTMORELAND. Faith, Sir John, 'tis more than time that
I were there, and you too, but my powers are there
already. The King, I can tell you, looks for us all, we
must away all night. 55

FALSTAFF. Tut, never fear me, I am as vigilant as a cat to
steal cream.

PRINCE. I think, to steal cream indeed, for thy theft hath
already made thee butter. But tell me, Jack, whose fellows are these that come after? 60

FALSTAFF. Mine, Hal, mine.

PRINCE. I did never see such pitiful rascals.

---

33. *prodigals* (as in the parable, Luke 15:11 ff.)   34. *draff* pig-swill   39.
gyves leg-irons   44, 45. *Saint Albans, Daventry* (both on the main road
from London to Coventry)   46. *hedge* (where clothes were laid to dry,
and from which they were often stolen)   47. *blown* (i) swollen, (ii)
short-winded   *quilt* (because a "jack" is a soldier's quilted jacket)   49.
Warwickshire (see 3.2.173-6, end note)

FALSTAFF. Tut, tut, good enough to toss; food for powder,
food for powder, they'll fill a pit as well as better; tush,
man, mortal men, mortal men.   65
WESTMORELAND. Ay, but, Sir John, methinks they are ex-
ceeding poor and bare, too beggarly.
FALSTAFF. Faith, for their poverty, I know not where they
had that, and for their bareness, I am sure they never
learned that of me.   70
PRINCE. No, I'll be sworn, unless you call three fingers in
the ribs bare. But, sirrah, make haste; Percy is already
in the field.   *Exit.*
FALSTAFF. What, is the King encamped?
WESTMORELAND. He is, Sir John. I fear we shall stay too 75
long.
FALSTAFF. Well, to the latter end of a fray and the begin- ‡
ning of a feast fits a dull fighter and a keen guest.
                                               Exeunt.

[Scene 3. *The rebel camp, near Shrewsbury.*]

Enter Hotspur, Worcester, Douglas, Vernon.

HOTSPUR. We'll fight with him tonight.
WORCESTER.   It may not be.   ‡
DOUGLAS. You give him then advantage.
VERNON.   Not a whit.
HOTSPUR. Why say you so? Looks he not for supply?
VERNON. So do we.
HOTSPUR.   His is certain, ours is doubtful.
WORCESTER. Good cousin, be advised; stir not tonight.   5
VERNON. Do not, my lord.
DOUGLAS.   You do not counsel well.
You speak it out of fear and cold heart.
VERNON. Do me no slander, Douglas. By my life –

63. *toss* (i.e. on a pike, like fodder on a pitchfork) 71. *three fingers*
(i.e. of fat; a finger was a measure equal to three-quarters of an inch)
  4.3.3. *supply* reinforcements

And I dare well maintain it with my life —
If well-respected honour bid me on,   10
I hold as little counsel with weak fear
As you, my lord, or any Scot that this day lives;
Let it be seen tomorrow in the battle
Which of us fears.
DOUGLAS   Yea, or tonight.
VERNON.   Content.
HOTSPUR. Tonight, say I.
VERNON.   Come, come, it may not be.   15
I wonder much, being men of such great leading as
    you are,
That you foresee not what impediments
Drag back our expedition: certain horse
Of my cousin Vernon's are not yet come up,
Your uncle Worcester's horse came but today,   20
And now their pride and mettle is asleep,
Their courage with hard labour tame and dull,
That not a horse is half the half of himself.
HOTSPUR. So are the horses of the enemy
In general journey-bated and brought low.   25
The better part of ours are full of rest.
WORCESTER. The number of the King exceedeth ours.
For God's sake, cousin, stay till all come in.

The trumpet sounds a parley.

Enter Sir Walter Blunt.

BLUNT. I come with gracious offers from the King,
If you vouchsafe me hearing and respect.   30
HOTSPUR. Welcome, Sir Walter Blunt, and would to God
You were of our determination.
Some of us love you well, and even those some
Envy your great deservings and good name
Because you are not of our quality,   35
But stand against us like an enemy.

---

10. *well-respected* well-considered (i.e. "not your thoughtless sort")   16.
leading generalship 18. *expedition* moving fast (into battle) 25.
journey-bated travel-wearied 32. *determination* mind (i.e. "on our side")
35. *quality* fellowship, party

BLUNT. And God defend but still I should stand so,
  So long as out of limit and true rule
  You stand against anointed majesty.
  But to my charge. The King hath sent to know   40
  The nature of your griefs, and whereupon
  You conjure from the breast of civil peace
  Such bold hostility, teaching his duteous land
  Audacious cruelty. If that the King
  Have any way your good deserts forgot,   45
  Which he confesseth to be manifold,
  He bids you name your griefs, and with all speed
  You shall have your desires with interest
  And pardon absolute for yourself and these
  Herein misled by your suggestion.   50
HOTSPUR. The King is kind, and well we know the King
  Knows at what time to promise, when to pay.
  My father and my uncle and myself
  Did give him that same royalty he wears,
  And when he was not six and twenty strong,   55
  Sick in the world's regard, wretched and low,
  A poor unminded outlaw sneaking home,
  My father gave him welcome to the shore;
  And when he heard him swear and vow to God
  He came but to be Duke of Lancaster,   60
  To sue his livery, and beg his peace,
  With tears of innocency and terms of zeal,
  My father, in kind heart and pity moved,
  Swore him assistance, and performed it too.
  Now when the lords and barons of the realm   65
  Perceived Northumberland did lean to him,
  The more and less came in with cap and knee,
  Met him in boroughs, cities, villages,
  Attended him on bridges, stood in lanes,
  Laid gifts before him, proffered him their oaths,   70

37. *defend* forbid 38. *limit* boundary (of subjects' duty) 40. *my charge* i.e. what I have been charged to do 50. *suggestion* instigation 61. *sue . . . peace* sue for recovery of his inheritance (confiscated by Richard II) and make peace with the king 67. *cap and knee* i.e. cap in hand and on bended knee 69. *lanes* i.e. two facing rows (through which the triumphant Henry might pass)

Gave him their heirs as pages, followed him
Even at the heels in golden multitudes.
He presently, as greatness knows itself,
Steps me a little higher than his vow
Made to my father, while his blood was poor,   75
Upon the naked shore at Ravenspurgh;
And now, forsooth, takes on him to reform
Some certain edicts and some strait decrees
That lie too heavy on the commonwealth,
Cries out upon abuses, seems to weep   80
Over his country's wrongs; and by this face,
This seeming brow of justice, did he win
The hearts of all that he did angle for;
Proceeded further – cut me off the heads
Of all the favourites that the absent king   85
In deputation left behind him here
When he was personal in the Irish war.
BLUNT. Tut, I came not to hear this.
HOTSPUR.   Then to the point.
In short time after, he deposed the King,
Soon after that deprived him of his life,   90
And in the neck of that tasked the whole state;
To make that worse, suff'red his kinsman March
(Who is, if every owner were well placed,
Indeed his king) to be engaged in Wales,
There without ransom to lie forfeited;   95
Disgraced me in my happy victories,
Sought to entrap me by intelligence,
Rated mine uncle from the council board,
In rage dismissed my father from the court,
Broke oath on oath, committed wrong on wrong,   100
And in conclusion drove us to seek out
This head of safety, and withal to pry

73. *knows itself* appreciates its power   78. *strait* strict   86. *In deputation*
as deputies   87. *personal* personally engaged   91. *in . . . of that* i.e.
immediately afterwards   *tasked* taxed (technically, imposed a royal levy
authorized under the Magna Carta)   94. *engaged* held as hostage   97.
intelligence spies   98. *Rated* drove away by scolding (see 1.3.14-20)   99.
In rage . . . court (see 1.3.120-22)   102. *head* army

Into his title, the which we find
Too indirect for long continuance.
BLUNT. Shall I return this answer to the King?   105
HOTSPUR. Not so, Sir Walter. We'll withdraw awhile.
  Go to the King, and let there be impawned
  Some surety for a safe return again,
  And in the morning early shall mine uncle
  Bring him our purposes – and so farewell.   110
BLUNT. I would you would accept of grace and love.
HOTSPUR. And may be so we shall.
BLUNT.   Pray God you do.
                                                [*Exeunt.*]

[Scene 4. *York. The Archbishop's palace.*]   ‡

Enter [the] Archbishop of York [and] Sir Michael.   ‡

ARCHBISHOP. Hie, good Sir Michael, bear this sealèd brief
  With wingèd haste to the Lord Marshal,   ‡
  This to my cousin Scroop, and all the rest
  To whom they are directed. If you knew
  How much they do import, you would make haste.   5
SIR MICHAEL. My good lord, I guess their tenor.
ARCHBISHOP. Like enough you do.
  Tomorrow, good Sir Michael, is a day
  Wherein the fortune of ten thousand men
  Must bide the touch; for, sir, at Shrewsbury,   10
  As I am truly given to understand,
  The King with mighty and quick-raisèd power
  Meets with Lord Harry; and I fear, Sir Michael,
  What with the sickness of Northumberland,
  Whose power was in the first proportion,   15
  And what with Owen Glendower's absence thence,   ‡

104. *indirect* (i) roundabout, i.e. out of the direct line; but also suggesting,
(ii) morally irregular   107. *impawned* put in pawn
  4.4.1. *brief* letter   10. *bide the touch* i.e. stand the test ("touch" =
application of the touchstone to try for gold)   15. *proportion* magnitude
(i.e. larger in proportion than any of the others)

Who with them was a rated sinew too
And comes not in, overruled by prophecies –
I fear the power of Percy is too weak
To wage an instant trial with the King.　　　20
SIR MICHAEL. Why, my good lord, you need not fear,
　There is Douglas and Lord Mortimer.
ARCHBISHOP. No, Mortimer is not there.
SIR MICHAEL. But there is Mordake, Vernon, Lord Harry
　　Percy,
　And there is my Lord of Worcester, and a head　　25
　Of gallant warriors, noble gentlemen.
ARCHBISHOP. And so there is; but yet the King hath drawn
　The special head of all the land together:
　The Prince of Wales, Lord John of Lancaster,
　The noble Westmoreland, and warlike Blunt,　　30
　And many moe corrivals and dear men
　Of estimation and command in arms.
SIR MICHAEL. Doubt not, my lord, they shall be well
　　opposed.
ARCHBISHOP. I hope no less, yet needful 'tis to fear,
　And, to prevent the worst, Sir Michael, speed.　　35
　For if Lord Percy thrive not, ere the King
　Dismiss his power, he means to visit us,
　For he hath heard of our confederacy,
　And 'tis but wisdom to make strong against him.
　Therefore make haste; I must go write again　　40
　To other friends, and so farewell, Sir Michael.

Exeunt.

17. *rated sinew* highly regarded source of strength　25. *head* army　31.
moe corrivals more associates (see 1.3.205, gloss)　*dear* worthy

[ACT 5

Scene 1. *The King's camp, near Shrewsbury.*]

*Enter the King, Prince of Wales, Lord John of
Lancaster, Earl of Westmoreland, Sir Walter
Blunt, Falstaff.*

KING. How bloodily the sun begins to peer
  Above yon bulky hill! The day looks pale
  At his distemp'rature.
PRINCE.   The southern wind
  Doth play the trumpet to his purposes
  And by his hollow whistling in the leaves   5
  Foretells a tempest and a blust'ring day.
KING. Then with the losers let it sympathize,
  For nothing can seem foul to those that win.

*The trumpet sounds. Enter Worcester
[and Vernon].*

How now, my Lord of Worcester? 'Tis not well
That you and I should meet upon such terms   10
As now we meet. You have deceived our trust
And made us doff our easy robes of peace
To crush our old limbs in ungentle steel.
This is not well, my lord, this is not well.
What say you to it? Will you again unknit   15
This churlish knot of all-abhorrèd war,
And move in that obedient orb again
Where you did give a fair and natural light,
And be no more an exhaled meteor,

5.1.3. *his* i.e. the sun's *distemp'rature* ailment (cf. 3.1.33) 4. *play
. . . purposes* blow like a trumpeter; hence, serves as a herald, announcing the sun's intentions 17. *orb* orbit 19. *exhaled meteor* (meteors
were thought to be drawn up ["exhaled"] from the atmosphere, and since
they took irregular paths were feared as omens of future evil; cf. 1.1.10-11
and the end note)

463

A prodigy of fear, and a portent   20
Of broachèd mischief to the unborn times?
WORCESTER. Hear me, my liege:
 For mine own part, I could be well content
 To entertain the lag-end of my life
 With quiet hours. For I protest   25
 I have not sought the day of this dislike.
KING. You have not sought it? How comes it then?
FALSTAFF. Rebellion lay in his way, and he found it.
PRINCE. Peace, chewet, peace!
WORCESTER. It pleased your Majesty to turn your looks 30
 Of favour from myself and all our house,
 And yet I must remember you, my lord,
 We were the first and dearest of your friends.
 For you my staff of office did I break
 In Richard's time, and posted day and night 35
 To meet you on the way and kiss your hand,
 When yet you were in place and in account
 Nothing so strong and fortunate as I.
 It was myself, my brother, and his son
 That brought you home and boldly did outdare 40
 The dangers of the time. You swore to us,
 And you did swear that oath at Doncaster,
 That you did nothing purpose 'gainst the state,
 Nor claim no further than your new-fall'n right,
 The seat of Gaunt, dukedom of Lancaster.   45
 To this we swore our aid. But in short space
 It rained down fortune show'ring on your head,
 And such a flood of greatness fell on you —
 What with our help, what with the absent king,
 What with the injuries of a wanton time,   50
 The seeming sufferances that you had borne,
 And the contrarious winds that held the king
 So long in his unlucky Irish wars
 That all in England did repute him dead —

20. *prodigy* omen 21. *broachèd* i.e. started (literally: "to broach" is to tap a cask) 24. *lag-end* late years 29. *chewet* (i) chough, i.e. jackdaw, or "chatterbox", (ii) mince-meat pie 32. *remember* remind 44. *new-fall'n right* (i.e. rights recently fallen to him by the death of his father) 50. *wanton time* time of misgovernment

And from this swarm of fair advantages   55
You took occasion to be quickly wooed
To gripe the general sway into your hand,
Forgot your oath to us at Doncaster,
And, being fed by us, you used us so
As that ungentle gull, the cuckoo's bird,   60
Useth the sparrow – did oppress our nest,
Grew by our feeding to so great a bulk
That even our love durst not come near your sight
For fear of swallowing; but with nimble wing
We were enforced for safety sake to fly   65
Out of your sight and raise this present head,
Whereby we stand opposèd by such means
As you yourself have forged against yourself
By unkind usage, dangerous countenance,
And violation of all faith and troth   70
Sworn to us in your younger enterprise.
KING. These things indeed you have articulate,
Proclaimed at market crosses, read in churches,
To face the garment of rebellion
With some fine colour that may please the eye   75
Of fickle changelings and poor discontents,
Which gape and rub the elbow at the news
Of hurlyburly innovation.
And never yet did insurrection want
Such water-colours to impaint his cause,   80
Nor moody beggars, starving for a time
Of pell-mell havoc and confusion.
PRINCE. In both your armies there is many a soul
Shall pay full dearly for this encounter,
If once they join in trial. Tell your nephew,   85
The Prince of Wales doth join with all the world
In praise of Henry Percy. By my hopes,

57. *gripe* grasp 60. *gull* nestling *cuckoo's bird* the young of the cuckoo
(the cuckoo lays its eggs in other bird's nests and its young, when
hatched, eat all the food, thus destroying the other nestlings) 69.
dangerous countenance menacing looks 71. *in your . . . enterprise* i.e.
at an earlier time in your undertaking 72. *articulate* specified in formal
articles 74. *face* decorate or line with colourful trimmings 77. *rub the
elbow* i.e. hug themselves with joy 78. *innovation* something new,
necessarily disturbing the accepted order, hence, a revolution 81. *moody*
sullen

This present enterprise set off his head,
I do not think a braver gentleman,
More active-valiant or more valiant-young,   90
More daring or more bold, is now alive
To grace this latter age with noble deeds.
For my part, I may speak it to my shame,
I have a truant been to chivalry,
And so I hear he doth account me too.   95
Yet this before my father's majesty –
I am content that he shall take the odds
Of his great name and estimation,
And will, to save the blood on either side,
Try fortune with him in a single fight.   100

KING. And, Prince of Wales, so dare we venture thee,
Albeit, considerations infinite
Do make against it. No, good Worcester, no,
We love our people well; even those we love
That are misled upon your cousin's part,   105
And, will they take the offer of our grace,
Both he, and they, and you, yea, every man
Shall be my friend again, and I'll be his.
So tell your cousin, and bring me word
What he will do. But if he will not yield,   110
Rebuke and dread correction wait on us,
And they shall do their office. So be gone;
We will not now be troubled with reply;
We offer fair; take it advisedly.

Exit Worcester [with Vernon].

PRINCE. It will not be accepted, on my life.   115
The Douglas and the Hotspur both together
Are confident against the world in arms.

KING. Hence, therefore, every leader to his charge;
For, on their answer, will we set on them,
And God befriend us as our cause is just!   120

Exeunt. Manent Prince [and] Falstaff.

88. *set . . . head* not counted in his record   96. *this before* I say this in the
presence of   102. *Albeit* although (on the other hand)   103. *make
against* oppose   111. *wait on us* are at our command   112. *office* duty
120 s.d. *Manent* they remain (Latin)

FALSTAFF. Hal, if thou see me down in the battle and
  bestride me, so; 'tis a point of friendship.
PRINCE. Nothing but a colossus can do thee that friendship. Say thy prayers, and farewell.
FALSTAFF. I would 'twere bedtime, Hal, and all well.   125
PRINCE. Why, thou owest God a death.   [*Exit.*]
FALSTAFF. 'Tis not due yet, I would be loath to pay him
  before his day. What need I be so forward with him that
  calls not on me? Well, 'tis no matter, honour pricks me
  on. Yea, but how if honour prick me off when I come 130
  on? How then? Can honour set to a leg? No. Or an
  arm? No. Or take away the grief of a wound? No. Honour hath no skill in surgery then? No. What is honour?
  A word. What is in that word honour? What is that
  honour? Air. A trim reckoning! Who hath it? He that 135
  died a Wednesday. Doth he feel it? No. Doth he hear
  it? No. 'Tis insensible then? Yea, to the dead. But will
  it not live with the living? No. Why? Detraction will not
  suffer it. Therefore I'll none of it. Honour is a mere
  scutcheon – and so ends my catechism.   *Exit.* 140

[Scene 2. *The rebel camp, near Shrewsbury.*]

Enter Worcester [and] Sir Richard Vernon.

WORCESTER. O no, my nephew must not know, Sir Richard,
  The liberal and kind offer of the King.
VERNON. 'Twere best he did.
WORCESTER.   Then are we all undone.
  It is not possible, it cannot be,
  The King should keep his word in loving us;
  He will suspect us still and find a time
  To punish this offence in other faults.

123. *colossus* a huge statue, like the Colossus of Rhodes which was
supposed to have stood astride the harbour so that ships sailed between
its legs 126. *death* (pronounced like "debt"; compare 1.3.183-4 and
gloss) 129. *pricks* spurs 130. *prick me off* check me off (the list of the
living) 132. *grief* pain 135. *trim* pretty (ironically) 138. *Detraction*
slander 140. *scutcheon* a shield bearing a painted coat of arms and
displayed at a funeral

Supposition all our lives shall be stuck full of eyes,
For treason is but trusted like the fox,
Who, never so tame, so cherished and locked up,   10
Will have a wild trick of his ancestors.
Look how we can, or sad or merrily,
Interpretation will misquote our looks,
And we shall feed like oxen at a stall,
The better cherished still the nearer death.   15
My nephew's trespass may be well forgot;
It hath the excuse of youth and heat of blood,
And an adopted name of privilege –
A hare-brained Hotspur, governed by a spleen.
All his offences live upon my head   20
And on his father's. We did train him on,
And, his corruption being ta'en from us,
We, as the spring of all, shall pay for all.
Therefore, good cousin, let not Harry know,
In any case, the offer of the King.   25
VERNON. Deliver what you will, I'll say 'tis so.
Here comes your cousin.

Enter Hotspur [and Douglas].

HOTSPUR.   My uncle is returned;
Deliver up my Lord of Westmoreland.
Uncle, what news?
WORCESTER. The King will bid you battle presently.   30
DOUGLAS. Defy him by the Lord of Westmoreland.
HOTSPUR. Lord Douglas, go you and tell him so.
DOUGLAS. Marry, and shall, and very willingly.   *Exit.*
WORCESTER. There is no seeming mercy in the King.
HOTSPUR. Did you beg any? God forbid!   35
WORCESTER. I told him gently of our grievances,
Of his oath-breaking, which he mended thus,

5.2.8. *Supposition* suspicion   *stuck . . . eyes* i.e. will have eyes everywhere (allegorical figures of rumour, ill-report, etc. were often depicted
as full of eyes)   11. *trick* trait   12. *or . . . or* whether sad or   18. *an . . .
privilege* a nickname that gives him a privilege (to be rash)   20. *live*
will still be alive on my record   21. *train* lure   22. *ta'en* caught (like an
infection)   28. *Westmoreland* (see 5.1 s.d., end note)   34. *seeming*
appearance of

By now forswearing that he is forsworn.
He calls us rebels, traitors, and will scourge
With haughty arms this hateful name in us.   40

Enter Douglas.

DOUGLAS. Arm, gentlemen, to arms, for I have thrown
    A brave defiance in King Henry's teeth,
    And Westmoreland, that was engaged, did bear it,
    Which cannot choose but bring him quickly on.
WORCESTER. The Prince of Wales stepped forth before
        the King   45
    And, nephew, challenged you to single fight.
HOTSPUR. O would the quarrel lay upon our heads,
    And that no man might draw short breath today
    But I and Harry Monmouth! Tell me, tell me,
    How showed his tasking? Seemed it in contempt?   50
VERNON. No, by my soul. I never in my life
    Did hear a challenge urged more modestly,
    Unless a brother should a brother dare
    To gentle exercise and proof of arms.
    He gave you all the duties of a man,   55
    Trimmed up your praises with a princely tongue,
    Spoke your deservings like a chronicle,
    Making you ever better than his praise
    By still dispraising praise valued with you;
    And, which became him like a prince indeed,   60
    He made a blushing cital of himself,
    And chid his truant youth with such a grace
    As if he mast'red there a double spirit
    Of teaching and of learning instantly,
    There did he pause, but let me tell the world,   65

38. *forswearing* taking a false oath 43. *engaged* held as hostage 49.
Monmouth (a by-name, like "Bolingbroke", from Prince Hal's place of
birth, Monmouth, on the Wye River near the Welsh border) 50. *tasking*
challenging 55. *all . . . man* all that is due from one man to another
57. *like a chronicle* i.e. in the detailed manner of a chronicle-history (and
as the chronicle-histories did, in fact, do) 59. *By . . . with you* i.e. by
disparaging praise itself since it could not do justice to your worth 61.
cital citation (in the senses of both "mention" and "indictment") 64.
instantly simultaneously

If he outlive the envy of this day,
England did never owe so sweet a hope,
So much miscónstrued in his wantonness.
HOTSPUR. Cousin, I think thou art enamourèd
On his follies. Never did I hear   70
Of any prince so wild a liberty.
But be he as he will, yet once ere night
I will embrace him with a soldier's arm,
That he shall shrink under my courtesy.
Arm, arm with speed! And, fellows, soldiers, friends,   75 ⸸
Better consider what you have to do
Than I, that have not well the gift of tongue,
Can lift your blood up with persuasion.

Enter a Messenger.

MESSENGER. My lord, here are letters for you.
HOTSPUR. I cannot read them now.   80
O gentlemen, the time of life is short!
To spend that shortness basely were too long
If life did ride upon a dial's point,
Still ending at the arrival of an hour.
And if we live, we live to tread on kings;   85
If die, brave death, when princes die with us!
Now for our consciences, the arms are fair
When the intent of bearing them is just –

Enter another [Messenger].

MESSENGER. My lord, prepare; the King comes on apace.
HOTSPUR. I thank him that he cuts me from my tale,   90
For I profess not talking: only this –
Let each man do his best; and here draw I
A sword whose temper I intend to stain
With the best blood that I can meet withal
In the adventure of this perilous day.   95
Now, Esperance! Percy! and set on.

66. *envy* malice   67. *owe* own   71. *liberty* reckless freedom   82-4. *To spend . . . hour* i.e. If life lasted only an hour, that would still be too long if it were spent basely   83. *dial's point* clock hand   96. *Esperance* (see 2.3.71, gloss)

Sound all the lofty instruments of war,
And by that music let us all embrace,
For, heaven to earth, some of us never shall
A second time do such a courtesy.   100
               Here they embrace. The trumpets sound.
                             [Exeunt.]

      [Scene 3. *Shrewsbury. The battlefield.*]

*The King enters with his power. Alarum to the
battle. [Exeunt.] Then enter Douglas, and Sir
Walter Blunt [disguised as the King].*

BLUNT. What is thy name, that in battle thus thou crossest
    me?
What honour dost thou seek upon my head?
DOUGLAS. Know then my name is Douglas,
And I do haunt thee in the battle thus
Because some tell me that thou art a king.   5
BLUNT. They tell thee true.
DOUGLAS. The Lord of Stafford dear today hath bought
Thy likeness, for instead of thee, King Harry,
This sword hath ended him: so shall it thee,
Unless thou yield thee as my prisoner.   10
BLUNT. I was not born a yielder, thou proud Scot,
And thou shalt find a king that will revenge
Lord Stafford's death.

       *They fight. Douglas kills Blunt. Then
             enter Hotspur.*

HOTSPUR. O Douglas, hadst thou fought at Holmedon thus,
I never had triumphed upon a Scot.   15
DOUGLAS. All's done, all's won: here breathless lies the
    King.
HOTSPUR. Where?
DOUGLAS. Here.

99. *heaven to earth* the odds are as heaven to earth, i.e. as infinity to
nothing
    5.3 s.d. *Alarum* sound effects, here specifically the call to arms, sounded
by trumpets and drums

HOTSPUR. This, Douglas? No, I know this face full well.
A gallant knight he was, his name was Blunt,   20
Semblably furnished like the King himself.
DOUGLAS. A fool go with thy soul, whither it goes!
A borrowed title hast thou bought too dear.
Why didst thou tell me that thou wert a king?
HOTSPUR. The King hath many marching in his coats.   25
DOUGLAS. Now, by my sword, I will kill all his coats;
I'll murder all his wardrobe, piece by piece,
Until I meet the King.
HOTSPUR.   Up and away!
Our soldiers stand full fairly for the day.   [*Exeunt.*]

Alarum. Enter Falstaff solus.

FALSTAFF. Though I could scape shot-free at London, I   30
fear the shot here; here's no scoring but upon the pate.
Soft! Who are you? Sir Walter Blunt. There's honour
for you! Here's no vanity! I am as hot as molten lead,
and as heavy too. God keep lead out of me; I need no
more weight than mine own bowels. I have led my rag-   35 ‡
of-muffins where they are peppered. There's not three
of my hundred and fifty left alive, and they are for the
town's end, to beg during life. But who comes here?

Enter the Prince.

PRINCE. What, stands thou idle here? Lend me thy sword.
Many a nobleman lies stark and stiff   40
Under the hoofs of vaunting enemies, whose deaths are
yet unrevenged. I prithee lend me thy sword.
FALSTAFF. O Hal, I prithee give me leave to breathe
awhile. Turk Gregory never did such deeds in arms as

21. *Semblably* similarly 22. *A fool* i.e. may the name of "fool" 25.
coats i.e. sleeveless tunics bearing his coat of arms 29. *stand . . . day*
have a good chance of winning the day 30. *shot-free* without paying the
"shot" or bill 31. *scoring* (i) keeping the score, or bill, (ii) making
gashes 33. *Here's no vanity* (ironic) this is vanity, i.e. futility, for you
("vanity" is also used here in the sense of "lightness" as opposed to his
own weightiness) 44. *Turk Gregory* ("Turk" = any cruel or violent
man; "Gregory" might suggest either of two popes, Gregory VII and
Gregory XIII, who were regarded with special horror in Protestant
countries)

I have done this day. I have paid Percy, I have made 45
him sure.
PRINCE. He is indeed, and living to kill thee.
I prithee lend me thy sword.
FALSTAFF. Nay, before God, Hal, if Percy be alive thou
gets not my sword, but take my pistol if thou wilt. 50
PRINCE. Give it me. What, is it in the case?
FALSTAFF. Ay, Hal. 'Tis hot, 'tis hot. There's that will sack
a city.   *The Prince draws it out and finds*
                                        it to be a bottle of sack.
PRINCE. What, is it a time to jest and dally now?
                                He throws the bottle at him. Exit.
FALSTAFF. Well, if Percy be alive, I'll pierce him. If he do 55
come in my way, so; if he do not, if I come in his willingly, let him make a carbonado of me. I like not such
grinning honour as Sir Walter hath. Give me life, which
if I can save, so; if not, honour comes unlooked for,
and there's an end.   [*Exit.*] 60

[Scene 4. *Shrewsbury. The battlefield.*]

Alarum. Excursions. Enter the King, the Prince,
Lord John of Lancaster, Earl of Westmoreland.

KING. I prithee, Harry, withdraw thyself, thou bleedest
too much.
Lord John of Lancaster, go you with him.
JOHN. Not I, my lord, unless I did bleed too.
PRINCE. I beseech your Majesty make up,
Lest your retirement do amaze your friends.   5
KING. I will do so. My Lord of Westmoreland, lead him
to his tent.

52. *hot* (i.e. from much firing; the gun has been put in its holster to cool)
55. *pierce* (pronounced "perse")   57. *carbonado* a piece of meat slashed
across for broiling
  5.4 s.d. *Alarum* sound effects   *Excursions* groups of men running
across the stage (see 5.3, end note)   4. *make up* move to the front   5.
amaze dismay

WESTMORELAND. Come, my lord, I'll lead you to your
    tent.
PRINCE. Lead me, my lord? I do not need your help,
    And God forbid a shallow scratch should drive   10
    The Prince of Wales from such a field as this,
    Where stained nobility lies trodden on,
    And rebels' arms triumph in massacres!
JOHN. We breathe too long. Come, cousin Westmoreland,
    Our duty this way lies. For God's sake, come.   15
            [*Exeunt Lancaster and Westmoreland.*]
PRINCE. By God, thou hast deceived me, Lancaster!
    I did not think thee lord of such a spirit.
    Before, I loved thee as a brother, John,
    But now I do respect thee as my soul.
KING. I saw him hold Lord Percy at the point   20
    With lustier maintenance than I did look for
    Of such an ungrown warrior.
PRINCE. O this boy lends mettle to us all!   *Exit.*

            [*Enter Douglas.*]

DOUGLAS. Another king? They grow like Hydra's heads.
    I am the Douglas, fatal to all those   25
    That wear those colours on them. What art thou
    That counterfeit'st the person of a king?
KING. The King himself, who, Douglas, grieves at heart
    So many of his shadows thou hast met,
    And not the very King. I have two boys   30
    Seek Percy and thyself about the field,
    But, seeing thou fall'st on me so luckily,
    I will assay thee, and defend thyself.
DOUGLAS. I fear thou art another counterfeit,
    And yet, in faith, thou bearest thee like a king.   35
    But mine I am sure thou art, whoe'er thou be,
    And thus I win thee.

      They fight, the King being in danger. Enter Prince
                  of Wales.

14. *breathe* rest for breath 24. *Hydra* a mythological monster which
grew two heads for each one cut off

PRINCE. Hold up thy head, vile Scot, or thou art like
   Never to hold it up again. The spirits
   Of valiant Shirley, Stafford, Blunt are in my arms.   40
   It is the Prince of Wales that threatens thee,
   Who never promiseth but he means to pay.

                     They fight: Douglas flieth.

   Cheerly, my lord. How fares your Grace?
   Sir Nicholas Gawsey hath for succor sent,
   And so hath Clifton. I'll to Clifton straight.   45
KING. Stay and breathe awhile.
   Thou hast redeemed thy lost opinion,
   And showed thou mak'st some tender of my life
   In this fair rescue thou hast brought to me.
PRINCE. O God, they did me too much injury   50
   That ever said I heark'ned for your death.
   If it were so, I might have let alone
   The insulting hand of Douglas over you,
   Which would have been as speedy in your end
   As all the poisonous potions in the world,   55
   And saved the treacherous labour of your son.
KING. Make up to Clifton; I'll to Sir Nicholas Gawsey.

                            Exit.

               Enter Hotspur.

HOTSPUR. If I mistake not, thou art Harry Monmouth.
PRINCE. Thou speak'st as if I would deny my name.
HOTSPUR. My name is Harry Percy.   60
PRINCE. Why, then I see a very valiant rebel of the name.
   I am the Prince of Wales, and think not, Percy,
   To share with me in glory any more.
   Two stars keep not their motion in one sphere,
   Nor can one England brook a double reign   65
   Of Harry Percy and the Prince of Wales.

---

40. *Shirley, Stafford, Blunt* (all killed by Douglas while he was seeking
the King) 47. *opinion* reputation 48. *thou mak'st some tender* you
have some concern for 53. *insulting* (because contemptuously exulting)
64. *Two . . . sphere* (in the Ptolemaic astronomy each heavenly body had
its own crystalline shell, or "sphere") 65. *brook* endure

HOTSPUR. Nor shall it, Harry, for the hour is come
  To end the one of us, and would to God
  Thy name in arms were now as great as mine!
PRINCE. I'll make it greater ere I part from thee,   70
  And all the budding honours on thy crest
  I'll crop to make a garland for my head.
HOTSPUR. I can no longer brook thy vanities.

                                 They fight.

               Enter Falstaff.

FALSTAFF. Well said, Hal! To it, Hal! Nay, you shall find
  no boy's play here, I can tell you.   75

        Enter Douglas. He fighteth with Falstaff [who]
        falls down as if he were dead. [Exit Douglas.]
            The Prince killeth Percy.

HOTSPUR. O Harry, thou hast robbed me of my youth!
  I better brook the loss of brittle life
  Than those proud titles thou hast won of me;
  They wound my thoughts worse than thy sword my
    flesh.
  But thoughts, the slaves of life, and life, time's fool,   80 ‡
  And time, that takes survey of all the world,
  Must have a stop. O I could prophesy,
  But that the earthy and cold hand of death
  Lies on my tongue. No, Percy, thou art dust,
  And food for –   *[Dies.]* 85 ‡
PRINCE. For worms, brave Percy. Fare thee well, great
    heart.
  Ill-weaved ambition, how much art thou shrunk!
  When that this body did contain a spirit,
  A kingdom for it was too small a bound,
  But now two paces of the vilest earth   90
  Is room enough. This earth that bears thee dead
  Bears not alive so stout a gentleman.
  If thou wert sensible of courtesy,
  I should not make so dear a show of zeal,

92. *stout* valiant   94. *dear* heartfelt

But let my favours hide thy mangled face,   95
And, even in thy behalf, I'll thank myself
For doing these fair rites of tenderness.
Adieu, and take thy praise with thee to heaven.
Thy ignominy sleep with thee in the grave,
But not rememb'red in thy epitaph.   100
                    He spieth Falstaff on the ground.
What, old acquaintance, could not all this flesh
Keep in a little life? Poor Jack, farewell!
I could have better spared a better man.
O I should have a heavy miss of thee
If I were much in love with vanity.   105
Death hath not struck so fat a deer today,
Though many dearer, in this bloody fray.
Embowelled will I see thee by-and-by,
Till then in blood by noble Percy lie.   *Exit.*
                              Falstaff riseth up.

FALSTAFF. Embowelled? If thou embowel me today, I'll 110 ‡
give you leave to powder me and eat me too tomorrow.
'Sblood, 'twas time to counterfeit, or that hot termagant
Scot had paid me scot and lot too. Counterfeit? I lie; I
am no counterfeit. To die is to be a counterfeit, for he
is but the counterfeit of a man who hath not the life of 115
a man; but to counterfeit dying when a man thereby
liveth, is to be no counterfeit, but the true and perfect
image of life indeed. The better part of valour is discre-   ‡
tion, in the which better part I have saved my life.
Zounds, I am afraid of this gunpowder Percy, though 120
he be dead. How if he should counterfeit too, and rise?
By my faith, I am afraid he would prove the better
counterfeit. Therefore I'll make him sure; yea, and I'll
swear I killed him. Why may not he rise as well as I?
Nothing confutes me but eyes, and nobody sees me. 125

95. *favours* (either the scarf in his personal colours or the plumes from
his helmet)   105. *vanity* frivolity, "lightness" (parallel with "heavy"
miss, above)   107. *dearer* (i) nobler, (ii) better loved   108. *Embowelled*
i.e. disembowelled (i) (for embalming), and (ii) as is a slain deer at the
end of the hunt (continuing the metaphor of Falstaff as a deer)   111.
powder salt   112. *termagant* violent; fire-eating   113. *scot and lot* parish
taxes (to pay "scot and lot" was to pay in full)

Therefore, sirrah [*stabs him*], with a new wound in
your thigh, come you along with me.

He takes up Hotspur on his back. Enter Prince
[and] John of Lancaster.

PRINCE. Come, brother John, full bravely hast thou
  fleshed
Thy maiden sword.
JOHN.   But soft! whom have we here?
Did you not tell me this fat man was dead?   130
PRINCE. I did; I saw him dead,
Breathless and bleeding on the ground. Art thou alive?
Or is it fantasy that plays upon our eyesight?
I prithee speak. We will not trust our eyes
Without our ears. Thou art not what thou seem'st.   135
FALSTAFF. No, that's certain, I am not a double man; but
  if I be not Jack Falstaff, then am I a Jack. There is
  Percy. If your father will do me any honour, so; if not,
  let him kill the next Percy himself. I look to be either
  earl or duke, I can assure you.   140
PRINCE. Why, Percy I killed myself, and saw thee dead.
FALSTAFF. Didst thou? Lord, Lord, how this world is
  given to lying. I grant you I was down, and out of
  breath, and so was he, but we rose both at an instant
  and fought a long hour by Shrewsbury clock. If I may 145
  be believed, so; if not, let them that should reward
  valour bear the sin upon their own heads. I'll take it
  upon my death, I gave him this wound in the thigh. If
  the man were alive and would deny it, zounds! I would
  make him eat a piece of my sword.   150
JOHN. This is the strangest tale that ever I heard.
PRINCE. This is the strangest fellow, brother John.
Come, bring your luggage nobly on your back.
For my part, if a lie may do thee grace,
I'll gild it with the happiest terms I have.   155

                    A retreat is sounded.

136. *double man* (i) ghost-like *alter ego*, but also (ii) "two fold" man
137. *Jack* fellow, knave

The trumpet sounds retreat; the day is ours.
Come, brother, let us to the highest of the field,
To see what friends are living, who are dead.
                    Exeunt [Prince and John of Lancaster].
FALSTAFF. I'll follow, as they say, for reward. He that
rewards me, God reward him. If I do grow great, I'll 160
grow less; for I'll purge, and leave sack, and live cleanly,
as a nobleman should do.
                    Exit [bearing off the body].

[Scene 5. *Shrewsbury. The battlefield.*]

*The trumpets sound. Enter the King, Prince of
Wales, Lord John of Lancaster, Earl of Westmoreland, with Worcester and Vernon prisoners.*

KING. Thus ever did rebellion find rebuke.
    Ill-spirited Worcester, did not we send grace,
    Pardon, and terms of love to all of you?
    And wouldst thou turn our offers contrary?
    Misuse the tenor of thy kinsman's trust?   5
    Three knights upon our party slain today,
    A noble earl, and many a creature else
    Had been alive this hour,
    If like a Christian thou hadst truly borne
    Betwixt our armies true intelligence.   10
WORCESTER. What I have done my safety urged me to,
    And I embrace this fortune patiently,
    Since not to be avoided it falls on me.
KING. Bear Worcester to the death, and Vernon too;
    Other offenders we will pause upon.   15
                    [*Exeunt Worcester and Vernon, guarded.*]
    How goes the field?

159. *follow* a hunting term (now Falstaff is the hound who has brought
down the deer and will be rewarded with portions of the kill)   161.
purge (literally, by taking medicines, and figuratively, by repenting)
    5.5.5. *tenor* nature, character   10. *intelligence* information

PRINCE. The noble Scot, Lord Douglas, when he saw
  The fortune of the day quite turned from him,
  The noble Percy slain, and all his men
  Upon the foot of fear, fled with the rest,   20
  And, falling from a hill, he was so bruised
  That the pursuers took him. At my tent
  The Douglas is, and I beseech your Grace
  I may dispose of him.
KING.   With all my heart.
PRINCE. Then, brother John of Lancaster, to you   25
  This honourable bounty shall belong;
  Go to the Douglas and deliver him
  Up to his pleasure, ransomless and free.
  His valours shown upon our crests today
  Have taught us how to cherish such high deeds,   30
  Even in the bosom of our adversaries.
JOHN. I thank your Grace for this high courtesy,
  Which I shall give away immediately.
KING. Then this remains, that we divide our power.
  You, son John, and my cousin Westmoreland,   35
  Towards York shall bend you with your dearest speed
  To meet Northumberland and the prelate Scroop,
  Who, as we hear, are busily in arms.
  Myself and you, son Harry, will towards Wales
  To fight with Glendower and the Earl of March.   40
  Rebellion in this land shall lose his sway,
  Meeting the check of such another day,
  And since this business so fair is done,
  Let us not leave till all our own be won.

                               Exeunt.

20. *Upon . . . fear* fleeing in panic   36. *dearest* best   43. *business* (trisyllabic, pronounced "busy-ness")

For the material of his English history plays, Shakespeare turned to readily available sources. As is generally known, he depended most heavily on Raphael Holinshed's *Chronicles of England, Scotland, and Ireland*, of which the second edition appeared in 1587. There is evidence, however, that he supplemented what he found in Holinshed with matter from other sources, such as the Chronicle of Edward Halle. Specifically, for *1 Henry IV*, he also used the *Civil Wars*, a poetic account by Samuel Daniel, and an old play – either the one which has come down to us as *The Famous Victories of Henry the fifth* or an antecedent of it. It must be remembered, too, that a good many legends had grown up around the character of Prince Hal, which would be known both to Shakespeare and to his audience; there may well have been similar folk-history about other elements in the story. Finally, there was very great contemporary interest in English history – particularly in that segment which Shakespeare treated – both from a growing sense of national identity and pride and from a sense that the key to present problems might be found in the past. Hence, historical information or legend might crop up anywhere – in pamphlet literature, ballads, even in tavern conversation.

We cannot know how accurately Shakespeare or his audience knew the history that lay behind his plays, and the account that follows therefore makes little or no attempt (except in the first paragraph) to reflect the story as it was known in Shakespeare's day; some of the points in which the play differs from historical fact are noted.

Eight of the ten plays which Shakespeare wrote on English history form a kind of loosely connected sequence dealing with the period from 1398, just prior to the deposition of Richard II, to 1485, when Richard III lost both the crown of England and his life on Bosworth Field. In very broad terms, it might be said that for Shakespeare and his audience the story of what happened in those years was the story of a curse. Not only the rivals who fought for the throne – the Houses of Lancaster and York – but all England fell under the scourge of "Disorder, horror, fear, and mutiny" (*Richard II*, 4.1.142) which was God's vengeance for the sacrilegious act of deposing and then murdering Richard II, the "anointed king", "The deputy elected by the Lord" (*Richard II*, 3.2.55, 57).

To understand the part of this story that is told in *1 Henry IV*, it is necessary to know something of what had gone before, and of who the historical personages in it were and how they were related. A chart showing the principal descendants of Edward III follows this section. Edward III died in 1377 after a reign of fifty years. Five of his seven sons lived to maturity, but in 1377, when their father died, the two oldest of his remaining five sons were also dead. The crown thus passed to the grandson of Edward III, the only surviving son of the famous "Black Prince", who became King Richard II when he was a child of ten. But the three younger sons of Edward III were still living, and they were powerful and ambitious. Indeed, in view of the fate of other children who inherited the throne of England and were unfortunate enough to have aspiring uncles – such as Arthur of Brittany, whose uncle was King John, or the Princes in the Tower, whose uncle was Richard III – it is perhaps surprising that Richard II lived to his majority. He may have been lucky in that he had three uncles rather than just one.

The wealthiest and most influential of these uncles was John of Gaunt, Duke of Lancaster. John's policies seem to have helped to bring on the Peasants' Revolt of 1381, and for a time thereafter he prudently kept in the background, staying, in fact, out of England altogether for considerable periods. Thus it was the youngest son of Edward III, Thomas of Woodstock, Duke of Gloucester (whose chance of getting the crown by peaceful inheritance was most remote), who made the first move against Richard. He did gain power briefly, but then Richard, having turned twenty-one, asserted himself, and Woodstock (as he is most often called in the plays) was eventually imprisoned at Calais, where he died, probably murdered, and probably with Richard's consent, if not at his order.

Parliament meanwhile had declared that, since Richard had as yet no children, the heir apparent was Roger Mortimer, fourth Earl of March and grandson of Edward III's son Lionel. When Roger Mortimer was killed in 1398, Parliament recognized his son, the seven-year-old Edmund Mortimer, fifth Earl of March, as the rightful heir. The difficulty here lay not only in the youth and relative powerlessness of Edmund Mortimer, but in the fact that his claim to the throne was through a woman, Lionel's daughter Philippa. Not for another 150 years, until the accession of the Tudor queens, was it established that a woman might rule England, or even that a valid claim to the throne could be based on descent in the female line.

The nearest heir in the male line was John of Gaunt, and he and his warrior son, Henry, called "Bolingbroke", were the most immediate threats to Richard. In 1398 Henry was charged with treason and banished, and in 1399, when John of Gaunt died, Richard seized Henry's patrimony. But then Richard blundered. In May of 1399 he set off on an expedition to Ireland, and contrary winds prevented his quick return. In the meantime, on July 4, 1399, Henry landed at Ravenspurgh, ostensibly returning from banishment only to claim his inheritance. He found, in effect, an empty throne, and with help from the Percy family he so ensconced himself that when Richard returned he had no alternative but to submit, which he did at Flint Castle on August 19. On September 29 Richard abdicated, and the next day he was declared by Parliament deposed in favour of Henry. Richard was imprisoned in Pontefract Castle where he died in 1400, again probably murdered, quite possibly at Henry's order.

Henry was to find the throne more easily taken than peacefully kept. At the point where Shakespeare takes up the story in *1 Henry IV*, it is in the autumn of 1402, and Henry has been having trouble on his borders. A great guerilla fighter, Owen Glendower, had stirred Welsh nationalist spirit and defeated an

English army under Edmund Mortimer, taking Mortimer prisoner. This Mortimer was not the young claimant to the throne, but his uncle. On the Scottish border, however, things went better; Henry Percy, famous as "Hotspur", won a victory at Holmedon on September 14, 1402. Despite the fact that the Percy family had helped Henry IV gain the throne, they also had an interest in the Mortimer line; Hotspur was married to a Mortimer. The Percies chose this moment to defy Henry IV, perhaps feeling that they had not been sufficiently rewarded for their part in making him King. They entered into a kind of grand alliance against him, joining forces with Glendower, the Scots, and the Mortimers. A royal army commanded by Henry's eldest son, "Prince Hal", then not quite sixteen years old, surprised the Percy forces on their way to join Glendower, and in the ensuing Battle of Shrewsbury, July 21, 1403, the Percies were defeated, Hotspur was killed, and his uncle, Thomas Percy, Earl of Worcester, taken prisoner and summarily executed. The head of the Percy family, the Earl of Northumberland, was not present at this battle (with which the action of Shakespeare's *1 Henry IV* ends), and he continued to make trouble for Henry IV, as did Glendower and others, through much of Henry's reign. As the genealogical chart shows, the Mortimer claim was eventually allied with that of the descendants of still another son of Edward III, Edmund, the Duke of York, to found the powerful House of York, rival dynasty to the House of Lancaster in the fifteenth-century Wars of the Roses.

There exists, of course, little in the way of factual history to support Shakespeare's story of the association of Prince Hal with the tavern gang led by Sir John Falstaff. Falstaff was originally called Sir John Oldcastle, both in the old play *The Famous Victories*, and in the first productions of Shakespeare's plays (see Hal's reference to him as "my old lad of the castle" at 1.2.40). There had been a real Oldcastle, whose story Holinshed tells, and who, though reputed to have been high in Henry V's regard, was burned for heresy. After the Reformation he came to be thought of as a Protestant martyr, and his descendants understandably protested comic treatment of him on the stage. Shakespeare responded by changing the name, adapting that of another historical figure who had earlier been shown as a "cowardly knight" in *1 Henry VI*, Sir John Fastolfe. The Oldcastle association was long-lived, however. Shakespeare tried to end it in the Epilogue to *2 Henry IV* by expressly declaring that "Oldcastle died a martyr, and this is not the man." None the less, there are numerous later allusions to him as Oldcastle.

Whatever one may make of Oldcastle, it is likely that most of the legend about Hal's wild youth was fiction. Indeed, this sort of tradition often attaches itself to the biography of a national hero. Many royal princes in English history have behaved ill toward their fathers, and it is entirely possible that in the later years of the reign of Henry IV, when he was seriously ill and his son was impatient to take the throne, there was some estrangement between them.

Apart from the comic subplot, Shakespeare portrayed history as faithfully as any dramatist might be expected to. He fore-shortens time, but nothing like as inordinately as in some of the other histories; there elapsed only about ten months from the Battle of Holmedon, with which the play opens, to that of Shrewsbury, with which it closes. Shakespeare felt no need here, as he did in the Prologue to *Henry V*, to apologize to his audience for "Turning the accomplishment of many years/ Into an hourglass". He did, to be sure, confuse the two Edmund Mortimers – a natural enough mistake and one that seems to have already existed in his sources. But he might have done it deliberately, even if he was aware of the distinction, because what he needed for dramatic purposes was one character to symbolize the Mortimer claim and its alliance with the Percy faction and Glendower's movement, and for this purpose the elder Edmund Mortimer was far more appropriate. A few other details are erroneous; for example Hotspur was married to Elizabeth Mortimer, but Shakespeare calls her Kate (a name he seems to have liked).

The most striking change made by Shakespeare and the one that best illustrates what must be done to make drama out of history is the alteration of Hotspur's age. Historically, Hotspur was of Henry IV's generation; indeed, he was three years older than the King. But in the play Prince Hal and Hotspur are to be the principal vehicles of the dramatic conflict; to emphasize this, Shakespeare makes them seem to us much more of an age. Such a conflict ought to end with direct confrontation; thus Shakespeare also takes the historical liberty of showing Hotspur killed by Hal. Hal did lead the King's army, and Hotspur was killed, but history does not record whose hand dealt the fatal blow.

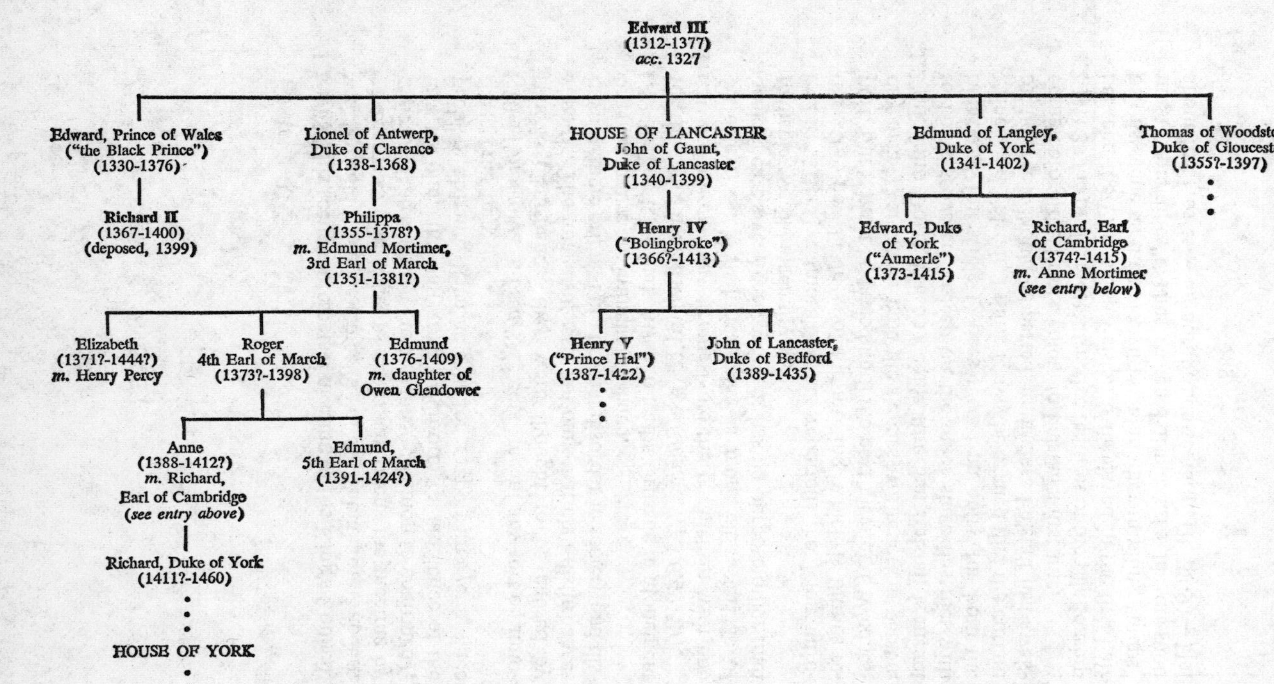

Edward III
(1312-1377)
acc. 1327

Edward, Prince of Wales
("the Black Prince")
(1330-1376)

Lionel of Antwerp,
Duke of Clarence
(1338-1368)

HOUSE OF LANCASTER
John of Gaunt,
Duke of Lancaster
(1340-1399)

Edmund of Langley,
Duke of York
(1341-1402)

Thomas of Woodstock,
Duke of Gloucester
(1355?-1397)

Richard II
(1367-1400)
(deposed, 1399)

Philippa
(1355-1378?)
m. Edmund Mortimer,
3rd Earl of March
(1351-1381?)

Henry IV
("Bolingbroke")
(1366?-1413)

Edward, Duke
of York
("Aumerle")
(1373-1415)

Richard, Earl
of Cambridge
(1374?-1415)
m. Anne Mortimer
(see entry below)

Elizabeth
(1371?-1444?)
m. Henry Percy

Roger
4th Earl of March
(1373?-1398)

Edmund
(1376-1409)
m. daughter of
Owen Glendower

Henry V
("Prince Hal")
(1387-1422)

John of Lancaster,
Duke of Bedford
(1389-1435)

Anne
(1388-1412?)
m. Richard,
Earl of Cambridge
(see entry above)

Edmund,
5th Earl of March
(1391-1424?)

Richard, Duke of York
(1411?-1460)

HOUSE OF YORK

1.1.1-33 This scene represents a meeting of the King's Council, which would resemble a meeting of the Cabinet of a modern government. The King, as chairman, opens the meeting by reviewing the situation (in a manner common to chairmen), thus enabling the playwright to inform the audience of the problem at hand. Then he calls for a report on events since the last meeting.

1.1.10-11 *meteors . . . bred* "Meteors" meant any sort of atmospheric disturbance; they were thought to be caused by vapours. The image suggests not only that civil disturbances have a single origin, but also that disorder in society and disorder in nature are intimately related.

1.1.19-21 The King had vowed to lead a Crusade in atonement for the murder of Richard II (see *Richard II*, 5.6.49-50).

1.1.50 *uneven and unwelcome* Note the parallelism with line 66 below. Such rhetorical play is more characteristic of Shakespeare's very early work. It has no purpose other than to display verbal ingenuity.

1.1.62 ff. After Westmoreland has reported, the King introduces the new business of the meeting, which is Blunt's report. But it must be tabled until the next meeting ("Wednesday next"), at which time the Percies will report in person.

1.2 s.d. John Dover Wilson's conjecture that Falstaff is meant to be "discovered" asleep on the inner stage has met with objection. But while Q does record an entry for both the Prince and Falstaff, I think it may be argued that the curtain of the recess should be parted, to disclose Falstaff just awakening before the Prince enters to Falstaff's first line.

1.2.1-102 One of the most attractive features of the relationship between the Prince and Falstaff is displayed in the first half of this scene as they vie with one another in piling "quips" upon "quiddities". Thus, when Falstaff asks his question about the Hostess – an abrupt non-sequitur (ll. 38-9) – Hal is quick to play up with a rejoinder of the same kind. Later, in the piling up of similes for Falstaff's melancholy (ll. 71-6), they play another round of this word-game. Such verbal fencing was much to the taste of the young men in Shakespeare's audience who were studying law at the Inns of Court, but Shakespeare also seems to have enjoyed it thoroughly, and he makes us like characters who have a witty command of language.

1.2.79-95 This is the first of many occasions on which Falstaff adopts what is perhaps his favourite comic pose – that of the scripture-quoting, hymn-singing Puritan. It is a devastating parody, the more hilarious as it is such an absurd contrast to the real Falstaff. Falstaff does see to have a genuine familiarity with some passages from the Bible, gained, perhaps, without having read it (see note to 4.2.24-5, 32-4 below).

At the time Shakespeare wrote *1 Henry IV*, two English translations of the Bible were current – the Geneva (1560) and the Bishops' (1568). Though the celebrated King James translation did not appear until 1611, biblical citations in the glossary notes have been taken from this most familiar version.

1.2.81-5 In *2 Henry IV*, the Lord Chief Justice does scold Falstaff in the streets, but about his own misdeeds.

1.2.103 *Gadshill* In the anonymous *Famous Victories of Henry the fifth*, Cuthbert Cutter, a thief, is nicknamed "Gadshill" because he operated at this favourite haunt of highwaymen on the Kentish Road, near Rochester. Shakespeare has caused confusion by adopting the same name for both man and place.

1.2.135 *royal* Here, as elsewhere in the glosses, values of obsolete coins are given in terms of British coinage. Because of inflation, already accelerating in Shakespeare's time and fairly continuous since, the real value of these coins, in terms of their purchasing power, was 50 to 100 times as much as their modern equivalents. No simple equation for translating Elizabethan money or prices into modern equivalents can be given; textiles, for instance, for which prices are suggested in the glosses to 3.4.68 and 3.4.70, were relatively much more expensive in Shakespeare's day than in ours, for they were then made by hand and many were imported.

1.2.186-208 See the Introduction for a discussion of this soliloquy, about which there has been much controversy. My own view is that it does not warrant condemnation of the Prince as a prig and hypocrite, but that it evidences his always purposeful character.

1.3.28-68 As much as possible the punctuation of Q_1 has been retained for this speech by Hotspur on the assumption that it was *dramatic*, designed to guide the actor's voice, not the reader's eye. This speech is all in three sentences, though modern editors usually break it up into five or six. In keeping with the implications of his nickname, Hotspur when he is emotionally roused tends to speak in breathless, rapid-fire fashion, and the light punctuation of Q_1 emphasizes the way in which his words tumble together without pause. Indeed, it is virtually impossible to read the speech any way but breathlessly.

1.3.45 *holiday . . . terms* Hotspur is one of a number of Shakespeare's characters who are maddened by pompous mangling of language; Hamlet is another notable example. Hotspur's attitude toward poetic flights may seem inconsistent; on the one hand, he can be contemptuous of "mincing poetry", as in Act 3, scene 1, but on the other, he can rise to heights of passion himself. This has led some commentators to feel that Worcester's remark about his "world of figures" after lines 199 to 206 in this scene is a disparaging reference, implying that Hotspur's extravagant figures were already clichés. But the inconsistency is resolved, I think, by the realization that it is a "mincing" quality that Hotspur objects to — affectation about anything. Later on, he will chide his wife for her mincing, "lady-like" oaths (see 3.1.248-58).

1.3.69-75 There may be a question whether Blunt, who reported to the council on the victory at Holmedon in scene 1, is the "certain lord" described by Hotspur. If he is, then Hotspur is surely exaggerating, since Blunt gives otherwise a good impression — his speech is not full of "holiday and lady terms" when *we* hear him, his name suggests forthrightness, and he eventually dies nobly in battle. The director of a performance must decide how he wants to play it; if he decides that Hotspur *was* describing Blunt, then Hotspur will appear somewhat less admirable than otherwise. Blunt is of the court, it is true, and Hotspur affects plain speech and dress. If Hotspur does mean Blunt, then there is special irony in Blunt's phrase,

"To such a person", and in his offer to Hotspur to forget the whole thing *if* Hotspur will now yield his prisoners.

1.3.143 ff. The Mortimer claim to the throne, discussed here by the Percies, would have been well known to all of them, and especially to Hotspur, who was related to the claimant by marriage (see the genealogical chart). But this information would have been known to Shakespeare's audience only confusedly – if at all – and so Hotspur is made to seem unaware of it. Shakespeare and many other playwrights have often made use of this device to explain something that the audience needs to know. By fusing the two Edmund Mortimers, Shakespeare may have eliminated an unnecessary complication, but there are some untidy loose ends, as for example the reference by this "brother" Mortimer to Hotspur's wife as "my aunt Percy" (3.1.195). For reasons of his own, apparently – perhaps because he liked the name – Shakespeare calls Lady Percy "Kate"; her real name was Elizabeth.

1.3.156-85 There is more than a little hypocrisy in the sentiment expressed here by Hotspur (and by the Percies generally, at this point) in reference to King Richard – "that sweet lovely rose" – and to the circumstances of his deposition and murder. Hotspur himself makes only a brief, incidental appearance in *Richard II*, but his father is shown there as one of the chief architects of Henry's coup – an arrogant, harsh prosecutor of Richard's "crimes". One is tempted to think, at this juncture, that the Percies misjudge King Henry, that Hotspur's belief that he "studies day and night" to encompass their deaths is ill-founded. But kingmakers can be uncomfortable to have around, once the king-making is done – particularly when, as in this instance, they have another candidate to put forward, should their first creation prove intractable. The Percies *are* dangerous, and in the end (*2 Henry IV*, 4.5.210) the King admits that he "cut them off". The Percy view is that the feudal baronage, having made Henry king, might unmake him. Hotspur's reversion, here, to the by-name of "Bolingbroke" for Henry already implies withdrawal of his right to the title of "King". Later on (4.3.102-4), Hotspur will put forward this feudal theory of the kingship quite explicitly. Despite Tudor and Stuart assertions about the divine rights of kings, the feudal theory had not been forgotten in Shakespeare's time.

1.3.193-6, 199-206 These lines are the most direct statement by Hotspur of his code of honour. Personal honour – not political advantage, the common good, or any other end – is what matters to him. He *must* be the bravest, the champion, and the tragedy of his final defeat is, for him, not that he has been fatally wounded, but that his "championship" will pass to the man who beat him. Worcester, it may be noted, plays skilfully on Hotspur's love of derring-do, but in the end this quixotic chivalry of Hotspur's is perhaps the conspiracy's undoing.

1.3.248-9 *candy . . . greyhound* Shakespeare consistently associated candy with the excessive fawning of dogs (see *Hamlet*, 3.2.65). There is a suggestion of cowardice in at least one etymology proposed for "greyhound".

1.3.280-7 Worcester puts very clearly here the viewpoint of the Percies, alluded to in the note to lines 156 to 185 above, regarding the King's discomfort at being in their debt. A complex theorizing about motives is going on: "The King will think that we think . . . " etc. *Both* the King and Worcester are what Hotspur calls "politicians", i.e. cunning schemers. ("Policy" and words derived from it, like "politician", always carried sinister connotations for the Elizabethans.) Worcester involves Hotspur in his scheming by cleverly appealing to his love of adventure and danger, and by investing the conspiracy with the glamour of a "plot". Compare the way Cassius plays on Brutus's sense of honour in *Julius Caesar* to involve him in the conspiracy against Caesar.

2.1 This scene, often omitted in production, is a sharply and realistically drawn vignette of contemporary life. But attention should also be drawn to the thematic significance, which is suggested in some of the notes below.

2.1.19-21 Elizabethan sanitary conditions were crude, at best. But the practice described by the carrier here was often condemned.

2.1.75-82 Gadshill's remarks about the aristocrats and wealthy bourgeoisie who prey on the commonwealth are not just commonplace rationalizations by a criminal. They are part of the system of parallels and contrasts that forms the essential structure of the play. There is an obvious parallel between the highwaymen and the rebels, both of whom seek to plunder the commonwealth, but it should be remembered that Gadshill is actually referring here to the fact that the Prince is a member of his gang. Henry IV had, indeed, already claimed the commonwealth as his "booty" by deposing and murdering Richard II, and Hal, even if he took less part in this robbery than in the one on Gadshill, stood in a fair way to inherit the profit from it.

2.1.86-7 *We have . . . invisible* Since the fern reproduces by means of spores, not seeds, fernseed would be indeed invisible. This botanical fact was not known till later, however; earlier, the tiny spores were taken to be seeds, and since they were small and hard to see, invisibility was associated with them. The mental process involved was very common in the folk culture of medieval times, and even much later. To make the compounding of the "recipe" for invisibility still more difficult, the fernseed in it was supposed to be gathered on St. John's Day (June 24) only.

2.1.92-7 One of the overarching themes of this play has to do with the problem of appearance and reality, the distinction of true and false, genuine and counterfeit. It is put before us here in startling clarity, in this chaffing between rogues. What is it, for instance, to be a *false* thief? Prince Hal himself is a false thief, in that he only pretends to rob the travellers, yet in a larger sense (see note to ll. 75-82 above), is he not the falsest thief of all? Or is the larger sense that "true" and "false" are only relative terms, as Gadshill implies? In the last analysis can one say any more than Gadshill does, that all men are alike?

2.2.82, 86 Another of Falstaff's comic poses, like that of the snuffling Puritan, is that of youth. He *is* ageless; as he says of himself in *2 Henry IV*, "I was born about three of the clock in the afternoon, with a white head and something a round belly" (1.2.210-12). His agelessness is the reason that his opening line, asking Hal the time of day, strikes the Prince as so absurd.

2.2.90-105 The trick played on Falstaff by the Prince and Poins seems likely to make good the Prince's prophecy that it would be "a good jest forever". It has also been "argument" (in a somewhat different sense than that intended by the Prince) for much more than a week. Whether, or to what degree, Falstaff is a coward has long been debated, and this scene furnishes much of the evidence. He does run away, "roaring" (presumably with fright) according to Poins. But he did strike a blow or two; no one supported him, however, and Falstaff was never one to fight against odds – even of two to one. He tells us himself, later on, of his conviction that "the better part of valour is discretion".

2.3.52 The artillery pieces named are Elizabethan: the eight-inch "cannon" fired 60-pound shot; the basilisk and culverin were smaller guns, measuring about five inches, and fired 15- to 17-pound shot. These references, and Falstaff's to his "pistol" in Act 5, scene 3, are of course anachronistic, though by 1400 gunpowder had been introduced to Europe, and primitive guns, often firing stones rather than iron shot, were in use.

2.4 location: The tavern in Eastcheap frequented by Falstaff and his crew is never actually named in this play, though references in *2 Henry IV* imply that Shakespeare had in mind the Boar's Head. This inn existed in the time of Richard II, boasting itself the "chief tavern in London", and it was still well known in Shakespeare's day. In his edition of *Piers Plowman*, W. W. Skeat suggested that this same Boar's Head might have been the tavern frequented by Glutton in that work. If so, it has the distinction, surely unique, of figuring in two great classics of English literature.

2.4.1 ff. It seems clear that Hal has been drinking heartily with the "leash of drawers". He does not usually talk (to others) with this note of pride, and his speech is usually less rambling (note l. 106, *he* is the drunkard). But it is precisely because he is a little tipsy that he can reveal as much as he does of his real motives, though Poins does not appear to be any the wiser about Hal afterwards. The time is to come when he will indeed command all the good lads in Eastcheap, who will follow him all the more willingly because he seems one of them – able to "drink with any tinker in his own language". Hal no doubt enjoys his tavern revelry, but he is none the less coolly aware of its political usefulness.

2.4.21-78 The joke played on Francis by the Prince and Poins is an ancient comic routine, still highly amusing. But there is just a hint of cruelty in it, as perhaps there is in most practical joking. It may be thought that the Prince finds his amusement rather frequently in the discomfiture of those who cannot very well hit back, and his displays of verbal wit descend often to the level of calling someone a lot of unsavoury names. In any event, while it does not do to sentimentalize over him, one may feel that Francis has been unkindly repaid for his gift of the pennyworth of sugar.

2.4.97-106 This has already been noted in the Introduction as an example of Shakespeare's remarkable application of parody. Hal's burlesque version of the tender, bantering relationship between Hotspur and his wife – shown "straight" in Act 2, scene 3, and in Act 3, scene 1 – is a *possible* view of it, coming close enough to the truth about Hotspur's character to put us on guard against being seduced by his charm. But it may also reveal something of the real hardness in the Prince, who has contempt for what he recognizes as a brutish quality in his unruly rival. It is apparent from his suggestion here that he and his tavern companions often amuse themselves with impromptu take-offs on the serious business of the state.

2.4.108 ff. Here begins the great comic culmination of the trick played upon Falstaff at Gadshill by the Prince and Poins. Falstaff opens by taking the offensive and denouncing the Prince and Poins as cowards, since, as far as he knows, they ran away even before he did. When they at last get him to begin telling his tale (l. 150), he first claims that his gang was set upon by an indefinitely large number ("a hundred", "a dozen", "fifty"), but happening upon a turn of phrase – "two or three and fifty" – and reinforcing it by speaking of himself as a "two-legged creature" (ll. 179, 180) it is probable that he suddenly grasps the truth. As he well knows, there were only *two*, while two of the gang were strangely missing. The two in buckram suits must surely have been the two he is presently addressing. That seems the likeliest explanation of his three-times repeated "two" in quick succession, in his next speech. He knows, however, that his part in the Prince's jokes is always to be the apparent "fall guy" who, at the last instant, turns the tables. At any rate, he now sets out on a very different account of the incident, quite deliberately multiplying the "two rogues in buckram suits", and then, with seeming innocence, allows the trap to be sprung with his reference to Kendal green and the absolute darkness. This now allows the Prince and Poins to face him down with their "plain tale", but the whole game is to see what card Falstaff has up his sleeve. It turns out to be an unbeatable trump. To his claim that he recognized the Prince – even if only by instinct – and ran not to save his own life but the Prince's, there is no possible rejoinder. Of course it is a lie, but it is such a magnificent one that it truly caps the jest, and it is precisely this that the contrivers of the comedy, Hal and Poins, were waiting for. Not all commentators will agree that Falstaff realizes the truth as early as I have suggested here, and it is true that, if he did not, his ultimate response proves him an even quicker wit. But this same quick-witted Falstaff could hardly have made such an obvious blunder as saying that he discerned Kendal green in the pitch darkness.

2.4.110-11, 124-5 Falstaff sometimes actually assumes a Puritan pose, sometimes, as here, merely threatens to turn Puritan. The connection with sewing "netherstocks" or becoming a weaver is that many in the cloth trade were Puritanically inclined refugees from persecution on the continent; their influx created a social and economic disturbance that aroused considerable bitterness in sixteenth-century England.

2.4.113-15 The primary image is of Falstaff making the sack disappear like the sun (Titan) melting butter. But it would appear that "pitiful-hearted" should describe the butter rather than the merciless sun. Theobald emended to "pitiful-hearted Butter", which perhaps makes a more sensible reading.

2.4.260 The belief that "the lion will not touch the true prince" is very old, going back at least to Pliny. It is founded on the ancient analogical concept of the universe, according to which corresponding ranks in every order of beings were intimately associated. The lion among animals, the eagle among birds, fire among the elements, the rose among flowers, the sun among the heavenly bodies – all were kings of their respective realms. They were interchangeable, at least in the mind, and hence imagery of lion, eagle, fire, rose, or sun had more than a simple metaphorical application to the king. This habit of mind had not disappeared, though it was weakening, in Shakespeare's time. (It was once suggested, when two individuals claimed the French throne, that to decide which was the true prince both should be exposed to a lion; the one not eaten would thus have his title ratified. The experiment does not seem to have been carried out, however.)

2.4.343-4, 359 *instinct* Despite the triumph which Falstaff enjoys with his answer to the charge that he ran away, he does not enjoy being reminded of it, and the Prince badgers him a good deal by returning to the topic of "instinct". He needs more than the mere escape from discredit to get his own back in full. As is suggested in the Introduction, it is at Shrewsbury that he settles the score by accusing Hal of lying.

2.4.367-9 *Thy state . . . crown* It has been suggested that these lines by Hal should be spoken "aside", and that he is referring to his father, the King, rather than to Falstaff. Spoken thus, the lines would be a comment on the disrespect shown for the King, not only by this tavern crowd, but similarly by the rebels; they would also let us glimpse a filial affection in Hal not outwardly displayed in this play.

2.4.382-3 The Hostess quite probably speaks affectionately of the "harlotry players", but another little jibe at the Puritans may be intended, too. Actors in Shakespeare's day were classed by statute with rogues and vagabonds, and they and their productions were under constant attack by Puritan preachers and pamphleteers. One of the chief grounds for Puritan objections was that the players deliberately portrayed lewdness and bawdiness, which induced "whoredom and uncleanness" in the spectators (see, for example, Philip Stubbes, *The Anatomie of Abuses* [1583]).

2.4.384 ff. Falstaff has promised that he will speak "in King Cambyses' vein" (1. 374), i.e. in the ranting style used by actors of the period of Thomas Preston's *Cambyses, King of Persia* (about 1570). To do so would be a pointed take-off on the style of the opposition star, Edward Alleyn, who was famous for his acting of the bombastic parts in Marlowe's plays. But the speech Shakespeare gives him is actually a parody of something else — the "euphuistic" prose style, which takes its name from the title of John Lyly's "novel", *Euphues* (1578). Lyly's work was popular at court, where grandiose or affected speech was a natural tendency in any event. The euphuistic style is marked by highly artificial structure, elaborately balanced sentences, extended alliteration, and high-flown similes drawn from the "ancient writers", particularly writers on natural history. All these tricks are employed in Falstaff's speech. Indeed, the "camomile" sentence seems to be based on a particular model in *Euphues*. Since Lyly's original sentence connects its antithetical elements with a logical "yet", some editors have felt constrained to emend Shakespeare's "so". But part of the fun, I think, is that in Falstaff's parody the elaborate parallels and antitheses become confused, completely garbling the sense.

2.4.389-96 There is elaborate play here on the various senses of the sun–son homonyms. The sun of heaven is both the sun in the skies and the Son of Heaven – Christ. But, as was noted above (l. 260), in the medieval system of analogies the sun is a symbol of the king. There had also been a long tradition that kings were, if not divine, more or less direct deputies of Christ on earth ("The deputy elected by the Lord" is the phrase used in *Richard II*, 3.2.57). English kings since Henry VIII, of course, have been the official heads of the Church of England.

2.4.465-82 This passage comes at a critical moment in the action of the play. The gaiety of the tavern had been disturbed a little earlier by the messenger from the Court, come to summon Hal. On that occasion, the Prince let Falstaff "send him packing". Now there is another summons, this time for Falstaff. The sheriff with a large force is at the door; Falstaff and his gang are caught with the stolen goods in their possession, and it will be the hangman's cart for them unless the Prince, in his turn, sends them packing. But will he? He has appeared to grow more critical of Falstaff, and he has just said, "I do, I will [banish Falstaff]." There is time only for a brief plea "in the behalf of that Falstaff". Into it, Falstaff introduces the theme of "true" and "counterfeit" which he will canvass again in Act 5, scene 4 (see Introduction). His exact words have been blurred by a textual crux (see 2.4.475, textual variants), but what he says is clearly meant to suggest that he and Hal are alike, that both have true gold under the "seeming" false exterior. Hal's reply to this is challenging; he returns to the charge that Falstaff is only a coward. Falstaff's rejoinder is courageous enough, though he has perhaps no alternative. He denies the charge, but it is up to Hal to decide whether *he* will deny the sheriff entry; if he does not, Falstaff is ready to take his punishment. It is, perhaps, a test; if so, Falstaff passes it, and Hal intervenes. The validity of Falstaff's claim to likeness with Hal in being no counterfeit, but true gold, is left undecided.

3.1 location: When Shakespeare came to be edited, in the eighteenth century, the editors felt it necessary to specify a location for each scene. For this one, unfortunately, they turned to their Holinsheds and found there that the historical meeting of the rebels had taken place at the Archdeacon of Bangor's house, though it is obvious from the content of the scene that Glendower is playing the host throughout and behaving very much as though he were in his own home. Actually, Shakespeare was not concerned with the precise location; what he does emphasize is that the scene is laid in Wales.

3.1.49 *there's no . . . Welsh* Glendower is exactly the kind of stuffy, punctilious person to put the mercurial Hotspur beside himself. Unerringly, Hotspur finds the tenderest spots in Glendower's make-up to jab away at. Glendower is perhaps most sensitive about being thought a crude provincial who speaks English with a thick accent, and Hotspur continually needles him with remarks about his Welshness. The line here about no man speaking better Welsh means not only that what he says is unintelligible (as though it were spoken in that uncouth Welsh language), but also that he cannot speak understandably in English and perhaps, too, that he is a great braggart, the Welsh having been thought to be much given to boasting.

3.1.69 ff. The squabble over the division of the spoils, though it gives us another comic encounter between Glendower and Hotspur, has a quite serious significance. Not only does it suddenly disclose a naked greediness among these charming personages (notice how even the gentle Mortimer is aroused by the prospect of losing part of his share), but also it puts the conspiracy in a light which the Elizabethans could not fail to recognize as abhorrent. The success of the rebels would mean a divided nation, and whatever else men of Shakespeare's day might quarrel about, they were agreed that a divided kingdom was an unthinkable catastrophe. Indeed, in *Henry V* Shakespeare anticipates history by showing England, Scotland, Ireland, and Wales united in support of Henry against the French. The tragic consequence of dividing a kingdom is all too obvious in *King Lear*.

3.1.148 ff. Prophecies attributed to Merlin have cropped up at various points in British history. The Tudors, for instance, liked to regard themselves as the fulfilment of Merlin's prophecy that Arthur (or at least his line) would return to rule Britain. The prophecy which is referred to by scoffing Hotspur was bruited about in Richard II's and Henry IV's time; it spoke of Henry as the "moldwarp" or mole (condemned as unclean by the Bible; see Lev. 11:29-30) and referred also to the dragon, lion, and boar, which were the heraldic emblems, respectively, of Glendower, Percy, and Mortimer. The other beasts seem to have been thrown in by Shakespeare for good measure.

3.1.196 s.d. Obviously, Shakespeare had no Welsh; he does not write lines for Glendower and Lady Mortimer in Welsh but signifies in the stage directions that they speak or she sings in Welsh. There must have been an older actor and a boy among the Lord Chamberlain's Men at this time who knew at least a little Welsh. The actor's personality may have contributed something to the characterization of Glendower, in which Shakespeare departs radically from his sources. The need to speak Welsh poses a problem for modern productions of the play, particularly by school or amateur groups. The song most frequently used is the familiar one known in English as "All Through the Night".

3.1.213-21 These lines aptly display Glendower's ability to frame "an English ditty lovely well". Like Mortimer's, just preceding, they are in the extravagant style favoured by young men "trained up in the English court". Well-bred English gentlemen in Elizabethan England were expected to be able to turn out a sonnet or a song; their effusions tended to be overgrown with classical allusions, euphuistic phrases, and ornate diction. They represent one of the types of "mincing" poetry that Hotspur detested; these lines contrast sharply with Hotspur's own energetic speech.

3.2.39 ff. This is Henry's cold appraisal of his "courtship to the common people", described by Richard in *Richard II*, 1.4.23-36 (see Introduction).

3.2.60-84 "The skipping King" described here with such contempt by King Henry is not at all like the King Richard shown in Shakespeare's earlier play, nor is he to be found in Holinshed (though there is perhaps a basis for this portrait in the anonymous play, *Woodstock* [*c.* 1591-4]). Possibly Henry exaggerates on purpose to drive home his lesson – "As thou art to this hour was Richard then" – but he may also be thinking particularly of the scene of Richard's deposition (*Richard II*, 4.1), in which Richard's wit and playfulness sparkled, to Henry's discomfort. The King does not understand that Hal, though a "companion to the common streets", has by no means "enfeoffed" himself, but remains in control of his destiny.

3.2.98-9 *He . . . succession* The question of the succession to Queen Elizabeth is reflected in numerous places in the history plays, particularly when, as here, theoretical bases for the title to the throne are canvassed. King Henry himself had taken the crown from one whose right to it was based only on birth; he may be expected, therefore, to argue that ability to rule is a better foundation for title. A further qualification, not referred to by Henry here but implied by the play generally, might be moral integrity. (See the discussions of the Elizabethan succession problem and the theme of political morality in the Introduction.)

3.2.129-61 Hal's promise to "redeem all this on Percy's head" apparently moves his father to forgiveness and brings about a reconciliation (ll. 160-61). Since the promise is kept (whether the King knows who killed Hotspur, he is certainly aware of Hal's bravery, and in particular he knows that Hal rescues him from the Douglas in 5.4), the reconciliation would appear to be complete by the end of the play. In Part II, however, Hal seems to have slid back into his old ways. See the Introduction, footnote 2, for reference to the controversy over the unity of the two plays.

3.2.173-6 Since the Prince is being sent through Gloucestershire, by a rather longer route, he is given a day's start. Later, however, Shakespeare apparently forgot that Hal was to go by Gloucestershire, for he meets Falstaff in Act 4, scene 2, on the other route, near Coventry.

3.3.1-10 It is significant that promptly upon the impassioned vow of repentance by Prince Hal in Act 3, scene 2, there should follow Falstaff in his comic penitent pose. Indeed, the real and mock reformations are continuously paralleled.

Hal's promise of reformation is made privately (in the soliloquy of 1.2, and in confidence to his father in 3.2), but its fulfilment is more and more nearly at hand as this sequence of plays approaches its culmination in *Henry V*. Falstaff's threats to reform are always public, but of course quite hypocritical. It is an entirely comic hypocrisy, made more pointed by his continuing parody of the scripture-spouting Puritan. None the less, the juxtaposition of the two vows to repent invites a more searching inspection of Hal's reformation than might otherwise be undertaken.

3.3.14-20 The actor playing Falstaff will probably find it natural to give this mock confession added comic effect by pausing significantly after "times", "quarter", and "borrowed"; indeed, many editors punctuate in this fashion, though the original texts do not. This trick of changing the meaning by adding, after a delay, an unexpected completing phrase is an old comic routine. Some critics have reduced Falstaff's role to nothing more than a series of such *lazzi*, the standardized "gags" of traditional clowns (see E. E. Stoll, *Shakespeare Studies, Historical and Comparative in Method* [New York: Macmillan, 1927]). Without going so far, it is possible to remark on the obvious opportunities in this part for stock comic business. It is generally assumed that Shakespeare wrote the part of Falstaff for Will Kempe, a famous clown who was a leading member of the Lord Chamberlain's Company and who seems to have depended a good deal on broad comic action for his effects (compare the part of Bottom in *A Midsummer Night's Dream*). Kempe eventually left the company, perhaps after disagreement with Shakespeare over *ad lib* comic business (see *Hamlet*, 3.2.42 ff.). Since Falstaff has come to be the star part in these plays (Maurice Evans and Sir Ralph Richardson have had notable successes in it), it has been suggested that possibly the role was originally created, not by Kempe, but by the leading actor of Shakespeare's company, Richard Burbage.

3.3.26-7 Falstaff's language is thickly studded with tags from the Bible, old plays, ballads, and, as in this instance, the romances of chivalry. He is not necessarily jibing here at the sobriquets of knights in these romances (as Beaumont and Fletcher were to do a few years later in *The Knight of the Burning Pestle*, which probably has in mind the same original as Falstaff's "Knight of the Burning Lamp"). He reflects a genuine popular taste for romantic literature, a taste to which Shakespeare's plays in general obviously cater. Humanists, who preferred more polished classical literature, and Puritans, who thought all fiction wicked, alike denounced the old romances, without, however, notably checking the popular appetite for them. Indeed, Falstaff's relish for plays, ballads, and romances marks him as anathema to Puritans, for all these types of entertainment came under Puritan attack. Nor would the Puritans have enjoyed his clever twisting of the Bible to his own disreputable purposes.

3.3.51 ff. The pocket-picking episode provides another instance (on a less epic scale than the Gadshill robbery) of the Prince and Falstaff in their customary roles – the Prince attempting to pin Falstaff down in a lie, Falstaff nimbly eluding him and ending by turning the tables so that Hal can only ruefully admit the truth – that he is the pickpocket. Falstaff then turns in expansive good humour and "forgives" the Hostess, who is hustled off, with no prospect of her money.

3.3.60-62, 114-28 The Hostess is so anxious to defend her good name against what sound like calumnies by Falstaff that she is trapped into making ludicrous (and sometimes double-meaning) comments on herself.

3.3.180-81 Falstaff's suggestion about what Hal should do now that he is back in favour is the first hint of his vain expectations for the future. Shakespeare has already told the audience, through the Prince's soliloquy at the end of Act 1, scene 2, that Falstaff and his gang are to be cast off eventually; now he is showing why this must be so, if Hal's reign is not to be complete anarchy. The remark here is meant only as a joke, but it is given more significance by the attitude expressed a few lines later, that rebellion is a good thing since it provides opportunity for men like Falstaff to satisfy their greed. In Part II, Falstaff's delusion about what it will be like when Hal is King culminates in the exultant cry, "Let us take any man's horses; the laws of England are at my commandment" (5.3.142). He discovers the unpleasant truth very shortly thereafter, when the Lord Chief Justice commits him to Fleet prison.

4.1.1-5 Hotspur says, in effect, that if Douglas had the praise he deserves, no soldier of recent times would be more generally recognized throughout the world. The image is of a newly minted coin ("of this season's stamp") which is accepted at its full value everywhere (goes "general current").

4.1.28 ff. Shakespeare allows us to see Hotspur passing through the stages from his first bewildered shock at the news of his father's dereliction to his eventual conviction that this is the best thing that could have happened. It is entirely in character for Hotspur to see fighting against odds as a way to gain more glory. Shakespeare manipulated history a bit to enhance the isolation of Hotspur and heighten the odds against him. The sickness of Northumberland was transferred from an earlier incident, and the Welsh are made to be absent (as in Daniel's account, rather than Holinshed's). Holinshed says Hotspur had 14,000 men, but does not estimate the King's force. Actually, the King caught the rebel army by surprise; in the ensuing battle, according to Holinshed, 5,000 were killed on the rebel side and 1,600 on the King's.

4.1.31-41 Hotspur reads his father's letter half aloud, half to himself, putting it into the third person as he goes, but using words and phrases from the letter. Some editors feel that the end of line 31 is defective and supply some phrase, but this is not required if we imagine him picking out words from the letter to emphasize and skimming the rest. The tone of what he reads is unmistakably that of the cautious, evasive Northumberland, not of the forthright and vigorous Hotspur.

4.1.68-71 A little later, the rebels will be putting their grievances before the King with great show of righteousness. Here, however, politic Worcester acknowledges that their rebellion will not stand up to critical examination by the "eye of reason". The motives of the various leaders of this confederacy are different: Douglas and Glendower are nationalists whose enemy is England, not Henry IV in particular; Worcester and Northumberland are politicians, as much as anything seeking to save their own skins; Hotspur is a daredevil who loves fighting for its own sake.

4.1.96-109 Vernon's description of the Prince of Wales and his companions is a rich combination of images suggesting royalty, brilliant pageantry, and vital energy. Vaulting fully-armed into the saddle was a feat requiring no mean skill and strength. Had Shakespeare's stage permitted him to show such scenes, the plays would be the poorer for many passages of vivid poetry. (In Sir Laurence Olivier's film of *Henry V*, Vernon's description of the Prince was brilliantly realized.)

4.2.11-46 Elizabethan captains were notorious for the practices which Shakespeare has Falstaff describe here. Not only did they take bribes to let conscripted men off (rounding up such strays as Falstaff speaks of in their places), but since soldiers' pay went to the captain for disbursing, on the basis of the latest muster-roll, the practice was to lead the men into battle as soon as possible, so that the dead soldiers' pay would go into the captain's pocket. This accounts for Falstaff's nonchalance about his "mortal men" (l. 68; see also 5.3.35-8). In Part II, Falstaff is again in the country, "recruiting", but this time the impressment of reluctant men, the bribe-taking, and the consequent acceptance of worthless substitutes are all comically acted out. These scenes from Part II are often transferred to Part I, when only the latter is being produced, being substituted for this descriptive passage.

4.2.24-5, 32-4 The "painted cloth" or similar pictorial representations were a principal means by which unlettered medieval and Renaissance men came to know scriptural stories. Falstaff's acquaintance with the Bible is wide, but this need not mean he read it; it is difficult now to realize how much of men's lives once was filled by religion and the Scriptures, which they met in liturgical ceremony, sermons, and even in drama. The parable of the Prodigal Son was a highly popular story; it is mentioned more frequently than any other parable in Shakespeare's plays and is, of course, most apt in *1 Henry IV*.

4.2.77-8 Some editors give Westmoreland an exit before these lines, so that Falstaff may speak them alone on the stage, with a knowing wink to the audience. However this is staged, the point is that Falstaff, meeting the Prince and Westmoreland far behind the lines, assumes that they are hypocritical in their talk about the need for haste and that they, like himself, hope to come in to the battle too late for the danger but in time for glory and spoils. The sentiment is apt for Falstaff's mercenary attitude toward war, but would probably be wrongly attributed to the others.

4.3.1-28 This can hardly be called a "quarrel" scene, as is the one in *Julius Caesar* between Brutus and Cassius, but the divided counsel here may well suggest the weakness and the confusion visited by God upon sinful rebellion.

4.3.31-6 Hotspur's praise of Blunt here accords with Blunt's honourable death in battle and militates against the suggestion (see 1.3.69-75, end note) that Blunt was the "popingay" Lord at Holmedon.

4.3.51-104 In the two parts of *Henry IV*, and to some extent in *Henry V* as well, there is recurring discussion of key events that took place in the first play in the series, *Richard II*. Richard's throwing down of the warder in the lists at Coventry, Bolingbroke's departure into exile and attendant "courtship" of the common people, and his landing at Ravenspurgh, to be welcomed by the Percies, are each recalled on several occasions. Hotspur here, and Worcester in the following scene describe in considerable detail the circumstances of Bolingbroke's homecoming. The effect of such recollections is obviously to give unity to the cycle, but a more subtle purpose is also being accomplished. The events are not merely recollected; they are reflected upon, debated, presented from various viewpoints. Eventually, then, they come to be seen with something like the historian's perspective; if Shakespeare is not himself rendering a historian's judgement, he is inviting one. These plays, much more than those of the other cycle (*1 Henry VI* to *Richard III*) are truly *history* plays, not mere chronicles.

4.4 This brief scene is often omitted in production. It serves, however, several purposes. One of these is certainly to connect events in this play to those of its sequel in which the Archbishop and Northumberland, with others mentioned here, will carry on the struggle against King Henry. Another is to give a different, more distant perspective on the impending battle, one that will not only suggest the apprehension with which all England awaited the event, but also provide some idea of its dimensions and even its likely outcome, as they appeared to non-participants. Finally, this glimpse of the busily scheming Archbishop reminds us again of the darker side of this conspiracy – the side that is represented by politic Worcester and evasive Northumberland and that is in such sharp contrast to the dash and spirit of Hotspur and Douglas.

4.4 s.d. This "Sir Michael" is unknown to history. He may be either a priest or a knight, since "Sir" was a courtesy title for a priest as well as the designation of a knight and since either a priest or a knight might have been employed by this warrior-prelate.

4.4.2-3 The Lord Marshal was Thomas Mowbray, Duke of Norfolk, who is one of the insurgent leaders in Part II. "Scroop" may have been one of the several members of the Scrope family who were Bolingbroke's enemies; most probably he was Sir Stephen, younger brother of the Scrope executed by Bolingbroke at Bristol (see 1.3.268 and gloss).

4.4.16-18 Shakespeare follows Daniel rather than Holinshed in having Glendower absent from Shrewsbury (see 4.1.28 ff., end note). The prophecies which keep Glendower away are a touch of pure invention by Shakespeare; they are, however, in keeping with the characterization of Glendower as a magician and visionary in Act 3, scene 1, which was likewise unhistorical.

5.1 s.d. The inclusion of the Earl of Westmoreland in this stage direction represents a slip by Shakespeare, since Westmoreland is the hostage held by the rebels against Worcester's return (see 4.3.108 and 5.2.28). Probably, as Shakespeare wrote out this entry, he did not realize that he would later name the hostage. When he did, he failed to make a correction here.

5.1.30-71 Hotspur's earlier recital, to Blunt, of the rebels' grievances had emphasized a shade more the feudal concept that the nobility, having created the King, might sit in judgement on his title and find against him. Worcester, covering much the same ground, suggests that the rebels have armed themselves for safety against the King's evident desire to be rid of his erstwhile allies. Both attitudes are suggested in Act 1, scene 3 (see notes to 1.3.156-85 and 1.3.280-87 above).

5.2.1-27 Shakespeare found an account of Worcester's treachery in Holinshed and supplied Worcester with a plausible motive for it. Since Worcester himself speaks here of the "liberal and kind offer of the King" and conspires with Vernon to conceal it with the unheroic purpose of saving his own skin, we tend to regard the King's offer as bona fide and Worcester as a villain. The King's offer of amnesty appears in a better light for having been made in the context of Prince Hal's manly challenge to Hotspur, but no one can say how sincerely the offer was made, since it was not taken up. However, in Part II, the situation recurs with almost uncanny exactness. *There* the rebels accept the offer (issued by Prince John of Lancaster) and, once their arms are laid down, they are arrested and led off to execution. After that, one is a little more inclined to think Worcester may have been right. The recurring circumstance permits yet another form of new perspective on history (see note to 4.3.51-104 above).

5.2.51-68 Vernon's account of Hal's challenge is a highly coloured version of what Hal actually said (5.1.83-100). But Vernon is not currying favour with Hotspur. Shakespeare has allowed these adversaries, Hotspur and Hal, to speak contemptuously of one another on earlier occasions; now that they are to meet in honourable combat, he can enhance the stature of both by showing their own respect for one another. He is also pointing up Hal's newly displayed decorousness, and this can be done more fittingly by another than in Hal's own words.

5.2.75-100 Shakespeare generally allows his leaders to exhort their armies before going into battle. These battle orations are often bravura passages, playing upon all too familiar propaganda themes – the justness of the cause, the beastliness of the enemy, and so on. Hotspur here seems about to begin just such a conventional address when he is interrupted by news of the King's advance (l. 89); we may join Hotspur in giving thanks that he has time only for the sounding of his battle-cry.

5.3 On the Elizabethan stage, perhaps forty feet wide and some thirty feet deep, mounting a full-scale battle would be manifestly impossible. Yet in the historical material of which so many plays were made (not just the "histories") battles were key events; Elizabethan theatre-goers demanded the noise, colour, and excitement of a battle as a fitting climax to the afternoon's entertainment. Shakespeare was conscious of the inadequacy of his stage for these effects (see the Prologue to *Henry V*); his solution to the problem was to combine "alarums" (sound effects) and "excursions" (groups of soldiers running – or fighting their way – across the stage) with brief scenes which may be compared to "close-ups" of incidents in the battle. The whole battle scene obviously was meant to run continuously; modern scene divisions are quite arbitrary. The division between scene 2 and scene 3 here was made by Edward Capell in the eighteenth century, obeying the neo-classical principle that there must be a scene break when all the actors leave the stage. This division is now retained for convenience of scene and line reference; in every other respect it should be ignored.

5.3.1 ff. Down to the sixteenth century it was obligatory for kings to lead their armies in person; if the king did not fight in his own cause, no one else would. The main object of the enemy was to capture or kill the king, for this would end the battle, victoriously, no matter what happened otherwise. The king was the more vulnerable in that he was astride the largest, handsomest horse (often white), wearing the most brilliant and colourful insignia. Near him was displayed his personal flag, and the next best thing to killing the king was to cut down his standard, at which his supporters might flee, thinking him taken. The standard-bearers were thus also in a most vulnerable position. At Shrewsbury, in fact, Sir Walter Blunt was the King's standard-bearer, and Holinshed records that the standard was cut down and that Blunt, the Earl of Stafford, and others near by were killed. Under these circumstances, the stratagem of dressing a number of men in the King's colours was an obvious method of bettering the odds for the King. Shakespeare found mention of this strategy in Holinshed, but he developed it, both to exploit the grim comedy of Douglas seeking to kill all the King's "coats" and to imply yet another contrast between the King and Hotspur – the one operating on the principle that "all's fair in war", the other adhering to a stricter code of chivalry. The effect is not unlike the well-known convention of the Western film in which the villain draws his gun first, or attempts to shoot the hero from ambush, while the hero must fight fair.

5.3.35-8 *I have . . . life* Falstaff led his men into the thick of battle, not from any heroic motive but so that he might collect the dead men's pay (see 4.2.11-46, end note). We may assume that he himself was in little danger of being "peppered".

5.3.49 ff. See the Introduction for remarks about the Elizabethan pistol. Falstaff is guilty of trying to evade censure by implying that he has it in the holster (instead of primed and ready) because it is hot from much firing and must be allowed to cool. The real point of the incident lies in Hal's question: "What, is it a time to jest and dally now?" For Hal (in this play, at any rate) the time for jesting and dalliance is over, but Falstaff, now and later, does not appreciate this. For him, there is no moment in life so serious that it cannot bear a jest.

5.4.27 It is significant that Douglas should use the word "counterfeit'st" in reference to the King himself. The importance of this expression to the theme of the play is discussed in the Introduction. Douglas uses the word again in line 34.

5.4.80-82 *But . . . stop* The sense is that thoughts, which are subjects to life, and life, which is the sport of time, and even time, which has dominion over all the world, all alike must come to an end. Many editors have followed the F version, which makes three separate clauses in the sentence (see 5.4.80-82, textual variants).

5.4.85 An old tradition has it that some members of the Percy family suffered from a minor speech defect, involving a tendency to stammer on the sound of the letter "w". When Sir Laurence Olivier played Hotspur at the Old Vic he made capital of this. In the earlier speeches, Olivier's occasional stumble at the "w" sound seemed a natural concomitant of Hotspur's breathless manner; when he struggled to pronounce the final "worms", the effect was exquisitely pathetic.

5.4.110-27 See the Introduction for a discussion of the significance of "counterfeit" to the theme of the play.

5.4.118-19 *The . . . discretion* The original meaning of this maxim was that "discretion" was a necessary ingredient of true valour; without it, a man would be simply reckless (like Hotspur). But Falstaff's version has now become the accepted meaning.

5.4.127 s.d. The business of Falstaff carrying the dead Hotspur like a sack of potatoes on his back was made necessary by the lack of a curtain on the Elizabethan stage. It would spoil the effect if "dead" bodies rose and ran off; they had either to die in the recess at the back or be borne off. Here Shakespeare makes capital of this necessity, not only allowing Falstaff to perpetrate a rather lugubrious joke, but emphasizing the contrast between this "counterfeit of a man" now lugged rudely about and the intense life that once breathed in Hotspur.

5.4.142-55 This is Falstaff's final revenge for the embarrassment he suffered about the incident at Gadshill. Hal is not deceived, of course, but he cannot very well deny Falstaff's claim without himself appearing a braggart, eager for glory. Perhaps it suits Hal's purpose anyway to let Falstaff have the credit; he has sufficiently proved himself to himself, and he is not ready yet to undergo his final and complete reformation. The lie does not appear to do Falstaff grace; he grows more and more presumptuous in Part II, blindly heading for his final, fatal encounter with the newly crowned Henry V.

5.5.34-44 The King's final speech "is a conclusion in which nothing is concluded", as Hartley Coleridge remarked (*Essays* [1851]). But this does not necessarily imply that Shakespeare was deliberately pointing to a sequel. There were obvious loose ends which were not tidied up at Shrewsbury; Northumberland, Scroop, Glendower, and Mortimer had all figured in the play but were left out of the closing action. Nevertheless, as the King suggests, the back of the rebellion is now broken, and what remains is a mopping-up operation. There is also reflected here the fact that the material for this play was history — not an invention by the author. The difference between the "fables" of tragedy or comedy and history, as Alfred Harbage points out (*As They Liked It* [London: Macmillan, 1947], p. 158), is that in history, "The story is not over when the play ends."

BIBLIOGRAPHY

Invaluable guides for the detailed study of *1 Henry IV* are provided by the New Variorum Edition and its Supplement, listed below. Both offer excerpts from or summaries of the principal critical works:

Shakespeare, William, *Henry the Fourth, Part 1*, ed. S. B. Hemingway (A New Variorum Edition of Shakespeare). Philadelphia: Lippincott, 1936.

Evans, G. Blakemore (ed.), "Supplement to *Henry IV, Part I*: A New Variorum Edition of Shakespeare", *Shakespeare Quarterly*, VII (1956), i-iv, 1-121.

The reader may trace the differing approaches to Falstaff in a number of the works listed below or in the General Bibliography. The remarks of Dr. Johnson and the works by E. E. Stoll and John Dover Wilson will illustrate objections to Falstaff; the essays of Maurice Morgann and A. C. Bradley defend him. John Masefield combines defence of Falstaff with the most extreme attack on Prince Hal.

Auden, W. H., "The Fallen City: Some Reflections on Shakespeare's *Henry IV*", *Encounter*, XIII (1959), 21-31.

Beck, Richard J., *Shakespeare: "Henry IV"* (Studies in English Literature No. 24). London: Edward Arnold, 1965.

Bradley, A. C., "The Rejection of Falstaff", *Oxford Lectures on Poetry*. London: Macmillan, 1909.

Brooks, Cleanth, and Robert B. Heilman, *Understanding Drama*. New York: Henry Holt, 1945.

Campbell, Lily B., *Shakespeare's "Histories": Mirrors of Elizabethan Policy*. San Marino, Calif.: Huntington Library, 1947.

Charlton, H. B., "Falstaff", *Shakespearian Comedy*. London: Methuen, 1938.

Dickinson, Hugh, "The Reformation of Prince Hal", *Shakespeare Quarterly*, XII (1961), 33-46.

Doran, Madeleine, "Imagery in *Richard II* and in *Henry IV*", *Modern Language Review*, XXXVII (1942), 113-22.

Evans, Gareth Lloyd, "The Comical-tragical-historical Method – *Henry IV*", *Early Shakespeare* (Stratford-upon-Avon Studies 3), eds. John R. Brown and Bernard Harris. London: Edward Arnold, 1961.

Hemingway, S. B., "On Behalf of that Falstaff", *Shakespeare Quarterly*, III (1952), 307-11.

Hunter, G. K., "Shakespeare's Politics and the Rejection of Falstaff", *The Critical Quarterly*, I (1959), 229-36.

Jenkins, Harold, *The Structural Problem in Shakespeare's "Henry the Fourth"*. London: Methuen, 1956.

Kris, Ernst, "Prince Hal's Conflict", *Psychoanalytic Quarterly*, XVII (1948), 487-506.

Masefield, John, *William Shakespeare*. London: Williams & Norgate, 1911. Pp. 109-114.

McLuhan, Herbert Marshall, "*Henry IV*, A Mirror for Magistrates", *University of Toronto Quarterly*, XVII (1948), 152-60.

Palmer, John L., *Political Characters in Shakespeare*. London: Macmillan, 1945.

Quiller-Couch, Arthur T., "The Story of Falstaff", *Shakespeare's Workmanship*. London: Fisher Unwin, 1918.

Ribner, Irving, "Bolingbroke, a True Machiavellian", *Modern Language Quarterly*, IX (1948), 177-84.

——, *The English History Play in the Age of Shakespeare* (revised ed.). London: Methuen, 1965.

Rossiter, A. P., "Ambivalence: the Dialectic of the Histories", *Talking of Shakespeare*, ed. John Garrett. London: Hodder & Stoughton, 1954.

Sprague, Arthur C., "Gadshill Revisited", *Shakespeare Quarterly*, IV (1953), 125-37.

Stewart, J. I. M., "The Birth and Death of Falstaff", *Character and Motive in Shakespeare*. London: Longmans, Green, 1949.

Stoll, E. E., *Shakespeare Studies, Historical and Comparative in Method*. New York: Macmillan, 1927.

Tillyard, E. M. W., *Shakespeare's History Plays*. London: Chatto & Windus, 1944.

Toliver, Harold E., "Falstaff, the Prince, and the History Play", *Shakespeare Quarterly*, XVI (1965), 63-80.

Traversi, Derek, *Shakespeare, from "Richard II" to "Henry V"*. Stanford University Press, 1957.

Unger, Leonard, "Deception and Self-Deception in Shakespeare's *Henry IV*", *The Man in the Name*. Minneapolis: University of Minnesota Press, 1956.

Waith, Eugene M. (ed.), *Shakespeare: The Histories, a Collection of Critical Essays*. Englewood Cliffs, N.J.: Prentice-Hall, 1965.

Williams, Philip, "The Birth and Death of Falstaff Reconsidered", *Shakespeare Quarterly*, VIII (1957), 359-65.

Wilson, John Dover, *The Fortunes of Falstaff*. Cambridge University Press, 1943.

Zeeveld, W. Gordon, " 'Food for Powder'–'Food for Worms' ", *Shakespeare Quarterly*, III (1952), 249-53.

GENERAL BIBLIOGRAPHY

General Criticism

Each work in this section has been remarkably influential in its time. These books constitute, of course, only a handful of the many that might be included in a history of Shakespearian criticism. The student with a special interest in the subject will find that Frank E. Halliday's *Shakespeare and his Critics* (London: Duckworth, 1950) provides a useful introduction, with bibliography.

Bradley, A. C., *Shakespearean Tragedy*. London: Macmillan, 1904.

Coleridge, Samuel Taylor, *Coleridge's Shakespearean Criticism*, ed. T. M. Raysor. 2 vols. Cambridge, Mass.: Harvard University Press, 1930. (The criticism in this volume is drawn from various writings and lectures originally published during the first half of the nineteenth century.)

Granville-Barker, Harley, *Prefaces to Shakespeare* (originally published separately between 1927 and 1947). 2 vols. Princeton University Press, 1946-7.

Hazlitt, William, *Characters of Shakespear's Plays* (originally published 1817). London: Dent, 1907.

Johnson, Samuel, *Johnson on Shakespeare*, ed. Walter A. Raleigh. London: Oxford University Press, 1908. (The criticism in this volume is drawn from various writings originally published between about 1747 and 1765.)

Knight, G. Wilson, *The Wheel of Fire* (4th ed., revised and enlarged). London: Methuen, 1949.

Morgann, Maurice, *An Essay on the Dramatic Character of Sir John Falstaff* (originally published 1777), ed. W. A. Gill. London: Oxford University Press, 1912.

516   *General Bibliography*

Spurgeon, Caroline F. E., *Shakespeare's Imagery and What It Tells Us.* Cambridge University Press, 1935.

Stoll, E. E., *Art and Artifice in Shakespeare.* Cambridge University Press, 1933.

Shakespeare's Life and Work

Alexander, Peter, *Shakespeare.* London: Oxford University Press, 1964.

Bentley, Gerald E., *Shakespeare: A Biographical Handbook.* New Haven, Conn.: Yale University Press, 1961.

Chambers, E. K., *William Shakespeare: A Study of Facts and Problems.* 2 vols. Oxford: Clarendon Press, 1930. (Abridged: C. Williams, *A Short Life of Shakespeare with Sources.* Oxford: Clarendon Press, 1933.)

Quennell, Peter C., *Shakespeare, A Biography.* New York: World Publishing, 1963.

Raleigh, Walter A., *Shakespeare.* London: Macmillan, 1907.

Wilson, John Dover, *The Essential Shakespeare.* Cambridge University Press, 1932.

The Times

Bindoff, Stanley T., *Tudor England* (The Pelican History of England, 5). Harmondsworth: Penguin Books, 1950.

Black, John B., *The Reign of Elizabeth, 1558-1603* (The Oxford History of England, 8) (2nd ed.). Oxford: Clarendon Press, 1959.

Byrne, Muriel St. Clare, *Elizabethan Life in Town and Country* (8th ed., revised). London: Methuen, 1961.

Elton, Geoffrey R., *England Under the Tudors.* London: Methuen, 1955. (Reprinted with a new bibliography, 1962.)

Harrison, G. B., *The Elizabethan Journals . . . 1591-1603.* 3 vols. London: Routledge & Sons, 1938.

———, *A Jacobean Journal . . . 1603-1606.* London: Routledge & Sons, 1941.

———, *A Second Jacobean Journal . . . 1607-1610.* London: Routledge & Kegan Paul, 1958.

Hurstfield, Joel, *Elizabeth the First and the Unity of England.* London: English Universities Press, 1960.

Neale, John E., *Queen Elizabeth.* London: Jonathan Cape, 1934.

Nicoll, Allardyce, *The Elizabethans*. Cambridge University Press, 1957.

Pearson, Lu E., *Elizabethans at Home*. Stanford University Press, 1957.

Intellectual Background

Craig, Hardin, *The Enchanted Glass*. London: Oxford University Press, 1936.

Morris, Christopher, *Political Thought in England: Tyndale to Hooker*. London: Oxford University Press, 1953.

Spencer, Theodore, *Shakespeare and the Nature of Man* (2nd ed.). New York: Macmillan, 1949.

Tillyard, E. M. W., *The Elizabethan World Picture*. London: Chatto & Windus, 1943.

Winny, James (ed.), *The Frame of Order: An Outline of Elizabethan Belief Taken from Treatises of the Late Sixteenth Century*. London: Allen & Unwin, 1957.

The Theatre

Beckerman, Bernard, *Shakespeare at the Globe, 1599-1609*. New York: Macmillan, 1962.

Bentley, Gerald E., *Shakespeare and his Theatre*. Lincoln: University of Nebraska Press, 1964.

Chambers, E. K., *The Elizabethan Stage*. 4 vols. Oxford: Clarendon Press, 1923.

Harbage, Alfred B., *Shakespeare's Audience*. New York: Columbia University Press, 1941.

Hodges, Cyril W., *The Globe Restored*. London: Benn, 1953.

————, *Shakespeare's Theatre*. London: Oxford University Press, 1964.

Wickham, Glynne W. G., *Early English Stages, 1300-1660*. 2 vols. London: Routledge & Kegan Paul, 1959-63.

Works on Language and Other Special Topics

Armstrong, Edward A., *Shakespeare's Imagination*. London: Lindsay Drummond, 1946.

Clemen, Wolfgang H., *The Development of Shakespeare's Imagery*. Cambridge, Mass.: Harvard University Press, 1951.

Coghill, Nevill, *Shakespeare's Professional Skills*. Cambridge University Press, 1964.

Crane, Milton, *Shakespeare's Prose*. University of Chicago Press, 1951.

Evans, B. Ifor, *The Language of Shakespeare's Plays*. London: Methuen, 1952.

Halliday, Frank E., *The Poetry of Shakespeare's Plays*. London: Duckworth, 1954.

Harbage, Alfred B., *As They Liked It: An Essay on Shakespeare and Morality*. London: Macmillan, 1947.

Play Production

Odell, George C. D., *Shakespeare from Betterton to Irving*. 2 vols. New York: Scribner, 1920.

Sprague, Arthur C., *Shakespeare and the Actors*. Cambridge, Mass.: Harvard University Press, 1945.

Trewin, John C., *Shakespeare on the English Stage, 1900-1964*. London: Barrie & Rockliff, 1964.

The Authorship Controversy

Friedman, William F. and Elizabeth S., *The Shakespearian Ciphers Examined*. Cambridge University Press, 1957.

Gibson, H. N., *The Shakespeare Claimants*. London: Methuen, 1962.

McMichael, George L., and E. M. Glenn (eds.), *Shakespeare and his Rivals*. New York: Odyssey Press, 1962.

Reference Works

Bartlett, John, *A Complete Concordance . . .* (originally published under the title *A New and Complete Concordance . . .* in 1894). London: Macmillan, 1960.

Bullough, Geoffrey (ed.), *Narrative and Dramatic Sources of Shakespeare*. 6 vols. to date. London: Routledge & Kegan Paul, 1957-66.

Campbell, Oscar J., and Edward G. Quinn (eds.), *The Reader's Encyclopedia of Shakespeare*. New York: Thomas Y. Crowell, 1966.

Granville-Barker, Harley, and G. B. Harrison (eds.), *A Companion to Shakespeare Studies*. Cambridge University Press, 1934.

Halliday, Frank E., *A Shakespeare Companion, 1564-1964* (revised ed.). Harmondsworth: Penguin Books, 1964.
Lee, Sidney, C. T. Onions, and Walter A. Raleigh (eds.), *Shakespeare's England*. 2 vols. Oxford: Clarendon Press, 1916.
Onions, C. T., *A Shakespeare Glossary* (2nd ed., revised and enlarged). Oxford: Clarendon Press, 1958.

Periodicals

Shakespeare Quarterly. New York: Shakespeare Association of America, since 1950.
Shakespeare Survey. Cambridge University Press, annually since 1948.